Learn iOS 8 App Development

Second Edition

James Bucanek

Apress®

Learn iOS 8 App Development

ISBN-13 (pbk): 978-1-4842-0209-8

ISBN-13 (electronic): 978-1-4842-0208-1

Managing Director: Welmoed Spahr
Lead Editor: Michelle Lowman
Development Editor: Douglas Pundick
Technical Reviewer: Charles Cruz
Editorial Board: Steve Anglin, Mark Beckner, Gary Cornell, Louise Corrigan, Jim DeWolf, Jonathan Gennick, Robert Hutchinson, Michelle Lowman, James Markham, Matthew Moodie, Jeff Olson, Jeffrey Pepper, Douglas Pundick, Ben Renow-Clarke, Gwenan Spearing, Matt Wade, Steve Weiss
Coordinating Editor: Kevin Walter
Copy Editor: Kim Wimpsett
Compositor: SPi Global
Indexer: SPi Global
Artist: SPi Global
Cover Designer: Anna Ishchenko

Distributed to the book trade worldwide by Springer Science+Business Media New York, 233 Spring Street, 6th Floor, New York, NY 10013. Phone 1-800-SPRINGER, fax (201) 348-4505, e-mail orders-ny@springer-sbm.com, or visit www.springeronline.com. Apress Media, LLC is a California LLC and the sole member (owner) is Springer Science + Business Media Finance Inc (SSBM Finance Inc). SSBM Finance Inc is a Delaware corporation.

For information on translations, please e-mail rights@apress.com, or visit www.apress.com.

Apress and friends of ED books may be purchased in bulk for academic, corporate, or promotional use. eBook versions and licenses are also available for most titles. For more information, reference our Special Bulk Sales–eBook Licensing web page at www.apress.com/bulk-sales.

Any source code or other supplementary material referenced by the author in this text is available to readers at www.apress.com. For detailed information about how to locate your book's source code, go to www.apress.com/source-code/.

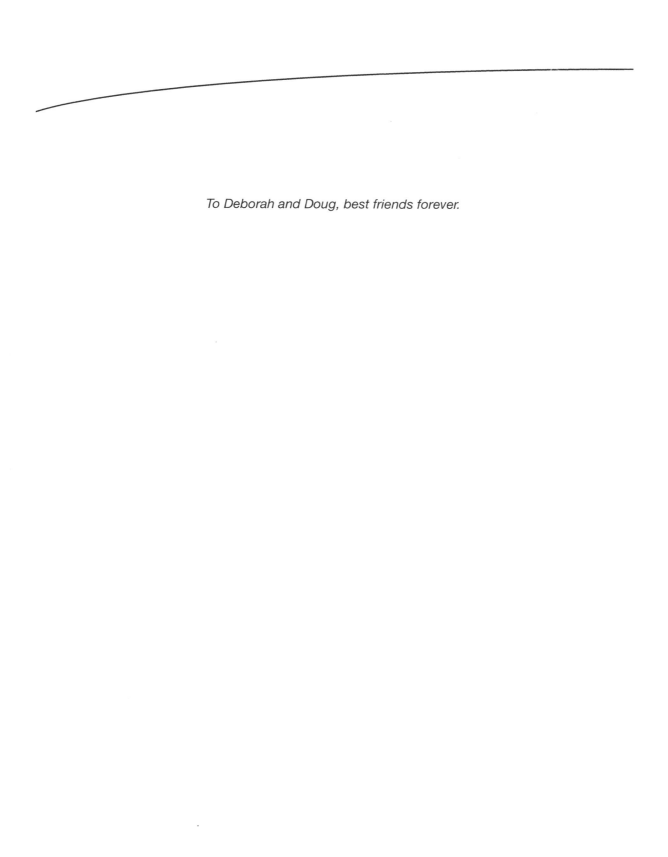

To Deborah and Doug, best friends forever.

Contents at a Glance

Contents

About the Author

James Bucanek has spent the past 30 years programming and developing microprocessor systems. He has experience with a broad range of computer hardware and software, from embedded consumer products to industrial robotics. His development projects include the first local area network for the Apple II, distributed air-conditioning control systems, a piano teaching system, digital oscilloscopes, silicon wafer deposition furnaces, and collaborative writing tools for K-12 education. James holds a Java Developer Certification from Sun Microsystems and was awarded a patent for optimizing local area networks. James is currently focused on OS X and iOS software development, where he can combine his deep knowledge of UNIX and object-oriented languages with his passion for elegant design. James holds an associate's degree in classical ballet from the Royal Academy of Dance and can occasionally be found teaching at Adams Ballet Academy.

About the Technical Reviewer

Charles Cruz is a mobile application developer for the iOS, Windows Phone, and Android platforms. He graduated from Stanford University with bachelor's and master's degrees in engineering. He lives in Southern California and runs a photography business with his wife (www.bellalentestudios.com). When not doing technical things, he plays lead guitar in an original metal band (www.taintedsociety.com). Charles can be reached at codingandpicking@gmail.com and @CodingNPicking on Twitter.

Acknowledgments

This edition of *Learn iOS 8 App Development* is largely a continuation of the previous edition. I would be remiss not to acknowledge the giants who created *Learn iOS 7 App Development*, on whose shoulders we now stand. Charles Cruz, my technical editor, checked every line of code and symbol to ensure complete accuracy. This was made all the more challenging because the Swift language was literally changing from one day to the next. Any technical errors are ultimately my responsibility, but there are significantly fewer thanks to Charles. Kim Wimpsett dotted my i's, crossed my t's, and corrected my (egregious) spelling. If you find this book easy to read, you have Kim's blue pencil to thank.

The entire project was stewarded by my coordinating editor, Kevin Walter, who juggled schedules, liaised between editors, tracked production, and herded everyone toward a common goal. Assisting us was a phalanx of production specialists, artists, and managing editors. To all the folks at Apress, thank you, thank you, thank you!

Finally, I want to shout a "thank-you" to Apple's Xcode development team for creating the most advanced mobile app development tool in the world.

Introduction

I'm standing on a street corner in San Francisco, a city I visit far too infrequently. In my hand I hold an electronic device. The device is receiving status updates about the city's public transportation system in real time. It is telling me that the F-line rail will arrive at the Market and 5th Street station in seven minutes. It displays a map of the city and, by timing radio waves it receives from outer space, triangulates and displays my exact location on that map. A magnetometer determines which direction I'm holding the device and uses that information to indicate the direction I should walk to meet the rail car in time to board it. My friends call me, wondering when I will arrive. A tiny video camera and microphone share my image and voice with them as I walk. I'm meeting them at a gallery opening. It's an exhibition of new artwork, by artists from all over the world, created entirely using devices similar to the one I hold in my hand. When I arrive, I use my device to share my experiences with friends and family back home, exchange contact information with people I meet, and look up restaurant suggestions for where we might eat later.

This is a true story. A couple of decades ago, it would have been science fiction.

We live in a time in which personal electronics are changing how we work, travel, communicate, and experience the world. A day doesn't go by without someone discovering another novel use for them. And while I'm sure you enjoy benefiting from this new technology, you're reading this book because you want to participate in this revolution. You want to create apps.

You've come to the right place.

Who Is This Book For?

This book is for anyone who wants to learn the basic tools and techniques for creating exciting, dynamic applications for Apple products that run the iOS operating system. As of this writing, that includes the iPad, iPhone, and iPod Touch.

This book assumes you are new to developing iOS apps and that you have limited programming experience. If you've been learning Swift—Apple's new programming language—that's perfect. If you know Objective-C, C, Java, C#, or C++, you shouldn't have too much trouble following along, and there's a Swift primer in Chapter 20 that you'll want to read. If you are completely new to programming computers, I suggest getting a basic Swift programming book—say, *Swift for Absolute Beginners* by Gary Bennett and Brad Lees—and read that first or in parallel. iOS app are developed using Objective-C or Swift, but this book uses Swift exclusively.

This book will explain the fundamentals of how iOS apps are designed, built, and deployed. You'll pick up some good design habits, get some core programming skills, and learn your way around the development tools used to create apps.

This book is not an in-depth treatise on any one technology. It's designed to stimulate your imagination by giving you a firm grounding in building apps that use a variety of device capabilities, such as finding your location on a map, using the accelerometer, taking pictures with the built-in camera, creating dynamic animation, participating in social networks, and storing information in the cloud. From there, you can leap beyond these examples to create the next great iOS app!

Too Cool for School

I'm an "old-school" programmer. I learned programming from the bit up (literally). At the risk of dating myself, the first program I wrote was on a 4-bit microcontroller using toggle switches to input the machine instructions. So, I pretty much knew everything there was to know about machine code before I started to program in "high-level" languages like BASIC and C. All that was well behind me before I wrote my first graphical user interface (GUI) application for the (then-revolutionary) Macintosh computer.

While I value this accumulated knowledge, and much of it is still useful, I realize that a strict "ground-up" approach isn't necessary to develop great apps for iOS today. Many of the advances in software development over the past few decades have been in insulating the developer—that's you—from the nitty-gritty details of CPU instructions, hardware interfaces, and software design. This frees you to concentrate on harnessing these technologies to turn your idea into reality, rather than spending all of your time worrying about register allocations and memory management.

So, the exciting news is that you can jump right in and create full-featured iOS apps with only a minimal knowledge of computer programming or the underlying technologies that make them possible. And that's what this book is going to do in the first couple of chapters—show you how to create an iOS app without any traditional programming whatsoever.

That's not to say you don't need these skills in order to master iOS development. On the contrary; the more you know about programming, performance, and memory management, the more proficient you're going to be. What's changed is that these skills aren't the prerequisites that they once were. Now, you can learn them in parallel while you explore new avenues of iOS development.

How to Use This Book

This book embraces an "explore as go" approach. Some chapters will walk you through the process of creating an iOS app that uses the camera or plays music. These chapters may gloss over many of the finer details. In between, you'll find chapters on basic software development skills. There are chapters on good software design, making the most of sample code and the Swift programming language.

So, instead of the "traditional" order of first learning all of the basic skills and then building apps using those skills, this book starts out building apps and then explores the details of how that happened.

You can read the chapters in any order, skipping or returning to chapters as you need. If you really want to know more about objects in an earlier chapter, jump ahead and read the chapter on objects. If you're already familiar with the Model-View-Controller design pattern, skip that chapter when you get to it. Treat this book as a collection of skills to learn, not a series of lessons that have to be taken in order.

Here's a preview of the chapters ahead:

- *Got Tools?* shows you how to download and install the Xcode development tools. You'll need those.

- *Boom! App* walks you through the core steps for creating an iOS app—no programming needed.

- *Spin a Web* creates an app that leverages the power of iOS's built-in web browser.

- *Coming Events* discusses how events (touches, gestures, and movement) get from the device into your app and how you use them to make your app respond to the user.

- *Table Manners* shows you how data gets displayed in an app and how it gets edited.

- *Object Lesson* dishes the straight dope on objects and object-oriented programming.

- *Smile!* shows you how to integrate the camera and photo library into your app.

- *Model Citizen* explains the magic incantation that software engineers call Model-View-Controller.

- *Sweet, Sweet Music* jazzes up your mix by showing you how to add music, sounds, and iTunes to your apps.

- *Got Views?* takes you on a brief survey of the view objects (buttons, sliders, and so on) available in the Cocoa Touch framework.

- *Draw Me a Picture* shows you how to create your own views, unlocking the power to draw just about anything in an iOS app.

- *There and Back Again* lays out the basics of app navigation: how your users get from one screen to another and back again.

- *Sharing Is Caring* is all about getting your content out to the 'net, through services such as Twitter, SMS, and e-mail.

- *Game On!* dishes out a fun game with real-time animation.

- *If You Build It . . .* explains some of the magic behind Interface Builder.

- *Apps with Attitude* shakes up your apps with the accelerometer.

- *Where Are You?* draws you a map—literally.

- *Remember Me?* shows you how user preferences are set and saved and how to share them with other iOS devices using iCloud.

- *Doc, You Meant Storage* explains how app documents are stored, read, and updated.

- *See Swift, See Swift Run* is a crash course on the Swift programming language.

- *Frame Up* escapes the confines of your app to create an extension and teaches you a little about frameworks in the process.

Got Tools?

If you want to build something, you are probably going to need some tools: hammer, nails, laser, crane, and one of those IKEA hex wrenches. Building iOS apps requires a collection of tools called *Xcode*.

This chapter will show you how to get and install Xcode and give you a brief tour of it, so you'll know your way around. If you've already installed and used Xcode, check the "Requirements" section to make sure you have everything you need, but you can probably skip most of this chapter.

Requirements

In this book, you will create apps that run on iOS version 8. Creating an app for iOS 8 requires Xcode version 6. Xcode 6 requires OS X version 10.9 (a.k.a. Mavericks), which requires an Intel-based Mac. Did you get all of that? Here's your complete checklist:

- Intel-based Mac
- OS X 10.9 (or newer)
- A few gigabytes of free disk space
- An Internet connection
- At least one iOS device (iPad Touch, iPhone, or iPad) running iOS 8.0 (or newer)

Make sure you have an Intel-based Mac computer with OS X 10.9 (Mavericks), or newer, installed, enough disk space, and an Internet connection. You can do all of your initial app development right on your Mac, but at some point you'll want to run your apps on a real iOS device (iPhone, iPod Touch, or iPad), and for that you'll need one.

> **Note** As a general rule, newer versions are better. The examples in this book were developed for iOS 8.0, built using Xcode 6.1, running on OS X 10.10 (Yosemite). By the time you read this, there will probably be a newer version of all of these, and that's OK. Read the Xcode and iOS release notes to see what has changed.

Installing Xcode

Apple has made installing Xcode as easy as possible. On your Mac, launch the App Store application—not to be confused with the App Store for iOS, which you find in iTunes. Find the Developer Tools category or just search for *Xcode*. Figure 1-1 show the Xcode app in the Mac App Store.

Figure 1-1. Xcode in the App Store

Click the Install button to start downloading Xcode. This will take a while (see Figure 1-2). You can monitor its progress from the Purchases tab of the App Store. Be patient. Xcode is huge, and even with a fast Internet connection, it will take some time to install.

Figure 1-2. Downloading Xcode

While Xcode is downloading, let's talk about it and some related topics.

What Is Xcode?

So, what is this huge application you're downloading?

Xcode is an *integrated development environment* (IDE). Modern software development requires a dizzying number of different programs. To build and test an iOS app, you're going to need editors, compilers, linkers, syntax checkers, cryptographic signers, resource compilers, debuggers, simulators, performance analyzers, and more. But you don't have to worry about that; Xcode orchestrates all of those individual tools for you. All you have to do is use the Xcode interface to design your app, and Xcode will decide what tools need to be run and when. In other words, Xcode puts the *I* in IDE.

As well as including all of the tools you'll need, Xcode can host a number of *software development kits* (SDKs). An SDK is a collection of files that supply Xcode with what it needs to build an app for a particular operating system, like iOS 8. Xcode downloads with an SDK to build iOS apps and with an SDK to build OS X apps, for the most recent versions of each. You can download additional SDKs as needed.

An SDK will consist of one or more *frameworks*. A framework tells Xcode exactly how your application can use an iOS service. This is called an *application programming interface* (API). While it's possible to write code in your app to do just about anything, much of what it will be doing is making requests to iOS to do things that have already been written for you: display an alert, look up a word in the dictionary, take a picture, play a song, and so on. Most of this book will be showing you how to use those built-in services.

> **Note**　A framework is a bundle of files in a folder, much like the app bundles you'll be creating in this book. Instead of containing an app, however, a framework contains the files your app needs to use a particular segment of the operating system. For example, all of the functions, constants, classes, and resources needed to draw things on the screen are in the Core Graphics framework. The AVFoundation framework contains classes that let you record and playback audio. Want to know where you are? You'll need the functions in the CoreLocation framework. There are scores of these individual frameworks.

Wow, that's a lot of acronyms! Let's review them.

- ▦ *IDE*: Integrated development environment. Xcode is an IDE.
- ▦ *SDK*: Software development kit. The supporting files that let you build an app for a particular operating system, like iOS 8.
- ▦ *API*: Application programming interface. A published set of functions, classes, and definitions that describe how your app can use a particular service.

You don't need to memorize these. It's just good to know what they mean when you hear them or talk to other programmers.

Becoming an iOS Developer

The fact that you're reading this book makes you an iOS developer—at least in spirit. To become an official iOS developer, you need to join Apple's iOS Developer program.

You must be an iOS developer if you want to do any of the following:

- ▦ Sell, or give away, your apps through Apple's App Store
- ▦ Gain access to Apple's Developer Forums and support resources
- ▦ Give your apps to people directly (outside of the App Store)
- ▦ Develop apps that use Game Kit, in-app purchases, push notifications, or other technologies that depend on Apple-operated services
- ▦ Test your apps on a real iOS device

The first reason is the one that prompts most developers to join the program and is probably the reason you'll join. You don't, however, have to join to build, test, and run your apps in Xcode's simulator. If you never plan to distribute your apps through the App Store or run your app on an iOS device, you may never need to become an official iOS developer. You can get through most of this book without joining.

Another reason for joining is to gain access to the iOS Developer's community and support programs. Apple's online forums contain a treasure trove of information. If you run into a problem and can't find the answer, there's a good chance someone else has already bumped into the same problem. A quick search of the Developer Forums will probably reveal an answer. If not, post your question and someone might have an answer for you.

Even if you don't plan to sell or give away your masterpiece on the App Store, there are a couple of other reasons to join. If you want to install your app on a device, Apple requires that you become a registered developer. Apple will then generate special files that will permit your app to be installed on an iOS device.

As a registered developer, Apple will also allow you to install your apps on someone else's device directly (that is, not through the App Store). This is called *ad hoc distribution*. There are limits on the number of people you can do this for, but it is possible, and it's a great way to test your app in the field.

Finally, some technologies require your app to communicate with Apple's servers. Before this is allowed, you must register yourself and your app with Apple, even just to test them. For example, if you plan to use Game Kit in your app—and this book includes a Game Kit example—you'll need to be an official iOS developer.

As I write this book, the cost of becoming an iOS developer is $99. It's an annual subscription, so there's no point in joining until you need to join. Go to `http://developer.apple.com/` to find more information about Apple's developer programs.

So, is there anything at `http://developer.apple.com/` that's free? There's quite a lot actually. You can search through all of Apple's published documentation, download example projects, read technology guides, find technical notes, and more—none of which requires you to be an iOS developer. Some activities may require you to log in with your Apple ID. The Apple ID you use with iTunes or your iCloud account will work, or you can create a new Apple ID for free.

Paid registration also gives you the opportunity to buy tickets to the World Wide Developers Conference (WWDC) held by Apple each year. It's a huge gathering, and it's just for Apple developers.

Getting the Projects

Now would be a good time to download the project files for this book. There are numerous projects used throughout this book. Many can be re-created by following the steps in each chapter, and I encourage you to do that whenever possible so you'll get a feel for building your apps from scratch. There are, however, a number of projects that don't explain every detail, and some projects include binary resources (image and sound files) that can't be reproduced in print.

Go to this book's page at `www.apress.com` (you can search for it by name, ISBN, or author name). Below the book's description, you'll see some folder tabs, one of which is labeled Source Code/ Downloads. Click that tab. Now find the link that downloads the projects for this book. Click that link and a file named `Learn iOS Development Projects.zip` will download to your hard drive.

Locate the file `Learn iOS Development Projects.zip` in your Downloads folder (or wherever your browser saved it). Double-click the file to extract its contents, leaving you with a folder named `Learn iOS Development Projects`. Move the folder wherever you like.

Launching Xcode the First Time

After the Xcode application downloads, you will find it in your `Applications` folder. Open the Xcode application, by double-clicking it, using Launchpad, or however you like to launch apps. I recommend adding Xcode to your Dock for easy access.

Xcode will present a licensing agreement (see Figure 1-3), which you are encouraged to at least skim over but must agree to before proceeding. Xcode then may then request an administrator's account and password to finish its installation. Once it has authorization, it will finish its installation, as shown on the right in Figure 1-3.

Figure 1-3. License agreement

Once you've gotten through all of the preliminaries and Xcode has put everything where it belongs, you'll see Xcode's startup window, as shown in Figure 1-4.

Figure 1-4. Xcode's startup window

The startup window has several self-explanatory buttons to help you get started. It also lists the projects you've recently opened.

A new feature of Xcode 6 is playgrounds. A *playground* is a blank page where you can try code in Swift, the language you'll be using in this book. You don't have to create a project or run a compiler; just type some Swift code and Xcode will show you what it did or why it didn't. You'll use playgrounds in Chapter 20 to explore the Swift language in detail, but don't be shy about creating a playground whenever you want to try some code.

The interesting parts of Xcode don't reveal themselves unless you have a project open, so start by creating a new project. Click the Create a new Xcode project button in the startup window (or choose File ➤ New ➤ Project from the menu). The first thing Xcode will want to know is what kind of project you want to create, as shown in Figure 1-5.

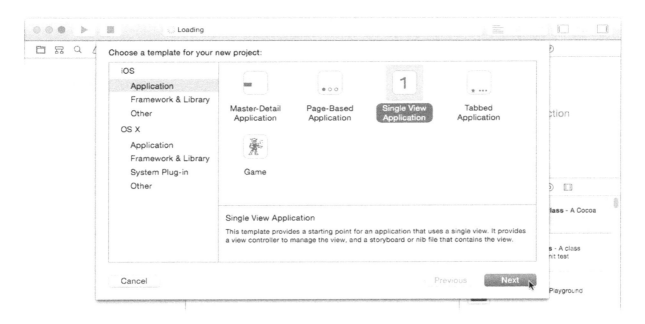

Figure 1-5. Project template browser

The template browser lets you select a project template. Each template creates a new project preconfigured to build something specific (application, library, plug-in, and so on) for a particular platform (iOS or OS X). While it's possible to manually configure any project to produce whatever you want, it's both technical and tedious; save yourself a lot of work and try to choose a template that's as close to the final "shape" of your app as you can.

In this book, you'll only be creating iOS apps, so choose the Application category under the iOS section—but feel free to check out some of the other sections. As you can see, Xcode is useful for much more than just iOS development.

With the Application section selected, click the Single View Application template, and then click the Next button. In the next screen, Xcode wants some details about your new project, as shown in Figure 1-6. What options you see here will vary depending on what template you chose.

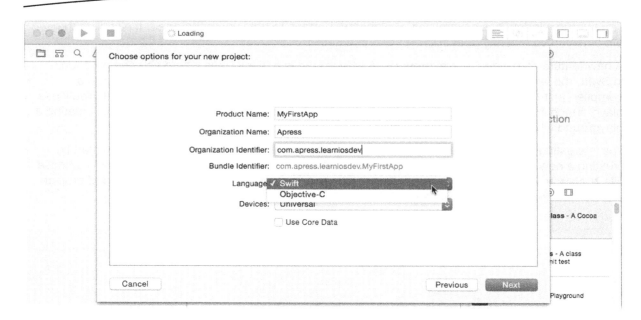

Figure 1-6. New project options

For this little demonstration, give your new project a name in the Product Name field. It can be anything you want—I used MyFirstApp for this example—but I recommend you keep the name simple. The organization name is optional, but I suggest you fill in your name (or the company you're working for, if you're going to be developing apps for them).

The organization identifier and product name, together, create a *bundle identifier* that uniquely identifies your app. The organization identifier is a reverse domain name, which you (or your company) should own. It isn't important right now because you'll be building this app only for yourself, so use any domain name you like. When you build apps that you plan to distribute through the App Store, these values will have to be legitimate and unique.

Finally, choose Swift for the project's language. Objective-C is the traditional language for iOS (and most OS X) development. At the 2014 World Wide Developers Conference, Apple unveiled the Swift language. Swift is a, highly efficient, succinct computer language with a lot of features that promote effortless, bug-free development. Swift is the future of iOS development, and it's the language you'll be using throughout this book.

Note   While you've chosen Swift as the project's language, you're not limited to just Swift. Xcode and iOS can seamlessly mix Swift, Objective-C, C++, and C in the same project. You can always add Objective-C to a Swift project, and vice versa.

The rest of the options don't matter for this demonstration, so click the Next button. The last thing Xcode will ask is where to store your new project (see Figure 1-7) and if you want to create a source control repository. Source control is a way to maintain the history of your project. You can later go back and review what changes you've made. Xcode's preferred source control system is Git, and Xcode will offer to create a local Git repository for your project. If you don't know what to do, say "yes"; it doesn't really cost anything, and it's easier to do now than later. Xcode also supports remote Git repositories as well older source control systems, like Subversion. Now let's get back to creating that project.

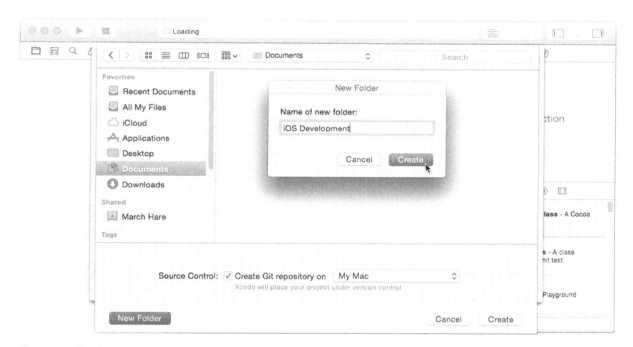

Figure 1-7. *Creating a new project*

Every project creates a *project folder*, named after your project. All of the documents used to create your app will (should) be stored in that project folder. You can put your project folder anywhere (even on the Desktop). In this example (see Figure 1-7), I'm creating a new iOS Development folder so that I can keep all of my project folders together.

Welcome to Xcode

With all of the details about your new project answered, click the Create button. Xcode will create your project and open it in a *workspace window*. Figure 1-8 shows an exploded view of a workspace window. This is where the magic happens and where you'll be spending most of your time in this book.

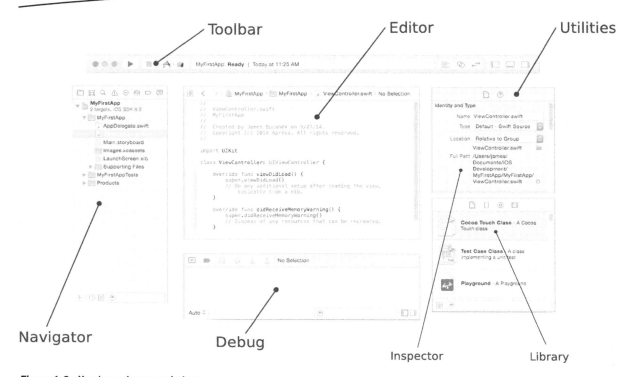

Figure 1-8. Xcode workspace window

A workspace window has five main parts.

- Navigator area (left)
- Editor area (center)
- Utility area (right)
- Debug area (bottom)
- Toolbar (top)

You can selectively hide everything except the editor area, so you may not see all of these parts. Let's take a brief tour of each one, so you'll know your way around.

Navigation Area

The navigators live on the left side of your workspace window. There are eight navigators:

- Project
- Symbol
- Find
- Issue

- Test
- Debug
- Breakpoint
- Report

Switch navigators by clicking the icons at the top of the pane or from the View ➤ Navigator submenu. You can hide the navigators using the View ➤ Navigator ➤ Hide Navigator command (Command+0) or by clicking the left side of the View button in the toolbar (as shown on the right in Figure 1-9). This will give you a little extra screen space for the editor.

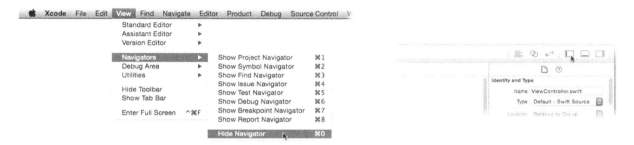

Figure 1-9. *Navigator view controls*

The project navigator (see Figure 1-8) is your home base and the one you'll use the most. Every source file that's part of your project is organized in the project navigator, and it's how you select a file to edit.

> **Note**   A *source file* is any original document used in the creation of your app. Most projects have multiple source files. The term is used to distinguish them from *intermediate files* (transient files created during construction) and *product files* (the files of your finished app). Your product files appear in a special `Products` folder, at the bottom of the project navigator.

The symbol navigator keeps a running list of the symbols you've defined in your project. The search navigator will find text in multiple files. The issues, debug, breakpoint, and report navigators come into play when you're ready to build and test your app.

Editor Area

The editor area is where you create your app—literally. Select a source file in the project navigator, and it will appear in the editor area. What the editor looks like will depend on what kind of file it is.

> **Note**   Not all files are editable in Xcode. For example, image and sound files can't be edited in Xcode, but Xcode will display a preview of them in the editor area.

What you'll be editing the most are program source files, which you edit like any text file (see Figures 1-8 and 1-10), and Interface Builder files, which appear as graphs of objects (see Figure 1-11) that you connect and configure.

The editor area has three modes.

- Standard editor
- Assistant editor
- Version editor

The standard editor edits the selected file, as shown in Figure 1-10. The assistant editor splits the editor area and (typically) loads a *counterpart* file on the right side. For example, you can edit your interface design in the left pane and preview what that interface will look like on different devices in the right pane. When editing a Swift source file, you can elect to have the source for its superclass automatically appear in the right, and so on.

Figure 1-10. The editor

The version editor is used to compare a source file with an earlier version. Xcode supports several version control systems. You can check in files into your version control system or take a "snapshot" of your project. You can later compare what you've written against an earlier version of the same file. We won't get into version control in this book. If you're interested, read the section "Save and Revert Changes to Projects" in the Xcode Users Guide.

To change editor modes, click the Editor control in the toolbar or use the commands in the View menu. You can't hide the editor area.

Utility Area

On the right side of your workspace window is the utility area. As the name suggests, it hosts a variety of useful tools, as shown on the right in Figure 1-11.

Figure 1-11. Editing an Interface Builder file

At the top of the utilities area are the *inspectors*. These will change depending on what kind of file is being edited and possibly what you have selected in that file. As with the navigators, you can switch between different inspectors by clicking the icons at the top of the pane or from the View ➤ Utilities submenu (shown on the left of Figure 1-11). You can hide the utility area using the View ➤ Utilities ➤ Hide Utilities command or by clicking the right side of the View control in the toolbar (also shown at the upper right of Figure 1-11).

At the bottom of the utility area is the library. Here you'll find ready-made objects, resources, and code snippets that you can drag into your project. These too are organized into tabs by type: file templates, code snippets, interface objects, and media assets.

Debug Area

The debug area is used to test your app and work out any kinks. It usually doesn't appear until you run your app—and isn't much use until you do. To make it appear, or disappear, use the View ➤ Debug Area ➤ Show/Hide Debug Area command. You can also click the close drawer icon in the upper-left corner of the debug pane.

Toolbar

The toolbar contains a number of useful shortcuts and some status information, as shown in Figure 1-12.

Figure 1-12. Workspace window toolbar

You've already seen the Editor and View buttons on the right. On the left are buttons to run (test) and stop your app. You will use these buttons to start and stop your app during development.

Next to the Run and Stop buttons is the Scheme control. This multipart pop-up menu lets you select how your project will be built (called a *scheme*) and your app's destination (a simulator, an actual device, the App Store, and so on).

In the middle of the toolbar is your project's status. It will display what activities are currently happening, or have recently finished, such as building, indexing, and so on. If you've just installed Xcode, it is probably downloading additional documentation in the background, and the status will indicate that.

You can hide the toolbar, if you want, using the View ➤ Show/Hide Toolbar command. All of the buttons and controls in the toolbar are just shortcuts to menu commands, so it's possible to live without it. This book, however, will assume that it's visible.

If you're interested in learning more about the workspace window, the navigators, editor, and inspectors, you will find all of that (and more) in the Xcode Overview, under the Help menu.

Running Your First App

With your workspace window open, click on the Scheme control and choose one of the iPhone choices from the submenu, as shown in Figure 1-13. This tells Xcode where you want this app to run when you click the Run button.

Figure 1-13. Choosing the scheme and target

Click the Run button. OK, there's probably one more formality to attend to. Before you can test an application, Xcode needs to be granted some special privileges. The first time you try to run an app, Xcode will ask if it can have those (see Figure 1-14). Click Enable and supply your administrative account name and password.

Figure 1-14. *Enabling developer mode*

Once you're past the preliminaries, Xcode will assemble your app from all of the parts in your project—a process known as a *build*—and then run your app using its built-in iPhone simulator, as shown on the left in Figure 1-15.

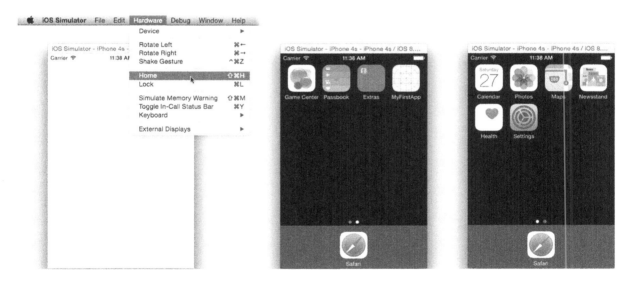

Figure 1-15. *The iPhone simulator*

The simulator is just what it sounds like. It's a program that pretends—as closely as possible—to be a real iPhone or iPad. The simulator lets you do much of your iOS app testing right on your Mac, without ever having to load your app into a real iOS device. It also allows you to test your app on different kinds of devices, so you don't have to go buy one of each.

Congratulations, you just created, built, and ran an iOS app on a (simulated) iPhone! This works because Xcode project templates always create a runnable project; what's missing is the functionality that makes your app do something wonderful. That's what the rest of this book is about.

While you're here, feel free to play around with the iPhone simulator. Although the app you created doesn't have any functionality—beyond that of a lame "flashlight" app—you'll notice that you can simulate pressing the home button using the Hardware ➤ Home command (shown on the left in Figure 1-15) and return to the springboard (the middle and right in Figure 1-15). There you'll find your new app, the Settings app, Game Center, and more, just as if this were a real iPhone. Sorry, it won't make telephone calls.

When you're finished, switch back to the workspace window and click the Stop button (next to the Run button) in the toolbar.

Summary

You now have all of the tools you need to develop and run iOS apps. You've learned a little about how Xcode is organized and how to run your app in the simulator.

The next step is to add some content to your app.

Chapter 2

Boom! App

In this chapter you'll create an iOS app that does something. Not much—these are early days—but enough to call it useful. In the process, you will do the following:

- Use Xcode's Interface Builder to design your app
- Add objects to your app
- Connect objects
- Customize your objects to provide content
- Add resource files to your project
- Use storyboards to create segues
- Control the layout of visual elements using constraints

Amazingly, you're going to create this app without writing a single line of computer code. This is not typical, but it will demonstrate the flexibility of Xcode.

The app you're going to create presents some interesting facts about women surrealists of the 20th century. Let's get started.

Design

Before firing up Xcode and typing furiously, you need to have a plan. This is the design phase of app development. Over the lifetime of your app, you may revise your design several times as you improve it, but before you begin you need a basic idea of what your app will look like and how you want it to work.

Your design may be written out formally, sketched on a napkin, or just be in your head. It doesn't matter, as long as you have one. You need to, at the least, be able to answer some basic questions. What kinds of devices will your app run on (iPhone/iPod, iPad, or both)? Will your app run in portrait mode, sideways, or both? What will the user see? How will the user navigate? How will they interact with it?

Figure 2-1 shows a rough sketch of this app. The app is simple, so it doesn't require much in the way of initial design. The surrealist app will have an opening screen containing portraits of famous women surrealists. Tapping one will transition to a second screen showing a representative painting and a scrollable text field with information about the artist's life. You've decided this is going to run only on an iPhone or iPod Touch and only in portrait orientation. This will simplify your design and development.

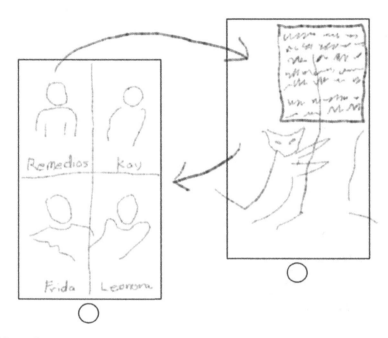

Figure 2-1. Sketch of Surrealist app

Creating the Project

The first step is to create your project. Click the New Project button in the startup window or choose the File ➤ New Project command. Review the available templates, as shown in Figure 2-2.

Figure 2-2. iOS project templates

Your design gives you a basic idea of how your app will work, which should suggest which Xcode project template to start with. Your app's design isn't a perfect fit with any of these, so choose the Single View Application template—it's the simplest template that already has a view. Click the Next button.

The next step is to fill in the details about your project (see Figure 2-3). Name the project Surrealists and fill in your organization name and identifier. Consistent with your design choices, change the Devices option from Universal to iPhone, as shown in Figure 2-3. The choice of language doesn't matter since, as I already mentioned, you won't be writing any code for this app.

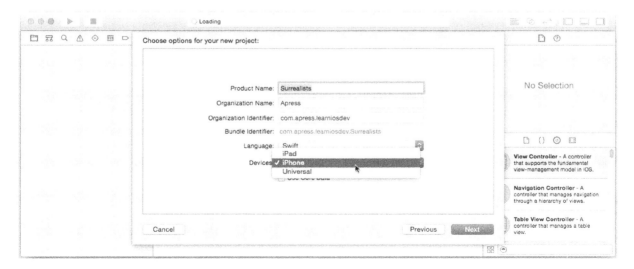

Figure 2-3. Setting the project details

> **Note**   Developing for the iPhone is the same as developing for the iPod Touch (unless your app uses features available only on the iPhone). From here on, I'll mention the iPhone only, but please remember that this also includes the iPod Touch.

Click the Next button. Pick a location on your hard drive to save the new project and click Create.

Setting Project Properties

You now have an empty Xcode project; it's time to start customizing it. Begin with the project settings by clicking the project name (Surrealists) in the project navigator, as shown in the upper left of Figure 2-4. The editor area will display all of the settings for this project. If your project's targets are collapsed, pick the Surrealist target from the pop-up menu, in the upper-left corner of the editor (see the left side of Figure 2-4). If your project's targets are expanded, simply select the target from the list, as shown in the middle of Figure 2-4. Once you've picked the target, select the General tab in the middle, as shown on the right in the same figure.

Figure 2-4. Target settings

Scroll down the target settings until you find the Deployment Info section. Uncheck the Landscape Left and Landscape Right boxes in Device Orientation so that only the Portrait orientation is checked.

To review, you've created an iPhone-only app project that runs exclusively in portrait orientation. You're now ready to design your interface.

Building an Interface

Click the `Main.storyboard` file in the project navigator. Xcode's Interface Builder editor appears in the edit area, as shown in Figure 2-5.

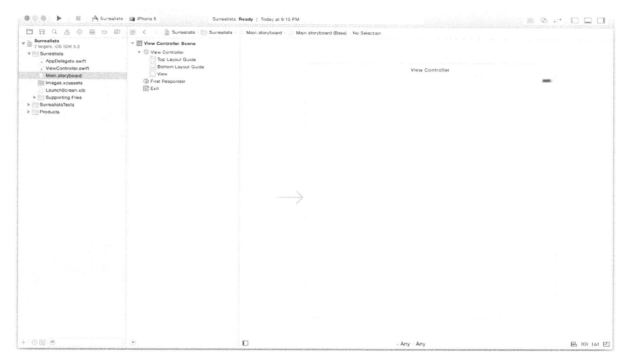

Figure 2-5. Interface Builder

Interface Builder is the secret sauce in Apple's app kitchen. In a nutshell, it's a tool that adds, configures, and interconnects objects within your app—without writing any code. You can define most of the visual elements of your app in Interface Builder. Interface Builder edits storyboard, xib, and (legacy) nib files.

> **Note**   Modern Interface Builder files have extensions of `.xib` or `.storyboard`. Legacy Interface Builder files have a `.nib` (pronounced "nib") extension, and you'll still hear programmers refer to all of them generically as "nib" files. The NIB acronym stands for Next Interface Builder because the roots of Xcode, Interface Builder, and the Cocoa Touch framework stretch all the way back to Steve Job's "other" company, NeXT. Later in this book, you'll see a lot of class names that begin with NS, which is an abbreviation for NeXTStep, the name of NeXT's operating system.

Interface Builder displays the objects in the file in two views. On the left (see Figure 2-5) are the objects organized into a hierarchical list, called the *outline*. Some objects can contain other objects, just as folders can contain other folders, and the outline reflects this. Use the disclosure triangles to reveal contained objects.

> **Tip**   The outline can be collapsed to a *dock* of just the top-level object icons. Click the expand button, in the lower left of the canvas pane (bottom center in Figure 2-5), to toggle between the two views.

The view on the right is called the *canvas*. Here you'll find the visual objects in your Interface Builder file. Only visual objects (such as buttons, labels, images, and so on) appear in the canvas. Objects that don't have a visual aspect will be listed only the outline. If an object appears in both, it doesn't matter which one you work with—they're the same object.

> **Note**   If you've been learning an object-oriented programming language, then you know what an object is. If you don't know what an object is, don't panic. For now, just think of objects as Lego bricks—a discrete bundle that performs a specific task in your app and can be connected to others to make something bigger. Feel free to skip ahead to Chapter 6 if you want to learn about objects right now.

Adding Objects

You get new objects from the library. Choose the View ➤ Utilities ➤ Show Object Library command. This will simultaneously make the utility area on the right visible and switch to the object library (the little round thing), like this:

To add an object to your app, drag it from the library and drop it into the Interface Builder editor. Your app needs a navigation controller object, so scroll down the list of objects until you find the Navigation Controller. You can simplify your search by entering a term (like *nav*) into the search field at the bottom of the library pane (see Figure 2-6).

Figure 2-6. *Adding a navigation controller*

Drag the navigation controller object from the library into the canvas, as shown in Figure 2-6, and drop it anywhere in the blank space. You just added an object—several, actually—to your app.

Deleting and Connecting Objects

The library's navigation controller object is really a cluster of objects. A navigation controller, as the name implies, manages how a user moves between multiple screens, each screen being controlled by a single view controller object. The navigation controller is connected to the view controller of the first screen that will appear, called its *root view controller*. Don't worry about the details; you'll learn more about navigation controllers in upcoming chapters.

For your convenience, the navigation controller in the library creates both a navigation controller object and the root view controller that it starts with. This root view controller happens to be a table view controller. This is a popular choice; navigation controllers and table views go together like bread and butter. Your project, however, doesn't need a table view controller. Instead, you want this navigation controller to use the no-frills view controller you already have.

Start by discarding the superfluous table view controller. Select just the table view controller that's connected to the navigation controller on the right, as shown in Figure 2-7. Press the Delete key, or choose Edit ➤ Delete.

Figure 2-7. *Deleting the table view controller*

Now you need to connect your new navigation controller to the plain-vanilla view controller your project came with. Drag the original view controller and position it to the right of the navigation controller (see Figure 2-8). I tend to lay out my storyboards so they progress from left to right, but you can organize them however you want.

Figure 2-8. Designating the initial view controller

The unconnected arrow attached to the view controller indicates the initial view controller for your app. You want to make the navigation controller the first controller, so drag the arrow away from the original view controller and drop it into the navigation view controller, as shown in Figure 2-8.

The last step is to reestablish the navigation controller's connection with its root view controller. There are numerous ways of making connections in Interface Builder. I'll show you the two most popular. Right-click the navigation controller (or hold down the Control key and click) and then drag a line from it to the view controller, as shown in Figure 2-9.

Figure 2-9. Setting the root view controller connection

When you release the mouse, a pop-up menu will appear listing all of the possible connections between these two objects. Click the root view controller connection. Now the navigation controller will present this view controller as the first screen when your app starts.

I did promise to teach you two ways of connecting objects. The second method is to use the connections inspector in the utility area. Choose View ➤ Utilities ➤ Show Connections Inspector, or click the little arrow icon in the utilities pane, as shown in Figure 2-10.

Figure 2-10. *Using the connections inspector*

To use the inspector, first choose an object. In this case, choose the navigation controller. The connections inspector will show all of the connections for that object. Find the connection labeled root view controller. To the right of each connection is a little circle. To set a connection, click and drag that circle to the object you want it connected to—in this case, the view controller. To clear (or "break") a connection, click the small *x* next to the connection.

So far, you've created a new project. The project template included a simple view controller. You added a new navigation controller object (along with an unneeded table view controller, which you discarded) to your app. You designated the navigation controller as the one that takes control of your app when it starts, and you connected that controller to the empty view controller. Now it's time to put something in that empty view.

Adding Views to a View

Now you get to the fun part of this project: creating your app's content. Start by adding four buttons, which you'll customize, to your opening screen. To do that, you need to work in your initial screen's view object.

The view controller object is not a single object; it's a bag of objects. I said earlier that some objects may contain other objects; view controllers and views are two such objects. Start by selecting the view object. There are two ways of doing this in Interface Builder. You can find the object in the outline on the left (see Figure 2-11) and select it. The other is to select the object directly in the canvas. Click in the center of the view controller (in the middle of Figure 2-11) to select its root view object—every view controller has a single root view object. You can confirm that you've selected the desired object in the outline.

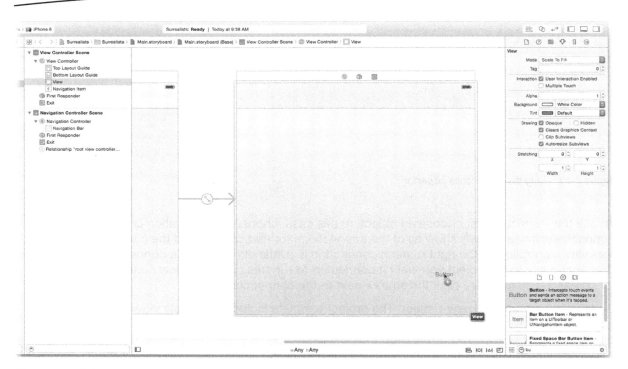

Figure 2-11. *Selecting the view object*

> **Tip** Some visual objects are nested. A toolbar, for example, is a view object that contains individual button items. "Drill down" to select a nested object, click once to select the outer object (the toolbar), and then click again to select the nested object (an individual button item in that toolbar). If you're unsure about what you're selecting, use the outline.

Now it's time to add some new view objects to your design. In the object library, find the Button object—type **bu** in the search field to make this easier. Grab a button object and drag it into the view object, as shown in Figure 2-11.

Repeat this three more times so you have four button objects inside the view, approximately like those shown in Figure 2-12. Now you want to resize these buttons so that each one approximately fills one-quarter of the screen. Figure 2-12 shows one button being resized—the background of the button was temporarily changed to gray so that it would be easier to see.

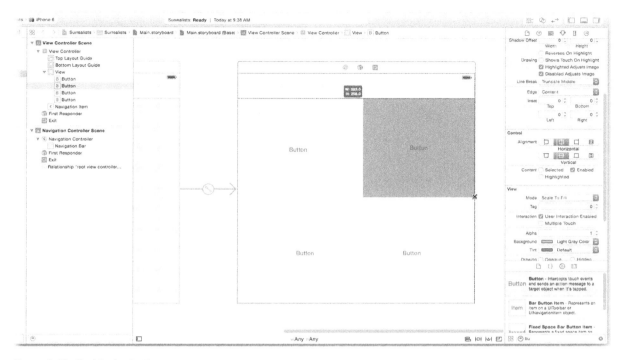

Figure 2-12. Positioning buttons

Editing Object Properties

Now it's time to customize your buttons. Select all four buttons—click one button and then, while holding down the Shift key, click once on each of the other three. Choose View ➤ Utilities ➤ Show Attributes Inspector, or click the small control icon in the inspector pane, as shown in Figure 2-13.

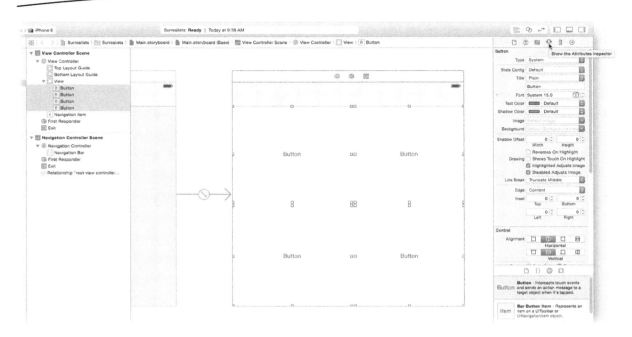

Figure 2-13. *Customizing button objects*

The attributes inspector is used to change various properties about an object (or objects). The properties in the inspector will change depending on what kind of object you have selected. If you select multiple objects, the inspector will present just those properties that all of those objects have in common.

With the four buttons selected, make the following changes using the attributes inspector:

- Change Type to Custom.

- Click the Font attribute and set it to System Bold 18.0.

- Click the Text Color pop-up menu and choose White Color.

- Find the Control group and select the bottom vertical alignment icon.

When you're all done, your view should look like the one in Figure 2-14. The next step is to add an image and a label to each one, individually. To do that, you're going to need to add some resources to your project.

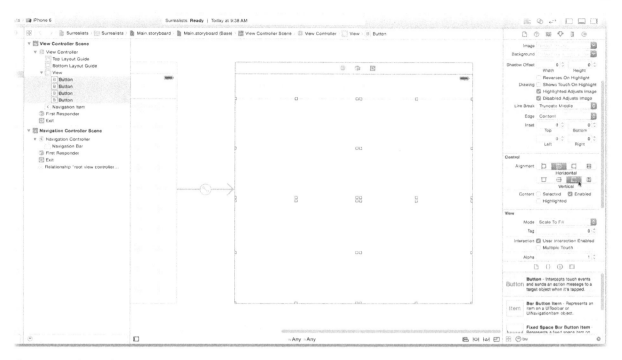

Figure 2-14. *Customized buttons*

Adding Resources

Everything that your app needs to run must be part of the app that you build. If your app needs an image, that image must be included in its resources. Image files, Interface Builder files, sound files, and anything else that's not computer code are collectively referred to as *resources*.

You can add virtually any file as a resource to your app. Resource files are copied into your app's *bundle* when it is built and are available to your app when it runs.

Xcode has a special way of organizing commonly used media resources, such as images, into a single resource called an *asset catalog*. To add new images to an asset catalog, select the catalog in the project navigator, as shown in Figure 2-15. Locate the resource files you want to add in the Finder. You'll find these in the Learn iOS Development Projects folder you downloaded in Chapter 1. Inside the Ch 2 folder you'll find the Surrealists (Resources) folder, which contains eight image files. With the files and your workspace window visible, drag the eight image files into the group list (left side) of the asset catalog, as shown in Figure 2-15.

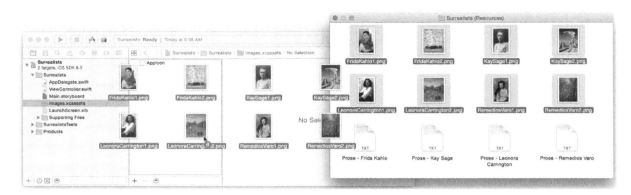

Figure 2-15. *Dragging resource files into an asset catalog*

The files will be copied to your project folder, added to the project navigator, and added to your app as a resource. Xcode can't edit these files, but the preview pane (see Figure 2-16) lets you review thumbnails of them.

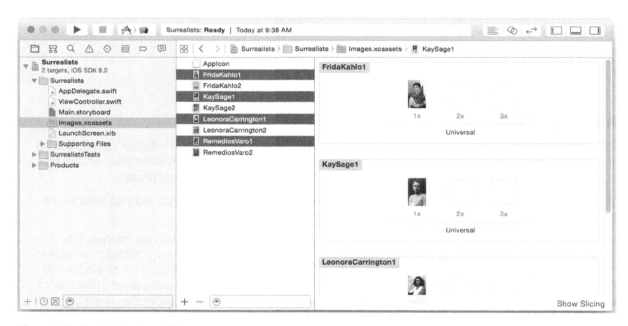

Figure 2-16. *Previewing image files*

THE RESOLUTION OF IMAGE ASSETS

Older iOS devices display one pixel per coordinate point of the interface. Newer iOS devices have Retina and Retina HD displays that have two or three pixels per coordinate point. To accommodate these higher-density displays, an assets catalog will organize multiple versions of each resource image.

In Figure 2-16, notice that each image has a 1x, 2x, and 3x version—the latter two being blank in this project. I supplied you only with 1x versions of these images, which is sufficient to get the app to work. Ideally, you should also include 2x and 3x versions of every asset image in your app so your app looks pin sharp on newer devices.

To add resolutions, simply prepare two more image files—one at exactly twice the resolution (pixel dimensions) and one at thrice the resolution. Drop these into the 2x and 3x image wells, respectively. The Cocoa Touch view classes work with the asset catalog to automatically load the version of the image that matches the resolution of the device your user is running. You don't even have to write any code.

Customizing Buttons

With the necessary resource files added, it's time to customize your buttons. Select the Main.storyboard file again and select the upper-left button. Reveal the attributes inspector (View ➤ Utilities ➤ Show Attributes Inspector) and change the title property to Remedios Varo and the background property to RemediosVaro1.png, as shown in Figure 2-17.

Figure 2-17. Customizing the first button

The background property is the resource name of the image you want the button to use for its background. You can type it in, but Xcode recognizes common image types and includes the image resources you just added to the drop-down list. Just select the filename from that list.

> **Note** The background image will look distorted in your layout. Don't worry about this; it will look OK in the running app. You'll understand why later.

Customize the remaining three buttons (working clockwise), setting their title and background image as follows:

- Kay Sage, `KaySage1.png`

- Leonora Carrington, `LeonoraCarrington1.png`

- Frida Kahlo, `FridaKahlo1.png`

As a finishing touch, select Kay Sage's button and change the Text Color to Black Color (so it's easier to read). When you're all done, your interface should look like Figure 2-18.

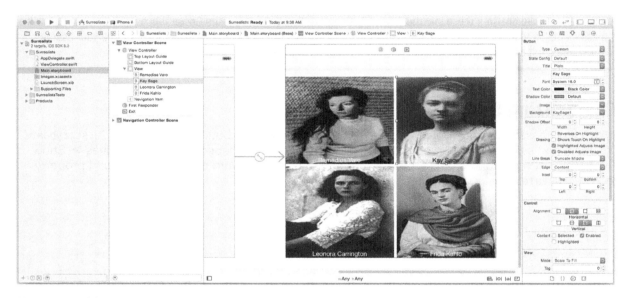

Figure 2-18. Finished buttons

Using Storyboards

Storyboards simplify your app development by allowing you to plan your app's screens and define how the user will navigate between them. Before storyboards, you could design your screens in Interface Builder, but each was in a separate file, and you had to write code to move between them. It wasn't a lot of code, and it wasn't complex, but it was a chore. With storyboards, you can see everything in one document and connect them—often without writing any code at all.

FRICTIONLESS DEVELOPMENT

Repetitive code is a drag on development. The time you spend writing the same code, over and over again, is time you don't have to develop cool new features. What you want is a *frictionless* development environment, where the simple tasks are taken care of for you, leaving you time to work on the stuff that makes your app special.

Apple works hard on making iOS and Xcode as frictionless as possible. Every release adds new classes and development tools to make developing high-quality apps easier. For example, before the introduction of gesture recognizers, writing code to detect multitouch gestures (such as a pinch or a three-fingered swipe) was a complicated task, often requiring a page or more of code. Today—as you might have guessed already—your app can detect these gestures simply by dropping a gesture recognizer object into your design and connecting it to an action.

Let's use storyboards to define the remaining screens of your app and how the user will navigate between them.

Adding New Scenes

Before you can create a transition between two screens, called a *segue* (pronounced "seg-way"), you must first create another view controller (called a *scene* in storyboard-speak). Return to the object library and drag in a new view controller object into your `Main.storyboard` file, as shown in Figure 2-19.

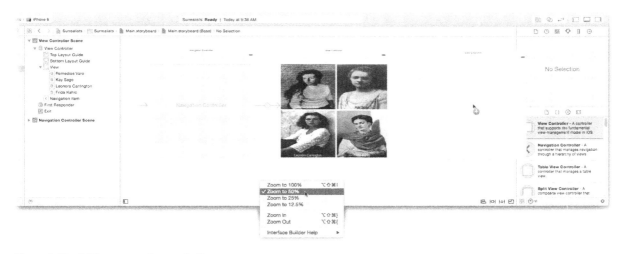

Figure 2-19. *Adding a new view controller*

> **Tip** Sometimes storyboards can be a little unwieldy, especially on smaller screens like a laptop. To get a bird's-eye view, zoom out by Control+clicking or right-clicking any blank portion of the Interface Builder canvas and choosing one of the zoom commands, as shown in Figure 2-19.

Locate the image view object in the library. Drag one into the empty view, as shown in Figure 2-20.

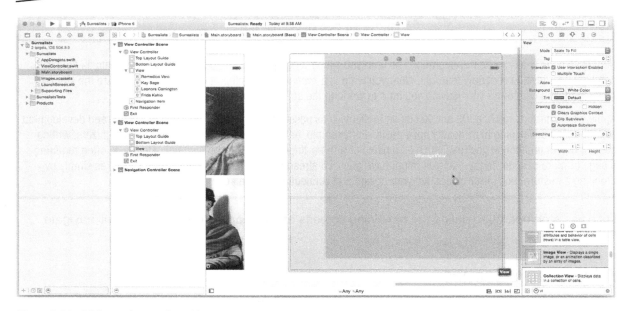

Figure 2-20. Adding an image view object

If the image view object didn't snap to fill the whole view, drag it around until it does. With the new image view object still selected, switch to the attributes inspector. Change the Image property to RemediosVaro2.png and change the image mode to Aspect Fill, as shown in Figure 2-21.

Figure 2-21. Customizing the image view

Now add a scrolling text field to this screen. Locate the text view (not the text field!) object in the library. Drag a new text view into the window and position it, using the automatic user interface guides, in the upper-right corner of the scene, as shown in Figure 2-22.

Figure 2-22. *Adding a text view*

With the text view selected, use the attributes inspector to change the following properties:

- Set text color to White Color.

- Reduce the font size to 12.0.

- Uncheck the Editable option.

- Further down, uncheck Shows Horizontal Indicator.

- Click the Background Color's color well (the sample color on the left side of the pop-up). This will reveal a color picker palette. Use the gray slider to choose 50 percent gray with a 33 percent alpha or opacity (see Figure 2-23).

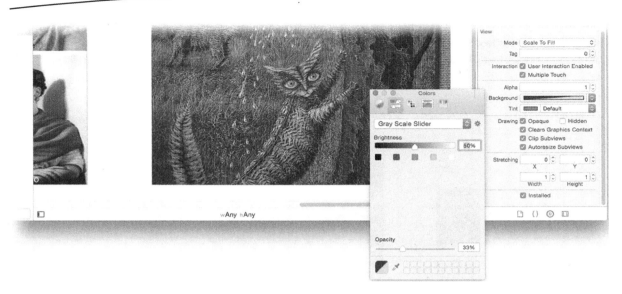

Figure 2-23. *Setting a semitransparent background color*

You can find the text for this object in the Surrealists (Resources) folder where you found the image files. You won't add these files to your project, however. Instead, open the file named Prose - Remedios Varo, copy the text, switch back to Xcode, and paste it into the object's Text property using the attributes inspector, as shown in Figure 2-24.

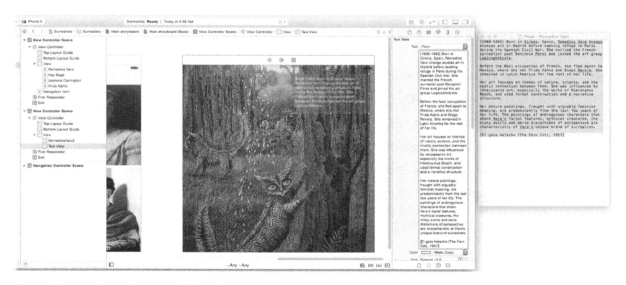

Figure 2-24. *Pasting text into a text field object*

Creating a Segue

With your initial scenes designed, it's time to define the segue between the main screen and this one. You want this screen to appear when the user taps the Remedios Varo button. To create this segue, Control+click or right-click the Remedios Varo button, drag the connection to this new view controller, and release the mouse, as shown in Figure 2-25.

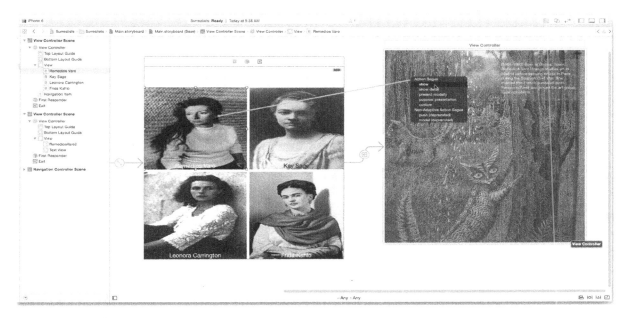

Figure 2-25. Creating a segue

When you release the mouse button, a pop-up menu will appear with the possible segue types. Choose show (see Figure 2-25). When your user taps the Remedios Varo button, your segue will perform a "show" transition. It works with the navigation controller to slide the new screen into view.

Setting Navigation Titles

The initial view controller is, itself, under the control of the navigation controller object you created at the beginning. The job of the navigation controller is to present a series of views underneath a *navigation bar*. The navigation bar—which you've seen a hundred times—displays the title of the screen you're looking at and optionally has a back button to return you to the screen you came from. The navigation controller handles all of the details.

When you added a show segue to the second screen, the second screen falls under the control of the navigation controller too. When a show segue is used with a navigation controller, it replaces one view with another and makes the original view the target of the back button in the new view. This is called a *push*.

So that this is meaningful to your user, you'll want to set the titles for each screen. This will make the navigation bar intelligible.

Select the navigation bar in the initial view controller and have the attributes inspector handy. Change the title of the navigation bar to Woman Surrealists and set the back button property to Surrealists. Most Interface Builder objects with a title can be edited simply by double-clicking the title in the canvas, as shown in Figure 2-26. Alternatively, you can select the object and edit its title property in the attributes inspector, also shown on the right of Figure 2-26. Setting the optional back button property will assign a more succinct title to the back button on screens that return to this one.

Figure 2-26. *Editing the navigation bar title*

Finally, select the view controller in the second scene and change its title to Remedios Varo, as shown in Figure 2-27.

Figure 2-27. *Setting the view controller's title*

Testing Your Interface

You've been very patient, but the moment of truth has finally arrived. You have now built enough of your app to see it in action! Make sure the run target is set to one of the iPhone simulators, as shown in Figure 2-28.

Figure 2-28. Selecting the run target

Click the Run button. Xcode will build your app and start it running in the simulator. If, for some unexpected reason, there are problems building your app, messages describing those problems can be found in the issue navigator (View ➤ Navigator ➤ Show Issue Navigator).

Your app will appear in the iPhone simulator and should look like the one on the left in Figure 2-29.

Figure 2-29. The first test of your app

Tap the button in the upper left, and the second screen slides smoothly into view. A navigation bar appears at the top with the name of the screen and a back button. Tap the back button to return to the initial screen. Your app has all of the standard behavior of an iOS app: a touch interface, title bars, animation, navigation, and everything works exactly as you expect it to. Well, not exactly.

Debugging Your App

You can run your app, and it—more or less—functions the way you designed it. But wow, does it look bad! The buttons on the first screen don't fit, and there are weird gaps between some of them. The second screen shows the painting, but the text view isn't anywhere to be seen. What's going on?

I hate to tell you this, but your app has bugs. A *bug* is usually used to describe a flaw in computer code, but any defect in how your app behaves or operates is a bug, and you need to fix it. The process of tracking down and fixing bugs is called *debugging*. In this case, the issue has to do with how your views are resized, or repositioned, for different devices. The problem is that your interface didn't adapt to the display size of the iPhone.

> **Note**   The term *bug* originated from a moth that expired in one of the earliest digital computers, causing it to malfunction. I'm not kidding. There's a picture of the moth on Grace Hopper's Wikipedia page (http://en.wikipedia.org/wiki/Grace_hopper).

iOS 8 introduces a new philosophy in interface design. Instead of designing your interface for specific devices, you design it once for a kind of "generic" device—the big square you've been working with in Interface Builder. This isn't intended to represent any particular device or any particular orientation. It's just a container you use to organize your views. When it comes time to present that view in your app, the view must be adapted to the actual device, screen size, resolution, and orientation. You haven't told iOS how to do that yet.

There are lots of ways of adapting an interface, and you'll explore most of them in later chapters, but the tool of choice is auto-layout. *Auto-layout* positions and resizes your view objects based on a set of constraints. A *constraint* is a rule describing some aspect of your view's geometry. A constraint can be as simple as "the height of this view is 20 points." Constraints can also be relative to other views, as in "the left edge of this view is exactly 8 points from the right edge of that button." Create the right set of constraints, and iOS can reorganize your views no matter how big, small, tall, or wide the user's device is.

Switch back to Xcode and select your `Main.storyboard` file. You'll add some constraints to your interface so they adapt to an iPhone's display.

Adding Basic Constraints

Even a "simple" interface, with only a few views, may require a dozen or more constraints to communicate your intent to auto-layout. Fortunately, Xcode provides lots of smart ways to add constraints and can often guess which ones you need, with some hints here and there.

Let's start with the image view object (the one with the cat painting) in your second view controller. When you dropped a new image view into your design, Xcode took a guess that you wanted it to fill the entire view, which was correct. You need four constraints to have that image view fill the entire interface no matter what size the device display size is.

- The top edge of the view must be at the same position as the top edge of its enclosing view.

- The left edge of the view must be at the same position as the left edge of its enclosing view.

- The right edge of the view must be at the same position as the right edge of its enclosing view.

- The bottom edge of the view must be at the same position as the bottom edge of its enclosing view.

The image view's enclosing view is the root view of the view controller. (You can see this relationship in the Interface Builder outline.) This root view is always the size of the display area for the view controller. You can't change that, even if you try. The root view's size becomes the first set of constants from which you can build constraints. When you give auto-layout a constraint that says "the top edge of the image view must be at the same position as the top edge of its superview," it will move the position of the top edge of the image view to the top of the display. That's its only choice; the superview is immovable, so moving the image view is the only solution. With all four constraints, the image view will always be the exact size of its superview.

At the bottom right of the canvas area you'll find four controls (also shown in Figure 2-30). They are, from left to right, as follows:

- Alignment constraints

- Pin constraints

- Resolve auto-layout issues

- Reposition constraint preferences

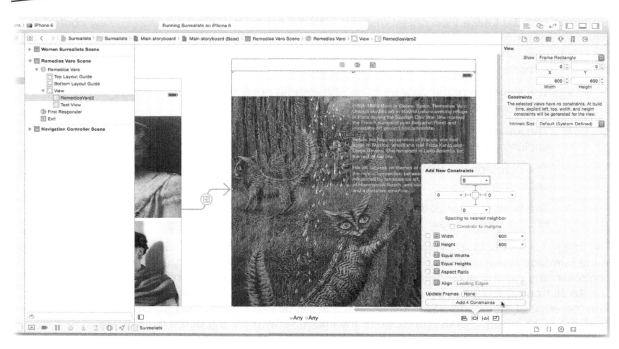

Figure 2-30. *Adding edge constraints to the image view*

With the image view selected, click the pin constraints control (second from the left). The pin constraints control lets you add common constraints that express either a fixed dimension or a fixed distance to another view. In the pop-up panel (see Figure 2-30) start by unchecking the Constrain to margins option. The margins are for content that's inset from the edge, and that's not the case here. Click the struts to add top, left, right, and bottom distance constraints, all set to 0 (also shown in Figure 2-30). If any default value is not 0, change it so it is. Click the Add 4 Constraints button.

With the image still selected, reveal the size inspector in the utility area (View ➤ Utilities ➤ Show Size Inspector). The size inspector displays all of the constraints that relate to this view. As you see, Xcode has added four new constraints: Top Space to, Leading Space to, Trailing Space to, and Bottom Space to. These are the four constraints listed earlier. Congratulations, you're done with the constraints for the image view.

> **Note**   The left and right edges of a view can also be referred to as the *leading* and *trailing* edges. When your user's language is one that reads from left to right (such as English), the leading edge is the left edge. If your user's language reads from right to left (such as Hebrew), the leading edge is the right edge. This allows constraints to reverse the layout and alignment of your views for right-to-left readers. Xcode prefers to create leading/trailing constraints, but you can change them to right/left edge constraints if your layout should not be transposed for right-to-left languages.

Adding Missing Constraints

Now try a slightly different set of constraints. Drag the text view down a little and position it so it "snaps" to the human interface guidelines close to the right edge and just below the placeholder for the navigation bar at the top, as shown in Figure 2-31.

Figure 2-31. *Repositioning text view*

> **Tip**   When adding constraints, I recommend placing your views as close to their ultimate layout as you can. Xcode makes it easy to define constraints for relationships that already exist in your design.

With the text view still selected, choose the pin constraints control (second from the left) again. This time add a height of 270 points and a width constraint of 230 points, as shown on the left in Figure 2-32. Click the Add 2 Constraints button.

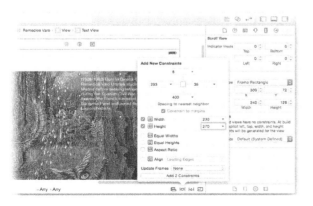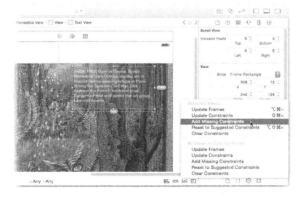

Figure 2-32. *Adding size constraints*

With the text view still selected, choose the resolve auto-layout issues control (third button from the left) and choose the Add Missing Constraints command, as shown on the right in Figure 2-32. Xcode can often infer what constraints your views needs if you first position it where they should be in the layout. By positioning the text view using the top and right layout guides, Xcode guessed (correctly) that you would like top and trailing edge constraints attached to the top layout guide and right margin. If your layout is obvious, the Add Missing Constraints command will save you a lot of time.

The layout objects are special view objects just to assist constraints. Each represent the position where the usable content of your view begins. Some visual elements are outside your view controller, like the status bar that's normally at the top of the iPhone's screen. Some visual elements, however, are inserted into your view, like the navigation bar that will be added by the navigation controller when your view is presented. In those cases, the top and bottom layout guides move to accommodate the new elements. Making your view relative to these guides keeps them visible and neatly positioned.

> **Tip**   If you have a view that disappears underneath a navigation or search bar, make sure you're aligning to the top layout guide and not the edge of another view.

Editing Constraint Objects

Now take a moment to see how your design has changed, as shown in Figure 2-33. Constraints are objects, and they appear several different ways in Interface Builder. Select a view and the constraints associated with that view appear in both the size inspector (on the right in Figure 2-33) and the canvas. Distance and size constraints appear as struts, while alignment and zero-length distance constraints show up as straight lines.

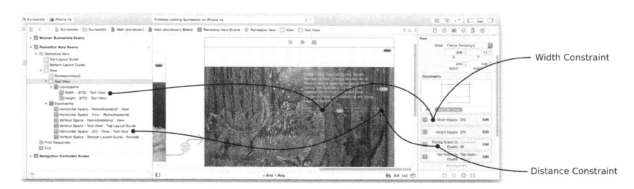

Figure 2-33. Examining view constraints

You can select a constraint in the canvas—although this can require a steady mouse hand because they can be very small. Constraint objects can also be selected in the outline (shown on the left in Figure 2-33). Edit the selected constraint with the attributes inspector or find the constraint in the size inspector and click its edit button.

Some constraints in your design appear orange and have a number attached to them. Xcode is telling you that the size or position of the object in your design doesn't agree with the constraints. The number tells you how many points Xcode would like to adjust your view so it agrees. Specifically, you added a 270-point width constraint to the text view, but the text view in the canvas isn't 270 points wide. When you run your app, that text view *will* be 270 points wide because that's what the constraint demands. If you want to see your text view the same size in your design too, choose the Update Frames command from the resolve auto-layout issues control, as shown in Figure 2-34. These warnings are purely informational—ignoring them won't change how your app runs.

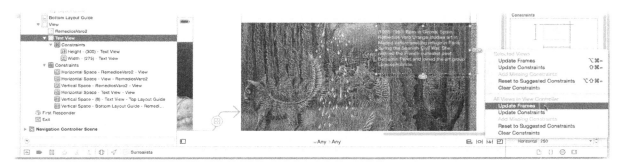

Figure 2-34. *Updating frames to match their constraints*

Note   If you have insufficient or conflicting constraints, these will appear (in red) in the object outline.

Let's try the constraints you've added so far. Run your app again, as shown in Figure 2-35, using the iPhone 6 simulator. The initial screen is still ugly—no surprise there. Tap the Remedios Varo button. This time, you have an attractive and usable interface, as shown in the middle of Figure 2-35.

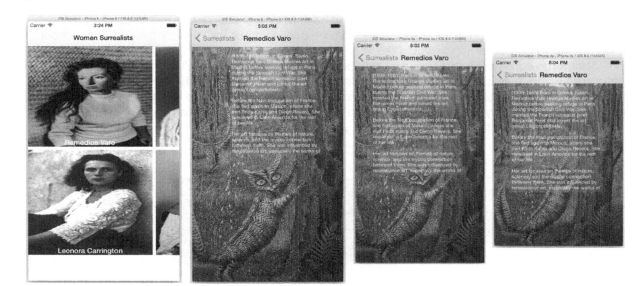

Figure 2-35. *Testing constraints*

More importantly, if you run your app again using the iPhone 5s and iPhone 4s simulators, your interface looks OK on those devices as well, as shown on the right in Figure 2-35. Now let's fix those buttons.

Adding Relationship Constraints

The buttons present a little more of a challenge. You want to them fill the interface, and you want them to tile evenly. Filling the interface sounds a lot like the constraints you just added to the image view. And a few distance constraints between their inner edges should cause them to be flush and tile. That sounds like a plan.

Luckily, you can create all of these constraints in a single step. You essentially want the same constraints for all four buttons: the top, left, right, and bottom edges should touch the closest view or interface edge. Select all four button and click the pin constraints control, as shown in Figure 2-36.

Figure 2-36. *Pinning the buttons*

Again, uncheck the Constrain to Margins option. Click the struts to add top, left, right, and bottom distance constraints to all four views. Edit the distances so that all four are 0, as shown in Figure 2-36. Click the Add 14 Constraints button.

Voilà! You're done, right? Try selecting the Update Frames command from the resolve auto-layout issues control. You'll probably get something that looks like Figure 2-37.

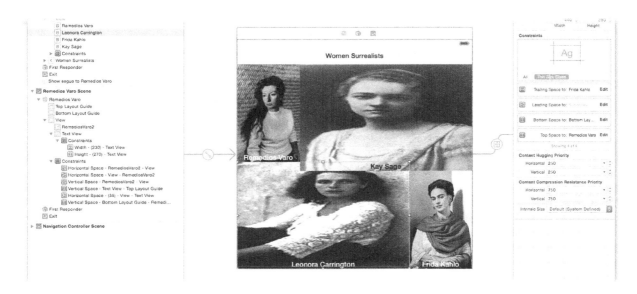

Figure 2-37. *An unacceptable layout solution*

Hilariously, the layout in Figure 2-37 satisfies all of the constraints but is clearly not what you want. You'll need more, or different, constraints to get the desired geometry. Thinking about the problem, you want all four buttons to be the same size—and there's a constraint for that.

Select the top two buttons and click the pin constraints control again. With multiple views selected, the Equal Widths constraint is available, as shown in Figure 2-38. Check the Equal Widths constraint and click the Add 1 Constraints button. You've now added a constraint that tells auto-layout that the width of these two view should be the same, whatever that is.

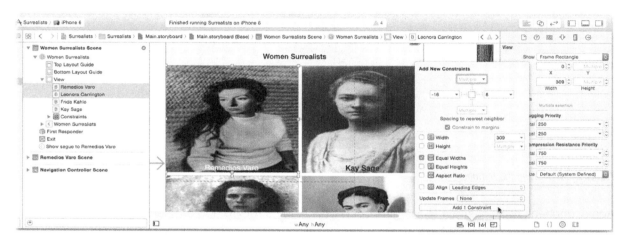

Figure 2-38. Adding an equal widths constraint

Now repeat with the bottom two buttons. Continuing the pattern, select the left two buttons and add an equal heights constraint. Repeat with the right two buttons.

Run your app again. Now things are looking like they should, as shown in Figure 2-39. Even on different devices, the buttons align and size to the available display.

Figure 2-39. *Tiled buttons using constraints*

This isn't the only solution to this problem. In fact, I can think of at least five different sets of constraints that would achieve the same layout. Like programming, that there is no single set of constraints that's "correct." Some constraint sets might be more elegant than others, but in the end either they work or they don't. But enough about constraints, let's wrap this app up.

Finishing Your App

Return to the Xcode workspace window and click the Stop button in the toolbar to stop your app. You could finish you app by repeating the steps in the "Adding New Scenes" section for each of the other three artist. But that sounds too much like work to me.

Select the view controller for Remedios Varo and copy it the clipboard, as shown in Figure 2-40. Click a blank portion of the canvas (to unselect any object) and paste in three more copies of the view controller. Arrange them so they don't overlap.

Figure 2-40. Copying the first view controller

Everything in the view controller has been duplicated. What didn't get duplicated are objects and segues outside the view controller. Create three more segues by Control+clicking or right-clicking the other buttons and connecting each to one of the new view controllers, as shown in Figure 2-41. Choose the show segue, as before.

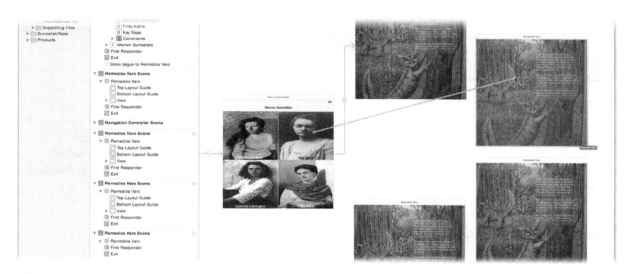

Figure 2-41. Connecting buttons to new view controllers

Now edit the contents of the new controllers with the information about the artist it's connected to. Start with the scene connected to the Key Sage button. Edit its content as follows:

1. Select the image view and change its Image property to KeySage2.

2. Locate the `Prose - Kay Sage` text file and copy the text into the text view object.

3. Select the view controller object and change its title to Kay Sage.

Repeat with the remaining two view controllers, using the image, text, and title appropriate to the button it's connected to. When you're done, your design should look like Figure 2-42.

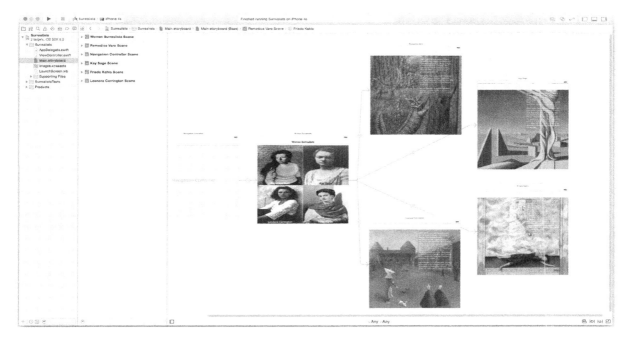

Figure 2-42. *Finished app design*

Now run your app and make sure everything works, as shown in Figure 2-43.

Figure 2-43. *The working Surrealist app*

This is a pretty simple app, but there are still a number of things you'll want to test before pronouncing it finished.

- See that the layout of all screens looks pleasing on different devices.
- Make sure each button segues to the correct screen.
- Test that the text is correct and can be scrolled.
- Check all of the titles.

Does everything check out? Then your first iOS app is a success!

Summary

Give yourself a round of applause; you've covered a lot of ground in this chapter. You learned your way around Xcode, added resources to a project, and used Interface Builder to create, configure, and connect the objects of your interface; you also learned a lot about auto-layout constraints. Amazingly, you did that all without writing a single line of computer code.

The point of this chapter wasn't to avoid writing Swift code. We are, after all, computer programmers. If we're not writing code, what are we getting paid for? The point was to illustrate how much functionality you can add, and how much tedious detail you can avoid, using Interface Builder and iOS objects.

Are your coding fingers itchy? In the next chapter you'll write a more traditional app—one with code.

Chapter 3

Spin a Web

Warm up your coding fingers. This chapter will introduce you to some of the core skills of iOS app development, along with a healthy dose of Swift code. The app you'll create in this chapter and the steps you'll take are typical of the way iOS apps are built. From that perspective, this will be your first "real" iOS app.

You've already learned to use Interface Builder to add library objects to your app, customize them, and connect them. In this chapter, you will do the following:

- Customize a Swift class
- Add outlets and actions to your custom class using Swift
- Connect those outlets to objects using Interface Builder
- Connect objects to your custom actions using Interface Builder
- Alter the behavior of a library object by connecting it to a delegate

The app you're going to build is a URL shortening app. This app relies on one of the many URL shortening services available. These services take a URL of any length and generate a much shorter URL, which is far more convenient to read, recite over the phone, or use in a tweet. A URL shortening service works by remembering the original URL. When anyone in the world attempts to load the web page at the short URL, the service returns a *redirect* response, directing the browser to the original URL.

To make this app, you'll learn how to embed a web browser in it—a trick that has many uses. It will also show you how to programmatically send and receive an HTTP request from your app, a useful tool for creating apps that use Internet services.

> **Note**   To computer programmers, the word *programmatically* means "by writing computer code." It means you accomplished something by writing instructions in a computer language, such as Swift, as opposed to any other way. As an example, Interface Builder will let you connect two objects by dragging a line between those objects. You can write Swift code to connect those same two objects. If you used the latter method, you could say that you "set the connection programmatically."

Design

This app needs some basic elements. The user will need a field to type in and edit a URL. It would be nice to have a built-in web browser so they can see the page at that URL and tap links to go to other URLs. It needs a button to convert the long URL into a short one and some place to display the shortened URL.

That's not a particularly complicated design, and everything should easily fit on one screen, like the sketch in Figure 3-1. Let's toss in one extra feature: a button to copy the shortened URL to the iOS clipboard. Now the user has an easy way to paste the shortened URL into another app.

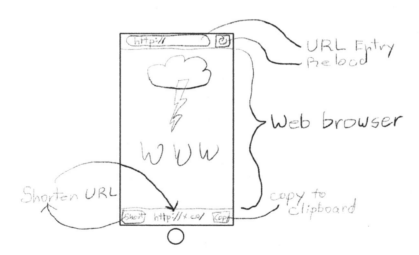

Figure 3-1. Sketch of Shorty app

Your app will run on all iOS devices and work in both portrait and landscape orientations. Now that you have a basic design, it's time to launch Xcode and get started.

Creating the Project

As with any app, start by creating a new project in Xcode. This is a one-screen app, so the obvious choice is the Single View Application template.

Fill in the project details, as shown in Figure 3-2. Name the project Shorty, set the language to Swift, and choose Universal for devices.

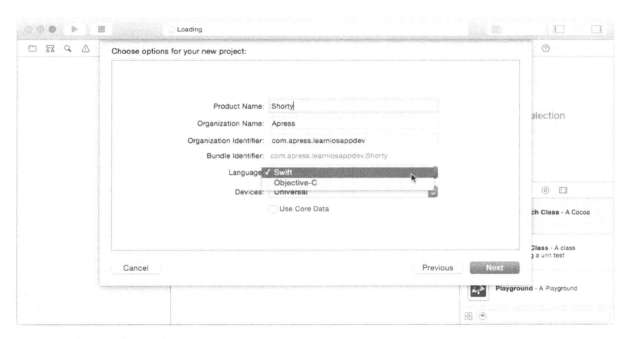

Figure 3-2. Shorty project details

Click the Next button. Choose a location to save your new project and click Save.

Building a Web Browser

Start by building the web browser portion of your app. This will consist of a text field, where the user enters the URL they want to visit/convert, and a web view that will display that page. Let's also throw in a refresh button to reload that page at the current URL.

Select the `Main.storyboard` file in the navigator. In the object library, find the navigation bar object and drag it into the view, toward the top, as shown in Figure 3-3. Navigation bar objects are normally created by navigation controllers to display a title, a back button, and so on. You saw this in the Surrealist app. Here, however, you're going to use one on its own.

Figure 3-3. *Adding a navigation bar*

Position the navigation bar so it's the full width of the view. Make sure it's still selected and click the pin constraints control (the second of four) in the lower-right corner of the canvas. In the pin constraints pop-up, click to set the top, left, and right edge constraints, as shown in Figure 3-4.

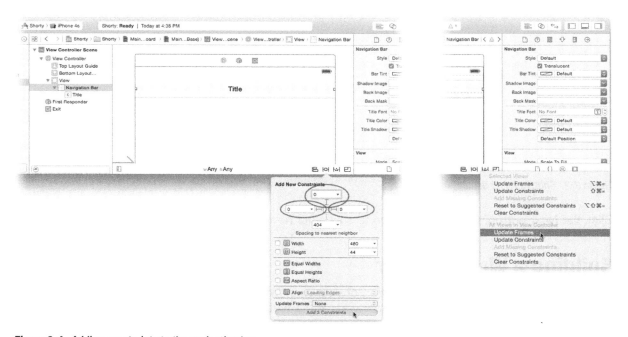

Figure 3-4. *Adding constraints to the navigation bar*

Make sure the value for all three constraints is 0. This tells iOS to position the navigation bar at the recommended spot at the top of the screen, just below the system's status bar, and it will be the full width of the display. Click the Add 3 Constraints button. Click the Resolve Auto Layout Issues control (the third of four), as shown on the right in Figure 3-4, and choose the Update Frames command. This will reposition the view in Interface Builder based on the constraints you just set.

Now add the web view. Find the Web View object in the library and drag one into the lower portion of the screen. Move and resize the web view so it exactly fills the rest of the view, from the navigation bar to the bottom of the screen, as shown in Figure 3-5.

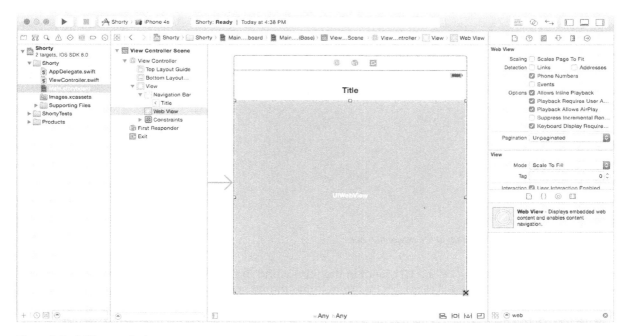

Figure 3-5. Adding a web view

Click the Resolve Auto Layout Issues control again, but this time choose Add Missing Constraints in View Controller. Interface Builder uses the constraints you've already established and fills in any additional constraints needed to establish this layout for all devices.

Find the bar button item object in the library and drag one into the right side of the navigation bar, as shown in Figure 3-6. Bar button items are button objects specifically designed to be placed in a navigation bar or toolbar.

Figure 3-6. Adding a button to the navigation bar

Once there, select it. Switch to the attributes inspector and change the Identifier setting of the new button to Refresh (see Figure 3-7). The icon of the button will change to a circular arrow.

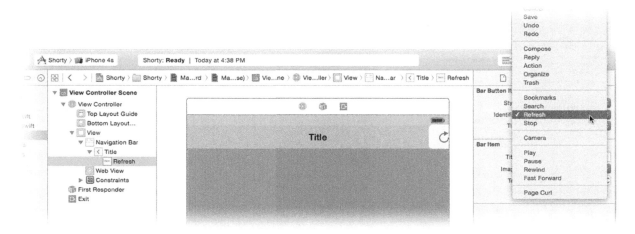

Figure 3-7. *Making a refresh button in the navigation bar*

Find the text field (not the text view!) object in the library and drag one into the middle of the navigation bar. This object will displace the default title that is normally displayed. Grab the resize handle on the right or left and stretch the field so it fills most of the free space in the navigation bar, as shown in Figure 3-8.

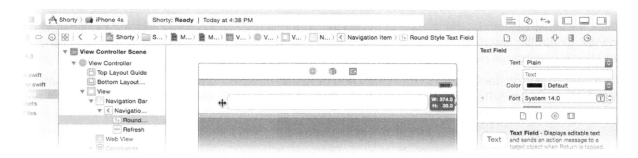

Figure 3-8. *Resizing the URL field*

The user will type their URL into this field. Configure it so it is optimized for entering and editing URLs. Select the new text field object and, using the attributes inspector, change the following properties:

- Set text to http://.
- Set Placeholder Text to http://.
- Change Clear Button to Appears while editing.

- Change Correction to No.

- Change Keyboard Type to URL.

- Change Return Key to Go.

These settings set the initial content of the field to `http://` (so the user doesn't have to type that), and if they clear the field, a ghostly `http://` will prompt them to enter a web URL. Turning spelling correction off is appropriate (URLs are not a spoken language). When the keyboard appears, it will be optimized for URL entry, and the Return key on the keyboard will display the word *Go*, indicating that the URL will load when they tap it.

You've created and laid out all of the visual elements of your web browser. Now you need to write a little code to connect those pieces and make them work together.

Coding a Web Browser

Select the `ViewController.swift` file in the project navigator (see Figure 3-9). This file defines your `ViewController` class. This is a custom class, which you created—well, technically, it was created on your behalf by the project template, but you can take credit for it. I won't tell anyone. The job of your `ViewController` object is to add functionality to and manage the interactions of the view objects it's connected to. Your app has only one view, so you need only one view controller.

Figure 3-9. Adding properties to ViewController.swift

Different objects have different roles to play in your app. These roles are explained in Chapter 8. When you add code to your app, you need to decide what class to add it to. This app is simple; you'll add all of your customizations to the ViewController class.

> **Tip**   Are the terms *class* and *object* confusing? Read the first part of Chapter 6 for an explanation.

Your ViewController class is a subclass of the UIViewController class, which is defined by the Cocoa Touch framework. This means your ViewController class inherits all of the features and behavior of a UIViewController—which is a lot because UIViewController is quite sophisticated. If you did nothing else, your ViewController objects would behave exactly like any other UIViewController object.

The fun is in editing ViewController.swift to add new features or change the behavior it inherited.

Adding Outlets to ViewController

Start by adding two new properties to ViewController. A *property* defines a value associated with an object. In its simplest form, it merely creates a new variable that the object will remember. Add these properties to ViewController.swift (new code in bold):

```
class ViewController: UIViewController {
    @IBOutlet var urlField: UITextField!
    @IBOutlet var webView: UIWebView!
```

When you're done, your class definition should look like the one in Figure 3-9. So, what does all this mean? Let's examine these declarations in detail:

- @IBOutlet is an important keyword that makes this property appear as an *outlet* in Interface Builder.

- var defines a *var*iable property.

- urlField/webView is the *name* of the property.

- UITextField/UIWebView is the *type* of the property. In this case, it's the class of the object this property stores.

- The ! means it's an optional variable, but it is assumed to contain a valid object reference. Optionals are explained in Chapter 20.

By adding these properties to ViewController, you enable any ViewController object to be directly connected to one text field object (via its urlField property) and one web view object (via its webView property).

You've defined the potential for being connected to two other objects, but you haven't connected them. For that, you'll use Interface Builder.

Connecting Custom Outlets

Click the `Main.storyboard` file in the project navigator. Find and select the view controller object in the outline or in the dock above the view, both shown in Figure 3-10.

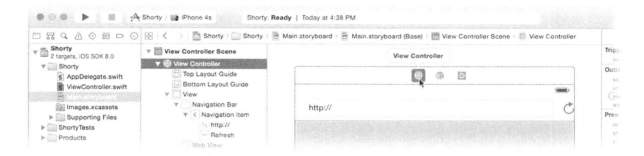

Figure 3-10. *Selecting the view controller object for a scene*

In most cases, a screen in iOS is defined by a single view controller object and a collection of view objects. When it's time to display that screen, iOS reads the information from the `.storyboard` file and uses that to construct new instances of all the objects in that scene. In addition to creating the objects, it also connects the objects, using the outlets and connections you set. When it's done, your view controller and all of its view objects will have been created, initialized, and connected.

> **Note** Don't worry if you don't get this concept right away. Interface Builder is elegant and simple, but it takes most people a while to fully grasp how it works. Check out Chapter 15 for an in-depth explanation of how Interface Builder works its magic.

So far, you've added the objects to the scene, but you've yet to connect them. Do that now. Select the view controller object and show the connections inspector. In it, you'll see the `urlField` and `webView` properties you just added to `ViewController.swift`. These appear in Interface Builder because you included the `@IBOutlet` keyword in your property declarations.

Drag the connection circle to the right of `urlField` and connect it to the text field in the navigation bar, as shown in Figure 3-11. Now, when the `ViewController` scene is loaded, the `urlField` property of your view controller object will refer to the text field in your interface. Pretty cool, huh?

Figure 3-11. *Connecting an outlet to an object*

Another handy way of setting connections is to Control+drag or right-click+drag from the object with the connection to the object you want it connected to. Holding down the Control key, click the view controller object (either in the sidebar or at the top of the scene) and drag down to the web view object, as shown in Figure 3-12.

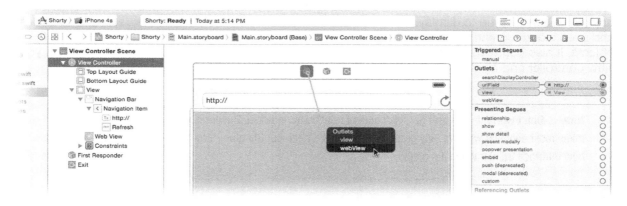

Figure 3-12. *Connecting the web view outlet*

When you release the mouse button, a pop-up menu will appear asking you to choose which outlet to set. Choose webView.

Adding Actions to ViewController

Why did you do all of this (creating outlets and connecting them in Interface Builder)? Your controller object needs to get the value of the URL typed by the user and communicate that to the web view object so the web view knows what URL to load. Your view controller object is acting as a liaison or manager, getting data from one object (the text field) and assigning tasks to another (the web view). Do you see now why it's called a *controller*?

It's a simple task, but there has to be some code that will make it happen. Select the ViewController.swift file in the project navigator. After the existing functions included by the project template and just before the closing } of the class declaration, add this new function:

```
func loadLocation( AnyObject ) {
    var urlText = urlField.text

    if !urlText.hasPrefix("http:") && !urlText.hasPrefix("https:") {
        if !urlText.hasPrefix("//") {
            urlText = "//" + urlText
        }
        urlText = "http:" + urlText
    }

    let url = NSURL(string: urlText)
    webView.loadRequest(NSURLRequest(URL: url))
}
```

This function does one simple task: it loads the web page at the URL entered by the user. This will require three basic steps.

1. Get the string of characters the user typed into the text field.

2. Convert that string of characters into a URL object.

3. Request that the web view object load the page at that URL.

Here's the breakdown of this code:

```
var urlText = urlField.text
```

The first line declares a new string object variable, named urlText, and assigns it the value of the text property of the urlField property of this object. The urlField property is the one you just added to this class. Your urlField refers to the UITextField object in your interface because you connected it in Interface Builder. A UITextField object has a text property that contains the characters currently in the field—either ones the user typed or those you put there programmatically. (See, I used the word *programmatically* again).

Tip   To see the documentation for any class or constant, hold down the Option key and single-click (quick view) or double-click (full documentation) its name. To see the properties and functions of the UITextField class, hold down the Option key and double-click the word UITextField in the .swift file.

The first part of your task is already accomplished; you've retrieved the text of the URL using the `urlField` property you defined and connected. The next few lines might look a little strange.

```
if !urlText.hasPrefix("http:") && !urlText.hasPrefix("https:") {
    if !urlText.hasPrefix("//") {
        urlText = "//" + urlText
    }
    urlText = "http:" + urlText
}
```

If you're comfortable with Swift, take a close look at this code. It isn't critical to your app; you could leave it out, and your app would still work. It does, however, perform a kindness for your users. It checks to see whether the string the user typed starts with `http://` or `https://`, the standard protocols for a web page. If these standard URL elements are missing, this code inserts one automatically.

Computers tend to be literal, but you want your app to be forgiving and friendly. The previous code allows the user the type in just www.apple.com (for example), instead of the correct http://www.apple.com, and the page will still load. Does that make sense? Let's move on.

Object-oriented programming is all about encapsulating the complexity of things in objects. While a string object can represent the characters of a URL, it's still just a string (an array of characters). Most functions that work with URLs expect a URL object. In Cocoa Touch, the class of URL objects is `NSURL`. How do you turn the `String` you got from the text field into an `NSURL` you can use with the web view? I thought you'd never ask.

```
let url = NSURL(string: urlText)
```

This line of code creates a new URL object from a string object. In Swift, you create a new object using the class of the object (`NSURL`) followed by a set of parentheses (`()`), just as if you were calling a function. This creates a new instance of the class and executes its initializer. A class can declare a variety of ways in which it can be created, and the `NSURL` class provides an initializer that creates an `NSURL` object directly from a `String` object. As you can see, it's pretty easy to convert a string object into a URL object, and there are functions that convert the other way too, which you'll use later in this chapter.

With the second step accomplished, the last thing left to do is display the web page at that URL in the web view. That's accomplished with the last line in your function.

```
webView.loadRequest(NSURLRequest(URL: url))
```

`webView` is the `webView` property you created earlier, and it's connected to the web view object on the screen. You call that object's `loadRequest()` function to load the page. It turns out, however, that a web view needs a URL request (`NSURLRequest`) object, not just a simple URL object. A URL request not only represents a URL but also describes how that URL should be transmitted over the network. For your purposes, a plain-vanilla HTTP GET request is all you need, and the expression `NSURLRequest(URL:url)` creates a new `NSURLRequest` object from the given URL, which you pass on to `loadRequest(_:)`. The rest of the work is done by the web view.

Setting Action Connections

Let's review what you've accomplished so far.

- You created a text field object where the user can type in a URL.
- You created a web view object that will display the web page at that URL.
- You added two outlets (properties) to your ViewController class.
- You connected the text field and web view objects to those outlets.
- You wrote a loadLocation(_:) function that takes the URL in the text view and loads it in the web view.

What's missing? The question is "How does the loadLocation(_:) function get called?" That's a really important question, and, at the moment, the answer is "never." The next, and final, step is to connect the loadLocation(_:) function to something so it runs and loads the web page.

Start by adding the @IBAction keyword to your function. In your ViewController.swift file, locate the func loadLocation() declaration and edit it so it looks like this:

```
@IBAction func loadLocation( AnyObject ) {
```

The @IBAction keyword tells Interface Builder that this function can be called by an interface object, just as the @IBOutlet keyword told Interface Builder that the property could refer to an interface object. A function that can be invoked by objects (such as buttons and text fields) in your interface is called an *action*.

Select the Main.storyboard file again. Select the text field object and switch to the connections inspector. Scroll down until you find Did End On Exit in the Sent Events section. Drag the connection circle to the View Controller object and release the mouse, as shown in Figure 3-13. A pop-up menu will ask you what action you want this event connected to; choose loadLocation: (which is currently the only action).

Figure 3-13. Setting the Did End On Exit action connection

You also want the web page loaded when the user taps the refresh button, so connect the refresh button to the same action. The refresh button is simpler than the text field and sends only one kind of event ("I was tapped"). Use an Interface Builder shortcut to connect it. Hold down the Control key, click the refresh button, and drag the connection to the View Controller object. Release the mouse button and select the loadLocation: sent action, as shown in Figure 3-14.

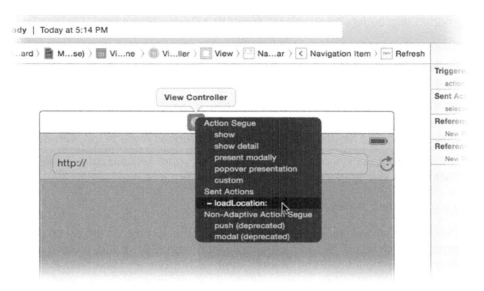

Figure 3-14. Setting the action for the refresh button

Testing the Web Browser

Are you excited? You should be. You just wrote a web browser app for iOS! Make sure the build destination is set to an iPhone simulator (see Figure 3-15) and click the Run button.

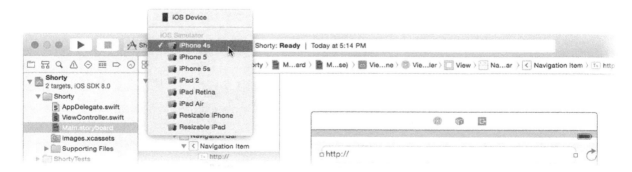

Figure 3-15. Setting the iPhone simulator destination

Your app will build and launch in the iPhone simulator, as shown on the left in Figure 3-16. Tap the text field, and a URL-optimized keyboard appears. Tap out a URL (I'm using `www.apple.com` for this example) and tap the Go button. The keyboard retracts, and Apple's home page appears in the web view. That's pretty darn nifty.

Figure 3-16. *Testing your web browser*

So, how does it work? The text field object fires a variety of events, depending on what's happening to it. You connected the `Did End On Exit` event to your `loadLocation(_:)` function. This event is sent when the user "ends" editing by tapping the action button in the keyboard (Go). When you ran the app and tapped Go, the text field triggered its `Did End On Exit` event, which called your `ViewController`'s `loadLocation(_:)` function. Your function got the URL the user typed in and told the web view to load it. *Voilá*! The web page appears.

> **Note**   The iOS simulator uses your computer's Internet connection to emulate the device's Wi-Fi or cellular data connection. If you're working through this chapter on a desert island, your app might not work.

Debugging the Web View

What you've developed so far is pretty impressive. Go ahead—try any web page, I'll wait. Only two things about it bother me. First, when you tap a link in the page, the URL in the text field doesn't change. Second, the web pages are crazy big.

The second problem is easy to fix. Quit the simulator or switch back to Xcode and click the Stop button in the toolbar. Select the web view object in the Main.storyboard file and switch to the attributes inspector, as shown in Figure 3-17. Find and check the Scale Page to Fit option. Now, when the web view loads a page, it will zoom the page so you can see the whole thing.

Figure 3-17. Setting the Scale Page to Fit property

The first problem is a little trickier to solve and requires some more code. I'll address that one as you add the rest of the functionality to your app.

Adding URL Shortening

You now have an app that lets you enter a URL and browse that URL in a web browser. The next step, and the whole purpose of this app, is to convert the long URL of that page into a short one.

To accomplish that, you'll create and lay out new visual objects in Interface Builder, create outlets and actions in your controller class, and connect those outlets and actions to the visual object, just as you did in the first part of this chapter. If you haven't guessed by now, this is the fundamental app development workflow: design an interface, write code, and connect the two.

Start by fleshing out the rest of the interface. Edit Main.storyboard, select the web view object, grab its bottom resizing handle, and drag it up to make room for some new view objects at the bottom of the screen, as shown in Figure 3-18. Select the vertical constraint beneath the view (also shown in Figure 3-18) and delete it (press the Delete key or choose Edit ➤ Delete). You no longer want the bottom edge of the web view to be at the bottom edge of its superview; you now want it to snuggle up to the toolbar view, which you'll add in a moment.

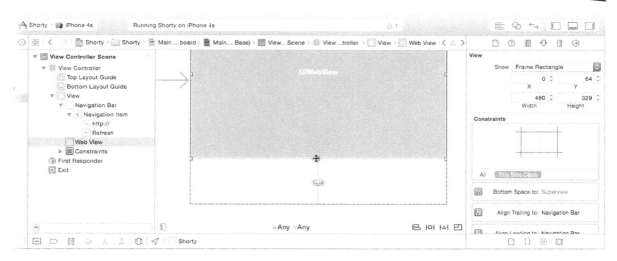

Figure 3-18. Making room for new views

In the library, find the toolbar object (not a navigation bar object, which looks similar) and drag it into the view, as shown in Figure 3-19. Position it so it fits snugly at the bottom of the view.

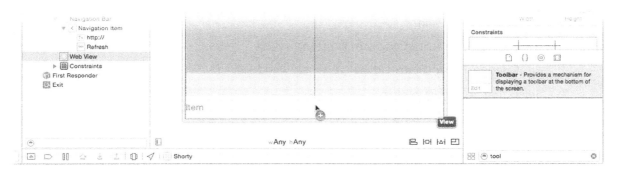

Figure 3-19. Adding a toolbar

Find the bar button item object in the library and add new button objects to the toolbar, as shown in Figure 3-20, until you have three buttons.

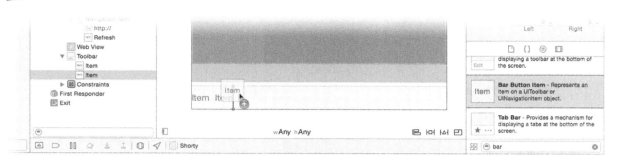

Figure 3-20. Adding additional button objects to the toolbar

You're going to customize the look of the three buttons to prepare them for their roles in your app. The left button will become the "shorten URL" action, the middle one will be used to display the shortened URL, and the right one will become the "copy short URL to clipboard" action. Switch to the attributes inspector and make these changes:

1. Select the leftmost button.

    a. Change Identifier to Play.

    b. Uncheck Enabled.

2. Select the middle button.

    a. Set Style to Plain.

    b. Change Title to Tap arrow to shorten.

    c. Change Tint to Black Color.

3. Select the rightmost button.

    a. Change Title to Copy.

    b. Uncheck Enabled.

Now select and resize the web view so it touches the new toolbar. Finish the layout by choosing Add Missing Constraints in View Controller from the Resolve Auto Layout Issues button. The final layout should look like Figure 3-21.

Figure 3-21. *Finished interface*

Just like before, you'll need to add three outlets to the `ViewController` class so your object has access to these three buttons. Select the `ViewController.swift` file in the project navigator and add these three declarations immediately after your existing outlets:

```
@IBOutlet var shortenButton: UIBarButtonItem!
@IBOutlet var shortLabel: UIBarButtonItem!
@IBOutlet var clipboardButton: UIBarButtonItem!
```

Select the `Main.storyboard` Interface Builder file, select the view controller object, and switch to the connections inspector. The three new outlets will appear in the inspector. Connect the `shortenButton` outlet to the left button, the `shortLabel` outlet to the middle button, and the `clipboardButton` to the right button, as shown in Figure 3-22.

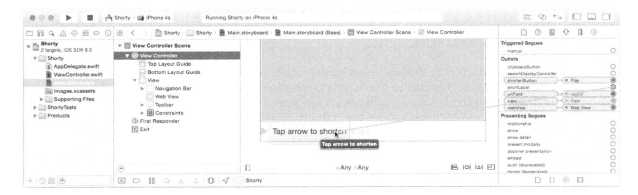

Figure 3-22. *Connecting outlets to toolbar buttons*

Designing the URL Shortening Code

With your interface finished, it's time to roll up your sleeves and write the code that will make this work. Here's how you want your app to behave:

1. The user enters a URL into the text field and taps Go. The web view loads the web page at that URL and displays it.

2. When the page is successfully loaded, two things happen.

    a. The URL field is updated to reflect the actual URL loaded.

    b. The "shorten URL" button is enabled, allowing the user to tap it.

3. When the user taps the "shorten URL" button, a request is sent to the URL shortening service.

4. When the URL shortening service sends its response, two things happen:

    a. The shortened URL is displayed in the toolbar.

    b. The "copy to clipboard" button is enabled, allowing the user to tap it.

5. When the user taps on the "copy to clipboard" button, the short URL is copied to the iOS clipboard.

You can already see how most of this is going to work. The "shorten URL" and "copy to clipboard" button objects will be connected to actions that perform those functions. The outlets you just created will allow your code to alter their state, such as enabling the buttons when they're ready.

The pieces in between these steps are a little more mysterious. The "When the page is successfully loaded" makes sense, but how does your app learn when the web page has loaded or whether it was successful? The same is true with the "when the URL shortening service sends its response." When does that happen? The answer to these questions is found in multitasking and delegates.

"Multi-what?" you ask. *Multitasking* is doing more than one thing at a time. Usually, the code you write does one thing at a time and doesn't perform the next thing until the first is finished. There are, however, techniques that enable your app to trigger a block of code that will execute in parallel so that both blocks of code are running, more or less, concurrently. This is explained in more detail in Chapter 24. You've already done this in your app, probably without realizing it.

```
webView.loadRequest(NSURLRequest(URL: url))
```

The loadRequest(_:) function of the web view object doesn't load the URL; it simply *starts the process* of loading the URL. The call to this function returns immediately, and your code continues, doing other things. This is called an *asynchronous* function. One of those things you want to keep doing is responding to user touches—something that's covered in Chapter 4. This is important because it keeps your app responsive.

Meanwhile, code that's part of the UIWebView class started running on its own, quietly sending requests to a web server, collecting and interpreting the responses, and ultimately displaying the rendered page in the web view. This is often referred to as a *background thread* or *background task* because it does its work silently, and independently, of your main app (called the *foreground thread*).

Becoming a Web View Delegate

All of this multitasking theory is great to know, but it still doesn't answer the question of how your app learns when a web page has, or has not, loaded. Tasks can communicate with one another in several ways. One of those ways is to use a *delegate*. A delegate is an object that agrees to undertake certain decisions or tasks for another object or would like to be notified when certain events occur. It's this last aspect of delegates that you'll use in this app.

The web view class has a `delegate` outlet. You connect that to the object that's going to be its delegate. Delegates are a popular programming pattern in iOS. If you poke around the Cocoa Touch library, you'll see that a lot of classes have a `delegate` outlet. Chapter 6 covers delegates in some detail.

Becoming a delegate is a three-step process.

1. In your custom class, adopt the delegate's protocol.

2. Implement the appropriate protocol functions.

3. Connect the `delegate` outlet of the object to your delegate object.

A *protocol* is a contract, or promise, that your class will implement specific functions. This lets other objects know that your object has agreed to accept certain responsibilities. A protocol can declare two kinds of functions: *required* and *optional*. All required functions must be included in your class. If you leave any out, you've broken the contract, and your project won't compile.

It's up to you to decide which optional functions you implement. If you implement an optional function, that function will get called. If you don't, it won't. It's that simple. Most Cocoa Touch delegate functions are optional.

> **Tip**   A few older classes rely on what is called an *informal protocol*. It really isn't a protocol at all but a documented set of functions that your delegate is expected to implement. The documentation for the class will explain which you should use. All of the steps for using an informal protocol are the same, except that there's no formal protocol name to add to your class.

The first step is to decide what object will act as the delegate and adopt the appropriate protocol. Select your `ViewController.swift` file. Change the line that declares the class so it reads as follows:

```
class ViewController: UIViewController, UIWebViewDelegate {
```

The change is adding the `UIWebViewDelegate` to the end of the class declaration. Adding this to your class definition means that your class agrees to define the functions required by the `UIWebViewDelegate` protocol and is prepared to be connected to a `UIWebView`'s `delegate` outlet.

Looking up the UIWebViewDelegate protocol, you find that it lists four functions, all of which are optional.

```
optional func webView(webView: UIWebView!, ⏎
                    shouldStartLoadWithRequest request: NSURLRequest!, ⏎
                    navigationType: UIWebViewNavigationType) -> Bool
optional func webViewDidStartLoad(webView: UIWebView!)
optional func webViewDidFinishLoad(webView: UIWebView!)
optional func webView(webView: UIWebView!, ⏎
                    didFailLoadWithError error: NSError!)
```

The first function, webView(_:,shouldStartLoadWithRequest:...), is called whenever the user taps a link. It allows your delegate to decide whether that link should be taken. You could, for example, create a web browser that kept the user on a particular site, like a school calendar. Your delegate could block any link that took the user to another site or maybe just warn them that they were leaving. This app doesn't need to do anything like that, so just ignore this function. By omitting this function, the web view will let the user tap and follow any link they want.

The next three functions are the ones you're interested in. webViewDidStartLoad(_:) is called when a web page begins to load. webViewDidFinishLoad(_:) is called when it's finished. And finally, webView(_:,didFailLoadWithError:) is called if the page could not be loaded for some reason.

You want to implement all three of these functions. Get started with the first one. Select your ViewController.swift file and find a place to add this function:

```
func webViewDidStartLoad( UIWebView ) {
    shortenButton.enabled = false
}
```

When a web page begins to load, this function will disable (by setting the enabled property to false) the button that shortens a URL. You do this simply so the short URL button can't be triggered between pages, and also you're not yet sure if the page can be loaded successfully. You'd like to limit the URL shortening to URLs you know are good.

After that function, add this one:

```
func webViewDidFinishLoad( UIWebView ) {
    shortenButton.enabled = true
    urlField.text = webView.request.URL.absoluteString
}
```

This function is invoked after the web page is finished loading. The first line uses the shortenButton outlet you created earlier to enable the "shorten URL" button. So, as soon as the web page loads, the button to convert it to a short URL becomes active.

The second line fixes up an issue I brought up earlier in the "Debugging" section. You want the URL in the text field at the top of the screen to reflect the page the user is looking at in the web view. This code keeps the two in sync. After a web page loads, this line digs into the webView object to find the URL that was actually loaded. The request property (an NSURLRequest) contains a URL property (an NSURL), which has a property named absoluteString. This property returns a plain string object that describes the loaded URL. In short, it turns a URL into a string, the reverse of what you did in loadLocation(_:). The only thing left to do is to assign it to the text property of the urlField object, and the new URL appears in the text field.

The last function is called only if the web page couldn't be loaded. It is, ironically, the most complicated function because you want to take the time to tell the user why the page wasn't loaded—instead of just making them guess. Here's the code:

```
func webView( webView: UIWebView, didFailLoadWithError error: NSError! ) {
    var message = "That page could not be loaded. " + ↩
                  error.localizedDescription
    let alert = UIAlertController(title: "Could not load URL",
                                  message: message,
                         preferredStyle: .Alert )
    let okAction = UIAlertAction(title: "That's Sad",
                                 style: .Default,
                               handler: nil)
    alert.addAction(okAction)
    presentViewController(alert, animated: true, completion: nil)
}
```

The first statement creates a message that says "That page could not be loaded…" and appends a description of the problem from the error object the web view passed to the function. The next few statements create an alert view—a pop-up dialog—presenting the message to the user.

You've now done everything you need to make your ViewController class a web view delegate, but it isn't a delegate yet. The last step is to connect the web view to it. Select the Main.storyboard file. Holding down the Control key, drag from the web view object and connect it to the view controller object. When you release the mouse button, choose the delegate outlet, as shown in Figure 3-23.

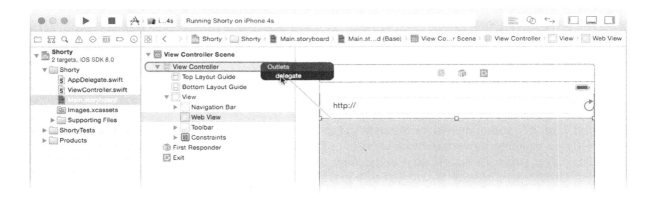

Figure 3-23. *Connecting the web view delegate*

Now your view controller object is the delegate for the web view. As the web view does its thing, your delegate receives calls about its progress. You can see this working in the simulator. Run your app, go to a URL (the example in Figure 3-24 uses http://developer.apple.com), and now follow a link or two in the web view. As each page loads, the URL in the text field is updated.

Figure 3-24. URL field following links

> **Tip** Also try loading a URL or two that can't be loaded by entering an invalid domain name or nonexistent path, as shown on the right in Figure 3-24. It's important to test how your app handles failure too.

Shortening a URL

You've finally arrived at the moment of truth: writing the code to shorten the URL. But first, let's review what has happened so far.

1. The user has entered a URL and loaded it into a web view.

2. When the web view loaded, your `ViewController` object's `webViewDidFinishLoad(_:)` function was called, where your code enabled the "shorten URL" button.

What you want to happen next is for the user to tap the "shorten URL" button and have the long URL be magically converted into a short one. That sounds like an action. Select your `ViewController.swift` file again and add this new code:

```
let GoDaddyAccountKey = "0123456789abcdef0123456789abcdef"
var shortenURLConnection: NSURLConnection?
var shortURLData: NSMutableData?

@IBAction func shortenURL( AnyObject ) {
    if let toShorten = webView.request.URL.absoluteString {
        let encodedURL = toShorten.stringByAddingPercentEscapesUsingEncoding(↵
                                        NSUTF8StringEncoding)

        let urlString = ↵
        "http://api.x.co/Squeeze.svc/text/\(GoDaddyAccountKey)?url=\(encodedURL)"
```

```
        shortURLData = NSMutableData()
        let request = NSURLRequest(URL:NSURL(string:urlString))
        shortenURLConnection = NSURLConnection(request:request, delegate:self)
        shortenButton.enabled = false
    }
}
```

The shortenURL(_:) action function sends a request to the X.co URL shortening service. iOS includes a number of classes that make complicated things—such as sending and receiving an HTTP request to a web server—relatively easy to write.

X.CO URL SHORTENING SERVICE

I chose to use the X.co URL shortening service in this project for several reasons. First, the service is free. Second, it has a well-documented and straightforward application programming interface (API) that can be used by performing a simple HTTP request. Finally, it has some debugging and management features. The service lets you log in and see what URLs your app has shortened, which is useful while you're trying to debug it.

The X.co service is provided by GoDaddy!. To use X.co, go to the X.co web page and either create a free account or log in with your existing GoDaddy! account (if you're already a customer). In your X.co account settings, you'll find an account key—a 32-character hexadecimal string—that uniquely identifies you to the X.co service. This key must be included in your requests. Once you have your key, edit the following line in your ViewController class, replacing the dummy number between the quotes with your account key:

```
let GoDaddyAccountKey = "0123456789abcdef0123456789abcdef"
```

There are other URL shortening services out there, and you could easily adapt this app to use almost any of them. Some services, such as Bit.ly, even offer an iOS SDK that you can download and include in your project!

The X.co services will accept an HTTP GET request that includes the URL to be shortened and replies with a shortened URL. It's that simple. A GET request is particularly easy to construct because all of the needed information is in the URL.

Writing shortenURL(_:)

Now let's walk through shortenURL(_:) one line at a time. You begin by constructing the request URL. You'll need three pieces of information.

■ The service request URL

■ Your GoDaddy! account key

■ The long URL to shorten

The first piece of information is documented at the X.co web site. To convert a long URL into a short one and have the service return the shortened URL as plain text, submit a URL with this format:

```
http://api.x.co/Squeeze.svc/text/<YourAccountKey>?url=<LongURL>
```

To construct this URL, you'll need the values for the two placeholders, `<YourAccountKey>` and `<LongURL>`. Get your account key from GoDaddy and use it to define the `GoDaddyAccountKey` value (see the "X.co URL Shortening Service" sidebar).

The last bit of information you need is the URL to shorten. Start with that, just as you did in the `webViewDidFinishLoad(_:)` function, and assign it to the `toShorten` variable.

```
if let toShorten = webView.request.URL.absoluteString {
```

The next two lines of code are the most complicated statements in your app. It constructs the entire X.co request URL using *string interpolation*—a fancy term for assembling a new string from other values.

```
    let encodedURL = ↩
toShorten.stringByAddingPercentEscapesUsingEncoding(NSUTF8StringEncoding)
    let urlString = ↩
"http://api.x.co/Squeeze.svc/text/\(GoDaddyAccountKey)?url=\(encodedURL)"
```

Notice that you don't use the `toShorten` value directly. Instead, the `stringByAddingPercentEscapesUsingEncoding(_:)` function is used to replace any characters that have special meaning in a URL with a character sequence that won't be confused for something important. The sidebar "URL String Encoding" explains why this is done and how it works. The result is kept in the `encodedURL` value.

URL STRING ENCODING

Computers, and thus computer programmers, deal with strings a lot. A string is a sequence of characters. Often, some characters in a string have special meaning. A URL can be represented as a string. Special characters separate the various parts of the URL. Here's a generic URL with the special characters in bold:

```
scheme://some.domain.net/path?param1=value1&param2=value2#anchor
```

The colon, forward slash, question mark, ampersand, equals, and pound sign (hash) characters all have special meaning in a URL; they're used to identify the various parts of the URL. All of the characters following the question mark are the query string portion of the URL. The ampersand character separates multiple name-value pairs. The fragment ID follows the pound sign character, and so on.

So, how do you write a URL that has a question mark character in the path or an ampersand character in one of the query string values? You can't write the following; it won't make any sense:

```
http://server.net/what?artcl?param=red&white
```

This is the problem you're faced with when sending a URL to the X.co service. The query string of your URL contains another URL—it's full of special characters, all of which have to be ignored. What you need is a way to write a character that normally has special meaning, without its special meaning. What you need is an escape sequence.

An *escape sequence* is a special sequence of characters used to represent a single character, so it's treated like any other character, instead of something special. (Read that again until it makes sense.) URLs use the percent character (%) followed by two hexadecimal digits. When a URL sees a percent character followed by two hex digits, as in %63, it treats it as a single character, determined by the value of the two digits. Converting characters into escape sequences to preserve their values is called *encoding* a string.

The sequence %63 represents a single question mark character (?), and %38 means a single ampersand character (&). Now you can encode that pesky URL, and it will make sense to the recipient:

```
http://server.net/what%63artcl?param=red%38white
```

The `stringByAddingPercentEscapesUsingEncoding(_:)` function converts any characters that might be confusing to a URL and replaces them with escape sequences that mean the same character but without any special meaning. Now you have a string you can safely append to the query portion of the URL without confusing anyone, especially the server.

The next line constructs the entire URL (as a string) and stores it in the `urlString` value. The string is constructed using string interpolation. When you include the sequence \(any+expression) in a string literal, Swift replaces it with the value of the expression—assuming Swift knows how to convert results of the expression into a string. In your program, this is trivial because `GoDaddyAccountKey` and `encodedURL` are already strings, so the placeholders in the literal string are simply replaced with the actual strings.

This next line of code might seem like a bit of a mystery:

```
shortURLData = NSMutableData()
```

It sets an instance variable named `shortURLData` to a new, empty, `NSMutableData` object. Don't worry about it now. It will make sense soon.

This next line of code is similar to what you used earlier to load a web page:

```
let request = NSURLRequest(URL: NSURL(string:urlString))
```

Just like the web view, the `NSURLConnection` class (the class that will send the URL for you) needs an `NSURLRequest`. The `NSURLRequest` needs an `NSURL`. Working backward, this line creates an `NSURL` from the URL string you just constructed and uses that to create a new `NSURLRequest` object, saving the final results in the `request` variable.

This next statement is what does (almost) all of the work:

```
shortenURLConnection = NSURLConnection(request:request, delegate:self)
```

Creating a new `NSURLConnection` object immediately starts the process of sending the requested URL. Just like the web view's `loadRequest(_:)` function, this is an asynchronous function—it simply starts a background task and returns immediately. And just like the web view, you supply a delegate object that will receive calls about its progress, as they occur.

Unlike a web view, however, the delegate for an NSURLConnection is passed (programmatically) when you create the request. That's what the delegate:self part of the call does; it tells NSURLConnection to use this object (self) as its delegate.

What's that you say? You haven't made the ViewController class a URL connection delegate? You're absolutely right. You should get on that.

Becoming an NSURLConnection Delegate

You can now follow the same steps you took to make ViewController a delegate of the web view to turn it into an NSURLConnection delegate as well. There's no practical limit on how many objects your object can be a delegate for.

The first step is to adopt the protocols that make your class a delegate. NSURLController declares a couple of different delegate protocols, and you're free to adopt the ones that make sense to your app. In this case, you want to adopt the NSURLConnectionDelegate and NSURLConnectionDataDelegate protocols. Do this by adding those protocol names to your ViewController class, in your ViewController.swift file, like this:

```
class ViewController: UIViewController, UIWebViewDelegate,
                      NSURLConnectionDelegate,
                      NSURLConnectionDataDelegate {
```

The NSURLConnectionDelegate defines functions that get sent to your delegate when key events occur. There are a slew of messages that deal with how your app responds to authenticated content (files on the web server that are protected by an account name and password). None of that applies to this app. The only function you're interested in is connection(_:,didFailWithError:). That message is sent if the request fails for some reason. Open your ViewController.swift file and add this new function:

```
func connection( connection: NSURLConnection!, ↩
                 didFailWithError error: NSError! ) {
    shortLabel.title = "failed"
    clipboardButton.enabled = false
    shortenButton.enabled = true
}
```

It's unlikely that a URL shortening request would fail. The only likely cause would be that your iPhone has temporarily lost its Internet connection. Nevertheless, you want your app to behave itself and do something intelligent under all circumstances. This function handles a failure by doing three things.

- Sets the short URL label to "failed," indicating that something went wrong

- Disables the "copy to clipboard" button because there's nothing to copy

- Turns the "shorten URL" button back on so the user can try again

With the unlikely stuff taken care of, let's get to what should happen when you send a request. The NSURLConnectionDataDelegate protocol functions are primarily concerned with how your app gets the data returned from the server. It, too, defines a bunch of other functions you're not interested in. The two you are interested in are connection(_:,didReceiveData:) and connectionDidFinishLoading(_:). Start by adding this connection(_:,didReceiveData:) function to your class:

```
func connection( connection: NSURLConnection!, didReceiveData data: NSData! ) {
    shortURLData?.appendData(data)
}
```

The X.co service returns the shortened URL in the body of the HTTP response as a simple string of ASCII characters. Your delegate object will get a connection(didReceiveData:) call every time new body data has been received from the server. In this app, that's probably going to be only once since the amount of data you're requesting is so small. If your app requested a lot of data (such as an entire web page), this function would get called multiple times.

The only thing this function does is take the data that was received (in the data parameter) and add it to the buffer of data you're maintaining in shortURLData. Remember the shortURLData = NSMutableData() statement in shortenURL()? That statement set up an empty buffer (NSMutableData) before the request was started. As you receive the answer to that request, it accumulates in your shortURLData variable. Does that all make sense? Let's move on to the final function.

The last function should be self-explanatory by now. The connectionDidFinishLoading(_:) function is called when the transaction is complete: you've sent the URL request, you've received all of the data, and the whole thing was a success. Add this function to your implementation:

```
func connectionDidFinishLoading( connection: NSURLConnection! ) {
    if let data = shortURLData {
        let shortURLString = NSString(data:data, encoding:NSUTF8StringEncoding)
        shortLabel.title = shortURLString
        clipboardButton.enabled = true
    }
}
```

The first two statements turn the ASCII bytes you received in connection(_:,didReceiveData:) into a string object. String objects use Unicode character values, so turning a string of *bytes* into a string of *characters* requires a little conversion.

Tip   If you need to convert string objects to or from other forms, such as character or byte arrays, it would help to learn a little about Unicode characters. There's a great article for beginners, titled "The Absolute Minimum Every Software Developer Absolutely, Positively Must Know About Unicode and Character Sets (No Excuses!)," by Joel Spolsky at http://joelonsoftware.com/articles/Unicode.html.

The third line sets the title of the shortLabel toolbar button to the short URL you just received (and converted). This makes the short URL appear at the bottom of the screen.

The last step is to turn on the "copy to clipboard" button. Now that your app has a valid short URL, it has something to copy.

Testing the Service

You're almost ready to test your app; there's just one tiny detail to attend to first. You've written the code that sends the request to the X.co service, you've set up delegate functions to collect the data that comes back, and you've written code to deal with any problems. The only thing left to do is connect the "shorten URL" button in the interface to your shortenURL(_:) function, so all that happens when you tap the button.

Select the Main.storyboard file. Holding down the Control key, click the "shorten URL" button and connect its action to the view controller. Release the mouse button and choose the shortenURL: action, as shown in Figure 3-25.

Figure 3-25. *Connecting the "shorten URL" button*

Run your app and enter a URL. In the example shown in Figure 3-26, I've entered http://www.apple.com. When the page loads, the "shorten URL" button becomes active. Tap it and, within a second or two, a short URL to this page appears in the toolbar (on the right in Figure 3-26).

Figure 3-26. *The Shorty app in action*

This calls for a celebration! You've created a remarkably sophisticated app by leveraging the power of existing iOS classes, judiciously connecting the right objects, and writing action and delegate functions to handle the details.

Final Touches

You're still not quite done. You've yet to write the action that copies the short URL to the system clipboard. Fortunately, that's not difficult to code either. In your ViewController.swift file, add this function:

```
@IBAction func clipboardURL( AnyObject ) {
    let shortURLString = shortLabel.title
    let shortURL = NSURL(string: shortURLString)
    UIPasteboard.generalPasteboard().URL = shortURL
}
```

The first line gets the text of the URL from the `shortLabel` button that was set by `connectionDidFinishLoading(_:)`. The second line turns the text of the short URL into a URL object, just as you did in the `loadLocation(_:)` function you wrote at the beginning of the chapter. Finally, the `UIPasteboard.generalPasteboard()` function returns the systemwide pasteboard for "general" data—what most people think of as the clipboard. You set the `URL` property of that pasteboard object to the URL object you just created. And almost as if by magic, the short URL is now on the clipboard.

Now you can use Interface Builder to connect the "copy to clipboard" button to the `clipboardURL(_:)` function. Do this the same way you connected the "shorten URL" button (refer to Figure 3-25).

With everything hooked up, run your app again. You should get in the habit of running your app as you write it, testing each new feature and function as it is developed. In the simulator, go to a URL and generate a shortened one, as shown on the left in Figure 3-27. Once you have a shortened URL, tap the Copy button.

Figure 3-27. *Testing the clipboard*

Tap in the text field again and clear the field. Hold down your mouse (simulated finger) until the Paste pop-up button appears (second image in Figure 3-27). Tap the paste button, and the shortened URL will be pasted into the field. This would also work with any other app that allows you to paste text.

As a final test, tap the Go button. The shortened URL will be sent to the X.co server, the server will redirect your browser to the original URL, and the web page you started at will reappear in the browser, along with the original URL in the text field.

Cleaning Up the Interface

Your app is fully functional, but there are still a few quirks in the interface. With the simulator still running, choose the Hardware ➤ Rotate Left command. This simulates turning the device 90° counterclockwise, as shown in Figure 3-28. Most of it still looks OK, but the buttons in the bottom toolbar get squished over to the left, which looks cheesy.

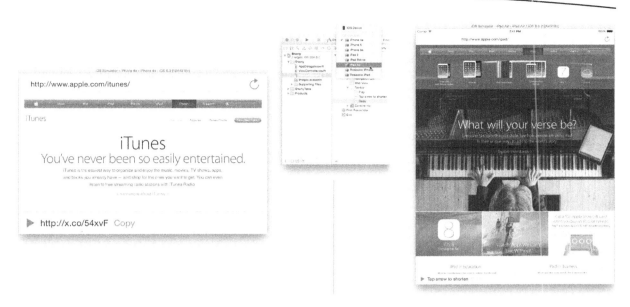

Figure 3-28. Testing device rotation

Quit the simulator, change the project destination in the toolbar to iPad simulator, and run your app again. Not too bad, but again all of the toolbar buttons are piled up on the left.

Quit the simulator or click the stop button in Xcode. Select the `Main.storyboard` file. In the library, find Flexible Space Bar Button Item. This object, with a ridiculously long name, acts as a "spring" that fills the available space in a toolbar so the button objects on either side get pushed to the edge of the screen.

Drag one flexible space item object and drop it between the "shorten URL" button and the short URL field. Drop a second between the URL field and the "copy the clipboard" button, as shown in Figure 3-29.

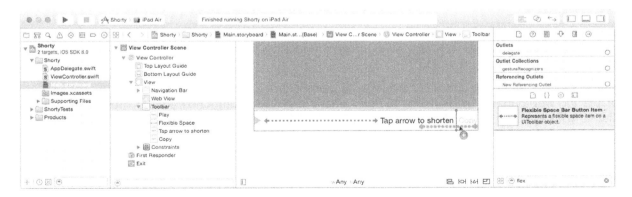

Figure 3-29. Adding flexible space bar button items

With two flexible items, the "springs" share the empty space, causing the label in the middle to be centered and the copy button to shift all the way to the right. It's not obvious in portrait orientation, but if you rotate the device to landscape, it works perfectly. Switch back to the iPhone simulator, run your app (see Figure 3-30), and rotate the device to the left (or right). Now the toolbar looks much nicer (on the right in Figure 3-30).

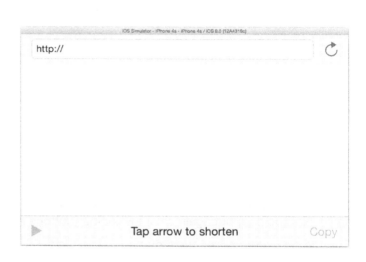

Figure 3-30. Testing iPhone rotation

Summary

This was a really important chapter, and you made it through with flying colors. You learned a lot about the fundamentals of iOS app development and Xcode's workflow. You will use these skills in practically every app you develop.

You learned how to whip up a web browser, something that can be used in a lot of ways, not just displaying web pages. For example, you can create static web content by adding .html resource files to your app and have a web view load those files. The web view class will also let you interact with its content using JavaScript, opening all kinds of possibilities.

Learning to create, and connect, outlets is a crucial iOS skill. As you've discovered, an iOS app is a web of objects, and outlets are the threads that connect that web.

Most importantly, you learned how to write action functions and create delegates. These two patterns appear repeatedly throughout iOS.

In the next chapter, I'll explain how events turn a finger touch into an action.

Chapter 4

Coming Events

Now that you've seen an iOS app in action, you might be wondering what keeps your app "alive," so to speak. In the Shorty app, you created action functions that were called when the user tapped a button or pressed the Go key on the keyboard. You created delegate objects that received messages when certain milestones were reached, such as when a web page had problems loading or the URL shortening service responded. You never wrote any code to see whether the user had touched something or checked to see whether the web page had finished loading. In other words, you didn't go out and get this information; your app waited for this information to come to it.

iOS apps are *event-driven* applications. An event-driven application doesn't (and shouldn't!) spin in a loop checking to see whether something has happened. Event-driven applications set up the conditions they want to respond to (such as a user's touch, a change in the device's orientation, or the completion of a network transaction). The app then sits quietly, doing nothing, until one of those things happen. All of those things are collectively referred to as *events* and are what this chapter is all about.

In this chapter, you'll learn about the following:

- Events
- Run loops
- Event delivery
- Event handling
- The first responder and the responder chain
- Running your app on a real iOS device

I'll start with some basic theory about how events get from the device's hardware into your application. You'll learn about the different kinds of events and how they navigate the objects in your app. Finally, you'll create two apps: one that handles high-level events and one that handles low-level events.

Run Loop

iOS apps sit perfectly still, waiting for something to happen. This is an important feature of app design because it keeps your app efficient; the code in your app runs only when there's something important to do.

This seemingly innocuous arrangement is critical to keeping your users happy. Running computer code requires electricity, and electricity in mobile devices is a precious commodity. Keeping your code from running at unnecessary times allows iOS to conserve power. It does this by turning off or minimizing the amount of power the CPU and other hardware accessories use when they are not needed. This power management happens hundreds of times a second, but it's crucial to the battery life of mobile devices, and users love mobile devices with long battery life.

The code in your app is at the receiving end of two mechanisms: a run loop and an event queue. The run loop is what executes code in your app when something happens and stops your app from running when there's nothing to do. The event queue is a data structure containing the list of events waiting to be processed. As long as there are events in the queue, the run loop sends them—one at a time—to your app. As soon as all of the events have been processed and the event queue is empty, your app stops executing code.

Conceptually, your app's run loop looks like this:

```
while true {
    let event: UIEvent = iOS.waitForNextEvent()
    yourApp.processEvent(event)
}
```

The magic is in the `waitForNextEvent()` function (which doesn't exist; I made it up). If there's an event waiting to be processed, that event is removed from the queue and returned. The run loop passes it to your app for processing. If there's no event, the function simply doesn't return; your app is suspended until there's something to do. Now let's look at what those events are and where they come from.

Event Queue

Events waiting to be processed are added to a first in, first out (FIFO) buffer called the *event queue*. There are different kinds of events, and events come from different sources, as shown in Figure 4-1.

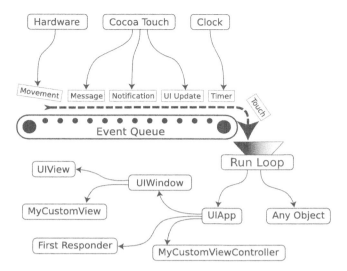

Figure 4-1. *The event queue*

Let's follow one event through your app. When you touch your finger to the surface of an iOS device, here's what happens:

1. Hardware in the screen detects the location of the touch.

2. This information is used to create a touch event object, which records the position of the touch, what time it occurred, and other information.

3. The touch event object is placed in the event queue of your app.

4. The run loop pulls the touch event object from the queue and passes it to your application object.

5. Your application object uses the geometry of the active views in your app to determine which view your finger "touched."

6. An event message containing the touch event is sent to that view object.

7. The view object decides what the touch event means and what it will do. It might highlight a button or send an action message.

When you touched the "shorten URL" button in the Shorty app from Chapter 3, that's how the physical act of touching the screen turned into the shortenURL(_:) call your view controller received.

Different event types take different paths. The next few sections will describe the different delivery methods, along with the types of events that each delivers.

Event Delivery

Event delivery is how an event gets from the event queue to an object in your app. Different types of events take different paths, befitting their purpose. The actual delivery mechanism is a combination of logic in the Cocoa Touch framework, your application object, and various functions defined by your app objects.

Broadly speaking, there are three delivery methods.

- Direct delivery
- Hit testing
- First responder

The next few sections will describe each of these three methods and the events that get delivered that way.

Direct Delivery

Direct delivery is the simplest form of event delivery. A number of event types target specific objects. These events know which objects will receive them, so there's not much to know about how these events are delivered, beyond that they're dispatched by the run loop.

For example, a Swift function call can be placed in the event queue. When that event is pulled from the queue, the call is performed on its target object. That's how the web view told your Shorty app when the web page had loaded. When the network communications code (running in its own thread) determined the page had finished loading, it pushed a `webViewDidFinishLoad()` call onto the main thread's event queue. As your main thread pulled events from its event queue, one of those events made that call on your web view delegate object, telling it that the page had loaded.

> **Note**   That isn't exactly how asynchronous delegate messages are delivered. But from an app developer's perspective—which is you—it's conceptually accurate; the details aren't important.

Other events that are sent to specific objects, or groups of objects, are notifications, timer events, and user interface updates. All of these events know, either directly or indirectly, which objects they will be sent to. As an app developer, all you need to know is that when those events work their way to the end of the event queue, the run loop will call a Swift function on one or more objects.

Hit Testing

Hit testing delivers events based on the geometry of your user interface, and it applies only to touch events. When a touch event occurs, the `UIWindow` and `UIView` objects work together to determine which view object corresponds to the location of the touch. Messages are then sent to that view object, which interprets those events however it chooses; it may flip a switch, scroll a shopping list, or blow up a spaceship. Let's take a quick look at how hit testing works.

When a touch event is pulled from the event queue, it contains the absolute hardware coordinates where the touch occurred, as shown on the left in Figure 4-2. This example will use a stylized representation of the Shorty app from the previous chapter.

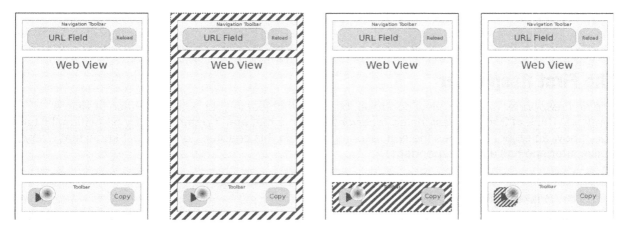

Figure 4-2. *Hit testing a touch event*

Your `UIApplication` object uses the event coordinates to determine the `UIWindow` object that's responsible for that portion of the screen. That `UIWindow` object receives a `sendEvent(_:)` call containing the touch event object to process.

The `UIWindow` object then performs hit testing. Starting at the top of its view hierarchy, it calls the `hitTest(_:,withEvent:)` function on its top-level view object, as shown in the second panel of Figure 4-2.

The top-level view first determines whether the event is within its bounds. It is, so it starts to look for any subviews that contain the touch coordinate. The top-level view contains three subviews: the navigation toolbar at the top, the web view in the middle, and the toolbar at the bottom. The touch is within the bounds of the toolbar, so it passes on the event to the `hitTest(_:,withEvent:)` function of the toolbar.

The toolbar repeats the process, looking for a subview that contains the location, as shown in the third frame of Figure 4-2. The toolbar object discovers that touch occurs inside the leftmost bar button item bounds. The bar button item is returned as the "hit" object, which causes `UIWindow` to begin sending it low-level touch event messages.

Being a "button," the bar button item object examines the events to determine whether the user tapped the button (as opposed to swiping it or some other irrelevant gesture). If they did, the button sends its action, in this case `shortenURL()`, to the object its connected to.

> **Tip**   Hit testing is highly customizable, should you ever need to modify it. By overriding the `pointInside(_:,withEvent:)` and `hitTest(_:,withEvent:)` functions of your view objects, you can literally rewrite the rules that determine how touch events find the view object they will be sent to. See the *Event Handling Guide for iOS*, which can be found in Xcode's Documentation and API Reference, for the details.

The First Responder

The *first responder* is a view, view controller, or window object in your active interface (a visible window). Think of it as the *designated receiver* for events that aren't determined by hit testing. I'll talk about how an object becomes the first responder later in this chapter. For now, just know that every active interface has a first responder.

The following are the events that get delivered to the first responder:

- Shake motion events
- Remote control events
- Key events

The shake motion event tells your app that the user is shaking their device (moving it rapidly back and forth). This information comes from the accelerometer hardware.

So-called remote control events are generated when the user presses any of the multimedia controls, which include the following:

- Play
- Pause
- Stop
- Skip to Next Track
- Skip to Previous Track
- Fast Forward
- Fast Backward

These are called *remote* events because they could originate from external accessories, such as the play/pause button on the cord of many headphones. In reality, they most often come from the play/pause buttons you see on the screen.

Key events come from tapping the virtual keyboard or from a hardware keyboard connected via Bluetooth.

To review, direct delivery sends event objects or Swift calls directly to their target objects. Touch events use hit testing to determine which view object will receive them, and all other events are sent to the first responder. Now it's time to do something with those events.

Event Handling

You've arrived at the second half of your event processing journey: event handling. In simple terms, an object *handles* or *responds* to an event if it contains code to interpret that event and decide what it wants to do about it.

I'll get the direct delivery events out of the way first. An object receiving a direct delivery event *must* have a function to process that event, call, or notification. This is not optional. If the object doesn't implement the expected function, your application will malfunction and could crash. That's all you need to know about directly delivered events.

> **Caution**   When requesting timer and notification events, make sure the object receiving them has the correct functions implemented.

Other event types are much more forgiving. Much like optional delegate functions, if your object overrides the function for handling an event, it will receive those events. If it isn't interested in handling that type of event, you simply omit those functions from its implementation, and iOS will go looking for another object that wants to handle them.

To handle touch events, for example, you override the following functions in your class:

```
override func touchesBegan(touches: NSSet, withEvent event: UIEvent)
override func touchesMoved(touches: NSSet, withEvent event: UIEvent)
override func touchesEnded(touches: NSSet, withEvent event: UIEvent)
override func touchesCancelled(touches: NSSet!, withEvent event: UIEvent)
```

If hit testing determines that your object should receive touch events, it will receive a touchesBegan (_:,withEvent:) call when the hardware detects a physical touch in your view, a touchesMoved (_:,withEvent:) call whenever the position changes (a dragging gesture), and a touchesEnded(_:,withEvent:) call when contact with the screen is removed. As the user taps and drags their fingers across the screen, your object may receive many of these calls, often in rapid succession.

> **Note**   The touchesCancelled(_:,withEvent:) function is the oddball of the group. This function is called if something interrupts the sequence of touch events, such as your app changing to another screen in the middle of a drag gesture. You need to handle the cancel call only if an incomplete sequence of touch events (such as receiving a "began" but no "ended" message) would confuse your object.

If you omit all of these functions from your class, your object will not handle any touch events.

All of the methods for handling events are inherited from the UIResponder class, and each type of event has one or more functions that you must implement if you want to handle that event. The UIResponder class documentation has a complete list of event handling functions.

So, what happens if the hit test or first responder object ignores the event? That's a good question, and the answer is found in the responder chain.

The Responder Chain

The *responder chain* is a string of objects that represent the focus of your user interface. What I mean by *focus* is those objects controlling the currently visible interface and those view objects that are most relevant to what the user is doing. Does that sound all vague and confusing? A picture and an explanation of how iOS creates and uses the responder chain will make things clear.

The responder chain starts with the *initial responder* (see Figure 4-3). When delivering motion, key, and remote events, the first responder is the initial responder object. For touch events, the initial responder is the view object determined by hit testing.

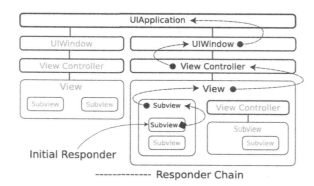

Figure 4-3. *First responder chain*

> **Note**   All objects in the responder chain are subclasses of UIResponder. So, technically, the responder chain consists of UIResponder objects. UIApplication, UIWindow, UIView, and UIViewController are all subclasses of UIResponder. By extension, the initial responder (first responder or hit test result) is always a UIResponder object.

iOS begins by trying to deliver that event to the initial responder. *Trying* is the key word here. If the object provided functions to handle that event, it does so. If not, iOS moves onto the next object in the chain until either it finds an object that wants to process the event or it gives up and throws the event away.

Figure 4-3 shows the conceptual organization of view objects in an app with two screens. The second screen is currently being shown to the user. It consists of a view controller object, a number of subviews, some nested inside other subviews, and even a subview controller. In this example, a sub-subview has been designated the initial responder, which would be appropriate after a hit test determined that the user touched that view.

iOS will try to deliver the touch event to the initial responder (the sub-subview). If that object doesn't handle touch events, iOS sees whether that view has a view controller object (it doesn't) and tries to send the event to its controller. If neither the view nor its controller handles touch events, iOS finds the view that contains that view (its superview) and repeats the entire process until it runs out of views and view controllers to try.

After all the view and view controller objects have been given a chance to handle the event, delivery moves to the window object for that screen and finally to the single application object.

What makes the responder chain so elegant is its dynamic nature and ordered processing of events. The responder chain is created automatically, so your object doesn't have to do anything to be a part of the responder chain, except to make sure that either it or a subsidiary view is the initial responder. Your object will receive event messages while that portion of your interface is active and won't receive events when it's not.

The other aspect is the specific-to-general nature of responder chain event handling. The chain always starts at the view that's most relevant to the user: the button they touched, an active text input field, or a row in a list. That object always receives the events first. If the event has specific meaning to those views, it's processed accordingly. At the same time, your view controller or UIApplication object could also respond to those events, but if one of the subviews handles it first, those objects won't receive it.

If the user moves to another screen, as shown in Figure 4-4, and presses the pause button on their headphones, a new responder chain is established. This chain starts at the first responder, which in this case is a view controller. The chain doesn't include any view objects at all because the top-level view controller object is the first responder.

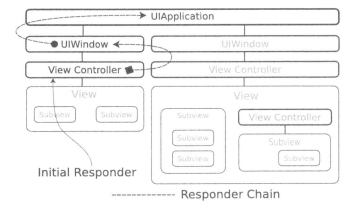

Figure 4-4. Second responder chain

If the view controller handles the "pause" event, then it goes ahead and does so. The view controllers in other interfaces never see the event. By implementing different "pause" event handling code in the various controllers, your app's response to a "pause" event will be different, depending on which screen is active.

Your application object could also handle the "pause" event. If none of the view controllers handled the "pause" event, then all "pause" events would trickle down to the application object. This would be the arrangement you'd use if you wanted all "pause" events to be handled the same way, regardless of what screen the user was looking at.

Finally, you can mix these solutions. A "pause" event handler in the application could handle the event in a generic way, and then specific view controllers could intercept the event if pressing the pause button has special meaning in that screen.

> **Tip**   It's rare to create a custom subclass of UIApplication and even rarer to subclass UIWindow. In a typical app, all of your event handling code will be in your custom view and view controller objects.

CONDITIONALLY HANDLING EVENTS

In practical terms, you override an event handling function (such as touchesBegan(_:,withEvent:)) to handle that event type, or you omit the function to ignore it. In reality, it's a little more nuanced.

Events are handled by receiving specific Swift function calls (such as touchesBegan(_:,:withEvent:)). Your object inherits these functions from the UIResponder base class. So, every UIResponder object has a touchesBegan(_:,:withEvent:) function and will receive the touch event object via a function call. So, how does the object ignore the event?

The secret is in UIResponder's implementation of these functions. The inherited base class implementation for all event calls simply passes the event up the responder chain. So, a more precise description is this: To handle events, you override UIResponder's event handler function and process the event. To ignore it, you let the event go to UIResponder's function, which ignores the event and passes it to the next object in the responder chain.

That brings up an interesting feature: conditionally handling events. It's possible to write an event handler function that decides whether it wants to handle an event. It can arbitrarily choose to process the event itself or pass it along to the next object in the responder chain. Passing it on is accomplished by forwarding the event to the base class's implementation, like this:

```
override func touchesBegan(touches: NSSet, withEvent event: UIEvent) {
    if iWantToHandleTheseTouches(touches) {
        // handle event
        doSomethingWithTheseTouches(touches)
    } else {
        // ignore event and pass it up the responder chain
        super.touchesBegan(touches, withEvent: event)
    }
}
```

Using this technique, your object can dynamically decide which events it wants to handle and which events it will pass along to other objects in the responder chain.

Now that you know how events are delivered and handled, you're ready to build an app that uses events directly. To do that, you'll need to consider what kind of events you want to handle and why.

High-Level vs. Low-Level Events

Programmers are perpetually labeling things as high level or low level. Objects in your app form a kind of pyramid. A few complex objects at the top are constructed from more primitive objects in the middle, which are themselves constructed from even more primitive objects. The complex objects on top are called the *high-level* objects (UIApplication, UIWebView). The simple objects at the bottom are called the *low-level* objects (NSNumber, String). Similarly, programmers will talk about high- and low-level frameworks, interfaces, communications paths, and so on.

Events, too, come in different levels. Low-level events are the nitty-gritty, moment-by-moment, details that are happening right now. The touch events are examples of low-level events. Another example is the instantaneous force vector values that you can request from the accelerometer and gyroscope hardware.

At the other end of the scale are high-level events, such as the shake motion event. Another example is the UIGestureRecognizer objects that interpret complex touch event patterns and turn those into a single high-level action, such as "pinched" or "swiped."

When you design your app, you must decide what level of events you want to process. In the next app, you're going to use the shake motion event to trigger actions in your app.

To do that, you could request and handle the low-level accelerometer events. You would have to create variables to track the force vectors for each of the three movement axes (x, y, and z). When you detected that the device was accelerating in a particular direction, you would record that direction and start a timer. If the direction of travel reversed, within a reasonable angle of trajectory and within a short period of time, and then reversed two or three more times, you could conclude that the user was shaking the device.

Or, you could let iOS do all of those calculations for you and simply handle the shake motion events generated by the Cocoa Touch framework. When the user starts to shake their device, your first responder receives a motionBegan(_:,withEvent:) call. When the user stops shaking it, your object receives a motionEnded(_:,withEvent:) call. It's that simple.

That doesn't mean you'll never need low-level events. If you were writing a game app where your user directed a star-nosed mole through the soil of a magical garden by tilting the device from side to side, then interpreting the low-level accelerometer events would be the correct solution. You'll use the low-level accelerometer events in Chapter 16.

Decide what information you need from events and then handle the highest-level events that give you that information. Now you're ready to start designing your app.

Eight Ball

The app you'll create mimics the famous Magic Eight Ball toy from the 1950s (http://en.wikipedia.org/wiki/Magic_Eight_Ball). The app works by displaying an eerily prescient message whenever you shake your iOS device. Start by sketching out a quick design for your app.

Design

The design for this app is the simplest so far: a screen containing a message is displayed in the center of a "ball," as shown in Figure 4-5. When you shake the device, the current message disappears. When you stop shaking it, a new message appears.

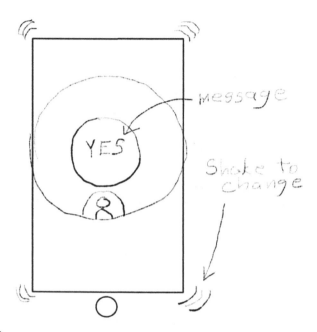

Figure 4-5. EightBall app design

Create the Project

Launch Xcode and choose File ➤ New Project. Select the Single View iOS app template. In the next sheet, name the app EightBall, set the language to Swift, and choose iPhone for the device, as shown in Figure 4-6.

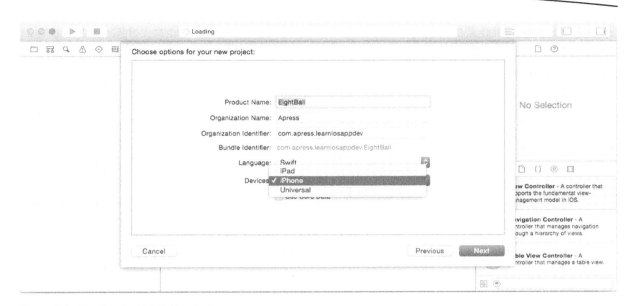

Figure 4-6. *Creating the EightBall project*

Choose a location to save the new project and create it. In the project navigator, select the project, select the EightBall target from the pop-up menu (if needed), select the General tab, and then turn off the two landscape orientations in the Supported Interface Orientation section so only the portrait orientation is enabled.

Create the Interface

Select the `Main.storyboard` Interface Builder file and select the single view object. Using the attributes inspector, set the background color to Black, as shown in Figure 4-7.

Figure 4-7. *Setting the main view background color*

From the library, drag a new image view object into the interface. With the new image object selected, click the pin constraints control (the second button in the lower-right corner of the canvas). Check the Width and Height constraints, as shown on the left in Figure 4-8, and set both of their values to 320. Click the Add 2 Constraints button.

Figure 4-8. *Setting the image view constraints*

Click the align constraints control (leftmost button). Check the Horizontal Center in Container and Vertical Center in Container constraints, as shown in the middle of Figure 4-8. Make sure both of their values are set to 0. Click the Add 2 Constraints button. Finally, click the Resolve Auto Layout Issues control (third button) and choose the Update Frames command, as shown on the right in Figure 4-8. The image view object will now have a fixed size (320x320 points) and will always be centered in the view controller's root view.

> **Tip**   When adding new constraints via the pin constraints or align constraints control, choose an option from the Update Frames pop-up menu before clicking the add button. Xcode will apply the constraints and then update the frames in a single step.

Just as you did in Chapter 2, you're going to add some resource image files to your project. In the project navigator, select the Images.xcassets assets catalog. In the Finder, locate the Learn iOS Development Projects folder you downloaded in Chapter 1. Inside the Ch 4 folder you'll find the EightBall (Resources) folder, which contains five image files. Select the files eight-ball.png and eight-ball@2x.png. With these files and your workspace window visible, drag the two image files into the assets catalog, as shown in Figure 4-9.

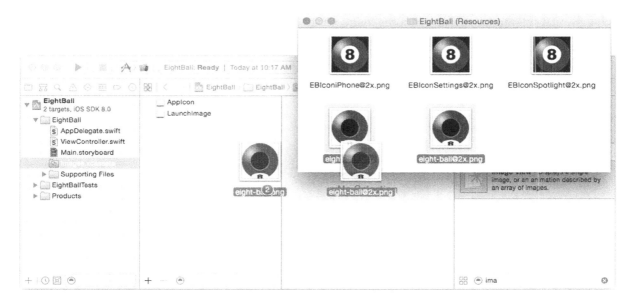

Figure 4-9. Adding eight-ball images to the assets catalog

Returning to your project, select `Main.storyboard` and select the image view object. Using the attributes inspector, set the image property to eight-ball, as shown in Figure 4-10.

Figure 4-10. Setting the image

Now you need to add a text view to display the magic message. From the object library, drag in a new text view (not a text field) object, placing it over the "window" in the middle of the eight ball. Almost exactly as you did for the eight-ball image view (see Figure 4-8), add the following constraints:

1. Pin Width to 160 and Height to 112.

2. Align Horizontal Center in Container and Vertical Center in Container.

The text view now has a fixed size and is centered right on top of the eight-ball image view. With the text view still selected, use the attributes inspector to set the following properties:

1. Set the text to SHAKE FOR ANSWER, on three lines (see Figure 4-11). Hold down the Option key when pressing the Return key to insert a literal "return" character into the text property field.

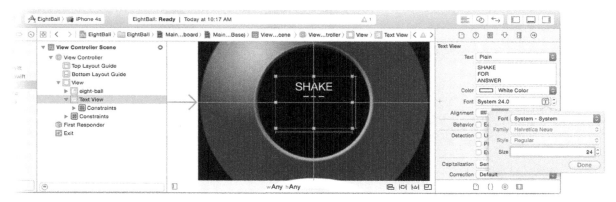

Figure 4-11. *Finished EightBall interface*

2. Make the text view color white.

3. Click the up arrow in the Font property until it reads System 24.0.

4. Choose the centered (middle) alignment.

5. Uncheck the Editable behavior property.

6. Further down, find the Background property and set it to default (no background).

7. Uncheck the Opaque property.

Your interface design is finished and should look like the one in Figure 4-11. Now it's time to move on to the code.

Writing the Code

Your ViewController object will need a connection to the text view object. Select your ViewController.swift file and add the following property:

```
@IBOutlet var answerView: UITextView!
```

You'll also need a set of answers, so add this immediately after the new property:

```
let answers = [ "\rYES", "\rNO", "\rMAYBE",
                "I\rDON'T\rKNOW", "TRY\rAGAIN\rSOON", "READ\rTHE\rMANUAL" ]
```

This statement defines an immutable array of String objects. Each object is one possible answer to appear in the eight ball. The \r characters are called an *escape* sequence. They consist of a backslash (left leaning slash) character followed by a code that tells the compiler to replace the sequence with a special character. In this case, the \r is replaced with a literal "carriage return" character—something you can't type into your source without starting a new line.

Now you're going to add two functions to update the message display: fadeFortune() and newFortune(). Add this code after the array:

```
func fadeFortune() {
    UIView.animateWithDuration(0.75) {
        self.answerView.alpha = 0.0
    }
}

func newFortune() {
    let randomIndex = Int(arc4random_uniform(UInt32(answers.count)))
    answerView.text = answers[randomIndex];
    UIView.animateWithDuration(2.0) {
        self.answerView.alpha = 1.0
    }
}
```

The fadeFortune() function uses iOS animation to change the alpha property of the answerView text view object to 0.0. The alpha property of a view is how opaque the view appears. A value of 1.0 is completely opaque, 0.5 makes it 50 percent transparent, and a value of 0.0 makes it completely invisible. fadeFortune() makes the text view object fade away to nothing, over a period of ¾ of a second.

> **Note**   Animation is covered in more detail in Chapter 11.

The newFortune() function is where all the fun is. The first statement does these three things:

1. The arc4random_uniform(_:) function is called to pick a random number between 0 and a number less than the number of answers. So if answers.count is 6, the function will return a random number between 0 and 5 (inclusive).

2. The random number is used as an index into the answers array to pick one of the constant string objects.

3. The random answer is used to set the text property of the text view object. Once set, the text view object will display that text in your interface.

Finally, iOS animation is used again to change the alpha property slowly back to 1.0, going from invisible to opaque over a period of 2 seconds, causing the new message to gradually appear.

There's one minor detail remaining: connecting the answerView outlet to the text view object in the interface. Switch to the Main.storyboard Interface Builder file. Select the view controller object and then use the connections inspector to connect the answerView outlet, as shown in Figure 4-12.

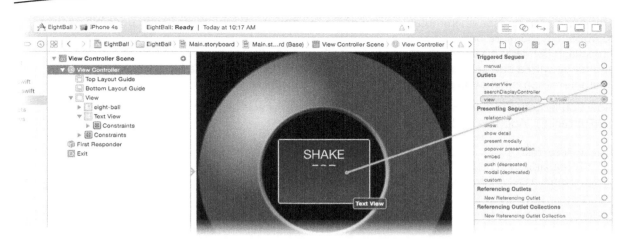

Figure 4-12. Connecting the answerView outlet

Handling Shake Events

Your app now has everything it needs to work, except the event handling that will make it happen. In the Xcode documentation (Help ➤ Documentation and API Reference), take a look at the documentation for UIResponder. In it, you'll find documentation for three functions.

```
func motionBegan(motion: UIEventSubtype, withEvent event: UIEvent)
func motionEnded(motion: UIEventSubtype, withEvent event: UIEvent)
func motionCancelled(motion: UIEventSubtype, withEvent event: UIEvent)
```

Each function is called during a different phase of a motion event. Motion events are simple— remember, these are "high-level" events. Motion events begin, and they end. If the motion is interrupted or never finishes, your object receives a motion canceled message.

To handle motion events in your view controller, add these three event handler functions to your ViewController:

```
override func motionBegan(motion: UIEventSubtype, withEvent event: UIEvent) {
    if motion == .MotionShake {
        fadeFortune()
    }
}

override func motionEnded(motion: UIEventSubtype, withEvent event: UIEvent) {
    if motion == .MotionShake {
        newFortune()
    }
}

override func motionCancelled(motion: UIEventSubtype, withEvent event: UIEvent) {
    if motion == .MotionShake {
        newFortune()
    }
}
```

Each function begins by examining the motion parameter to see whether the motion event received describes the one you're interested in (the shake motion). If not, you ignore the event. This is important. Future versions of iOS may add new motion events; your object should pay attention only to the ones it's designed to work with.

The `motionBegan(_:,withEvent:)` function calls `fadeFortune()`. When the user starts to shake the device, the current message fades away.

The `motionEnded(_:,withEvent:)` function calls `newFortune()`. When the shaking stops, a new fortune appears.

Finally, the `motionCancelled(_:,withEvent:)` function makes sure a message is visible if the motion was interrupted or interpreted to be some other gesture.

Testing Your EightBall App

Make sure you have an iPhone simulator selected in the scheme and run your app. It will appear in the simulator, as shown in Figure 4-13.

Figure 4-13. Testing EightBall

Choose the Hardware ➤ Shake Gesture command in the simulator, as shown in the middle of Figure 4-13. This command simulates the user shaking their device, which will cause shake motion events to be sent to your app.

Congratulations, you've successfully created a shake-motion event handler! Each time you shake your simulated device, a new message appears, as shown on the right in Figure 4-13.

FIRST RESPONDER AND THE RESPONDER CHAIN

Technically, it isn't necessary that your view controller be the first responder. What's required is that your view controller be *in the responder chain*. If any view, or subview, in your interface is the first responder, your view controller will be in the responder chain and will receive motion events—unless one of those other views intercepts and handles the event first.

By default, your view controller isn't the first responder and can't become the first responder. An object that wants to be a first responder must return `true` from its `canBecomeFirstResponder()` function. The base class implementation of `UIResponder` returns `false`. Therefore, any subclass of `UIResponder` is ineligible to be the first responder unless it overrides its `canBecomeFirstResponder()` function.

After making your object eligible to be the first responder, the next step is to explicitly request to be the first responder. This is often done in your `viewDidAppear()` function, using code like this:

```
becomeFirstResponder()
```

Specific Cocoa Touch classes—most notably the text view and text field classes—are designed to be first responders, and they return `true` when `canBecomeFirstResponder()` is called. These objects establish themselves as the first responder when touched or activated. As the first responder, they handle keyboard events, copy and paste requests, and so on.

At this point you might be wondering why your view controller is getting motion events, if it's not the first responder and it's not in the responder chain. You can thank iOS 7 for that. Recent changes in iOS deliver motion events to the active view controller if there is no first responder or the window is the first responder. If you want your app to work with earlier versions of iOS too, you'd need to make sure your view controller can become the first responder (by overriding `canBecomeFirstResponder()`) and then request that it is (`becomeFirstResponder()`) when the view loads.

Here's an experiment that demonstrates the responder chain in action. In the `Main.storyboard` file, select the text view object and use the attributes inspector to check the Editable behavior. Run the app, tap and hold the text field, and when the keyboard pops up, edit the fortune text. Now choose the simulator's Hardware ➤ Shake Gesture command. What happens? The text in the field changes, just as you programmed it to.

Return to the `ViewController.swift` file and comment out all three of your motion event handling functions. Do this by selecting the text of all three functions and choosing Editor ➤ Structure ➤ Comment Selection (Command+/). Now run your app again, select the text, change it, and shake the simulator. What happens? This time you see an Undo dialog, asking if you want to undo the changes you made to the text.

Motion events are initially sent to the first responder (the text field), eventually pass through the view controller, and ultimately land in the UIApplication object. The UIApplication object interprets a shake event to mean "undo typing." By intercepting the motion events in your view controller, you overrode the default behavior supplied by the UIApplication object.

Put your app back the way it was returning to ViewController.swift and choosing Edit ➤ Undo. Do the same to Main.storyboard.

Finishing Touches

Put a little spit and polish on your app with a nice icon—well, at least with the icon you'll find in the EightBall (Resources) folder. In your project navigator, select the images.xcassets file and then select the AppIcon group. With the EightBall (Resources) folder visible, drag the three icon images files into the AppIcon preview area, as shown in Figure 4-14. Xcode will automatically assign the appropriate image file to each icon resource, based on its size.

Figure 4-14. *Importing app icons*

With that detail taken care of, let's shake things up—literally—by running your app on a real iOS device.

Testing on a Physical iOS Device

You can test a lot of your app using Xcode's iPhone and iPad simulators, but there are few things the simulator can't emulate. Two of those things are multiple (more than two) touches and real accelerometer events. To test these features, you need a real iOS device, with real accelerometer hardware, that you can touch with real fingers.

The first step is to connect Xcode to your iOS Developer account. Choose Xcode ➤ Preferences and switch to the Accounts tab. Choose Add Apple ID from the + button at the bottom of the window, as shown in Figure 4-15.

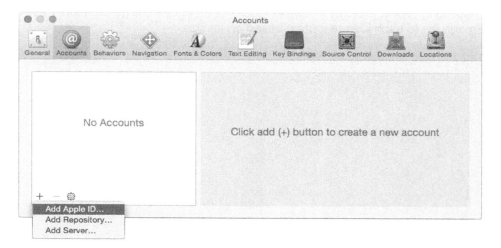

Figure 4-15. *Adding a new Apple ID to Xcode*

Supply your Apple ID and password and then click the Add button. If you're not a member of the iOS Developer Program yet, there's a convenient Join Program button that will take you to Apple's website.

> **Note**   Before you can run your app on a device, you must first become a member of the iOS Developer Program. See `http://developer.apple.com/programs/ios` to learn how to become a member. Once you are a member, Xcode will use your Apple ID to download and install the necessary security certificates required to provision a device.

Plug an iPhone, iPad, or iPod Touch into your computer's USB port. Open the Xcode devices window (Window ➤ Devices). The iOS device you plugged in will appear on the left, as shown in Figure 4-16. If a "trust" dialog appears on your device, as shown on the right in Figure 4-16, you'll need to grant Xcode access to your device.

Figure 4-16. *Device management*

Select your iOS device in the sidebar. If a Use for Development button is displayed, click it, and Xcode will prepare your device for development, a process known as *provisioning*. This will allow you to build, install, and run most iOS projects directly through Xcode.

Once your device is provisioned, return to your project workspace window. Change the scheme setting from one of the simulators to your actual device. I provisioned an iPad named iPad 4, so iPad 4 now appears as one of the run destinations in Figure 4-17.

Figure 4-17. *Selecting an iOS device to test*

Run the EightBall app again. This time, your app will be built, it will be copied onto your iOS device, and the app will start running there. Pretty neat, isn't it?

The amazing thing is that Xcode is still in control—so don't unplug your USB connection just yet! You can set breakpoints, freeze your app, examine variables, and generally do anything you could do in the simulator.

With EightBall app running, shake your device and see what happens. When you're done, click the Stop button in the Xcode toolbar. You'll notice that your EightBall app is now installed on your device. You're free to unplug your USB connection and take it with you; it is, after all, your app.

Other Uses for the Responder Chain

While the responder chain concept is still fresh in your mind, I want to mention a couple of other uses for the responder chain, before you move on to low-level events. The responder chain isn't used solely to handle events. It also plays an important role in actions, editing, and other services.

In earlier projects, you connected the actions of buttons and text fields to specific objects. Connecting an action in Interface Builder sets two pieces of information.

- The object that will receive the action (ViewController)
- The action function to call (shortenURL(_:))

It's also possible to send an action to the responder chain, rather than a specific object. In Interface Builder you do this by connecting the action to the first responder placeholder object, as shown in Figure 4-18.

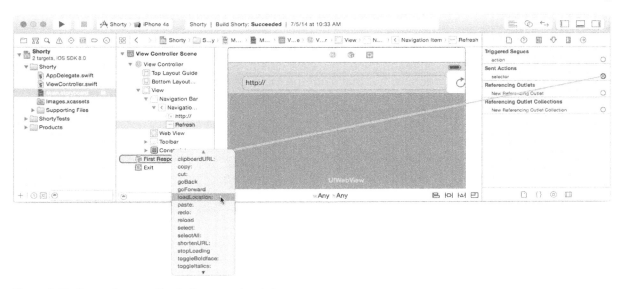

Figure 4-18. *Connecting an action to the responder chain*

When the button's action is sent, it goes initially to the first responder object—whatever that object is. For actions, iOS tests to see whether the object implements the expected function (loadLocation(_:), in this example). If it does, the object receives that message. If not, iOS starts working its way through the responder chain until it finds an object that does.

This is particularly useful in more complex apps where the recipient of the action message is outside the scope of the Interface Builder file or storyboard scene. You can make connections between objects only in the same scene. If you need a button to send an action to another view controller or the application object itself, you can't make that connection in Interface Builder. But you can connect your button to the first responder. As long as the intended recipient is in the responder chain when the button fires its action, your object will receive it.

Editing also depends heavily on the responder chain. When you begin editing text in iOS, like the URL field in the Shorty app, that object becomes the first responder. When the user types using the keyboard—virtual or otherwise—those key events are sent to the first responder. You can have several text fields in the same screen, but only one is the first responder. All key events, copy and paste commands, and so on, go to the active text field.

Touchy

You've learned a lot about the so-called high-level events, the initial responder, and the responder chain. Now it's time to dig into low-level event handling, and you're going to start with the most commonly used low-level events: touch events.

The Touchy app is a demonstration app. It does nothing more than show you where you're touching the screen. It's useful both to see this in action and to explore some of the subtleties of touch event handling. You'll also learn a new and really important Interface Builder skill: creating custom objects in your interface.

Design

The Touchy app also has a super-simple interface, as depicted in Figure 4-19. Touchy will display the location, or locations, where you're touching your view object. So the app isn't too boring, you'll jazz it up a little with some extra graphics, but that's not the focus of this outing.

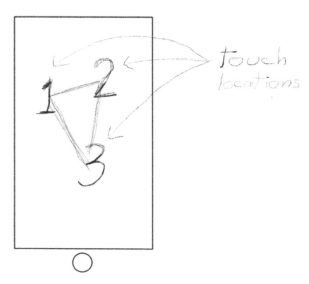

Figure 4-19.   Sketch of Touchy app

The app will work by intercepting the touch events using a custom view object. Your custom view object will extract the coordinates of each active touch point and use that to draw their positions.

Creating the Project

As you've done several times already, start by creating a new Xcode project based on the Single View iOS Application template. Name the project Touchy, set the language to Swift, and choose Universal for the device.

Select a location to save the new project and create it. In the project navigator, select the project, select the Touchy target, select the Summary tab, and change the device orientations so that only the portrait orientation is enabled.

Creating a Custom View

You're going to depart from the development pattern you've used in previous apps. Instead of adding your code to the ViewController class, you'll create a new custom subclass of UIView. "Why" is explained in Chapter 11. "How" will be explained right now.

Select the Touchy group (not the project) in the project navigator. From the file template library, drag in a new Swift file and drop it into your project, just below the ViewController.swift file. See Figure 4-20. Name the file TouchyView and add it to your project.

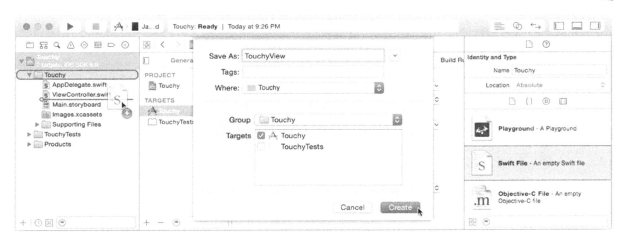

Figure 4-20. *Adding a new Swift source file*

Replace the single `import Foundation` statement with an `import UIKit` statement, followed by a `class TouchyView: UIView { }` declaration, as shown in Figure 4-21.

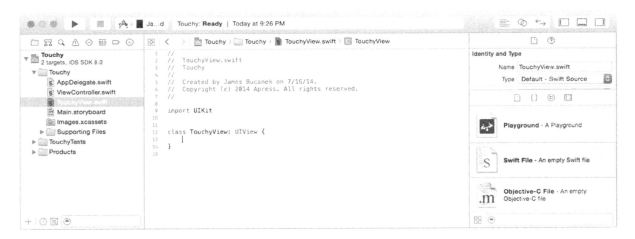

Figure 4-21. *Defining a new Swift class*

You've successfully created a new Swift class! Your class is a subclass of `UIView`, so it inherits all of the behavior and features of a `UIView` object and can be used anywhere a `UIView` object can.

Handling Touch Events

Now you're going to customize your `UIView` object to handle touch events. Remember that the base classes `UIResponder` and `UIView` don't handle touch events. Instead, they just pass them up the responder chain. By implementing your own touch event handling functions, you're going to change that so your view responds directly to touches.

As you already know, touch events will be delivered to the view object they occurred in. If you didn't know that, go back and read the section "Hit Testing." All you have to do is add the appropriate event handling functions to your class. Add the following code to your TouchyView class:

```
override func touchesBegan(touches: NSSet, withEvent event: UIEvent) {
    updateTouches(event.allTouches())
}

override func touchesMoved(touches: NSSet, withEvent event: UIEvent) {
    updateTouches(event.allTouches())
}

override func touchesEnded(touches: NSSet, withEvent event: UIEvent) {
    updateTouches(event.allTouches())
}

override func touchesCancelled(touches: NSSet!, withEvent event: UIEvent) {
    updateTouches(event.allTouches())
}
```

> **Note**   Xcode will be showing some errors in your source code. Ignore them for now; you'll fix that when you add the updateTouches(_:) function.

Each touch event message includes two objects: an NSSet object, containing the touch objects of interest, and a UIEvent object that summarizes the event that caused the function to be called.

In a typical app, your function would be interested in the touches set. This set, or unordered collection, of objects contains one UITouch object for every touch relevant to the event. Each UITouch object describes one touch position: its coordinates, its phase, the time it occurred, its tap count, and so on.

For a "began" event, the touches set will contain the UITouch objects for the touches that just began. For a "moved" event, it will contain only those touch points that moved. For an "ended" event, it will contain only those touch objects that were removed from the screen. This is convenient from a programming perspective because most view objects are interested only in the UITouch objects that are relevant to that event.

The Touchy app, however, is a little different. Touchy wants to track all of the active touches all of the time. You're not actually interested in what just happened. Instead, you want "the big picture": the list of all touch points currently in contact with the screen. For that, move over to the event object.

The UIEvent object's main purpose is to describe the single event that just occurred, or, more precisely, the single event that was just pulled from the event queue. But UIEvent has some other interesting information that it carries around. One of those is the allTouches property that contains the current state of all touch points on the device, regardless of what view they are associated with.

Now I can explain what all of your event handling functions are doing. They are waiting for any change to the touch state of the device. They ignore the specific change and dig into the event object to find the state of all active touch objects, which it passes to your updateTouches(_:) function. This function will record the position of all active touches and use that information to draw those positions on the screen.

So, I guess you need write that function! Immediately after the touch event handler functions you just added in TouchyView.swift, add this function:

```
var touchPoints = [CGPoint]()

func updateTouches( touches: NSSet? ) {
    touchPoints = []
    touches?.enumerateObjectsUsingBlock() { (element,stop) in
        if let touch = element as? UITouch {
            switch touch.phase {
                case .Began, .Moved, .Stationary:
                    self.touchPoints.append(touch.locationInView(self))
                default:
                    break
            }
        }
    }
    setNeedsDisplay()
}
```

The updateTouches(_:) function starts by setting the touchPoints array object to an empty array. This is where you'll store the information you're interested in. updateTouches(_:) then loops through each of the UITouch objects in the set and examines its *phase*. The phase of a touch is its current state: "began," "moved," "stationary," "ended," or "canceled." Touchy is interested only in the states that represent a finger that is still touching the glass ("began," "moved," and "stationary"). The switch statement matches these three states and obtains the coordinates of the touch relative to this view object. That CGPoint value is then added to the touchPoints array.

Once all of the active touch coordinates have been gathered, your view object calls its setNeedsDisplay() function. This function tells your view object that it needs to redraw itself.

Drawing Your View

So far, you haven't written code to draw anything. You've just intercepted the touch events sent to your view and extracted the information you want about the device's touch state. In iOS, you don't draw things when they happen. You make note of when something needs to be drawn and wait for iOS to tell your object when to draw it. Drawing is initiated by the user interface update events I mentioned at the beginning of this chapter.

How drawing works is described in Chapter 11, so I won't go into any of those details now. Just know that when iOS wants your view to draw itself, your object's drawRect(_:) function will be called. Add this drawRect(_:) function to your class:

```
override func drawRect(rect: CGRect) {
    let context = UIGraphicsGetCurrentContext()
    UIColor.blackColor().set()
    CGContextFillRect(context,rect)

    var connectionPath: UIBezierPath?
    if touchPoints.count>1 {
        for location in touchPoints {
            if let path = connectionPath {
                path.addLineToPoint(location)
            }
            else {
                connectionPath = UIBezierPath()
                connectionPath!.moveToPoint(location)
            }
        }
        if touchPoints.count>2 {
            connectionPath!.closePath()
        }
    }

    if let path = connectionPath {
        UIColor.lightGrayColor().set()
        path.lineWidth = 6
        path.lineCapStyle = kCGLineCapRound
        path.lineJoinStyle = kCGLineJoinRound
        path.stroke()
    }

    var touchNumber = 0
    let fontAttributes = [
            NSFontAttributeName:              UIFont.boldSystemFontOfSize(180),
            NSForegroundColorAttributeName: UIColor.yellowColor()
            ];
    for location in touchPoints {
        let text: NSString = "\(++touchNumber)"
        let size = text.sizeWithAttributes(fontAttributes)
        let textCorner = CGPoint(x: location.x-size.width/2,
                                 y: location.y-size.height/2)
        text.drawAtPoint(textCorner, withAttributes: fontAttributes)
    }

}
```

Wow, that's a lot of new code. Again, the details aren't important, but feel free to study this code to get a feel for what it's doing. I'll merely summarize what it does.

The first part fills the entire view with the color black.

The middle section is a big loop that creates a Bezier path, named after the French engineer Pierre Bézier. A Bezier path can represent practically any line, polygon, curve, ellipsis, or arbitrary combination of those things. Basically, if it's a shape, a Bezier path can draw it. You'll learn all about Bezier paths in Chapter 11. Here, it's used to draw light gray lines between the touch points, when there are two or more. It's pure eye candy, and this part of the `drawRect(_:)` function could be left out and the app would still work just fine.

The last part is the interesting bit. It loops through the touch coordinates and draws a big "1," "2," or "3" centered underneath each finger that's touching the screen, in yellow.

Now you have custom view class that collects touch events, tracks them, and draws them on the screen. The last piece of this puzzle is how to get your custom object into your interface.

Adding Custom Objects in Interface Builder

Select your `Main.storyboard` Interface Builder file and select the one and only view object in the view controller scene. Switch to the identity inspector. The identity inspector shows you the class of the object selected. In this case, it's the plain-vanilla `UIView` object created by the project template.

Here's the cool trick: you can use the identity inspector to change the class of a generic view object to any subclass of `UIView` that you've created. Change the class of this view object from `UIView` to `TouchyView`, as shown in Figure 4-22. You can do this either by using the pull-down menu or by just typing in the name of the class.

Figure 4-22. Changing the class of an Interface Builder object

Now instead of creating a `UIView` object as the root view, your app will create a `TouchyView` object, complete with all the functions, properties, outlets, and actions you defined. You can do this to any existing object in your interface. If you want to create a new custom object, find the base class object in the library (`NSObject`, `UIView`, and so on), add that object, and then change its class to your custom one.

There are still a few properties of your new `TouchyView` object that need to be customized for it to work correctly. With your `TouchyView` object still selected, switch to the attributes inspector and check the Multiple Touch option under Interaction. By default, view objects don't receive multitouch events. In other words, the `touchesSomePhase(_:,withEvent:)` function will never contain more than one `UITouch` object, even if multiple touches exist. To allow your view to receive all the touches, you must turn on the multiple touch option.

> **Note**   If you want, give Touchy an icon too. Open the Touchy (Resources) folder, locate the five TouchyIcon....png files, and drag them into the AppIcon group of the images.xcassets asset catalog, just as you did for the EightBall app.

Testing Touchy

Set your scheme to the iPhone or iPad simulator and run your project. The interface is completely—and ominously—black, as shown on the left in Figure 4-23.

Figure 4-23. Running Touchy in the simulator

Click the interface and the number "1" appears, as shown in the middle of Figure 4-23. Try dragging it around. Touchy is tracking all changes to the touch interface, updating it, and then drawing a number under the exact location of each touch.

Hold down the Option key and click again. Two positions appear, as shown on the right in Figure 4-23. The simulator will let you test simple two finger gestures when you hold down the Option key. With just the Option key, you can test pinch and zoom gestures. Hold down both the Option and Shift keys to test two-finger swipes.

But that's as far as the simulator will go. To test any other combination of touch events, you have to run your app on a real iOS device. Back in Xcode, stop your app, and change the scheme to iOS Device (iPhone, iPad, or iPod Touch—whatever you have plugged in). Run your app again.

Now try Touchy on your iOS device. Try touching two, three, four, or even five fingers. Try moving them around, picking one up, and putting it down again. It's surprisingly entertaining.

Advanced Event Handling

There are a couple of advanced event handling topics I'd like to mention, along with some good advice. I'll start with the advice.

Keep your event handling timely. As you now know, your app is "kept alive" by your main thread's run loop. That run loop delivers everything to your app: touch events, notifications, user interface updates, and so much more. Every event, action, and message that your app handles must execute and return before the next event can be processed. That means if any code you write takes too long, your app will appear to have died. And if code you write takes a really, really long time to finish, your app *will* die—iOS will terminate your app because it's stopped responding to events.

I'm sure you've had an app "lock up" on you; the display is frozen, it doesn't respond to touches or shaking or anything. This is what happens when an app's run loop is off doing something other than processing events. It's not pleasant. Most iOS features that can take a long time to complete have asynchronous functions (like the ones you used in Shorty), so those time-consuming tasks won't tie up your main thread. Use these asynchronous functions, pay attention to how long your program takes to do things, and be prepared to reorganize your app to avoid "locking up" your run loop. I'll demonstrate all of these techniques in later chapters.

Second, handling multiple touch events can be tricky, even confusing. iOS does its best to untangle the complexity of touch events and present them to your object in a rational and digestible form. iOS provides five features that will make your touch event handling simpler.

- Gesture recognizers
- Filtering out touch events for other views
- Prohibiting multitouch events
- Providing exclusive touch event handling
- Suspending touch events

Gesture recognizers are special objects that intercept touch events on behalf of a view object. Each recognizer detects a specific touch gesture, from a simple tap to a complex multifinger swipe. If it detects the gesture it's programmed to recognize, it sends an action—exactly like the button objects you've used in earlier projects. All you need to do is connect that action to an object in Interface Builder, and you're done. This feature alone has saved iOS developers tens of thousands of lines of touch event handling code. I'll show you how to use gesture recognizer objects in later chapters.

As I described earlier, the touch events (such as touchesMoved(_:,withEvent:)) include only the relevant touch objects—those touches that originated in your view object—in the touches parameter. Your code doesn't have to worry about other touches in other views that might be happening at the same time. In Touchy, this was actually a disadvantage, and you had to dig up the global set of touch objects from the UIEvent object. But normally, you pay attention only to the touches in your view.

You've also seen how iOS will prohibit multitouch events using UIView's multipleTouchEnabled property. If this property is false, iOS will send your view object events associated only with the first touch—even if the user is actually touching your view with more than one finger. For the Touchy app to get events about all of the touches, you had to set this property to true. Set this property to false if your view interprets single touch events only and you won't have to write any code that worries about more than one touch at a time.

If you don't want iOS to be sending touch events to two view objects simultaneously, you can set UIView's exclusiveTouch property to true. If set, iOS will block touch events from being sent to any other views once a touch sequence has begun in yours (and vice versa).

Finally, if your app needs to, you can temporary suspend all touch events from being sent to a specific view or even your entire app. If you want to make an individual view "deaf" to touch events, set its userInteractionEnabled property to false. You can also call your application object's beginIgnoreingInteractionEvents() function, and all touch events for your app will be silenced. Turn them back on again by calling endIgnoringInteractionEvents(). This is useful for preventing touch events from interfering with something else that's going on (say, a short animation), but don't leave them turned off for long.

Summary

By now you have a pretty firm grasp on how messages and events get into your app and how they are handled. You know about the event queue and the run loop. You know that events in the queue are dispatched to the objects in your app. You know that some of them go directly to your objects, touch events use hit testing, and the rest get sent to the first responder.

You've learned a lot about the responder chain. The responder chain performs a number of important tasks in iOS, beyond delivering events.

You know how to configure an object to handle or ignore specific types of events. You've written two apps, one that handled high-level events and a second that tracked low-level touch events.

Possibly even more astounding, you built and ran your app on a real iOS device! Feel free to run any other projects on your device too. Creating your own iOS app that you can carry around with you is an impressive feat!

In the next chapter, you're going to learn a little about data models and how complex sets of data get turned into scrolling lists on the screen.

EXERCISES

According to the instructions that come with the Magic Eight Ball, you should not shake the ball; it causes bubbles to form in the liquid. Of course, this never stopped my brother and I from shaking the daylights out of it. Instead, you were supposed to place the ball with the "8" up on a table, ask a question, gently turn it over, and read the answer.

For extra credit, rewrite the EightBall app so it uses the device orientation events, instead of shake motion events, to make the message disappear and appear. A device's orientation will be one of portrait, landscape left, landscape right, upside down, face up, or face down.

Changes in device orientation are delivered via notifications. You haven't used notifications yet, but think of them as just another kind of event (at least in this context). Unlike events, your object must explicitly request the notifications it wants to receive. Whenever the device changes orientation, such as when the user turns their iPhone over, your object will receive a notification message.

All of the code you need to request and handle device orientation change notifications is shown in the *Event Handling Guide for iOS*, in the section "Getting the Current Device Orientation with UIDevice." In Xcode, choose Help ➤ Documentation and API Reference and search for *Event Handling Guide*.

Change EightBall so it requests device orientation notifications instead of handling shake motion events. When your app receives an orientation change notification, examine the current orientation of the current UIDevice object. If the orientation property is UIDeviceOrientationFaceUp, make a new message appear. If it's anything else, make the message disappear. Now you have a more "authentic" Magic Eight Ball simulator! You can find my solution to this exercise in the EightBall E1 folder.

Chapter 5

Table Manners

Tables are a powerful and flexible iOS interface element. They are so flexible that—in many applications—table views *are* the interface. In this chapter, you'll learn about table views and pick up some class organization and interobject communication skills in the process. By the end of this chapter, you'll know about the following:

- Table views
- Table cells
- Cell caching
- Table editing
- Notifications

The app you'll create in this chapter will depend a lot more on Swift code than Interface Builder. This is typical of table view interfaces because the table view classes already provide much of the look of your table, so there's not much for you to design. (That doesn't mean you *can't* design your own, and I'll discuss that too.) First, you need to know what a table view looks like.

Table Views

A *table view* is a `UITableView` object that presents, draws, manages, and scrolls a single vertical list of rows. Each *row* is one element in the table. Rows can all be alike (homogeneous) or can be substantially different (heterogeneous) from one another. A table can appear as a continuous list of rows, or it may organize rows into groups.

If you've used an iPhone, iPad, or iPod for more than a few minutes, you've seen table views in action. In fact, there are probably more than a few iOS app interfaces that you didn't realize were table views. By the time you're done with this section, you'll be able to spot them from a mile away.

The overall appearance of a table is set by the *table style* you choose when the table view is created. Its contents can be further refined by the style and layout of the individual rows. I'll start by describing the overall table styles.

Plain Tables

The plain table style (UITableViewStyle.Plain) is the one you're most likely to recognize as a table view or list. The list of keyboard choices on the left of Figure 5-1 shows a plain (.Plain) table style view.

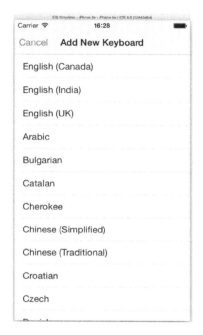
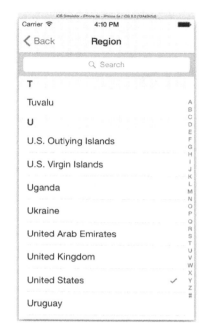
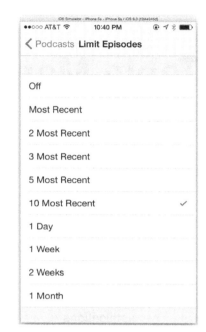

Figure 5-1. Plain table styles

In the middle of Figure 5-1 is a plain table style with an index, a common embellishment for long lists. An index adds section labels that group similar items and provides a quick way of jumping to a particular group in the list, using the index on the right.

Another, somewhat obscure, plain table style is the selection list style (shown on the right in Figure 5-1). It looks just like a plain table style with section titles but has no index. It's used to choose one or more options from a (potentially long) list of options.

Grouped Tables

The grouped table style (UITableViewStyle.Grouped) is the other table style. This style groups sets of rows together. Each group has an optional header and footer, allowing you to surround the group with a title, description, or even explanatory text. You should immediately recognize the examples in Figure 5-2.

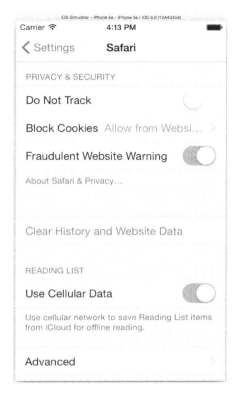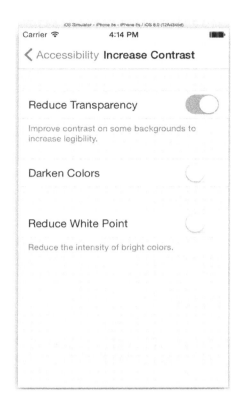

Figure 5-2. *Grouped table style*

The Settings app is built almost entirely of table views. The title above each group is a *group header*. The text below is a *group footer*. The individual setting controls are each one row of the table. It almost doesn't look like a table at all, but it uses the same UITableView object that Figure 5-1 does. Grouped lists cannot have indexes.

The style you choose for the list sets the overall tone of your table. You then have a lot of choices when it comes to how each row looks.

Cell Styles

A *table view cell* object controls the appearance and content of each row. iOS comes with several styles of table cells.

- Default
- Subtitle
- Value1 (Right Detail)
- Value2 (Left Detail)

The default style (UITableViewCellStyle.Default) is the basic one, as shown in Figure 5-3.

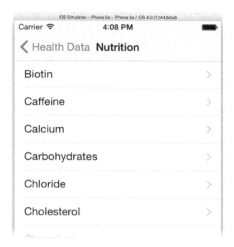

Figure 5-3. Default cell style

The default style has a bold title. It may optionally include a small image, which appears on the left. The arrow, check mark, or control on the right is called an *accessory view*, and I'll talk about them shortly.

The second major cell style is the subtitle style (UITableViewCellStyle.Subtitle), shown in Figure 5-4. Almost identical to the default style, it can include a deemphasized line of text below each title—the subtitle. The subtitle text is optional. If you leave out the subtitle, it will look like the default style.

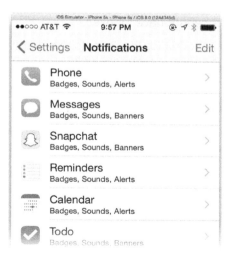

Figure 5-4. Subtitle cell style

The last two styles are the value1 and value2 styles (UITableViewCellStyle.Value1 and UITableViewCellStyle.Value2), as shown in Figure 5-5. The value1 style, also called the *right detail* style (on the left in Figure 5-5), is typically used to display a series of values or settings; the title of the cell describes the value, and the field on the right shows the current value.

Figure 5-5. *Value1 and value2 cell styles*

The alternate .Value2 style, also called the *left detail* style, puts more emphasis on the value and less on its title, as shown on the right of Figure 5-5. You'll see this style of cell used in the Contacts app. Neither the .Value1 nor .Value2 cell style allows an image.

Cell Accessories

On the right of all cell styles is the optional accessory view. iOS provides three standard accessory views, as shown in Figure 5-6.

Figure 5-6. *Standard accessory views*

The standard accessory views are (from left to right in Figure 5-6) the disclosure indicator, detail disclosure button, and check mark. The first two are used to indicate that tapping the row or the button will *disclose*—navigate to—another screen or view that displays details about that row. Nested lists are often organized this way. For example, in a table of countries, each row might navigate to another table listing the major cities in that country.

The disclosure indicator is not a control. It's an indication that tapping anywhere in the row will navigate you to some additional information, as in the country/city example. The detail disclosure button, however, is a regular button. You must tap the accessory view button to navigate to the details. This frees the row itself to have some other purpose. The Phone app's recent calls table works this way (see the middle of Figure 5-6); tapping a row places a call to that person, while tapping the detail disclosure button navigates to their contact information.

The check mark is just that and is used to indicate when a row has been selected or marked, for whatever purpose.

A cell's accessory view can also be set to a control view of your choosing (such as a toggle switch). This is common in tables that display settings (see Figure 5-2).

Custom Cells

The two table view styles, four cell styles, and various accessory views provide a remarkable amount of flexibility. If you peruse the Contacts, Settings, and Music apps from Apple, it's almost stunning the number of interfaces (dozens, by my count) that are just different combinations of the built-in table and cell styles, with judicious use of optional images, subtitles, and accessory views.

You'll also notice cells that don't fit any of the styles I've described. There's a wildcard in the table cell deck: you can design your own cell. A UITableCell object is a subclass of UIView. So, in theory, a table cell can contain *any* view objects you want, even custom ones you've designed yourself using Swift and Interface Builder. So, don't fret if the standard styles don't exactly fit your needs; you can always make your own. I'll go into the details of that in Chapter 11.

Now that you have an idea of what's possible, it's time to take a closer look at how tables work.

How Table Views Work

Up to this point, every visual element in your apps has been a view object. In other words, there's been a one-to-one relationship between what you see on your device and a UIView object in your app. Table views, however, have a few issues with that arrangement, and the table view class comes with an ingenious solution.

A table view that creates a cell object for every row runs into a number of problems when the number of rows is large. It's not hard to imagine a contact list with several hundred names or a music list with several *thousand* songs. If a table view had to create a cell object for every single song, it would overwhelm your app, consume a ridiculous amount of memory, require a long time to create, and generally result in a sluggish and cumbersome interface. To avoid all of these problems, table views use some clever sleight of hand.

Table Cells and Rubber Stamps

If you've ever filed papers with the county clerk or shopped in a supermarket in the days before UPC bar codes, you're familiar with the idea of a rubber stamp that can be altered to stamp a particular date or price, using a dial or movable segments. It would be ludicrous if your county clerk had to have a different rubber stamp for every date. Similarly, table views don't create cell objects for every row. They create one cell object—or at least a small number—and reuse that cell object to draw each row in the table, kind of like a rubber stamp.

Figure 5-7 shows the concept of reusing a cell object. In this figure, there are only three (principal) view objects: a `UITableView` object, a `UITableViewCell` object, and a data source object. The table view reuses the one cell object to draw each row.

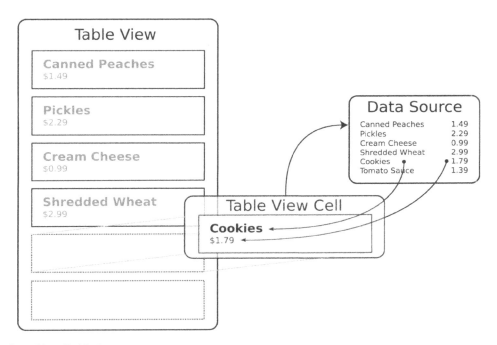

Figure 5-7. *Reusable cell object*

The table view does this using a delegate object, just like the delegate object you used in the Shorty app. When you create a table view object, you must provide it with a *data source* object. Your data source object implements specific delegate functions that the table view object will send when it wants a cell object configured to draw a particular row.

Continuing with the rubber stamp analogy, pretend you have a table view that wants to print a list of products and their prices. It starts by handing your (data source) object the rubber stamp (cell object) and saying, "Please configure this stamp for the first product in the list." Your object then sets the properties of the stamp (product name and price) and hands the configured stamp back to the table view. The table view uses the stamp to print the first row. It then turns around and repeats this process for the second row, and so on, until all of the rows have been printed.

Using this technique, a table view can draw tables that are thousands of rows tall using only a few objects. It's fast, flexible, and wickedly efficient.

MyStuff

You're going to create a personal inventory app named MyStuff. It's a relatively simple app that manages a list of items you own, recording the name of each item and where you keep it (living room, kitchen, and so on).

Design

This app's design is slightly more involved than the last two. It's complicated, a little, by the differences between the iPhone and iPad. Apple's Mail app looks substantially different on the iPhone versus the iPad. That's because the iPhone is a compact interface and has only enough screen space to comfortably display one thing at a time—either the list of messages or the content of a message. The iPad is a regular-sized interface where there's plenty of room for both. The underlying app logic is similar, but the visual design is quite different. Fortunately, the `UISplitViewController` class manages most of these differences for you. I'll describe how some of it works in this chapter and go into more detail in Chapter 12. Figure 5-8 shows the compact (iPhone) design.

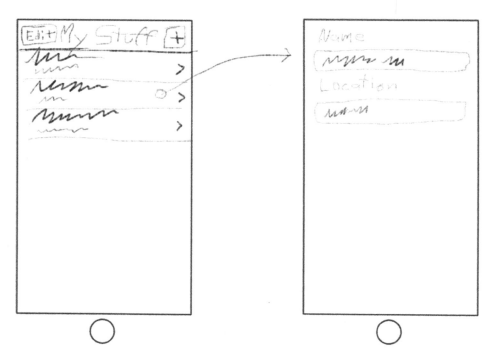

Figure 5-8. Sketch of MyStuff for iPhone

The compact design is simple and typical of how table views work. The main screen is a list of your items, with their description and location. Tapping an item navigates to a second screen where you can edit those values.

The regular design is less structured. In landscape orientation, the list of items will appear on the left, as shown in Figure 5-9. Tapping an item makes the details of that item appear on the right, where they can be changed. In portrait orientation (not shown), the item detail consumes the screen while the list of items becomes a pop-up that the user accesses via a button in the upper-left corner of the screen.

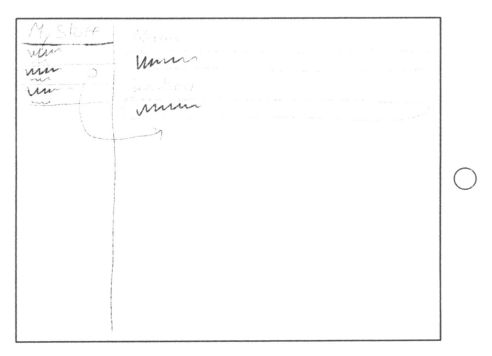

Figure 5-9. *Sketch of MyStuff for iPad*

If this interface looks familiar, it's the same one used by Apple's Mail app. This is not a trivial interface to program, but you're in luck; Xcode has an app template that includes all of the code needed to make this design work. You just have to fill in the details, which is exactly what you're going to do next.

Creating the Project

As with all apps, begin by creating a new project in Xcode. This time, choose the Master-Detail Application template, as shown in Figure 5-10.

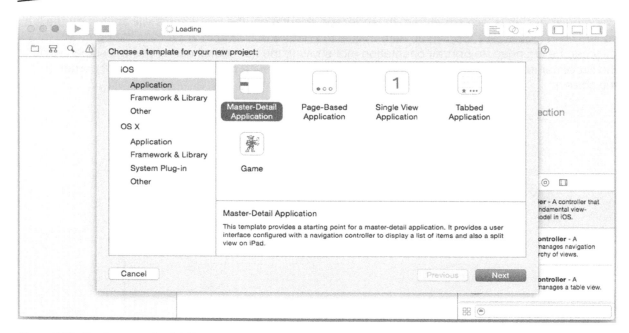

Figure 5-10. Creating a master-detail app

The master-detail template is so named because it's what computer developers call this kind of interface. The list is your *master* view, displaying a summary of all the data. The master view segues to a secondary *detail* view that might show more specifics about that item or provide tools for editing it.

Name the project MyStuff, choose the Swift language, and make sure Use Core Data is turned off. Set the devices option to Universal. Click Next and save your new project folder somewhere.

The first thing you'll notice is that there's a lot of code in this project already. The master-detail template includes all of the code needed to display a list of items, navigate to a detail interface, create new items, delete items, and handle orientation changes. The content of its table is simple NSDate objects. Your job is to replace those placeholder objects with something of substance.

> **Tip** You'd do well to spend some time looking over the code included by the project template. It does "all the right things" when it comes to navigation, orientation changes, and so on. You'll read more about navigation in Chapter 12.

Creating Your Data Model

You know that you want to display a list of "things"—the individual items you own. And you know that each thing is going to need at least two properties, a name property and a location property, which are both strings. So, what object is going to represent each thing? That's an important question because this mysterious object (or objects) is what's called your *data model*. Your data model comprises the objects that represent whatever concept your table view is displaying.

> **Note**   The theory and practice behind data models are described in Chapter 8.

Clearly the Cocoa Touch framework doesn't include such an object, so you'll have to create one! In the library, choose the file templates tab and drag a new Swift file into your project, as shown on the left in Figure 5-11. You can also add a new file by using the New File command from the File menu or by Control+right-clicking a group in the navigator. Use whichever you find most convenient.

Figure 5-11. *Creating the MyWhatsit class*

Name the new file MyWhatsit, as shown on the right in Figure 5-11. Accept the default location (the `MyStuff` project folder), make sure the new file is a member of the MyStuff target, and click Create. Now you have a new Swift file in your app named `MyWhatsit.swift`. Select the `MyWhatsit.swift` file in the navigator. It's pretty bleak. In fact, it doesn't define anything at all. Get started by declaring a new `MyWhatsit` class of objects.

```
class MyWhatsit {
}
```

This is the class of objects that will represent each item you own. Each one will need a `name` property and a `location` property. Define those now by adding these properties to your new class:

```
var name: String
var location: String
```

Congratulations, you now have a data model. You'll also want to create your `MyWhatsit` objects with something other than nothing for a name and location, so define an initializer function that creates an object and sets both properties in a single statement.

```
init( name: String, location: String = "" ) {
    self.name = name;
    self.location = location
}
```

This initializer function lets you create a new MyWhatsit object with a name and location (MyWhatsit("Lightsaber","guest bedroom")) or just a name (MyWhatsit("Lightsaber")). Initializers and default parameter values are described in Chapter 20.

When you're finished, your file should look like the one in Figure 5-12.

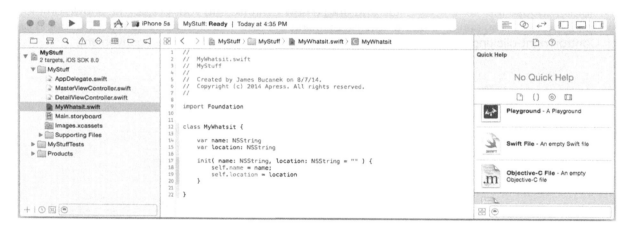

Figure 5-12. *Complete MyWhatsit.swift file*

Now that you have a data model, your next task is to teach the table view class how to use it.

Creating a Data Source

A table view object (UITableView) has *two* delegate properties. Its delegate property works just like the delegates you used in earlier chapters. The table view delegate is optional. If you choose to use one, it must be connected to an object that adopts the UITableViewDelegate protocol.

The table view's other delegate is its *data source* object. For a table view to work, you must set its dataSource property to an object that adopts the UITableViewDataSource protocol. This delegate is not optional—without it, your table won't display anything.

The data source's job is to provide the table view with all the information it needs to arrange and display the contents of the table. At a minimum, your data source must do the following:

- Report the number of rows in the table
- Configure the table view cell (rubber stamp) object for each row

A data source can also provide lots of optional information to the table view. Here are the kinds of things you can customize:

- Organize rows into groups
- Display section titles
- Provide an index (for indexed lists)
- Provide custom header and footer views for grouped tables

- Control which rows are selectable

- Control which rows are editable

- Control which rows are movable

As you saw in Shorty, a single class can adopt multiple protocols and can be the delegate for more than one object. In a similar vein, your view controller object can adopt both the UITableViewDelegate and UITableViewDataSource protocols and act as both the delegate and the data source for a table view. This arrangement is so common that iOS provides a class—UITableViewController—designed just for this purpose. UITableViewController is a subclass of UIViewController that's also a table view delegate and a table view data source. All you have to do is subclass UITableViewController and override a few functions. And you don't even have to do the first part because the master-detail project template already did that for you.

> **Note** UITableViewController can also control a table view that uses different objects for its delegate and/or data source. When UITableViewController loads its view, it examines the delegate and dataSource properties. If they weren't explicitly connected in Interface Builder to some other object, it automatically makes itself the table's delegate and data source.

Select the MasterViewController.swift file and take a look at the functions defined there. For a table view to work, your data source object must implement these two required functions:

```
func tableView(tableView: UITableView, numberOfRowsInSection section: Int) -> Int
func tableView(tableView: UITableView, cellForRowAtIndexPath indexPath: NSIndexPath) -> UITableViewCell
```

The first function is called on your data source object whenever the table view wants to know how many rows are in a particular section of your table. Remember, some tables can be grouped into sections, with each section having a different number of rows. For a simple table (like yours), there's only one section (0), so just return the total number of rows.

You're going to store your MyWhatsit objects in an array. One has already been defined in MSMasterViewController, but let's rename it. At the top of the MasterViewController.swift file, find the objects variable. Position (hover) your cursor over the variable name for a second or two. A pop-up list control will appear just to the right of the symbol name. Gently slide over, click it, and choose the Edit All In Scope command, as shown in Figure 5-13.

Figure 5-13. *Renaming a variable*

Xcode selects the symbol name and highlights every other occurrence of that symbol in your file. Type the name things, and Xcode replaces all references to objects with things in a single step.

Note   Xcode's Edit All In Scope feature uses Swift's language parser to intelligently find references to your variable. If the word *objects* appears in a comment or as a local variable in a loop, those instances won't be altered.

Finally, replace the initialization of the variable with a Swift array (modified code in bold):

```
var things = [MyWhatsit]()
```

This presets the things variable to an empty array capable of storing MyWhatsit objects. Now it's time to visit those two required data source functions.

Implementing Your Rubber Stamp

Find the tableView(_:,numberOfRowsInSection:) function. Here's what it looks like:

```
override func tableView(tableView: UITableView,
                        numberOfRowsInSection section: Int) -> Int {
    return things.count
}
```

There's nothing to change here. The function already does exactly what you need it to do: return the number of rows (MyWhatsit objects) in your table.

Move on to the tableView(_:,cellForRowAtIndexPath:) function. The code currently looks like this:

```
override func tableView(tableView: UITableView, cellForRowAtIndexPath indexPath:
                                          NSIndexPath) -> UITableViewCell {
    let cell = tableView.dequeueReusableCellWithIdentifier("Cell", ↵
                            forIndexPath: indexPath) as UITableViewCell
    let object = things[indexPath.row] as NSDate
    cell.textLabel.text = object.description
    return cell
}
```

This is your rubber stamp. This function is called every time the table view wants to draw a row. Your job is to prepare a UITableViewCell object that will draw that row and return it to the caller. This happens in two steps. The first step is to get the UITableViewCell object to use. Ignore that step for the moment; I'll describe this process in the next section ("Table Cell Caching").

The second step is to configure the cell so it draws the row correctly. The last three statements are where that happens. Right now, it expects to get an NSDate object from the array and set the label of the cell to its description. This is the code you need to replace. Replace the last three statements in the function with this (modified code in bold):

```
let thing = things[indexPath.row] as MyWhatsit
cell.textLabel?.text = thing.name
cell.detailTextLabel?.text = thing.location
return cell
```

Now your rubber stamp gets the MyWhatsit object for the row to be drawn (from the indexPath object) and stores it in the thing variable. It then uses the name and location properties to set the textLabel.text (title) and detailTextLabel.text (subtitle) of the cell.

> **Note**   Table views use NSIndexPath objects to identify rows in a table. The NSIndexPath objects used by UITableView have a section property and a row property that unambiguously identifies each row. Since your table has only one section, you can ignore the section property; it will always be 0.

The cell you return will be used to draw the row. That was the easy part. Now take one step back and look at the first part of that function again.

Table Cell Caching

In the rubber stamp analogy, I said that the table view "gives you a rubber stamp and asks you to configure it." I lied—at least a little. The table view doesn't give you the cell object to use because it doesn't know what kind of cell object you need. Instead, a cell object is created by either the storyboard or the code you write, and the table view hangs onto it so you can reuse it again next time. This is called the *table cell cache*.

There are three ways of using the table cell cache:

- Let your storyboard create the cell objects

- Lazily create cell objects programmatically, as needed

- Ignore the cache entirely

In this app, you'll take the first approach. The master-detail project template has already defined a single table cell object, with the unimaginative identifier Cell. Select the Main.storyboard file and select the table view object in the Master Scene, as shown in Figure 5-14.

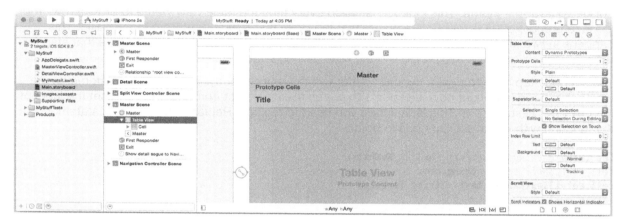

Figure 5-14. Table view with prototype table cell

At the top of the table view you'll see a Prototype Cells region. This is where Interface Builder lets you design the rubber stamps, er, cell objects, your table view will use. The Prototype Cells count (shown in the attributes inspector on the right of Figure 5-14) declares how many different cell objects your table defines. You need only one.

Click the one and only prototype cell template, as shown in Figure 5-15. Now you're editing a single table cell object. Notice that the Identifier property is set to Cell; this identifies the cell in the cache and must exactly match the identifier you pass in the dequeueReusableCellWithIdentifier(_:, forIndexPath:) call.

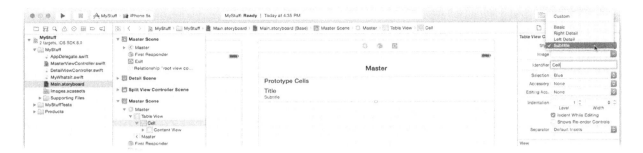

Figure 5-15. *Editing a table cell prototype*

Your table will display the name of the object and its location. The standard cell type that fits that description is the subtitle style (UITableViewCellStyle.Subtitle). Change the cell's style to Subtitle, as shown in the upper right of Figure 5-15.

Your table view design is complete. You've defined a single cell object, it has an identifier of Cell, and it uses the subtitle table cell style.

CELL OBJECT IDENTIFIERS AND REUSE

The table view cell cache makes it easy for your tableView(_:,cellForRowAtIndexPath:) function to efficiently reuse table cell view objects, and there are a variety of different ways to use it.

The traditional way of using the table cell cache is to programmatically create your table cell view objects, as needed. This is also called *lazy* object creation. You do this by checking to see whether the cell object you need is already in the cache and create one only if it isn't. The code to do that looks like this:

```
let cellIdent = "LazyCell"
var cell = tableView.dequeueReusableCellWithIdentifier(
                                    cellIdent) as? UITableViewCell
if cell == nil {
    cell = UITableViewCell(style: .Subtitle, reuseIdentifier: cellIdent)
    cell!.accessoryType = .DisclosureIndicator
}
```

This code asks the table cell cache if a cell with the identifier LazyCell has already been added. If not, the message will return nil, indicating there's no such cell in the cache. Your code responds by creating a new cell object, assigning it the same cell identifier. When you return this cell object to the table view, it will automatically add it to its cache. The next time, that cell view object will be in the cache.

A more modern approach is to register a cell view class or Interface Builder file with the table using the registerClass (_:,forCellReuseIdentifier:) or registerNib(_:,forCellReuseIdentifier:) function. After you do that, requests for a cell with that identifier that's not in the cache will automatically create one for you using the prototype cell defined in the storyboard file. This happens automatically when you design prototype cells using the storyboard and is the technique you're using in MyStuff.

Using cell identifiers, you can also maintain a small stable of different cell objects. In your MyStuff app, you might one day decide to have a different row design for *Star Wars* memorabilia and another row design for stuff you got from your grandmother. You would assign each cell object its own identifier ("Cell", "Star Wars", "Me Ma"). The table view cell cache would then keep all three cell objects, returning the appropriate one when you call any of the dequeueReusableCellWithIdentifier(_:...) functions. To do this using a storyboard, set the Prototype Cells count to 3 and assign a unique identifier to each prototype cell.

At the other extreme, you don't have to use the cache at all. Your tableView(_:,cellForRowAtIndexPath:) function could return a new cell object every time it's called. This would be appropriate for a tiny number of rows, where each row was completely different, or the number of rows is fixed—the kind of interface you see in the Settings app, for example.

Xcode lets you create this kind of table right in Interface Builder. Using the attributes inspector, change the table view's Content property from Dynamic to Static. Now the cells you add to your table are exactly the cells the table will display. For this kind of table, you don't override the tableView(_:,numberOfRowsInSection:) or tableView(_:,cellForRowAtIndexPath:) function.

You are free to mix and match any of these techniques. A single table could have some cell view objects that are defined in the storyboard and others registered to be created by class name, and your code could lazily create the rest.

While you're here, change the name in the navigation bar from Master to My Stuff. Do this by double-clicking the Master title in navigation bar above the table view or locating the navigation item object (see Figure 5-16). You've now implemented all of the code needed to display your MyWhatsit objects in a table view, but there are still a few problems. You changed the type (and name) of the original objects array, and there's still some stray code—from the project template—using that as if it were an array of NSDate objects. Swift is very precise about the types of values and won't compile that code.

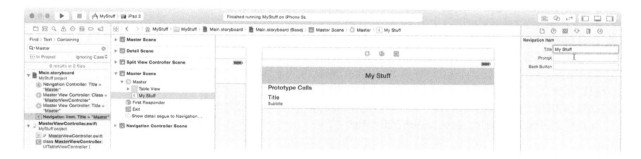

Figure 5-16. Renaming the master view

The code that's giving you problems is not important now; let's just ignore it. Locate the insertNewObject(sender:) and prepareForSegue(_:,sender:) functions in the MasterViewController.swift file and "comment out" their code; select the statements inside the outer { and } braces and choose the Editor ➤ Structure ➤ Comment Selection command, as shown in Figure 5-17.

Figure 5-17. *"Commenting out" a block of code*

There's one more tiny problem. When you replaced NSMutableArray() with an [MyWhatsit]() array, you inadvertently changed the type of the array from a foundation NSArray object to a native Swift array object. These two array types are largely interchangeable, but (again) Swift is picky about how you use them. NSArray has a removeObjectAtIndex() function. Swift arrays have the same function, but it's called removeAtIndex(). Locate the tableView(_:,commitEditingStyle:,forRowAtIndexPath:) function and change the removeObjectAtIndex() line so it reads as follows (modified code in bold):

```
things.removeAtIndex(indexPath.row)
```

Finally, your project builds! There's only one thing missing…

Where's the Beef?

You can run your app right now, but it won't display anything. That's because you don't have any MyWhatsit objects to display. To make things worse, you haven't written any of the code to create or edit objects yet.

My solution in these situations is to cheat; programmatically create a few test objects so the interface has something to display. Find the var things property in MasterViewController.swift. Replace the initialization statement so it looks like this (modified code in bold):

```
var things: [MyWhatsit] = [
    MyWhatsit(name: "Gort",                       location: "den"),
    MyWhatsit(name: "Disappearing TARDIS mug",    location: "kitchen"),
    MyWhatsit(name: "Robot USB drive",            location: "office"),
    MyWhatsit(name: "Sad Robot USB hub",          location: "office"),
    MyWhatsit(name: "Solar Powered Bunny",        location: "office")
    ]
```

This code preinitializes the things array with five new MyWhatsit objects. Now when your controller is first created, it will have a set of MyWhatsit objects to show.

Testing MyStuff

Set your scheme to one of the iPhone simulators and run your app. Your table view of MyWhatsit objects appear, as shown on the left in Figure 5-18.

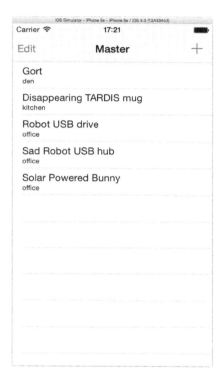 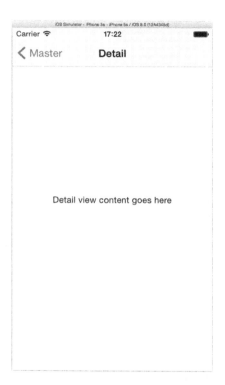

Figure 5-18. *Working table view*

That's pretty cool! You've created your own data model object and implemented everything required to display your custom set of objects in a table view, using a cell format of your choosing.

But it's clear that this app isn't finished yet. If you tap one of the rows, you get a new screen (on the right in Figure 5-18) that doesn't have much and certainly isn't part of your design.

While you're at it, stop the app and change the simulator to one of the iPad devices. Run your app again. This time your interface looks substantially different, as shown in Figure 5-19.

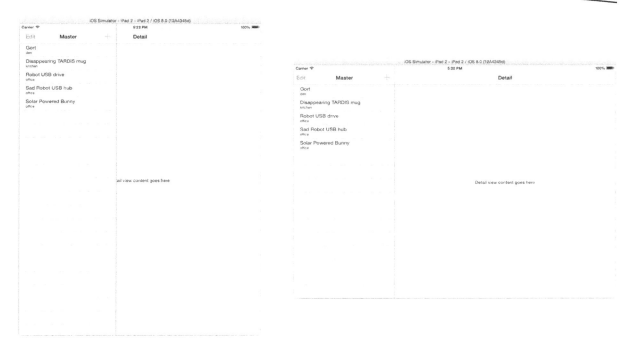

Figure 5-19. Working table view on an iPad

The iOS classes are working behind the scenes to adapt your interface to the size class of the user's device. On an iPad you have plenty of room for both the table view and the detail view. The split view controller steps in to show both.

The next step is to design your details view. After that, you'll implement the code needed to edit the list, change an item, and add new ones.

Adding the Detail View

Now you're at the second half of the master-detail design. Your detail view is controlled by the DetailViewController object. DetailViewController is a plain old UIViewController in the Detail scene. You need to create label and text field objects to display and edit your MyWhatsit properties. You'll need to create Interface Builder outlets in DetailViewController to connect with those text fields, and you'll need to connect them to their objects in Interface Builder. This should be familiar territory by now, so let's get started.

Creating the Detail View

Select the `Main.storyboard` file and then select Detail View Controller in the Detail Scene, as shown in Figure 5-20. Select and delete the label object in the view. You don't need it.

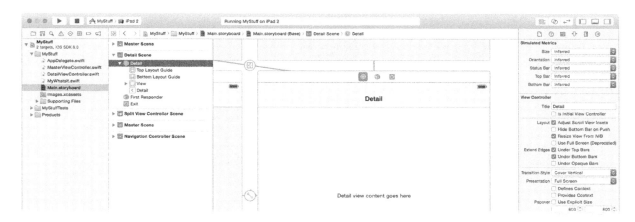

Figure 5-20. *Template detail view*

In the object library, locate the label object and add two of them to your view. Find the text field object and add two of them. Set the text of one label to *Name* and the other to *Location*. Arrange and resize them so your interface looks like the one in Figure 5-21.

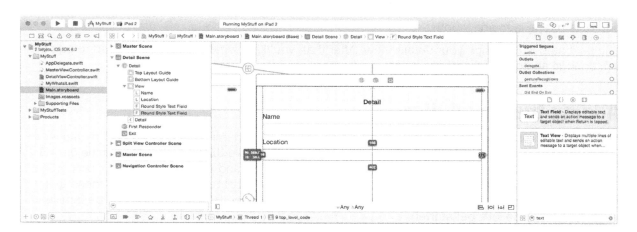

Figure 5-21. *Finished detail view*

Choose the Editor ➤ Resolve Auto Layout Issues ➤ Clear All Constraints in View Controller command to discard any stray constraints from the previous design. Simultaneously select all four of the view objects you just added and click the pin constraints control in the lower-right corner of the canvas, as shown in Figure 5-22. Click the three struts to add top, leading, and trailing edge constraints to all of the views, as shown on the right in Figure 5-22.

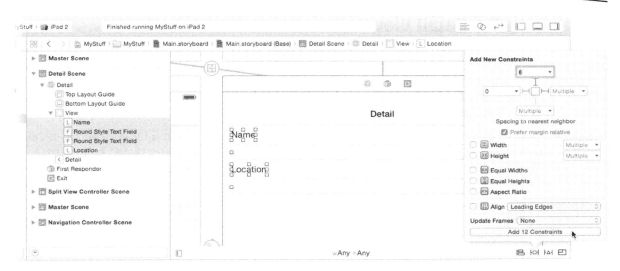

Figure 5-22. *Adding detail view constraints*

Switch to the `DetailViewController.swift` file. Change the type of the `detailItem` property so it's specifically a `MyWhatsit` object (modified code in bold):

```
var detailItem: MyWhatsit? {
```

Delete the existing `detailDescriptionLabel` property and replace it with two new outlet properties.

```
@IBOutlet var nameField: UITextField!
@IBOutlet var locationField: UITextField!
```

Switch back to the `Main.storyboard` file. Select the Detail View Controller object and use the connections inspector to connect the two new outlets (`nameField` and `locationField`) to the appropriate text field objects in the interface, as shown in Figure 5-23.

Figure 5-23. *Connecting the text field outlets*

Configuring the Detail View

You might be asking how the values of a MyWhatsit object are going to get into the two UITextField objects you just created. That's an excellent question. It's going to happen when the user taps a row in the table view. Most of the mechanism to get from that tap to your detail view has already been written for you (as part of the master-detail project template), but it's helpful to understand how it all works. Let's walk through the process of tapping a row.

There are a couple of different ways to respond to the user tapping a row in a table. The "old-school" method is to override the table view delegate function tableView(_:,didSelectRowAtIndexPath:). This rather obviously named function is called when the user selects (taps) a row in your table. Your code can decide what it wants to do about that.

Using storyboards, however, you don't have to write any code to respond to taps. The master-detail template provided a prototype cell that already had a seque—with an identifier of showDetail—attached to it. That seque presents the detail view controller when the user taps a row.

> **Note**   Attaching a seque to a prototype cell automatically sets the cell's accessory type to
> .DisclosureIndicator—that right-facing arrow on the right side of the row. If you're not using seques,
> remember to set the accessory type so the user knows what will happen when they tap a row.

Using the seque method, you can intercept the transition from the table view to the detail view in the prepareForSeque(_:,sender:) function. Locate that function in the MasterViewController.swift file. Hey, it looks like someone commented out all of its code! No problem. Select the commented lines and choose the Editor ➤ Structure ➤ Comment Selection command again. This will "uncomment" the previously commented lines.

Now that you've fixed the type of the detailItem property in the details view controller, you can modify this code so it will compile. Edit the code so it looks like this (modified code in bold):

```
if segue.identifier == "showDetail" {
    if let indexPath = tableView.indexPathForSelectedRow() {
        let thing = things[indexPath.row]
        let controller = (segue.destinationViewController as ↵
            UINavigationController).topViewController as DetailViewController
        controller.detailItem = thing
        controller.navigationItem.leftBarButtonItem = ↵
                        self.splitViewController?.displayModeButtonItem()
        controller.navigationItem.leftItemsSupplementBackButton = true
    }
}
```

The code compiles successfully because the detailItem property is now a MyWhatsit object, the same type you retrieve from the things array.

The prepareForSeque(_:,sender:) function is your opportunity to do anything that needs to be done before the interface transitions to the next view controller. For this app, you catch that seque (named showDetail) and set the detailItem property of the detail view controller to the

MyWhatsit object displayed in the row the user tapped. That information is obtained from the indexPathForSelectedRow() function.

The didSet observer for the detailItem property calls the configureView() function. That function's job is to populate the text fields in the interface with the properties of the MyWhatsit object being edit. Edit the configureView() function, in the DetailViewController.swift file, so it looks like this (modified code in bold):

```
func configureView() {
    if let detail = detailItem {
        if nameField != nil {
            nameField.text = detail.name
            locationField.text = detail.location
        }
    }
}
```

The mystery of how you get from a tap in a table to a detail view is solved. When the user taps a row, the following steps happen:

1. The table cell triggers a seque to the details view controller.

2. prepareForSeque(_:,sender:) is called.

3. prepareForSeque gets the row index the user tapped.

4. It uses the row index to obtain the MyWhatsit object and sets the detailItem of the detail view controller.

5. The detailItem property observer calls configureView().

6. configureView() sets up the text fields from the MyWhatsit object.

This completes the detail view! Run your app and tap a row, as shown on the right in Figure 5-24.

Figure 5-24. Working detail view

You may notice that while you can edit the text fields, they don't change anything. The last part of your app development will be to set up editing of your MyWhatsit objects—allow the user to create new ones, change them, and delete ones they don't want.

Editing

I'm not going to lie to you; editing is hard. That's not to say you can't tackle it, and you're going to add editing to MyStuff. But don't fret, you already have a huge head start. The table view and collection classes do most of the heavy lifting, and most of the code you need to write to support table editing has already been included in your app, thanks to the master-detail project template. There's still code you need to write, but mostly you need to understand what's already been written and how the pieces fit together.

Editing tables can be reduced to a few basic tasks.

- Creating and inserting a new item into the table
- Removing an item from the table
- Reorganizing items in a table
- Editing the details of an individual item

Your app will allow new items to be added, existing items to be removed, and the details of an item to be edited. By default, items in a table can't be reordered. You can enable that feature if you need to, but you won't here.

iOS has a standard interface for deleting and reordering items in a table. You can individually delete items by swiping the row, as shown on the left in Figure 5-25, or you can tap the Edit button and enter editing mode, as shown in the middle of Figure 5-25. In editing mode, tapping the minus button next to a row will delete it. Tapping the Done button returns the table view to regular viewing. iOS also provides a standard "plus" button for you to use to trigger adding a new item, as shown on the right in Figure 5-25.

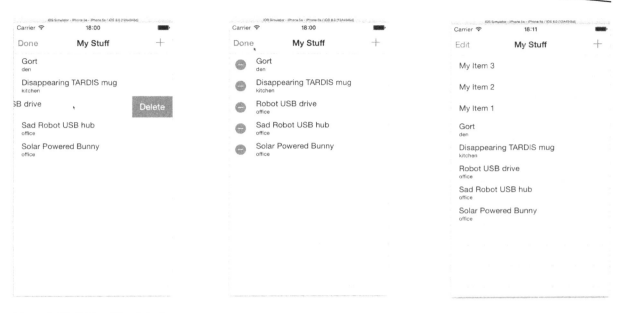

Figure 5-25. *Table editing interface*

These interfaces are part of the table view classes. The only work you need to do is to set up the interface objects to trigger these actions. You'll start by providing the code to add new objects, then I'll describe the setup that enables editing of your table, and finally you'll write the code to edit the properties of a single MyWhatsit object.

Inserting and Removing Items

Inserting a new item into your list is a two-step process:

1. Create new objects and add them to your collection.

2. Inform that table view that you added new objects, and where.

The master-detail template includes an action function, insertNewObject(_:), that does this. The template code, however, doesn't know about your data model, so you'll need to make some small adjustments to create the correct kind of object.

In the MasterViewController.swift file, find the insertNewObject(_:) function. Wow, it looks like someone commented out all of its code too. Uncomment the code and edit the function so it looks like this (modified code in bold):

```
var itemNumber = 0
func insertNewObject(sender: AnyObject) {
    let newThing = MyWhatsit(name: "My Item \(++itemNumber)")
    things.insert(newThing, atIndex: 0)
    let indexPath = NSIndexPath(forRow: 0, inSection: 0)
    self.tableView.insertRowsAtIndexPaths( [indexPath],
                        withRowAnimation: .Automatic)
}
```

Your code generates a unique name for each new item (starting with My Item 1), uses that name to create a new MyWhatsit object, and inserts that new object into the collection, at index 0.

The next step, which is important, is to tell the table view what changed in your data model—the table view isn't psychic. Note that the first parameter to the insertRowsAtIndexPaths(_:, withRowAnimation:) call is an array of NSIndexPath objects. If you've added more than one item to the table, make sure each one is accounted for in the array. You've inserted only one here, so you need to pass only one NSIndexPath.

Tip   If you want your new items to appear at the end of the list, instead of the beginning, append that new object at the end of the array (using things.append(newThing)) and then tell the table view it was added at the end (using let indexPath = NSIndexPath(forRow: things.count-1, inSection: 0)).

Run your app again and tap the + button a few times, as shown on the right in Figure 5-25. Now you may be wondering when, and how, the insertNewObject(_:) function gets called. After all, you don't call it, and it's not an object created in any of the Interface Builder files. The answer to that question can be found in the next section.

Enabling Table Editing

To allow any row in your table to be deleted (via the standard iOS editing features, that is), your data source object must tell the table view that it's allowed. If you don't, iOS won't permit that row to be deleted. Your data source does this via its optional tableView(_:,canEditRowAtIndexPath:) function. The master-detail template provided one for you (in MasterViewController.swift).

```
override func tableView(tableView: UITableView, ↩
                        canEditRowAtIndexPath indexPath: NSIndexPath) -> Bool {
    return true
}
```

The function provided by the template allows all rows in your table to be editable. By default, "editable" means it can be deleted. If you don't want a row to be editable, return false.

Note   Technically, the tableView(_:,canEditRowAtIndexPath:) function determines only whether a row *could* be edited. If it is, then the table view delegate object gets to determine how—or if—via its optional tableView(_:,editingStyleForRowAtIndexPath:) function. The default edit style, which you're using here, allows the row to be deleted (UITableViewCellEditingStyle.Delete).

If `tableView(_:,canEditRowAtIndexPath:)` returns `true` for a row, iOS allows the swipe gesture to delete the row. If you also want to enable "editing mode" for the entire list (where minus signs appear in each row), you hook that up in the navigation bar, provided by the `UITableViewController` (which your `MasterViewController` inherits). iOS provides all the needed button objects, and most of the behavior, that you need. All you have to do is turn them on. In your `MasterViewController` code, find the `viewDidLoad()` function. The beginning of the function should look like this:

```
override func viewDidLoad() {
    super.viewDidLoad()
    self.navigationItem.leftBarButtonItem = self.editButtonItem()

    let addButton = UIBarButtonItem(barButtonSystemItem: .Add,
                                        target: self,
                                        action: "insertNewObject:")
    self.navigationItem.rightBarButtonItem = addButton
```

The first line calls the superclass's `viewDidLoad()` function, so the superclass can do whatever it needs to do when the view objects load.

The next line creates the Edit button you see on the left side of the navigation bar (see Figure 5-24). It sets the left button to the view controller's `editButtonItem`. The `editButtonItem` property is a preconfigured `UIBarButtonItem` object that's already set up to start and stop the edit action for its table. All you need to do is get the button and add it to your interface.

The button to create and insert a new item requires a little more setup, but not much. The next line creates a new `UIBarButtonItem`. It will have the standard iOS + symbol (`UIBarButtonSystemItem.Add`). When the user taps it, it will call the `insertNewObject(_:)` function on this object (`self`). The last line adds the new toolbar button to the right side of the navigation bar.

That's it! This is the code that adds the Edit and + buttons to your table's navigation bar. The Edit button takes care of itself, and you configured the + button to call your controller object's `insertNewObject(_:)` function when it's tapped.

There's one last detail you should be aware of. When adding a new object, your code created the object, added it to your data model, and then told the table view what you'd done. When deleting a row, the table view is deciding what rows to delete. So, how does the actual `MyWhatsit` object get removed from the `things` array? That happens in this data source delegate function, which was already written for you.

```
override func tableView(tableView: UITableView, ↩
            commitEditingStyle editingStyle: UITableViewCellEditingStyle, ↩
            forRowAtIndexPath indexPath: NSIndexPath) {
    if editingStyle == .Delete {
        things.removeAtIndex(indexPath.row)
        tableView.deleteRowsAtIndexPaths([indexPath], withRowAnimation: .Fade)
    } ...
```

When a user edits a table and decides to delete (or insert) a row, that request is communicated to your data source object by calling this function. Your data source object must examine the `editingStyle` parameter to determine what's happening—a row is being deleted, for example—and take appropriate action. The action to take when a row is deleted is to remove the corresponding MyWhatsit object from the array and let the table view know what you did.

That's all of the code needed to edit your table. Now it's time to put the last big piece of the puzzle into place: editing the details of a single item.

Editing Details

To edit the details of an item, you're going to need to do the following:

1. Create a view where the user can see all of the details.

2. Set the values of that view with the properties of the selected item in the table.

3. Record changes to those values.

4. Update the table with the new information.

The good news is that you've already done half of this work. You already modified the DetailViewController to display the name and location properties of a MyWhatsit object, and you added code to fill in the text fields with the property values of the selected item (in configureView()). Now you just have to add some code to do the next two steps, and your app is nearly done.

Create an action that will respond to changes made to the name and location text fields. Add this function to DetailViewController.swift:

```
@IBAction func changedDetail(sender: AnyObject!) {
    if sender === nameField {
        detailItem?.name = nameField.text
    } else if sender === locationField {
        detailItem?.location = locationField.text
    }
}
```

This action function will be called when either the name or location text field is edited. Since both fields call the same function, you must figure out which one sent the action by comparing the sender object with well-known view objects. If one is a match, you know which text field sent the action and can update the appropriate MyWhatsit property with the new value.

Connect the action of the two text fields to this function in Interface Builder. Select the Main.storyboard file. Select the name property text field. Control+drag from the text field to the view controller object, release the mouse button, and choose the changedDetail: action—which is currently your only action, as shown in Figure 5-26. Repeat with the location text field.

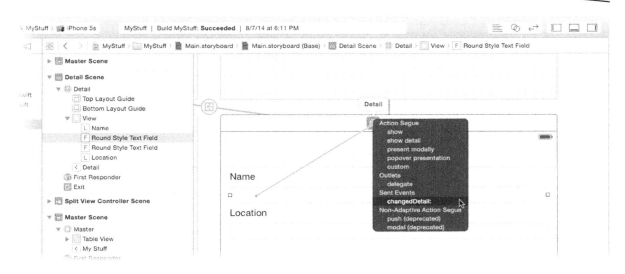

Figure 5-26. *Connecting text field to changedDetail: action*

Now when you edit one of the text fields in the detail view, it will change the property values of the original object, updating your data model. Give it a try.

Make sure your scheme is still set to an iPhone simulator and run your app. Your items appear in the list, shown on the left in Figure 5-27.

Figure 5-27. *Testing detail editing*

Tapping the Gort item shows you its details. Edit the details of the first row. In the example in Figure 5-27, I'm changing its location to "living room." Clicking the My Stuff button in the navigation bar returns you to the list. But wait! The Gort row wasn't updated.

Or was it? You could test this theory by setting a debugger breakpoint in the changedDetail(_:) function to see whether it was called (it was). No, the problem is a little more insidious. With your cursor (or finger, if you're testing this on a real device), drag the list up so it causes the Gort row to disappear briefly underneath the navigation toolbar, as shown on the left in Figure 5-28.

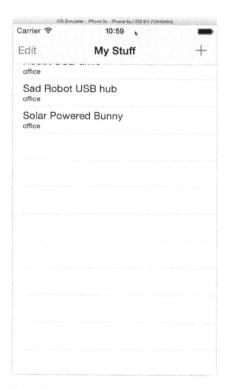
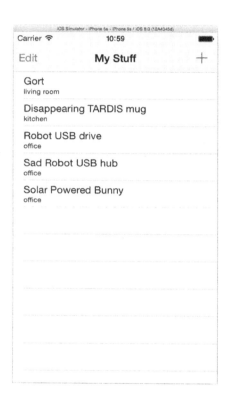

Figure 5-28. Redrawing the first row

Release your mouse/finger and the list snaps back. Notice that the first row now shows the updated values. That's because your changedDetail(_:) function changed the property values in your data model, but you never told the table view, so it didn't know to redraw that row. You need to fix that.

Observing Changes to MyWhatsit

In Chapter 8 I'll explain the rationale behind data model and view object communications. For now, all you need to know is that when the properties of a MyWhatsit object change, the table view needs to know about it so it can redraw that row.

In theory, this is an easy problem to solve: when the MyWhatsit property is updated, something needs to call a table view function to redraw the table, just like you did when you added or removed an object. In practice, it's a little trickier. The problem is that neither the MyWhatsit object nor DetailViewController have a direct connection to the table view object of the MasterViewController view. While there's nothing stopping you from adding one and connecting it in Interface Builder or programmatically, there's a cleaner solution.

> **Note**   In a good model-view-controller design, it would be completely inappropriate for a data model object (such as MyWhatsit) to have a direct connection to a view object (such as a table view). So, this isn't just a clever solution; it's actually good software design.

There's a software design pattern called the *observer pattern*. It works like this:

1. Any object interested in knowing when something happens registers as an observer.

2. When something happens, the object responsible posts a notification.

3. That notification is then distributed to all interested observers.

The real beauty of this arrangement is that neither the observers nor the objects posting notifications have to know anything about each other. You'll use notifications to communicate changes in MyWhatsit objects to the MasterViewController. The first step is to design a notification and have MyWhatsit post it at the appropriate time.

Posting Notifications

Toward the top of your MyWhatsit.swift file, add this constant definition, before the class declaration:

```
let WhatsitDidChangeNotification = "MyWhatsitDidChange"
```

In the body of the class, add this new function:

```
func postDidChangeNotification() {
    let center = NSNotificationCenter.defaultCenter()
    center.postNotificationName(WhatsitDidChangeNotification, object: self)
}
```

When called, this function posts a notification named "MyWhatsitDidChange". The object of the notification is itself. The name of the notification can be anything you want; you just want to make sure it's unique so it isn't confused with a notification used by another object.

Of course, you have to call this function at some point. You want to post your notification whenever anyone changes a property of your MyWhatsit object. You'll do that by adding property observers to your two properties (new code in bold).

```
var name: String {
    didSet {
        postDidChangeNotification()
    }
}
var location: String {
    didSet {
        postDidChangeNotification()
    }
}
```

A property observer is a block of code executed whenever that property value is set (that is, something.name = anyValue). The didSet observer is executed after the property is set, which is a perfect place to fire your notification. (There's also a willSet observer that executes before, should you need that.)

> **Note**   Property observers are never executed during object initialization. So, the self.name = name statement in your init(name:,location:) initializer won't post a notification.

Now whenever you change the details of your MyWhatsit object, it will post a notification that it changed. Any object interested in that fact will receive that notification. The last step is to make MasterViewController observe this notification.

Observing Notifications

The basic pattern for observing notifications is as follows:

1. Create a function to receive the notification.

2. Become an observer for the specific notifications your object is interested in.

3. Process any notifications received.

4. Stop observing notifications when you don't need them anymore or before your object is destroyed.

The first step is simple enough. In your MasterViewController.swift file, add a whatsitDidChange(_:) function.

```
func whatsitDidChange(notification: NSNotification) {
    if let changedThing = notification.object as? MyWhatsit {
        for (index,thing) in enumerate(things) {
            if thing === changedThing {
                let path = NSIndexPath(forItem: index, inSection: 0)
                tableView.reloadRowsAtIndexPaths( [path], ↩
                            withRowAnimation: .None)
            }
        }
    }
}
```

All notification functions follow the same pattern: func *myNotification*(notification: NSNotification) -> *Void*. You can name your function whatever you want, but it must expect a single NSNotification object as its only parameter.

The notification parameter has all the details about the notification. Often you don't care, particularly if your object wants to know only that the notification happened and not exactly why. In this case, you're interested in the object property of the notification. Every notification has a name and an object it's associated with—often it's the object that caused the notification.

The first line of your function gets the notification's object and, assuming the property is set and contains a MyWhatsit object, assigns it to the changedThing constant.

The loop then looks through your array of MyWhatsit objects. If the MyWhatsit object that changed is part of your data model, notify the table view that one of its rows needs to be updated. If the object that was modified isn't in your data model, ignore it.

Now you just have to register MasterViewController with the notification center so it will receive this notification.

Locate the viewDidLoad() function. At the end of the function, add these statements:

```
let center = NSNotificationCenter.defaultCenter()
center.addObserver( self,
        selector: "whatsitDidChange:",
            name: WhatsitDidChangeNotification,
          object: nil)
```

This call tells the notification center to register this object (self) and call the function (whatsitDidChange (_:)) whenever a notification with the name WhatsitDidChangeNotification is posted for any object (nil).

NOTIFICATION MATCHING

Registering to be a notification observer is very flexible. By passing `nil` for either the `name` parameter or the `object` parameter in `addObserver(_:,selector:,name:,object:)`, you can request to receive notifications with a given name, for a specific object, or both. The following table shows the effect of the `name` and `object` parameters when becoming an observer:

name	object	Notifications received
"Name"	object	Receive only notifications named Name for the object object
"Name"	nil	Receive all notifications named Name for any object
nil	object	Receive every notification for the object object
nil	nil	Receive every notification (not recommended)

In this situation, you want to be notified when any `MyWhatsit` object is edited. Your code then looks at the specific object to determine whether it's interesting. In other situations, you'll want to receive notifications only when a specific object sends a specific notification, ignoring similar notifications from unrelated objects.

Just as important as registering to receive notifications is to unregister when your object should no longer receive them. For this app, there's no point at which the notifications are irrelevant, but you should still make sure that your object is no longer an observer before it's destroyed. Leaving a destroyed object registered to receive notifications is a notorious cause of app crashes in iOS. So, make absolutely sure your object is removed from the notification center before it ceases to exist.

It's really easy to ensure this, so you don't have any excuses for not doing it. Add a deinitializer to your `MasterViewController` class.

```
deinit {
    NSNotificationCenter.defaultCenter().removeObserver(self)
}
```

The special deinitializer function is called just before the object is destroyed. In it, you should clean up any "loose ends" that wouldn't be taken care of automatically. This statement tells the notification center that this object is no longer an observer for any notification. You don't even have to remember what notifications or objects you'd previously ask to observe; this call will deregister them all.

Run your app in an iPhone simulator again. Edit an item and return to the list. This time your changes appear in the list!

Modal vs. Modeless Editing

You're in the home stretch. In fact, you're so close to the finish line that you can almost touch it. There's only one vexing detail to fix: the iPad interface.

The iPhone interface uses what software developers call a *model interface*: when you tap a row to edit an item, you're transported to a screen where you can edit its details (editing mode), and then you exit that screen and return to the list (browsing mode).

The iPad interface doesn't work like that. Particularly in landscape orientation, you can jump between the master list and the detail view at will. This means you can start editing a title or location and then switch immediately to another item in the list. This is called a *modeless interface*

While this makes for a fluid user experience, it's a disaster for your app, as shown in Figure 5-29. Tap an item ("Gort" in this example), edit one of the fields, and then switch to another item. Go ahead; give it a try. I'll wait.

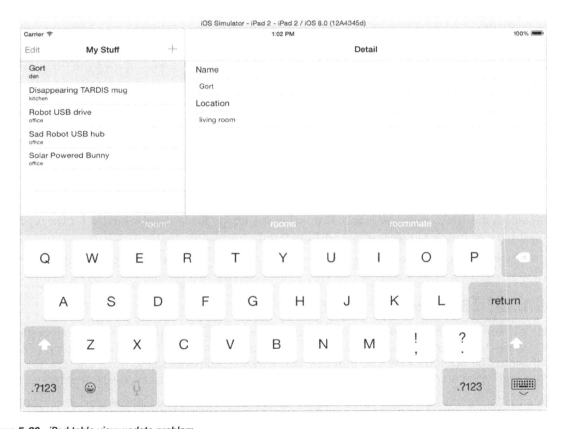

Figure 5-29. iPad table view update problem

The problem is that the editing of the text field never gets a chance to "end" before you can change to another MyWhatsit object in the list. Fortunately, there's an easy out. When you connected your text field to the details view controller, you connected the Editing Did End event. This is the default action event for text fields. But there are many other events. Try connecting the Editing Changed event instead.

Select a text field in your details view controller, as shown on the left in Figure 5-30. Using the connections inspector, click the little (x) next to the Editing Did End event to disconnect that action. Now drag the Editing Changed event connector to the view controller, connecting it to the changedItem: action, as shown on the right in Figure 5-30. This event is a "lower-level" event that's sent whenever the user makes *any* change in the text field. Now the rows in the table view will update as the user edits the details.

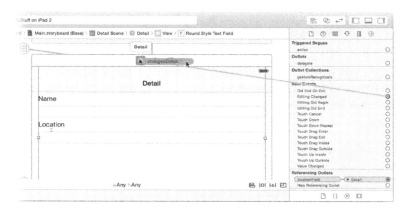

Figure 5-30. Reconnecting the text field action

Little Touches

Polish your app by giving it an icon, just as you did for the EightBall app in the previous chapter. Locate the Learn iOS Development Projects folder you downloaded in Chapter 1. Inside the Ch 5 folder you'll find the MyStuff (Icons) folder. Select the images.xcassets item in the navigator and then select the AppIcon image group. Drag all of the image files from the MyStuff (Icons) folder and drop them into the group. Xcode will sort them out.

Your app is finished, but I'd like to take a moment to direct you to other table-related topics.

Advanced Table View Topics

You can now see that table views are used for a lot more than just listing contacts and song titles. The table view classes are powerful and flexible, but that means they are—at times—complicated and confusing. The good news is that they are extensively documented, and there are lots of sample projects, which you can download from Apple, that demonstrate various table view techniques.

The place to start is the *Table View Programming Guide for iOS*. Choose Help ➤ Documentation and API Reference, in the search field enter **Table View Programming**, and click the Table View Programming Guide for iOS in the autocompletion list, as shown in Figure 5-31.

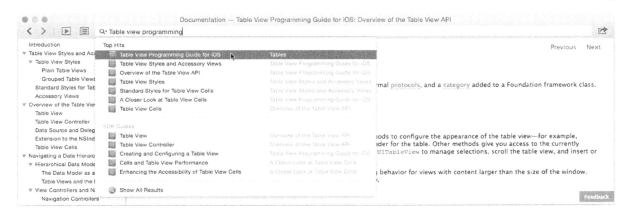

Figure 5-31. *Locating the Table View Programming Guide for iOS*

This guide will explain every major feature of table views and how to use them. It's not a short read, but if you want to know how to do something specific—such as create an indexed list—this is where you should start.

Most major iOS classes have links in their documentation that will take you to a guide explaining how to use it and related classes. In the overview section for the UITableView class, for example, there are several links to table-specific programming guides.

Summary

Give yourself a big "high five!" You've taken another huge step in iOS app development. You've learned how table views works and how to use cell objects. You know what messages your app receives when a user taps a row, how to handle editing of rows, and how to create new rows. You created a data model, and you learned how to post and observe notifications between unconnected objects.

This app still falls short in a few categories. The details of a particular item could be, well, more detailed. But probably the most annoying issue is that your app doesn't remember anything. If you restart your app, any changes you made are lost. So, for an app that's supposed to keep track of your stuff, it doesn't do a very good job.

Don't worry; you'll attack those shortcomings in future chapters. Before you get there, take a well-deserved rest from app development and take a brief stroll through the theory of object-oriented programming.

Chapter 6

Object Lesson

I'd like to take a break from app development for a chapter. Good iOS development requires conceptual and design skills that go beyond just knowing how to write for loops or connect a button to an outlet. Software engineers call these *design patterns* and *design principles*. To appreciate these philosophies, I'll start with the foundation for it all: the object.

"Hey!" you say, "I've been using objects; what's to understand?" You'd be surprised at the number of programmers who can't describe exactly what an *object* is. If you haven't had any questions about the terms used in this book so far (*class*, *object*, *instance*, *function*, *stored property*, and so on) and you're already familiar with design patterns and principles, feel free to skip or skim this chapter. If you have questions, keep reading.

In this chapter, I will do the following:

- Give a brief history of objects and object-oriented programming
- Explain exactly what classes, objects, and instances are
- Describe inheritance and encapsulation
- Explain delegation and a few other design patterns
- Touch on a few key design principles

To appreciate objects, it helps to know what came before them and why they're such a big deal.

Two Houses, Both Alike in Dignity

There are two basic types of information rattling around inside a computer. *Data* consists of the binary values that represent values and quantities, such as your name, a URL, or the airspeed velocity of an unladen swallow. *Code* consists of the binary values that represent instructions that tell the computer to do things such as draw your name on the screen, load a URL, or choose your favorite color.

It's easy to see this division in computer languages. The syntax of a programming language, like Swift, is largely divided between statements that define, retrieve, and store values and statements that change values, make decisions, and invoke other statements. Think of them as the nouns and verbs of the computer's language.

Like the Montagues and the Capulets,[1] these two aspects of programming stayed separate for a long time. As computers got bigger and faster and computer programs got longer and more complicated, a number of problems began to develop.

Programmers encountered more solutions where multiple pieces of information needed to be kept together. A person doesn't just have a name; they also have a height, an age, a tax identification number, and so on. To keep these related facts together, they started combining multiple values into a single block of memory called a *structure*. In the Swift programming language, a structure looks like this:

```
struct Person {
    var name: String
    var female: Bool
    var birthdate: Date
    var height: Float
    var taxNumber: Int
}
```

These structures became so handy that programmers started to use them as if the whole thing was a single value. They would pass a `Person` to a function or store a `Person` in a file. They would write functions that operated on a `Person` structure (as opposed to a single value, like a date). An example is a function that determines whether it is that person's birthday, like `IsBirthdayToday( Person person ) -> Bool`.

Programmers also started to encounter situations where there were lots of structures that resembled one another. A `Player` structure has all the same properties that a `Person` structure does, except that it has more variables for things like the player's high score. They quickly figured out that they could create structures from structures, like this:

```
struct Player {
    var person: Person
    var gamesPlayed: Int
    var highScore: Int
}
```

What got programmers really excited was that they could now reuse the functions they wrote for the `Person` structure for the `Player` structure![2] They even gave this idea a name: *subtype polymorphism*. You'll get extra credit if you work that into a conversation at your next party.

---

[1] The Montagues and the Capulets were the two alienated families in the play *Romeo and Juliet*. I mention this in case your reading list is skewed toward Jules Verne and not William Shakespeare.

[2] You can't pass a `Player` structure to a function that expects a `Person` structure in Swift, even though the `Player` structure begins with a `Person` structure. You can do that in more primitive languages, like C, which is where many of these early programming ideas germinated.

Things should have been swell, but they weren't. The number of structures and functions grew at a dizzying pace. Projects would have thousands and thousands of individual functions and nearly as many different structures. Some functions would work with `Person` structures, but most wouldn't.

The problem was that data structures and functions were still in separate families; they didn't mix. Trying to figure out what functions should be used with what structures became unmanageable. Programs didn't work. Large software projects were failing. Something needed to happen—and it did.

Romeo Meets Juliet

In the late 1960s something magical happened: structures and functions got together, and the object was born. An *object* is the fusion of property values (the data structure) and the methods that act on those values (the functions) into a single entity that owns both. It seems so simple, but it was a dramatic turning point in the evolution of computer languages.

Before objects, programmers spent their days writing and calling functions (also called *procedures*), passing them the correct data structures. Computer languages that work this way are called *procedural* languages. When the concept of an object was introduced, it turned the way programmers wrote and thought about programs inside-out. Now the center of the programmer's world is the object; you take an object and invoke its methods. These new computer languages are called *object-oriented* languages.

Objects also created programs that felt "alive." A data structure is an inert collection of values, and a function is an abstract sequence of instructions, but an object is both; it's an entity that has both characteristics and can do things when told. In this sense, objects are much more analogous to the kinds of things you deal with in the real world.

Now that you know what an object is, I'm going to give you a short course in how objects are defined and created and what that looks like in Swift. Chapter 20 describes this in much more detail.

Classes and Cookies

An object is the tangible embodiment of a *class*. An object's class defines what properties that object can have and what actions it can perform. Objects are the things you actually work with. Think of it this way: classes are the cookie cutters, and objects are the cookies. See Figure 6-1.

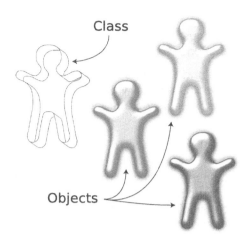

Figure 6-1. Classes and objects

In Swift, a class is defined using a class declaration.

```
class MyClass {
    // Class definition goes here
}
```

A class doesn't do much by itself. A class is simply the "shape" used to create new objects. When you create an object, you do so by specifying the class of object you want to create and then telling the class to create one. In Swift, that code looks like this:

```
let object = MyClass()
```

The result of that expression is a new *instance of a class*, which is synonymous with *an object*. The object includes its own storage (data structure) where all of its individual property values are kept; changing the properties of one object won't change the properties of any other object in the system.

Each object is also associated with a number of functions that act only on that class of objects. The class defines those functions, and every object of that class is endowed with those actions. In Swift, the code for those functions appears in the definition of the class.

```
class MyClass {
    func doSomething() {
        // Do something here
    }
}
```

Functions that do their thing on a particular object (instance) of a class are called *instance functions*, *instance methods*, or just *methods*. Methods always execute in the context of a single object. When the code in a method refers to a property value or the special `self` variable, it's referring to the property of the specific object it was invoked for. In Swift, methods are always called "on" an object, like this:

```
object.doSomething()
```

You'll write and use methods almost exclusively in this book and in your day-to-day programming. You can also define methods for structures, where they work exactly like they do for classes. You can also define global functions that don't execute in the context of an object (or structure) and work just like plain old C functions—back in the days before objects. These are described in more detail in Chapter 20.

Classes and Objects and Methods, Oh My!

A continual source of confusion for new developers is the profusion, and confusion, of terms used in object-oriented programming. Every programming language seems to pick a slightly different set of terms to use. Computer scientists use yet another vocabulary. Terms are often mixed up, and even seasoned programmers will use terms incorrectly, saying "object" when they really mean "class."

Table 6-1 will help you navigate the world of object-oriented programming terms. It lists common Swift programming terms, their meaning, and some synonyms that you'll encounter. I'll explain most in more detail later in this chapter.

Table 6-1. Common Swift Terms

Term	Meaning	Similar Terms
Class	The definition of a class of objects. It defines what property values those objects can store and what functions they implement.	Interface, type, definition, prototype
Object	An instance of a class.	Class instance, instance
Property	A value stored in, or produced by, an object. (See *stored property* and *computed property*.)	Attribute
Stored property	A value stored in an object.	Instance variable (sometimes *ivar*)
Computed property	A value calculated or generated by an object.	Synthetic property
Method	A function that executes in the context of a single object.	Instance method, function, instance function, procedure, business logic
Global function	A function that executes outside the context of any particular object.	Class function, static function

(*continued*)

Table 6-1. (*continued*)

Term	Meaning	Similar Terms
Override	Supplanting the implementation of an inherited method with a different one.	
Selector	A value that chooses a particular method (instance function) of an object.	Message
Send	Using a selector to invoke an object's method.	Perform a function
Responds	Having a function that executes when sent a particular selector.	Implements, conforms
Client code	The code outside of the class that is using the public interface of that class or its objects.	User, client
Abstract	A class, property, or function that is defined or declared but has no useful functionality. This is used to define a concept that subclasses will implement in a meaningful way.	Abstraction layer, placeholder, stub
Concrete	A class, property, or method that does something and is usable.	

By now you should have a solid understanding of the relationship between a class, its objects, and its properties and methods.

Inheritance

Earlier I mentioned that programmers found many situations where a class or structure that they needed was similar, possibly with only minor additions, to another object or structure that already existed. Furthermore, the methods they'd written for the existing object/structure were all applicable to the new one. This idea is called *inheritance* and is a cornerstone of object-oriented languages.

The idea is that classes can be organized into a tree, with the more general classes at the top, working down to more specific classes at the bottom. This arrangement might look like something in Figure 6-2.

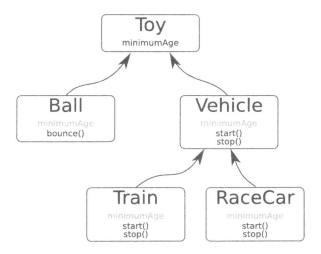

Figure 6-2. *A class hierarchy*

In Figure 6-2, the generic Toy class serves as the base class of all the other classes. Toy defines a set of properties and methods common to all Toy objects. The subclasses of Toy are Ball and Vehicle. The subclasses of Vehicle are Train and RaceCar.

> **Note**   In Swift, inheritance is the bright line that separates classes from structures. A class inherits from other classes. A structure cannot inherit from another structure.

The Toy class defines a minimumAge property that describes the youngest age the toy is appropriate for. All subclasses of Toy inherit this property. Therefore, a Ball, Vehicle, Train, and RaceCar all have a minimumAge property.

Similarly, classes inherit methods too. The Vehicle class defines two functions: start() and stop(). All subclasses of Vehicle inherit these two functions, so you can call the start() function on a Train and the stop() function on a RaceCar. The bounce() function can be called only on a Ball.

Through inheritance, every object of type Vehicle and every object of every subclass of type Vehicle will have a start() and stop() function. This is what computer scientists call *subtype polymorphism*. It means that if you have an object, parameter, or variable of a specific type (say, Vehicle), you can use or substitute any object that's a subclass of Vehicle. You can pass a function that expects a Vehicle parameter a Train or a RaceCar object, and that function can call start() on the more complex object just as effectively. A variable that refers to a Toy can store a Toy, a Ball, or a Train. A variable that refers to a Vehicle, however, cannot be set to a Ball because a Ball is not a subclass of Vehicle.

You've already seen this in the apps you've written. NSResponder is the base class for all objects that respond to events. UIView is a subclass of NSResponder, so all view objects respond to events. The UIButton is a subclass of UIView, so it can appear in a view, and it responds to events. A UIButton object can be used in any situation that expects a UIButton object, a UIView object, or an NSResponder object.

Abstract and Concrete Classes

Programmers refer to the Toy and Vehicle classes as *abstract classes*. These classes don't define usable objects; they define the properties and methods common to all subclasses. You'll never find an instance of a Toy or Vehicle object in your program. The objects you'll find in your program are Ball and Train objects, which inherit common properties and methods from the Toy and Vehicle classes. The classes of usable objects are called *concrete classes*.

Overriding Methods

Starting a train is a lot different than starting a car. A class can supply its own code for a specific function, replacing the implementation it inherited. This is called *overriding* a method.

As an example, all subclasses of UIViewController inherit a supportedInterfaceOrientation() function. This returns an Int describing which device orientations (portrait, landscape left, landscape right, or upside down) that view controller supports. The version of supportedInterfaceOrientations() supplied by UIViewController is generic and assumes your view controller supports all orientations on a regular device and all but upside down on a compact device. As a programmer, you can override supportedInterfaceOrientations() to describe exactly what orientations your view controller allows.

Sometimes a class—particularly abstract classes—will define a function that doesn't do anything at all; it's just a placeholder for subclasses to override. The Vehicle class methods start() and stop() don't do anything. It's up to the specific subclass to decide what it means to start and stop, as shown in Figure 6-3.

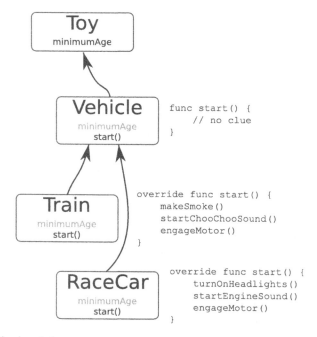

Figure 6-3. Overriding a function in subclasses

You've been doing this since Chapter 3. The `UIViewController` class defines the function `viewDidLoad()`. This function doesn't do anything. It's just a placeholder function that gets called just after the view controller's view objects have been created. If *your* view controller subclass needs to do something else to set up your view objects, your class would override `viewDidLoad()` and perform whatever it is you need it to do.

If your class's method also needs to invoke the method defined by its superclass, Swift has a special syntax for that. The `super` keyword means the same thing as `self`, but functions called on `super` go to the function defined by the superclass (ignoring the function defined in your class), as if that function had not been overridden.

```
super.viewDidLoad()
```

This is a common pattern for extending (rather than replacing) the behavior of a function. The overriding function calls the original function and then performs any additional tasks.

> **Caution**   Sometimes the superclass's implementation does do something important, so your override function must call the superclass's version before it returns. These cases are usually noted in the function's documentation.

Design Patterns and Principles

With the newfound power of objects and inheritance, programmers discovered that they could build computer programs that were orders of magnitude more complex than what they had achieved in the past. They also discovered that if they designed their classes poorly, the result was a tangled mess, worse than the old way of writing programs. They began to ponder the question "What makes a good class?"

A huge amount of thought, theory, and experimentation has gone into trying to define what makes a good class and the best way to use objects in a program. This has resulted in a variety of concepts and philosophies, collectively known as design patterns and design principles. *Design patterns* are reusable solutions to common problems—a kind of programming best practices. *Design principles* are guidelines and insights into what makes a good design. There are dozens of these patterns and principles, and you could spend years studying them. I'll touch on a few of the more important ones.

Encapsulation

An object should hide, or *encapsulate*, its superfluous details from clients—the other classes that use and interact with that class. A well-designed class is kind of like a food truck. The outside of the truck is its interface; it consists of a menu and a window. Using the food truck is simple: you choose what you want, place your order, and receive your food through the window. What happens inside the truck is considerably more complicated. There are stoves, electricity, refrigerators, storage, inventory, recipes, cleaning procedures, and so on. But all of those details are encapsulated inside the truck.

Similarly, a good class hides the details of what it does behind its public interface. Properties and methods that the clients of that object need should be declared normally. Everything else should be "hidden" using the `private` keyword. You can also "hide" functions in extensions. Access scope and extensions are explained in Chapter 20.

This isn't just for simplicity, although that's a big benefit. The more details a class exposes to its clients, the more entangled it becomes with the code that uses it. Computer engineers call this a *dependency*. The fewer dependencies, the easier it is to change the inner workings of a class without disrupting how that class is used. For example, the food truck can switch from using frozen French fries to slicing fresh potatoes and cooking them. That change would improve the quality of its French fries, but it wouldn't require it to modify its menu or alter how customers place their order.

Singularity of Purpose

The best classes are those that have a single purpose. A well-designed class should represent exactly one thing or concept, encapsulate all of the information about that one thing, and nothing else. A method of a class should perform one task. Software engineers call this the *single responsibility principle*.

A button object that starts a timer has limited functionality. Sure, if you need a button that starts a timer, it would work great. But if you need a button that resets a score or a button that turns a page, it would be useless. On the other hand, a `UIButton` object is infinitely useful because it does only one thing: it presents a button the user can tap. When a user taps it, it sends a message to another object. That other object could start a timer, reset a score, or turn a page.

Great objects are like Lego blocks. Create objects that do simple, self-contained tasks and connect them to other objects to solve problems. Don't create objects that solve whole problems. I'll discuss this more in Chapter 8.

Stability

A ball should be usable all of the time. If you picked up a ball, you would expect it to bounce. It would be strange to find a ball that wouldn't bounce until you first turned it over twice or had to paint it a color.

Strive to make your objects functional regardless of how they were created or what properties have been set. In the ball example, the `bounce()` function should work whether the `minimumAge` property has been set or not. Software engineers call these *preconditions*, and you should keep them to a minimum.

Open/Closed

There are two corollaries to the single responsibility principle. The first is the so-called open/closed principle: classes should be *open* to extension and *closed* to change. Are you thinking "Huh?" Well, you're not alone; this is a strange one to grasp. It basically means that a class is well designed if it can be reused to solve other problems by *extending* the existing class or methods, rather than *changing* them.

Programmers abhor change, but it's the one constant in software development. The more things you have to change in a class, the more chance that it's going to affect some other part of your project adversely. Software engineers call this *coupling*. It's a polite way of saying that by changing one thing, you'll create a bug somewhere else. The open/closed principle tries to avoid changing things by designing your classes and methods so you don't have to change them in the future. This takes practice.

Using the toy classes again, let's pretend your app has been getting great reviews and now you want to add two new vehicle toys: an electric dune buggy and an electric Transformer robot. Both will be subclasses of Vehicle, but both also need new properties common to electric vehicles, like a battery level.

It might be tempting to add a batteryLevel property to your Vehicle class, as shown on the left in Figure 6-4, and then create your new subclasses. This changes your existing Vehicle class. Because of inheritance, it indirectly changes your Train and RaceCar classes too. There's now a real possibility that you've introduced a bug or other complication into three classes that were previously working just fine.

Instead, consider creating a new ElectricVehicle subclass with the new batteryLevel property and then make DuneBuggy and Transformer subclasses of this new intermediary class. See the right side of Figure 6-4. Notice that you've added the new batteryLevel property for all the subclasses that need it and created your new toy classes, but without making any changes to your existing Vehicle, RaceCar, and Train classes. If these classes were working correctly before, they should still be after the addition.

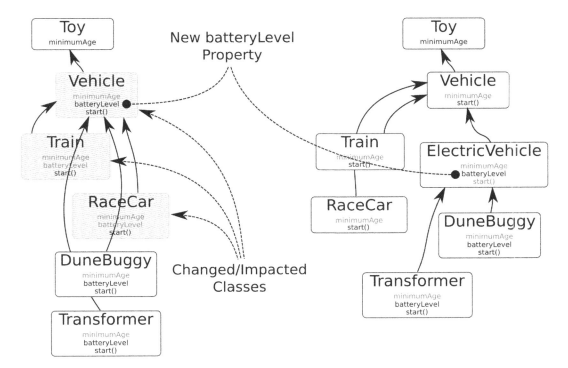

Figture 6-4. Imact of changing existing classes

The open/closed principle invites you to think about how your app will grow in the future. The trick is to design your classes so that new classes and features can be added without modifying the classes you've already written and debugged. So, as you design your classes, think a little beyond the code you're writing today to the code you might want to add tomorrow. If you have a class that handles four different record types or twenty different shapes, ask yourself, "How would I add a fifth record type or nine new shapes *without* altering the class I just finished?"

Delegation

Another lesson of the single responsibility principle is to avoid mixing in knowledge or logic that's beyond the scope of your object. A ball has a bounce() function. To know how high the ball will bounce, the function must know what kind of surface the ball is bouncing against. Since this calculation has to be made in the bounce() function, it's tempting to include that logic in the Ball class. You might do this by adding a howHigh() function that calculates the height of a bounce.

That design decision, unfortunately, leads you down a crazy path. Since the bounce calculation varies depending on the environment, the only way to modify the calculation is to override the bounce() method in subclasses. This forces you to create subclasses such as BallOnWood, BallOnConcrete, BallOnCarpet, and so on. If you then want to create different kinds of balls, such as a basketball and a beach ball, you end up subclassing all of those subclasses (BeachBallOnWood, BasketBallOnWood, BeachBallOnCarpet, and on and on). Your classes are spiraling out of control, as shown in Figure 6-5.

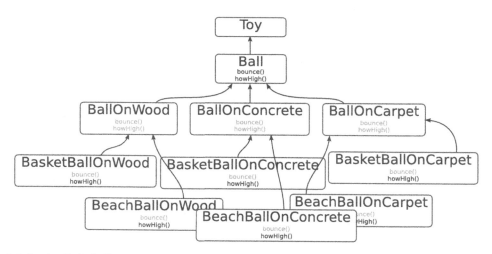

Figure 6-5. *Subclassing "solution"*

A design pattern that avoids this mess is the delegate pattern. As you've seen, the delegate pattern is used extensively in the Cocoa Touch framework. The *delegate pattern* defers—delegates—key decisions to another object so that logic doesn't distract from the single purpose of the class.

Using the delegate pattern, you would create a surface property for the ball. The surface property would connect to an object that implements a bounceHeight(ball:) function. When the ball wants to know how high it should bounce, it calls the delegate function bounceHeight(ball:), passing itself as the ball in question. The Surface object would perform the calculation and return the answer. Subclasses of Surface (ConcreteSurface, WoodSurface, CarpetSurface, GrassSurface) would override bounceHeight(ball:) to adjust its behavior, as shown in Figure 6-6.

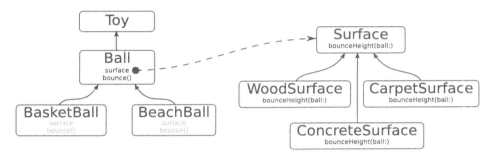

Figure 6-6. Delegate solution

Now you have a simple, and flexible, class hierarchy. The abstract Ball class has BasketBall and BeachBall subclasses. Any of these can be connected to any of the Surface subclasses (ConcreteSurface, WoodSurface, CarpetSurface, GrassSurface) to provide the correct physics. This arrangement also preserves the open/closed principle: you can *extend* Ball or Surface to create new balls or new surfaces, without *changing* any of the existing classes.

Other Patterns

There are many, many other design patterns and principles. I don't expect you to memorize them—just be aware of them. With an awareness of design patterns, you'll begin to notice them as you see how classes in the Cocoa Touch framework and elsewhere are designed; iOS is a very well-designed system.

Here are other common patterns you'll encounter:

- *Singleton pattern*: A class that maintains a single instance of an object for use by the entire program. The UIApplication.sharedApplication() function returns a singleton.

- *Lazy initialization pattern*: Waiting until you need an object (or a property) before creating it. Lazy initialization makes some things more efficient and reduces preconditions. UITableView lazily creates table cell objects; it waits until the moment it needs to draw a row before asking the data source delegate to provide a cell for that row.

■ *Factory pattern and class clusters*: A method that creates objects for you (instead of you creating and configuring them yourself). Often, your code won't know what object, or even what class of objects, needs to be created. A factory method handles (encapsulates) those details for you. The `NSURL.URLWithString(_:)` function is a factory method. The class of the `NSURL` object returned will be different, depending on what kind of URL the string describes.

■ *Decorator pattern*: Dress up an object using another object. A `UIBarButtonItem` is not, ironically, a button object. It's a decorator that may cause a button, cause a special control item, or even change the positioning of controls in a toolbar.

There are, of course, many others.

The first major book of design patterns (*Design Patterns: Elements of Reusable Object-Oriented Software*) was published in 1994 by the so-called "Gang of Four": Erich Gamma, Richard Helm, Ralph Johnson, and John Vlissides. Those patterns are still applicable today, and design patterns have become a "must-know" topic for any serious programmer. The original book is not specific to any particular computer language; you could apply these principles to any language, even non-object-oriented ones. Many authors have since reapplied, and refined, these patterns to specific languages. So if you're interested in learning these skills primarily for Swift, for example, look for a book on design patterns for Swift.

> **Note**   An interesting offshoot of design patterns has been the emergence of *anti-patterns*: programming pitfalls that developers repeatedly fall into. Many anti-patterns have entertaining names like "God object" (an object that does too much) and "Lasagna code" (a software design with too many layers). See `http://en.wikipedia.org/wiki/Anti-patterns` for their history and other examples.

Summary

That was a lot of theory, but it's important to learn these basic concepts. Understanding design pattern and principles will help you become a better software designer, and you'll also appreciate the design of the iOS classes. Observe how iOS and other experienced developers solve problems, identify the principles they used, and then try to emulate that in your own development.

Theory is fun, but do you know what's even more fun? Cameras!

Chapter 7

Smile!

Pictures and video are a big part of mobile apps. This is made possible by the amazing array of audio/video hardware built into most iOS devices. Your apps can take advantage of this hardware—and it's not that difficult. Apple has made it exceptionally easy to present an interface where your user can take a picture, or choose an existing picture from their photo library, and use that image in your app.

In this chapter you'll add pictures to MyStuff. You'll allow a user to choose, or take, a picture for each item they own and display that image in both the detail view and the master list. In doing that, you'll learn how to do the following:

- Create a camera or image picker controller and display it
- Retrieve the image the user took or chose
- Use Core Graphics to crop and resize the image
- Save the image to the user's camera roll
- Show image thumbnails in the rows of a table view

Along the way, you'll learn a few other useful skills:

- Add a tap gesture recognizer to a view object
- Present a view controller in a popover
- Dismiss the keyboard

This chapter will extend the MyStuff app you wrote in Chapter 5. You can continue working on the version you wrote in Chapter 5 or locate the finished version in the Ch 7 folder of the Learn iOS Developer Projects folder. If you're adding to the project in Chapter 5—which I highly recommend—you will need the resource file in the Ch 7 ➤ MyStuff (Resources) folder.

Design

Expanding your MyStuff app won't be difficult. You've already created the master-detail interface, and you have the table views and editing working. All of the hard work is done; you just need to embellish it a little. In the detail view you'll add a `UIImageView` object to display an image of the item, and in the table view you'll add icons to show a smaller version in the list, as shown in Figure 7-1.

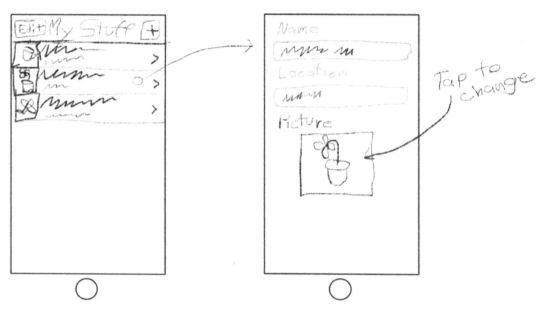

Figure 7-1. *Updated MyStuff design*

When the user taps the image in the detail view, your app will present either a camera or a photo picker interface. The camera interface will allow the user to take a picture with the device's built-in camera. The photo picker interface lets the user choose an existing image from their photo library. The new image will appear in both the detail view and the master list. Let's get started!

Extending Your Design

To extend your design, you'll need to make small alterations to a number of existing classes and interface files. Whether you realize it or not, your MyStuff app uses a model-view-controller design pattern. I describe the model-view-controller design in the next chapter, but for now just know that some of the objects in your app are "data model" objects, some are "view" objects, and others are "controller" objects. Adding pictures to MyStuff will require the following steps:

1. Extending your data model to include image objects

2. Adding view objects to display those images

3. Expanding your controller objects to take a picture and update the data model

Revising the Data Model

The first step is to extend your data model. Locate your MyWhatsit.swift interface file and add two new properties.

```
var image: UIImage? {
    didSet {
        postDidChangeNotification()
    }
}

var viewImage: UIImage {
    return image ?? UIImage(named: "camera")
}
```

The first adds an optional stored UIImage property to each MyWhatsit object. It includes a didSet observer that posts a "did change" notification whenever it's modified, just like your other stored properties. Now every MyWhatsit object has an image, and changing that image will notify its observers. Gee, that was easy!

The second property requires a little more explanation. In all of the view objects (both in the details view and in the table view) you want to display the image of the item. If there is no image, however, you want to display a placeholder image—an image that says "there's no image." The computed viewImage property will return either the item's image or a placeholder image. It's an immutable property, which means that clients of this object can't change it; in other words, the statement something.viewImage = newImage is not allowed.

This property also uses some Swift syntax you might not recognize. The ?? is the weirdly named *nil coalescing operator*. It's used with optional values to return a substitute value when the value is nil. If the value on the left has a value, the expression evaluates to that value. If the value on the left doesn't have a value, it evaluates to the expression on the right.

VIEWIMAGE IS BAD

Adding the viewImage property to the MyWhatsit class is actually poor software design. The problem is that the MyWhatsit class is a data model class and the viewImage property is in the domain of the view classes. In plain English, it solves a problem with displaying the image, not with storing the image. You're adding view-specific functionality to a data model object, which is something you should avoid.

In a well-organized model-view-controller (MVC) design, the domain of each class should be pure: the data model classes should have only data model–related properties and functions—nothing else. The problem here is that it's so darned convenient to add a viewImage property to the MyWhatsit class: it encapsulates the logic of providing a consistent and predictable display image for that item, which simplifies the code elsewhere. Code that encapsulates logic and makes the object easier to use can't be bad, right?

It isn't bad. In fact, it's good. But is there a way to avoid the architectural "flaw" of adding viewImage directly to the MyWhatsit class? The solution is to use an extension. An extension is an unusual feature of Swift that solves thorny domain issues like this, without making your objects more difficult to use. Using an extension, you can still add a `viewImage` property to your `MyWhatsit` objects but do it in a different module—a view module, separate from your `MyWhatsit` data model class. You get the benefits of adding a `viewImage` property to `MyWhatsit` while keeping your data model code separate from your view code. I explain extensions in Chapter 20.

At runtime (when your app runs) your `MyWhatsit` object still has a `viewImage` property, just as if you'd added it directly to your `MyWhatsit` class. So, what does it matter? Not much, and for a small project like this the ramifications are negligible, which is why I didn't have you create an extension for `viewImage`. Sometimes pragmatism trumps a fanatic adherence to design patterns. Just know that in a much more complex project, defining `viewImage` in `MyWhatsit` could become an obstacle, and the solution would be to move it into an extension.

For the computed `viewImage` property to work, you need to add that placeholder image file to your project. Find the `camera.png` file in the `MyStuff` (`Resources`) folder and drag it into the group list of your `Images.xcassets` asset catalog, as shown in Figure 7-2.

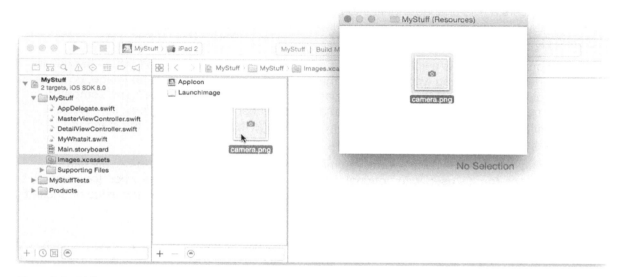

Figure 7-2. Adding camera.png resource

`MyWhatsit` is finished, so it's time to add the new view objects to your interface.

Adding an Image View

The next step is to add the view objects to your detail interface. This should feel like familiar territory by now.

1. Add an `imageView` outlet to your `DetailViewController` class.

2. Add label and image view objects to your `DetailViewController` interface file.

3. Connect the `imageView` outlet to the image view object.

Start in your DetailViewController.swift file. Add the following property:

```
@IBOutlet var imageView: UIImageView!
```

Now switch to the Main.storyboard file. From the object library, add a new label object. Position it below the Location text field, as shown in Figure 7-3. Change the label's title to Picture. Click the pin constraints control and add a top and leading edge constraint, as shown on the right in Figure 7-3.

Figure 7-3. *Adding the Picture label*

Add an image view object and position it underneath the new label. Select it. Click the pin constraints control, add a top constraint, and add height and width constraints, both set to 230, as shown in Figure 7-4. Finally, click the alignment constraint control and add a Center Horizontally in Container View constraint (with a value of 0). Your image view is now 230 by 230 pixels in size, centered, and just below the Picture label.

Figure 7-4. *Adding size constraints to the image view*

With the image view still selected, switch to the attributes inspector and change its Image property to camera. This will display the placeholder image when there's no MyWhatsit object being edited. (This is mostly for the benefit of the split-view iPad interface.)

The last step is to select Detail View Controller. Switch to the connections inspector and locate the imageView outlet you added to the controller. Connect it to the image view object, as shown in Figure 7-5.

Figure 7-5. Connecting the imageView outlet

> **Note**   The layout of the image view could be adapted so it filled out a regular-width (iPad) interface better. You can define constraints that adapt to different size classes, and I show you how in Chapter 9. After you've read that chapter, come back and make this layout smarter.

With the view objects in place, it's time to add the code to make your item images appear.

Updating the View Controller

You need to modify the code in the master view controller to add the image to the table cell and modify the code in the detail view controller to make the image appear in the new image view. Start with MasterViewController.swift. Locate the following code in tableView(_:,cellForRowAtIndexPath:) and add the bold text:

```
cell.textLabel?.text = thing.name
cell.detailTextLabel?.text = thing.location
cell.imageView?.image = thing.viewImage
return cell
```

The new code sets the image for the cell (cell.imageView.image) to the viewImage of the row's MyWhatsit object. Remember that the view image will be either the item's actual image or a placeholder. The act of setting the cell's image view will alter the cell's layout so the image appears on the left. (Refer to the "Cell Styles" section in Chapter 5.)

You're all done with `MasterViewController`. Click `DetailViewController.swift` and locate the `configureView()` function. Find the following code and add the one bold line:

```
if nameField != nil {
    nameField.text = detail.name
    locationField.text = detail.location
    imageView.image = detail.viewImage
}
```

This new line sets the image of the `UIImageView` object (connected to the `imageView` outlet) to the image of the `MyWhatsit` object being edited.

From a data model and view standpoint, everything is ready to go, so give it a try. Set the scheme to the iPhone simulator and run the project. You'll see the placeholder images appear in the table and the detail view, as shown in Figure 7-6.

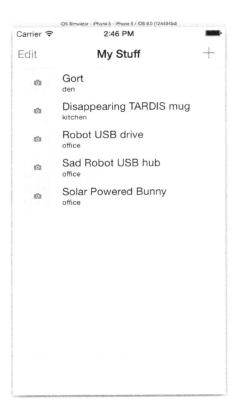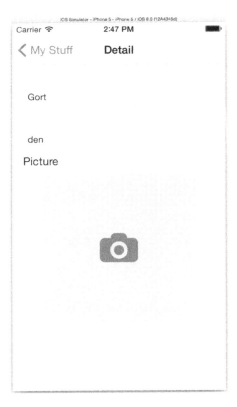

Figure 7-6. Placeholder images

So far everything is working great—there's just no way to change the picture. To accomplish that, you'll need to create an action.

Connecting a Choose Image Action

You want the camera, or photo library picker, interface to appear when the user taps the image in the detail view. That's simple enough to hook up: create an action method and connect the image view to it. Start by defining a new action in `DetailViewController.swift` (you don't need to write it yet; just declare it).

```
@IBAction func choosePicture(_: AnyObject!) {
}
```

Now switch back to the `Main.storyboard` interface, select the image view object, and connect its action outlet to the `choosePicture:` action in the `DetailViewController`.

Uh-oh, we seem to have a problem. The image view object isn't a button or any other kind of control view; it doesn't send an action message. In fact, by default, it ignores all touch events (its User Interaction Enabled property is false). So, how do you get the image view object to send an action to your view controller?

There are a couple of ways. One solution would be to subclass `UIImageView` and override its touch event methods, as described in Chapter 4. But there's a much simpler way: attach a gesture recognizer object to the view.

In the object library, locate the tap gesture recognizer. Drag a new tap gesture recognizer object into the interface and drop it into the image view object, as shown in Figure 7-7.

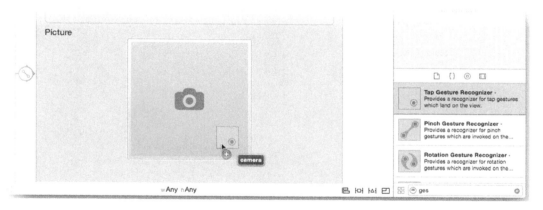

Figure 7-7. Attaching a tap gesture recognizer to the image view

When you drop a gesture recognizer into a view object, Interface Builder creates a new gesture recognizer object and connects the view object to it. This is a one-to-many relationship: a view can be connected to multiple gesture recognizers, but a recognizer works only on a single view object. To see the relationship, select the view object and use the connections inspector to see its recognizers. Hover your cursor over the connection, and Interface Builder will highlight the object it's connected to, shown at the bottom of Figure 7-8.

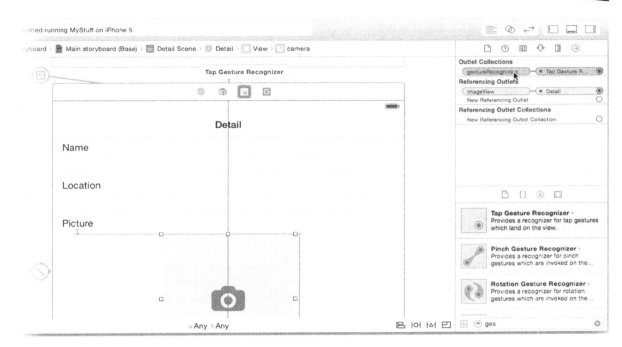

Figure 7-8. *Examining the gesture recognizer connection of the image view object*

> **Tip**   You can also see the inverse connections in the connections inspector. Select a recognizer object. Toward the bottom of the inspector you'll find the *referencing outlet collections* section. This section shows the connections from other view objects *to* this recognizer object. This works with all objects in Interface Builder.

By default, a new tap gesture recognizer is configured to recognize single-finger tap events, which is exactly what you want. You do, however, need to change the attributes of the image view object. Even though you have it connected to a gesture recognizer, the view object is still set to ignore touch events, so it will never receive any events to recognize. Rectify this by selecting the image view object and use the attributes inspector to check the User Interaction Enabled property, as shown in Figure 7-9.

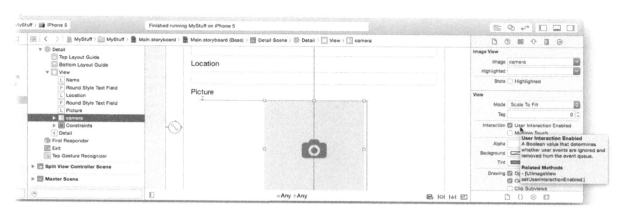

Figure 7-9. Enabling touch events for the image view

The last step is to connect the gesture recognizer to the choosePicture: action. Holding down the Control key, drag from the gesture recognizer in the scene's dock, as shown in Figure 7-10, or from the object outline. Both represent the same object. Drag the connection to the DetailViewController object and connect it to the choosePicture: action, also shown in Figure 7-10.

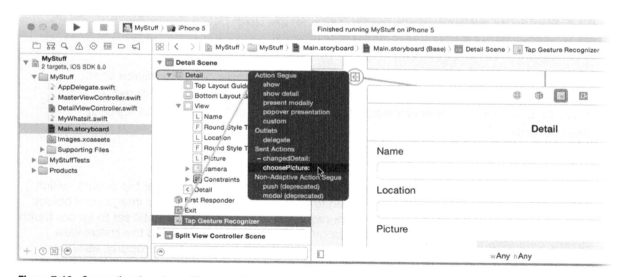

Figure 7-10. Connecting the -choosePicture: action

A choosePicture: action will now be sent to the detail view controller when the user taps the image. Now you have to implement the choosePicture(_:) function, which brings you to the fun part: letting the user take a picture.

Taking Pictures

The UIImagePickerController class provides simple, self-contained interfaces for taking a picture, recording a movie, or choosing an existing item from the user's photo library. The image picker controller does all of the hard work. For the most part, all your app has to do is create a UIImagePickerController object and present it as you would any other view controller. The delegate of the controller will receive messages that contain the image the user picked, the photo they took, or the movie they recorded.

That's not to say the image picker controller can do everything. There are a number of decisions and considerations that your app must make before and after the image picker has done its thing. This will be the bulk of the logic in your app, and I'll explain these decisions as you work through the code. Start by filling out the choosePicture(_:) function you started in your DetailViewController.swift file.

```
@IBAction func choosePicture(_: AnyObject!) {
    if detailItem == nil {
        return
    }
}
```

The first decision is easy: this action does something only if the detail view is currently editing a MyWhatsit object. If not (detailItem == nil), then return and do nothing. This can happen in the iPad interface when the detail view is visible, but the user has yet to select an item to edit.

You Can't Always Get What You Want

Now you get to the code that deals with deciding what image picker interfaces are available to your app. Continue writing the choosePicture(_:) function in DetailViewController.swift.

```
let hasPhotos = UIImagePickerController.isSourceTypeAvailable(.PhotoLibrary)
let hasCamera = UIImagePickerController.isSourceTypeAvailable(.Camera)
```

This is the intersection of what your user wants to do and what your app can do. The UIImagePickerController has the *potential* to present a still camera, video camera, combination still and video camera, photo library picker, or camera roll (saved) photo picker. That doesn't, however, mean it can do all of those things. Different iOS devices have different hardware. Some have a camera, some don't, and some have two. Some cameras are capable of taking movies, while others aren't. Even on devices that have cameras and photo libraries, security or restrictions may prohibit your app from using them.

The first step to using the image picker is to decide what you want to do and then find out what you can do. For this app, you want to either present a still camera interface or present a picker interface to choose an existing image from the photo library. Use the UIImagePickerController class function isSourceTypeAvailable(_:) to find out whether you can do either of those. You pass the function a constant indicating the kind of interface you'd like to present, and the method tells you whether that interface can be used.

The result of asking whether the photo library picker interface can be used is saved in the hasPhotos value. The hasCamera value will remember if the live camera interface is available.

> **Note**   There's a third interface, `UIImagePickerControllerSourceType.SavedPhotosAlbum`. This presents the same interface as the photo library picker but allows the user to choose images only in their camera roll—called the Saved Photos album on devices that don't have a camera.

The `switch` statement that follows decides what to do in each of the four possible situations:

```
switch (hasPhotos,hasCamera) {
    case (true,true):
        let alert = UIAlertController(title: nil,
                                   message: nil,
                            preferredStyle: .ActionSheet)
        alert.addAction(UIAlertAction(title: "Take a Picture",
                                      style: .Default,
                                    handler: { (_) in
                                        self.presentImagePicker(.Camera)
                                    }))
        alert.addAction(UIAlertAction(title: "Choose a Photo",
                                      style: .Default,
                                    handler: { (_) in
                                        self.presentImagePicker(.PhotoLibrary)
                                    }))
        alert.addAction(UIAlertAction(title: "Cancel",
                                      style: .Cancel,
                                    handler: nil))
        if let popover = alert.popoverPresentationController {
            popover.sourceView = imageView
            popover.sourceRect = imageView.bounds
            popover.permittedArrowDirections = ( .Up | .Down )
        }
        presentViewController(alert, animated: true, completion: nil)
    case (true,false):
        presentImagePicker(.PhotoLibrary)
    case (false,true):
        presentImagePicker(.Camera)
    default: /* (false,false) */
        break
}
```

The `switch` statement considers the tuple (`hasPhotos,hasCamera`). In the first case, both are `true`, which means you don't know which interface to present. When in doubt, ask the user using an action sheet.

The action sheet has three buttons: Take a Picture, Choose a Photo, and Cancel. A `UIAlertAction` object defines each choice with properties for the button's `title`, its `style`, and—most importantly—the code that will execute should the user tap that button.

The second and third cases of the `switch` statement ((`true,false`) and (`false,true`)) handle the situations where only one of the interfaces is available and simply presents the one that is. The final case does nothing since there's nothing to do.

> **Tip**   In the real world, it would be a good idea to put up an alert message telling the user that there are no available image sources, rather than just ignoring their tap—but I'll leave that as an exercise you can explore on your own.

To review, you've queried the `UIImagePickerController` to determine which interfaces, in the subset of interfaces you'd like to present, are available. If none, do nothing. If only one is available, present that interface immediately. If more than one is available, ask the user which one they would like to use, wait for their answer, and present that. The next big task is to present the interface.

Presenting the Image Picker

Now add the `presentImagePickerUsingCamera(_:)` function to your `DetailViewController` class.

```
func presentImagePicker(source: UIImagePickerControllerSourceType) {
    let picker = UIImagePickerController()
    picker.sourceType = source
    picker.mediaTypes = [kUTTypeImage as NSString]
    picker.delegate = self
    presentViewController(picker, animated: true, completion: nil)
}
```

This method starts by creating a new `UIImagePickerController` object, a special subclass of `UIViewController`.

The `sourceType` property determines which interface the image picker will present. It should be set only to values that returned `true` by `isSourceTypeAvailable(_:)`. In your app, it's set to either `UIImagePickerControllerSourceType.Camera` or `UIImagePickerControllerSourceType.PhotoLibrary`, which you've already determined is available.

The `mediaTypes` property is an array of data types that your app is prepared to accept. The valid choices in iOS 8 are (currently) kUTTypeImage, kUTTypeMovie, or both. This property modifies the interface (camera or picker) so that only those image types are allowed. Setting only kUTTypeImage when presenting the camera interface limits the controls so the user can only take still images. If you included both types (kUTTypeImage and kUTTypeMovie), then the camera interface would allow the user to switch between still and movie capture as they please.

> **Tip**   To find out which media types are actually supported for a particular picker interface (say, for the `.Camera` interface), call the `availableMediaTypesForSourceType(_:)` function. Some cameras can record movies, while others can take only still photographs. And future versions of iOS may sport new media types, so it's a good practice to check.

The kUTTypeImage value is also an odd duck. First, it's not part of the standard UIKit framework. It's defined in the Mobile Core Services framework. To use it, add this import statement at the beginning of the DetailViewController.swift file:

```
import MobileCoreServices
```

Another quirk is that the constants kUTTypeImage and kUTTypeMovie aren't native Swift values. They're Core Foundation literals, which is why you had to coerce it into a Cocoa string object (kUTTypeImage as NSString). Core Foundation types and the toll-free bridge are explained in Chapter 20.

> **Tip**   There are a number of other UIImagePickerController properties that you could set before you start the interface. For example, set its allowsEditing property to true if you'd like to give the user the ability to refine pictures or trim movies.

The last two lines of presentImagePicker(_:) set your controller as the delegate for the picker and start its interface. The controller slides into view and waits for the user to take a picture, pick an image, or cancel the operation. When one of those happens, your controller receives the appropriate delegate message. But to be the image picker delegate, your controller must adopt both the UIImagePickerControllerDelegate and UINavigationControllerDelegate protocols. Add those to your DetailViewController class declaration now.

```
class DetailViewController: UIViewController, UIImagePickerControllerDelegate,
                                              UINavigationControllerDelegate {
```

> **Note**   Your DetailViewController isn't interested in, and doesn't implement, any of the UINavigationControllerDelegate functions. It adopts the protocol simply to avoid the compiler error that results if it doesn't.

With the picker up and running, you're now ready to deal with the image the user takes or picks.

Importing the Image

Ultimately, the user will take or choose a picture. This results in a call to your imagePickerController (_:,didFinishPickingMediaWithInfo:) delegate function. This is the function where you'll take the image the user took/selected and add it to the MyWhatsit object. All of the information about what the user did is contained in a dictionary, passed to your function via the info parameter. Add this code to your DetailViewController.swift file. The function starts out simply enough.

```
func imagePickerController(_: UIImagePickerController,
                didFinishPickingMediaWithInfo info: [NSObject : AnyObject]) {
    var image: UIImage! = info[UIImagePickerControllerEditedImage] as? UIImage
    if image == nil {
        image = info[UIImagePickerControllerOriginalImage] as UIImage
    }
```

The first task is to obtain the image object. There are, potentially, two possible images: the original one and the edited one. If the user cropped, filtered, or performed any other in-camera editing, the one you want is the edited version. Start by requesting that one (UIImagePickerControllerEditedImage) from the info dictionary. If that value is nil, then the original (UIImagePickerControllerOriginalImage) is the only image supplied.

> **Note** If you configured a picker interface that allowed the user to use more than one media type (kUTTypeImage and kUTTypeMovie), the info[UIImagePickerControllerMediaType] value will tell you which was chosen.

The next block of code considers the case where the user has taken a picture. When users take a picture, most expect their photo to appear in their camera roll. This isn't a requirement, and another app might act differently, but here you meet the user's expectations by saving the picture they just took to their camera roll:

```
if picker.sourceType == .Camera {
    UIImageWriteToSavedPhotosAlbum(image,nil,nil,nil)
}
```

You don't want to do this if the user picked an existing image from their photo library; you'd just duplicate the picture that was already in their library.

> **Tip** Many apps allow users to save an image to their camera roll. You can do this at any time using the UIImageWriteToSavedPhotosAlbum() function. This function isn't limited to being used in conjunction with the image picker interface.

Cropping and Resizing

Now that you have the image, what do you do with it? You could just set the MyWhatsit image property to the returned image object and return. While that would work, it's a bit crude. First, modern iOS devices have high-resolution cameras that produce big images, consuming several megabytes of memory for each one. It won't take too many such pictures before your app will run out of memory and crash. Also, the images are rectangular, and both the details interface and the table view would look better using square images.

To solve both of these problems, you'll want to scale down and crop the user's image. Start by cropping the image with this code, which is the next part of your imagePickerController (_:,didFinishPickingMediaWithInfo:) function:

```
let cgImage = image.CGImage
let height = Int(CGImageGetHeight(cgImage))
let width = Int(CGImageGetWidth(cgImage))
var crop = CGRect(x: 0, y: 0, width: width, height: height)
if height > width {
    crop.size.height = crop.size.width
    crop.origin.y = CGFloat((height-width)/2)
} else {
    crop.size.width = crop.size.height
    crop.origin.x = CGFloat((width-height)/2)
}
let croppedImage = CGImageCreateWithImageInRect(cgImage, crop)
```

The first step is to get a Core Graphics image reference from the UIImage object. UIImage is a convenient and simple-to-use object that handles all kinds of convoluted image storage, conversion, and drawing details for you. It does not, however, let you manipulate or modify the image in any significant way. To do that, you need to "step down" into the lower-level Core Graphics frameworks, where the real image manipulation and drawing functions reside. The cgImage value contains a CGImageRef—Core Graphics Image Reference. This is a reference (think of it like an object reference) that contains primitive image data.

The next step is to get the height and width (in pixels) of the image. That's accomplished by calling the functions CGImageGetHeight() and CGImageGetWidth().

PROGRAMMING IN C VS. SWIFT

Much of Cocoa Touch framework is actually written in C and Objective-C, not Swift. C is a procedural language that's been around a long time and is probably the world's most commonly used computer language. Objective-C is built on top of C, adding the concept of objects to C.

In Chapter 6 I spoke of writing programs entirely by defining structures and passing those structures to functions. This is exactly how you program using C and the framework of C functions called Core Foundation.

While C is not an object-oriented language, you can still write object-oriented programs; it's just more work. In Core Foundation, a class is called a *type*, and an object is a *reference*. Instead of calling the functions of an object, you call a global function and pass it a reference (typically as the first parameter). In other words, instead of writing myImage.height to get the height of an image, you write CGImageGetHeight(myImage). In C there are no classes, and structs and enums can't have functions the way they can in Swift.

While most Core Foundation types will work only with Core Foundation functions, a few fundamental types are interchangeable with Swift (and Objective-C) objects. These include String/NSString/CFStringRef, NSNumber/CFNumberRef, Array/NSArray/CFArrayRef, Dictionary/NSDictionary/CFDictionaryRef, NSURL/CFURLRef, and others. Any C, Objective-C, or Swift function that expects one will accept the other as is. This is called the *toll-free bridge*, and you've already used it in this app. The kUTTypeImage string is really a CFStringRef, not an NSString object. But since the two are interchangeable, it was possible to pass the Core Foundation kUTTypeImage string value in the parameter that expected an NSString object.

The `if` block decides whether the image is landscape (width > height) or portrait (height > width). Based on this, it sets up a `CGRect` that describes a square in the middle of the image. If landscape, it makes the rectangle the height of the image and insets the left and right edges. If portrait, the rectangle is the width of the image, and the top and bottom are trimmed.

The function after the `if/else` block does all of the work. The `CGImageCreateWithImageInRect()` function takes an existing Core Graphics image, picks out just the pixels in the rectangle, and copies them to a new Core Graphics image. The end result is a square Core Graphics image with just the middle section of the original image.

The next step is to turn the `CGImageRef` back into a `UIImage` object so it can be stored in the `MyWhatsit` object. At the same time, you're going to scale it down so it's not so big.

```
let maxImageDimension: CGFloat = 640.0
image = UIImage(CGImage: croppedImage,
                scale: max(crop.height/maxImageDimension,1.0),
          orientation: image.imageOrientation)
```

The `UIImage` class function `imageWithCGImage(_:,scale:,orientation:)` creates a new `UIImage` object from an existing `CGImageRef`. At the same time, it can scale the image and change its orientation. The scale calculates a ratio between the size of the original image and a 640-pixel one. This scales down the (probably) larger image size from the device's camera to a 640x640 pixel image, which is a manageable size. The `max()` function is used to keep the ratio from dropping below `1.0` (1:1); this prevents an image that's already smaller than 640 pixels from being made larger.

> **Note** `UIImage` has an `orientation` property. Core Graphic images do not. Images taken with the camera are all in landscape format. When you take a portrait (vertical) picture, you get a `UIImage` with a landscape image and an `orientation` that tells `UIImage` to draw the image vertically. When you started working with the `CGImageRef`, that orientation information was lost. If you step through the program with the Xcode debugger, you'll see that the code crops a landscape image (width > height), even if you took a portrait photo. So to make the photo draw the way it was taken, you have to supply the original orientation when creating the new `UIImage`.

Winding Up

All of the hard part is over. The only thing left for this function to do is store the cropped and resized image in the `MyWhatsit` object and dismiss the image picker controller.

```
    detailItem?.image = image
    imageView.image = image
    dismissViewControllerAnimated(true, completion: nil)
}
```

The first line stores the cropped image in the new `image` property of the `MyWhatsit` object. The second updates the image view in the detail view, so it reflects the same change. Finally, you must dismiss the picker view since the user is done with it.

But what if the user didn't take a picture or refused to choose a photo from their library? If the user taps the cancel button in the picker, your `imagePickerControllerDidCancel(_:)` delegate function is called instead. You need to handle that too. Add this function right after your new `imagePickerController(_:,didFinishPickingMediaWithInfo:)` function:

```
func imagePickerControllerDidCancel(_: UIImagePickerController!) {
    dismissViewControllerAnimated(true, completion: nil)
}
```

This method does nothing but dismiss the controller, making no change to your `MyWhatsit` object.

Testing the Camera

You're ready to test your image picker interface—for real. The simulator, unfortunately, does not emulate the camera hardware or come with any images in its photo library. To test this app, you'll need to run it on a real iOS device.

> **Note**   Ideally, you have an iPhone, iPod Touch, or similar compact iOS device to test with. If not, you'll need to read through the "Handling Regular Interfaces" section before your app will work.

Plug in your device and set the project's scheme to it. Run it. Your app's interface should look like that in Figure 7-11.

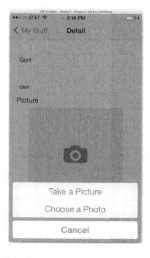

Figure 7-11. Testing the iPhone interface

Tap an item, tap the placeholder image in the detail view, tap Take a Picture, and take a picture. The cropped image should appear in the detail view and again back in the master table, as shown on the right in Figure 7-11.

Congratulations, you've added picture taking to your app! Enjoy the moment and have fun with the camera. iPad users, however, aren't feeling the love. Let's see whether we can figure out why.

Handling Regular Interfaces

Regular iOS devices, and by "regular" I mean ones you can't stuff in your jeans pocket, have a lot more screen real estate. They take advantage of that with some alternative interface techniques. On compact devices (iPhone, iPod, and so on) almost all views controllers are presented full-screen—your master table view, your detail view, the alert sheet, and the image picker all take over the entire screen. You just move from one screen to another.

On regular devices (like the iPad) there are popover windows, form sheets, split view controllers, and other techniques that don't consume the entire screen. They show multiple views simultaneously or overlay a smaller interface on top of the existing one.

So, how do you know which interface style to use or which one will be used? I'll talk a lot more about this in Chapter 12, but here's the short lesson: every view controller has a modalPresentationStyle property that hints to iOS how that view controller would like to be presented, size permitting. You can set this property, but iOS might choose to ignore it on compact devices.

Run your app on an iPad and try to tap the image view. Nothing seems to happen. Actually, something disastrous happened; your app just crashed. Back in Xcode, look at the console pane (at the bottom of the workspace window). You'll see a message like this one:

```
2014-08-12 15:24:47.429 MyStuff[494:211871] *** Terminating app due to uncaught
exception 'NSGenericException', reason: 'UIPopoverPresentationController
(<_UIAlertControllerActionSheetRegularPresentationController: 0x15683b00>) should have a
non-nil sourceView or barButtonItem set before the presentation occurs.'
```

Huh?

Let me explain. The action sheet has a preferred presentation style of "popover." On an iPhone, there's not enough room, so iOS ignores the style and presents the action sheet as an overlay (see Figure 7-11). On the iPad, a popover is a much tidier interface—much nicer than consuming the entire screen just to show three buttons—and iOS presents the alert in a popover.

And here's the rub. A popover requires some additional information. At a minimum, you have to tell the popover where the focus of the interface is so it can be positioned intelligently. Find your choosePicture(_:) function in the DetailViewController.swift file and insert this new code, shown in bold:

```
alert.addAction(UIAlertAction(title: "Cancel",
                              style: .Cancel,
                              handler: nil))
if let popover = alert.popoverPresentationController {
    popover.sourceView = imageView
    popover.sourceRect = imageView.bounds
    popover.permittedArrowDirections = ( .Up | .Down )
}
presentViewController(alert, animated: true, completion: nil)
```

The popoverPresentationController property returns a UIPopoverPresentationController if (and only if) that controller is, or will, be presented in a popover. This object does exactly what you think it would do—manages the appearance of the popover. At a minimum, you must tell the presentation controller either the view rectangle or the bar button item the popover should appear next to. If you're setting a rectangle, you set the rectangle's coordinates (sourceRect) along with the view object (sourceView) those coordinates are in. In this app, you use imageView and imageView.bounds, which defines the frame of imageView. (You could just as easily have used view and imageView.frame, which also defines the frame of imageView.)

UIPopoverPresentationController has lots of optional properties. A particularly useful one is permittedArrowDirections. Here you set that to (.Up|.Down), so the popover always tries to appear above, or below, the image view. Run your app again on an iPad and check out the results, shown on the left in Figure 7-12.

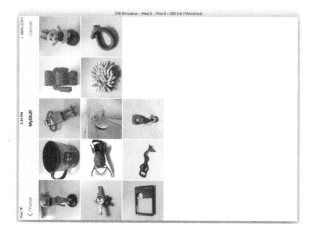

Figure 7-12. Regular alert controller in a popover

Your alert now appears in a popover with two buttons. Notice that the third action (Cancel) isn't shown. Tapping anywhere outside the popover dismisses it. This makes a Cancel button redundant. The alert controller knows this and omitted it.

Choosing to take a picture presents a full-screen camera interface. That's perfect. (Apple's human interface guidelines recommend always presenting the camera interface full-screen.)

The photo library picker (shown on the right in figure 7-12), however, leaves something to be desired. Taking over the entire screen is heavy handed, and it supports only portrait orientation—awkward to say the least. I think it can be improved; what do you think? Find your `presentImagePicker(_:)` function and change it to this (new code in bold):

```swift
func presentImagePicker(source: UIImagePickerControllerSourceType) {
    let picker = UIImagePickerController()
    picker.sourceType = source
    picker.mediaTypes = [kUTTypeImage as NSString]
    picker.delegate = self
    if source == .PhotoLibrary {
        picker.modalPresentationStyle = .Popover
    }
    if let popover = picker.popoverPresentationController {
        popover.sourceView = imageView
        popover.sourceRect = imageView.bounds
    }
    presentViewController(picker, animated: true, completion: nil)
}
```

If you're going to present the library picker interface, change its preferred presentation style to `UIModalPresentationStyle.Popover`. If your recommended style isn't ignored by iOS (which it will be on compact devices), get the popover presentation controller—exactly as you did for the alert—and configure it. Now the library picker interface is much more iPadish, as shown in Figure 7-13.

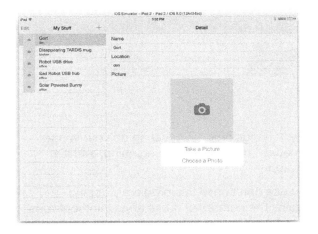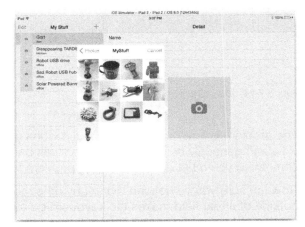

Figure 7-13. Presenting the photo picker interface in a popover

There are even more ways to customize the presentation of view controllers, but I'll save that for Chapter 12.

Sticky Keyboards

One quirk of your app, if you haven't noticed, is the sticky keyboard. No, I'm not talking about the kind you get from eating chocolate while programming. I'm talking about the virtual keyboard in iOS. Figure 7-14 shows the virtual keyboard that appears when you tap in a text field.

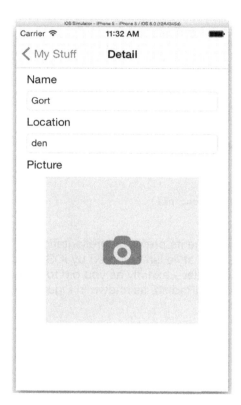

Figure 7-14. iOS's virtual keyboard

The problem is that, once summoned, it won't go away. It hangs around, covering up your image view and generally being annoying. This has been a "feature" of iOS from its beginning, and it's something you must deal with if it's a problem for your app.

Now I'm sure you've noticed that many other apps you use don't have this problem. Tapping outside of a text field makes the keyboard go away again. The authors of those apps intercept taps outside of the text field and dismiss the keyboard. There have been a wide variety of solutions to this problem, and you'll find many of them floating around the Internet. I'm going to show you a particularly simple one that will take only a minute to add to your app.

The "trick" is to catch touch events outside any of the text field objects and translate those events into an action that will retract the keyboard. Start with the second part first: create an action to retract the keyboard. In your DetailViewController.swift file, add the following method to your file:

```
@IBAction func dismissKeyboard(_: AnyObject!) {
    view.endEditing(false)
}
```

This simple method calls the endEditing(_:) function on the root view of your interface. The endEditing(_:) function is ready-built to solve this problem; it searches through the view's subviews looking for an editable object that's currently being edited. If it finds one, it asks the object to resign its first responder status, ending the editing session, and retracting the keyboard.

> **Tip**   The single value passed to the endEditing(_:) function is the force parameter. If true, it forces the view to end editing, even if it doesn't want to. Passing false lets the view decide and might not end the editing session. I elected to be polite and let the view decide.

Now you're going to add another tap gesture recognizer. In the Main.storyboard file, find the tap gesture recognizer in the object library. Drag one into your interface and drop it into the root view object, by dropping it either into the empty space in the interface, as shown in Figure 7-15, or directly into the root view object in the outline.

Figure 7-15. Adding a tap gesture recognizer to the root view

Control+right-click the new gesture recognizer, drag it to the Detail View Controller, and connect it to the new dismissKeyboard: action. (If you can't figure out which gesture recognizer object belongs to the root view, use the connections inspector, as shown in Figure 7-8, in the section "Connecting a Choose Image Action.") Now any tap that occurs outside a specific subview will pass those touch events to the root view, dismissing the keyboard. If you're not sure why that happens, review the section "Hit Testing" in Chapter 4.

Give it a try. Run your app, tap inside a text field, and then tap outside the text field. You should see the keyboard appear and then disappear.

This happens anywhere you tap, except in the image view. That's easy to fix. Find the point in the choosePicture(_:) function where the app intends to present an interface and add this one bold line of code:

```
dismissKeyboard(self)
let hasPhotos = UIImagePickerController.isSourceTypeAvailable(.PhotoLibrary)
...
```

This will cause the keyboard to retract when the user taps the image view to change it. Remember that in hit testing, it's the most specific view object that gets the touch events. Since the image view object receives touch events, those events won't make their way to the root view.

Advanced Camera Techniques

I'm sure you're excited to add camera and photo library features to your app. But there are more features to UIImagePickerController than you've explored in this chapter. There are properties to adjust the flash and capture modes, show or hide the camera controls, add your own custom views to the interface, and programmatically take a picture or start recording a movie. Check out the details in the UIImagePickerController documentation.

If your goal, however, is to create the next Hipstamatic or Instagram, the UIImagePickerController isn't what you want; you want the low-level camera controls. You'll find that kind of control in the AVCaptureDevice object. That object represents a single image capture device (aka a camera) and gives you excruciatingly precise control over every aspect of it, from controlling the focus to setting the white balance of the exposure.

This is part of the much larger AV Foundation framework, which also encompasses video capture, video playback, audio recording, and audio playback. You'll explore some parts of this framework later in this book. Some of its features are object-oriented, while others are C functions.

The advantage of using a class like UIImagePickerController is that so many of the picture-taking details are taken care of for you. But it also constrains your app's functionality and design. The lower-level classes and functions open up a world of design and interface possibilities but require that you deal with those details yourself. To learn more, start with the *AV Foundation Programming Guide* you'll find in Xcode's Documentation and API Reference.

Summary

Adding picture taking to your MyStuff app spiffed it up considerably and made it much more exciting to use. You also learned a little about presenting view controllers and manipulating images. You now know how to export an image to the user's camera roll, add tap gesture recognizers to an existing view, and get that pesky keyboard out of the way. You're also getting comfortable with outlets, connections, and delegates; in other words, you're turning into an iOS developer!

Throughout the past few chapters, I've constantly referred to *view*, *controller*, and *data model* objects. The next chapter is going to take another short recess from development to explain what that means and explore an important design pattern.

EXERCISES

If there's no camera or photo library, it would be nice to tell the user that, rather than just ignoring them. In the Shorty app, you put up an alert when a web page couldn't be loaded for some reason. Use the same technique to present a dialog if neither the camera nor the photo library picker interface is available.

Also consider how to test this code. In the devices you're likely to own, and in the simulator, one of those interfaces is always going to be available. You can find a modified MyStuff project, with comments, in the `MyStuff E1` project folder for this chapter.

Chapter 8

Model Citizen

This chapter is all about the model-view-controller design pattern. Design patterns, which I talked about in Chapter 6, are reusable solutions to common programming problems. The model-view-controller (MVC) design pattern is, arguably, the most important and wide-ranging design pattern used today. In this chapter, you'll learn about the following:

- What the model-view-controller design pattern is
- What makes a good data model
- What makes a good view object
- What makes a good controller object
- How MVC objects communicate with each other
- When you can cheat

You might be thinking that all of this MVC stuff is a bunch of esoteric computer science theory that won't really help you write your Death Star Laser Cannon Control app. On the contrary, learning (even a little) about the MVC design pattern will not only make your Death Star Laser Cannon Control app more reliable, it will actually make it easier to write and maintain. Good MVC design might require a little more thought and consideration up front but you save a whole lot of work in the end—and your app is likely to have fewer bugs.

So, feel free to skip this chapter, but when you press the Destroy Alderaan button on your app and nothing happens, you'll have to answer to Lord Vader, not me.

The Model-View-Controller Design Pattern

In Chapter 6 I talked about the single responsibility principle, encapsulation, and the "open-closed" principle. All of these can be distilled into a simple concept.

An object should do one thing and do it well.

To do anything useful, your app must store data, display that data in an interface, and allow the user to interact with it. The model-view-controller design pattern organizes what your app must do (store, display, and interact) into objects (data objects, view objects, and controller objects) that do just one thing, and it describes how those objects work together. Let's start with the simplest of the three:

Data Model Objects

Your data model consists of the objects that store your app's information. Data model objects should do the following:

- Represent the data in your app
- Encapsulate the storage of that data
- Avoid assumptions about how the data is displayed or changed

The data of your app is whatever values, information, or concepts your app uses. In your MyStuff app, your data model was simply the names, locations, and images of the things you own. A chess app would have a slightly more complex data model; there would be an object that represented the chess board, objects for each player, objects for each piece, objects that recorded the moves, and so on. An astronomical catalog app might require dozens of classes and hundreds of thousands of objects to keep track of the visible stars.

The first job of your data model classes is to represent the data for your app, while hiding (encapsulating) how that data is stored. It should present the rest of your app with a simple interface so the other classes can get the information they need, without needing to know exactly how that data is represented or stored.

Even for "simple" apps, like MyStuff, encapsulation is important for the future of your app. For example, the image property of MyWhatsit stored a UIImage object with the picture of that item. Simple, right? But images can take up a lot of memory, and if your app is going to inventory hundreds, instead of dozens, of items, your app can't keep all of those images in memory—it will run out of memory and crash.

You could address this problem by changing your data model so images that you're not currently displaying—after all, you can't display them all at once—are written to flash memory as individual image files. The next time an object requests the image property of a MyWhatsit object, your data model can determine whether it has that image in memory or whether it needs to retrieve it from flash storage.

The key concept is that all of these decisions are encapsulated in your data model. The other classes that use your MyWhatsit object just request the image property; they don't know how, or where, that information is stored, and they shouldn't care. Review the food truck analogy in the "Encapsulation" section of Chapter 6 if that isn't clear.

The other really important aspect of the data model is what it is *not*. The data model is at the bottom of the MVC design, and it shouldn't contain any properties or logic not directly related to your app's data or how that data is maintained.

Specifically, it shouldn't know anything about, or make any assumptions about, the view or controller objects it works with. It shouldn't contain references to view objects, have methods that present the data in the user interface, or directly handle user actions. In this respect, the data model is the purest of the three MVC roles; it's all about the data and nothing else.

View Objects

View objects sit in the middle of the MVC design. A good view object does the following:

- Presents some aspect of the data model to the user
- Understands the data it displays and how to display it, but nothing more
- May interpret user interface events and send actions to controller objects

A view object's primary purpose is to display the values in your data model. View objects must, by necessity, understand at least some aspects of your data model, but they know nothing about controller objects.

How much does a view object know about the data model? That depends on the complexity of what's being displayed. In general, it should know just enough to do its job and no more. A view that displays a string needs to know only the string value to display. A view that draws an animated picture of the night sky needs a lot of information: the list of visible stars, their magnitude and color, the coordinates of the observer, the current time, the azimuth, the elevation, the angle of view, and so on. To find examples, you have to look no further than the Cocoa Touch framework, which is full of view objects that display everything from the simplest string (UILabel) to entire documents (UIWebView).

It's common for view objects, especially complex ones, to maintain a reference to the data model objects they display. Such a view object not only understands how to display the data but also knows what data to display.

View objects may also interpret user interface events (such as a "swipe" or a "pinch" gesture) and translate those into action messages (nextPage(_:) or zoomOut(_:)), which it sends to a controller object. A view object should not act on those actions; it should simply pass them on to a controller.

> **Note** View objects that interpret user interaction and send action messages are called *controls*—not to be confused with controllers. Most control views (text field, button, slider, toggle switch, and so on) are subclasses of UIControl.

Controller Objects

Controllers are at the top of the MVC design and are the "business end" of your app. Controller objects are supervisors that oversee, and often coordinate, the data model and view objects. Controller objects do the following:

- Understand, and often create, the data model objects
- Configure, and often create, the view objects
- Perform the actions received from view objects
- Make changes to the data model
- Coordinate communications between the data model and view objects
- May take responsibility for keeping the view objects updated

It's almost easier to explain what a controller is not than what it is. It is not your data model; a controller object does not store, manage, or convert your app's data.[1] It is not a view object; it does not draw the interface or interpret low-level events. It is, essentially, everything else.

Controllers can be involved in the initialization of your data model and view objects, often creating the data model objects and loading your view objects from an Interface Builder file.

Controller objects contain all of the business logic of your app. They perform the commands initiated by the user, respond to high-level events, and instigate changes to the data model. In complex apps, there are often multiple controller objects, each responsible for a particular feature or interface.

Your controller objects are also either the recipient or source of most of the messages within your app. How they are involved depends on your design, which brings us to the topic of interobject communications.

MVC Communications

In its simplest form, the communications between MVC objects form a loop (see Figure 8-1).

- Data model objects notify view objects of changes.
- View objects send actions to controller objects.
- Controller objects modify the data model.

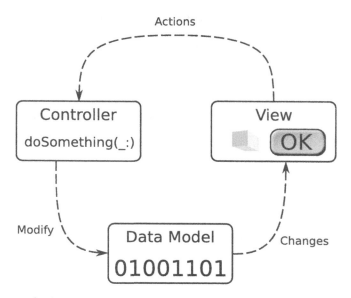

Figure 8-1. Simple MVC communications

---

[1]There's an exception to this rule that I'll describe toward the end of this chapter.

In this arrangement, the data model is responsible for notifying any observers of changes. The view objects are responsible for observing and displaying those changes and sending actions to the controller objects. The controller objects perform the actions, often making changes to the data model, and the whole cycle starts again.

Counterintuitively, this simplified arrangement happens only in fairly sophisticated apps. Most of the time, the data model is not set up to post notifications, and the view objects don't observe changes directly. Instead, the controller object steps in and takes responsibility for notifying the view objects when the data model changes, as shown in Figure 8-2.

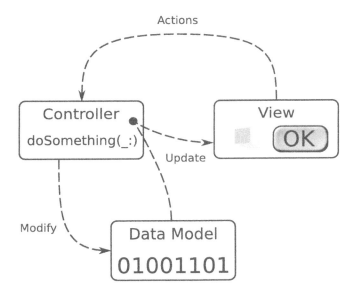

Figure 8-2. Typical MVC communications

Now that you have the basics of the MVC design pattern, let's put together another iOS app. Instead of focusing on a particular iOS technology, such as the motion events or the camera, I want you to pay attention to the roles of your objects, their design, and how they change as your app evolves.

Color Model

You're going to develop a new app called ColorModel. It's an app that lets you choose a color using the hue-saturation-brightness (HSB) color model. Its initial design is simple, as shown in Figure 8-3. The interface consists of three sliders, one for each of the HSB values, and a view where the chosen color appears.

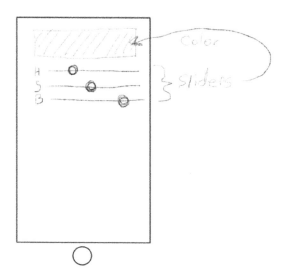

Figure 8-3. Initial design of ColorModel

Note   A color model, or color space, is a mathematical representation of a visible color. There are several common models, suited to different applications. Computer displays and televisions use the red-green-blue (RGB) model, artists like to use the hue-saturation-brightness model, while printers use the cyan-magenta-yellow-black (CMYK) model. See http://en.wikipedia.org/wiki/Color_model.

Start by launching Xcode. Create and configure a new project by following these steps:

1. Use the Single View Application template.

2. Name the project ColorModel.

3. Set the language to Swift.

4. Set the device to iPhone.

5. Create the project.

6. On the General tab of the ColorModel target, uncheck the Landscape Left and Landscape Right orientations so only Portrait orientation is checked.

Creating Your Data Model

The first step (after design) of almost any app is to develop your data model. The data model in this app is remarkably simple; it's a single object that maintains the values for hue, saturation, and brightness. It also translates those values into a color object suitable for display and other uses. Start by adding a new Swift source file to your project. Grab a Swift file from the file template library and drag it into the ColorModel group of your project. Name the new file Color. Replace the code in the file with this:

```swift
import UIKit

class Color {

    var hue: Float = 0.0
    var saturation: Float = 0.0
    var brightness: Float = 0.0

    var color: UIColor {
        return UIColor(hue: CGFloat(hue/360),
                saturation: CGFloat(saturation/100),
                brightness: CGFloat(brightness/100),
                    alpha: 1.0)
    }

}
```

You now have a data model class. Its first three properties are floating-point values, one each for the color's hue, saturation, and brightness. The hue is in degrees and can range between 0° and 360°. The other two are expressed as a percentage and can range between 0 percent and 100 percent.

The last property is a computed property—which just means it's a value that's calculated rather than stored. It returns a UIColor object that represents the same color as the current hue/saturation/brightness triplet.

The conversion from the hue-saturation-brightness values into a UIColor object (which uses the red-green-blue model, by the way) is thoughtfully provided by the UIColor class. I'm glad. There are formulas for converting between various color models, but it requires a lot more math than I want to explain.

> **Note**   It's possible to make the color property settable too; you'd just need to add code to update the hue, saturation, and brightness values to match. Data models should be consistent; if the color property always represents the color of the current hue, saturation, and brightness properties, then changing the color should also change the hue, saturation, and brightness so they still agree.

The values that UIColor uses to express hue, saturation, and brightness are, however, different from the one you choose (OK, I choose) for the data model. In your data model, hue is a Float value between 0.0 and 360.0. UIColor expects a CGFloat value between 0.0 and 1.0. Likewise, UIColor saturation and brightness values are also between 0 and 1. To convert between your model and the one used by UIColor, you must scale the values by dividing them by their range and converting from Float to CGFloat. This is the kind of detail that data models encapsulate (hide) from the rest of your app.

With your data model complete, it's time to move on to the view objects.

Creating View Objects

Select your Main.storyboard Interface Builder file. In the object library, find the plain view object and drag one into your interface. Resize and position it so it occupies the top of the display, as shown in Figure 8-4. This will be the view where the user's chosen color appears.

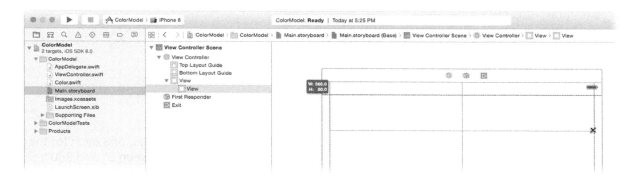

Figure 8-4. *Adding a simple view object*

Select the new view object and click the pin constraints control. Add top (Standard), left (20), and right (20) edge constraints, as shown in Figure 8-5. Also add a height constraint of 80 pixels.

Figure 8-5. *Setting the view object constraints*

Find the label object in the library and drag one into your interface. Position it immediately below the lower-left corner of the view object. Set its title to H. Locate the slider object in the library and drag one into your interface, positioning it just below the color view and immediately to the right of the label you just added, as shown in Figure 8-6.

Figure 8-6. *Adding the first label and slider*

Align the label and slider so they are vertically centered. Size the slider so it extends from the right edge of the label to the right edge of the view.

You need two more label/slider pairs, so let's quickly duplicate the ones you just created. Select both the label and slider views (by holding down the Shift key or by dragging out a selection rectangle that selects both). Now press the Option key. While holding down the Option key, click and drag the pair down. The Option key turns the drag into a copy operation. Position the pair immediately below the first two, as shown in Figure 8-7, and release the mouse.

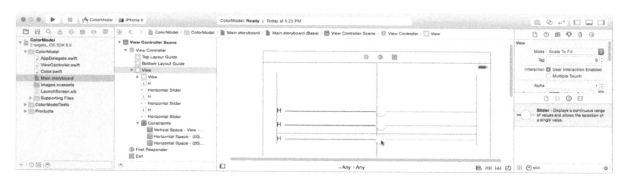

Figure 8-7. *Duplicating the label and slider*

Repeat the copy again so you have three labels and three slider controls. Control/right-click the top slider, drag down to the middle slider, release, and choose Equal Widths from the constraints menu. Repeat, dragging to the bottom slider, as shown in Figure 8-8. This adds constraints to keep the three slider controls the same width.

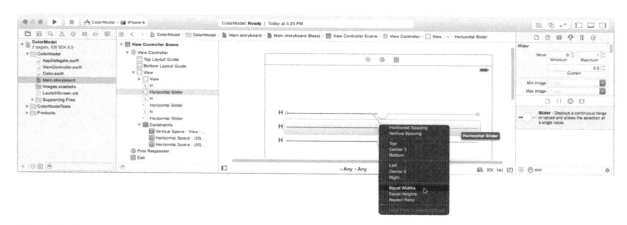

Figure 8-8. *Constraining the widths of the sliders*

Retitle the second and third labels to S and B. You now have all of the view objects you need. Flesh out the constraints by choosing Add Missing Constraints in View Controller from the Resolve Auto Layout Issues control.

In your data mode, the hue value ranges from 0° to 360° and saturation and brightness range from 0 percent to 100 percent. Change the value range of the three sliders to match. Select the top (hue) slider and use the attributes inspector to change its Maximum value from 1 to 360, as shown in Figure 8-9. Change the maximum value of the other two sliders to 100.

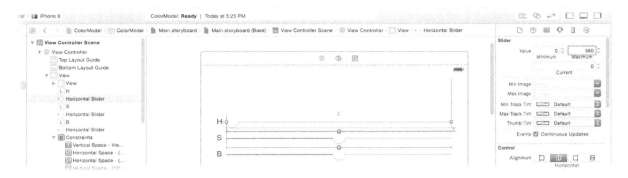

Figure 8-9. *Establishing value range of slider control*

Writing Your Controller

The Xcode project template already provides you with a controller class; you just need to fill it out. Select your ViewController.swift interface file. Your controller will need a reference to your data model object, along with outlets and actions to connect with your interface. Start by adding the properties to your ViewController class.

```
var colorModel = Color()
@IBOutlet var colorView: UIView!
```

The first is your controller's connection with your data model. The second is an outlet that you'll connect to your color view. This will let your controller update the color displayed in the view.

Finally, your controller will need three actions, one for each slider control, that will adjust one value in the data model. While still in your ViewController.swift file, add these three functions:

```
@IBAction func changeHue(sender: AnyObject!) {
    if let slider = sender as? UISlider {
        colorModel.hue = slider.value
        colorView.backgroundColor = colorModel.color
    }
}

@IBAction func changeSaturation(sender: AnyObject!) {
    if let slider = sender as? UISlider {
        colorModel.saturation = slider.value
        colorView.backgroundColor = colorModel.color
    }
}

@IBAction func changeBrightness(sender: AnyObject!) {
    if let slider = sender as? UISlider {
        colorModel.brightness = slider.value
        colorView.backgroundColor = colorModel.color
    }
}
```

Each action message will be received from one of the slider controls whenever it changes. Each method simply modifies the corresponding value in the data model with the new value of the slider. It then updates the color view to reflect the new color in the data model. In this implementation, your controller is taking responsibility for updating the view whenever the data model changes (see Figure 8-2).

Wiring Your Interface

The last step is to connect your controller's outlets and actions to the view objects. Select the `Main.storyboard` Interface Builder file again. Select the View Controller object and use the connections inspector to connect your controller's `colorView` outlet to the `UIView` object, as shown in Figure 8-10.

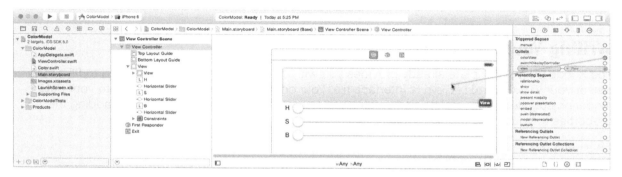

Figure 8-10. *Connecting the colorView outlet*

Now connect the actions of the three sliders to the controller's `changeHue(_:)`, `changeSaturation(_:)`, and `changeBrightness(_:)` functions. Select the top slider. Using the connections inspector, connect the `Value Changed` event to the controller's `changedHue:` action. Repeat, connecting the middle slider to the `changeSaturation:` action and connecting the bottom slider to the `changeBrightness:` action, as shown in Figure 8-11.

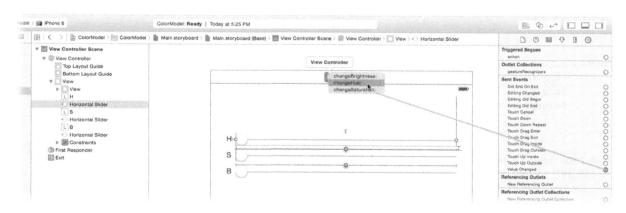

Figure 8-11. *Connecting slider actions*

Tip You could have made these connections by Control/right-clicking a slider and dragging to the controller. This works because the `Value Changed` event is the default event for control objects when connecting an action.

There's one last, cosmetic detail to attend to. The values for the `hue`, `saturation`, and `brightness` in the data model all initialize to 0.0 (black). The default color in the color view is not black, and the initial positions of the sliders are all 0.5. So that your view objects are consistent with your data model from the beginning, select the sliders and use the attributes inspector to set the Current property to 0.0. Select the color view object and set its background attribute to Black Color, as shown in Figure 8-12.

Figure 8-12. Finished ColorModel interface

Run your app in the iPhone simulator. It appears with the color black and all three sliders set to their minimum values. Change the values of the sliders to explore different combinations of hue, saturation, and brightness, as shown on the right in Figure 8-13.

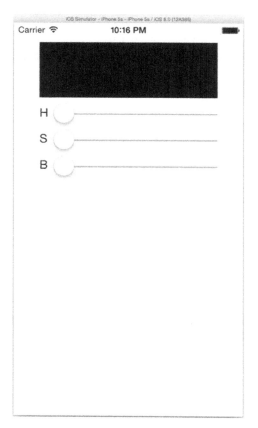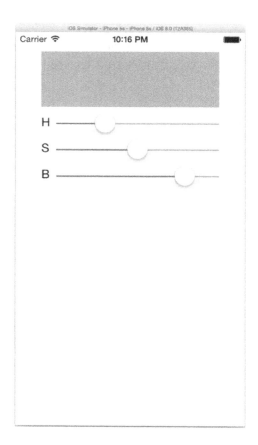

Figure 8-13. First ColorModel app

Having Multiple Views

One reason the MVC design pattern separates the data model from the view objects is to avoid a one-to-one relationship between the two. With MVC you can create a one-to-many, or even a many-to-many, relationship between your data model and view objects. Exploit this by creating more view objects that display the same data model and in different ways. (You'll find this version of the project in the Learn iOS Development Projects ➤ Ch 8 ➤ ColorModel-2 ➤ ColorModel folder).

Start by selecting your Main.storyboard Interface Builder file. Using the right resizing handle, make the width of the three sliders considerably shorter. You want to temporarily create some room to add new view objects to their right, as shown in Figure 8-14.

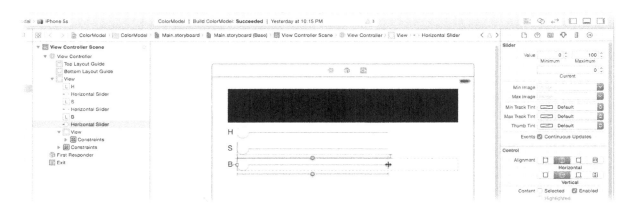

Figure 8-14. Making room for new view objects

Find the label object in the library and add three new labels, to the right of each slider and aligned with the right edge of the color view, as shown in Figure 8-15.

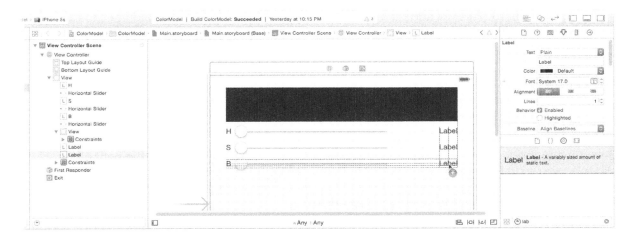

Figure 8-15. Adding HSB value labels

Each label will display the textual value of one property. Edit the text property of the three labels, either by using the attributes inspector or by double-clicking the label object. Change the top label to 360° (press Shift+Option+8 to get the degrees symbol), and the other two to 100%, as shown in Figure 8-16.

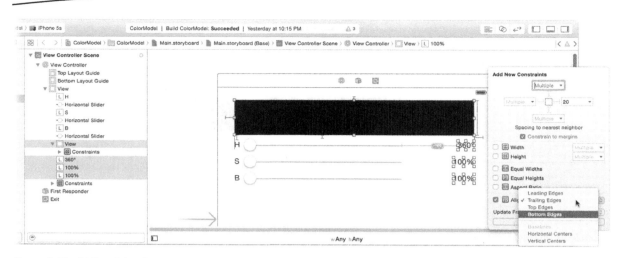

Figure 8-16. *Adding right-alignment constraints for labels*

Now create some constraints to right-justify the labels. Select all three new labels and the view object above them. Click the pin constraints control and add a right align edges constraint, also shown in Figure 8-16. This will add three new constraints to keep the right edge of the labels horizontally aligned with the right edge of the color view.

To vertically position the labels, select the "H" label and the "360" label, click the pin constraints control, and add a top edge alignment constraint. Repeat with the "S" and "100%" pair and the "B" and "100%" pair. Now the three labels on the right will now match the vertical position of the ones on the left. You could have also centered them to the sliders or added the same vertical spacing constraints the labels on the left are using. There are a million different combinations of constraints that will create the same layout. Use the one that makes sense to you.

Select the top slider. Select the right-edge constraint, created by Xcode, just to the right of the slider, as shown in Figure 8-17. Using the attributes inspector, set its value to -60. This changes the constraint so the right edge of the top slider is now inset from the right edge of the color view by 60 pixels, leaving room for the labels you just added.

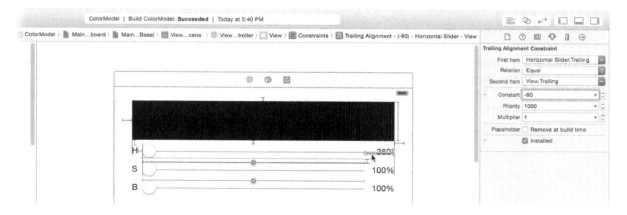

Figure 8-17. *Adjusting the slider constraint*

> **Note** See how you made less work for yourself by adding equal width constraints for the second and third sliders, rather than simply setting the same right edge constraint for all three? By making the width of your sliders dependent on each other, you only have to modify the width of one and the others fall into line, literally.

You'll need outlets to use these three labels, so add these to your `ViewController.swift` file:

```
@IBOutlet var hueLabel: UILabel!
@IBOutlet var saturationLabel: UILabel!
@IBOutlet var brightnessLabel: UILabel!
```

Connect these three outlets in Interface Builder. Switch back to the `Main.storyboard` file, select the view controller, and use the connections inspector to connect the outlets to their respective `UILabel` objects.

Switch back to your `ViewController.swift` file and modify the three actions so each also updates its respective label view, by adding the following code in bold:

```
@IBAction func changeHue(sender: AnyObject!) {
    if let slider = sender as? UISlider {
        colorModel.hue = slider.value
        colorView.backgroundColor = colorModel.color
        hueLabel.text = NSString(format: "%.0f°", colorModel.hue)
    }
}

@IBAction func changeSaturation(sender: AnyObject!) {
    if let slider = sender as? UISlider {
        colorModel.saturation = slider.value
        colorView.backgroundColor = colorModel.color
        saturationLabel.text = NSString(format: "%.0f%%", ↵
                                        colorModel.saturation)
    }
}

@IBAction func changeBrightness(sender: AnyObject!) {
    if let slider = sender as? UISlider {
        colorModel.brightness = slider.value
        colorView.backgroundColor = colorModel.color
        brightnessLabel.text = NSString(format: "%.0f%%", ↵
                                        colorModel.brightness)
    }
}
```

These three new statements change the text in the label fields to display the textual value of each property. The `%.0f` format specifier rounds the data model's floating-point value to the nearest integer. Literally translated, it means "Format (%) the floating-point value (f) so there are zero (.0) digits to the right of its radix point."

> **Note**   The %% escape sequence means a single % character. Format string specifiers begin with % (such as %u or %02x). To include a single percent character in a format string, you use %%.

Now run your app again. This time, whenever you adjust the value of one of the sliders, both the color and the textual HSB value are updated too, as shown in Figure 8-18.

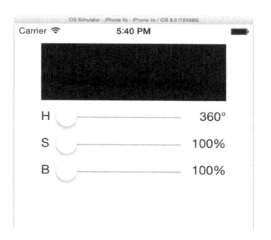 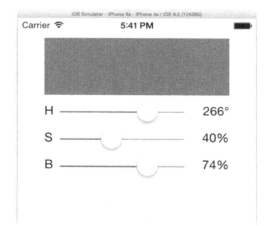

Figure 8-18. ColorModel with HSB values

One of the advantages of the MVC design pattern is that data model objects aren't coupled to their view objects. If you want to display the same data model information in a second view or want to display the same information three different ways, you just add the appropriate view objects. The data model never changes. Let's add yet another way to display the color and see how that affects your design.

Consolidating Updates

Now your data model appears, in different forms, in four different views. But why stop there? In the Main.storyboard file—you're now working toward the project in the ColorModel-3 folder—add two more labels. Set the text of one to #000000 and the other to Web:. Position them as shown in Figure 8-19. Choose Add Missing Constraints in View Controller from the Resolve Auto Layout Issues control.

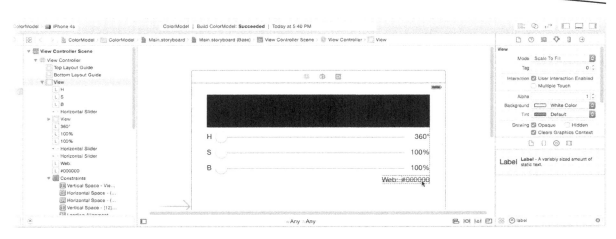

Figure 8-19. *Adding web-safe color view*

You'll use this label to display the "web" color selected. This is the RGB value of the chosen color, as an HTML short color constant. You should be able to do the next two steps in your sleep. Add the following outlet property to `ViewController.swift`:

```
@IBOutlet var webLabel: UILabel!
```

Switch back to `Main.storyboard` and connect the `webLabel` outlet to the #000000 label object, as shown in Figure 8-20.

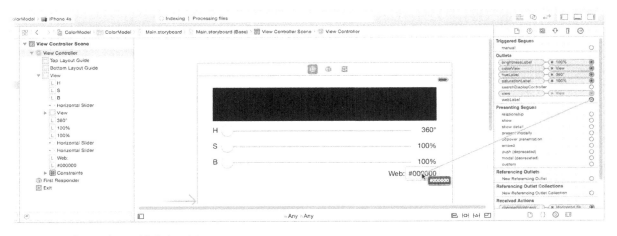

Figure 8-20. *Connecting webLabel outlet*

Now return to the ViewController.swift file and consider what needs to change. Here's the code to set the webLabel view to display the hex value of the color:

```
var red: CGFloat = 0.0
var green: CGFloat = 0.0
var blue: CGFloat = 0.0
var alpha: CGFloat = 0.0
color.getRed(&red, green: &green, blue: &blue, alpha: &alpha)
webLabel.text = NSString(format: "#%02X%02X%02X", ⏎
                       CInt(red*255),CInt(green*255),CInt(blue*255))
```

This code extracts the individual red, green, and blue values from the UIColor object. It then uses those values (in the range of 0.0 to 1.0) to create a string of six hexadecimal digits, two for each color, in the range of 00 to ff, rounding down to the closest integer.

While that's not a lot of code, it is a lot of code to repeat three times, because each action method (changeHue(_:), changeSaturation(_:), changeBrightness(_:)) must also update the new web value view.

There's an old programming adage that says

If you're repeating yourself, refactor.

This means if you find yourself writing the same code, again and again, it's probably a good time to reorganize and consolidate your code. It's a truism that the more code you write, the more chance you have of introducing a bug. A common goal of software engineers is to minimize the amount of code they write—not just because they're lazy (at least, many of us are) but because it results in more succinct solutions.

Consolidate the updates to your various view objects into a single function named updateColor(). Replace the code in the three action methods that update the color view with a call to this new function (modified code in bold).

```
@IBAction func changeHue(sender: AnyObject!) {
    if let slider = sender as? UISlider {
        colorModel.hue = slider.value
        updateColor()
    }
}

@IBAction func changeSaturation(sender: AnyObject!) {
    if let slider = sender as? UISlider {
        colorModel.saturation = slider.value
        updateColor()
    }
}

@IBAction func changeBrightness(sender: AnyObject!) {
    if let slider = sender as? UISlider {
        colorModel.brightness = slider.value
        updateColor()
    }
}
```

Finally, write the `updateColor()` function.

```
func updateColor() {
    let color = colorModel.color
    colorView.backgroundColor = color
    hueLabel.text = "\(Int(colorModel.hue))°"
    saturationLabel.text = "\(Int(colorModel.saturation))%"
    brightnessLabel.text = "\(Int(colorModel.brightness))%"
    var red: CGFloat = 0.0
    var green: CGFloat = 0.0
    var blue: CGFloat = 0.0
    var alpha: CGFloat = 0.0
    color.getRed(&red, green: &green, blue: &blue, alpha: &alpha)
    webLabel.text = NSString(format: "#%02X%02X%02X",
                    CInt(red*255),CInt(green*255),CInt(blue*255))
}
```

The first line updates the background color of the color view object, a task that had been repeated in each of the three actions. The next three statements update the three HSB label views, and the remaining code calculates the hexadecimal RGB value and updates `webLabel`.

Run your app again, as shown in Figure 8-21. Each change to the data model updates five different view objects, and your controller code is arguably simpler and easier to maintain than it was before. You can easily add new actions that update the data model; all you have to do is call `updateColor()` before returning. Similarly, new view objects could be added and you'd only have to add an outlet and modify `updateColor()`.

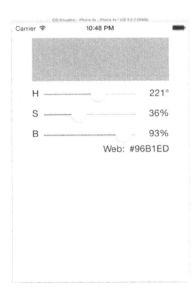
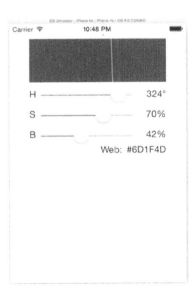

Figure 8-21. ColorModel with web value

Complex View Objects

So far, the view objects you've used in ColorModel display relatively trivial (String or UIColor) values. Sometimes view objects display much more complex data types. It's not uncommon for complex view objects to maintain a reference to the data model. This gives them direct access to all of the information they need.

To make ColorModel a little more interesting, you're going to replace the simple UIView object with a custom view object that displays a hue/saturation color chart, in addition to identifying the exact color selected by the hue, saturation, and brightness sliders. Revising your design, your new app should look like the one in Figure 8-22.

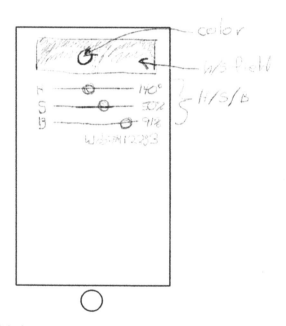

Figure 8-22. *Updated ColorModel design*

Replacing UIView with ColorView

Your new design will replace the UIView object in your current design with your own custom ColorView object. Start by adding a new Swift class to your project. Drag in a new Swift file from the file template library and name it ColorView. (Alternatively, you can drag the finished ColorView.swift file from this version of the project in the Learn iOS Development Projects ➤ Ch 8 ➤ ColorModel-4 ➤ ColorModel folder).

If you're starting from scratch, define the skeleton of the class in your new file so Interface Builder knows it exists.

```
import UIKit

class ColorView : UIView {
}
```

Upgrade the plain view in your interface from a UIImage object to your new ColorView object. In Main.storyboard, select the UIImage view object. Use the identity inspector to change the class of the object from UIView to ColorView, as shown in Figure 8-23.

Figure 8-23. *Changing the UIView into a ColorView*

In your ViewController.swift file, find the colorView property that refers to this object. Change the type of the colorView property from UIView to ColorView (modified code shown in bold). Now your controller is connected to a ColorView object instead.

```
@IBOutlet var colorView: ColorView!
```

Connecting the View to Your Data Model

Your fancy new ColorView object will have a direct connection its data model (the Color object). Add that property in your ColorView.swift file.

```
var colorModel: Color?
```

> **Note**   The colorModel property is not an Interface Builder outlet (IBOutlet) because you'll be setting this property programmatically rather than in Interface Builder. That's not to say it couldn't be an outlet; it just doesn't need to be for this project.

Drawing ColorView

While still in your ColorView.swift file, you're going to add a drawRect(_:) function that draws a 2D hue/saturation color chart at the current brightness level. At the position within the color chart that represents current hue/saturation, the view draws a circle filled with that color.

It's a fair amount of code, and it's not the focus of this chapter, so I'll gloss over the details. The code for the drawRect(_:) function you need to add to ColorView.swift is in Listing 8-1. If you're writing this app as you work through this chapter, I applaud you. If you're not and you didn't import the complete ColorView.swift file earlier, at least save yourself a lot of typing and copy the code for the drawRect(_:) function from the ColorView.swift file that you'll find in the Learn iOS Development Projects ➤ Ch 8 ➤ ColorModel-4 ➤ ColorModel folder.

Listing 8-1. ColorView.swift drawRect(_:) Function

```
override func drawRect(rect: CGRect) {
    if let color = colorModel {
        let bounds = self.bounds
        if hsImage != nil && ( brightness != color.brightness || ⤶
                            bounds.size != hsImage!.size ) {
            hsImage = nil
            }

        if hsImage == nil {
            brightness = color.brightness
            UIGraphicsBeginImageContextWithOptions(bounds.size, true, 1.0)
            let imageContext = UIGraphicsGetCurrentContext()
            for y in 0..<Int(bounds.height) {
                for x in 0..<Int(bounds.width) {
                    let uiColor = UIColor(hue: CGFloat(x)/bounds.width,
                                saturation: CGFloat(y)/bounds.height,
                                brightness: CGFloat(brightness/100.0),
                                    alpha: 1.0)
                    uiColor.set()
                    CGContextFillRect(imageContext,CGRect(x: x, y: y, width: 1, height: 1))
                }
            }
            hsImage = UIGraphicsGetImageFromCurrentImageContext()
            UIGraphicsEndImageContext()
        }

        hsImage!.drawInRect(bounds)

        let circleRect = CGRect(x: bounds.maxX*CGFloat(color.hue/360)-radius/2,
                                y: bounds.maxY*CGFloat(color.saturation/100)-radius/2,
                            width: radius,
                            height: radius)
```

```
        let circle = UIBezierPath(ovalInRect: circleRect)
        color.color.setFill()
        circle.fill()
        circle.lineWidth = 3.0
        UIColor.blackColor().setStroke()
        circle.stroke()
    }
}
```

In a nutshell, the ColorView draws a two-dimensional graph of the possible hue/saturation combinations at the current brightness level. (When iOS devices come out with 3D displays, you can revise this code to draw a 3D image instead!)

The point of interest (for this chapter) is that the ColorValue has a direct reference to the Color data model object, so your controller doesn't have to explicitly update it with a new color value anymore. All your controller needs to do is tell the ColorView object when it needs to redraw; the ColorView will use the data model directly to obtain whatever information it needed to draw itself.

For this to happen, your controller needs to establish this connection when it creates the data model and view objects. In your ViewController.swift file, find the viewDidLoad() function and add this one bold line:

```
override func viewDidLoad() {
    super.viewDidLoad()
    colorView.colorModel = colorModel
}
```

When the view objects are created (when the Interface Builder file loads), the controller creates the data model object and connects it to the colorView object.

Now replace the code that you used to set the color to draw (via colorView's backgroundColor property) with code that simply tells the colorView object that it needs to redraw itself, shown in bold.

```
func updateColor() {
    colorView.setNeedsDisplay()
    let color = colorModel.color
    ...
```

Run your new app and try it. This is a dramatically more interesting interface, as shown in Figure 8-24.

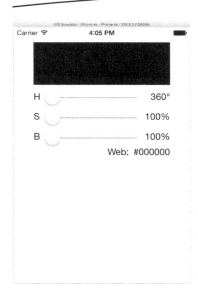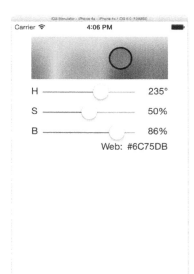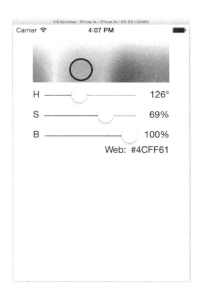

Figure 8-24. ColorModel with ColorView

This version of your app represents the next level of MVC sophistication. Instead of spoon-feeding simple values to your view objects, you now have a view object that understands your data model and obtains the values it needs directly. But the controller still has to remember to refresh all of the views whenever it changes the data model. Let's take a different approach and have the data model tell the controller when it changes.

Being a Keen Observer

Way back in the "MVC Communications" section, I described a simple arrangement where the data model sent notifications to view objects (see Figure 8-1) letting them know when they need to update their display. You've already done this in your MyStuff app. You added a postDidChangeNotification() function to your MyWhatsit class. That method notified any interested parties that an item in your data model had changed. Your table view controller observed those notifications and redrew its table, as needed.

Using NSNotificationCenter to communicate data model changes to views is a *perfect* example of MVC communications. Save that in your bag of "iOS solutions I know." I won't repeat that solution here. Instead, I'm going to show you an even more sophisticated method of observing changes in your data model.

Key-Value Observing

I told you that design patterns run deep in iOS. You're about to find out just how deep. MVC communications is based, in part, on the observer pattern. The *observer pattern* is a design pattern in which one object (the observer) receives a message when some event in another object (the subject) occurs. In MVC, the data model (the subject) notifies view or controller objects (the observers) whenever it changes. This relieves the controller from having to remember to update the view objects (that is, calling updateColor()) whenever it changes the data model. Now it—or any other object—can just change the data model at will; any changes will send notifications to its observers.

In MyStuff you accomplished this using NSNotifcation objects. In ColorModel you're going to use some Cocoa Touch magic called *key-value observing* (KVO). KVO is a technology that notifies an observer whenever the property of an object is set. That's right. All you do is set a property value, and any object observing that property is automatically notified.

Observing Key Value Changes

Observing property changes in a Swift object is a three-step process.

1. Make sure your properties are observable.

2. Become an observer for the property (identified by a *key*).

3. Implement an observeValueForKeyPath(_:,ofObject:,change:,context:) function.

The first step is to make the Color class eligible for KVO. (You'll find the finished project in the Learn iOS Development Projects ➤ Ch 8 ➤ ColorModel-5 ➤ ColorModel folder.) Switch to the Color.swift file and make the following change to the class (new code in bold):

```
class Color: NSObject {
    dynamic var hue: Float = 0.0
    dynamic var saturation: Float = 0.0
    dynamic var brightness: Float = 0.0
```

If you want to know why you needed to make these changes, see the sidebar "Swift and KVO."

SWIFT AND KVO

Key-value observing depends on dynamically dispatched methods. In English, when you call an instance function of an object, either the CPU can jump directly to that code (*static calling*) or the caller can query the object and ask for the address of the code that should be run (*dynamic dispatching*). The latter is more flexible because an object can spontaneously alter the code that executes when you call its method. In Objective-C, Swift's predecessor, all methods and properties are dynamically dispatched.

The disadvantage of dynamically dispatched methods is performance. It takes time to ask that question ("What code should I execute for method X?"), and it has to be asked and answered every time a method is called or a property is accessed. Swift prefers to use static dispatching, when it can, which is why it's typically faster than Objective-C. The problem is that technologies like KVO—that depend on dynamic dispatching—simply won't work with statically called functions.

But that's not to say that Swift is incapable of using dynamically dispatched methods. In fact, it uses them all the time. Swift is also compatible with any Objective-C object, all of which use dynamically dispatched methods. To use KVO with a Swift object, you just need to get Swift to use dynamic dispatching on the properties and methods you're interested in.

The first step is to make your class a subclass of NSObject. NSObject is the base class for all Objective-C classes. (Swift doesn't have a common base class.) By making your object a subclass of NSObject, you've turned it into an Objective-C class, rather than a purely Swift class. This makes no real difference to the rest of your app; as I said, Swift will use an Objective-C object as effortlessly as a native Swift object. In fact, it doesn't even change your object that much. But it has the important side effect of inheriting all of the standard KVO methods defined in NSObject.

The second step is to tell Swift to specifically use dynamic dispatching on the properties you want to observe. This is accomplished with the dynamic keyword. Placing dynamic before a var or func tells Swift that you want this property or function to always use dynamic dispatching. Behind the scenes, a dynamic property creates two hidden functions (both dynamically dispatched): a *getter* function called to obtain that value and a *setter* function called to change it. It's this setter function that KVO intercepts to work its magic.

I honestly don't know what the future of KVO in Swift will be. As of this writing, Swift is still at version 1.0 and is very much a work-in-progress. The official documentation for Swift simply states that KVO is "To be determined." You can still use KVO in your Swift projects by leveraging Swift's support for Objective-C, where KVO and similar technologies are a given. But I don't know what the fate will be for KVO and native Swift classes. There's a natural tug-of-war between Swift's desire to be fast and efficient and the power of features like KVO. My hope is that Apple will find a way to efficiently support KVO in Swift—fingers crossed.

The second step is simple enough. In your ViewController.swift file, find the viewDidLoad() function and change the following code, adding the new code in bold:

```
super.viewDidLoad()
colorModel.addObserver(self, forKeyPath: "hue",        options: .allZeros, context: nil)
colorModel.addObserver(self, forKeyPath: "saturation", options: .allZeros, context: nil)
colorModel.addObserver(self, forKeyPath: "brightness", options: .allZeros, context: nil)
colorModel.addObserver(self, forKeyPath: "color",      options: .allZeros, context: nil)
colorView.colorModel = colorModel
```

Each statement registers your ViewController object (self) to observe changes to one property (the key path) of the receiving object (colorModel).

Thereafter, every time one of the observed properties of colorModel changes, your controller will receive an observeValueForKeyPath(_:,ofObject:,change:,context:) call. The first parameter identifies the property that changed on the ofObject parameter. Use these parameters to determine what changed and take the appropriate action.

Your new observeValueForKeyPath(_:,ofObject:,change:,context:) function will replace your old updateColor() function because it serves the same purpose. Replace updateColor() with the code in Listing 8-2. The code in bold shows what's different.

Listing 8-2. observeValueForKeyPath(_:,ofObject:,change:,context:)

```
override func observeValueForKeyPath(keyPath: String!, ofObject object: AnyObject!, ↵
              change: [NSObject : AnyObject]!, context: UnsafeMutablePointer<Void>) {
    switch keyPath {
        case "hue":
            hueLabel.text = "\(Int(colorModel.hue))°"
        case "saturation":
            saturationLabel.text = "\(Int(colorModel.saturation))%"
        case "brightness":
            brightnessLabel.text = "\(Int(colorModel.brightness))%"
        case "color":
            colorView.setNeedsDisplay()
            var red: CGFloat = 0, green: CGFloat = 0, blue: CGFloat = 0, alpha: CGFloat = 0
```

```
                    colorModel.color.getRed(&red, green: &green, blue: &blue, alpha: &alpha)
                    webLabel.text = NSString(format: "#%02X%02X%02X",
                                             CInt(red*255),CInt(green*255),CInt(blue*255))
            default:
                break
        }
    }
}
```

The code is straightforward. It checks to see whether the keyPath parameter matches one of the property names you expect to change. Each case updates the view objects affected by changes to that property.

You can now remove all of the references to updateColor(). Now your changeHue(_:) function looks like the following:

```
@IBAction func changeHue(sender: AnyObject!) {
    if let slider = sender as? UISlider {
        colorModel.hue = slider.value
    }
}
```

None of your methods that change the properties of your data model have to remember to update the view because the data model object will notify your controller automatically whenever that happens. Run your app to try it, as shown in Figure 8-25.

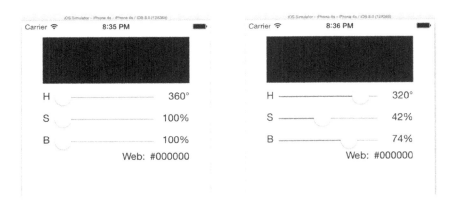

Figure 8-25. *Defective KVO*

Some parts of it work, but clearly something is wrong. Let's think about the problem for a moment.

Creating KVO Dependencies

Your controller is receiving changes for the hue, saturation, and brightness properties because the three label objects are getting updated. The colorView and webLabel objects, however, never change. Your controller is not receiving change notifications for the color property.

That's because nothing ever changes the color property. (It's not even allowed to change because it's an immutable property.) The problem is that color is a synthesized property value: code, that you wrote, makes up the color value based on the values of hue, saturation, and brightness. Swift and iOS don't know that. All they know is that no one ever sets the color property (colorModel.color = newColor), so it never sends any notifications.

There are two straightforward ways to address this. The first would be to add code to your controller so that it updates the color-related views whenever it receives notifications that any of the other three (hue, saturation, or brightness) changed. That's a perfectly acceptable solution, but there's an alternative.

You can teach the KVO system about a property (the *derived key*) that is affected by changes to other properties (its *dependent keys*). Open your Color.swift file and add this special class function:

```
class func keyPathsForValuesAffectingColor() -> NSSet {
    return NSSet(array: ["hue", "saturation", "brightness"])
}
```

Now run your app again and see the difference (see Figure 8-26) that one function makes.

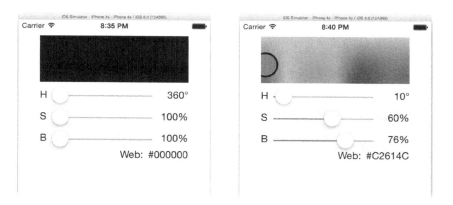

Figure 8-26. Working KVO updates

So, what's happening? The special class function keyPathsForValuesAffectingColor()[2] tells the KVO system that there are three properties (key paths) that affect the value of the color property: hue, saturation, and brightness. Now, whenever the KVO mechanism sees one of the first three properties change, it knows that color changed too and sends a second notification for the "color" key path.

---

[2]The name of the derived property is actually part of the function name. When you observe a property key (say, anyProp), KVO looks to see whether you've implemented a class function named keyPathsForValuesAffectingAnyProp(). If you did, it calls it to discover its dependent keys.

> **Tip**   KVO is very flexible, and there are several ways to describe dependent keys. You can also write code that determines exactly what property change notifications are sent, when, and what information those notifications include. For a much more in-depth explanation, check out the *Key-Value Observing Programming Guide* that you'll find in Xcode's Documentation and API Reference.

I'm sure you're thinking this is pretty cool, but you might also be thinking that it's not that much less work than the updateColor() function you wrote in the previous section. And you're right; it's not. But that's also because all of your data model changes come from one source (the slider controls), and there's a relatively small number of places where your data model is altered. If that were to change, however, it becomes a whole new ball game.

Multivector Data Model Changes

As your app matures, it's likely to get more complex, and changes to your data model can occur in more places. The beauty of KVO is that the change notifications happen in the same place the changes occur—in the data model.

It was OK to call changeColor() when the only places that changed the color were the three slider actions. But what if you added a fourth control view object that also changed them—or five or nine?

Here's an example. The sliders in your app are nice, but they're sooooo twentieth century. We live in the age of the touch interface. Wouldn't it be nicer to just touch the hue/saturation graph and point to the color you want? Let's do it.

Handling Touch Events

You should already know how to implement this—unless you skipped Chapter 4. If you did, go back and read it now. Add touch event handler methods to your custom ColorView class. The handlers will use the coordinates within the color chart to choose a new hue and saturation. Since you know what you're doing, get started by adding three touch event handlers to ColorView.swift. (You'll find the finished project in the Learn iOS Development Projects ➤ Ch 8 ➤ ColorModel-6 ➤ ColorModel folder).

```swift
override func touchesBegan(touches: NSSet, withEvent event: UIEvent) {
    changeColorTo(touch: touches.anyObject() as? UITouch)
}

override func touchesMoved(touches: NSSet, withEvent event: UIEvent) {
    changeColorTo(touch: touches.anyObject() as? UITouch)
}

override func touchesEnded(touches: NSSet, withEvent event: UIEvent) {
    changeColorTo(touch: touches.anyObject() as? UITouch)
}
```

These three handlers catch all touch began, moved, and ended events; extract the one touch object; and pass it to the changeColorTo(touch:) function.

> **Note**   Remember that, by default, a view object's `multipleTouchEnabled` property is `false`, which means that its touch event handler methods will never see more than one touch object in `touches`, even if your user is touching the view with more than one finger.

Clearly, the `changeColorTo(touch:)` function is where the action is. Add these two functions to your class:

```
func changeColorTo(# touch: UITouch? ) {
    if let contact = touch {
        changeColorTo(point: contact.locationInView(self))
    }
}

func changeColorTo(# point: CGPoint ) {
    if let color = colorModel {
        let bounds = self.bounds
        if bounds.contains(point) {
            color.hue = Float((point.x-bounds.minX)/bounds.width*360)
            color.saturation = Float((point.y-bounds.minY)/bounds.height*100)
        }
    }
}
```

The `changeColorTo(touch:)` function simply checks to see whether a usable `UITouch` object is present. If so, it extracts the location of the touch in the coordinate system of the color view and passes it on to `changeColorTo(point:)`.

The `changeColorTo(point:)` function does the interesting work. It converts the local coordinate into the hue and saturation at that location in the view and uses those values to update the data model.

Notice that this is all it has to do. It didn't send an action message to the controller. It could have—that would be a perfectly reasonable implementation too. But since you have KVO, you don't need to. Any object can make changes to the data model directly, and all the observers will receive the necessary notifications.

Try it. Run your app. Move the brightness slider off of 0 percent and then use your finger (or mouse) to drag around inside the color chart. The hue and saturation change as you drag your finger around, as shown in Figure 8-27.

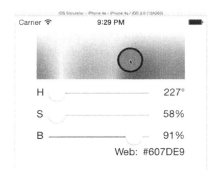 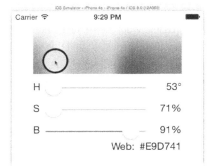

Figure 8-27. Turning ColorView into a control

Binding the Sliders

The only thing that doesn't work is the hue and saturation sliders don't move when you touch the color view. That's because they're still acting only as inputs. Up until this point, the only way the hue and saturation could have changed was to move the slider. Now that there are other pathways to changing these properties, you need to keep the sliders in synchronization with the data model too.

You'll need a connection to the three sliders, so add that to your `ViewController.swift` file:

```
@IBOutlet var hueSlider: UISlider!
@IBOutlet var saturationSlider: UISlider!
@IBOutlet var brightnessSlider: UISlider!
```

Switch to the `Main.storyboard` Interface Builder file and connect these new outlets from your view controller object to the three `UISlider` controls.

Find the `observeValueForKeyPath(_:,ofObject:,change:,context:)` function in `ViewController.swift` and insert these three lines of bold code:

```
switch keyPath {
    case "hue":
        hueLabel.text = "\(Int(colorModel.hue))°"
        hueSlider.value = colorModel.hue;
    case "saturation":
        saturationLabel.text = "\(Int(colorModel.saturation))%"
        saturationSlider.value = colorModel.saturation
    case "brightness":
        brightnessLabel.text = "\(Int(colorModel.brightness))%"
        brightnessSlider.value = colorModel.brightness
```

Now when the hue value changes, the hue slider will be changed to match, even if the change came from the hue slider.

> **Caution**   Moving a slider won't cause an infinite loop of messages: the slider sends an action to the controller, which changes the data model, which updates the slider, which sends an action to the controller, and so on. That's because slider controls send action messages only when the user drags them around, not when their value is set programmatically. Not all views, however, are so clever, and it's possible to create infinite MVC message loops. The way to solve that is to send actions or notifications only when the value actually changes.

The color view and the sliders now update whenever the data model changes, and the color view can directly change the data model. Software engineers would say that these views are *bound* to properties of the data model. A *binding* is a direct, two-way linkage between a data model and a view.

Final Touches

You can now also easily fix an annoying bug in your app. The display values for the hue, saturation, and brightness are wrong (360°, 100%, and 100%) when the app starts. The values in the data model are 0°, 0%, and 0%. Switch to `ViewController.swift` and at the end of `viewDidLoad()`, add this code:

```
colorModel.hue = 60
colorModel.saturation = 50
colorModel.brightness = 100
```

Since this code executes after your controller starts observing changes to your data model, these statements will not only initialize your data model to a color that's not black but will also update all relevant views to match. Try it!

There's also some icon resources in the `Learn iOS Development Projects` ➤ `Ch 8` ➤ `ColorModel` (`Icons`) folder. Add them to the `AppIcon` group of the `Images.xcassets` item, just as you did for earlier projects.

Cheating

The model-view-controller design pattern will improve the quality of your code, make your apps simpler to write and maintain, and give you an attractive, healthy glow. Do not, however, fall under its spell and become its slave.

While the use of design patterns gives you an edge in your quest to become a master iOS developer, I caution against using them just for the sake of using them. Pragmatic programmers call this *over engineering*. Sometimes the simple solutions are the best. Take this example:

```
class MyScoreController {
    var score = 0
    @IBOutlet var scoreView: UILabel!
```

```
    @IBAction func incrementScore(sender: AnyObject!) {
        score += 1
        scoreView.text = "\(score)"
    }
}
```

What's wrong with this controller? MVC purists will point out that there's no data model object. The controller is also acting as the data model, storing and manipulating the score property. This violates the MVC design pattern as well as the single responsibility principle.

Do you want my opinion? There's nothing wrong with this solution; it's just one #@$%&* integer! There's nothing to be gained in creating a new class to hold just one number, and you'll waste a whole lot of time doing it.

If someday, maybe, your data model grew to three integers, a string, and a localization object, then sure: refactor your app, pull the integer out of your controller, and move it to a real data model object. But until that day arrives, don't worry about it.

There's a programming discipline called *agile development* that values finished, working software over plans and pristine design. In these situations, my advice is to use the simplest solution that does the job. Be aware when you're taking shortcuts in your MVC design, and have a plan to fix it when (and if) that becomes a problem, but don't lash yourself to a design philosophy. Design patterns should make your development easier, not harder.

Summary

To summarize, MVC is good.

Is all of this computer science study making you want to take a break and listen to your favorite tunes? Well then, the next chapter is for you.

EXERCISE

While your ColorModel app came very close to the idealized MVC communications, it still relied on the controller to observe the changes and forward update events the view objects. Given the work you've done so far, how difficult would it be to make the color view observe data model changes directly?

It wouldn't be that hard, and that's your exercise for this chapter. Modify ViewController and ColorView so that ColorView is the direct observer of "color" changes in the Color object.

This is a common pattern in fairly extensive apps that have complex data models and lots of custom view objects. The advantage is that each view object takes on the responsibility of observing the data model changes specific to that view, relieving your controller objects from this burden.

You'll find my solution to this exercise in the Learn iOS Development Projects ➤ Ch 8 ➤ ColorModel ➤ E1 folder.

Chapter 9

Sweet, Sweet Music

Choosing and playing music from your iPod library is a great way to add some toe-tapping fun to your app. You can also add your own music and audio effects to actions and games. Both are relatively easy to do, and I'll get to those straightaway. But don't stop reading this chapter at that point. Sound in iOS apps exists in a larger world of competing audio sources, real-world events, and an ever-changing configuration of hardware. Making audio work nicely in this demanding, and sometimes complex, environment is the real test of your iOS development skills. This chapter covers the following:

- Choosing tracks from the iPod music library
- Playing music in the iPod music library
- Obtaining the details (title, artist, album, artwork) of a track
- Playing sound files
- Configuring the behavior of audio in your app
- Mixing music with other sounds
- Responding to interruptions
- Responding to hardware changes

Along the way, you'll pick up some timesaving Xcode tricks, manage view objects without an outlet connection, and learn some mad constraint skills. Are you ready to make some noise?

> **Note**   The app you're about to create will run in the simulator, but the simulator does not have any music in its iPod library. If you want to pick a song and play music, you'll need a provisioned iOS device.

Making Your Own iPod

The two most common sources for prerecorded sounds in an iOS app are audio resource files and audio files in the user's iPod library. The app you'll develop in this chapter plays both—at the same time! It's a dubbing app that lets you play a track from your iPod's music library and then spontaneously add your own percussive instrument sounds. So if you've ever felt that Delibes' Flower Duet (Lakmé, Act 1) would sound so much better with a tambourine, this is the app you've been waiting for.

Design

Your app design is a simple, one-screen affair that I've named DrumDub. At the bottom are controls for choosing a track from your music library and for pausing and resuming playback. At the top you'll find information about the track that's playing. In the middle are buttons to add percussive sounds, all shown in Figure 9-1.

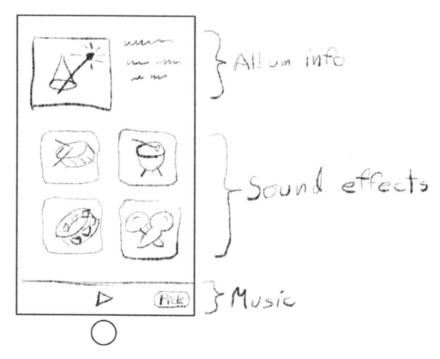

Figure 9-1. DrumDub rough sketch

You'll start by building the iPod music playback. Later you'll add the album artwork, and finally you'll mix in the percussion sounds. As always, start by creating a new Xcode project.

1. Use the Single View Application template.

2. Name the project DrumDub.

3. Set the language to Swift.

4. Set the device to Universal.

5. Save the project.

6. In the project's supported interface orientations, find the iPhone/iPod section and turn off landscape left and right, leaving only portrait enabled. (The iPad version can run in any orientation.)

Adding a Music Picker

The first step is to create an interface so the user can choose a song, or songs, from their iPod music library. After Chapter 7 (where you used the photo library picker), you shouldn't be surprised to learn that iOS provides a ready-made music picker interface. All you have to do is configure it and present it to the user.

You'll present the music picker interface when the user taps the Song button in the interface. For that you'll need an action. Start by adding this stub function to your `ViewController.swift` file:

```
@IBAction func selectTrack(sender: AnyObject!) {
}
```

Switch to the `Main.storyboard` Interface Builder file. In the object library, find the Toolbar object. Drag a toolbar into your interface, positioning it at the bottom of the view. The toolbar already includes a bar button item. Select it and change its Title property to Song. Connect its sent action (Control+right-drag) to the view controller's `selectTrack:` action, as shown in Figure 9-2.

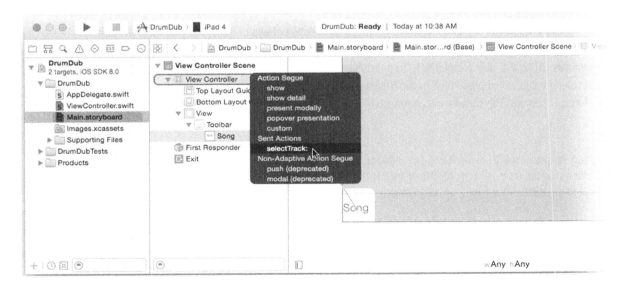

Figure 9-2. Connecting Song action

Switch back to the ViewController.swift file and finish your selectTrack(_:) function (new code in bold).

```
@IBAction func selectTrack(sender: AnyObject!) {
    let picker = MPMediaPickerController(mediaTypes: .AnyAudio)
    picker.delegate = self
    picker.allowsPickingMultipleItems = false
    picker.prompt = "Choose a song"
    presentViewController(picker, animated: true, completion: nil)
}
```

This code creates a new MPMediaPickerController object that will let the user choose any audio type. The media picker is rather flexible and can be set up to present various types of audio and/or video content on the device. The categories for audio content are as follows:

- Music (MPMediaType.Music)

- Podcasts (MPMusicType.Podcast)

- Audiobooks (MPMediaType.AudioBook)

- iTunes U (MPMediaType.AudioITunesU)

By combining these binary values, you can configure your media picker to present any combination of those categories you desire. The constant MPMediaType.AnyAudio includes all categories, allowing the user to choose any audio item in their library. A similar set of flags allows video content to be selected.

> **Tip**   Some parameters, like the mediaTypes parameter in MPMediaPickerController(mediaTypes:), are interpreted not as a single integer value but as a collection of bits or flags. The raw value of each individual MPMediaType constant is a power of 2—a single 1 bit in the integer. You can combine them by logically ORing the values together to form arbitrary combinations, such as (.Music | .AudioBook). The resulting value would present all music tracks and audiobooks but would not let the user pick podcasts or iTunes U content. The convenient .AnyAudio constant is just all-possible audio flags ORed together.

You then make your ViewController object the picker's delegate. For that to work, your view controller needs to conform to the MPMediaPickerControllerDelegate protocol. Add that to your class declaration now (new code in bold).

```
class ViewController: UIViewController, MPMediaPickerControllerDelegate {
```

Next, the option to allow picking multiple tracks at once is disabled. The user will be able to choose only one song at a time. And set a prompt, or title, so the user knows what you're asking them to do.

Finally, the controller is presented, allowing it to take over the interface and choose a song. This is enough code to see it working, so give it a try. Set the project's scheme to your iOS device and click the Run button, as shown on the left in Figure 9-3. The toolbar appears, and you can tap the Song button to bring up the music picker, browse your audio library, and choose a song, as shown on the right in Figure 9-3. If you run the app in the simulator, the picker will work, but there won't be anything to pick (as shown on the middle of Figure 9-3).

Figure 9-3. *Testing the audio picker*

QUERYING THE IPOD MUSIC LIBRARY

You don't have to use the media picker to choose items from the user's iPod library. It's just the most convenient method.

It's possible to create your own interface or not have an interface at all. The iPod framework provides classes that allow your app to explore and search the user's media collection as if it was a database. (Come to think of it, it is a database, so that description is literally true.)

You do this by creating a query object that defines what you're searching for. This can be as simple as "all R&B songs" or more nuanced, such as "all tracks longer than 2 minutes, belonging to the 'dance' genre, with a BPM tag between 110 and 120." The result is a list of media items matching that description, which you can present any way you like (*cough*—table—*cough*).

You can read more about this in the *iPod Library Access Programming Guide* that you will find in Xcode's Documentation and API Reference. Read the section "Getting Media Items Programmatically" to get started.

Using a Music Player

What happens next is, well, nothing happens next. When the user picks a track or taps the Cancel button, one of these delegate functions is called:

```
mediaPicker(_:,didPickMediaItems:)
mediaPickerDidCancel(_:)
```

Nothing happened because you haven't written either. Start by writing mediaPicker(_:,didPickMediaItems:). This method will retrieve the audio track the user picked and start it playing using an MPMusicPlayerController object.

Add the first delegate method to your ViewController class.

```
func mediaPicker(mediaPicker: MPMediaPickerController!, ↵
            didPickMediaItems mediaItemCollection: MPMediaItemCollection!) {
    if let songChoices = mediaItemCollection {
        if songChoices.count != 0 {
            musicPlayer.setQueueWithItemCollection(songChoices)
            musicPlayer.play()
        }
    }
    dismissViewControllerAnimated(true, completion: nil)
}
```

The mediaItemCollection parameter contains the list of tracks, books, or videos the user picked. Remember that the picker can be used to choose multiple items at once. Since you set the allowsPickingMultipleItems property to false, your picker will always return a single item.

We double-check to see that at least one track was chosen (just to be sure) and then use the collection to set the music player's playback queue. The *playback queue* is a list of tracks to play and works just like a playlist. In this case, it's a playlist of one. The next statement starts the music playing. It's that simple.

> **Note** While the music player's playback queue works just like a playlist, it isn't an iPod playlist. It won't appear in the iPod interface as a playlist, and iOS won't save it for you. If you want this functionality in your app, you can do it yourself. Using what you learned in Chapter 5, present the items in the media collection as a table, allowing the user to reorder, delete, or add new items (using the media picker again) as they like. Call the music player's setQueueWithItemCollection(_:) function again with the updated collection.

So, what's the problem with this code? The problem is there is no `musicPlayer` property yet! Write a read-only computed property for `musicPlayer` that lazily creates the object.

```
var musicPlayer: MPMusicPlayerController {
   if musicPlayer_Lazy == nil {
      musicPlayer_Lazy = MPMusicPlayerController()
      musicPlayer_Lazy!.shuffleMode = .Off
      musicPlayer_Lazy!.repeatMode = .None
      }
   return musicPlayer_Lazy!
}
private var musicPlayer_Lazy: MPMusicPlayerController?
```

> **Note** This code follows two well-used design patterns: singleton and lazy initialization. The code implements a computed `musicPlayer` property; any code that requests that property (`myController.musicPlayer`) invokes this code. The code checks to see whether an `MPMusicPlayerController` object—stored in `musicPlayer_Lazy`—has already been created. If not, it creates one, configures it, and saves it in the `musicPlayer_Lazy` instance variable. This happens only once. All subsequent requests to get `musicPlayer` see that the `musicPlayer_Lazy` variable is already set and immediately return the (single) object.

When you construct an application music player (see the "Application and iPod Music Players" sidebar), the player inherits the current iPod playback settings for things such as shuffle and repeat modes. You don't want any of that, so you turn them off.

APPLICATION AND IPOD MUSIC PLAYERS

Your app has access to two different music player objects. The *application music player* belongs to your app. Its current playlist and settings exist only in your app, and it stops playing when your app stops.

You can also request the *system music player* object, using `MPMusicPlayerController.systemMusicPlayer()`. The system music player object is a direct connection to the iPod player in the device. It reflects the current state of music playing in the iPod app. Any changes you make (such as pausing playback or altering shuffle mode) change the iPod app. Music playback continues after your app stops.

There's only one quirk. The system music player object won't report information about media that's being streamed, say via home sharing. But other than that, the system music player object is a transparent extension of the built-in iPod app and allows your app to participate in, and integrate with, the user's current music activity.

Only one music player can be playing at a time. If your app starts an application music player, it takes over the music playback service, causing the built-in iPod player to stop. Likewise, if your application music player is playing and the user starts the system player, your music player is stopped.

Now toss in a delegate function to handle the case where the user declines to choose a track.

```
func mediaPickerDidCancel(mediaPicker: MPMediaPickerController!) {
    dismissViewControllerAnimated(true, completion: nil)
}
```

Your basic playback code is now complete. Run your app, choose a track, and enjoy the music.

The `MPMusicPlayerController` object is self-contained. It takes care of all the standard iPod behavior for you. It will, for example, automatically fade out if interrupted by an alarm or incoming call or stop playback when the user unplugs their headphones. I'll talk a lot more about these events later in this chapter.

That's not to say you can't influence the music player. In fact, you have a remarkable amount of control over it. You can start and stop the player, adjust the volume, skip forward or backward in the playlist, set shuffle and repeat modes, change the playback rate, and more. The player will also tell you a lot about what it's doing and playing. Using these properties and methods, you could create your own, full-featured music player.

For this app, you don't need a full-featured music player. But it would be nice to at least know what's playing and be able to pause it. Get ready to add that next.

Adding Playback Control

Start by adding some buttons to pause and play the current song. These buttons will need actions, so add these two methods to your `ViewController.swift` file:

```
@IBAction func play(sender: AnyObject!) {
    musicPlayer.play()
}

@IBAction func pause(sender: AnyObject!) {
    musicPlayer.pause()
}
```

You'll also need to update the state of the play and pause buttons, so add some connections for that.

```
@IBOutlet var playButton: UIBarButtonItem!
@IBOutlet var pauseButton: UIBarButtonItem!
```

Switch to your `Main.storyboard` file and add the following objects to the toolbar, inserting them to the left of the Song button, in order, as shown in Figure 9-4:

1. A Flexible Space Bar Button Item

2. A Bar Button Item, changing its style to Plain, changing its identifier to Play, and unchecking Enabled

3. A Bar Button Item, changing its style to Plain, changing its identifier to Pause, and unchecking Enabled

4. A Flexible Space Bar Button Item

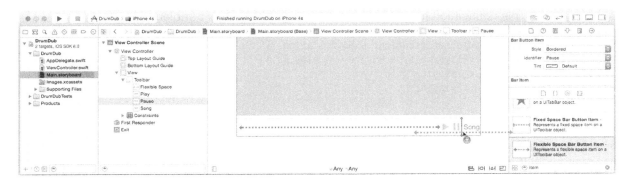

Figure 9-4. *Adding controls to the toolbar*

Finally, set all of the connections. Control+right-click the play button and connect its action to the play: action (in the View Controller) and connect the pause button to the pause: action. Select the View Controller object and use the connections inspector to connect the playButton outlet to the play button and to connect the pauseButton outlet to the pause button.

With the interface objects created and connected, consider for a moment how these buttons should work. You want the following:

- The play button to be active (tappable) when the music player is not currently playing
- The play button's action to start the music playing
- The pause button to be active when the music player is playing
- The pause button's action to pause the music player

The button's actions will start and stop the music player. You'll need to update the enabled state of the buttons whenever the player starts or stops playing. The first part you've already done, in the play(_:) and pause(_:) functions. The second half is updating the button states (enabling or disabling them) at the appropriate times, and for that you'll need to get some information from the music player.

Receiving Music Player Notifications

The music player runs in a background thread. Normally, it plays tracks in its playlist until it runs out and stops. It can also pause in response to external events: the user presses the pause button on their headphone cable, or they unplug the iPod from a dock. How do you think your app will learn about these events?

If you said, "From delegate functions or notifications," give yourself a big round of applause! Reading the documentation for the MPMusicPlayerController class, you discover that the music player will *optionally* send notifications whenever important changes occur, which happen to include when it starts or stops playing. To be notified of those events, you'll need to register your controller object to receive them. As you remember from Chapter 5, to receive notifications you must do the following:

1. Create a notification function.
2. Register with the notification center to become an observer for the notification.

Start by adding this notification function to your `ViewController.swift` implementation:

```swift
func playbackStateDidChange(notification: NSNotification) {
    let playing = ( musicPlayer.playbackState == .Playing )
    playButton!.enabled = !playing
    pauseButton!.enabled = playing
}
```

Your notification handler examines the current `playbackState` of your music player. The player's playback state will be one of stopped, playing, paused, interrupted, seeking forward, or seeking backward. In this implementation, the only likely states are playing, stopped, interrupted, and paused.

If the player is playing, the pause button is enabled, and the play button is disabled. If it's not playing, the opposite occurs. This presents the play button as an option whenever the player is not playing and presents the pause button when it is.

Your controller won't receive these notifications until two additional steps are taken. First, you must register to receive these notifications. In the `musicPlayer` getter block, add this immediately after the player object is created and configured (new code in bold):

```swift
musicPlayer_Lazy = MPMusicPlayerController()
musicPlayer_Lazy!.shuffleMode = .Off
musicPlayer_Lazy!.repeatMode = .None
let center = NSNotificationCenter.defaultCenter()
center.addObserver( self,
        selector: "playbackStateDidChange:",
            name: MPMusicPlayerControllerPlaybackStateDidChangeNotification,
          object: musicPlayer_Lazy)
```

The second step is to enable the music player's notifications. `MPMusicPlayerController` does not, by default, send these notifications. You must explicitly request that it does. Immediately after the previous code, add one more line.

```swift
musicPlayer_Lazy!.beginGeneratingPlaybackNotifications()
```

Your playback controls are now finished. Run your app and see that they work, as shown in Figure 9-5.

Figure 9-5. *Working playback controls*

Both buttons start out disabled. When you choose a track to play, the pause button becomes active (the middle of Figure 9-5). If you pause the song or let it finish playing, the play button becomes active (on the right in Figure 9-5).

MVC AT WORK

You're watching the model-view-controller design pattern at work—again. In this scenario, your music player (despite the fact it's called a "music controller") is your data model. It contains the state of the music playback. Whenever that state changes, your controller receives a notification and updates the relevant views—in this case, the play and pause buttons.

You didn't write any code to update the play or pause button when you start or stop the player. Those requests are just sent to the music player. If one of those requests results in a state change, the music player posts the appropriate notifications, and the affected views are updated.

While functional, your app lacks a certain *je ne sais quoi*. Oh, who are we kidding? This interface is as dull as dishwater! Let's spruce it up a bit.

Adding Media Metadata

A colorful aspect of the music player object is its `nowPlayingItem` property. This property returns an object containing metadata about the song that's playing. The object works like a dictionary, revealing all kinds of interesting tidbits about the current song. This includes information such as its title, the artist, the track number, the musical genre, any album artwork, and much more.

> **Note** *Metadata* is "data about data." A file, like a document, contains data. The name of that file, when it was created, and so on, is its metadata—it's data that describes the data in the file. A waveform stored in a song file is data. The name of the song, the artist, and its genre are all metadata.

For your app, you'll add an image view to display the album's cover and text fields to show the song's title, the album it came from, and the artist. Start by adding new interface objects to `Main.storyboard`.

Creating a Metadata View

You're going to add an image view and a few label views to the interface. The image view will display the song's album artwork, while the label views will show the song, artist, and album currently playing (see Figure 9-1). But this isn't a one-size-fits-all layout. The image and label views that would fit on an iPhone would look odd and puny on an iPad. And the layout that would look good on an iPad would look strange on an iPhone. So, what do you do?

The answer is in adaptive constraints, which are new in iOS 8. As you remember from Chapter 2, the view controller is associated with a size class. A *size class* is a broad indication of the space available for your interface. There are only two size classes: Regular (there's plenty of room for your interface to spread out) and Compact (your interface needs to be tight). These aren't indications of actual device sizes—although you can get that information if your app needs it. They're intended to make it easy to create alternate layouts that work in a variety of device sizes and orientations, without getting tangled up in the specifics.

Your interface has two size classes, one for horizontal and one for vertical. For example, if you're using an iPhone 5 in portrait orientation, your view's size class will be Compact/Regular. This means the horizontal size class is Compact, and the vertical size class is Regular.

The constraint sets you're about to create are the most complex ones in this book. But you'll also see that, with a little planning, it's not difficult to create sophisticated sets of layout constraints that intelligently adapt to different devices and orientations, without writing a single line of code.

Adding the Image View

Select the `Main.storyboard` file. Using the object library, find the `Image View` object and add one to the interface. Position it (roughly) in the upper-left corner of the view, as shown in Figure 9-6.

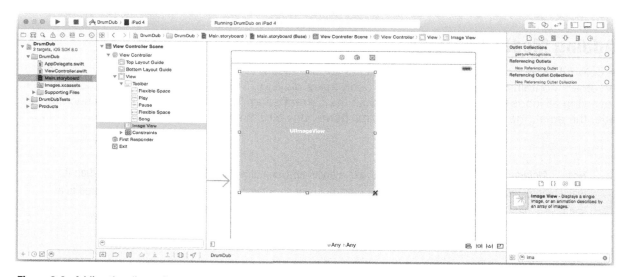

Figure 9-6. Adding the album view

The size and position of the image view will be determined by its constraints. There's only one rule for constraints; you must add enough constraints so that iOS can unambiguously determine the view's position (horizontal and vertical) and its size (height and width). And you can't add constraints that conflict. OK, that's two rules.

Coming up with constraints for a particular layout or device size is pretty easy. What's fun is coming up with sets of constraints so your interface will lay out nicely on all devices, in all supported orientations. For DrumDub, you need only two layouts:

- For the iPhone/iPod:
    - Artwork is smaller and nestled in the upper-left corner.
    - The song info labels fill the space to the right.

- For the iPad:
    - Artwork view is larger.
    - The artwork image and song info labels split the screen, so the image is to the left of center, and the labels are to the right.

This required two set of constraints, one for a Compact/Regular (iPhone) interface and one for a Regular/Regular (iPad) interface. Furthermore, there are some constraints that are common to both interfaces. All of the needed constraints are shown in Table 9-1.

Table 9-1. *Artwork Image View Constraint Sets*

Any/Any	Compact/Any	Regular/Any
Top of image is just below top layout guide	Left edge is against left edge of super view	Right edge is against the horizontal center of superview
	Size is 160x160	Size is 300x300

Constraints you add in Interface Builder form a hierarchy. The constraints you add to the Any/Any category will always be applied to your interface. Constraints that you add to the Compact/Any category will be applied to your interface only when it appears in a Compact/Regular or Compact/Compact environment. Likewise, constraints you add to the Regular/Any category will be applied only when your interface appears in a Regular/Regular environment. You can also get very specific, adding constraints that are active only when the interface is Compact/Regular or Compact/Compact. Let's get started.

Adding the Universal Constraints

You need one constraint—the top edge position—to be applied in all cases. Still in the Main.storyboard file, make sure the size class category at the bottom of the Interface Builder canvas is set to wAny/hAny (any width, any height). Select the UIImageView object and click the Pin Constraints control, as shown in Figure 9-7. Select the top constraint and set its value to Use Standard Value. Add the constraint.

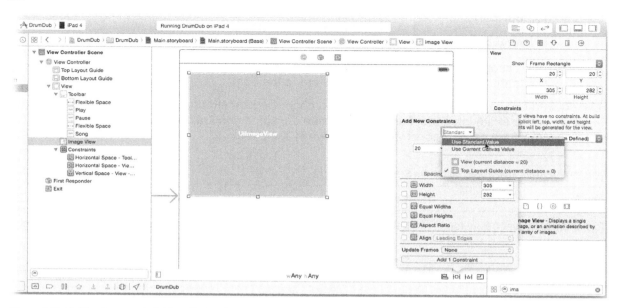

Figure 9-7. Setting top constraint for all size classes

Adding Compact/Any Constraints

The next step is to add the constraints that apply only when the horizontal size is compact. Click the size class control at the bottom of the canvas and drag until the matrix says Compact Width | Any Height, as shown on the left in Figure 9-8. Notice that the view controller canvas gets a little narrower, suggesting a more compact device.

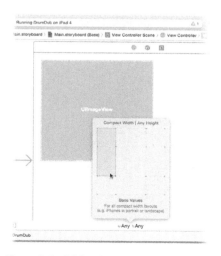
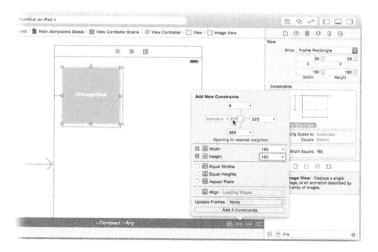

Figure 9-8. Adding Compact/Any constraints

Any constraints you add now will be applied only when the interface's horizontal size class is compact. Select the image view object, click the pin constraints control, add a leading edge constraint set to Use Standard Value, and add both Height and Width constraints set to 160 pixels, as shown on the right in Figure 9-8.

When the horizontal size class is compact (iPhone or iPod in any orientation), the image view will be positioned in the upper-left corner and be 160 pixels high and wide. Now let's move on to the iPad layout.

Adding Regular/Any Constraints

Repeat the steps you took for the iPhone interface. Change the size class control to wRegular/hAny, as shown on the left in Figure 9-9. Select the image view, click the pin constraints control, and add Height and Width constraints both set to 300 pixels (as shown in the middle in Figure 9-9). Click the align constraint control and add a Horizontal Center in Container constraint with a value of 150 (as shown on the right in Figure 9-9).

Figure 9-9. Adding Regular/Any constraints

When the horizontal size class is regular (iPad), the image view will be positioned to the left of center and be 300 x 300 pixels. If the value of the Horizontal Center in Container constraint was 0, the center of the view would be centered in the superview. Adding an offset of half the width positions the right edge of the view at the center of the superview instead. With the image view constraints for all possible size classes finished, turn your attention to the label views.

Adding the Song Labels

You're going to add three labels. You want those labels to align with the album art view and fill the right side of the interface, for all sizes and orientations.

Before adding the label objects, switch back to the wAny/hAny size class, as shown on the left in Figure 9-10. Drag in a label object, align it with the top edge of the image view, and stretch it so it fills the space to the right, as shown on the right in Figure 9-10. Set its font size to System 14.0.

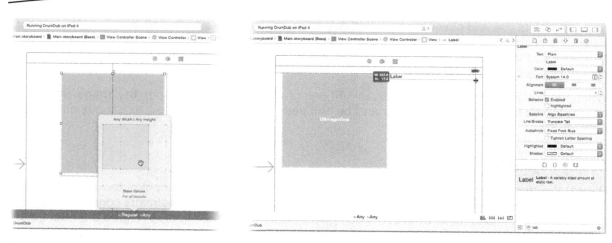

Figure 9-10. Adding the first song label object

> **Caution**   Make sure the size class is set to wAny/hAny before adding new objects to your interface, or you'll be adding those views to the layout only for that size class. Interface Builder allows you to add objects that will appear only in specific size classes, but that's not what you want here.

Make two duplicates of the first label—hold down the Option key and drag a copy to a new location—so you have three, as shown on the left in Figure 9-11. Select the top label and the image view, click the align constraints control, and add a Top Edges constraint, as shown on the right in Figure 9-11. This will vertically position the label view so its top edge is the same as the image view's top edge.

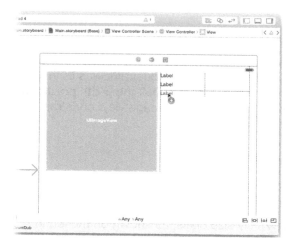
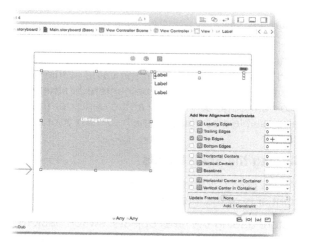

Figure 9-11. Duplicating label and top alignment

Select all three labels. Click the Pin Constraints control and add a leading edge, trailing edge, and height constraints for all three label objects, as shown on the left in Figure 9-12. Notice that the button says that you're about to add nine constraints—three constraints for three label objects.

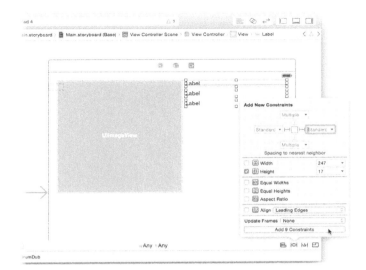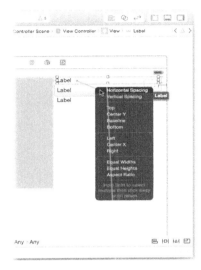

Figure 9-12. *Setting label constraints*

Now add vertical spacing constraints between the top label and the next two. You could do this using the constraint controls, as you have been doing, but here's another way. If you want to establish a constraint between two specific views, Control+click one view (the top label) and drag it to the other (the middle label), as shown on the right in Figure 9-12. When you release the mouse button, a pop-up menu will appear. Choose the constraint you want to establish. In this case, choose Vertical Spacing. Repeat, creating another vertical spacing constraint between the second and third labels.

> **Tip**   The Control+drag method of adding constraints is quick and specific, but you can't modify the value of the constraint at the same time. If you need to change its value after the fact, select the constraint and edit its value using the attributes inspector.

Your constraints are now complete. The constraints you added for the label objects are the same for all size classes. The beautiful thing is that those constraints are relative to the position of the image view, and that will change because it has a different set of constraints for compact and regular-width devices.

Previewing Your Layouts

It can sometimes be difficult to predict how constraints will affect your layout, and the effects of conditional constraints in different size classes can make your head start to spin. Fortunately, Xcode is here to help.

Switch to the assistant view. The right pane should display the ViewController.swift file. At the top of the editing pane on the right, choose Preview from the navigation menu, as shown at the top in Figure 9-13. The right pane will now show you how your layouts, as interpreted by Interface Builder, should appear on specific devices.

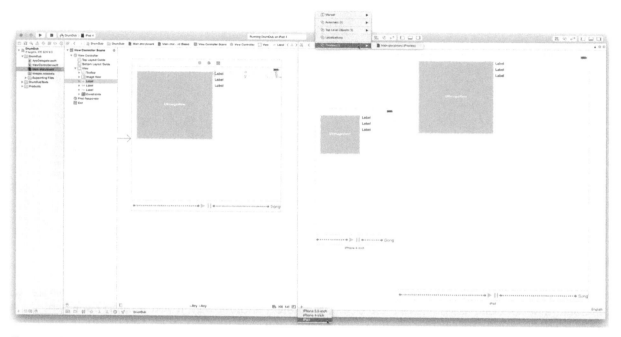

Figure 9-13. *Previewing layouts for different devices*

> **Note**   These are live previews. If your layouts are not looking the way they should, continue to edit your views and constraints in the left pane, and the effects will be immediately appear on the right.

Click the + button in the lower-left corner of the pane to add new devices to the preview. In Figure 9-13, I'm previewing this layout on both a 4-inch iPhone and an iPad simultaneously. You can rotate a preview to check landscape orientation or even add both portrait and landscape previews simultaneously—assuming you have a really big monitor. Click a preview and press the Delete key to remove it.

Finishing the Album Interface

For the final touch, select the three label views and use the attributes inspector to change their font color to White. Select the root view object and change its background color to Black.

While still in the assistant editor, use the navigation ribbon to switch back to the Automatic view. The ViewController.swift will reappear in the right-hand pane. Add these four outlets:

```
@IBOutlet var albumView: UIImageView!
@IBOutlet var songLabel: UILabel!
@IBOutlet var albumLabel: UILabel!
@IBOutlet var artistLabel: UILabel!
```

Now connect them to the image and label views, as shown in Figure 9-14.

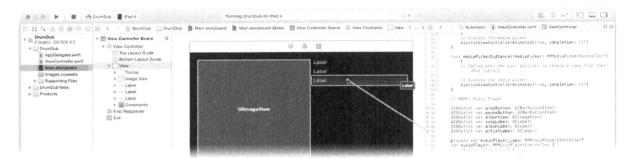

Figure 9-14. Connecting the album views

You've done a lot of cool work in this section. You've created a layout that uses adaptive constraints to adjust itself, automatically, for different devices sizes and orientations. Switch back to the standard editor (View ➤ Standard Editor ➤ Show Standard Editor) and select the ViewController.swift file. It's time to write the code to update these new interface objects.

Observing the Playing Item

The music player object also sends notifications when the item being played changes. This occurs when a new song starts playing or one finishes playing. The notification is different than the one your controller is currently observing, so you'll need to create another notification handler and register to observe it.

Near the playbackStateDidChange(_:) function, add your new notification handler function.

```
func playingItemDidChange(notification: NSNotification) {
    let nowPlaying = musicPlayer.nowPlayingItem

    var albumImage: UIImage!
    if let artwork = nowPlaying?.valueForProperty(MPMediaItemPropertyArtwork) ↵
                                           as? MPMediaItemArtwork {
        albumImage = artwork.imageWithSize(albumView.bounds.size)
    }
    if albumImage == nil {
        albumImage = UIImage(named: "noartwork")
    }
    albumView.image = albumImage

    songLabel.text = ↵
      nowPlaying?.valueForProperty(MPMediaItemPropertyTitle) as? NSString
```

```
albumLabel.text = ↵
    nowPlaying?.valueForProperty(MPMediaItemPropertyAlbumTitle) as? NSString
artistLabel.text = ↵
    nowPlaying?.valueForProperty(MPMediaItemPropertyArtist) as? NSString
}
```

The method gets the nowPlayingItem property object. Rather than have a bunch of fixed properties (like typical objects), the MPMediaItem object contains a variable number of property values that you request via a key. A key is a fixed value—typically a string—that identifies the value you're interested in.

The first thing you ask for is the MPMediaItemPropertyArtwork value. This value will be a MPMediaItemArtwork object that encapsulates the album artwork for the song. You then request a UIImage object, optimized for the size of your image view.

> **Tip** MPMediaItemArtwork objects may store multiple versions of the item's artwork, at different sizes and resolutions. When requesting a UIImage of the artwork, specify a size as close as possible to the size you plan on displaying the image, so the media item object can return the best possible image for that size.

The thing to remember about media metadata is that there are no guarantees. Any song in the iPod library might have values for title, artist, and artwork. Or, it might not have any of those values. Or, it might have a title and artist but no artwork, or artwork and no title. The bottom line is, be prepared for the case where something you ask for isn't available.

In this app, you test to see whether MPMediaItemArtwork declined to return a displayable image (albumImage==nil). In that case, replace the image with a resource image named "noartwork."

For that statement to work, you'll need to add the noartwork.png and noartwork@2x.png files to your project. Select the Images.xcassets item in the navigator. Find the Learn iOS Development Projects ➤ Ch 9 ➤ DrumDub (Resources) folder and drag the noartwork.png and noartwork@2x.png files into the asset catalog.

The last three statements repeat this process, obtaining the title, album title, and artist name for the item. In this code you don't have to worry about missing values. If an item doesn't have an album name (when requesting MPMediaItemPropertyAlbumTitle), the media item will return nothing. It just so happens that setting a UILabel's text property to nothing blanks the view—exactly what you want to happen if there's no album name.

The last step is observing the item changed notifications. Find the musicPlayer property getter code. Find the code that observes the playback state changes and insert this new statement:

```
center.addObserver( self,
        selector: "playingItemDidChange:",
            name: MPMusicPlayerControllerNowPlayingItemDidChangeNotification,
          object: musicPlayer_Lazy)
```

Now whenever a new song starts playing, your controller will receive a "playing item did change" notification and display that information to the user. Give it a try.

Run your app, select a song, and start it playing. The song information and artwork display, as shown in Figure 9-15. If you let the song play to its end, the information disappears again.

Figure 9-15. *Album artwork and song metadata*

The only thing I don't like about this interface is that the artwork view and the three label views are filled with the placeholder information when the app launches. Fix that in the `Main.storyboard` file by clearing the text property of the three label objects and setting the image view's initial image to `noartwork.png`.

Make Some Noise

So far, you've essentially created a (minimal) iPod app. That's an impressive feat, but it isn't the only way to add sound to your app. You may want to add sound effects to actions or play music files that you've bundled. Maybe you want to play live audio streams from a network data source. Those are all easy to do, even easier than playing songs from the iPod library—which was pretty easy.

I'll get the easy part out of the way first. To play and control almost any kind of audio data your app has access to, follow these steps:

1. Create an `AVAudioPlayer` object.

2. Initialize the player with the source of the audio data, typically a URL to a resource file.

3. Call its `play()` function.

And just like the `MPMusicPlayerController`, the `AVAudioPlayer` object takes care of all of the details, including notifying your delegate when it's done.

So, you might be thinking that it won't take more than a dozen lines of code and some buttons to finish this app, but you would be mistaken.

Living in a Larger World

What makes playing audio in this app complicated is not the code to play your sounds. The complication lies in the nature of iOS devices and the environment they exist in.

Consider an iPhone. It's a telephone and a videophone; audio is used to indicate incoming calls and play the audio stream from the caller. It's a music player; you can play your favorite music or audiobook, or stream Internet radio, even while using other apps. It's an alarm clock; timers can remind you of things to do any time of the day or night. It's a game console; games are full of sounds, sound effects, and ambient music. It's a pager; messages, notifications, and alerts can occur for countless reasons, interrupting your work (or play) at a moment's notice. It's also a video player, TV, answering machine, GPS navigator, movie editor, Dictaphone, and digital assistant.

All of these audio sources share a *single* output. To do that effectively—creating a pleasant experience for the user—all of these competing audio sources have to cooperate. Game sounds and music playback have to stop when a telephone call arrives. Background music needs to temporarily lower its volume[1] if the user is expected to hear a reminder or recorded message. iOS refers to these as *interruptions*.

Adding to this complexity, iOS devices have many different ways of producing sound. Consider the built-in speakers, the headphone jack, wireless Bluetooth devices, AirPlay, and the dock connecter; iOS calls these *audio routes*. Audio can be directed to any one of these and switched to a different one at any time (called a *route change*). Audio playback must be aware of this, and your app may need to react to those changes. For example, Apple recommends that unplugging the headphones should cause music playback to pause, but game sound effects should continue playing.

And just to add one more dash of complication, most iOS devices have a ring/silence switch. Audio that's intended as an alert, alarm, embellishment, or sound effect should play only when the ring switch is in its normal position. More deliberate audio, such as movies and audiobooks, should play normally, even when the silence switch is engaged.

Taken together, your app needs to do the following:

- Decide the intent and purpose of each source of audio in your app
- Declare this purpose so iOS can adjust its behavior to accommodate your audio
- Observe interruptions and audio route changes and take appropriate action

The good news is that not every audio-endowed app you write has to do all of these things. In fact, if you *only* use the iPod music player or *only* play incidental sounds using AVAudioPlayer objects, you probably don't have to do anything at all. Both of these classes will "do the right thing."

For an app like DrumDub, however, that wants to manage its own music playback while mixing in additional sound effects, all of these steps need to be taken. So, before you start adding sound effects to your app, lay some of the groundwork.

Configuring Your Audio Session

You communicate your intent—describe the kinds of sounds your app will make and how those will affect other audio sources—to iOS through an *audio session*. Every iOS app gets a generic audio session, preconfigured with a basic set of behaviors. That's why if you play music only through a music player controller, you don't have to do anything special; the default audio session is just fine.

DrumDub needs to both playback and mix audio. This is unusual, so it will need to reconfigure its audio session. Apps that only play audio can typically configure their audio session once and leave it.

---

[1]Temporarily lowering the volume of one audio source so you can hear a second audio source is called *ducking*.

> **Note** Apps that record audio, or record and playback audio, are more complicated. They must repeatedly reconfigure their audio session as they switch between recording, playback, and processing.

In your `AppDelegate.swift` file, you'll find the code for your app's delegate object. One of the functions in your app's delegate is the `application(_:,didFinishLaunchingWithOptions:)` function. As the name implies, it's called immediately after your app has loaded and initialized and is about to start running. It's the perfect place to put code that needs to run just once and run before anything else gets underway. Add the following code (in bold) to the beginning of that function:

```swift
func application(application: UIApplication!, didFinishLaunchingWithOptions
                                launchOptions: NSDictionary!) -> Bool {
    let audioSession = AVAudioSession.sharedInstance()
    audioSession.setCategory( AVAudioSessionCategoryPlayback,
                withOptions: .MixWithOthers,
                    error: nil)
    return true
}
```

An audio session has a category and a set of options. There are seven different categories to choose from, as listed in Table 9-2.

Table 9-2. Audio Session Categories

Session Categories	App Description
AVAudioSessionCategoryAmbient	Plays background audio or nonessential sound effects. The app will work just fine without them. App audio mixes with other audio (like your iPod) playing at the same time. The ring/silence switch silences the app's audio.
AVAudioSessionCategorySoloAmbient	Plays nonessential audio that does not mix with other audio; other audio sources are silenced when the app plays its audio. The ring/silence switch silences the app's audio. This is the default category.
AVAudioSessionCategoryPlayback	Plays music or other essential sounds. In other words, audio is the principle purpose of the app, and it wouldn't work without it. The ring/silence switch does not silence its audio.
AVAudioSessionCategoryRecord	Records audio.
AVAudioSessionCategoryPlayAndRecord	Plays and records audio.
AVAudioSessionCategoryAudioProcessing	Performs audio processing (using the hardware audio codecs), while neither playing nor recording.
AVAudioSessionCategoryMultiRoute	Needs to output audio to multiple routes simultaneously. A slideshow app might play music through a dock connector while simultaneously sending audio prompts through the headphones.

The default category is AVAudioSessionCategorySoloAmbient. For DrumDub, you've decided that audio is its *raison d'être*—its reason to exist—so you call the setCategory(_:,withOptions:,error:) function to change its category to AVAudioSessionCategoryPlayback. Now your app's audio won't be silenced by the ring/silence switch.

You can also fine-tune the category with a number of category-specific options. The only option for this playback category is AVAudioSessionCategoryOptionMixWithOthers. If set, this option allows audio played with your AVAudioPlayer objects to "mix" with other audio playing at the same time. This is exactly what you want for DrumDub. Without this option, playing a sound would stop playback of the song.

The code you just added is being flagged with errors. That's because all of these symbols are defined in the AVFoundation framework, so you'll need to import those definitions to use them. Add this statement before all the other import statements in AppDelegate.swift:

```
import AVFoundation
```

See, that wasn't too hard. In fact, there was a lot more explanation than code. With your audio session correctly configured, you can now add (mix in) sound effects with your music.

Playing Audio Files

You're finally at the heart of your app's design: playing sounds. You're going to have four buttons, each playing a different sound. To implement this, you will need the following:

- Four button objects
- Four images
- Four AVAudioPlayer objects
- Four sampled sound files
- An action function to play a sound

It will be easier to build the interface once you have added the resources and defined the action function, so start there. Find your Learn iOS Development Projects ➤ Ch 9 ➤ DrumDub (Resources) folder and locate the 12 files in this table:

Sound Sample	Button Image	Retina Display Image
snare.m4v	snare.png	snare@2x.png
bass.m4v	bass.png	bass@2x.png
tambourine.m4v	tambourine.png	tambourine@2x.png
maraca.m4v	maraca.png	maraca@2x.png

Begin by adding the button image files. Select the Images.xcassets asset catalog item. In it, you'll see the noartwork resource you added earlier. Drag the eight instrument image files (two each of snare, bass, tambourine, and maraca) into the asset catalog's group list, as shown in Figure 9-16.

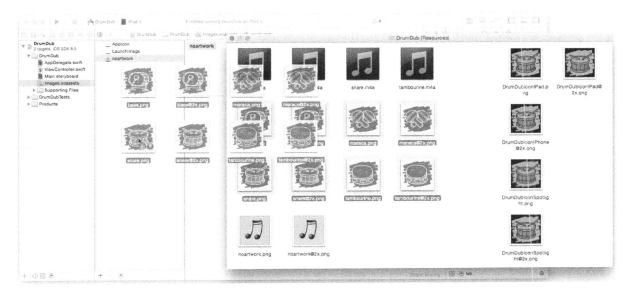

Figure 9-16. Adding image resources

While you're here, select the AppIcon group of the asset catalog and drag the app icon image files into it, as you've done for earlier projects.

The four sound files (bass.m4a, maraca.m4a, snare.m4a, and tambourine.m4a) will also become resource files, but they're not the kind of resources managed by an asset catalog. You can add any kind of file you want directly to a project and have that file included as a resource in your app's bundle.

For the sake of neatness, begin by creating a new group for these resource files. Control+click/right-click the DrumDub group (not the project) in the navigator and choose the New Group command, as shown on the left in Figure 9-17.

Figure 9-17. Adding nonimage resources

Name the group Sounds, as shown in the middle of Figure 9-17. Locate the four sound sample files in the Finder and drag them into the group, as shown on the right of Figure 9-17. If you miss and add the items to the DrumDub group instead, select them in the navigator and drag them into the Sounds group. You can always reorganize your project items as you please.

After dropping your items into the navigator, Xcode presents some options that determine how the items will be added to your project, as shown in Figure 9-18. Make sure the Copy items into destination group's folder (if needed) option is checked. This option copies the new items into your app's project folder. The second option (Create groups for any added folders) applies only when adding folders full of resource files.

Figure 9-18. Add project file options

> **Caution**   If you fail to check the Copy items into destination group's folder (if needed) option, Xcode will add only a *reference* to the original item, which is still outside your project's folder. This works fine, until you rename one of the original files, move your project, or copy it to another system—then your project suddenly stops building. Save yourself some grief and keep all of your project's resources inside your project folder.

Finally, make sure the DrumDub target is checked, as shown in Figure 9-14. This option makes these items *members* of the DrumDub app target, which means they'll be included as resource files in your finished app. (If you forget to check this, you can later change the target membership of any item using the file inspector.) Click Finish, and Xcode will copy the sound sample files into your project folder, add them to the project navigator, and include them in the DrumDub app target. These files are now ready to be used in your app.

Creating AVAudioPlayer Objects

You'll play the sound sample files using AVAudioPlayer objects. You'll need four. Rather than creating four AVAudioPlayer variables and writing four play actions, create one array to hold all of the objects and one function to play any of them. Start with the AVAudioPlayer objects. Add these statements to your ViewController.swift file:

```
let soundNames = [ "snare", "bass", "tambourine", "maraca" ]
var players = [AVAudioPlayer]()
```

The first statement declares a constant array of strings that contains the names of the sound resource files. The `players` variable is an array of AVAudioPlayer objects, initialized to an empty array. The syntax looks a little weird, but it's just creating a new object. The new object is an array containing AVAudioPlayer objects ([AVAudioPlayer]), created using the default object initializer (()).

Do those compiler errors look familiar? Just as you did for the `AppDelelgate` class, add this `import` statement to the beginning of your `ViewController.swift` file:

```
import AVFoundation
```

The functions `createAudioPlayers()` and `destroyAudioPlayers()` will create and destroy all four audio player objects at once. Add them now.

```
func createAudioPlayers() {
    destroyAudioPlayers()
    for soundName in soundNames {
        if let soundURL = NSBundle.mainBundle().URLForResource(soundName, ↵
                                              withExtension: "m4a") {
            let player = AVAudioPlayer(contentsOfURL: soundURL, error: nil)
            player.prepareToPlay()
            players.append(player)
        }
    }
}

func destroyAudioPlayers() {
    players = []
}
```

`createAudioPlayers()` loops through the array of sound name constants (soundNames) and uses that to create a URL that refers to the m4a sound resource file that you added earlier. This URL is used to create and initialize a new AVAudioPlayer object that will play that sound file.

Some optimization is then applied. The `prepareToPlay()` function is called on each sound player. This preps the player object so that it is immediately ready to play its sound. Finally, the new player object is appended to the `players` array. When the loop is finished, you'll have an array of AVAudioPlayer objects, each configured to play the corresponding sound file in the soundNames array.

> **Note**   Normally, player objects prepare themselves lazily, waiting until you request them to play before actually reading the sound sample data file, allocating their buffers, configuring hardware codecs, and so on. All of this takes time. When your user taps a sound button, they don't want to wait for the sound to play; they want it to play immediately. The `prepareToPlay()` function eliminates that initial delay.

The destroyAudioPlayers() function is self-explanatory, and you don't need it yet. It will come into "play" later.

Next up are the buttons to play these sounds and the action function to make that happen. Start by adding a stu.e bang(_:) action.

```
@IBAction func bang(sender: AnyObject!) {
}
```

Now you're ready to design the interface.

Adding the Sound Buttons

Return to your Main.storyboard Interface Builder file. Drag in a new UIButton object. Select it and do the following:

    1. Use the attributes inspector to

        a. Set its type property to Custom

        b. Clear its title text property (deleting *Button*)

        c. Set its image property to snare

        d. Scroll down to its tag property and change it from 0 to 1

    2. Select the button and use the Pin Constraints control to add both a height and a width constraint, both set to 100 pixels.

    3. Use the connections inspector to connect its Touch Down event to the new bang: action of the View Controller object (see Figure 9-19).

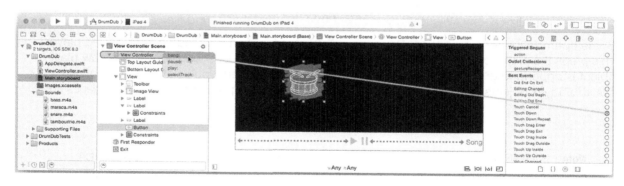

Figure 9-19. Creating the first bang button

There are a couple of noteworthy aspects to this button's configuration. First, you've connected the Touch Down event, instead of the more common Touch Up Inside event. That's because you want to call the bang(_:) action function the *instant* the user touches the button. Normally, buttons don't send their action message until the user touches them and releases again, with their finger still inside the button—thus, the name Touch Up Inside.

Second, you didn't create an outlet to connect to this button. You're going to identify, and access, the object via its `tag` property. All `UIView` objects have an integer `tag` property. It exists solely for your use in identifying views; iOS doesn't use it for anything else. You're going to use the `tag` to determine which sound to play and later to obtain the `UIButton` object in the interface.

Duplicate the new button three times, to create four buttons in all. You can do this either by using the clipboard or by holding down the Option key and dragging out new copies of the button.

All of the buttons have the same type, image, tag, constraints, and action connection. Use the attributes inspector to change the image and tag properties of the three duplicates, using the following table:

Image	Tag
bass	2
tambourine	3
maraca	4

Your interface should now look like the one in Figure 9-20.

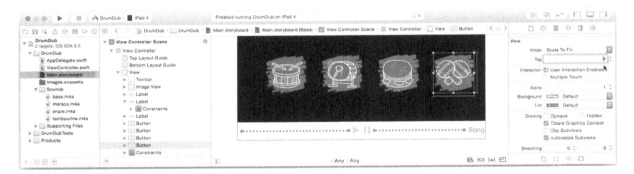

Figure 9-20. *Configured sound buttons*

Now you need to add constraints to position the button in the interface. The buttons are too wide to be in a single row on compact devices, like an iPhone. On the other hand, you wouldn't want them all bunched together in a tiny group on a big iPad. If only there were some way the layout could adapt itself to different devices and orientations….

Of course, I'm joking. You'll use the same technique you used earlier with the album artwork and song labels. This time, you'll create a completely different set of constraints that will fundamentally change how the buttons are laid out on different devices. Let's get started.

Button Layout for Compact Interfaces

You're already added height and width constraints for all four buttons in the wAny/hAny size class. Therefore, the buttons will be 100x100 pixels in all layouts. All you have to add now are the constraints to position them. Switch to the wCompact/hAny size class and add these constraints:

1. Select the button with tag 1 (the snare drum).

    a. Add a Horizontal Center in Container constraint with a value of 60.

    b. Add a Vertical Center in Container constraint with a value of -8 (left image in Figure 9-21).

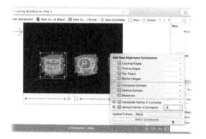 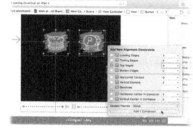 

Figure 9-21. Button constraints for the Compact/Any size class

These constraints are sufficient to position the first button just to the left, and slightly below, the center point of the interface. This will be your "anchor" button. All of the remaining constraints will be relative to that button.

2. Drag the button with tag 2 (the bass drum) so it's to the right of the first button.

3. Select both (or Control+drag between them) and add a Top Edges alignment constraint (middle of Figure 9-21) with a value of 0.

4. Select the right button and add a Leading Edge space constraint with a value of 20, as shown on the right in Figure 9-21. Make sure the leading edge is relative to the other button and not the container view.

You've positioned the second button 20 pixels to the right, and at the same vertical position, as the first button. Keep adding constraints to position the remaining two buttons:

5. Drag the third button below the first.

6. Select the first and third buttons and add a Leading Edge alignment constraint with a value of 0.

7. Add a Vertical Spacing constraint between the first and third buttons, with a value of 20.

8. Drag the last button in to fill out the square.

9. Add a Top (or Bottom, your choice) Edges alignment constraint with the third button with a value of 0.

10. Add a Trailing (or Leading, your choice) Edges alignment constraint with the second button with a value of 0.

> **Tip** Having trouble selecting a button? When the Interface Builder canvas is resized, view objects can "fall off" the edges where you can't see or select them. Don't worry. All of the scene's objects are listed to the left. Double-click the missing button object in the view hierarchy; this will select it in the canvas (even if you can't see it). Use the arrow keys to move the view (hold down the Shift key to move faster) or use the size inspector to change its origin so it's visible in the canvas again.

This final two constraints position the last button relative to the second (horizontally) and the third (vertically), completing the grid. The finished layout is shown in Figure 9-22.

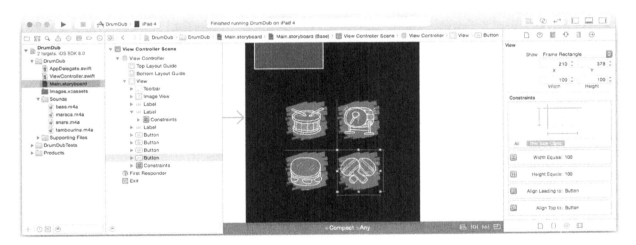

Figure 9-22. Finished compact button layout

Button Layout for Regular Interfaces

Now perform these steps again for regular width environments. For iPads, the buttons don't need to be grouped tightly together. Let's create a different set of constraints that let them breathe a little.

Switch to the wRegular/hAny size class. All of the constraints you just added disappear. This time start with the button with tag 2 (the bass drum). This will be the "anchor" for this layout.

1. Select the second button (the bass drum).

    a. Add a Horizontal Center in Container constraint with a value of 70.

    b. Add a Vertical Center in Container constraint with a value of -160 (see Figure 9-23).

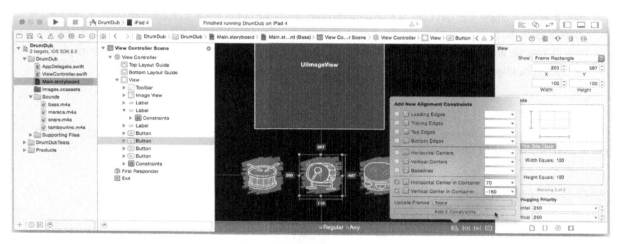

Figure 9-23. Button constraints for Regular/Any size class

Just as you did before, you've positioned this button to the left, and below, the relative center of the display. This time the distances are little more generous because the display is bigger.

2. Drag the other buttons so they make a rough line.

3. Select all of the buttons and add a Top Edges alignment constraint with a value of 0.

This tells iOS to position the other three buttons at the same (vertical) position as the second button. The only thing left is to assign horizontal positions to the remaining three buttons.

4. Add a Horizontal Spacing constraint between the first and second button with a value of 40.

5. Do the same between the second and third button.

6. Repeat, adding a horizontal spacing constraint between the third and final buttons.

Check your work using the assistant editor and the preview, as shown in Figure 9-24. If you did everything right, you should see pleasing button layouts for 4-inch iPhones, 3.5-inch iPhones, and iPads.

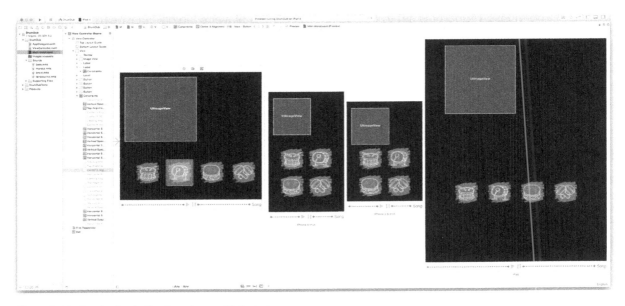

Figure 9-24. *Previewing button layout on multiple devices*

Your app can seamlessly morph between substantially different interface designs, accomplished simply by providing alternate sets of constraints. This was all very educational, but I'm sure you really want to get back to making those sound buttons work.

Making Noise

Return again to the regular editor and the ViewController.swift file. Finish writing your bang(_:) function (new code in bold).

```
@IBAction func bang(sender: AnyObject!) {
    if let button = sender as? UIButton {
        let index = button.tag-1
        if index >=0 && index < players.count {
            let player = players[index]
            player.pause()
            player.currentTime = 0.0
            player.play()
        }
    }
}
```

All four buttons send the same action. You determine which button sent the message using its tag property. Your four buttons have tag values between 1 and 4, which you use as an index (0 through 3) to obtain that button's AVAudioPlayer object.

Once you have the button's AVAudioPlayer, you first call its pause() function. This will suspend playback of the sound if it's currently playing. If not, it does nothing.

Then the currentTime property is set to 0. This property is the player's logical "playhead," indicating the position (in seconds) where the player is currently playing or will begin playing. Setting it to 0 "rewinds" the sound so it plays from the beginning.

Finally, the play() function starts the sound playing. The play() function is asynchronous; it starts a background task to play and manage the sound and then returns immediately.

There are just two more details to take care of before your sounds will play.

Activating Your Audio Session

It's not strictly required, but the documentation for the AVAudioSession class recommends that your app activate the audio session when it starts and again whenever your audio session is interrupted. You'll take this opportunity to prepare the audio player objects at the same time. You'll do that in an activateAudioSession() function, which you'll add in a moment. Call it once when the view first loads. Find the viewDidLoad() function and add that call (new line in bold).

```
override func viewDidLoad() {
    super.viewDidLoad()
    activateAudioSession()
}
```

Now write the activateAudioSession() function.

```
func activateAudioSession() {
    let active = AVAudioSession.sharedInstance().setActive(true, error: nil)
    if active {
        if players.count == 0 {
            createAudioPlayers()
        }
    } else {
        destroyAudioPlayers()
    }
    for i in 0..<soundNames.count {
        if let button = view.viewWithTag(i+1) as? UIButton {
            button.enabled = active
        }
    }
}
```

The first line obtains your app's audio session object (the same one you configured back in applica tion(_:,didFinishLaunchingWithOptions:)). You call its setActive(_:,error:) function to activate, or reactivate, the audio session.

The setActive(_:,error:) function returns true if the audio session is now active. There are a few obscure situations where this will fail (returning false), and your app should deal with that situation gracefully.

In this app, you look to see whether the session was activated and call `createAudioPlayers()` to prepare the `AVAudioPlayer` objects for playback. If the session couldn't be activated (which means your app can't use any audio), then you destroy any `AVAudioPlayer` objects you previously created and disable all of the sound effect buttons in the interface.

Since you don't have an outlet connected to those buttons, you'll get them using their `tag`. The `viewWithTag(_:)` function searches the hierarchy of a view object and returns the first subview matching that tag. Your bang buttons are the only views with tag values of 1, 2, 3, and 4. The loop obtains each button view and enables, or disables, it.

> **Tip**   Tags are a convenient way to manage a group of view objects, without requiring you to create an outlet for each one.

The functional portion of your app is now finished. By functional, I mean you can run your app, play music, and annoy anyone else in the room with cheesy percussion noises, as shown in Figure 9-25.

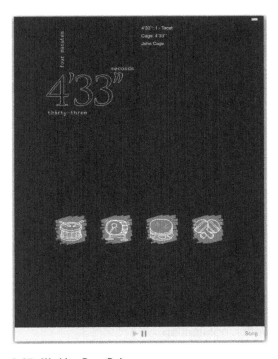 

Figure 9-25. Working DrumDub app

Interruptions and Detours

In the "Living in a Larger World" section, I described the multitude of events and situations that conspire to complicate your app's use of audio. Most people hate interruptions or being forced to take a detour, and I suspect app developers are no different. But dealing with these events gracefully is the hallmark of a finely crafted iOS app. First up are interruptions.

Dealing with Interruptions

An *interruption* occurs when another app or service needs to activate its audio session. The most common sources of interruptions are incoming phone calls and alerts (triggered by alarms, messages, notification, and reminders).

Most of the work of handling interruptions is done for you. When your app's audio session is interrupted, iOS fades out your audio and deactivates your session. The usurping session then takes over and begins playing the user's ring tone or alert sound. Your app, audio, and music player delegates then receive "begin interruption" messages.

Your app should do whatever is appropriate to respond to the interruption. Often, this isn't much. You might update the interface to indicate that you're no longer playing music. Mostly, your app should just make a note of what it was doing so it can resume when the interruption ends.

Interruptions can be short, such as a few seconds for alarms. Or they can be very (very) long, such as an hour or more, if you accept that incoming phone call from chatty aunt May. Don't make any assumptions on how long the interruption will last; just wait for iOS to notify your app when it's over.

When the interruption is over, your app will receive "end interruption" messages. This is where the work begins. First, your app should explicitly reactivate its audio session. This isn't a strict requirement, but it's recommended. It gives your app a chance to catch the (very rare) situation where your audio session can't be reactivated.

Then you need to resume playback, reload audio objects, update your interface, or whatever else your app needs to do so it is once again running, exactly as it was before the interruption occurred. In DrumDub, there's surprisingly little work to do because most of the default music and audio player behavior is exactly what you want. Nevertheless, there's still some rudimentary interruption handling you need to add.

Adding Your Interruption Handlers

Interruption notifications can be received in a number of different ways. Your app only needs to observe those it wants and are convenient; there's no need to observe them all. Begin and end interruption messages are sent to the following:

- Any observer of the audio session's interruption notification (AVAudioSessionInterruptionNotification)
- All audio player delegates (AVAudioPlayerDelegate)
- Any observer of music player state change notifications (MPMusicPlayerControllerPlaybackStateDidChangeNotification)

Decide how you want your app to respond to interruptions and then implement the handlers that conveniently let you do that. When something interrupts DrumDub, you want to do the following:

- Pause the playback of the music

- Stop any percussion sound that's playing (so it doesn't resume when the interruption is over)

When the interruption ends, you want DrumDub to do the following:

- Reactivate the audio session and check for problems

- Resume playback of the music

Pausing and resuming the music player requires no code. The MPMusicPlayerController class does this automatically in response to interruptions. You don't even need to add any code to update your interface. When the music player is interrupted, its playbackState changes to MPMusicPlaybackStateInterrupted, and your controller gets a playbackStateDidChangeNotification(_:) call, which updates your play and pause buttons. When the interruption ends, the music player resumes playing and sends another state change notification.

So, DrumDub's only nonstandard behavior is to silence any playing percussion sounds when an interruption arrives. That's so the "tail end" of the sound bite doesn't start playing again when the interruption is over (which is the default behavior). Start writing your audioInterruption(_:) function and handle that in its first case.

```
func audioInterruption(notification: NSNotification) {
    if let typeValue = ↵
        notification.userInfo?[AVAudioSessionInterruptionTypeKey] as? NSNumber {
        if let type = AVAudioSessionInterruptionType.fromRaw( ↵
                                            typeValue.unsignedLongValue) {
            switch type {
                case .Began:
                    for player in players {
                        player.pause()
                    }
```

The last task on the list is to reactivate the audio session when the interruption is over. You already wrote the code to do that in activateAudioSession(); you just need to call it. Do that in the second case.

```
                case .Ended:
                    activateAudioSession()
                }
            }
        }
    }
}
```

To get these notifications, add your view controller as an observer in your viewDidLoad() function (new code in bold).

```
override func viewDidLoad() {
    super.viewDidLoad()
    activateAudioSession()
    let center = NSNotificationCenter.defaultCenter()
    center.addObserver( self,
            selector: "audioInterruption:",
                name: AVAudioSessionInterruptionNotification,
              object: nil)
```

With the tricky business of interruptions taken care of, it's time to deal with detours (route changes).

Dealing with Audio Route Changes

An audio route is the path that data takes to get to the eardrum of the listener. Your iPhone might be paired to the speakers in your car. When you get out of your car, your iPhone switches to its built-in speakers. When you plug in some headphones, it stops playing through its speaker and begins playing through your headphones. Each of these events is an audio route change.

You deal with audio route changes exactly the way you deal with interruptions: decide what your app should do in each situation and then write handlers to observe those events and implement your policies. From DrumDub, you want to implement Apple's recommended behavior of stopping music playback when the user unplugs their headphones or disconnects from external speakers. If these were sound effects in a game, or something similar, it would be appropriate to let them continue playing. But DrumDub's music will stop playing when the headphones are unplugged, so the instrument sounds should stop too.

Audio route notifications are posted by the AVAudioSession object, all you have to do is observe them. Begin by requesting that your ViewController object receive audio route change notifications. At the end of the viewDidLoad() function, add this code:

```
center.addObserver( self,
        selector: "audioRouteChange:",
            name: AVAudioSessionRouteChangeNotification,
          object: nil)
```

Now add your route change handler function.

```
func audioRouteChange(notification: NSNotification) {
    if let reasonValue = ↵
        notification.userInfo?[AVAudioSessionRouteChangeReasonKey] as? NSNumber {
        if reasonValue.unsignedLongValue == ↵
            AVAudioSessionRouteChangeReason.OldDeviceUnavailable.toRaw() {
            for player in players {
                player.pause()
            }
        }
    }
}
```

The function begins by examining the reason for the audio route change. It gets this information from the notification's userInfo dictionary. If the value associated with the AVAudioSessionRouteChangeReasonKey is AVAudioSessionRouteChangeReasonOldDeviceUnavailable, it indicates that a previously active audio route is no longer available. This happens when headphones are unplugged, the device is removed from a dock connector, a wireless speaker system is disconnected, and so on. If that's the case, it stops playback of all four audio players.

That wraps up this app! Go ahead and run it again to make sure everything is working. You'll want to test your interruption and audio route change logic by doing things like the following:

- Setting an alarm to interrupt playback
- Calling your iPhone from another phone
- Plugging and unplugging headphones

While you do this, set breakpoints in your audioInterruption(_:) and audioRouteChange(_:) functions to verify that they are being called. Testing your app under as many situations as you can devise is an important part of app development.

Other Audio Topics

This chapter didn't even begin to approach the subjects of audio recording or signal processing. To get started with these, and similar topics, start with the *Multimedia Programming Guide*. It provides an overview and road map for playing, recording, and manipulating both audio and video in iOS.

If you need to perform advanced or low-level audio tasks (such as analyzing or encoding audio), refer to the *Core Audio Overview*. All of these documents can be found in Xcode's Documentation and API Reference.

Here's something else to look at: if you need to present audio or video in a view, want your app to play music in the background (that is, when your app is not running), or need to handle remote events, take a look at the AVPlayer and AVPlayerLayer classes. The first is a near-universal media player for both audio and video, similar to MPMusicPlayerController and AVAudioPlayer. It's a little more complicated but also more capable. It will work in conjunction with an AVPlayerLayer object to present visual content (movie) in a view, so you can create your own YouTube-style video player.

Summary

Sound adds a rich dimension to your app. You've learned how to play and control audio from the iPod library as well as resource files bundled in your app. You understand the importance of configuring your audio session and intelligently handing interruptions and audio route changes. "Playing nice" with other audio sources creates the kind of experience that users enjoy and will want to use again and again.

But is there more to iOS interfaces than labels, buttons, and image views? Join me in the next chapter to find out.

EXERCISE

Blend DrumDub further into the iOS experience by using the system music player, instead of an application music player. This will require a couple of subtle changes, listed here:

- Obtain the music player object by calling `systemMusicPlayer()`, instead of `applicationMusicPlayer()`.

- Create and initialize the music player as soon as the view loads, rather than doing it lazily when the user chooses a song.

- Don't arbitrarily change the player's settings (like the shuffle or repeat modes). Remember that you're changing the user's iPod settings; most people won't like your app fiddling with their iPod.

When you're done, DrumDub will be "plugged in" to the user's iPod app. If their iPod music is playing when they launch DrumDub, the song will appear the moment your app launches. If the user starts a song playing and quits DrumDub, the music plays on.

You'll find my solution to this exercise in the `Learn iOS Development Projects` ➤ `Ch 9` ➤ `DrumDub E1` folder.

Chapter 10

Got Views?

You now have a lot of experience adding view objects to your design, arranging them, connecting them to outlets and actions, and customizing them. You've created iOS apps using buttons, labels, image views, a few text fields, and the odd toolbar. While you probably haven't been yearning for other kinds of view objects, there are more available. The Cocoa Touch framework provides all kinds of switches, toggles, sliders, specialty buttons, pickers, indicators, doo-dads, and gizmos you can use to build your apps. And if that isn't enough, many of those objects can be customized in ways you haven't explored yet. In this chapter, you'll learn about the following:

- Downloading sample projects
- Button views
- Switches, sliders, and steppers
- Indicators
- Labels, text fields, and text views
- Pickers
- Grouped table views
- Scroll views
- Search controls
- Alerts and action sheets

Anyone who's spent time building Lego figures, Erector Set constructions, or experimental aircraft will know one thing: your ability to imagine what's possible is directly linked to your knowledge about what parts you have to work with. To that end, I invite you on a guided tour of iOS view objects.

Learning by Example

Software development is a lot like cooking. It's one thing to read recipes, talk about the process, and enjoy the results. It's another thing to actually do it. One of the best ways to learn how to cook is to watch someone who knows what they're doing and emulate them.

Apple provides many example projects—fully written, ready-to-run apps—that demonstrate the use of various technologies in iOS. All you have to do is download one, build it, run it, and then mine it for all of its secrets. These example projects are a great way to get started using, or at least understanding how to use, many of the frameworks and features in iOS.

Not only does Apple provide these example projects free of charge, it has made it ridiculously simple to download them. Xcode will search for, download, and open sample code projects with the click of a button. Start in Xcode's documentation window (Help ➤ Documentation and API Reference), as shown in Figure 10-1.

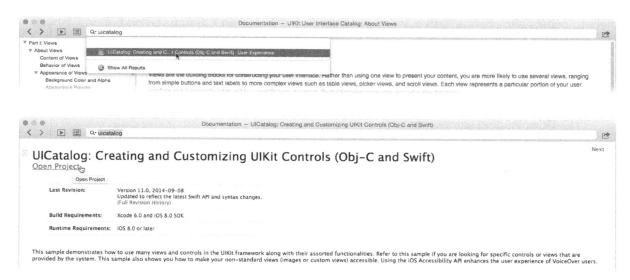

Figure 10-1. Searching for sample code

Search for the UICatalog project, as shown in Figure 10-1. Click it and the project's documentation page appears. Near the top is an Open Project link. Click it. Xcode downloads the project's archive file, un-archives it, and opens the project in a new workspace window, as shown in Figure 10-2. How easy was that?

Figure 10-2. UICatalog project

Note   Sample projects are not part of the Xcode installation package and require an Internet connection to download.

You'll find that the documentation for many classes contains links to sample projects, making it easy to download code that shows you those classes in action.

Tip   While Apple's so-called walled garden keeps most iOS app projects within the developer community (after all, you have to be a developer to build and run apps on your iOS device) that hasn't stopped the open source community. Many open source iOS projects are available to developers (like you) and to brave individuals who have "jailbroken" their device. A quick Internet search will turn up open source apps, as well as frameworks and code libraries, you can use in your own projects.

The UICatalog project is extra-special. It's an app that demonstrates every major view object supplied by iOS. So, not only is it a handy visual reference to the kinds of view objects iOS supplies, but you can see exactly how these objects are created and used in an app.

Run the UICatalog app in a simulator (or on your own device, if you like), as shown in Figure 10-3. As of this writing, UICatalog contains two projects: one app written in Objective-C and an identical app written in Swift. When you download them, Xcode will open both projects. It doesn't matter which one you run. For exploring the code, you'll be interested in the Swift version, so close the Objective-C project.

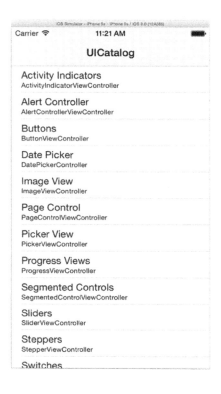

Figure 10-3. UICatalog app

The list consists of the core set of stand-alone UIKit view classes, in alphabetical order, followed by the specialty search and toolbar classes. Let's start with everyone's favorite control: the button.

Buttons

A button is a straightforward view object; it acts like a physical button. The UIButton class draws a button and observes touch events to determine how the user is interacting with it. It translates what the user is doing into action events, such as "user touched inside the button," "user moved their finger outside the button," "user moved back inside the button," and "user released their finger while still inside the button." That's pretty much all it does.

I know what you're thinking. Well, maybe I don't. But I hope you're thinking, "But a button does more than that! It sends action messages to another object, it remembers its state, it can be disabled, and it can have gesture recognizers attached to it. That's a lot!"

It is a lot, but the UIButton class doesn't do any of those things. UIButton is at the end of a chain of classes, each of which is responsible for one set of closely related behaviors. Software engineers say that each class performs a *role*. The role of a UIButton object is to act like a button. Its superclasses do all of that other stuff. So that you can get a clearer picture of what's going on, I think it's time for you to dissect a UIButton. This will help you understand not only how UIButton was built but how all control views are constructed.

Note No UIButton objects were harmed in the making of this book.

The Responder and View Classes

A UIButton is a subclass of UIControl, which is a subclass of UIView, which is a subclass of UIResponder, as shown in Figure 10-4. Each class adds one layer of functionality that, taken together, makes a button.

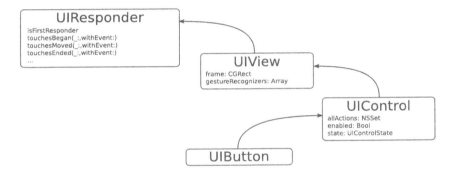

Figure 10-4. Anatomy of a button

The UIResponder class defines all the event-related functions of the objects, most notably the methods that handle touch events. You learned all about UIResponder in Chapter 4, and you created a custom UIView object that overrode the touch event handling methods with your own, so I won't repeat any of that here.

The next layer that UIButton inherits is UIView. UIView is a big, complicated class. It has dozens of properties and more than 100 methods. It's huge because it's responsible for every aspect of how every visible object in the iOS universe gets displayed on a screen. It handles the geometry of the view, its coordinate systems, transformations (such as rotation, scaling, and skewing), animation, how the view gets repositioned when the screen size changes, and hit testing. It's also responsible for drawing itself, drawing its subviews, deciding when those views need to be redrawn, and more. You'll get very intimate with UIView in Chapter 11.

One seemingly unrelated property of UIView is its gestureRecognizers property. The UIView class doesn't do anything with gesture recognizers directly. But a UIView defines a visible region of the display, and any visible region can have a gesture recognizer attached to it so that property exists in UIView.

HOW GESTURE RECOGNIZERS GET EVENTS

Gesture recognizers are fed events by the UIWindow object during touch event delivery. In Chapter 4, I explained that hit testing is used to determine the view that will receive the touch events. That description oversimplified the process somewhat.

Starting with iOS 3.2, the UIWindow first looks at the initial (hit test) view to see whether it has any gesture recognizer objects attached to it. If it does, the touch events are first sent to those gesture recognizer objects, instead of being delivered directly to the view object. If the gesture recognizers aren't interested, then the event eventually makes its way to the view object.

If you need to, there are a variety of ways to alter this behavior, but it's a tad complicated. For all of the details, read the "Gesture Recognizers" chapter of the *Event Handling Guide for iOS* that you'll find in Xcode's Documentation and API Reference window.

So, everything that's visual about the button is defined in the UIView class. Now move on to the next layer, the UIControl class.

The Control Class

UIControl is the abstract class that defines the properties common to all control objects. This includes buttons, sliders, switches, steppers, and so on. A control object does the following:

- Sends action messages to target objects
- Can be enabled or disabled
- Can be selected
- Can be highlighted
- Establishes how content is aligned

The first item in the previous list is the most important. The UIControl class defines the mechanism for delivering action messages to recipients, typically controller objects. Every UIControl object maintains a table of events that trigger actions, the object that will receive that action, and the action message it will send. When you're editing an Interface Builder file and you connect an event to an action method in another object, you're adding one entry to that object's event dispatch table.

> **Note**   Remember from Chapter 4 that an event can be associated with an action that is sent to the first responder. You do this by specifying the message to send and using nil as the target object for that message.

The other properties (enabled, selected, and highlighted) are general indicators of the control's appearance and behavior. Subclasses of UIControl determine exactly what those properties mean, if anything.

The enabled property is the most consistent. A control object interacts with the user when enabled and ignores touch events when disabled (control.enabled = false). Most control classes indicate that they are disabled by dimming, or graying, their image to show the user the control is inert.

The highlighted property is used to indicate that the user is currently touching the control. Many controls "light up" when touched, and this property reflects that.

The selected property is for controls that can be turned on or off, such as the UISwitch class. Controls that don't, such as buttons, ignore this property.

The UIControl class also introduces the concept of an alignment (vertical and horizontal) through the contentVerticalAlignment and contentHorizontalAlignment properties. Most control objects have some sort of title or image and use these properties to position that in the view.

Button Types

You've now worked your way back to the UIButton class. It's this class that implements the button-specific behavior of a control+view+responder object. The UIButton class supplies a handful of predefined button looks, along with a plethora of customizations so you can make it look just about any way you want.

The most important property of a button is its type. A button can be one of the following types:

- System
- Custom
- Detail disclosure
- An "info" button (light or dark)
- An "add contact" button

All of these button styles are shown in the UICatalog app, except for the detail disclosure and custom types, as shown in Figure 10-5. The important thing to remember is that a button's type is determined when it is created. Unlike all of its other properties, it cannot be changed afterward. An info button is an info button for life.

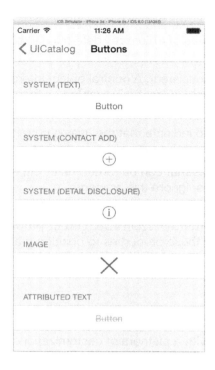

Figure 10-5. Buttons

The system button is the workhorse of iOS. It's the standard, default button style used throughout the iOS interface. The premiere properties that adjust your button's look are as follows:

- Tint color
- Title text (plain or attributed) and color
- Foreground image
- Background image or color

The tintColor property sets the highlight and accent color of the button. The standard color is blue.

The button's title can be a simple string value (which you've used in your projects so far), or it can be attributed string. An *attributed string* is a string that includes text attributes: font, size, italics, bold, subscript offset, and so on. Creating attributed strings is a bit complicated but allows you to create buttons with whatever font and style the system is capable of. I describe attributed strings in Chapter 20.

You can also use an image instead of text for your button's label by setting its image property. Similarly, the background can be set to an image or a solid color. You can also mix these in any combination you want: text title over an image background, image over a solid color background, image with no background (by setting the background color to UIColor's clearColor object), and so on.

Images used for a button's background can utilize an interesting feature that allows the graphic to resize its center portion independently of its edges. The cap insets (capInsets) property defines a margin around the edge of the image that is not scaled when the image is stretched to fit the size of the button. This property lets you design a single graphic image that will fill any button size, without distorting its edges.

At the other extreme is the custom type. This is a blank canvas, and iOS adds nothing to the look or behavior of the button. You can still use the title and image properties, but most of the standard button behavior (such as highlighting) is left up to you.

The detail disclosure type is the right-facing arrow button that normally appears only in the cells of a table view. The add contact button displays a plus (+) symbol, and the two info buttons present a localized symbol indicating more information is available. These four types have predefined appearances and sizes, and there's almost nothing about them that you can customize.

> **Note**   There's a rounded rectangle button type that is obsolete and should be ignored. If you use this type, your iOS 8 button will behave like the system type.

Control States

When creating and configuring the button's title, image, background image, and background color, you must consider the various states the button (control) can be in. The UIControl's enabled, highlighted, and selected properties combine to form a single state value (UIControlState) for that control. The state will always be one of normal, highlighted, disabled, or selected.

When the button is displaying normally, its state is .Normal. When the user is touching it, its state changes to .Highlighted. When it's disabled, its state becomes .Disabled.

When you set a button's title, image, background, or color, you do so for a particular state. This allows you to set one button image for when the button is enabled and alternate images for when it's disabled, highlighted, or selected. You see this reflected in the functions that set these properties:

```
setTitle(_:,forState:)
setTitleColor(_:,forState:)
setAttributedTitle(_:,forState:)
setImage(_:,forState:)
setBackgroundImage(_:,forState:)
```

You don't have to set values for every state. At a minimum, set the value for the normal (.Normal) state. If that's all you set, that value will be used for all other states. If you then want it to have a different title, image, background, or color for one of the other states, set that too.

There are lots of other, subtler properties for fine-tuning your button's look and feel. You can, for example, control the shadow thrown by the title text or change the position (inset) of the title, image, and background image. Read through the documentation for UIButton for all the available properties.

Button Code

You now know enough about button properties to take a peek at the button construction code in UICatalog. Up to now, you've created button objects using Interface Builder, which is fine—there's nothing wrong with that. But you can also create any iOS object programmatically, as you've done with other objects like arrays and images. And you can take a hybrid approach, letting Interface Builder create an object while you then customize or adapt it in code.

The UICatalog app takes this last approach. Most objects are created in a storyboard and then tweaked in the code. The project is meticulously organized to help you locate these. Each example in the app, such as Buttons, has a storyboard scene (Buttons Scene) and a view controller (ButtonsViewController) with similar names, as shown in Figure 10-6.

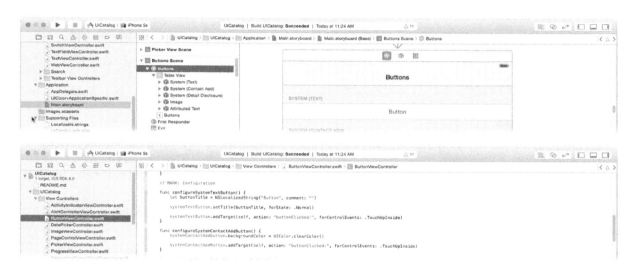

Figure 10-6. Organization of UICatalog project

Click the ButtonsViewController.swift file and find the configureImageButton() function. It should look something like the following code:

```
func configureImageButton() {
    imageButton.setTitle("", forState: .Normal)
    imageButton.tintColor = UIColor.applicationPurpleColor()
    let imageButtonNormalImage = UIImage(named: "x_icon")
    imageButton.setImage(imageButtonNormalImage, forState: .Normal)
    imageButton.accessibilityLabel = NSLocalizedString("X Button", comment: "")
    imageButton.addTarget(self, action: "buttonClicked:", forControlEvents: .TouchUpInside)
}
```

A basic button object is created in the storyboard and connected to the imageButton outlet. The configureImageButton() function then customizes it by clearing its title, assigning an image (for all states), adding explanatory text for the visually impaired, and connecting the button's action to the buttonClicked(_:) function.

If you want to try different button properties to see what they look like, fiddle with this code and run the app again. The UICatalog app is your UI playground.

Switches and Sliders

Next up on the tour are switches and sliders. Both are input devices. Unlike buttons, switches and sliders retain a value. A switch is just that, as shown on the left in Figure 10-7. It presents a sliding button that can change between on and off values by either tapping or swiping it with your finger. You see these everywhere in iOS, as shown on the right in Figure 10-7.

Figure 10-7. Switches, sliders, and the Settings app

A UISwitch object has a single Boolean value property named, appropriately enough, on. Getting that property will tell you which position the switch is in. Setting the property changes it. You can request that UISwitch perform a little animation eye-candy, when you change its value programmatically, by calling the setOn(_:,animated:) function and passing true for the animated parameter.

A number of properties let you customize your switch's appearance.

- tintColor, onTintColor, and thumbTintColor: The first two set the colors used when the switch is off and on. The thumbTintColor makes the "thumb" of the switch (the circle you drag) a different color than tintColor.

- onImage and offImage: Normally a switch displays either (localized) "On" or "Off" text titles next to the thumb. You can replace these with images of your choosing. There are important size restrictions, so read the documentation.

Like most controls with a value, a switch sends a "value changed" event (UIControlEvents.ValueChanged) whenever the user changes it. Connect this event to your controller to receive an action message when the switch is flipped.

Sliders, as shown in the middle of Figure 10-7, are another input control that lets the user choose a value by dragging a slider to a position within a predetermined range. While a switch's value is Boolean, a slider's value property is a floating-point value that represents a continuous range of numbers.

The slider's value property is constrained to the range set by the minimumValue and maximumValue properties. These default to 0.0 and 1.0, respectively. Unless you change those, value will be a fractional number between 0.0 and 1.0 (inclusive).

The key visual customization properties are as follows:

- minimumTrackTintColor, maximumTrackTintColor, and thumbTintColor: These change the colors of the tracks (to the left and right of the thumb), as well as the thumb itself. See the tinted slider in the UICatalog (Figure 10-7) for an example and the code that does it.

- minimumValueImage, maximumValueImage, thumbImage (per state): Like with the slider, you can change the image used to draw the tracks of the slider and the thumb itself. The thumb image works like UIButton's image, in that you can supply different images for different states (normal, highlighted, and disabled).

A slider sends a single "value changed" event when the user moves it, unless you set the continuous property to true. If you set continuous, the control fires a barrage of "value changed" messages as the user drags the slider. You used this setting in the ColorModel app in Chapter 8 so color changes happened "live" as you dragged around a slider.

Page Control

A page control (UIPageControl) object, as shown at the bottom of Figure 10-8, can be thought of as a discrete slider control. As its name implies, it's intended to indicate the user's position within a small (up to 20) number of pages or items. Apple's Weather app uses it to indicate which location the user is currently viewing, as shown on the right in Figure 10-8.

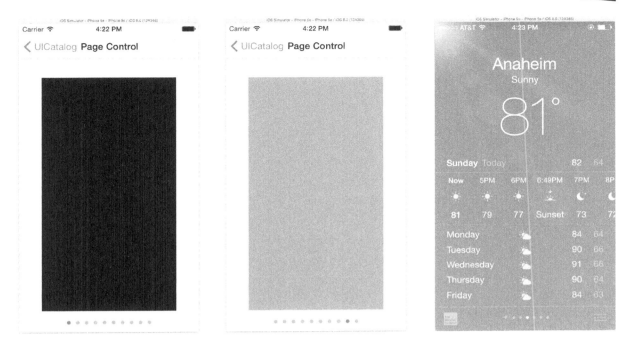

Figure 10-8. *Page control and Weather app*

UIPageControl's integer `currentPage` property is its value, and its `numberOfPages` property determines the former's range and the number of dots that appear. Its appearance can be slightly modified with these properties:

- `pageIndicatorTintColor`: This sets the color for the page indicator.
- `hidesForSinglePage`: If set to true, the control doesn't draw anything if there's only one page (`numberOfPages<=1`).

Tapping a page control object to the right or left of the current page either decrements or increments the `currentPage` property (moving forward or backward one page) and sends a "value changed" event.

Steppers

A stepper (`UIStepper`) has the face of `UIButton` and the heart of `UIPageControl`, as shown in Figure 10-9. It displays two buttons side by side. Use a stepper when your user needs to increase or decrease something—"something" is up to you; the stepper doesn't display a value—one step at a time.

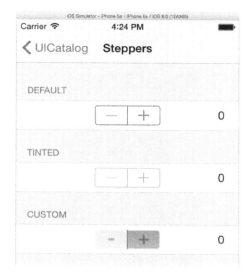

Figure 10-9. *Stepper*

Like a slider, the stepper's `minimumValue` and `maximumValue` properties set the range for its `value` property. The `stepValue` property determines what "one step" means. As an example, Table 10-1 would be the property values you'd set for a stepper with 11 possible values, between `1.0` and `6.0`.

Table 10-1. *Property Values for a Stepper with 11 Possible Values (1.0 to 6.0, Inclusive)*

Property	Value
minimumValue	1.0
maximumValue	6.0
stepValue	0.5

A stepper's visual appearance can be customized using increment, decrement, and background images, which you set the same way you do for a button. There's also a `UIButton`-ish `tintColor` property.

A stepper sends a "value changed" action every time the user taps the increment or decrement button. There are three properties that alter this behavior.

- `continuous`: The `continuous` property works just like it does for the slider.

- `autorepeat`: Setting `autorepeat` to `true` allows the user to continuously change the value (one step at a time) by holding down one of the buttons.

- `wraps`: This property lets the value "wrap" around the range. Using the example in Table 10-1, tapping + when the value was already a `6.0` would change the value back to `1.0`. When `wraps` is `true`, the buttons do not disable when the value is at the beginning or end of the range.

Segmented Controls

Closely related to steppers is the UISegmentedControl class. A segmented control displays multiple segments. Each segment acts as a button for a choice, as shown in Figure 10-10. Use a segmented control when you want the user to pick between a small number of mutually exclusive choices.

 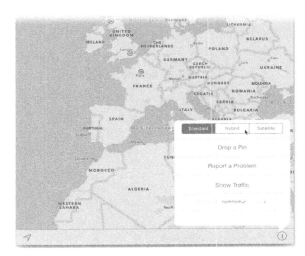

Figure 10-10. Segmented controls

To use a segmented control, first tell it how may segments there are by setting the numberOfSegments property. You can then set the label of each segment to either a string title or an image using one of these functions:

```
setTitle(_:,forSegmentAtIndex:)
setImage(_:,forSegmentAtIndex:)
```

Alternatively, you can choose to insert (or remove) segments one at a time. Using these functions, you have the option of having the view animate the change, sliding and resizing the other segments to make room.

```
insertSegmentWithTitle(_:,atIndex:,animated:)
insertSegmentWithImage(_:,atIndex:,animated:)
```

A segmented control sends a "value changed" event (UIControlEvents.ValueChanged) when the user changes it. Its selectedSegmentIndex property tells you which segment is selected or can be used to change that. The special value UISegmentedControlNoSegment means no segment is selected.

Normally, the buttons in a segment are "sticky"—they stay highlighted to indicate which segment is selected. If you set the momentary property to true, buttons don't stay down, and the selectedSegmentIndex goes back to UISegmentedControlNoSegment when the user removes their finger.

Progress Indicators

iOS provides two progress indicators, UIActivityIndicatorView and UIProgressView, that provide your users with feedback during time-consuming activities or to display relative quantities (such as the amount of storage used), as shown in Figure 10-11. Use these to let your user know that your app is hard at work; they should remain calm and stay in their seats, with their seatbelts securely fastened.

Figure 10-11. Activity and progress indicator

The UIActivityIndicatorView is often called a *spinner* or *gear*. Use it when space is limited or the duration of the activity is indeterminate. There are three spinner styles (UIActivityIndicatorViewStyle) to choose from: small gray (.Gray), small white (.White), and large white (.WhiteLarge).

Using a spinner is easy. Call startAnimating() to start it spinning, and call stopAnimating() to stop it again. Its hidesWhenStopped and color properties are self-explanatory.

The second indicator is the progress bar (UIProgressView), shown on the right in Figure 10-11. It presents a progress indicator, familiar to anyone who's had days of their life siphoned away waiting for computers to finish something. The view has two looks (UIProgressViewStyle).

- .Default: The regular style progress bar
- .Bar: A style designed to be used in a toolbar

You control the view by periodically setting its progress property to a value between 0.0 (empty) and 1.0 (full). Setting the progress property makes the indicator jump to that position. By calling setProgress(_:,animated:), you can ask the indicator to smoothly animate to the new setting, which is less jarring for big changes.

Use the trackImage or trackTintColor properties to customize the look of the unfinished segment of the view, and use the progressImage and progressTintColor properties to adjust the finished segment. In the UICatalog project, tint colors are set in the `configureTintedProgressView()` function, if you'd like to try some different colors.

Text Views

There are three species of text views in iOS: labels, text fields, and text views. The *label* is the simplest. It's used to place a single string of text in your interface, often next to another field or view to explain its purpose, which is where it gets its name. A *text field* is a general-purpose input field, providing full-featured editing for a single line of text. A *text view* can display, and edit, multiple lines of text. Let's start with the simple one.

Labels

You see labels everywhere in iOS (see practically any figure in this book), and you've used them numerous times in your own projects. Use a `UILabel` object wherever you simply want to display some text, for whatever purpose. Use label objects as labels by setting their text in Interface Builder and forgetting about them—no connection required. If you connect the label to an outlet, your controller can update the text, as you did in the ColorModel app.

Labels have a number of properties that let you alter how the text string is displayed, as listed in Table 10-2.

Table 10-2. Label Display Properties

Property	Description
`numberOfLines`	The maximum number of lines the label will display, normally 1. Set it to 0 to display as many lines as are needed.
`font`	The text's font (face, size, and style).
`textColor`	The color used to draw the text.
`textAlignment`	One of left, center, right, justified, or natural. Natural employs the native alignment of the font.
`attributedText`	Draws an attributed string, instead of the simple text property. Use this to display text with a mixture of different fonts, sizes, styles, and colors. The text attributes in the string override the other text style properties (font, textColor, shadowOffset, and so on).
`lineBreakMode`	Determines how an overly long string is made to fit in the available space of the view.
`adjustsFontSizeToFitWidth`	An alternative to shortening the string; it makes the text smaller so the whole string will fit.
`adjustLetterSpacingToFitWidth`	A third option to get a string to fit within the given space.

If you plan on displaying a variable amount of text, pay attention to the properties that control what happens when the string is too big to fit in the view. First are the numberOfLines and lineBreakMode properties. The line break mode (NSLineBreakMode) controls how the string is broken up across multiple lines. The choices for multiple-line labels (numberOfLines!=1) are to break text at the nearest character (.ByCharWrapping) or at the nearest word (.ByWordWrapping).

For single-line labels (numberOfLines==1), text that won't fit in the view is unceremoniously cut off (.ByClipping), or a portion of the beginning (.ByTruncatingHead), middle (.ByTruncatingMiddle), or end (.ByTruncatingTail) of the string is replaced by an ellipsis (...) character.

> **Note**   If the label's width is not fixed by constraints, changing its text will alter its intrinsic size. The auto-layout logic will then attempt to resize the label view. If you let a label resize itself to fit its text, the lineBreakMode and related properties have no effect.

The alternate method of getting text to fit is to set the adjustsFontSizeToFitWidth or adjustLetterSpacingToFitWidth property to true. These options cause either the spacing between words or the size of the font—you can also set both—to be reduced in an attempt to make the string fit in the available space. The spacing between words will never be reduced to nothing, and its size will never be shrunk below the minimumScaleFactor property. If the text still won't fit, the lineBreakMode is applied.

> **Caution**   Do not set adjustsFontSizeToFitWidth or adjustsLetterSpacingToFitWidth for a multiline (numberOfLines!=1) label or in conjunction with a multiline line break mode (char or word wrapping). Doing so is a programming error, and the behavior of the view will be unpredictable.

Text Fields

Use a text field (UITextField) when you want the user to enter or edit one line of text. The Shorty app used a text field to get an URL from the user.

The UICatalog app demonstrates five different text fields, as shown in Figure 10-12. Consistent with the complexity of editing almost any kind of text, you have a broad range of choices when it comes to the view's appearance and behavior.

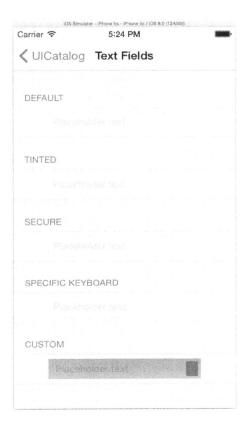

Figure 10-12. *Text fields*

Let's start with the appearance of the field. There are four styles (UITextBorderStyle) to choose from, controlled by the borderStyle property.

- .RoundedRect: Draws a simple rounded rectangle around the field
- .Line: Draws a thin gray rectangle around the field
- .Bezel: Surrounds the field with a chiseled border, giving the illusion of the field being inset
- .None: Does not draw a border

The UICatalog app demonstrates only the rounded rectangle and none styles, but the other two aren't hard to imagine. You can provide a more dramatic look by setting the background property to your own UIImage. The background property overrides the borderStyle property. In other words, you can't supply a background image for a chiseled border; if you want that look, your image will need to include a chiseled border.

The placeholder property shows a string (in light gray) when the field is empty (see Figure 10-12). Use this to prompt the user (like "Your Name Here") or possibly show a default value. Set the clearsOnBeginEditing to true if you want the text in the field to be automatically cleared before the user begins typing.

The font face, size, style, and color of the text in the field can be controlled either by setting the font and textColor properties or by using attributed text strings. The latter is considerably more complicated and commensurately more flexible.

You can also insert accessory views in three different places. Use these to add additional controls or indicators, such a button that pops up a set of options for the field or a progress indicator. The accessory view properties are as follows:

- leftView and leftViewMode
- rightView and rightViewMode
- inputAccessoryView

The left and right views can be any UIView object that will fit inside the text field. The UICatalog app demonstrates this by placing a purple UIButton in the rightView of the custom text field (see Figure 10-12) and inserting a small (invisible) UIView in the leftView; the latter is just used to create some padding on the left. The appearance of both right and left views are controlled by their companion rightViewMode and leftViewMode properties. Each can be set to never display the view, always display the view, display the view only when editing, or display the view only when not editing.

The input accessory view doesn't get attached to the text field. Instead, it gets attached to the top of the virtual keyboard that appears when the user begins editing. You can use an input accessory view to add special controls, presets, options, and so on, to your user's keyboard.

Text fields send a variety of events. The most useful are the "editing did end on exit" event (.EditingDidEndOnExit), which is sent when the user stops editing a field, and the "value changed" event (.ValueChanged), which is sent whenever the text in the field is modified. You connected actions to both of these events in the MyStuff app. To receive even more editing-related messages and exert some control over editing, create a delegate object for the text field (UITextFieldDelegate). The delegate receives messages when editing begins and ends, and it can also control if editing is allowed to begin, editing is allowed to end, or a specific change is allowed to be made.

Text Editing Behavior

There are a dizzying number of properties that affect how text in a field is edited. If you look in the documentation for UITextField, you won't find any of them. That's because they are defined in the UITextInput and UITextInputTraits protocols, which UITextField and UITextView both adopt. The number of properties and options are almost overwhelming, so I've listed the highlights in Table 10-3.

Table 10-3. *Important Text-Editing Properties*

Property	Description
autocapitalizationType	Controls the auto-capitalization mode: off or capitalize sentences, words, or characters.
autocorrectionType	Turns auto-correction on or off.
spellCheckingType	Turns spell checking, suggestions, and dictionary lookup on or off.
keyboardType	Chooses the virtual keyboard to use (normal, URL, just numbers, telephone dial, e-mail address, Twitter, and so on).
returnKeyType	If the keyboard has a "go" key, this property determines how it's labeled: Go, Google, Join, Next, Route, Search, Send, Yahoo!, Done, or Emergency Call.
secureEntry	Hides the characters as the user types them to discourage onlookers from seeing the contents. Set this option for sensitive information, such as passwords.

Text Views

Text view (UITextView) objects are the synthesis of labels and text fields, as shown in Figure 10-13. UITextView is not a subclass of either, but it essentially inherits the capabilities of both and adds a few extra features of its own. Whether a text view can be edited is controlled by its editable property.

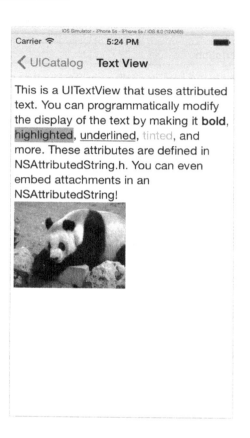

Figure 10-13. A text view

With `editable` set to `false`, a text view acts much like a multiline label. It displays multiple lines of text in a variety of fonts, sizes, and styles, with control over line breaks. To this it adds some additional talents: scrolling, selection, and data detectors.

Unlike a label, if the text won't fit in the vertical space of view, the user can scroll the text in the view to see the rest of it. You used this feature in the Surrealist app.

The user can select text in a text view (by touching and holding on the text), unless the `selectable` property is `false`. The selected text can be copied to the clipboard or used to look up words in the dictionary. In addition, you can enable data detectors. *Data detectors* are a technology that recognizes the purpose of certain text (such as a telephone number or someone's e-mail address). The user can then tap the text to do something useful (place a phone call, address a new e-mail message, and so on).

With the `editable` property set to `true`, the text view becomes a (miniature) word processor. The user can type, select, cut, copy, and paste to their heart's content. All of the editing features and options described in the "Text Fields" section apply to text views. About the only thing missing are the borders; text views do not draw a border.

A text view is also capable of editing styled (attributed) text, but you'll have to supply the additional user interface elements that allow the user to choose a font face, size, style, color, and so on. The text view will handle the mechanics of applying those styles to what the user is typing, but your controller will have to tell the text view what those styles are.

Use a text view, instead of a label or text field, when

- The user needs to edit multiline text
- There's more text than will fit in the view and you want it to scroll
- You want the user to have the ability to select and copy text or look up definitions
- You want to use data detectors

Search Bars

There are also specialty text fields. The UISearchBar view presents a text field specifically designed for performing searches. The UICatalog app neatly demonstrates the common ways you can embed a search bar into your design. I'll summarize your options here.

You can use a UISearchBar on its own, placing it in any view. The first example demonstrates the standard search bar look and feel (see the middle image of Figure 10-14). The basic search bar contains an embedded text field, prepopulated with a search icon (so the user knows what it is) and a cancel button.

Figure 10-14. Stand-alone search bar views

You can optionally display a segmented control below the search field, allowing the user to choose from a set of options. Enable this by setting the showScopeBar property to true and then setting two or more button titles in the scopeButtonTitles property.

The second demonstration, shown on the right in Figure 10-14, shows some ways in which the search field's presentation can be altered with custom backgrounds, different search bar styles (UIBarStyle), colored buttons, and so on.

The next three demonstrations show how to incorporate a search bar into a navigation bar or table view. iOS 8 adds several new ways of seamlessly integrating a search bar into these other elements.

First up, present the search bar on demand. In this technique, the search bar remains hidden (as shown in the upper left in Figure 10-15) until the user taps the search icon. The search bar is then presented over the navigation bar, replacing it until dismissed (see the lower-left image in Figure 10-15). The advantage is that your search feature doesn't consume any appreciable amount of screen real estate until the user wants it. The disadvantage is that, once summoned, it obscures your navigation bar until it is dismissed.

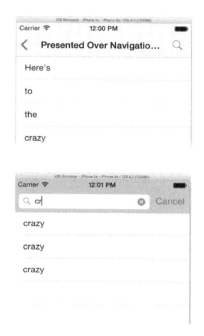

Figure 10-15. Search bars in navigation bars and table views

The second technique embeds the search bar right into the navigation bar so it is always visible, as shown in the middle of Figure 10-15. The search bar is readily apparent and immediately available but permanently displaces the title of your navigation bar.

The last example demonstrates how to embed a search bar into a table view, instead of a navigation bar, shown on the right of Figure 10-15. Use this to present a persistent search bar without interfering with the navigation bar or in the absence of a navigation bar.

Like `UIPickerView`, a `UISearchBar` is not a `UIControl` subclass and does not send action messages. You should create a `UISearchBarDelegate` object that will receive the user's input and related events.

Pickers

A *picker* is a user interface that lets the user choose something from a bounded set of choices. You used the image picker in your MyStuff to choose a picture from the photo library, and you used a media picker to choose a song from the iTunes library in DrumDub. These are both big interfaces that take over the entire user experience.

iOS also supplies a couple of smaller picker view objects. There's the specialty `UIDatePicker`, for choosing dates and times, and the customizable `UIPickerView`, for anything else. Both present a view containing a number of vertical "wheels" that the user spins to choose the value or item they want, as shown in Figure 10-16.

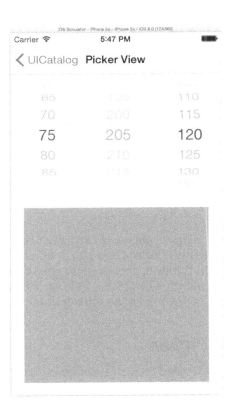

Figure 10-16. *Picker views*

Date Picker

Use the date picker when you want the user to choose a date, time, or duration. The date picker has four different interfaces, controlled by its `datePickerMode` property. This can be set to one of the four values listed in Table 10-4.

Table 10-4. *Date Picker Modes (UIDatePickerMode)*

Mode	Description
`.Time`	Choose a time of day.
`.Date`	Choose a calendar date.
`.DateAndTime`	Choose a date and time.
`.CountDownTimer`	Choose a duration (hours and minutes).

The picker's date property reports the value the user has selected. Setting it changes the date/time in the view. If you want to set the date and have the "wheels" spin to their new positions, call setDate(_:,animated:). The time portion of the date property is 0:00 when using the date-only interface. Similarly, the calendar day of the date property is meaningless when using the time-only or duration interface.

If you want to limit the range of values the user can choose from, set the minimumDate and/or maximumDate properties. For example, to force the user to choose a day in the future, set minimumDate to tomorrow.

You can also reduce the granularity of time choices with the minuteInterval property. When set to 1, the user can choose any time or duration in one-minute increments (2:30, 2:31, 2:32, and so on). Setting minuteInterval to 5 narrows the user's choices to five-minute intervals (2:30, 2:35, 2:40, 2:45, and so on).

Caution   The value of minuteInterval must divide evenly into 60 and can't be more than 30.

If you plan on using a date picker and your interface leaves the picker visible while time progresses, Apple recommends updating the picker in real time. For example, if your interface uses a duration picker and a start button, pressing the start button will probably cause some timer in your app to begin counting down. During that time, your app should periodically update the picker so it slowly (once a minute) changes as the time counts down to zero.

Anything Picker

What if you don't need to pick a date or a time? What if you need to pick an ice cream flavor, a model of car, or an arch nemesis? The UIPicker object is the catchall picker view. It looks and functions much like the date picker, except that you define the wheels and the content of each (shown on the right in Figure 10-16). This custom picker in UICatalog allows the user to "dial in" a color by selecting a value for the red, green, and blue color components, each on its own wheel.

A UIPicker uses a delegate and data source arrangement that's eerily similar to a table view (Chapter 5). A UIPicker needs a delegate object (UIPickerDelegate) and a data source object (UIPickerDataSource). The picker's data source determines the number of wheels (called *components*) and the number of choices (called *rows*) on each wheel. The delegate object provides the label for each choice. At a minimum, you must implement these UIPickerDataSource functions:

```
numberOfComponentsInPickerView(_:) -> Int
pickerView(_:,numberOfRowsInComponent:) -> Int
```

And you must implement *one* of these UIPickerDelegate functions:

```
pickerView(_:,titleForRow:,forComponent:) -> String
pickerView(_:,attributedTitleForRow:,forComponent:) -> NSAttributedString
pickerView(_:,viewForRow:,forComponent:,reusingView:) -> UIView
```

> **Tip**   Most often, a single object is both the delegate and the data source for a picker, in which case the division of functions between the two protocols doesn't matter.

The first data source function tells your picker how many wheels it has. The second function is then called once for each wheel; it returns the number of rows in that wheel.

Finally (much like the table view data source), a delegate function returns the label for each row in each wheel. You have three choices for which function you implement, depending on how sophisticated you want to be with the content of each row.

- Implement pickerView(_:,titleForRow:,forComponent:) to show plain-text labels. Your function returns a simple string value for each row. This is the most common.

- Implement pickerView(_:,attributedTitleForRow:,forComponent:) to display labels containing special fonts or styles. Your function returns an attributed string for each row, allowing each to have a mixture of fonts, sizes, and styles. This is the technique used in UICatalog. It cleverly creates an attributed string with a text color that matches the intensity of the color component for that row.

- Implement pickerView(_:,viewForRow:,forComponent:,reusingView:) to display anything you want in a row. Your function returns a UIView object, which is then used to draw that row.

The last function is the most like the table view's use of cell objects. For a picker, you can supply a different UIView object for each row or reuse a single UIView object over and over again. There's no row cell object cache like in the table view. Instead, the last UIView returned is passed to your delegate the next time pickerView(_:,viewForRow:,forComponent:,reusingView:) is called. If you're reusing a single UIView object, alter that view and return it again. If not (or the view parameter is nil), return a new view object.

If you want to control the width of each wheel or the height of the rows in a wheel, implement the optional pickerView(_:,widthForComponent:) or pickerView(_:,rowHeightForComponent:) function, respectively.

UIPickerView objects are not control objects; they are not subclasses of UIControl, and they don't send action messages. Instead, the picker's delegate gets a pickerView(_:,didSelectRow:, inComponent:) function call when the user changes one of the wheels.

Image Views

You've already used enough image views to know your way around them. There are, however, a couple of properties that I'd like to mention. The first is the contentMode. This property controls how the image (which may not be the same size as the view) gets arranged. The choices are listed in Table 10-5.

Table 10-5. View Content Mode

Mode (UIViewContentMode)	Description
.ScaleToFill	Stretches or squeezes the image to exactly fill the view. It may distort the image if the aspect ratio of the view is not the same as the image.
.ScaleAspectFit	Scales the image, without distorting it, so it just fits inside the view. Some parts of the view may not contain any image (think letterboxing).
.ScaleAspectFill	Scales the image, without distorting it, so it completely fills the view. Some parts of the image may get clipped.
.Center	Centers the image without scaling it.
.Top, .Bottom, .Left, or .Right	The middle of one edge of the image is aligned with the corresponding edge of the view. The image is not scaled. The image may not fill, or be clipped, in the other three directions.
.TopLeft, .TopRight, .BottomLeft, or .BottomRight	One corner of the image is aligned with the same corner of the view. The image is not scaled. The image may not fill the entire view or will be clipped if it overfills it.

> **Note**   The contentMode property is actually defined in the UIView class, but it's particularly germane to UIImageView.

UIImageView also has a quirky talent: it can show a sequence of images either quickly (like a flipbook or a really short movie) or slowly (like a slideshow), as shown in Figure 10-17. Put the images you want to display into an array and use that to set the animationImages property. Set the animationDuration and, optionally, the animationRepeatCount to control the speed of each frame and how many times the entire sequence plays. (Set animationRepeatCount to 0 to play forever.)

Figure 10-17. Image view slideshow

Once set up, call the view's `startAnimation()` function to begin the show, and call `stopAnimation()` to stop it again. Code that demonstrates this is in the `configureImageView()` function that you'll find in the `ImageViewController.swift` file.

Grouped Tables

Chapter 5 mentioned that you can create grouped table views, like those used in the Settings app. I didn't, however, actually show you how to do that. You already have all of the basics, but if you want a concrete example, look no further than the UICatalog project. Many of the sample views (activity indicators, buttons, text fields, and segmented controls) are presented in a group table view. Each group is a single example.

The `Main.storyboard` file in UICatalog uses the static table cell method I mentioned in Chapter 5. If you look at the table view for the Text Fields Scene, as shown in Figure 10-18, you'll see that all of the cells and their groups have been designed right in Interface Builder.

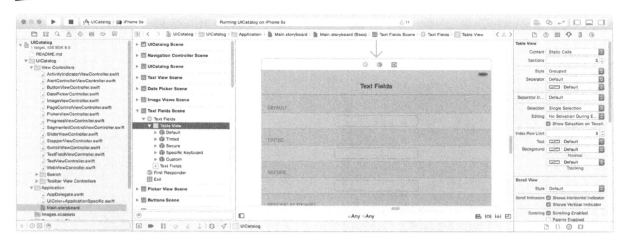

Figure 10-18. Statically designed table with groups

It's also possible to build a grouped table programmatically. Your table delegate simply needs to provide the group information, much the way it provides the row count and cells. Here are the delegate functions you'll need to write:

```
numberOfSectionsInTableView(_:) -> Int
tableView(_:,titleForHeaderInSection:) -> String
tableView(_:,numberOfRowsInSection:) -> Int
```

The View You Never See

That wraps up most of the important view objects in iOS. I'll talk about toolbars a little in Chapter 12 and a lot more about UIView in Chapter 11. But I want to mention a special view—one that's used a lot but you never see.

It's the UIScollView class. A scroll view adds the dynamics of scrolling to your interface. You never see the scroll view; you see its effects. A scroll view works by presenting a larger view inside a smaller view. The effect is like having a window into that larger view. When you drag inside the window, you are "sliding" the view behind it around so you can see different portions of it, as illustrated in Figure 10-19.

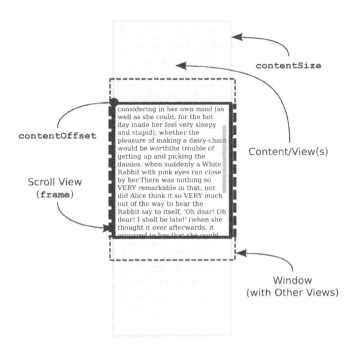

Figure 10-19. Conceptual arrangement a scroll view

It's easiest to think about a scroll view as being two views in one. For most view objects, the size of its content (called its *bounds*) and the size it occupies in your interface (called its *frame*) are the same. So, a view, say a button, that's 30 by 100 pixels will occupy a region of 30 by 100 pixels in your interface.

A scroll view breaks this relationship. A scroll view has a special contentSize property that's divorced from its frame size. Its frame becomes the "window" that appears in your interface. The contentSize defines the logical size of the view, only a portion of which is visible through the window.

The contentOffset property determines exactly what portion is visible. This property is the point in the content area that appears at the upper-left corner of the frame—the portion visible to the user. contentOffset is initially 0,0. This places the upper-left corner of the content at the upper-left corner of the frame. As the contentOffset moves down, the content appears to scroll up, keeping the contentOffset point at the upper-left corner of the frame.

Table views, web views, and text views all provide scrolling and are all subclasses of UIScrollView. You can subclass UIScrollView yourself to create a custom view that supports scrolling, or you can use a UIScrollView object on its own by simply populating its content view with whatever subviews you like. You can even have a scroll view inside another scroll view; it's weird, but there are notes in the *Scroll View Programming Guide for iOS* on how to do it.

A great place to get started with scroll views is the PhotoScroller example project. (As of this writing, this project is still in Objective-C.) Search Xcode's Documentation and API Reference for the PhotoScroller sample code project and click the Open Project button. The PhotoScroller project defines a subclass of `UIScrollView` used to display, pan, and zoom an image. This project demonstrates two of scroll view's three major talents.

- Scrolling a larger content view around inside a smaller view
- Pinching and zooming the content view
- Scrolling by "page"

The first is its basic function. It's for this ability that scroll views are most often used, which includes table views, web views, and text views. To use a scroll view in this fashion, you don't have to subclass it or use a delegate. Simply populate and size its content view with the views you want to display, and the scroll view will let the user drag it around.

The scroll view's second talent is pinching and zooming its content view, so it not only scrolls it but magnifies and shrinks it as well, as shown in Figure 10-20. This feature requires the use of a scroll view delegate (`UIScrollViewDelegate`) object. In the PhotoScroll project, the custom `ImageScrollView` is a `UIScrollView` subclass that's also its own delegate—an arrangement that's perfectly legitimate, if a little unusual. `UIScrollView` processes the touch events and handles the most of the panning and zooming details for you.

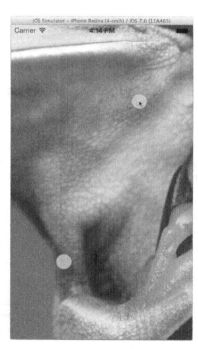

Figure 10-20. PhotoScroller app

You can also cause the view to scroll programmatically by setting its contentOffset property to any point in the content view you want. If you want to make the view animate its journey to the new position, call the setContentOffset(_:,animate:) function.

SCROLL VIEWS AND THE KEYBOARD

Scroll views can contain text fields—usually indirectly by placing a text field in a table view, which you now know is a scroll view. When the keyboard appears, it can cover up the very text field the user wants to edit. The solution is to cause the scroll view to scroll up so the text field is visible above the keyboard.

To do that, your controller will need to observe keyboard notifications (such as UIKeyboardDidShowNotification). These notifications contain the coordinates of the virtual keyboard on the screen. You use this information to determine whether the keyboard is covering your text field. If it is, use the scroll view's setContentOffset(_:,animate:) function to cause the text field to scroll to a position above the virtual keyboard.

The mechanics of this is described in the *Text, Web, and Editing Programming Guide for iOS*, which you'll find in Xcode's documentation. Look for the aptly named section "Moving Content That Is Located Under the Keyboard" in the "Managing the Keyboard" chapter.

The PhotoScroller project also demonstrates an advanced technique called *tiling*. In the beginning of Chapter 5, I explained that an iOS device doesn't have enough memory or CPU power to create thousands of individual row objects for a table. Instead, it draws just the portion of the table that is visible to the user, as the user scrolls through the list.

Any exceptionally large content view may fall into the same category. The PhotoScroller project demonstrates how to dynamically prepare only those view objects that are currently visible through the scroll view's "window." The table view—which, as you remember, is based on UIScrollView— already does this, preparing the view objects only for those rows that are visible in the table.

A much less common use of scroll views is to view content in "pages." This is enabled by setting the pagingEnabled property to true. When you do that, the scroll view forces the content view (technically, its contentOffset property) to move in discrete distances, exact multiples of its frame size. Conceptually, it divides your content view into a grid (the exact size of the window), and any scrolling eventually settles on one segment. There's a PageControl sample project that demonstrates this feature.

> **Note**   The PhotoScroller project lets you swipe between images, but it's not using UIScrollView's paging feature. Instead, it uses a UIPageViewController. You'll use UIPageViewController to create a similar interface in Chapter 12.

Advanced use of scroll views is not for the faint of heart. This can be really complex stuff, but it's the stuff of really cool apps. The now-famous "drag to update" gesture that has become the mainstay of iOS apps is all done with scroll views and scroll view delegates. If you need this feature in a table view, most of the work is already done for you; create a `UIRefreshControl` object and connect it to the table view controller's `refreshControl` property. Now the user can drag down to update the table. To dive into the power of scroll views, start with the *Scroll View Programming Guide for iOS*.

Alert Controllers

Alert controllers are the odd duck in the UICatalog project. They're out of place because they aren't view objects; they're view controllers. You have an exciting chapter on view controllers coming up (Chapter 12), so I really should defer alert controllers until then.

But, I won't. The reason is that alert controllers—while they are view controllers—are so specialized that you typically don't use, present, or adapt them the way you would other view controllers. So, while you have the UICatalog project running, let's explore how you use it right now.

An alert controller suspends the current interface and presents a choice, typically a button or two, that the user must tap to proceed. You can see examples in Figures 10-21 and 10-22. The user's choice executes a block of code, which you provide, and the controller is dismissed. It's that simple.

 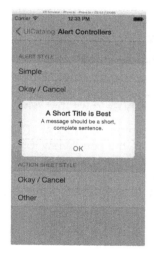  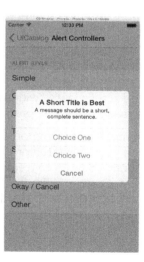

Figure 10-21. Alert examples

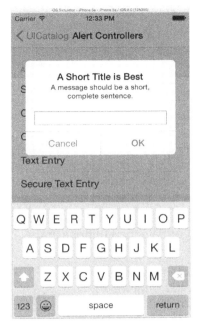
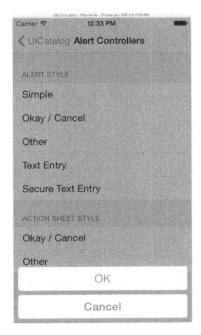
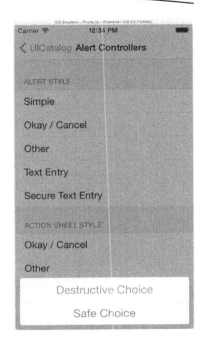

Figure 10-22. Alert and action sheet examples

UIAlertController is new in iOS 8 and replaces the UIAlertView and UIActionSheet classes, both now deprecated. This new class greatly simplifies, and unifies, the presentation of alerts and action sheets.

Note   You might encounter various deprecated classes, properties, or methods. APIs evolve over time. When better, more modern features are introduced, these often replace older classes and functions. These older interfaces may be *deprecated*, which means that Apple now discourages their use in new development, and Apple may someday eliminate them entirely—at which time any apps you have that still use them will stop running, or at least compiling. The Swift language was introduced alongside iOS 8, and there are no Swift APIs for deprecated functions. In other words, you can't write Swift code that uses an obsolete class or method from iOS 7 or earlier. So, for a brief period of iOS history, Swift programmers don't have to worry about deprecated features because, until iOS 9 comes out, there are none.

Using an alert controller is easy, and you've already done it several times in this book. The steps are as follows:

1. Create a `UIAlertController` object, choosing a preferred style and optionally assigning it a title and message.

2. Create one or more `UIAlertAction` objects and add them to the controller.

3. Optionally, set any special properties of the controller or add text fields.

4. Present the controller.

The preferred style (`UIAlertControllerStyle`) determines how you would like the alert presented. You choices are `.Alert` or `.ActionSheet`. It's a "preferred" style because, as you'll see in Chapter 12, a presentation controller may decide to present it in a different way—but I'm getting ahead of myself.

The `.Alert` style (on a compact device) appears as a floating window, as shown in Figure 10-21 and on the left in Figure 10-22. The `.ActionSheet` style appears as a set of detached buttons at the bottom of the interface, shown on the middle and right of Figure 10-22.

▪ Use an alert when you need to get the user's attention ("Something went horribly wrong!"), you need a confirmation to continue ("Are you sure you want me to delete all of your pictures?"), or you need to gather information ("What's the password?").

▪ Use an action sheet when offering a choice of possible actions ("Follow Obi Wan" or "Join the Dark Side").

The `title` and `message` can be anything you want, and either can be omitted, but they should be short and to the point. A message is presented only in an alert and is ignored by action sheets.

Tip As a rule, try to avoid alerts and action sheets. An interface that doesn't need them is almost always easier to use than one that does. They're great in a pinch, but overuse of modal interfaces—like alerts—is the hallmark of a poor user interface.

Once you've decided how it will appear, you need to add some actions. A `UIAlertAction` object represents one choice in the interface. Each action object defines the text of the button that will appear, the type of choice, and a block of code to be executed if the user taps that button. You did this in your MyStuff app in Chapter 7, so let's look at that code again.

```
let alert = UIAlertController(title: nil,
                           message: nil,
                     preferredStyle: .ActionSheet)
alert.addAction(UIAlertAction(title: "Take a Picture",
                          style: .Default,
                        handler: { (_) in
                            self.presentImagePicker(.Camera)
                            }))
```

```
alert.addAction(UIAlertAction(title: "Choose a Photo",
                              style: .Default,
                              handler: { (_) in
                                  self.presentImagePicker(.PhotoLibrary)
                              }))
alert.addAction(UIAlertAction(title: "Cancel",
                              style: .Cancel,
                              handler: nil))
presentViewController(alert, animated: true, completion: nil)
```

This code follows the formula to the letter. It creates a UIAlertController object. The action sheet has no title because the choices are self-explanatory. It creates three actions buttons: Take a Picture, Choose a Photo, and Cancel. It then presents the view controller.

Each action has a style. Your choices are .Default, .Destructive, and .Cancel. The default style presents a normal button. The destructive style presents an angry red button that should be used only for choices with negative consequences.

The cancel style is special and should be assigned to the single action that does nothing (if there is one). A cancel action can have a handler block, but it's not required if there's nothing to do. In some circumstances (again, you'll get to this in Chapter 12), the alert or action may be presented in a different form. For example, it could be presented in a popover on an iPad or similar device. In cases like that, the cancel button may be omitted because tapping outside a popover is an implied cancel.

Finally, there are a couple of special options you can set on the alert controller before presenting it. Most notably, an alert can also present one or more text entry fields, as shown on the left in Figure 10-22. You add these by calling the addTextFieldWithConfigurationHandler(_:) function. The alert controller goes to the trouble of creating and inserting the text field, and then your configuration handler block is given the opportunity to make any additional tweaks that your app might need. Locate the showSecureTextEntryAlert(_:) function in the AlertControllerViewController.swift file. You'll see the following code:

```
let alertController = UIAlertController(title: title,
                                        message: message,
                                        preferredStyle: .Alert)
alertController.addTextFieldWithConfigurationHandler { textField in
    textField.secureTextEntry = true
    }
```

After creating the alert controller, it requests the addition of a text field. After the field is added, the configuration handler block sets its secureTextEntry property, making it suitable for a password or other sensitive text.

Summary

Your command of the "language" of iOS is growing. You started with the syntax and grammar of iOS, learning to create objects, connect them, and send messages. In this chapter, you expanded your vocabulary, acquiring an impressive number of view and control objects you can add and customize. You also saw how grouped tables are made and got a glimpse of the magic behind scrolling. In the process, you learned how to download sample code and unlock its secrets.

You can go a long way using premade view and control objects. But there are limits, and at some point you're going to want a view that no one has created yet. Creating your own views is the next step of your journey and the next chapter in this book.

Chapter 11

Draw Me a Picture

You have arrived at a critical point in your mastery of iOS development. You have a good deal of experience adding existing view objects to your app. You've had them display your data, you've connected them to your custom controller logic, and you've customized their look and feel. But you've still been limited to the view classes that Apple has written for you. There's no substitute for creating your own view object—an object that will draw things no one else has imagined.

OK, that's not entirely true. You have created custom view objects, but in both cases I neglected to explain how they worked. Instead, there was a little note attached that read "Ignore the view behind the curtain; all will be explained in Chapter 11." Welcome to Chapter 11! In this chapter, you will learn (more) about the following:

- Creating view subclasses
- View geometry
- How and when views are drawn
- Core Graphics
- Bézier paths
- Animation
- Gesture recognizers
- Off-screen drawing

This chapter is going to get a little technical, but I think you're ready.

Creating a Custom View Class

You create a custom view by subclassing either `UIView` or `UIControl`, depending on whether your intent is to create a display object or something that acts like a control, like a new kind of switch. In this chapter, you'll be subclassing `UIView` only.

> **Caution**   Do not subclass concrete view classes, such as UIButton or UISwitch, in an attempt to "fiddle" with how they function. That is a recipe for disaster. Their internal workings are not public and often change from one iOS release to the next, meaning your class might stop working in the near future. View classes designed to be subclassed, such as UIControl, are clearly documented, usually with a section in their documentation titled "Subclassing Notes."

To create your own view class, you need to understand three things.

- The view coordinate system
- User interface update events
- How to draw in a Core Graphics context

Let's start at the top—literally.

View Coordinates

The device's screen, windows, and views all have a graphics *coordinate system*. The coordinate system establishes the position and size of everything you see on the device: the screen, windows, views, images, and shapes. Every view object has its own coordinate system. The origin of a coordinate system is at its upper-left corner and has the coordinates (0,0), as shown in Figure 11-1.

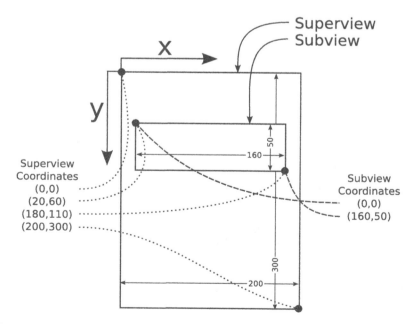

Figure 11-1. Graphics coordinate system

X coordinates increase to the right, and Y coordinates increase downward. The y-axis is upside-down from the Cartesian coordinate system you learned in school or maybe from reading geometry books in your spare time. For computer programs, this arrangement is more convenient; most content "flows" from the upper-left corner, so it's usually simpler to perform calculations from the upper-left corner than the lower-left corner.

> **Note**   If you've done any OS X programming, you'll notice a lot of similarities between iOS and OS X view objects. iOS, however, has no flipped coordinates—they're always flipped, from an OS X perspective.

There are four key types used to describe coordinates, positions, sizes, and areas in iOS, all described in Table 11-1.

Table 11-1. Coordinate Value Types

Type	Description
CGFloat	The fundamental scalar value. CGFloat is floating-point type used to express a single coordinate or distance.
CGPoint	A pair of CGFloat values that specify a point (x,y) in a coordinate system.
CGSize	A pair of CGFloat values that describe the dimensions (width,height) of something.
CGRect	The combination of a point (CGPoint) and a size (CGSize) that, together, describe a rectangular area.

Frame and Bounds

View objects have two rectangle (CGRect) properties: bounds and frame. The bounds property describes the coordinate system of the object. All of the view's graphic content, which includes any subviews, uses this coordinate system. The really important thing to understand is that all drawing of a view's content is performed by that view, and it's done using the view's coordinate system—often referred to as its *local coordinates*.

Moving the view around (in its superview) does not change the view's coordinate system. All of the graphics within the view remain the same, relative to the origin (upper-left corner) of that view object. In Figure 11-1, the subview is 160 points wide by 50 points high. Its bounds rectangle is, therefore, ((0,0),(160,50)); it has an origin (x,y) of (0,0) and a size (width,height) of (160,50). When the subview draws itself, it draws within the confines of that rectangle.

The frame property describes the view in the coordinates of its superview. In other words, the frame is the location of a subview in another view—often called its *superview coordinates*. In Figure 11-1, the origin of the subview is (20,60). The size of the view is (160,50), so its frame is ((20,60),(160,50)). If the view were moved down 10 points, its frame would become ((20,70),(160,50)). Everything drawn by the view would move down 10 points, but it wouldn't change the bounds of the view or the relative coordinates of what's drawn inside the view.

The size of the bounds and `frame` are linked. Changing the size of the `frame` changes the size of its bounds, and vice versa. If the `frame` of the subview in Figure 11-1 was 60 points narrower, its frame would become `((20,60),(100,50))`. This change would alter its bounds so it was now `((0,0),(100,50))`. Similarly, if the bounds were changed from `((0,0),(160,50))` to `((0,0),(100,40))`, the `frame` would automatically change to `((20,60),(100,40))`.

Note   There are a few exceptions to the "size of the frame always equals the size of the bounds" rule. You've already met one of those exceptions: the scroll view. The size of a scroll view's content (bounds) is controlled by its `contentSize` property that is independent of its frame size, the portion that appears on the screen. Other exceptions occur when transforms are applied, which I'll talk about later.

UIView also provides a synthetic `center` property. This property returns the center point of the view's `frame` rectangle. Technically, `center` is always equal to (`frame.midX`, `frame.midY`). If you change the `center` property, the view's `frame` will be moved so it is centered over that point. The `center` property makes it easy to both move and center subviews, without resizing them. You'll use this feature later in the chapter.

Converting Between Coordinate Systems

It will probably take you a while—it took me a long time—to wrap your head around the different coordinate systems and learn when to use bounds, when to use `frame`, and when to translate between them. Here are the quick-and-dirty rules to remember:

- The bounds are a view's *inner coordinates*: the coordinates of everything inside that view.

- The frame is a view's *outer coordinates*: the position of that view in its superview.

Should you need them, there are a number of functions that translate between the coordinate systems of views. The four most common are the UIView functions listed in Table 11-2. As an example, let's say you have the coordinates of the lower-right corner of the subview in Figure 11-1 in its local coordinates, (160,50). If you want to know the coordinate of that same point in the superview's coordinate system, call the function `superview.convertPoint(CGPoint(160,50), fromView: subview)`. That statement will return the point (180,110), which is the same point but in the superview's coordinate system.

Table 11-2. Coordinate Translation Functions in UIView

UIView function	Description
convertPoint(_:, toView:)	Converts a point in the view's local coordinate system to the same point in the local coordinates of another view
convertPoint(_:, fromView:)	Converts a point in another view's coordinates into this view's local coordinate system
convertRect(_:, toView:)	Converts a rectangle in the view's local coordinate system to the same rectangle in the local coordinates of another view
convertRect(_: fromView:)	Converts a point in another view's coordinates into this view's local coordinate system

Also, all of the event-related classes that deliver coordinates report them in the coordinate system of a specific view. For example, the UITouch class doesn't have a location property. Instead, it has a locationInView(_:) function that translates the touch point into the local coordinates of the view you're working with.

When Views Are Drawn

In Chapter 4, you learned that iOS apps are event-driven programs. Refreshing the user interface (programmer speak for drawing stuff on the screen) is also triggered by the event loop. When a view has something to draw, it doesn't just draw it. Instead, it remembers what it wants to draw, and then it requests a draw event message. When your app's event loop decides that it's time to update the display, it sends user interface update messages to all the views that need to be redrawn. A view's drawing life cycle, therefore, repeats this pattern:

1. Change the data to draw.

2. Call your view object's setNeedsDisplay() function. This marks the view as needing to be redrawn.

3. When the event loop is ready to update the display, iOS will call your view's drawRect(_:) function.

You rarely need to call another view's setNeedsDisplay() function. Most views send themselves that message whenever they change in a way that would require them to redraw themselves. For example, when you set the text property of a UILabel object, the label object calls its setNeedsDisplay() so the new label will appear. Similarly, a view automatically gets a setNeedsDisplay() call if it's changed in a way that would require it to redraw itself, such as adding it to a new superview.

This doesn't mean that every change to a view will trigger another drawRect(_:) call. When a view draws itself, the resulting image is saved, or *cached*, by iOS—like taking a snapshot. Changes that don't affect that image, such as moving the view around the screen (without resizing it), won't result in another drawRect(_:) call; iOS simply reuses the snapshot of the view it already has.

> **Note**   The `rect` parameter passed to your `drawRect(rect:)` function is the portion of your view that needs to be redrawn. Most of the time, it's the same as `bounds`, which means you need to redraw everything. In rare cases, it can be a smaller portion. Most `drawRect(rect:)` functions don't pay much attention to it and simply draw their entire view. It never hurts to draw more than what's required; just don't draw less than what's needed. If your drawing code is really complicated and time-consuming, you might try to save time by updating only the area in the `rect` parameter.

Now you know when and why views draw themselves, so you just need to know how.

Drawing a View

When your view object receives a `drawRect(_:)` call, it must draw itself. In simple terms, iOS prepares a "canvas" that your view object must then "paint." The resulting masterpiece is then used by iOS to represent your view on the screen—until it needs to be drawn again.

Your "canvas" is a *Core Graphics context*, also called your *current context* or just *context* for short. It isn't an object, per se. It's a drawing environment that is prepared before your object's `drawRect(_:)` function is called. While your `drawRect(_:)` function is executing, your code can use any of the Core Graphics drawing routines to "paint" into the prepared context. The context is valid until your `drawRect(_:)` function returns, and then it goes away.

> **Caution**   Your view's Core Graphics context exists only when your `drawRect(_:)` function is invoked by iOS. Because of this, you should never call your view's `drawRect(_:)` function, and you should never use any of the Core Graphics drawing functions outside of your `drawRect(_:)` function. (The exception is "off-screen" drawing, which I'll describe toward the end of this chapter).

For most of the object-oriented drawing functions, the current context is implied. That is, you call a paint function (`myShape.fill()`), and the function draws into the current context. If you use any of the C drawing functions, you'll need to get the current context reference and pass that as the call's first parameter, like this:

```
let currentContext = UIGraphicsGetCurrentContext()
CGContextSetAlpha(currentContext, 0.5)
```

A lot of the details of drawing are implied by the state of the current context. The context *state* consists of all the settings and properties that will be used for drawing in that context. This includes things such as the color used to fill shapes, the color of lines, the width of lines, the blend mode, the clipping regions, and so on.

Rather than specify all of these variables for every action, like drawing a line, you set up the state for each property first. Let's say you want to draw a shape (myShape), filling it with the red color and drawing the outline of the shape with the color black.

```
redColor.setFill()
blackColor.setStroke()
myShape.fill()
myShape.stroke()
```

The setFill() and setStroke() functions set the current fill and stroke colors of the context. The fill() function uses the context's current fill color, and stroke() uses the current stroke color. This arrangement makes it efficient to draw multiple shapes or effects using the same, or similar, parameters.

Now the only question remaining is what tools you have to draw with. Your fundamental painting tools are the following:

- Simple fill and stroke
- Bézier path (fill and stroke)
- Images

That doesn't sound like a lot, but taken together, they are remarkably flexible. Let's start with the simplest: the fill functions.

Fill and Stroke Functions

The Core Graphics framework includes a handful of functions that fill a region of the context with a color. The two principal functions are CGContextFillRect and CGContextFillEllipseInRect. The former fills a rectangle with the current fill color. The latter fills an oval that just fits inside the given rectangle (which will be a circle if the rectangle is a square).

CGContextFillRect is often used to fill in the background of the entire view before drawing its details. It's not uncommon for a drawRect(_:) function to begin something like this:

```
override func drawRect(rect: CGRect) {
    let context = UIGraphicsGetCurrentContext()
    backgroundColor.set()
    CGContextFillRect(context,rect)
```

This code starts by getting the current context (which you'll need for the CGContextFillRect call). It then obtains the background color for this view (backgroundColor) and makes that color the current fill color. It then fills the portion of the view that needs drawing (rect) with that color. Everything drawn after that will draw over a background painted with backgroundColor.

> **Tip** Drawing in a Core Graphics context works much like painting on a real canvas. Whenever you draw something, you're drawing over what's been drawn before. So, just like a painting, you typically start by covering the entire surface with a neutral color—artists call this a *ground*. You then paint with different colors and shapes on top of that, until you've painted everything.

The functions CGContextStrokeRect and CGContextStrokeEllipseInRect perform a similar function, but instead of filling the area inside the rectangle or oval, it draws a line over the outline of the rectangle or oval, using the current line color, line width, and line joint style. *Stroke* is the term used to describe the act of drawing a line.

Bézier Paths

You'll notice that there are hardly any Core Graphics functions for drawing really simple things, like straight lines. Or what about the rounded rectangles you see everywhere in iOS, triangles, or any other shape, for that matter? Instead of giving you a bazillion different functions for drawing every shape, the iOS gods provide you an almost magical tool that will let you draw all of those things and more: the Bézier path.

A Bézier path, named after the French engineer Pierre Bézier, can represent any combination of straight or curved lines, as shown in Figure 11-2. It can be as simple as a square or as complex as the coastline of Canada. A Bézier path can be closed (circle, triangle, pie chart), or it can be open (a line, an arc, the letter *W*).

Figure 11-2. Bézier paths

You define a Bézier path by first creating a UIBezierPath object. You then construct the path by adding straight and curved line segments. When you're done, you can use the path object to draw into the context by painting its interior (filling), drawing its outline (stroking), or both. You can reuse a path as often as you like.

> **Tip** For common shapes, such as squares, rectangles, circles, ovals, rounded rectangles, and arcs, the UIBezierPath class provides convenience initializers that will create a Bézier path with that shape in a single statement.

To show you how easy it is to create paths, you'll write an app that draws Bézier paths in a view. But before you get to that, let's briefly talk about the last major source of view content.

Images

An image is a picture and doesn't need much explaining. You've been using image (UIImage) objects since Chapter 2. Up until now, you've been assigning them to UIImageView objects (and other controls) that drew the image for you. But UIImage objects are easy to draw into the context of your own view too. The two most commonly used UIImage drawing functions are drawAtPoint(_:) and drawInRect(_:). The first draws an image into your context, at its original size, with its origin (upper-left corner) at the given coordinate. The second function draws the image into the given rectangle, scaling and stretching the image as necessary.

When I say an image is "drawn" into your context, I really mean it's copied. An image is a two-dimensional array of pixels, and the canvas of your context is a two-dimensional array of pixels. So really, "drawing" a picture amounts to little more than overwriting a portion of your view's pixels with the pixels in the image. The exceptions to this are images that have transparent pixels or if you're using atypical blend modes, both of which I'll touch on later.

I'll explain a lot about creating, converting, and drawing images in your custom view later in this chapter by revisiting an app you already wrote. But before I get to that, let's draw some Bézier paths.

Shapely

You're going to create an app that uses Bézier paths to draw simple shapes in a custom view. Through a few iterations of the app, you'll expand it to include movement and resizing gestures and learn about transforms and animation—along with a heap of UIView and Bézier path goodness. The design of the app is simple, as shown in Figure 11-3.

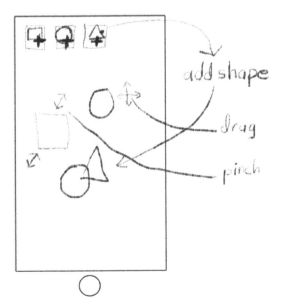

Figure 11-3. Shapely app design

The app will have a row of buttons that create new shapes. Shapes appear in the middle area where they can be moved around, resized, and reordered. Get started by creating a new project. In Xcode, do the following:

1. Create a new project based on the single-view app template.

2. Name the project Shapely.

3. Set the language to Swift.

4. Set the devices to Universal.

The next thing to do is to create your custom view class. You've done this several times already. Select the Shapely group in your project navigator, choose New File (from the File menu or by Control+right-clicking the group), and then do the following:

1. From the iOS group, choose the Swift class template.

2. Name the file ShapeView.

3. Add it to your project.

Creating Views Programmatically

In this app, you'll be creating your view objects programmatically, instead of using Interface Builder. In fact, you'll be creating just about everything programmatically. By the end of the chapter, you should be good at it.

When you create any object, it must be initialized. This is accomplished by using one of the class's *initializer functions*. Some classes, such as NSURL, provide a variety of initializers so you can create them in different ways: NSURL(string:), NSURL(scheme:, host:, path:), NSURL(string:, relativeToURL:), NSURL(fileURLWithPath:), and so on. Some of these initializers are called *convenience initializers*, for the obvious reason that they make object creation more convenient.

The UIView class has what is called a *designated initializer*. This initializer (UIView(frame:)) is the one you must use when constructing a subclass of UIView. Your subclass is free to define its own initializers, but it must call the designated initializer (via super.init(frame:)) so the UIView superclass gets set up correctly.

Note   The UIView class actually has two designated initializers. The other is used when creating an object defined in an Interface Builder file, which is described in Chapter 15. The designated initializer you're using here is for UIView objects created programmatically.

You're going to define a single initializer to create a new ShapeView object that will draw a specific shape (square, circle, and so on). The object's frame will be set to a predetermined placeholder frame, which you'll reposition later. So, you'll need a custom initializer function that tells the new object what kind of shape it's going to draw. Your view will draw its shape in a specific color, so you'll also need a property for its color. Start by editing the ShapeView.swift file. Change it so it looks like this:

```
import UIKit

enum ShapeSelector: Int {
    case Square = 1
    case Rectangle
    case Circle
    case Oval
    case Triangle
    case Star
}

class ShapeView: UIView {
}
```

The enum statement creates an enumeration that determines which shape the view will draw. An *enumeration* is a sequence of constant values assigned to names. You list the names, and the compiler assigns each a value. In this case, you've specified that the enumeration is compatible with the Int type, so all of the values assigned will have integer equivalents—you'll need that later. Often you don't care how the values are assigned, but for this app you want them to start at 1 (Square=1, Rectangle=2, Circle=3, and so on).

The next statement is the biggie; it declares a new class (ShapeView), which is a subclass of UIView. That's where all your work will go.

Start by adding some properties (new code in bold):

```
class ShapeView: UIView {
    let initialSize = CGSize(width: 100.0, height: 100.0)
    let alternateHeight: CGFloat = 100.0/2
    let strokeWidth = CGFloat(8.0)

    let shape: ShapeSelector
    var color: UIColor = UIColor.whiteColor()
```

The properties that begin with let are constants. They're immutable values that never change. You've defined constants for the initial dimensions of the view (initialSize, alternateHeight), the width of the line used to draw the shape (strokeWidth), and which shape to draw (shape). color is a variable property that stores the UIColor the shape will be drawn in. This permits you to later change the color of the shape. The default color is white.

You now have all the pieces you need to write your initializer function.

Initializing Your Object

Every class has at least one, and often several, initializer functions. Add a custom initializer that will construct a new ShapeView object for a given ShapeSelector.

```
init(shape: ShapeSelector) {
    self.shape = shape
    var frame = CGRect(origin: CGPointZero, size: initialSize)
    if shape == .Rectangle || shape == .Oval {
        frame.size.height = alternateHeight
    }
    super.init(frame: frame)
    opaque = false
    backgroundColor = nil
    clearsContextBeforeDrawing = true
}
```

This initializer function is called whenever you create a new ShapeView object from a ShapeSelector, like this: ShapeView(.Circle). The first statement sets the shape property to the value chosen by the caller.

Now at this point you might be saying "Just wait a second there, mister. The shape property is an immutable (let) value and can't be assigned!" And, you're almost correct. The shape property is immutable but only *after* the object is created. During the call to your object's initializer, there's a narrow window of opportunity to set up immutable properties, allowing you to determine their value for the lifetime of the object.

The next four lines construct an initial frame for the view. It will have an origin of (0.0,0.0) and will be 100.0 points wide by 100.0 points high, unless it's a rectangle or an oval, in which case it will be half as high.

The placeholder frame is then passed to the superclass's designated initializer by calling super.init(frame: frame). The superclass completes the process of constructing the object. When it returns, the object is now fully initialized, and you can start using it.

In fact, you can start using it before you return from your initializer. The next three lines change the default properties of the object (the property values that were just set up by super.init(frame:)). The most important is resetting the opaque property. If your view object will have transparent regions, you must declare that your view isn't opaque. The background property is set to nil because this view doesn't fill its background with a color. I'll explain the clearsContextBeforeDrawing property shortly.

> **Caution**   If your view leaves any portion of its image transparent, or even semitransparent, you *must* set the view's opaque property to false or it may not appear correctly on the screen.

Oddly, the compiler is now complaining that your class doesn't implement all of its required functions. As it turns out, there are a number of rules (explaining in Chapter 20) regarding what initializers you can, can't, and must implement. I won't go into the details here, but because you defined a custom initializer, there's now a required initializer that you must also define.

```
required init(coder decoder: NSCoder!) {
    shape = .Square
    super.init(coder: decoder)
}
```

This initializer is called whenever your object is constructed from a document or Interface Builder file. How that might happen is explained in Chapters 15 and 19. For now, just throw in this code, and the compiler will stop complaining.

The drawRect(_:) Function

I think it's time to write your drawRect(_:) function. This is the heart of any custom view class. Add this function to your ShapeView.swift file:

```
override func drawRect(rect: CGRect) {
    color.setStroke()
    path.stroke()
}
```

Whoa! That's it? Yes, that's all the code your class needs to draw its shape. It gets the Bézier path object from its path property. The Bézier path defines the outline of the shape this view will draw. You then set the color you want to draw with, and the stroke() function draws the outline of the shape. The details of how the line is drawn—its width, the shape of joints, and so on—are properties of the path object.

You'll also notice that you didn't have to first fill the context (as I explained in the "Fill and Stroke" section). That's because you set the view's clearsContextBeforeDrawing property. Set this to true, and iOS will prefill your context with (black) transparent pixels before it calls your drawRect(_:) function. For views that need to start with a transparent "canvas"—as this one does—why not let iOS do that work for you? If your view always fills its context with an image or color, set clearsContextBeforeDrawing to false; leaving it true will pointlessly fill the context twice, slowing down your app and wasting CPU resources.

Creating the Bézier Path

Clearly, the heavy lifting is creating that Bézier path object. Do that now. Add this computed property to your class:

```
var path: UIBezierPath {
    var rect = bounds
    rect.inset(dx: strokeWidth/2.0, dy: strokeWidth/2.0)
    var shapePath: UIBezierPath!
    switch shape {
        case .Square, .Rectangle:
```

```
            shapePath = UIBezierPath(rect: rect)
        default:
            // TODO: Add cases for remaining shapes
            shapePath = UIBezierPath()
    }
    shapePath.lineWidth = strokeWidth
    shapePath.lineJoinStyle = kCGLineJoinRound
    return shapePath
}
```

This code declares a read-only variable named path that bestows the object with a UIBezierPath property. code is a computed property. *Computed properties* don't store a value like the shape and color properties do. Instead, when you request the path property value, this block of code is executed. The code constructs a new UIBezierPath object that describes the shape this view draws (square, rectangle, circle, and so on), exactly fitting its current size (bounds).

> **Note** The path property provides code only to get the value, so you can't set the path property. While this makes the property immutable (it can't be set), it's still a var (variable) and not a let (constant) because the value it returns can change over the lifetime of the object.

The first two lines of code create a CGRect variable that describes the outer dimensions of the shape. The reason it is strokeWidth/2.0 pixels smaller than the bounds is explained in the "Avoiding Pixelitis: Coordinates versus Pixels" sidebar.

AVOIDING PIXELITIS POINTS VERSUS PIXELS

All coordinates in Core Graphics are mathematical points in space; they do not address individual pixels. This is an important concept to understand. Think of coordinates as infinitely thin lines between the pixels of your display or image. This has three ramifications.

- Points or coordinates *are not* pixels.
- Drawing occurs on and inside lines, not on or inside pixels.
- One point may not mean one pixel.

When you fill a shape, you're filling the pixels inside the infinitely thin lines that define that shape. In the following figure, a rectangle ((2,1),(5,2)) is filled with a dark color. A lower-resolution display will have one physical pixel per coordinate space, as shown on the left. On the right is a "retina" display, with four physical pixels per coordinate space.

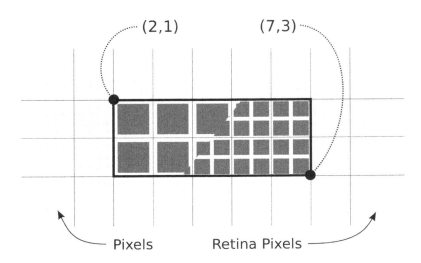

The rectangle defines a mathematically precise region, and the pixels that fall inside that region are filled with the color. This precision avoids a common programmer malady known as *pixelitis*: the anxiety of not knowing exactly what pixels will be affected by a particular drawing operation, common in many other graphic libraries.

This mathematical precision can have unanticipated side effects. One common artifact occurs when drawing a line with an odd width—"odd" meaning "not evenly divisible by 2." A line's stroke is centered over the mathematical line or curve. In the next figure, a horizontal line segment is drawn between two coordinates, with a stroke width of 1.0. The upper line in the next figure does not draw a solid line on a lower-resolution display because the stroke covers only half of the pixels on either side of the line. Core Graphics draws partial pixels using anti-aliasing, which means that the color of those pixels is adjusted using half the stroke's color value. On a 2.0 retina display, this doesn't occur because each pixel is half of a coordinate value.

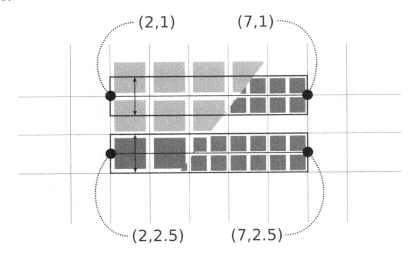

The lower line in the figure avoids the "half-pixel" problem by centering the line between two coordinates. Now the 1.0 width line exactly fills the space between coordinate boundaries, neatly filling the pixels and appearing to the user as a clean, solid line.

If pixel-prefect alignment is important to your app, you may need to consult the `contentScaleFactor` property of `UIView` or its trait collection. It discloses the number of physical screen pixels between two whole coordinate values. As of this writing, it can be one of three values: `1.0` for lower resolution displays, `2.0` for Retina displays, and `3.0` for Retina HD displays.

The next block of code declares a `UIBezierPath` variable and then switches on the `shape` constant to build the desired shape. For right now, the `case` statement only makes the paths for square and rectangular shapes, as shown in Figure 11-4. You'll fill in the other cases later.

Figure 11-4. *Unfinished -path function*

> **Tip**   If you start a `//`-style comment with `MARK:`, `TODO:`, or `FIXME:`, that comment will automatically appear in the file navigation menu at the top of the editing area, as shown in Figure 11-4. This is a really handy way to make a note about something you need to address later because it will appear prominently in your file's navigation menu until you remove it.

Sharp-eyed readers will notice that the code to create a square shape and a rectangular shape are the same. That's because the difference between these shapes is the aspect ratio of the view, and that was established in `init(shape:)` when the object was created. If you go back and look at `init(shape:)`, you'll see this code:

```
if shape == .Rectangle || shape == .Oval {
    frame.size.height = alternateHeight
}
```

When the view's frame was initialized, it was made half as high if the shape was a rectangle or oval. All other shape views begin life with a square frame.

Finally, the line width of the shape is set to strokeWidth, and the joint style is set to kCGLineJoinRound. This last property determines how a joint (the point where one line segment ends and the next begins) is drawn. Setting it to kCGLineJoinRound draws shapes with rounded "elbows."

Testing Squares

That's enough code to draw a square-shaped view, so let's hook this up to something and try it. The Shapely app creates new shapes when the user taps a button, so define a button to test it. The buttons get custom images, so start by adding those image resources to your project. Select the Images.xcassets asset catalog item in the navigator. Find the Learn iOS Development Projects ➤ Ch 11 ➤ Shapely (Resources) folder and drag all 12 of the image files (addcircle.png, addcircle@2x.png, addoval.png, addoval@2x.png, addrect.png, addrect@2x.png, addsquare.png, addsquare@2x.png, addstar.png, addstar@2x.png, addtriangle.png, and addtriangle@2x.png) into the asset catalog, as shown in Figure 11-5. There are also some app icons in the Shapely (Icons) folder, which you're free to drop into the AppIcon group.

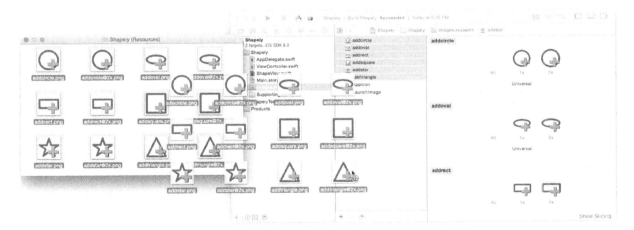

Figure 11-5. Adding button image resources

Select the Main.storyboard file. Bring up the object library (View ➤ Utilities ➤ Show Object Library) and drag a button into the upper-left corner of your interface, as shown in Figure 11-6.

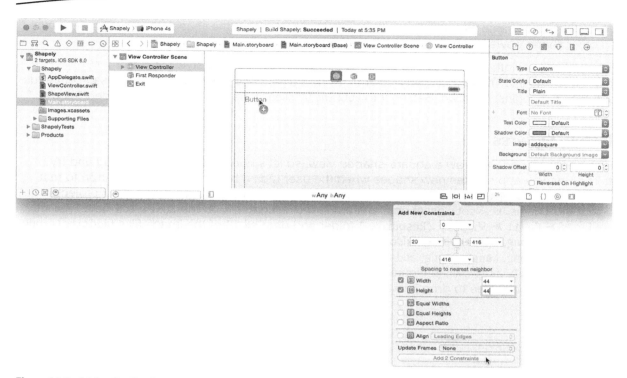

Figure 11-6. Adding the first button

Select the button and click the pin attributes control. Pin the height and width to 44 points, also shown in Figure 11-6. Choose the Add Missing Constraints in View Controller command, either from the layout issues control next to the pin constraints control or from the Editor menu.

Switch to the attributes inspector, select the root view object, and change its background property to Black Color. Select the new button again and make the following changes:

1. Change its type to Custom.

2. Erase its title (replacing *Button* with nothing).

3. Change its image to addsquare.png.

Now you're going to connect the button's action to a new Swift function, and you're going to use a really nifty Interface Builder trick to do it. Start by switching to the assistant view (View ➤ Assistant Editor ➤ Show Assistant Editor). The source for your view controller (ViewController.swift) will appear in the right-hand pane. If it doesn't, select the ViewController.swift file from the navigation ribbon immediately above the right-hand editor pane. In the ViewController.swift file (right-hand editing pane), add a new action.

```
@IBAction func addShape(sender: AnyObject!) {
    if let button = sender as? UIButton {
        let shapeView = ShapeView(shape: .Square)
        view.addSubview(shapeView)
```

```
        var shapeFrame = shapeView.frame
        let safeRect = CGRectInset(view.bounds, shapeFrame.width, ↵
                                              shapeFrame.height)
        var randomCenter = safeRect.origin
        randomCenter.x += CGFloat(arc4random_uniform(UInt32(safeRect.width)))
        randomCenter.y += CGFloat(arc4random_uniform(UInt32(safeRect.height)))
        shapeView.center = randomCenter
}
```

In brief, the first two lines of code create a new `ShapeView` object that draws a square. The new view object is then added to the root `view` so it will appear in your interface. If you did nothing else, a white square would be drawn at the upper-left corner of the display. The rest of the code simply picks a random location and moves the new view to that location. `safeRect` is inset by the height and width of the new view, so the randomly choosen position inside `safeRect` ensures the new view will be safely inside the bounds of the view.

Up until this point in this book, you've been creating and adding view objects using Interface Builder. This code demonstrates how you do it programmatically. Anything you add to a view using Interface Builder can be created and added programmatically, and you can create things in code that you can't create in Interface Builder.

Note The `addSubview(_:)` function adds a view to another view. The view being added becomes a subview of the other view (now its superview). The subview will appear at the coordinates of its frame, in the superview's local coordinate system. You can add a view to only one superview at a time; a view can't appear in two superviews simultaneously. To remove a view, call the view's `removeFromSuperview()` function.

Now for that Interface Builder trick. Notice that a little connection socket has appeared in the margin next to your addShape(_:) function. This acts exactly like the connectors in the connections inspector. Connect the button to the action by dragging the connection socket next to the addShape(_:) function into the new button, as shown in Figure 11-7.

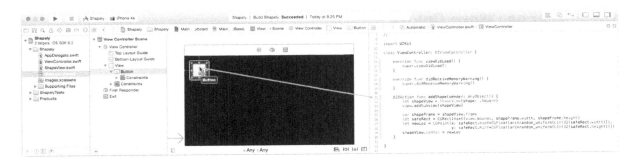

Figure 11-7. Connecting the first button

The assistant editor allows you to write the Swift code for properties and actions in your view controller and then connect them directly to the view objects in your interface, without switching files or windows. It's a great time-saver.

Fire up an iPad simulator and run your app, as shown in Figure 11-8. Tap the button a few times to create some shape view objects, as shown on the right in Figure 11-8.

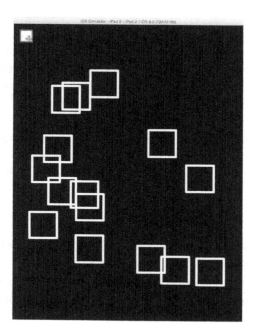

Figure 11-8. Working square shape views

So far, you've designed a custom UIView object that draws a shape using a Bézier path. You've created an action that creates new view objects and adds them to a view, programmatically. This is a great start, but you still want to draw different shapes, in different colors, so expand the app to do that.

More Shapes, More Colors

Back in Xcode, stop the app and switch to the Main.storyboard file again. Your app will draw six shapes, so create five more buttons. I did this by holding down the Option key and dragging out copies of the first UIButton object, as shown in Figure 11-9. You could, alternatively, copy and paste the first button. If you're a masochist, you could drag in new button objects from the library and individually change them to match the first one. I'll leave those decisions to you.

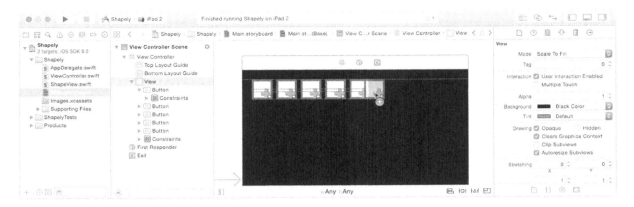

Figure 11-9. Duplicating the first button

Just as you did in DrumDub, you'll use the tag property of the button to identify the shape it will create. Since you duplicated the first button, all of the buttons are connected to the same addShape(_:) function in ViewController. (If not, connect them now.) Working from left to right, use the attributes inspector to set the tag and image properties of the buttons using Table 11-3.

Table 11-3. New Shape Button Properties

Tag	Image
1	addsquare.png
2	addrect.png
3	addcircle.png
4	addoval.png
5	addtriangle.png
6	addstar.png

You'll notice that the tag values, cleverly, match up with the enum constants you defined in ShapeView.swift. You'll change the first line of addShape(_:) (in ViewController.swift) to use the button's tag value instead of the .Square constant, so each button will create a different shape.

Of course, the path property in ShapeView still knows only how to create shapes for squares and rectangles; you'll correct that shortly. But before you leave ViewConroller.swift, modify your addShape(_:) function to choose the new shape based on the tag and give it a random color—just to make it pretty. Find your addShape(_:) function and make the following changes (in bold):

```
let colors = [ UIColor.redColor(), UIColor.greenColor(),
               UIColor.blueColor(), UIColor.yellowColor(),
               UIColor.purpleColor(), UIColor.orangeColor(),
               UIColor.grayColor(), UIColor.whiteColor() ]
```

```
@IBAction func addShape(sender: AnyObject!) {
    if let button = sender as? UIButton {
        if let shapeSelector = ShapeSelector(rawValue: button.tag) {
            let shapeView = ShapeView(shape: shapeSelector)
            shapeView.color = ↵
                        colors[Int(arc4random_uniform(UInt32(colors.count)))]
            view.addSubview(shapeView)
            ...
        }
    }
```

The modified function gets the tag of the button and uses the enumerator's built-in `fromRaw()` function to convert the integer into a `ShapeSelector` value, which is then passed to the `ShapeView` initializer. Now the shape will be determined by which button was tapped. A random color is then selected and assigned to the new shape.

> **Note**   The enumerator's `init(rawValue:)` initializer returns an optional. In other words, it won't return any value at all if there's no enumeration value that corresponds to the given integer value. So if the `tag` value is invalid (0 or 42, for example), the `if` statement fails and no code executes. Optionals are explained in Chapter 20.

To draw those shapes, your `ShapeView` object still needs some work. Switch to the `ShapeView.swift` file, find the `path` property's getter function, and finish it with the code shown in bold in Listing 11-1. Oh, and you might as well remove the `default:` case from the unfinished version; you don't need that anymore because the `switch` statement now covers all possible cases.

Listing 11-1. Finished Path Property Getter Function

```
var path: UIBezierPath {
    var rect = bounds
    rect.inset(dx: strokeWidth/2.0, dy: strokeWidth/2.0)

    var shapePath: UIBezierPath!
    switch shape {
        case .Square, .Rectangle:
            shapePath = UIBezierPath(rect: rect)
        case .Circle, .Oval:
            shapePath = UIBezierPath(ovalInRect: rect)
        case .Triangle:
            shapePath = UIBezierPath()
            shapePath.moveToPoint(CGPoint(x: rect.midX, y: rect.minY))
            shapePath.addLineToPoint(CGPoint(x: rect.maxX, y: rect.maxY))
            shapePath.addLineToPoint(CGPoint(x: rect.minX, y: rect.maxY))
            shapePath.closePath()
        case .Star:
            shapePath = UIBezierPath()
            let armRotation = CGFloat(M_PI)*2.0/5.0
            var angle = armRotation
            let distance = rect.width*0.38
```

```
            var point = CGPoint(x: rect.midX, y: rect.minY)
            shapePath.moveToPoint(point)
            for _ in 0..<5 {
                point.x += CGFloat(cos(Double(angle)))*distance
                point.y += CGFloat(sin(Double(angle)))*distance
                shapePath.addLineToPoint(point)
                angle -= armRotation
                point.x += CGFloat(cos(Double(angle)))*distance
                point.y += CGFloat(sin(Double(angle)))*distance
                shapePath.addLineToPoint(point)
                angle += armRotation*2
            }
            shapePath.closePath()
    }
    shapePath.lineWidth = strokeWidth
    shapePath.lineJoinStyle = kCGLineJoinRound
    return shapePath
}
```

The .Circle and .Oval cases use another UIBezierPath convenience initializer to create a finished path object that traces an ellipse that fits exactly inside the given rectangle.

The .Triangle case is where things get interesting. It shows a Bézier path being created, one line segment at a time. You begin a Bézier path by calling moveToPoint(_:) to establish the first point in the shape. After that, you add line segments by making a series of addLineToPoint(_:) calls. Each call adds one edge to the shape, just like playing "connect the dots." The last edge is created using the closePath() function, which does two things: it connects the last point to the first point and makes this a closed path—one that describes a solid shape.

> **Note** This app creates Bézier paths only with straight lines, but you can mix in calls to addArcWithCenter (_:,radius:,startAngle:,endAngle:,clockwise:), addCurveToPoint(_:,controlPoint1:, controlPoint2:), and addQuadCurveToPoint(_:,controlPoint:), in any combination, to add curved segments to the path too.

The .Star creates an even more complex shape. If you're curious about the details, read the comments in the finished Shapely project code that you'll find in the Learn iOS Development Projects ➤ Ch 11 ➤ Shapely folder. In brief, the code creates a path that starts at the top-center of the view (the top point of the star), adds a line that angles down to the interior point of the star, and then adds another (horizontal) line back out to the right-hand point of the star. It then rotates 72° and repeats these steps, four more times, to create a five-pointed star.

> **Tip** Trigonometric math functions perform their calculations in *radians*. If your trig skills are a little rusty, angles in radians are expressed as fractions of the constant π, which is equal to 180°. The iOS math library includes constants for π (M_PI or 180°), π/2 (M_PI_2 or 90°), and π/4 (M_PI_4 or 45°), as well as other commonly used constants (*e*, the square root of 2, and so on).

Run your app again (see Figure 11-10) and make a bunch of shapes!

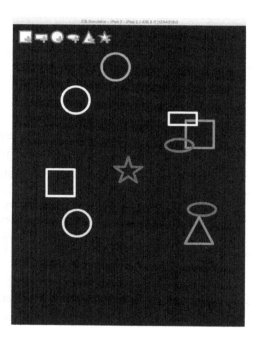

Figure 11-10. Multicolor shapes

Transforms

Next up on your app's feature list is dragging and resizing shapes. To implement that, you're going to revisit gesture recognizers and learn something completely new. Let's start with the gesture recognizer.

Like view objects, you can create, configure, and connect gesture recognizers programmatically. The concrete gesture recognizer classes supplied by iOS (tap, pinch, rotate, swipe, pan, and long-press) have all the logic needed to recognize these common gestures. All you have to do is create one, do a little configuration, and hook them up.

Return to your addShape(_:) function in ViewController.swift. At the end of the function, add this code:

```
let pan = UIPanGestureRecognizer(target: self, action: "moveShape:")
pan.maximumNumberOfTouches = 1
shapeView.addGestureRecognizer(pan)
```

The first two statements create a new pan (drag) gesture recognizer object. This recognizer will send its action message ("moveShape:") to your ViewController object (self). The maximumNumberOfTouches property is set to 1. This configures the object to recognize only single-finger drag gestures; it will ignore any two- or three-finger drags that it witnesses. Finally, the recognizer object is attached to the shape view that was just created.

> **Note**   This code is equivalent to going into an Interface Builder file, dragging a new Pan Gesture Recognizer into a ShapeView object, selecting it, changing its Maximum Touches to 1, and then connecting the recognizer to the moveShape(_:) action of the controller. And when I say "equivalent," I mean "identical to."

Now all you need is a moveShape(_:) function. In your ViewController class, add it now.

```
func moveShape(gesture: UIPanGestureRecognizer) {
    if let shapeView = gesture.view as? ShapeView {
        let dragDelta = gesture.translationInView(shapeView.superview)
        switch gesture.state {
            case .Began, .Changed:
                shapeView.transform = ⏎
                    CGAffineTransformMakeTranslation(dragDelta.x, dragDelta.y)
            case .Ended:
                shapeView.transform = CGAffineTransformIdentity
                shapeView.frame = ⏎
                    CGRectOffset(shapeView.frame, dragDelta.x, dragDelta.y)
            default:
                shapeView.transform = CGAffineTransformIdentity
        }
    }
}
```

Gesture recognizers analyze and absorb the low-level touch events sent to the view object and turn those into high-level gesture events. Like many high-level events, they have a *phase*. The phase of continuous gestures, such as dragging, progress through a predictable order: *possible*, *began*, *changed*, and finally *ended* or *canceled*.

Your moveShape(_:) function starts by getting the view that caused the gesture action; this will be the view the user touched and the one you're going to move. It then gets some information about how far the user dragged and the gesture's state. As long as the gesture is in the "began" or "changed" state, it means the user touched the view and is dragging their finger around the screen. When they release it, the state will change to "ended." In rare circumstances, it may change to "cancel" or "failed," in which case you ignore the gesture.

While the user is dragging their finger around, you want to adjust the origin of the shape view by the same distance on the screen, which gives the illusion that the user is physically dragging the view around the screen. (I hope you didn't think you could actually move things inside your iPhone by touching it.) The way you're going to do that uses a remarkable feature of the UIView class: the transform property.

> **Note**   Notice that you didn't need the @IBAction keyword at the beginning of the moveShape(_:) function. That's because you connected it to the gesture recognizer *programmatically*. The @IBAction keyword is needed only if you want your action to appear in, and be connected using, Interface Builder.

Applying a Translate Transform

iOS uses affine transforms in a number of different ways. An *affine transform* is a 3x3 matrix that describes a coordinate system transformation. In English, it's a (seemingly) magical array of numbers that can describe a variety of complex coordinate conversions. It can move, resize, skew, flip, and rotate any set of points. And since just about everything (view objects, images, and Bézier paths) is a "set of points," affine transforms can be used to move, flip, zoom, shrink, and spin any of those things. Even more amazing, a single affine transform can perform all of those transformations in a single operation.

AFFINE TRANSFORMS

iOS provides functions to create and combine the three common transforms: translate (shift), scale, and rotate. These are illustrated in the following figure. The gray shape represents the original shape and the dark figure its transformation:

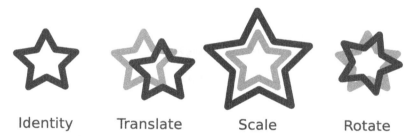

Identity   Translate   Scale   Rotate

You create a basic transform using the function CGAffineTransformMakeTranslation, CGAffineTransformMakeScale, or CGAffineTransformMakeRotation. If you're a hotshot math whiz, you can create any arbitrary transform using CGAffineTransformMake.

The special identity transform (CGAffineTransformIdentity) performs no translation at all. This is the default value for the transform property and the constant you use if you don't want any transformation performed.

Transforms can be combined. The effect of this is illustrated in the following figure:

To add transforms together, use the functions CGAffineTransformTranslate, CGAffineTransformScale, CGAffineTransformRotate, and CGAffineTransformConcat. These functions take one transform (which might already be the sum of other transforms), apply an additional transform, and return the combined transform. You would then use this combined transform value to perform all of the individual transforms, in a single operation.

The gesture cases for the "began" and "changed" states (in moveShape(_:)) take the distance the user dragged their finger and uses that to create a translate transform. Try to say "translate transform" three times fast. The transform property is set to this value, and you're done. But what, exactly, does this magic property do?

When you set the transform property of a view, all of the coordinates that the view occupies in its superview are transformed before they appear on the screen. The view's content and location (its frame) don't change. What changes is where the view's image appears in the superview. I like to think of the UIView transform as a lens that "projects" the view so it appears elsewhere or in a different way. If you apply a translate transform, as you just did in moveShape(_:), then the view will appear at a different set of coordinates.

> **Caution**   If you set the transform property to anything other than the identity transform, the value of the frame property becomes meaningless. It's not entirely meaningless, but it's unusable for most practical purposes. Just remember this: after you set a transform to anything other than the identity transform, don't use frame.

If you set the transform property back to the identity transform (CGAffineTransformIdentity), the view will reappear at its original location. Programmers call the transform property a *nondestructive translation* because setting it doesn't alter any of the object's other properties. Set it back, and everything returns to where it was. In the default: case, this is exactly what happens. The default: case handles the "canceled" and "failed" states by setting the transform property back to the identity transform.

The gesture "ended" case is where the work happens. First, the view's transform property is reset to the identity transform. Then, the view's frame origin is updated, based on the total distance the user dragged the view. The updated frame permanently relocates the view object to its new location.

> **Note**   The transform property of the view is set back to the identity transform *before* the frame property is used to change its location.

Run your project and try it. I didn't supply a figure because (as my publisher explained it to me) the illustration in the book wouldn't move. Create a few shapes and drag them around. It's a lot of fun. When you're done playing, get ready to add zooming and pinching to the mix.

But before you get to that, let me share a few nuggets about affine transforms. Transforms can be used in a variety of places, not just to distort the frame of a view. They can be used to transform the coordinate system of the current context while you draw your view. In essence, this use applies a transform to the bounds of your view, changing the effect of what you draw in your view, rather than translating the final results of your view. For example, you might have a complex drawing that you want to shift up or down in your view or maybe draw something upside down. Rather than recalculate all of the coordinates you want to draw, use the `CGContextTranslateCTM`, `CGContextRotateCTM`, or `CGContextScaleCM` function to shift, rotate, or resize all of the drawing operations. You'll use these functions in Chapter 16.

> **Tip**   You can also shift the drawing coordinates of your view by changing the `origin` of the bounds property.

Transforms can also be used to change the points in a Bézier path. Create the desired transform and then call the path's `applyTransform(_:)` function. All of the points in the path will be altered using that transform. This is a *destructive* translation; the original points in the path are lost.

Applying a Scale Transform

If one gesture recognizer is fun, then two must make a party. This time, you're going to add a pinch/zoom gesture that will resize your shape view. As before, start by creating and attaching a second gesture recognizer object at the end of the addShape(_:) function (in `ViewController.swift`).

```
let pinch = UIPinchGestureRecognizer(target: self, action: "resizeShape:")
shapeView.addGestureRecognizer(pinch)
```

The pinch gesture recognizer object doesn't need any configuration because a pinch/zoom is always a two-finger gesture.

Now add this resizeShape(_:) function:

```
func resizeShape(gesture: UIPinchGestureRecognizer) {
    if let shapeView = gesture.view as? ShapeView {
        let pinchScale = gesture.scale
        switch gesture.state {
            case .Began, .Changed:
                shapeView.transform = ↩
                    CGAffineTransformMakeScale(pinchScale, pinchScale)
            case .Ended:
                shapeView.transform = CGAffineTransformIdentity
                var frame = shapeView.frame
                let xDelta = frame.width*pinchScale-frame.width
                let yDelta = frame.height*pinchScale-frame.height
                frame.size.width += xDelta
                frame.size.height += yDelta
                frame.origin.x -= xDelta/2
                frame.origin.y -= yDelta/2
                shapeView.frame = frame
                shapeView.setNeedsDisplay()
```

```
        default:
            shapeView.transform = CGAffineTransformIdentity
        }
    }
}
```

This function follows the same pattern as moveShape(_:). The only significant difference is in the code to adjust the view's final size and position, which requires a little more math than the drag function.

Run the project and try it. Create a shape and then use two fingers to resize it, as shown in Figure 11-11.

Figure 11-11. Resizing using a transform

Tip If you're using the simulator, hold down the Option key to simulate a two-finger pinch gesture. You'll have to first position a shape in the middle of the view because the second "finger" in the simulator is always mirrored across the center point of the display, and you need to have both "fingers" inside the view to be recognized as a pinch gesture.

You'll notice that when you zoom the shape out a lot, its image gets the "jaggies": aliasing artifacts caused by magnifying the smaller image. This is because you're not resizing the view during the pinch gesture. You're just applying a transform to the original view's image. Bézier paths are resolution independent and draw smoothly at any size. But a transform has only the pixels of the view's current image to work with. At the end of the pinch gesture, the shape view's size is adjusted and redrawn. This creates a new Bézier path, at the new size, and all is smooth again, as shown on the right in Figure 11-11.

Your app is looking pretty lively, but I think it could stand to be jazzed up a bit. What do you think about adding some animation?

Animation: It's Not Just for Manga

Animation has become an integral and expected feature of modern apps. Without it, your app looks dull and uninteresting, even if it's doing everything you intended. Fortunately for you, the designers of iOS know this, and they've done a staggering amount of work, all so you can easily add animation to your app. There are (broadly) four ways to add movement to your app.

- The built-in stuff

- DIY

- Core Animation

- OpenGL, Sprite Kit, Scene Kit, and Metal

The "built-in stuff" includes those places in the iOS API where animation will be done for you. Countless functions, from view controllers to table views, include a Boolean animated parameter. If you want your view controller to slide over, your page to peel up, your toolbar buttons to resize smoothly, your table view rows to spritely leap to their new positions, or your progress indicator to drift gently to its new value, all you have to do is pass true for the animated parameter and the iOS classes will do all of the work. So, keep an eye out for those animated parameters and use them.

> **Tip**   Some view properties have two setters: one that's never animated and one that can be animated. For example, the UIProgressView class has a settable progress property (never animated) and a setProgress(_:,animated:) function (optionally animated). If you're setting a visual property, check the documentation to see whether there's an animated alternative.

In the do-it-yourself (DIY) animation solution, your code performs the frame-by-frame changes needed to animate your interface. This usually involves steps like this:

1. Create a timer that fires 30 times/second.

2. When the timer fires, update the position/look/size/content of a view.

3. Mark the view as needing to be redrawn.

4. Repeat steps 2 and 3 until the animation ends.

The DIY solution is, ironically, the method most often abused by amateurs. It might work "OK" in a handful of situations, but most often it suffers from a number of unavoidable performance pitfalls. The biggest problem is timing. It's really difficult to balance the speed of an animation so it looks smooth but doesn't run so fast that it wastes CPU resources, uses up battery life, and drags the rest of your app and the iOS system down with it.

Using Core Animation

Smart iOS developers—that's you since you're reading this book—use Core Animation. Core Animation has solved all of the thorny performance, load-balancing, background-threading, and efficiency problems for you. All you have to do is tell it what you want animated and let it work its magic.

Animated content is drawn in a *layer* (CALayer) object. A layer object is just like a UIView; it's a canvas that you draw into using Core Graphics. Once drawn, the layer can be animated using Core Animation. In a nutshell, you tell Core Animation how you want the layer changed (moved, shrunk, spun, curled, flipped, and so on), over what time period, and how fast. You then forget about it and let Core Animation do all of the work. Core Animation doesn't even bother your app's event loop; it works quietly in the background, balancing the animation work with available CPU resources so it doesn't interfere with whatever else your app needs to do. It's really a remarkable system.

Keep in mind that Core Animation doesn't change the contents of the layer object. It temporarily animates a copy of the layer, which disappears when the animation is over. I like to think of Core Animation as "live" transforms; it temporarily projects a distorted, animated version of your layer but never changes the layer.

Oh, did I say "a layer object is just like a UIView?" I should have said, "a layer object, *like the one* in UIView" because UIView is based on Core Animation layers. When you're drawing your view in drawRect(_:), you're drawing into a CALayer object. You can get your UIView's layer object through the layer property, should you ever need to work with the layer object directly. The takeaway lesson is this: *all* UIView objects can be animated using Core Animation. Now you're cooking with gas!

Adding Animation to Shapely

There are three ways to get Core Animation working for you. I already described the first: all of those "built-in" animated: parameters are based on Core Animation—that's no surprise. The second, traditional Core Animation technique is to create an animation (CAAnimation) object. An animation object controls an animation sequence. It determines when it starts, when it stops, the speed of the animation (called the *animation curve*), what the animation does, whether it repeats, how many times, and so on. There are subclasses of CAAnimation that will animate a particular property of a view or animate a transition (the adding, removal, or exchange of view objects). There's even an animation class (CAAnimationGroup) that synchronizes multiple animation objects.

Honestly, creating CAAnimation objects isn't easy. Because it can be so convoluted, there are a ton of convenience constructors and functions that try to make it as painless as possible—but it's still a hard row to hoe. You have to define the beginning and ending property values of what's being animated. You have to define timing and animation curves; then you have to start the animation and change the actual property values at the appropriate time. Remember that animation doesn't change the original view, so if you want a view to slide from the left to right, you have to create an animation that starts on the left and ends on the right, and then you have to set the position of the original view to the right, or the view will reappear on the left when the animation is over. It's tedious.

Fortunately, the iOS gods have felt your pain and created a really simple way of creating basic animations called the *block-based animation functions*. These UIView functions let you write a few lines of code to tell Core Animation how you want the properties of your view changed. Core Animation then handles the work of creating, configuring, and starting the CAAnimation objects. It even updates your view's properties, so when the animation is over, your properties will be at the end value of the animation—which is exactly what you want.

So, how simple are these block-based animation functions to use? You be the judge. Find your addShape(_:) function in ViewController.swift. Locate the code that randomly positions the new view and edit it so it looks like this (replacing the statement shapeView.center = randomCenter with the code in bold):

```
var shapeFrame = shapeView.frame
let safeRect = CGRectInset(view.bounds, shapeFrame.width, shapeFrame.height)
var randomCenter = safeRect.origin
randomCenter.x += CGFloat(arc4random_uniform(UInt32(safeRect.width)))
randomCenter.y += CGFloat(arc4random_uniform(UInt32(safeRect.height)))
shapeView.center = button.center
shapeView.transform = CGAffineTransformMakeScale(0.4, 0.4)
UIView.animateWithDuration(0.5) {
    shapeView.center = randomCenter
    shapeView.transform = CGAffineTransformIdentity
}
```

The new code starts by setting the center of the new view to the center of the button the user tapped, essentially positioning the new view right over the button. A transform is applied to shrink the size of the shape to 40 percent of its original size (approximately the same size as the button). If you stopped here, your shape view would appear right on top of the button you tapped, covering it.

The last statement is the magic. It starts an animation that will last a half second (0.5). The closure expression describes what you want animated, and by "describe" I mean you just write the code to set the properties that you want animated. It's that simple. UIView will automatically animate any of these seven properties:

- frame
- bounds
- center
- transform
- alpha
- backgroundColor
- contentStretch

If you want a view to move or change size, animate its center or frame. Want it to fade away? Animate its alpha property from 1.0 to 0.0. Want it to smoothly turn to the right? Animate its transform from the identity transform to a rotated transform. You can do any of these, or even multiple ones (changing the alpha and center), at the same time. It's that easy.

There are a number of variations on the animateWithDuration() function that provide different effects and even more control. With these functions you can easily do all of the following:

- Delay the start of the animation
- Animate a transition between two views

- Specify custom animation options, such as the following:

  - Start this animation at the currently animated value (interrupting another animation)

  - Select a different animation curve (ease in, ease out, and so on)

  - Choose a transition style (flip, page curl, cross dissolve, and so on)

  - Redraw the view's content during the animation

  - Reverse the animation

- Provide code that will be executed when the animation is finished, which can include code to start another animation, making it easy to create an animated sequence

See the "Animating Views with Block Objects" section of the `UIView` documentation for a complete list of functions.

Run your app again and create a few shapes. Pretty cool, huh? (Again, no figure). As you tap each add shape button, the new shape flies into your view, right from underneath your finger, like some crazy arcade game. If you're fast, you can get several going at the same time. And all it took was five lines of code.

What if you want to animate something other than these seven properties, create animations that run in loop, move in an arc, or run backward? For that, you'll need to dig into Core Animation and create your own animation objects. You can read about it in the *Core Animation Programming Guide* you'll find in Xcode's Documentation and API Reference.

OpenGL, Sprite Kit, Scene Kit, and Metal

Oops, I almost forgot about those other animation technologies. Modern computer systems, even a tiny one like an iPod, are actually two computer systems in one: a central processing unit (CPU) that does what computers do and a graphics processing unit (GPU) that does the work of putting bits on the screen. Each has its own set of processing units and memory. There's not much overlap between the two, save for some pathways that allow data and instructions to be exchanged. While the CPU is fast at a lot of tasks, it's not well suited to the kind of massively parallel computations needed to draw and animate graphics. That's where the GPU really shines. GPUs have dozens, sometimes hundreds, of small, simple, but blazingly fast processing units. I like to think of the GPU as "my army of pixel minions."

In the past two decades, most advances in computer graphics and animation have been made by shifting more and more of the data and computations from the CPU to the GPU. This requires a lot of coordination. Instead of having an object (like a `UIView`) that contains all of the data and logic to draw that view in the CPU, you create a hybrid solution where the CPU prepares the data needed to draw a view and hands that over to the GPU. The GPU can later render that view when told to. The CPU has only a reference to the image information (often called a *texture*), while the actual image data sits in the GPU.

An even more advanced solution is to write tiny programs, called *shaders*, that execute your code in the GPU. This is quite a different experience than programming in Swift, but the advantages are huge. All of the logic (data and computer code) needed to generate and draw figures and scenes is now entirely in the GPU. The CPU is just directing the show, telling the GPU what it needs to draw and when.

The results can be nothing less than stunning. If you've ever run a 3D flight simulator, shoot-'em-up, or adventure game, you're looking at code that's leveraging the power of the GPU.

The various animation technologies available to you on iOS can be broadly characterized by how much you (the programmer) are insulated from the details of what the GPU is doing. At one end is Core Animation, which you've already used. From your perspective, everything has been happening in the CPU. There's been no mention of texture buffers, shaders, or pipeline scheduling. Core Animation did those things for you. While ignorance might be bliss, there are also a lot of possibilities if you're willing to step into GPU-land. Here are your options.

Sprite Kit

Sprite Kit appeared in iOS 7, so it's a relatively recent addition to iOS. Sprite Kit's view classes are based on SKNode instead of UIView, but many of the properties and relationships will be familiar. You'll find a lot of what you've learned about UIView works with SKNode. (For example, SKNode is also a UIResponder subclass, so event handlers work the same way.)

Sprite Kit and UIView are both designed to draw and animate 2D graphics. Sprite Kit, however, is specifically designed for *continuous* animation and interaction. Core Animation tends to work best with short, simple sequences. Sprite Kit is designed to keep images moving around all the time, which is why it makes a great choice for 2D games. You'll create a Sprite Kit game in Chapter 14.

Sprite Kit also has an extensive physics simulation engine. You can program Sprite Kit nodes with a shape, mass, velocity, and collision rules, and then let Sprite Kit animate their behavior.

> **Note**   Cocoa Touch also has a physics simulation engine called View Dynamics that you can use with UIView objects. I'll show you how in Chapter 16.

Scene Kit

Scene Kit is new to iOS 8, although it's been around on OS X for a while. Like Sprite Kit, it's designed for high-speed rendering and animation. The big difference is that Scene Kit is primarily focused on 3D modeling and animation.

Scene Kit is Apple's replacement for OpenGL. It's designed on the same underlying technology but—like Sprite Kit—uses objects, structures, data, concepts, and programming languages that are familiar and convenient to Cocoa Touch programmers. Scene Kit and Metal are beyond the scope of this book, but Apple has excellent tutorials and guides to get you started.

Metal

New in iOS 8 is Metal. And, just like it sounds, Metal gives you direct access to all of the power of the GPU. Using Metal, it's possible to create 2D and 3D animations that exceed the performance of even Scene Kit and OpenGL. It's also terribly technical.

Metal can also be used for nongraphic computations. The number of floating-point calculations per second (known as a FLOP) that a GPU unit can perform is staggering. There are lots of applications that can exploit that. Cryptography, field calculations, and linear math problems can be greatly accelerated by running hundreds of small calculations in parallel—exactly what a GPU is designed to do. Metal provides an API for running and managing those calculations.

OpenGL

OpenGL is short for Open Graphics Library. It's a cross-language, multiplatform API for 2D and 3D animation and is the granddaddy of all GPU control libraries. Before Sprite Kit, Scene Kit, and Metal, OpenGL was the only way to fully realize the power of the GPU in iOS. The flavor of OpenGL included in iOS is OpenGL for Embedded Systems (OpenGL ES). It's a trimmed-down version of OpenGL suitable for running on small computer systems, like iOS devices.

The advantage of OpenGL is that it's an industry standard. There's a lot of OpenGL knowledge and code that will run on iOS. This gives you access to a vast reservoir of source code and solutions. And the OpenGL work you do on iOS will translate to other platforms as well.

The downside is that OpenGL is another world. An OpenGL view is programmed using a special C-like computer language called the OpenGL Shading Language (GLSL). To use it, you write *vertex* and *fragment* shader programs.[1] This is not like Swift at all. Even on the CPU side, OpenGL programming is typically written in C++—not Swift or even Objective-C. While some of the C APIs could be called from Swift, I would hesitate to write an OpenGL application entirely in Swift.

Having tried to steer you away from OpenGL, I must admit that it's a powerful technology and it works well in iOS—once you get past the learning curve and language barriers. Start with the *OpenGL ES Programming Guide for iOS* that you'll find in Xcode's Documentation and API Reference. But be warned, you'd need to learn a lot of OpenGL fundamentals before much of that document will make any sense.

The Order of Things

While you still have the Shapely project open, I want you to play around with view object order a little bit. Subviews have a specific order, called their *Z-order*. It determines how overlapping views are drawn. It's not rocket science. The back view draws first, and subsequent views draw on top of it (if they overlap). If the overlapping view is opaque, it obscures any views behind it. If portions of it are transparent, the views behind it "peek" through holes.

This is easier to see than explain, so add two more gesture recognizers to Shapely. Once again, go back to the addShape(_:) action function in ViewController.swift. Immediately after the code that attaches the other two gesture recognizers, insert this:

```
let dblTap = UITapGestureRecognizer(target: self, action: "changeColor:")
dblTap.numberOfTapsRequired = 2
shapeView.addGestureRecognizer(dblTap)
```

---

[1]Sprite Kit, Scene Kit, and Metal can also employ GPU shader programs, if you have them.

```
let trplTap = UITapGestureRecognizer(target: self, action: "sendShapeToBack:")
trplTap.numberOfTapsRequired = 3
shapeView.addGestureRecognizer(trplTap)
```

This code adds double-tap and triple-tap gesture recognizers, which call changeColor(_:) and sendShapeToBack(_:), respectively. Now add these two new functions:

```
func changeColor(gesture: UITapGestureRecognizer) {
    if gesture.state == .Ended {
        if let shapeView = gesture.view as? ShapeView {
            let currentColor = shapeView.color
            var newColor: UIColor!
            do {
                newColor = ↩
                    colors[Int(arc4random_uniform(UInt32(colors.count)))]
            } while currentColor == newColor
            shapeView.color = newColor
        }
    }
}

func sendShapeToBack(gesture: UITapGestureRecognizer) {
    if gesture.state == .Ended {
        view.sendSubviewToBack(gesture.view)
    }
}
```

The changeColor(_:) function is mostly for fun. It determines which color the shape is and picks a new color for it at random.

The sendShapeToBack(_:) function illustrates how views overlap. When you add a subview to a view (using UIView's addSubview(_:) function), the new view goes on top. But that's not your only choice. If view order is important, a number of functions will insert a subview at a specific index or immediately below or above another (known) view. You can also adjust the order of existing views using bringSubviewToFront(_:) and sendSubviewToBack(_:), which you'll use here. Your triple-tap gesture will "push" that subview to the back, behind all of the other shapes.

To make this effect more obvious, make a minor alteration to your drawRect(_:) function in ShapeView.swift, by adding the code in bold:

```
override func drawRect(rect: CGRect) {
    let shapePath = path
    UIColor.blackColor().colorWithAlphaComponent(0.4).setFill()
    shapePath.fill()
    color.setStroke()
    shapePath.stroke()
}
```

The new code fills the shape with black that's 40 percent opaque (60 percent transparent). It will appear that your shapes have a "smoky" middle that darkens any shapes that are drawn behind it. This will make it easy to see how shapes are overlapping.

Run your app, create a few shapes, resize them, and then move them so they overlap, as shown in Figure 11-12.

Figure 11-12. Overlapping shapes with semitransparent fill

The shapes you added last are "on top" of the shapes you added first. Now try double-tapping a shape to change its color. I'll wait.

I'm still waiting.

Is something wrong? Double-tapping doesn't seem to be changing the color of a shape? There are two probable reasons: the changeColor(_:) function isn't being called. Test that by setting a breakpoint in Xcode. Click once in the margin next to the first line of code in changeColor(_:). Double-tap the shape again. Xcode stops your app in the changeColor(_:) function, as shown in Figure 11-13, so that isn't the problem. Delete or disable the breakpoint and click the Continue button (in the debug control ribbon) to resume app execution.

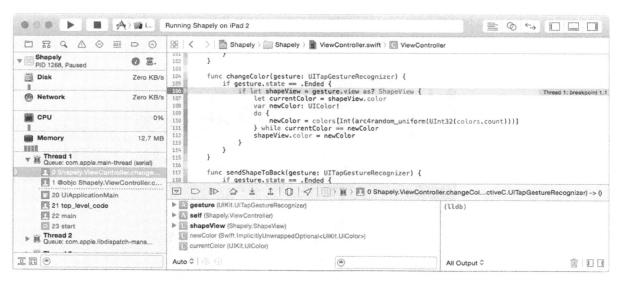

Figure 11-13. Determining whether changeColor(_:) is being called

The other possible problem is that the color is being changed but isn't showing up. You can test that by resizing the shape. If you double-tap a shape and then resize it, you'll see the color change. OK, it's the latter. Take a moment to fix this.

The problem is that the ShapeView object doesn't know that it should redraw itself whenever its color property changes. You could add a shapeView.setNeedsDisplay() statement to changeColor(_:), but that's a bit of a hack. I'm a strong believer that view objects should trigger their own redrawing when any properties that change their appearance are altered. That way, client code doesn't have to worry about whether to call setNeedsDisplay(); the view will take care of that automatically.

Return to ShapeView.swift and edit the color property so it looks like this (new code in bold):

```swift
var color: UIColor = UIColor.whiteColor() {
    didSet {
        setNeedsDisplay()
    }
}
```

You've added a *property observer* to the color property. The didSet code will be executed every time someone sets the color property of the object. The new code calls setNeedsDisplay() to indicate that this view needs to be redrawn since, we assume, its color has changed.

Run the app and try the double-tap again. That's much better!

Finally, you get to the part of the demonstration that rearranges the view. Overlap some views and then triple-tap one of the top views. Do you see the difference when the view is pushed to the back?

What is that, you say? The color changed when you triple-tapped it?

Oh, for Pete's sake, don't any of these gesture recognizer things works? Well, actually they do, but you've created an impossible situation. You've attached both a double-tap and a triple-tap gesture recognizer to the same view. The problem is that there's no coordination between the two. What's happening is that the double-tap recognizer fires as soon as you tap the second time, before the triple-tap recognizers gets a chance to see the third tap.

There are a number of ways to fix this bug, but the most common recognizer conflicts can be fixed with one line of code. Return to the ViewController.swift file, find the addShape(_:) function, and locate the code that adds the double- and triple-tap recognizers. Immediately after that, add this line:

```
dblTap.requireGestureRecognizerToFail(trplTap)
```

This message creates a dependency between the two recognizers. Now, the double-tap recognizer won't fire unless the triple-tap recognizer fails. When you tap twice, the triple-tap recognizer will fail (it sees two taps but never gets a third). This creates all of the conditions needed for the double-tap recognizer to fire. If you triple-tap, however, the triple-tap recognizer is successful, which prevents the double-tap from firing. Simple.

Now run your app for the last time. Resize and overlap some shapes. Triple-tap a top shape to push it to the back and marvel at the results, shown in Figure 11-14.

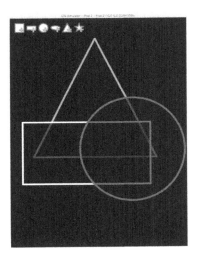
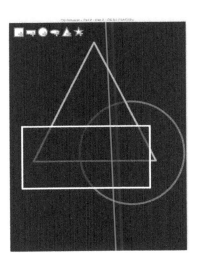

Figure 11-14. Working Shapely app

> **Note**   Hit testing knows nothing about the transparent portions of your view. So even if you can see a portion of one view in the middle, or near the edge, of the view on top of it, you won't be able to interact with it because the touch events are going to the view on top. It would be possible to change that by overriding the hitTest(_:,withEvent:) and pointInside(_:,withEvent:) functions of your view, but that's more work than I want to demonstrate. (Hint: use the hit test functions of UIBezierPath to determine whether a point is inside, or outside, of the view's shape).

By now you should have a firm grasp of how view objects get drawn, when, and why. You understand the context, Bézier paths, the coordinate system, color, a little about transparency, 2D transforms, and even how to create simple animations. That's a lot.

One thing you haven't explored much are images. Let's get to that by going back in time.

Drawing Images

As you've seen, drawing the content of your view is pretty straightforward. You draw your view's content into its context in response to a drawRect(_:) call. In addition to filling rectangles and drawing paths, you can also paint an image (UIImage) object into your context. You did this in the ColorView class in Chapter 8:

```
hsImage.drawInRect(bounds)
```

When you draw an image into a context, its pixels are copied into the context buffer. You can also have fun with the image, stretching, transforming, and blending its pixels, depending on the drawing mode and the context's state.

But it's possible to go the other direction too: capturing the pixels in a context and turning them into a UIImage object. This is called *off-screen drawing*, because you're drawing into a Core Graphics context that isn't destined to be displayed on the screen.

You also performed off-screen drawing in Chapter 8—I just glossed over the details. Let's take a closer look at that code now.

```
if !hsImage {
    brightness = colorModel!.brightness
    UIGraphicsBeginImageContextWithOptions(bounds.size, true, 1.0)
    let imageContext = UIGraphicsGetCurrentContext()
    for y in 0..<Int(bounds.height) {
        for x in 0..<Int(bounds.width) {
            let color = UIColor(hue: CGFloat(x)/bounds.width,
                        saturation: CGFloat(y)/bounds.height,
                        brightness: brightness/100.0,
                            alpha: 1.0)
            color.set()
            CGContextFillRect(imageContext,CGRect(x: x, y: y,
                                            width: 1, height: 1))
        }
    }
    hsImage = UIGraphicsGetImageFromCurrentImageContext()
    UIGraphicsEndImageContext()
}
```

Off-screen drawing begins with a call to either UIGraphicsBeginImageContext() or UIGraphicsBeginImageContextWithOptions(). Both initialize a new Core Graphics context with a size you specify. The latter function provides additional options to control the transparency and scale of the context.

Once created, you perform Core Graphics drawing, exactly as you would in your drawRect(_:) function. In fact, if you want to call your drawRect(_:) function and let it draw into your ad hoc context, that's fine. I'll show you an example of this in Chapter 13. (This is the one exception to the rule of never calling your own drawRect(_:) function.)

Once your context is drawn, you take a "snapshot" of the finished image and preserve that in a new UIImage object using the aptly named UIGraphicsGetImageFromCurrentImageContext() function. The returned UIImage can be retained in a property, converted to a file, copied to the clipboard, saved on the camera roll, drawn into another context, or whatever else you want to do with it.

> **Caution** UIGraphicsGetImageFromCurrentImageContext() works only with a context created by UIGraphicsBeginImageContext(). It can't be used with a normal "onscreen" context.

When you're all done, don't forget to call UIGraphicsEndImageContext(). This tears down the off-screen context and frees up its resources.

Advanced Graphics

Oh, there's more. Before your head explodes from all of this graphics talk, let me briefly mention a few more techniques that could come in handy.

Text

You can also draw text directly into your custom view. The basic technique is the following:

1. Create a UIFont object that describes the font, style, and size of the text.

2. Set the drawing color.

3. Call the drawAtPoint(_:...) or (drawInRect(_:...) function of any String object.

You can also get the size that a string would draw (so you can calculate how much room it will take up) using the various sizeWithFont(_:...) functions.

You'll find examples of this in the Touchy app you wrote in Chapter 4 and later in the Wonderland app in Chapter 12. The drawAtPoint(_:...) and drawInRect(_:,...) functions are just wrappers for the low-level text drawing functions, which are described in the "Text" chapter of the *Quartz 2D Programming Guide*. If you need really precise control over text, read the *Core Text Programming Guide*.

Shadows, Gradients, and Patterns

You've learned to draw solid shapes and solid lines. Core Graphics is capable of a lot more. It can paint with tiled patterns and gradients, and it can automatically draw "shadows" behind the shapes you draw.

You accomplish this by creating various pattern, gradient, and shadow objects and then setting them in your current context, just as you would set the color. You can find copious examples and sample code in the *Quartz 2D Programming Guide*.

Blend Modes

Another property of your context, and many drawing functions, is the blend mode. A blend mode determines how the pixels of what's being drawn affect the pixels of what's already in the context. Normally, the blend mode is kCGBlendModeNormal. This mode paints opaque pixels, ignores transparent ones, and blends the colors of partially transparent ones.

There are some two dozen other blend modes. You can perform "multiplies" and "adds," paint only over the opaque portions of the existing image, paint only in the transparent portion of the existing image, paint using "hard" or "soft" light, affect just the luminosity or saturation—the list goes on and on. You set the current blend mode using the CGContextSetBlendMode() function. A few drawing functions take a blend mode parameter.

The available blend modes are documented, with examples, in two places in the *Quartz 2D Programming Guide*. For drawing operations (shapes and fills), refer to the "Setting Blend Modes" section of the "Paths" chapter. For examples of blending images, find the "Using Blend Modes with Images" section of the "Bitmap Images and Image Masks" chapter.

The Context Stack

All of these settings can start to make your context hard to work with. Let's say you need to draw a complex shape, with a gradient, drop shadow, rotated, and with a special blend mode. After you've set up all of those properties and drawn the shape, now you just want to draw a simple line. Yikes! Do you now have to reset every one of those settings (drop shadow, transform, blend mode, and so on)?

Don't panic—this is a common situation, and there's a simple mechanism for dealing with it. Before you make a bunch of changes, call the CGContextSaveGState(_:) function to save almost everything about the current context. It takes a snapshot of your current context settings and pushes them onto a stack. You can then change whatever drawing properties you need (clipping region, line width, stroke color, and so on) and draw whatever you want.

When you're done, call CGContextRestoreGState(_:), and all of the context's setting will be immediately restored to what they were when you called CGContextSaveGState(_:). You can nest these calls as deeply as you need: save, change, draw, save, change, draw, restore, draw, restore, draw. It's not uncommon, in complex drawing functions, to begin with a call to CGContextRestoreGState(_:) so that later portions of the function can retrieve an unadulterated context.

Summary

I think it's time for a little celebration. What you've learned in this chapter is more than just some drawing mechanics. The process of creating your own views, drawing your own graphics, and making your own animations is like trading in your erector set for a lathe. You've just graduated from building apps using pieces that other people have made to creating anything you can imagine.

I just hope the next chapter isn't too boring after all of this freewheeling graphics talk. It doesn't matter how cool your custom views are; users still need to get around your app. The next chapter is all about navigation.

EXERCISE

If there's a big flaw in Shapely's interface, it's that it allows the user to make shapes that are so big they cover the entire interface and allow them to move shapes off the edge of the screen or cover the button views. Wouldn't it be nice if Shapely would gently slide, or shrink, shapes the user has dragged so this doesn't happen? I think so too.

Here's your challenge: add code to Shapely so that shapes can't be moved off the edge of the screen or cover the add shape buttons. There are a variety of ways to approach this problem. You could simply prevent the user from moving or resizing the shape too much during the drag or pinch gesture. Another solution would be to let them move it wherever they want and then gently "correct" it afterward. Whatever solution you choose, make it clear to the user what's happening so the user doesn't just think your app is broken.

You'll find my solution in the `Learn iOS Development Projects` ➤ `Ch 11` ➤ `Shapely E1` folder. (Hint: I added a `corralShape(_:)` function to `ViewController.swift`).

There and Back Again

Unless your app fits entirely on one screen, your users will need ways of getting around, not unlike the way people navigate cities and towns. We get around via roads, sidewalks, paths, and tracks. You'll need to lay down the "roads" between the screens of your app so your users can easily get around too. Closely related to organizing your view controllers is determining how they will appear once they are presented. In this chapter, you'll learn these three essential view controller development skills:

- Connecting view controllers
- Presenting view controllers
- Adapting view controller content

Urban planners have a proven set of solutions (expressways, one-way streets, roundabouts, intersections, overpasses) that they use to provide the best transportation solution for their populace. As an iOS app designer, you also have a rich set of navigation, presentation, and adaption tools that you and your users are already familiar with. The first step is to take stock of the view controllers iOS provides and understand how they work together.

Measure Twice, Cut Once

Like those urban planners, you need a plan. iOS navigation, just like city streets, is difficult to tear up and replace once built. So, begin your design by carefully considering how you want your users to navigate your app. You'll need to live with your decision or be willing to expend a fair amount of effort to change it in the future.

iOS navigation can also get complicated, which is ironic because the principal player (`UIViewController`) is a pretty straightforward class. The complication is not in the classes themselves but in how they combine to form larger solutions. I think of them like the elements. It's not difficult to explain the periodic table—each element has an atomic weight, a number of electrons, and so on. But it's quite a different matter to consider all of the ways those elements can combine into molecules and interact with one another. In this respect, iOS navigation is kind of like chemistry.

So, sharpen your No. 2 pencil and get ready to take notes because you're about to learn all about navigation: what it means, how it's done, the classes involved, and the roles they perform.

What Is Navigation?

Every screen in your app is defined and controlled by a view controller. If your app has three screens, then it has (at least) three view controllers. The base class for all view controllers is `UIViewController`.

In its simplest terms, *navigation* is the transition from one view controller to another. Navigation is an activity that view controllers participate in, and view controllers are its currency. Now this is where things begin to get interesting. Navigation is not a class *per se*, but there are classes that provide specific styles of navigation. While view controllers are the subjects of navigation, some view controllers *also* provide navigation, some *only* provide navigation, and some non–view controller classes provide navigation. Are you confused yet? Let's break it down.

View Controller Roles

View controllers come in two basic varieties. View controllers that contain just view objects are called *content view controllers*. This is the basic form of view controllers and what you've mostly dealt with in this book so far. The entire purpose of navigation is to get a content view controller to appear on the screen so the user can see and interact with it.

The other kind is a container view controller. A *container view controller* presents other view controllers. It may, or may not, have content of its own. Its primary job is to present, and navigate between, a set of view controllers.

The intriguing part is that both content view controllers and container view controllers are subclasses of `UIViewController` and are, therefore, all "view controllers." While a content view controller displays only views, a container view controller can present a parade of content view controllers and container view controllers, the latter of which may present other content view controllers or container view controllers, and so on, down the rabbit hole.

You won't get confused if you clearly understand the differences and relationship between container view controllers and content view controllers. So, let's review. Content view controllers display *only* tangible view objects. The following are examples of content view controllers:

- `UITableViewController`
- `UICollectionViewController`
- `MPMediaPickerController`
- `UIViewController`
- Every custom subclass of `UIViewController` you've created in this book

Note that `UIViewController` is on that list. The `UIViewController` base class is a content view controller. It has all of the basic properties and features needed to display a view, and it does not (implicitly) present any views owned by other view controllers.

Container view controllers present and provide navigation between the views in one or more other view controllers. The following are examples of container view controllers:

- UINavigationController
- UITabBarController
- UIPageViewController
- UIImagePickerController

These view controllers present other view controllers, provide some mechanism for navigating between them, and may decorate the screen with additional view objects that enable that navigation.

So, it's possible to have a tab bar (container view) controller that contains three other view controllers: a custom (content) view controller, a navigation (container view) controller, and a page (container) view controller. The navigation controller could contain a table (content) view controller and a detail (content) view controller. The page view controller could contain a series of custom (content) view controllers, one for each "page." Does that sound horribly complex? It's not. In fact, it's typical of a medium-sized app design, and it's exactly the organization of the app you're about to write. By the end of this chapter, this will seem like child's play.

Designing Wonderland

The app you're going to write is based on Lewis Carroll's famous book, *Alice's Adventures in Wonderland*. This seems appropriate given the (sometimes) confounding and convoluted nature of navigation. Here's a summary of the screens in your app:

- A title page
- The full text of the book
- Some supplementary information about the author
- A list of characters
- Detailed information about each character

The key is to organize the app's navigation in a way that makes sense, is obvious, is visually appealing, and is easy to use. Start thinking about how you would organize the content of your app while I review the basic styles of navigation available.

Weighing Your Navigation Options

To design your app, you need to know what styles of navigation are available and then what classes and methods provide what you need. Table 12-1 describes the major styles of navigation and the principal classes involved.

Table 12-1. Navigation Styles

Style	Class	Description
Modal	UIViewController	One view controller presents a second view controller. When the second view controller is finished, it disappears, and the first view controller reappears.
Stack or tree	UINavigationController	View controllers operate in a stack. View controllers modally present subview controllers, adding to the stack and navigating deeper into the "tree" of scenes. A navigation bar at the top takes the user to the previous view controller, removing the view controller from the stack and navigating up the "tree" toward the root.
Random	UITabBarController	A tab bar appears at the bottom of the screen. The user can jump immediately to any view controller by tapping one of the buttons in the tab bar.
Sequential	UIPageViewController	The user navigates through a linear sequence of view controllers, moving one view controller at a time forward or backward.
Concurrent	UISplitViewController	This presents two view controllers simultaneously, eliminating the need to navigate between them.
Custom	UIViewController subclass	You decide.

Modal navigation is the simplest and the one you've used the most in this book. When DrumDub presented the MPMediaPicker controller and MyStuff presented UIImagePickerController, these view controllers were presented modally. The new view controller took over the interface of the device until its task was complete. When it was done, it communicated its results to your controller (via a delegate message), which dismissed the modal controller and resumed control of the interface. The presented view controller is responsible for implementing an interface that signals when it's done.

> Use modal navigation when you need to "step out" of the current interface to present relevant details or controls or when you want to perform some task and then immediately return the user to where they were.

The second style of navigation is the stack or tree style, managed by a UINavigationController object. You see this style all over iOS. The Settings app is a particularly obvious example. The signature of the navigation controller is its navigation bar that appears at the top of the screen (see examples in Chapter 5). It shows users where they are and has a button to allow them to return to where they were. When a content view controller (modally) presents a new view controller, the navigation controller adds it to the stack of view controllers the user can step back through. This is called pushing a view controller. When used in the context of a navigation controller, a view doesn't have to provide a means for returning to the presenting view controller because the back button in the navigation bar provides that action.

You can (within strict limits) customize the navigation bar, adding your own titles, buttons, or even controls. The navigation controller can also add a toolbar at the bottom of the display, which you can populate with buttons and indicators. Both of these elements are owned and managed by the navigation controller.

■ Use a navigation controller when there are several layers of modal views in order to keep the user informed about where they are, tell them where they came from, and provide a consistent method of returning.

The UITabBarController manages a set of view controllers the user can maneuver through arbitrarily. Each view controller is represented by a button in a tab bar at the bottom of the screen. Tap a button and that view controller appears. The iOS Clock app is a perfect example.

■ Use a tab bar to allow quick and direct access to functionally different areas of your app.

The UIPageViewController is equally easy to understand. It presents a sequence of view controllers one at a time. The user navigates to the next or previous view controller in the sequence by tapping or swiping on the screen, as if leafing through the pages of a book. Apple's Weather app is the iconic example of a page view controller in action.

■ Use a page view controller, as an alternative to `UIScrollView`, when you have more information than can be presented on a single screen or an unbounded set of functionally similar screens that differ only in content.

The UISplitViewController is a navigation controller that eliminates the need for navigation. This special container view controller simultaneously presents two view controllers side by side. On compact devices with limited screen space (like an iPhone), the split view controller will naturally collapse to show only one view at a time, dynamically replacing the two views with a navigation view controller interface. You've already seen the split view controller in action in your MyStuff app.

■ Use a split view controller to present more content on a single screen (space permitting), reducing the need for navigation.

Finally, it's possible to create your own style of navigation. You can subclass UIViewController and create a container view controller with whatever new kind of navigation you invent. I would, however, caution you about doing this. The existing navigation styles are successful largely because they are familiar to users. If you start designing spiral sidewalks or streets that go backward on Tuesdays, you might be creating a navigation nightmare rather than navigation nirvana.

Wonderland Navigation

Figure 12-1 shows the design for the Wonderland app. The main screen—called the *initial view controller*—will be a tab view with three tabs. The first tab contains a content view with the book's title and an info button that (modally) presents some details about the author.

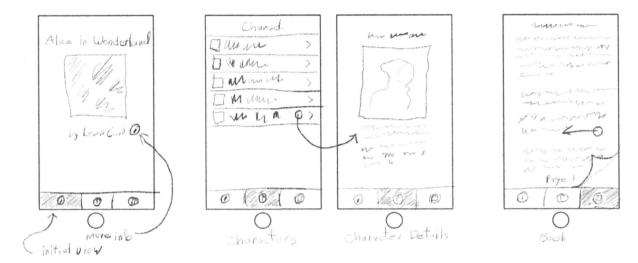

Figure 12-1. *Wonderland app design*

The middle tab lists characters in the book in a table view. Tapping a row transitions to a detail view with more information. This interface is under the control of a navigation controller, so a navigation bar provides a way back to the list.

The book appears in the last tab, a page view controller, where users can swipe and tap their way through the text.

Creating Wonderland

Launch Xcode and create a new project. (I'm sure you saw that one coming.) This time, create the project based on the Tabbed Application template, as shown in Figure 12-2. Name the app Wonderland, set the language to Swift, and make it Universal.

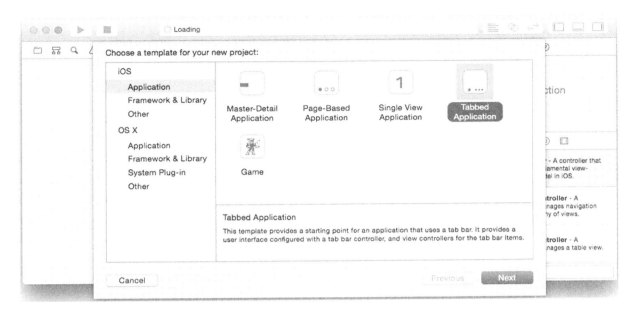

Figure 12-2. Project template for Wonderland

The initial view controller presented by your app will be a tab bar controller; the Tabbed Application template creates a project whose initial view controller is a tab bar controller. By cleverly choosing the Tabbed Application template, your first step is already done. You've created a `UITabBarController` object and installed it as the app's initial view controller.

Tip   The *initial view controller* is the view controller presented when your app starts. You can create it programmatically in the startup code of your application delegate object, or you can let iOS present it for you. For the latter to happen, you need to set its `Is Initial View Controller` property to `true`. You can set this in Interface Builder by checking the Is Initial View Controller option using the attributes inspector or by dragging around the initial view controller arrow (shown on the left side of the tab bar controller object in Figure 12-3) and attaching it to the view controller of your choice.

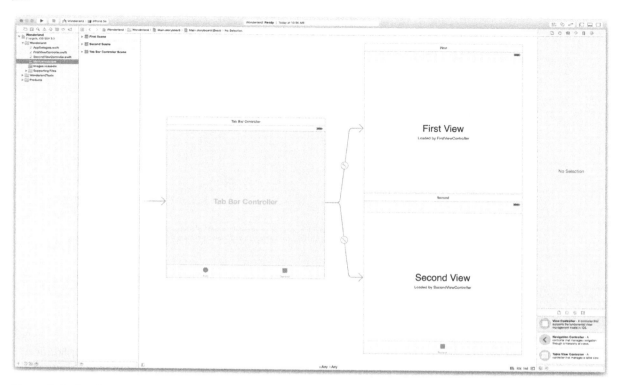

Figure 12-3. Starting tab bar configuration

Remember that a tab bar controller is a container view controller. It doesn't display (much) content of its own. Select the `Main.storyboard` Interface Builder file, as shown in Figure 12-3. The big blank area in the middle of the tab view controller is going to be filled in with the contents of some other view controller. The storyboard shows that your tab bar controller came preconfigured with two content view controllers, `FirstViewController` and `SecondViewController`.

To use a tab bar, you must provide a pair of objects for each tab: a view controller to display and a tab bar item (`UITabBarItem`) that configures that tab's button at the bottom of the screen. Each tab bar item defines a title and an icon. Icons smell suspiciously like resource files, so start there.

> **Note** A container view controller can show interface elements—like the tab bar—that is not part of or is outside of the content of the presented view controller. Everything inside a view controller's root view object is called its *content*. Everything outside is called the *chrome*.

Adding Wonderland's Resources

I'm going to have you cheat (a little bit) and add all of the resources for this project at once. This will save you (and me) from repeating these steps for each interface you're going to develop in this chapter. Just add them all now; I'll explain them as you need them.

In earlier projects, I had you add individual resource files to the main top-level group (the folder icon) in your project navigator or to the `Images.xcasset` asset catalog. There are a sufficient number of resource files in this project that I'm going to have you create subgroups so they don't become unwieldy. There are three ways you can organize source files in your project.

- Create a subgroup and then create or add new files to that group

- Import folders of source files and let Xcode create groups for each folder

- Wait until you have too many files cluttering up your navigator and then decide to organize them

To use the first or third method, create a new subgroup using the File ➤ New Group command (also available by Control+clicking or right-clicking in the project navigator). Name the new group and then import resource files, create new source files, or drag existing files into it. Developers tend to organize their groups either by file type (all of the data files in one group, with class source files in another) or by functional unit (all of the source and resources files for a table in a single group). It's a matter of style and personal preference.

> **Tip**   If you decide to use the third method, which is my personal favorite, make use of the File ➤ New Group from Selection command. Select the files you want to organize into a group and choose New Group from Selection. It creates a new subgroup and moves all of those items into it in one step.

The second method is handy when you're importing a large number of resource files at once. Find the `Learn iOS Development Projects` ➤ `Ch 12` ➤ `Wonderland (Resources)` folder. These resource files have been organized into subfolders: `Data Resources`, `Character Images`, `Info Images`, and `Tab Images`. Instead of dragging the individual files into the project navigator, you'll drag the folders into your project, importing all of the resource files at once. Begin with the data (nonimage) files in the `Data Resources` folder. Drag that folder and drop it into the Wonderland group, as shown in Figure 12-4.

Figure 12-4. Adding a folder of resource files

When the import dialog appears, make sure the Create groups option is selected, as shown on the left in Figure 12-5. This will turn each folder's worth of resource files into a group, as shown on the right in Figure 12-5.

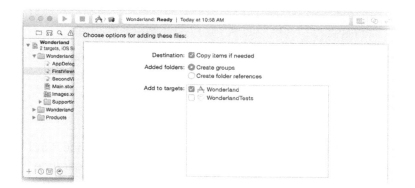

Figure 12-5. Copying and creating groups for new resource folders

To do something similar for your images, choose the Images.xcassets asset catalog item and drag all three folders of images (Character Images, Info Images, and Tab Images) into the catalog's group column, as shown on the left in Figure 12-5. This will automatically create three groups of images, as shown on the right of Figure 12-6.

Figure 12-6. Importing groups of image files

In the interests of neatness, let's discard some detritus you don't need. Select the `first` and `second` image sets in the asset catalog. While holding down the Command key, press the Delete key (or choose Edit ➤ Delete) to remove these items from your project.

> **Note**   You'll also find some app icons in the `Wonderland` (Icons) folder. Drop those into the `AppIcon` image set, if you like.

Configuring a Tab Bar Item

Now that you have all of your resources, configure the tab bar for the first tab. Each tab button in the tab bar is configured via a `UITabBarItem` object associated with its view controller. When a view controller is added to a tab bar controller, Interface Builder automatically creates this object in the scene that defines that view controller. Select the `Main.storyboard` file. Find and expand the first view controller group, as shown on the left in Figure 12-7. Select the tab bar item object, use the attributes inspector to change its title to Welcome, and set its image to `tab-info`, as shown on the right in Figure 12-7. When you change the name of the bar item, the name of the scene will change to Welcome Scene.

Figure 12-7. Configuring the first tab bar item

> **Note**   The image for the tab bar button is not displayed "as is." The image you supply is used like a stencil, creating a silhouette from the opaque pixels of the image. So, don't bother designing your tab bar button images with pretty colors; only the transparency matters.

You'll repeat these steps for each content view you add to the tab bar. Now move on to the content for this first tab.

The First Content View Controller

The first tab presents a simple content view controller, based on `UIViewController`. The Xcode template has already created a custom view controller (`FirstViewController`) and attached it as the contents of the first tab. This is almost exactly what you want, so gut it and make it your own.

Select the `Main.storyboard` file. Double-click the first view controller (upper right) in the canvas to make it the focus. The view already contains some label and text view objects. Select these and delete them.

Using the object library, add two labels and one image view object. Using the attributes and size inspectors, set their properties as follows:

1. First label
    a. Text: Alice's Adventures in Wonderland
    b. Font: System 16.0
2. Second label
    a. Text: by Lewis Carroll
    b. Font: System 13.0
3. Image view
    a. Image: `info-alice.png`
    b. Mode: Aspect Fit

> **Tip**   After changing the text, font, or image of an object, if its content no longer exactly fits its dimensions, select it and use the Editor ➤ Size to Fit Contents command. It will resize the object so it's exactly the same size as the image or text it contains, also called its *intrinsic size*.

Arrange the views so they look something like those in Figure 12-8.

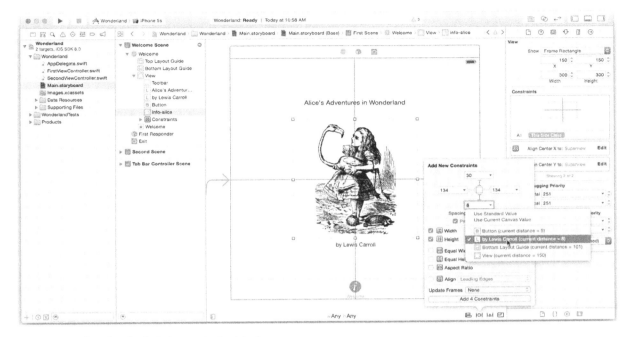

Figure 12-8. Creating the first view controller interface

Next add the constraints. Select all three view objects and use the alignment constraints control to add center horizontally constraints. Then select just the image view and center it vertically. With the image view still selected, use the pin constraints control to add vertical spacing constraints above (30 pixels) and below (8 pixels) and pin both the height and width to 300 pixels, as shown in Figure 12-8. The layout for your first tab view is finished. (Well, you're almost finished. Later in this chapter you'll return and add a button).

Choose a simulator and run your app. Your first view controller appears (as shown on the left in Figure 12-9), embedded in the tab view controller. You can switch between the two view controllers using the buttons at the bottom of the screen, as shown on the right in Figure 12-9.

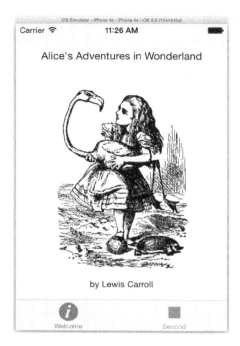 

Figure 12-9. Two view controllers in a tab view controller

To review, you've designed a content view controller (your welcome screen) and added it to a container view controller (the tab view). Now get crazy and add a container view controller to a container view controller.

Creating a Navigable Table View

The second tab of your Wonderland app presents a list of characters in a table view. Tapping a row navigates to a screen with some character details. Does this sound familiar? It should. You already built this app in Chapter 5. Well, you get to build it again. But this time, the focus is going to be on navigation.

You know from Chapter 5 that you're going to need the following:

- A navigation view controller
- A custom subclass of `UITableViewController` (for the table view)
- A data model
- A table view delegate object
- A data source object
- A table view cell object
- A custom subclass of `UIViewController` (for the detail view)
- View objects to display the detail view

Start with the navigation view controller. A navigation view controller is a container view controller. The view it initially displays is its *root view controller*. This view is its home base, which is the view that all navigation starts from and eventually returns to. To have the second tab of the Wonderland app present a navigable table view, you need to install a navigation controller as the second view controller in the tab bar and then install a table view controller as the root view controller of the navigation controller. This is easier than it sounds.

Start by clearing some room. Select the `Main.storyboard` file. A `SecondViewController` already occupies the second tab. You don't need it. Select the second view controller scene in the Interface Builder canvas and delete it. Then select the `SecondViewController.swift` file and delete it too.

From the object library, drag in a navigation controller and place it underneath the first view controller, as shown in Figure 12-10. A new navigation controller comes pre-installed with a table view controller, which is exactly what you want. (See, I told you this wouldn't be too hard.) You'll also need a detail view, so drop in another view controller object next to the table view, also shown in Figure 12-10.

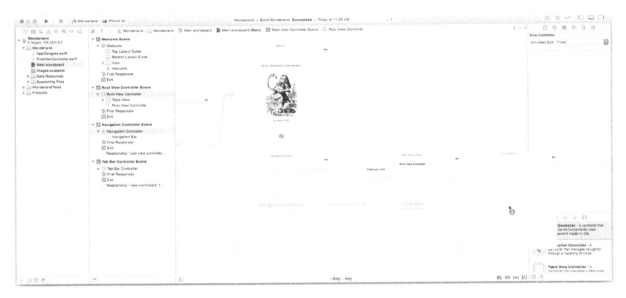

Figure 12-10. Adding a navigation controller, table view controller, and view controller

To add the navigation controller to the tab bar, Control+click or right-click the tab bar controller and drag to the navigation controller, as shown in Figure 12-11. When the pop-up appears, find the Relationship Segue category and choose view controllers. This special connection adds the view controller to the collection of controllers that the container view controller manages. A second tab appears in the tab view, and a companion tab bar item object is added to the navigation controller's scene.

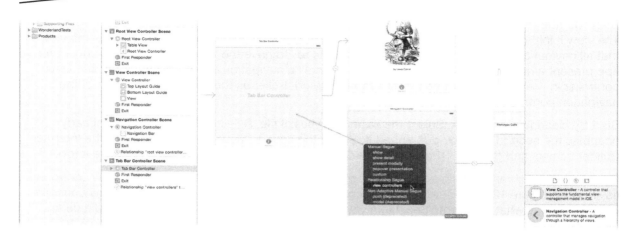

Figure 12-11. *Making the navigation controller the second tab*

Expand the Navigation Controller Scene group in the outline and select the tab bar item. Use the attributes inspector to set the title to Characters and the image to tab-chars.

You've now added a navigable view controller to your tab bar (container) view controller. It's the second tab. It has a title and icon. Tapping it will present the table (content) view controller inside the navigation (container) view controller. It sounds complicated, but the storyboard makes the organization easy to follow.

Breathing Data Into Your Table View

You can run your app right now, tap the Characters tab, and marvel at the raging emptiness of your table view. You know, from Chapter 5, that without a data source and some data, your table view has nothing to display. Let's tackle that now.

You're going to need a custom subclass of UITableViewController, so create one. You also know that you're going to need a custom subclass of UIViewController for your detail view. While you're here, you might as well create that too. Add (or drag in) a new Swift file. Name it CharacterTableViewController and edit it so it looks like this:

```
import UIKit

class CharacterTableViewController: UITableViewController {
}
```

Similarly, add (or drag in) a new Swift file, name it CharacterDetailViewController, and edit it so it looks like this:

```
import UIKit

class CharacterDetailViewController: UIViewController {
    @IBOutlet var nameLabel: UILabel!
    @IBOutlet var imageView: UIImageView!
    @IBOutlet var descriptionView: UITextView!
}
```

Reviewing the list of things you need to do to get the table view working, you now have a navigation controller and custom subclasses of the table and view controllers. But the objects in the interface aren't your custom subclasses yet. Select the `Main.storyboard` file, select the table view controller, and use the identity inspector to change its class to `CharacterTableViewController`. Do the same for the detail view controller, making its class `CharacterDetailViewController`.

Creating the Detail View

Since you're already in the character detail view controller, go ahead and create its interface. Use the object library to add a label, an image view, and a text view to the character detail view controller. Position the label view at the top, the image in the middle, and the text view below it, something like the arrangement shown in Figure 12-12. You're not going to add any constraints yet.

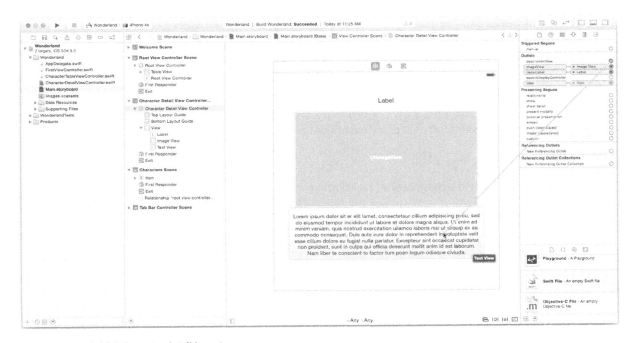

Figure 12-12. Initial character detail layout

Select the view controller object and switch to the outlets inspector. Connect the `nameLabel`, `imageView`, and `descriptionView` outlets to their respective objects in the interface, also shown in Figure 12-12.

Adding the Data Model

What's left? You still have to create a data model and provide the table view with a data source and table view cell object. Start with the data model.

I have a surprise for you. I created a data model for you. Isn't that nice of me? The character detail information is stored in an object array. Each element of the array contains a dictionary. Each dictionary has the name of the character, the filename of its image, and a brief description. All of this information is stored in the Characters.nsarray file, one of the resource files you added earlier in this chapter.

> **Note** The Characters.nsarray file is a serialized property list XML file. You can view it in Xcode or almost any plain-text editor, if you want to look at it. I created the file by writing an OS X command-line program that creates all of the dictionaries, assembles them into an array, and writes (serializes) the array to a file. The project that does this is in the Learn iOS Development Projects ➤ Ch 12 ➤ CharacterMaker folder. Property lists and serialization are explained in Chapter 18.

Add the data model to your table view controller by creating a property to hold the array. Add the following properties to your CharacterTableViewController.swift file:

```
var tableData: [[String: String]] {
    if tableData_Lazy == nil {
        if let url = NSBundle.mainBundle().URLForResource( "Characters", ↩
                                            withExtension: "nsarray") {
            tableData_Lazy = NSArray(contentsOfURL: url) as? [[String: String]]
        }
        assert(tableData_Lazy != nil, "Characters.nsarray did not load")
    }
    return tableData_Lazy!
}
private var tableData_Lazy: [[String: String]]?
```

You saw this sort of thing in Chapter 9. This declares a read-only property named tableData that returns an array of dictionaries, each of which maps a string key to a string value ([[String: String]]). This array is lazily read from the Character.nsarray file the first time it's requested, and it's stored in the private tableData_Lazy property for future use.

USING ASSERTS

Note the use of the `assert(_:,_:)` statement in the `tableData` property getter. Assert statements have two arguments: a Boolean condition and a string description. They're used during development to express any strong assumptions you're making. The first argument expresses something in your program that you always assume is true, and the message describes what might be wrong if it isn't. In most apps, there are lots of places where you assume something about values or relationships. You might assume that a size is always nonzero, a date is always in the future, or an outlet has always been set.

In this case, `tableData` should always return a value. This assumes that the `Characters.nsarray` file is a permanent resource of your app and can always be loaded. This really shouldn't be an issue. There's no point in writing code to consider the possibility that the `Characters.nsarray` file isn't there or can't be loaded. But if it's not true and `tableData` returns `nil`, your app is going to be a world of hurt. The `assert(_:,_:)` function catches that condition, terminates your app, and sends the message ("Characters.nsarray did not load") to your Xcode debug console. This helps you find these kinds of mistakes during development; maybe you forgot to include the `Characters.nsarray` resource file in the app's target or you accidentally renamed the file.

Sure, you could leave the assert statement out and let `tableData` return `nil`, but some random code in another part of your program will try to use that `nil` value and crash your app. You'll then spend five minutes trying to figure out what caused a memory segment fault. With the assert statement, you'll catch the problem immediately and know exactly what's wrong, shortening your debugging efforts.

Assert functions do not execute in production code. They test their conditional only when you build your app for debugging. When you compile your app for distribution, all of the assert statements turn off, almost as if they weren't there.

The keys for the dictionaries need to be defined as constants. Before the `class` `CharactersTableViewController` declaration, add these three global constants:

```
let nameKey = "name"
let imageKey = "image"
let descriptionKey = "description"
```

Declaring them outside the class definition makes them global properties, easily accessible from other classes (the `CharacterDetailViewController` will need these too). You now have a data model!

Implementing Your Data Source

Now you need to feed the table view this information via its data source object. While still in the `CharacterTableViewController.swift` file, add a `tableView(_:,numberOfRowsInSection:)` function.

```
override func tableView(tableView: UITableView, ↵
                        numberOfRowsInSection section: Int) -> Int {
    return tableData.count
}
```

This function provides the table view with the number of rows in the list, which is the number of objects in the array.

> **Note**   You might have noticed that you haven't connected the table view's `delegate` or `dataSource` outlet to your table view controller. That's because your controller is a subclass of `UITableViewController`, which is specifically designed to manage a table view. If you *do not* connect the `delegate` or `dataSource` outlets yourself, the controller makes itself both the delegate and the data source for the table automatically. Isn't that convenient?

Defining a Table View Cell Object

The last piece of the puzzle is to supply the table view with a table cell object for each row—the table view's rubber stamp. Add this `tableView(_:,cellForRowAtIndexPath:)` function immediately after your `tableView(_:,numberOfRowsInSection:)` function:

```
override func tableView(tableView: UITableView, ↵
            cellForRowAtIndexPath indexPath: NSIndexPath) -> UITableViewCell {
    let cellID = "Cell"
    let cell = tableView.dequeueReusableCellWithIdentifier( cellID, ↵
                                    forIndexPath: indexPath) as UITableViewCell
    let characterInfo = tableData[indexPath.row]
    cell.textLabel?.text = characterInfo[nameKey]
    return cell
}
```

This code should look familiar—unless you skipped Chapter 5. The cell's appearance is defined by the cell prototype in the storyboard, which you still need to define. Switch to the `Main.storyboard` file and locate the table view controller.

At the top of the table view you'll see an area labeled Prototype Cells, as shown in Figure 12-13. Select the first, blank cell and use the attributes inspector to change its style to Basic, set its identifier to Cell, and change its accessory to Disclosure Indicator (see Figure 12-13).

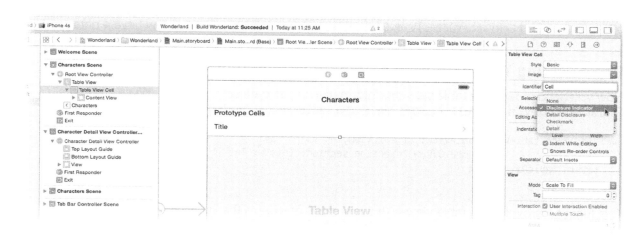

Figure 12-13. Defining a table cell

Now when your `tableView(_:,cellForRowAtIndexPath:)` function asks for the Cell table cell object, it's already there. Your code just configures the text of the cell and it's done.

Your table view now has data. Run the app in the simulator and tap the second tab, and this time your table is populated with the names from the data model, as shown in Figure 12-14.

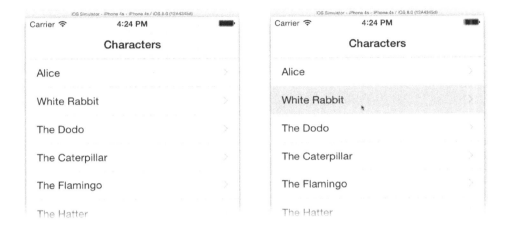

Figure 12-14. Working table view

Pushing the Detail View Controller

Tapping a row in the table, however, doesn't do much (on the right in Figure 12-14). That's because you haven't defined the action that presents the detail view.

You're going to add a segue from the table cell view to your detail view. Control+click or right-click on the prototype cell object and drag to the character detail view controller (also shown in Figure 12-15). When you release the mouse, choose the show option from the Selection Segue group. This configures all rows that use this cell object to "push" the character details view controller onto the navigation controller's stack, presenting it as the active view controller.

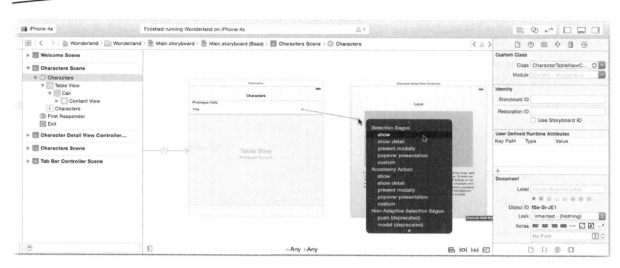

Figure 12-15. *Connecting a segue to the table cell view*

Just as you did in Chapter 5, you need some code to prepare the detail view based on the row the user tapped. For that to work, you'll need to know when the segue is triggered. Select the newly created segue and use the attributes inspector to change its identifier to detail, as shown in Figure 12-16.

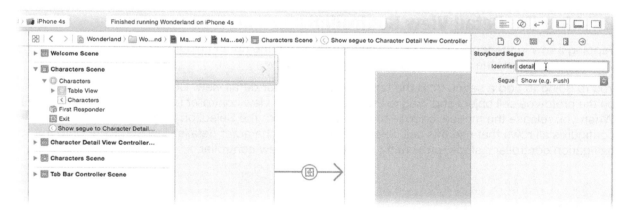

Figure 12-16. *Assigning a segue identifier*

Return to the `CharacterTableViewController.swift` file and add this function:

```
override func prepareForSegue(segue: UIStoryboardSegue, sender: AnyObject!) {
    if segue.identifier == "detail" {
        let detailsController = segue.destinationViewController ↩
                                        as CharacterDetailViewController
        if let selectedPath = tableView?.indexPathForSelectedRow() {
            detailsController.characterInfo = tableData[selectedPath.row]
        }
    }
}
```

This function is called whenever a segue is triggered in this view controller. The segue object contains information about the view controllers involved (both coming and going). Use it to get the details view controller object that the storyboard just created and loaded. You then use the `tableView` object to get the row number of the currently selected row—the one the user is tapping—and use that to get the character details from the data model and configure the new view controller (by setting `characterInfo`).

There are still a few loose ends. The detail view controller doesn't have a `characterInfo` property yet! Switch to your `CharacterDetailViewController.swift` file and add the following code:

```
var characterInfo = [String: String]()

override func viewWillAppear(animated: Bool) {
    super.viewWillAppear(animated)
    nameLabel?.text = characterInfo[nameKey]
    imageView?.image = UIImage(named: characterInfo[imageKey]!)
    descriptionView?.text = characterInfo[descriptionKey]
}
```

Your details view controller now has a `characterInfo` property. When the view controller is about to appear on the screen, this code will populate the view objects with details in `characterInfo`. Run the app in the simulator to try it, as shown in Figure 12-17.

Figure 12-17. Working character table

While the information is there, you'll notice that the views in the detail view controller aren't arranged nicely, nor do they adjust their size. If you're running this on an iPhone, it's going to look even worse. Don't worry. You'll fix that in the "Being Adaptable" section later in this chapter.

Your app is now two-thirds finished. In this section, you created a table view and a detail view, nested inside a navigation view controller, nested inside a tab view controller.

By now you should be getting pretty comfortable with content and container view controllers, connecting them and creating segues to define your app's navigation. The final section of this chapter is going to show you how to use a page view controller.

Creating a Page View Controller

You have arrived at the third, and final, tab of your Wonderland app. This tab will display the text of the book, one page at a time. This tab uses a page view controller (UIPageViewController) object. It's a container view controller that manages a (potentially huge) collection of content view controllers. Each "page" consists of one or two content view controllers. The page view controller provides gesture recognizers that perform and animate the navigation between pages in the collection.

Adding a page view controller to your design is simple enough. Getting it to work is another matter. Page view controllers are typically code intensive, and this app is no exception. To make the situation even more exciting, you have to get the bulk of your code working before the page view will do anything at all. So, settle in, this is going to be a long trip.

You're going to need a number of new classes, so create them all now. Use the New File command (or drag in Swift file template objects) to create new Swift files in your project's Wonderland group. As you create each new file, write a skeleton class definition. This will let Xcode know what classes you're going to write, what their superclasses are, and a few key outlets. This will let you design your interfaces before writing the bulk of the code.

Begin by creating a BookViewController.swift file. This class will be your custom page view controller.

```
import UIKit

class BookViewController: UIPageViewController {
}
```

Create a BookDataSource.swift file. This will become your page view controller's data source object.

```
import UIKit

class BookDataSource: NSObject, UIPageViewControllerDataSource {
}
```

Add a OnePageViewController.swift file to your project. This will be the view controller for each individual page of the book, and it needs some outlets to its views.

```
import UIKit

class OnePageViewController: UIViewController {
    @IBOutlet var textView: OnePageView!
    @IBOutlet var pageLabel: UILabel!
}
```

Finally, add a `OnePageView.swift` file. This is a custom `UIView` class that draws the text of one page. This one is so short, you might as well write the whole thing now.

```
import UIKit

class OnePageView: UIView {
    var text: NSString = "" { didSet { setNeedsDisplay() } }
    var fontAttrs: [String: AnyObject]! = nil

    override func drawRect(rect: CGRect) {
        super.drawRect(rect)
        text.drawInRect(bounds, withAttributes: fontAttrs)
    }
}
```

You should be able to decipher this, having read Chapter 11. When it's time to draw itself, a `OnePageView` object fills its view with the background color (`super.drawRect(rect)` does that for you) and then draws its `text` using the attributes stored in its `fontAttrs` property.

I've omitted the code for the last class you'll need. It's rather long and is not the focus of this chapter. Locate the source code you downloaded. In the `Learn iOS Development Projects` ➤ `Ch 12` ➤ Wonderland folder, find the `Paginator.swift` file and drag it into the Wonderland group of your project—remembering to check the Copy option when you import it.

The `Paginator` object is conceptually simple. It has three settable properties: the text of the entire book (as a single string), a font, and a view size. The object splits up the text into pages, each one of which will exactly fill the given view size using that font. If you're interested in the details, read the comments in the code.

> **Note**   This is hardly the most sophisticated way of implementing a paginator, but it's sufficient for this app.

You're now ready to add your view controllers and design the interface.

Adding the Page View Controllers

It's not all code. Use Interface Builder to create the two view controllers. Select the `Main.storyboard` file. Drag a new Page View Controller from the object library and add it to your design. Also add a new View Controller object, as shown in Figure 12-18. Arrange them below the other scenes.

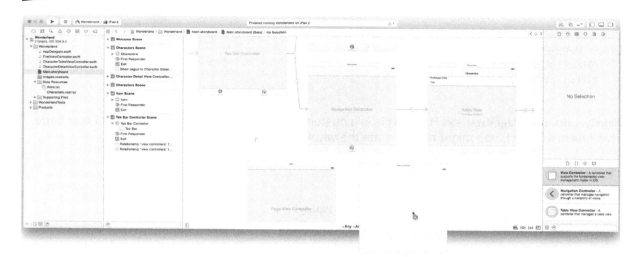

Figure 12-18. *Adding the page view controller and single page view controller*

Add the page view controller to the tab bar by Control+dragging or right-click-dragging from the tab bar controller to the new page view controller, as shown in Figure 12-19, just as you did earlier for the navigation view controller. Select the view controllers relationship.

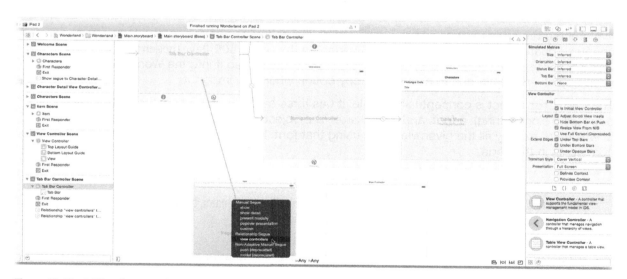

Figure 12-19. *Adding the page view controller to the tab bar*

As you did with the other tabs, select the tab bar item in the page view controller's scene. Use the attributes inspector to set its title to Book and its tab icon to tab-book.

Now configure the page view controller itself. Select the page view controller object and use the identity inspector to change its class to BookViewController. Switch to the attributes inspector and double-check that the following properties are set:

- Navigation: Horizontal
- Transition Style: Page Curl
- Spine Location: Min

These settings define a "book-like" interface where the user moves horizontally through a collection of view controllers, one per page. (If you set the Spine location to the Mid, you'd get two view controllers per page.) A transition between controllers emulates the turning of a paper page.

Designing a Prototype Page

Now move over to the plain view controller you just added. Use the identity inspector to change its class to OnePageViewController. Also change its Storyboard ID to OnePage. This last step is important. This controller won't be connected in Interface Builder; you're going to create instances of it programmatically. To do that, you need a way to refer to it, and you'll use its storyboard ID to do that.

With the preliminaries out of the way, create the interface for the one page view controller. From the object library, add three view objects as follows:

1. Label
   a. Font: System 15.0
   b. Text: Alice's Adventures in Wonderland
   c. Position at top center
2. Label
   a. Font: System 11.0
   b. Position at bottom center
3. View
   a. Center between the two labels to fill the available space.
   b. Use the identity inspector to change its class to OnePageView.
4. Constraints
   a. Select both label objects and add center horizontally constraints.
   b. Select the top label and add a vertical constraint to the top layout guide (standard distance).
   c. Select the bottom label and add a vertical constraint to the bottom layout guide (standard distance).
   d. Select the image view and add top, leading, trailing, and bottom constraints, all set to 20 pixels, as shown in Figure 12-20.

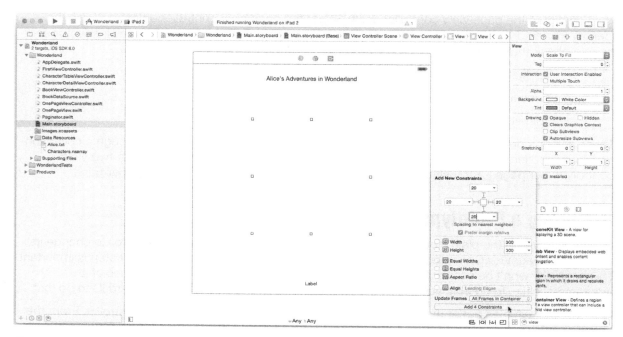

Figure 12-20. *One page view controller layout*

Select the one page view controller object and use the connections inspector to connect its two outlets to the OnePageView object and the label at the bottom (which will display the page number), as shown in Figure 12-21.

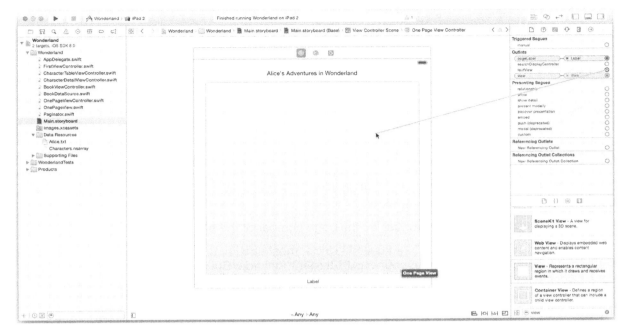

Figure 12-21. *Connecting the page view objects*

Coding the One Page View Controller

You've now done just about all you can do in Interface Builder. It's time to roll up your sleeves and start coding. This time, start from the "tail" end of this design and work back up to the page view controller, filling in the details as you go. The last object in the chain is OnePageView, the custom view that displays the text of a page. You've already written that, and it was pretty simple. (If you've already forgotten, sneak back to the "Creating a Page View Controller" section).

Let's move on to the view controller. You've already defined the class, added two outlets (textView and pageLabel), and connected those outlets to their view objects. Now add a couple of properties and a loadPageContent() function.

```
var pageNumber = 1
var paginator: Paginator? = nil

func loadPageContent() {
    if let tv = textView {
        if let pager = paginator {
            pager.viewSize = tv.bounds.size
            if !pager.pageAvailable(pageNumber) {
                pageNumber = pager.lastKnownPage
            }
```

```
            tv.fontAttrs = pager.fontAttrs
            tv.text = pager.textForPage(pageNumber)
        }
    }
    pageLabel?.text = "Page \(pageNumber)"
}
```

The pageNumber determines the page number of the book this view controller displays. It will be set by the data source when the controller is created. The paginator property connects this view controller to the book's content. The loadPageContent() function starts by configuring paginator with the actual size of the text view. It then simply asks the paginator for the text for this page and the font attributes that should be used to draw it. It transfers those values to the textView (OnePageView) object that will do that actual drawing. The OnePageViewController is really just "glue" between its OnePageView and the Paginator.

Finally, the pageLabel view is set to display the page number of the book.

So, when does loadPageContent() get called? Under most circumstances, this kind of first-time view setup code would be invoked from your viewDidLoad() function. But loadPageContent() needs to be called whenever the size of text view changes, and that can happen at any time, most notably when the user changes the display orientation. Solve that by overriding the viewDidLayoutSubviews() function and calling loadPageContent() whenever the controller's view layout is adjusted.

```
override func viewDidLayoutSubviews() {
    super.viewDidLayoutSubviews()
    loadPageContent()
}
```

I talk about viewDidLayoutSubviews() and the other adaption functions later in this chapter.

Coding the Page View Data Source

You finally get to the heart of the page view controller: the page view data source. A page view controller data source must conform to the UIPageViewControllerDataSource protocol and implement these two required functions:

```
pageViewController(_:,viewControllerBeforeViewController:) -> UIViewController
pageViewController(_:,viewControllerAfterViewController:) -> UIViewController
```

The page view starts with an initial view controller to display. When the user "flips" the page to the right or left, the page view controller sends the data source object one of these messages, depending on the direction of the page turn. The data source, using the current view controller as a reference, retrieves or creates the view controller that will display the next (or previous) page. If there is no page, it returns nil.

Your data source must implement these methods. It will also need a property that refers to the single paginator object used by all of the individual view controllers and a function to create the view controller for an arbitrary page. Your BookDataSource.swift file, therefore, should start like this:

```
let paginator = Paginator(font: UIFont(name: "Times New Roman", size: 18.0))

func load(# page: Int, pageViewController: UIPageViewController) ↵
                                        -> OnePageViewController? {
    if page < 1 || !paginator.pageAvailable(page) {
        return nil;
    }
    let controller = pageViewController.storyboard?.instantiateViewController ↵
    WithIdentifier("OnePage") as OnePageViewController
    controller.paginator = paginator
    controller.pageNumber = page
    return controller
}
```

The paginator property is initialized with a Paginator object that will use the Times New Roman font at 18 points to display the text.

The load(page:,pageViewController:) function is where all of the works gets done. You call this function with a page number, and it returns a view controller that will display that page. If the requested page doesn't exist, it returns nil. It asks the storyboard object (that it obtains via the page view controller) to create the controller and views contained in the scene with the identifier OnePage. This is done because segues and actions aren't used to navigate between view controllers in a page view. It's up to the data source to create them when requested.

> **Note**   Remember, earlier you assigned the view controller scene in the storyboard an identifier of OnePage. This is why. If you need to programmatically load a view controller and its view objects from a storyboard scene, the instantiateViewControllerWithIdentifier(_:) function is your ticket.

Once it has a new one page view controller object, it connects it to the paginator and sets the page number it should display.

All that's left to do is to implement the two required data source protocol methods. These also go in your BookDataSource class.

```
func pageViewController(bookViewController: UIPageViewController, ↵
        viewControllerAfterViewController viewController: UIViewController) ↵
                                        -> UIViewController? {
    if let pageController = viewController as? OnePageViewController {
        let pageAfter = pageController.pageNumber + 1
        return load(page: pageAfter, pageViewController: bookViewController)
    }
    return nil
}
```

```
func pageViewController(bookViewController: UIPageViewController, ↵
        viewControllerBeforeViewController viewController: UIViewController) ↵
                                        -> UIViewController? {
    if let pageController = viewController as? OnePageViewController {
        let pageBefore = pageController.pageNumber - 1
        return load(page: pageBefore, pageViewController: bookViewController)
    }
    return nil
}
```

Since each one page view controller stores the page number it displays, all these two functions have to do is request the page after or before the current one.

Initializing a Page View Controller

Your book implementation is almost complete. The only thing left to do is perform some initial setup of the page view controller and data model when the page view controller is created. Switch to the BookViewController.swift file. Begin by creating a property to store the data source object.

```
let bookSource = BookDataSource()
```

> **Note**   Why it's necessary to create a bookSource instance variable has to do with a quirk of the automatic reference counting (ARC) memory management system. Read the comments in the finished project and Chapter 20 for an explanation.

Now write a viewDidLoad() function to initialize the page view controller when it's created.

```
override func viewDidLoad() {
    super.viewDidLoad()
    if let textURL = NSBundle.mainBundle().URLForResource( "Alice",
                                        withExtension: "txt") {
        bookSource.paginator.bookText = NSString(contentsOfURL: textURL,
                                encoding: NSUTF8StringEncoding, error: nil)
    }
```

This first block of code reads in the text of the book, stored in the Alice.txt file. This was one of the resource files you added at the beginning. The file is a UTF-8 encoded text file with each line separated by a single carriage return (U+000d) character. This format is what the paginator expects. The entire text is read into a single string and stored in the paginator, which will use it to assign text to individual pages.

```
dataSource = bookSource
```

The next statement makes the bookSource object the data source for the page view controller.

```
let firstPage = bookSource.load(page: 1, pageViewController: self)!
setViewControllers( [firstPage],
        direction: .Forward,
        animated: false,
        completion: nil)
}
```

This last statement is probably the most important. It creates the initial view controller that the page view controller will present by explicitly creating the controller for page 1. This must be done programmatically before the page view controller appears.

> **Caution**   The initial view controller for a page view controller is an array. The number of view controllers must exactly match the number of view controllers the page view controller presents at one time. If you configure the page view controller with a spine location of .Mid, you must provide two initial view controllers: one for the left page and a second one for the right page.

That was a lot of code, but you're done! Run your app and test the third tab, as shown in Figure 12-22.

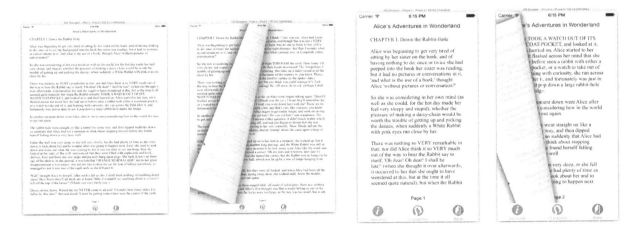

Figure 12-22. Working page view interface

Congratulations, you've created a truly complex app. You were aided, in part, by storyboards that allowed you to map out and define much of your app's navigation in a single file. But you also learned how to load storyboard scenes programmatically when needed.

I encourage you to take a moment and review the scenes in your storyboard file and the classes you created to support them. Once you're comfortable that you understand the organization of your view controllers, how they work together, and the roles of the individual classes you created, you can consider yourself a first-class iOS navigation engineer.

Now it's time to master the other two essential navigation skills: presenting view controllers and adapting view controllers.

Presenting View Controllers

Presenting a view controller makes the content of that view controller visible and allows the user to interact with it. You've been doing this since Chapter 2. Often, your view controllers are *implicitly* presented. That's the case with your initial view controller and the view controllers in container view controllers, like many of the ones you've created in this chapter. You didn't write any code to present the three view controllers in the tab view; you simply added them to the tab view controller and let it present them.

You *explicitly* present a view controller using the presentViewController(_:,animated:, completion:) function. This is almost always a *modal* presentation. That is, the presented view controller consumes the entire display (or overlays the existing interface) and takes over the user interaction until it is dismissed. At that time, it disappears, and the previous view controller becomes visible and active again.

You've been explicitly presenting modal view controllers since Chapter 3. You've presented alerts, the media picker, the photo library picker, and the camera interface. You've presented view controllers full-screen and in popovers. You've written code to collect the results of the presented controller and dismissed them when they were done.

So, you might be wondering what else there is to know about presenting view controllers. There's quite a lot actually. In this section you're going to learn about the different objects involved in presenting a view controller, the different presentation styles available, the default presentation behavior, the view controller transitions, and how you can override and customize presentations. Let's start by introducing the players.

Presentation Controllers

When presenting a view controller, there are a few key objects, as shown in Figure 12-23.

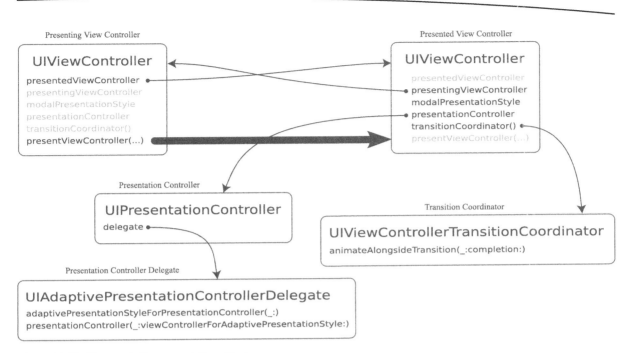

Figure 12-23. View controller presentation objects

The *presenting* view controller is the (currently active) view controller that wants to present a new view controller. The *presented* view controller is the new view controller that will be presented. When a presenting view controller wants to present another view controller, it calls presentViewController(_:,animated:,completion:).

The *presentation controller* is the object that manages the presentation. It's created at the same time as the view controller and exists until the view controller is dismissed. The presentation controller (UIPresentationController) determines how the new view controller appears on the screen. It might replace the entire screen with the new view controller, or it might put it inside a popover. This is a combination of the style the view controller would prefer to be presented in (its modelPresentationStyle), the style the presentation controller thinks it should be presented in, and the style the presentation controller delegate wants it to be presented in. There are a number of points in this decision chain where you can affect how your view controller is presented, which you'll explore in the next few sections.

Another object of interest is the *transition coordinator* (UIViewControllerTransitionCoordinator). This object is responsible for the transition between view controllers and the resizing of their content. When you tap a button and a new view controller slides up from the bottom, it's a transition coordinator directing that animation. And when you rotate the device, a transition coordinator orchestrates the smooth metamorphosis of the layout. Transition coordinators are created automatically at the beginning of a transition and disappear once it's over. You'll see how to use the transition coordinator later in this chapter.

To play around with view controller presentation, let's add a simple button that modally presents a custom view controller to your Wonderland app user. You can then explore different ways in which you can affect its presentation.

Presenting a Modal View Controller

Return to the Main.storyboard file and drag a button into the Welcome view, just to the right of the "by Lewis Carroll" text. Set its type to Info Dark, delete its title, and add a left horizontal constraint, as shown in Figure 12-24. Select both the button and the label and add an align vertical centers constraint.

Figure 12-24. Adding the author info button

Now add a new view controller to your storyboard. Drop it into the canvas right next to the Welcome Scene. Select the new view controller object, switch to the size inspector, and change its Simulated Size to Freeform. Give it a width of 250 and a height of 340 (see Figure 12-25).

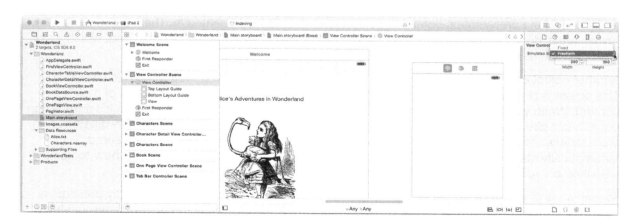

Figure 12-25. Creating a free-form view controller

Notice that the attribute is named Simulated Size. Interface Builder doesn't actually know how big your view controller will be when it's presented, but it will allow you to design it with a nontypical size.

Now you need to encourage it to be that size. Switch to the attributes inspector, find the Content Size properties, check the Use Preferred Explicit Size attribute, and set the width to 250 and the height to 340. This sets the view controller's preferredContentSize property. When a view controller is presented in such a way that its size can be variable (as in a popover as opposed to always being the size of the screen), this property is the size it would like to be. The presentation controller will try to accommodate it, but it isn't required to.

Add an image view and a label object to the new view controller, as follows:

1. Image view

    a. Set Image to info-charles.

    b. Set Mode to Aspect Fit.

    c. Add a vertical constraint (20 pixels) to the top layout guide.

    d. Add a center horizontally in superview constraint.

    e. Pin the height to 244 pixels and the width to 164 pixels.

2. Label view

    a. Set Text to "Lewis Carroll" and "a.k.a. Charles Lutwidge Dodgson" and "27 January 1832 – 14 January 1898" on three lines. (Hold the Option key down when pressing the Return key to create line breaks in the text.)

    b. Set Font to System 12.0.

    c. Set the alignment to centered.

    d. Set Lines to 3.

    e. Add top (8), leading (0), and trailing (0) constraints.

Your finished layout should look like the one in Figure 12-26.

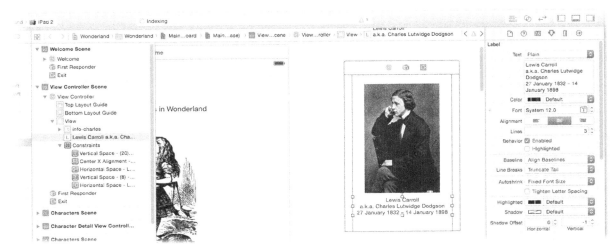

Figure 12-26. Finished author info layout

If you wanted to present this view controller modally and full-screen, you could do something like this:

1. Add an action to your FirstViewController (something like @IBAction func showInfo(_: AnyObject!)).

2. Connect the button to the new action.

3. Assign a storyboard ID to the new view controller.

4. In your showInfo(_:) function, instantiate your new view controller (using its storyboard ID).

5. Set the view controller's modalPresentationStyle to .FullScreen and its modalTransitionStyle to .Default.

6. Configure the presentation controller (if appropriate).

7. Call presentViewController(_:,animated:,completion:).

8. Create a new custom subclass of UIViewController (say, AuthorInfoViewController).

9. Add an @IBAction func done(_: AnyObject!) action.

10. Add a tap gesture recognizer or a Done button to the root view and connect it to the done(_:) function.

11. The done(_:) function will fetch the presenting view controller and dismiss itself.

When you tap the info button, the screen will be replaced with your new view controller. Tapping the Done button or root view will dismiss it.

You know all of this already; you've done all of these steps at one time or another in earlier projects. So, instead of repeating yourself, start with a shortcut and then use this as a foundation to explore some variations.

Modal Presentation Style

Begin by adding a segue from the button to the new view controller. Control+click or right-click the info button and drag to the new view controller, as shown in Figure 12-27.

Figure 12-27. *Connecting a model presentation segue*

If you select the present modally choice, you'll be performing steps 1 through 7 almost exactly. The key here is the modalPresentationStyle property (step 6). When a view controller's presentation style is set to .FullScreen, it's requesting to take over the entire screen, and the presentation controller generally honors that request.

But what are your other choices? You have several, as shown here:

- FullScreen
- OverFullScreen
- CurrentContext
- OverCurrentContext
- Popover
- PageSheet
- FormSheet
- Custom

The .OverFullScreen variation presents the view controller full-screen (exactly the same size as .FullScreen) but does not remove the presenting view controller. This subtle difference permits the new view controller to have a semitransparent or blurred background, allowing the presenting view controller's content to bleed through. It's a nice effect and has the sense of a temporary overlay rather than completely replacing the existing view. See the exercise in Chapter 17 for an example.

The two current context versions (.CurrentContext and .OverCurrentContext) place the presented view controller so it overlays or replaces the presenting view controller inside a container view controller, most notably a split view controller. In other words, it replaces or overlays a one view controller inside another view controller, instead of usurping the whole interface.

Popovers, page sheets, and form sheets are presentation modes specifically designed for the iPad. (Until iOS 8 they were available *only* on the iPad.) The presented view controller appears on top of the presenting view controller in a floating sheet (or "bubble"). The existing view controller never goes away but is often disabled and dimmed.

I'm sure your mouse button finger is getting tired deciding which option to pick. Go ahead and select the popover presentation segue choice (see Figure 12-27).[1] This segue will set the presented view controller's modalPresentationStyle to .Popover before the view is presented. Choose an iPad simulator (or device) and run your app. Tap the info button to present the new view controller, as shown on the left in Figure 12-28.

Figure 12-28. *The popover presentation style on an iPad and iPhone*

Hey, that looks pretty nice! Now switch to an iPhone (or similar compact device) and run your app again. Tap the info button. This time you get a full-screen view controller, as shown on the right in Figure 12-28.

While it doesn't look too bad, it's not a good interface. For one thing, you never implemented steps 8 through 11, so the user has no way to dismiss this view. Oops.

You could implement steps 8 through 11. That's a perfectly valid solution and completely appropriate for many circumstances. Instead, let's take a closer look at why you got a full-screen view controller instead of a popover and what you might do about that.

Making Presentation Suggestions

So, why did your view controller appear in .FullScreen mode on an iPhone? The modalPresentationStyle property is a suggestion of how the view controller wants to be presented, not a requirement. When the view controller is presented, the presentation controller considers the size of the interface, its current trait collection, and other information and decides the best way to present the view controller. This may, or may not, be what the view controller requested.

Generally, the presentation controller will present the view controller in whatever style it requested, *except* on horizontally compact devices. When the screen is small, the presentation controller turns popover, form sheet, and page sheet requests into the .FullScreen style, on the (sensible) assumption that there's not enough space on such a tiny device for those interface styles.

---

[1]If you already picked a different segue type, just select the segue and use the attributes inspector to change its Segue attribute to Present as Popover.

Guess what? The presentation controller has a `delegate` property (see Figure 12-23). The presentation controller's delegate is queried about what presentation style to use, and you can influence that decision. Let's do that now.

First, go back to the storyboard, select the info button's segue, and assign it an identifier of `info`. You'll need that to inject a little code into the presentation process. Now go to the `FirstViewController.swift` file and add the following function:

```
override func prepareForSegue(segue: UIStoryboardSegue, sender: AnyObject!) {
    if segue.identifier == "info" {
        let presented = segue.destinationViewController as UIViewController
        let presentationController = presented.presentationController
        presentationController?.delegate = self
    } else {
        super.prepareForSegue(segue, sender: sender)
    }
}
```

This function is called by the segue just before the new view controller is presented. It first obtains the view controller that will be presented and obtains its presentation controller. You then make this object the presentation controller's delegate.

For this to work, this view controller has to adopt the `UIAdaptivePresentationControllerDelegate` protocol, so add that now (new code in bold).

```
class FirstViewController: UIViewController,
                    UIAdaptivePresentationControllerDelegate {
```

Now add this adaptive presentation controller delegate function:

```
func adaptivePresentationStyleForPresentationController( ↵
        controller: UIPresentationController) -> UIModalPresentationStyle {
    return .None
}
```

Now select an iPhone simulator (or any other compact device) and run your app again. Tap the info button, and you get a popover, like the one on the right in Figure 12-29.

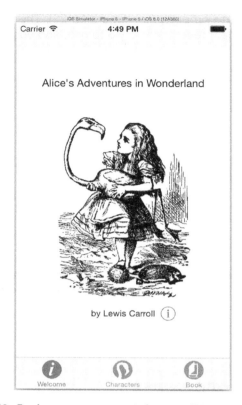
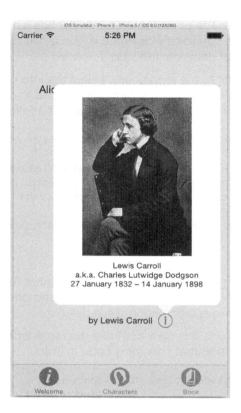

Figure 12-29. *Forcing a popover presentation on an iPhone*

So, what just happened? On a horizontally compact device, the presentation controller defers to its delegate object to determine how the interface should be adapted to the smaller device. If the delegate returns .None, it means "Don't adapt the interface. Present it exactly as it was requested." And that's what the presentation controller did, putting the new view controller in a popover—an interface you don't often see on an iPhone.

This particular interface is small enough that it actually works in a popover, even on the smallest mobile devices. But what if it didn't? Yes, you can still go back and implement steps 8 through 11, but the presentation controller delegate has one more trick up its sleeve.

Adapting a View Controller During Presentation

In addition to getting the delegate's opinion about the best way to present a view controller in a compact environment, the presentation controller also lets the delegate adapt the interface before presenting it. I'll talk a lot more about adapting in the next sections, but for now just know that "adapting" an interface means adjusting it so it fits its new home.

Return to the `FirstViewController.swift` file and adjust the delegate function so it reads like this (modified code in bold):

```
func adaptivePresentationStyleForPresentationController(
        controller: UIPresentationController) -> UIModalPresentationStyle {
    return .FullScreen
}
```

Now your delegate agrees with the presentation controller: when presented on a horizontally compact device, all view controllers (for this delegate) will be presented full-screen. That puts you right back into the pickle you had before—there's nothing that lets the user dismiss the view. Have no fear, there's a delegate method for that.

Before the view controller is presented, the presentation controller calls the `presentController` `(_:,viewControllerForAdaptivePresentationStyle:)` delegate function. Add one to your class.

```
func presentationController(controller: UIPresentationController, ↩
            viewControllerForAdaptivePresentationStyle style: ↩
                UIModalPresentationStyle) -> UIViewController? {
    let presentedVC = controller.presentedViewController
    let replacementController ↩
                = UINavigationController(rootViewController: presentedVC)
    let navigationItem = presentedVC.navigationItem
    let doneButton = UIBarButtonItem(barButtonSystemItem: .Done,
                                        target: self,
                                        action: "dismissInfo:")
    navigationItem.rightBarButtonItem = doneButton
    navigationItem.title = "Author"
    return replacementController
}
```

In this function, you can take the view controller to present and modify (adapt) it so it's ready to be presented full-screen—or whatever the `style` parameter says it's going to be presented as. This might entail adding a Done button or adding a tap gesture recognizer and a label that says "tap to dismiss." It's entirely up to you. Just make the modifications here and return the modified view controller.

Your function, however, goes one step further; it replaces the view controller with a completely different one! Actually, it creates a navigation view controller and makes the presented view controller its root view. It then configures the navigation bar so it has a Done button, which calls a `dismissInfo(_:)` function to dismiss the view controller. This neatly solves the need to provide a way to dismiss the view, with a standard and recognizable interface, without modifying the original view controller.

Oh, I guess you'll need that `dismissInfo(_:)` function.

```
@IBAction func dismissInfo(sender: AnyObject) {
    dismissViewControllerAnimated(true, completion: nil)
}
```

While still running an iPhone simulator, run your app again, as shown in Figure 12-30.

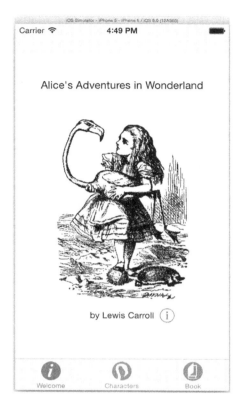
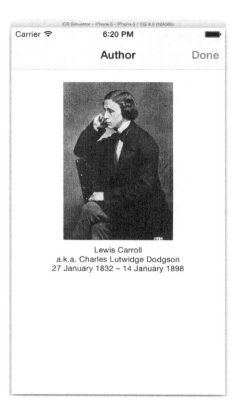

Figure 12-30. Adapted full-screen view controller presentation

Technically, this is adaption, which is the last section of this chapter. But before I segue to that topic (apologies for the pun), let's take stock about what you've learned about presentation controllers and talk about other reasons to use them.

- The view controller that wants to present another view controller is the *presenting* view controller.

- The view controlling being presented is the *presented* view controller.

- A *presentation controller* manages the presentation, adaption, and dismissal of a view controller.

- A view controller has a preferred presentation style, transition style, and size.

- The presentation controller considers these properties when presenting the view controller but may overrule them.

- The presentation controller's delegate may—in horizontally compact environments—overrule its style decisions and can alter or replace the view controller being presented.

Popover Presentation Controllers

Unless you plan to modify or customize how your view controller is presented, you normally don't need to mess with the presentation controller. But there's one notable exception: the popover presentation controller.

Depending on the modalPresentationStyle value, the presentation controller created for your view controller may be a subclass of UIPresentationController with additional features. Specifically, if your view controller's modalPresentationStyle is .Popover, its presentationController property will return a UIPopoverPresentationController object. This class has additional functions and properties that apply only to popover presentations—some of which you *must* set up or the presentation will fail.

You've already had to deal with this in earlier projects, so let's relive one of those moments. When you present a view controller in a popover, you must set its *source*. This is an object or rectangle that determines where the popover is anchored on the screen. You did this a couple of times in the MyStuff project, back in Chapter 9. Here's that code again:

```
if let popover = alert.popoverPresentationController {
    popover.sourceView = imageView
    popover.sourceRect = imageView.bounds
    popover.permittedArrowDirections = ( .Up | .Down )
}
```

The UIViewController's convenience property popoverPresentationController is the best way to get the popover controller. This property will be the presentationController if, and only if, it's a popover controller conveniently downcast to UIPopoverPresentationController. If not, it returns nil. Note that this is the same object returned by presentationController, just downcast.

At a minimum, you must set either the sourceView and sourceRect or the barButtonItem of the popover controller. When you use a segue, as you did earlier, the segue does this for you. You can optionally customize the allowed arrow directions, the color of the arrow (so it matches the background of your popover view's background), and other features.

Now that you know how to use the presentation controller, let's get back to adaption.

Adapting View Controller Content

The last essential view controller skill to master is how to adapt your view's content to different display environments. *Adapting* a view controller consists of modifying its view objects and layout to present a pleasing user interface for a specific device, screen size, orientation, or resolution. You've encountered this repeatedly throughout this book, but now it's time to dive into the details.

ADAPTION BEFORE IOS 8

Adaption isn't new to iOS, but iOS 8 introduces a radically different philosophy and a set of tools to help you. In the past, adaption was handled in a somewhat ad hoc fashion. There were properties that told you the broad category of device your app was running on (iPhone or iPad), properties and events that told you what orientation the device was in (portrait, landscape left, landscape right, upside down), properties that told you what size the screen was, and so on.

Your storyboard files were also split, with one storyboard file for iPhone and iPhone-like devices (`Main_iPhone. storyboard`) and a second storyboard file for iPad and iPad-like devices (`Main_iPad.storyboard`). Would you like to add a button? You'd have to add the button, connect it to an outlet, connect its action, and create its constraints. And then you'd have to do that all over again in the second storyboard file. Your code would also be riddled with statements such as `if deviceIdiom == .iPhone {` *do this for an iPhone* `} else {` *do that for an iPad* `}`. As new types of devices emerged, with new screen sizes and with new resolutions, managing your app's interface became untenable. iOS 8 changes all of that.

---

iOS 8 abstracts the interface environment into a set of generic traits and provides a consistent set of methods for adjusting your content. There are no longer separate functions for resizing the view controller and handing device rotation. Now, all view controller size changes are handled the same way. Broadly, you have four different ways of adapting your views, from the broad to the specific:

- Being clever
- Traits
- Sizes
- Layout events

Let's explore each one and see how and why you'd use it to adapt your interface.

Smarter Than the Average Bear

I listed "being clever" as one technique for adapting your views. If you're ingenious, you can often design your interface in such a way that it doesn't need adapting. It will just adjust itself to fit the available display, whatever that is. I think of these as "self-adapting" interfaces, and it's always the technique I try to apply first. Return to the `Main.storyboard` file of your Wonderland app and let's take a crack at adapting the character detail scene. Add the following constraints:

1. Label
   a. Top edge to top layout guide (40 pixels)
   b. Center horizontally in container
2. Image view
   a. Top edge to label (8 pixels)
   b. Bottom edge to text view (standard)
   c. Leading and trailing edges to superview (40 pixels each)

3. Text view

   a. Pin height at 128 pixels

   b. Leading and trailing edges to superview (30 pixels each)

   c. Bottom edge to bottom layout guide (standard), as shown in Figure 12-31

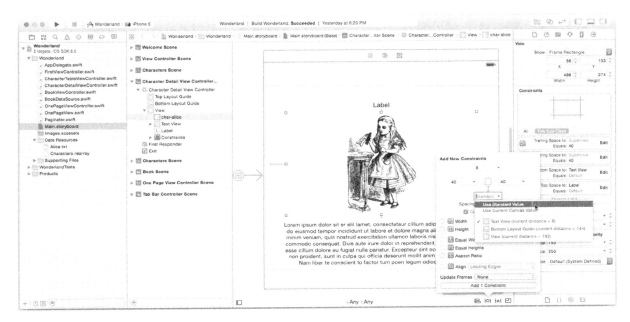

Figure 12-31. Initial constraints for character detail view

If you study these constraints or just run them in the simulator, you'll see that they work but not all that well (see Figure 12-32).

Figure 12-32. *Testing character detail constraints*

The constraints in a layout define a kind of algebraic equation. The auto-layout logic first finds all the constants in the equation (the size of the superview, the pinned height of a text view, a constraint that says "this label's top edge must be exactly 40 pixels below the top layout guide," and so on). It then identifies the properties that are variable (the height of the image view, the top-edge position of the text view, and so on). It then "solves" the equation by providing values for the variables that satisfy all of the constants. The layout in your character detail view "solves" the equation, but it doesn't look that great.

So far in this book you've created only simple, constant, invariable constraints. Most of the time that's all you need, but sometimes you need something more flexible, and the auto-layout system is both willing and able. Here are some additional tools at your disposal:

- Constraints can express inequalities.
- Constraints can be prioritized.
- View content is compressible.
- View content "hugs" its margins.

First, constraints don't have to express an unequivocal rule. You can create a constraint that says "The height of this view must be 80 pixels *or more*" or "The left edge of this button must be *more than* 6 pixels beyond the right edge of that label." The first change you're going to make is to alter the constraint for the bottom edge of the text view. Select the text view. This will reveal[2] the constraints attached to it. Select the small constraint at the bottom (between it and the bottom layout guide), as shown in Figure 12-33. In the attributes inspector, change the Relation property from Equal to Greater Than or Equal.

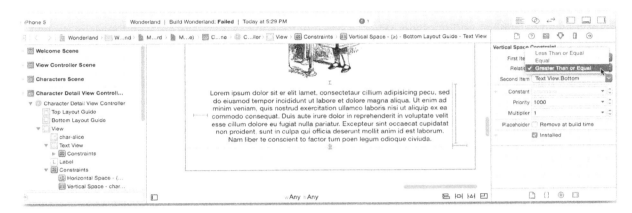

Figure 12-33. Creating a constraint inequlity

Now the auto-layout logic has a new variable to play with. No longer is the bottom edge of the text view required to be exactly 8 pixels above the bottom layout guide. The layout engine can now move it around, as long as it is *at least* 8 pixels above the bottom layout guide.

Prioritizing Constraints

Constraints are also prioritized. By default, the priority of a new constraint is `UILayoutPriorityRequired`. This value is 1,000, the highest priority. It means the constraint is required; it must be satisfied. But you can create constraints with lower priorities. If you do, the layout logic will "sacrifice" lower-priority constraints in order to satisfy high-priority ones. iOS defines two other handy priorities, `UILayoutPriorityDefaultHigh` (750) and `UILayoutPriorityDefaultLow` (250), for important but not required constraints and nice to have but not important constraints, respectively. You can assign any priority from 1 to 1,000—just avoid 50, that's reserved for another use.

Intrinsic Size

The auto-layout logic also considers a view's intrinsic size. View objects with content (labels, text views, image views, buttons, and so on) all have an *intrinsic size*. This is the size the view needs to be to exactly display its content. For an image view, it's the size of its image. For a label, it's the drawn size of its text. If you don't add constraints that dictate the height or width of a view, auto-layout looks to its intrinsic size and starts with that.

---

[2]If you've turned this feature off, select the view and then click the Edit button for the constraint in the size inspector.

> **Note**   If you create a custom subclass of `UIView` and need auto-layout to consider its intrinsic size, you must override the `intrinsicContentSize() -> CGSize` function and supply that value.

If the view's intrinsic size won't satisfy the other constraints, auto-layout will override its intrinsic size to resolve the layout. When it does this, auto-layout encounters two more sets of priorities: *compression resistance* and *hugging*. When the layout tries to make a view smaller, the view "resists" compression, and when it tries to make it bigger, the view's content "hugs" its margins—in other words, it "resists" expansion.

These priorities are properties of the view. Select the image view in the character detail view and use the size inspector to change its vertical compression resistance to 250 (`UILayoutPriorityDefaultLow`), as shown in Figure 12-34.

Figure 12-34. Changing the compression resistance of an image view

> **Note**   Compression resistance and hugging each have two priorities, one for vertical and one for horizontal, making for four priorities in all. A `UIButton` view, by default, has a low horizontal hugging priority because a button doesn't mind being made wider. But it has a high vertical hugging priority because it strongly resists being made taller.

Run the app again, as shown in Figure 12-35, and compare the results to those in Figure 12-32. With the lower vertical compression resistance, the layout is more inclined to reduce the size of the image view to satisfy all of the layout constraints. With a variable bottom constraint, the text view is free to float up to join the image view.

Figure 12-35. *Layout with modified constraint and compression resistance*

The priorities assigned to the compression resistance and hugging are the same ones used to rank constraints. For example, if a width constraint is narrower than a view's intrinsic width, the priority of its horizontal compression resistance is compared to the priority of the constraint to determine which width prevails.

> **Tip**   Setting the compression resistance and hugging priority to 1,000 (`UILayoutPriorityRequired`) is equivalent to pinning the view to its intrinsic size.

Now that you understand a little about how constraints, inequality constraints, intrinsic sizes, and priorities work together, you can begin to design complex layout solutions that smoothly adapt to a variety of environments.

But if auto-layout still isn't sufficient for your needs, you have lots of other options. The next tool to reach for is adaptive constraints. These depend on traits, so let's talk about traits next.

Using Trait Collections

A *trait* is one generic aspect of the interface. Is it roomy or cozy? Is it high resolution or low resolution? Every device, window, and view controller has a set of these traits, called its *trait collection*, that you can examine to make broad decisions about how your interface should appear. Your view controller's current trait collection can be obtained through its `traitCollection` property. Table 12-2 lists the properties of a trait collection.

Table 12-2. *Traits in a Trait Collection*

Trait	Possible Values
Horizontal size class	Regular or Compact
Vertical size class	Regular or Compact
Interface idiom	iPad or iPhone
Display scale	1.0, 2.0, or 3.0

The two most useful traits are the horizontal and vertical size class. A *size class* indicates how "roomy" the interface is in that direction. An iPad has a Regular size class in both directions, in all orientations. That's because an iPad's display is large and there's rarely any need to make big changes to your interface to make it fit. An iPhone, in contrast, is Compact horizontally and Regular vertically when it's in portrait orientation. When in landscape, it's considered Compact in both directions.

So, why doesn't an iPhone have a Regular horizontal size class when it's in landscape? Size classes are more about expectations and usability than physical display sizes. As you learned earlier in this chapter, the presentation controller makes decisions about whether to present a view controller as a popover or in full-screen based on the horizontal size class of the device. Keeping the horizontal size class Compact means your photo picker won't suddenly appear in a popover on your iPhone. It also means that split view controllers will stay collapsed. Think of size classes as "expectation" classes.

As you've seen already, the presentation controller uses size classes to make decisions about what presentation style to use. But they're used in many more places, and one of those is Interface Builder.

Adding Adaptive Constraints (and Objects)

You can define constraints (and view objects) in Interface Builder that appear in your interface only when they occur in conjunction with a specific combination of size classes. You've already done this several times in earlier chapters, and you'll do it a few more before you're done. Let's review one of those.

In Chapter 9, you created multiple sets of alignment constraints for the "bang" buttons in the DrumDub projects, as shown in Figure 12-36.

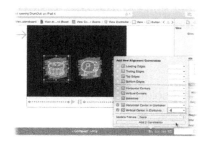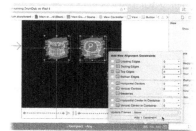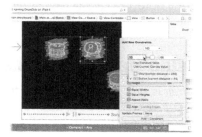

Figure 12-36. *Adding constraints for the wCompact/hAny size classes*

Since you've already gone through this process in detail, I won't rehash it here. But I will make two points.

First, be careful not to create conflicting constraints. If you add a width constraint to the wCompact/hAny set and a different width constraint (for the same view) in the wCompact/hCompact set, when your view is presented on an iPhone 5 in landscape orientation, your view will have a pair of conflicting constraints. Constraints do not override similar constraints in other sets. The constraints in your view are the union of every set that matches the current environment.

> **Caution**   A set of conflicting or incomplete constraints will cause your view's layout process to fail. Views may be pushed off screen, set with a zero size, or not positioned at all. The results are usually a jumbled mess of view objects.

Another feature is the ability to design view objects that appear only in certain trait environments. Just like constraints, objects added to your design when the size class selector is set to wRegular/hRegular will appear only when your view has a size class of wRegular/hRegular.

While this is handy feature, there are a couple of caveats. Adding one button to the wRegular/hAny set and a different button to the wCompact/hAny set creates two button objects. Both button objects exist for the lifetime of your view controller. When the display appears in a horizontally compact environment, the second button is automatically added to your view, and the first button is removed.

Because they are two different objects, *you can't connect them to the same outlet*. If you need an outlet for your button, create two outlets and synthesize a property that returns whichever one is installed, something like the following code:

```
@IBOutlet var button_Regular: UIButton!
@IBOutlet var button_Compact: UIButton!
var button: UIButton {
    if button_Regular.superview != nil {
        return button_Regular
    }
    return button_Compact
}
```

Probably the best feature of adaptive constraints and objects is that they're managed for you. If the device changes from a regular to a compact environment, the appropriate constraints are automatically added or removed. Doing this yourself in code requires overriding the appropriate functions. That's also a good thing to know how to do, so let's look at that now.

Adapting View Programmatically

You can also adapt your views programmatically in response to a number of environmental changes. Broadly, there are the following three strategies, in increasing order of granularity:

- Trait changes
- Size changes
- Layout changes

You'll need to consider programmatic adaption when you need to adjust the properties of views or make other layout changes that can't be expressed as constraints. The adaptive constraints in Interface Builder are great, but you can only add or remove constraints and objects. Interface Builder won't let you define adaptive properties or actions. You can't, for example, have an image view left-justify its image in a horizontally regular environment and center it in a compact environment. For that, you'll need a bit of code.

Adapting When Traits Change

The text of your book looks better when the font is little smaller on compact devices, like an iPhone. Modify the code in BookViewController.swift to adjust the font size based on the horizontal size class of the device.

The first step is to create the code to adapt your views. Add this function to your BookViewController class:

```
func adaptViewsToTraitCollection(traits: UITraitCollection) {
    let compactWidth = ( traitCollection.horizontalSizeClass == .Compact )

    var fontSize: CGFloat = 18.0
    if compactWidth {
        fontSize = 14.0
    }
    let paginator = bookSource.paginator
    let currentFont = paginator.font
    if currentFont.pointSize != fontSize {
        paginator.font = currentFont.fontWithSize(fontSize)
    }
}
```

The function examines the horizontal size class of the trait collection. If it is horizontally compact, it changes the font size the paginator uses to 14.0 points. Otherwise, it's changed to 18.0 points.

When the traits for your view controller changes, iOS calls your controller's willTransitionToTraitCollection(_:,withTransitionCoordinator:) function. Override that with this code:

```
override func willTransitionToTraitCollection(newCollection:UITraitCollection, ↵
 withTransitionCoordinator coordinator:UIViewControllerTransitionCoordinator) {
    super.willTransitionToTraitCollection(newCollection, ↵
                                    withTransitionCoordinator: coordinator)
    adaptViewsToTraitCollection(newCollection)
}
```

This is the function to override to adapt your interface to a new trait environment. All this code does is call your adaptViewToTraitCollection() function to adjust your interface.

> **Note**   The adaptViewToTraitCollection() function is called only when the traits for your view controller change. Rotating an iPad, for example, does not trigger this function because an iPad is wRegular/hRegular in both portrait and landscape orientations.

This function is also not called when your view first appears. So that it adapts to its initial environment, you'll need to call your adaption function once when the view is first loaded. While still in your BookViewController class, add a viewWillAppear(_:) function.

```
override func viewWillAppear(animated: Bool) {
    super.viewWillAppear(animated)
    adaptViewsToTraitCollection(traitCollection)
}
```

When the view is about to appear, the code obtains its current trait collection and uses that to adapt the view. Run the app in both iPad and iPhone simulators and compare the results, as shown in Figure 12-37.

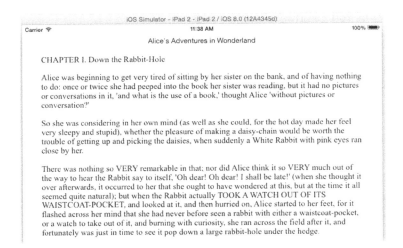

Figure 12-37. Adaptable font size

Adapting When Size Changes

If you need to adapt your interface more precisely, the next level of granularity is size changes. When the size of your view controller changes, iOS calls its viewWillTransitionToSize(_:withTransition Coordinator:) function. This happens whenever the device is rotated (resizing from portrait to landscape). It can also occur in other circumstances. For example, when the in-progress call status banner at the top of the iPhone display disappears, your view controller is subtly resized.

> **Note**   The `willTransitionToTraitCollection(...)` and `willTransitionToSize(...)` functions are defined by the `UIContentContainer` protocol. Both the view controller and the presentation controller adopt this protocol. You can intercept these events on either object, but since you typically subclass `UIViewController` and not `UIPresentationController`, they're usually overridden in the view controller.

This is the function to override to perform more precise layout and layout changes that depend on being in portrait or landscape orientation.

Adapting When Layout Occurs

The most fine-grained adaption occurs at the layout level. A view controller has two functions.

```
viewWillLayoutSubviews()
viewDidLayoutSubviews()
```

The first is called before your views are laid out, and the second one after. The presentation controller has a comparable set of functions, with slightly different names.

```
containerViewWillLayoutSubviews()
containerViewDidLayoutSubviews()
```

Override these functions when you need to adapt your design to any change in its layout.

> **Caution**   The will/did layout subviews functions can be called numerous times, so be careful about what code you put there. For example, let's say you have a label that displays a countdown and it's being updated once a second. Setting a label's text changes its intrinsic size, which triggers a layout, which will call `viewWillLayoutSubviews()` and `viewDidLayoutSubviews()` every second. You must also be careful not to make any changes in `viewDidLayoutSubviews()` that would trigger a new layout.

Animating Layout Changes

The last step in adapting your view is to make the actual layout changes that reposition and resize the views in your interface. If you're using constraints or adaptive constraints, this happens automatically. (That's one more reason to love constraints.) Your views will be gracefully resized to their new layout as the screen rotates.

But what if you're adapting your view programmatically? Some changes don't need to be animated. It would be impractical, for example, to animate the font size change for the book. So, the code you just wrote for that is fine.

On the other hand, if you are positioning views programmatically (without using constraints), you'll need to reposition them when the view size changes, and you'll want them to animate along with the rest of the changes. To accomplish that, reach for the object in Figure 12-23 that I've ignored so far: the transition coordinator.

A transition coordinator is another helper object, used only during transitions. It's an ephemeral object that's created just before the view controller is initially presented or before it transitions to a new trait collection or size. Once the transition is complete, the object goes away.

The transition coordinator has one supremely useful function: `animateAlongsideTransition(_:,completion:)`. Call this function from your `willTransitionToTraitCollection(...)` or `willTransitionToSize(...)` function with two blocks. The first block is the code that makes the animatable changes to your view. This will make more sense after you read Chapter 11. But in a nutshell, if you change any animatable properties of your view within this code block—notably, its size or position—that change will be smoothly animated.

You'll do this in Chapter 16, where you'll create a "dial" view that is positioned programmatically, without using any constraints. When the interface resizes, it will be your responsibility to reposition them.

Oh, I can't stand it! Let's jump ahead to Chapter 16 and peek at that code now (the interesting stuff is in bold).

```
override func viewWillTransitionToSize(size: CGSize, ↵
 withTransitionCoordinator coordinator: UIViewControllerTransitionCoordinator!) {
    super.viewWillTransitionToSize(size, ↵
        withTransitionCoordinator: coordinator)
    animator?.removeAllBehaviors()
    coordinator.animateAlongsideTransition( {
            (context) in self.positionDialViews()
        },
        completion: {
            (context) in self.attachDialBehaviors()
        })
}
```

Whenever the view controller is resized, this function relocates the "dial" views to their new position. That part is handled by the cleverly named `positionDialViews()` function. The thrilling bit is that this function is being called inside a code block passed to the `animateAlongsideTransition(_:,completion:)` function. When you do this, the transition coordinator will make sure your animated view changes occur in perfect synchronization with the rest of the view changes.

You don't have to do this. You're free to *not* animate your changes—lame. And you're free to set up your own animation that runs close to, or even after, the transition animation; the transition coordinator can help you with that too. But most of the time you want your interface to morph seamlessly to its new layout, and `animateAlongsideTransition(_:,completion:)` makes that easy.

Advanced View Controller Topics

This chapter is already ridiculously long, so if you made it this far, you deserve some kind of reward. But before I release you, let me touch on a couple of advanced topics, just so you'll be aware of them.

Custom Presentations and Transitions

You can customize your view controller presentation and transitions *far* beyond what I've described in this chapter. Would you like your presented view controller to appear from a puff of smoke? When you dismiss it, would you like it to crumple up like a discarded piece of paper? You can do that, and anything else you can think of, by providing your own presentation controller and/or transition coordinator objects.

There are a lot of details, but the basic technique is to set your view controller's modalPresentationStyle to .Custom. When you do that, iOS expects your view controller to supply a delegate object in its transitioningDelegate property. This object must conform to UIViewControllerTransitioningDelegate, the methods of which may provide your own custom subclass of UIPresentationController and other animation and transitioning objects that will do the work to presenting, transitioning, and dismissing your view controller.

Refer to the *View Controller Programming Guide* in Xcode's Documentation and API Reference window for all of the details. I also highly suggest downloading the sample projects that demonstrate these techniques.

Appearance Proxies

You've already seen how you can write code, in functions such as viewWillAppear() and viewWillTransitionToTraitCollection(...), to programmatically adjust the contents of your views. You do this for properties that can't be set in Interface Builder.

But what if you have the same adjustment to the same kind of view object in lots of different places? Do you have to write code to modify every one in every view controller? Let's say you're writing a multiplayer game and a player is on either the Rose team or the Periwinkle team. You'd like to background color of all of your buttons and navigation bars to be light red for Rose players and light blue for Periwinkle players every place those views appear in every view controller.

There's actually a way to do this with appearance proxies. An *appearance proxy* is an object that will adjust one or more properties of every view object in its class at once. Here's how it works.

You ask a specific view object class for its appearance proxy.

```
let navBarAppearanceProxy = UINavigationBar.appearance()
```

If you set a display property of the proxy object, it sets that property in every UINavigationBar object in your app, even ones that haven't been loaded yet.

```
navBarAppearanceProxy.barTintColor = roseTeamColor
```

> **Note**   You can also request an appearance proxy that applies only to objects in a specific trait environment or are contained in a particular view hierarchy.

A proxy cannot affect every property. The properties that are tagged with `UI_APPEARANCE_SELECTOR` in the framework headers are the ones it can change. I've never found an official list, but most of the visual properties (background, tint, font, and so on) that would apply uniformly to multiple view objects can be customized this way.

You can implement your own appearance properties in custom subclasses of `UIView`, and your class's appearance proxy will adjust those too. See the documentation for `UIAppearance` for the details.

Summary

You've traveled far in your quest to master iOS app development. View controllers are the foundation of your user interface. And mastering navigation is a key step in developing your app's user experience.

In this chapter you used all of the major view controller classes: `UIViewController`, `UITableViewController`, `UINavigationController`, `UITabBarController`, and `UIPageViewController`. More importantly, you learned the difference between content and container view controllers and how to assemble and connect them using storyboards. You created view controllers stored in a storyboard file programmatically and used that to create a page view controller data source. You also learned the fundamentals of presenting modal view controllers, the objects involved, and how presentation decisions are made. Finally, you explored all the major techniques for adapting your view to ever-changing display environments.

This is a huge accomplishment. It's so exciting that you should share it with your friends. The next chapter will show you how to do just that.

Chapter 13

Sharing Is Caring

Social networking has exploded in recent years, and mobile apps have played a huge part in that revolution. Not too long ago, it was quite difficult to add social networking features to your app. Today, recent additions to iOS have made it so easy that—given what you know about view controllers—the process can be accurately described as "trivial." In this, rather short, chapter, you will learn how to do the following:

- Share content via Facebook, Twitter, Sina Weibo, Tencent Weivo, Flickr, Vimeo, e-mail, SMS, and more
- Customize content for different services

Choosing which app to modify will probably be the most difficult decision in this chapter. Would people you know want to learn interesting facts about the Surrealists in Chapter 2? Of course you'd want to share a shortened URL from Chapter 3. Do your friends want to know what your Magic Eight Ball prediction was in Chapter 4? You took pictures of your cool stuff in Chapter 7; what if someone wants to see them? It would be easy to add sharing features to all of these apps. In the end, I chose to expand on the ColorModel app from Chapter 8. You've spent a lot of time and effort picking just the right color, and I'm sure your friends will appreciate you sharing it with them.

Color My (Social) World

Start with the final ColorModel app from Chapter 8. You'll find that project in the Learn iOS Development Projects ➤ Ch 6 ➤ ColorModel-6 ➤ ColorModel folder. You will add a button that shares the chosen color with the world. iOS includes a standard "activity" button item, just for this purpose, so use that. In the Main.storyboard interface file, add a toolbar to the bottom of the view controller's interface, as shown in Figure 13-1.

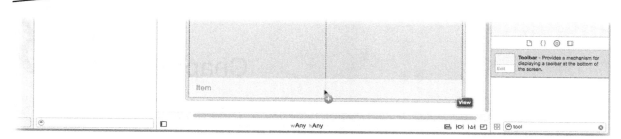

Figure 13-1. Adding a toolbar and toolbar button item

Select the new toolbar and click the pin constraints control, as shown in Figure 13-2. Add left, right, and bottom constraints, accepting the default values. This will keep the toolbar positioned at the bottom of the layout. Toolbars have an intrinsic height that never changes, so you don't need to pin its height.

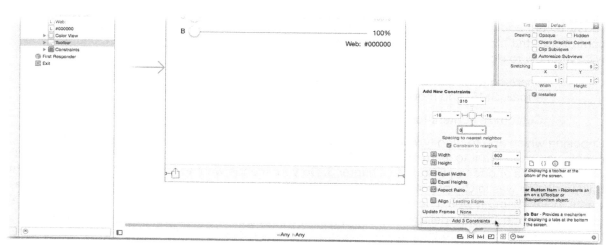

Figure 13-2. Adding the toolbar constraints

The toolbar comes with one bar button item pre-installed. Select that bar button item and change its identifier property to Action. It will now look like this:

Switch to the assistant editor view (View ➤ Assistant Editor ➤ Show Assistant Editor). Make sure the ViewController.swift file appears in the right pane. Add the following action stub:

```
@IBAction func share(sender: AnyObject!) {
}
```

Connect the action function to the activity button by dragging the action's connection to the button. I won't include a figure for that because if you don't know what that looks like by now, you've clearly skipped most of the earlier chapters.

Having Something to Share

Start by sharing the red-green-blue code for the color. Currently, the HTML value for the color is generated by the observeValueForKeyPath(_:,ofObject:,change:,context:) function (ViewController.swift). You now have a second method (share(_:)) that needs that conversion; consider reorganizing the code so this conversion is more readily accessible. Translating the current color into its equivalent HTML value feels as if it lies in the domain of the data model, so add this computed property to Color.swift:

```
var rgbCode: String {
    var red: CGFloat = 0, green: CGFloat = 0, blue: CGFloat = 0, alpha: CGFloat = 0
    color.getRed(&red, green: &green, blue: &blue, alpha: &alpha)
    return NSString(format: "%02X%02X%02X",CInt(red*255),CInt(green*255),CInt(blue*255))
}
```

Now that your data model object will return the color's HTML code, replace the code in ViewController.swift to use the new property. Edit the end of observeValueForKeyPath (_:,ofObject:,change:,context:) so it looks like the following (replacement code in bold):

```
case "color":
    colorView.setNeedsDisplay()
    webLabel.text = "#\(colorModel.rgbCode)"
```

Note   I've mentioned it once already, but it bears repeating. If you're repeating yourself (writing the same code in multiple places), stop and think about how you could consolidate that logic.

Presenting the Activity View Controller

While still in the ViewController.swift file, finish writing the new action method.

```
@IBAction func share(sender: AnyObject!) {
    let shareMessage = "I wrote an iOS app to share a color! RGB=#\(colorModel.rgbCode)"
    let itemsToShare = [shareMessage]
    let activityViewController = UIActivityViewController(activityItems: itemsToShare,
                                            applicationActivities: nil)
    if let popover = activityViewController.popoverPresentationController {
        popover.barButtonItem = sender as UIBarButtonItem
    }
    presentViewController(activityViewController, animated: true, completion: nil)
}
```

The method starts by collecting the items to share. Items can be a message (string), an image, a video, a document, a URL, and so on. Basically, you can include any message, link, media object, or attachment that would make sense to share. You then collect them in an array.

The next section is just as straightforward. You create a `UIActivityViewController`, initializing it with the items you want to share. You then modally present the view controller. (The code in between handles the popover case for iPads and the like; if you've read Chapter 12, you know all about that).

That's all there is to it! Run the project and tap the share button, as shown in Figure 13-3.

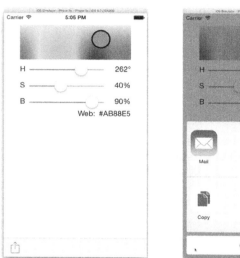
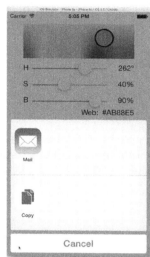
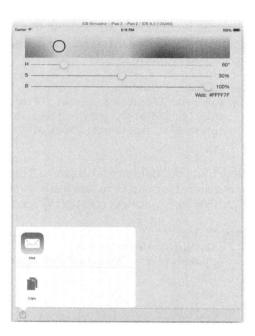

Figure 13-3. Sharing a String message

Tapping the share button presents a picker that lets the user decide how they want to share this message. While your goal is to add sharing to your app, the motivation behind the `UIActivityViewController` is to allow the user to do any number of things with the data items you passed in, all external to your application. This includes actions such as copying the message to the clipboard, which is why it's named `UIActivityViewController` and not `UIPokeMyFriendsViewController`.

Tapping Mail composes a new mail message containing your text. Each activity has its own interface and options. Some, such as the copy to clipboard action, have no user interface at all; they just do their thing and dismiss the controller.

> **Note** This is one of those rare cases where the modal controller dismisses itself.
> UIActivityViewController does not use a delegate to report what it did, and you are not responsible
> for dismissing it when it's done. In fact, the only way to find out whether it performed an activity is to
> assign a code block to its completionWithItemsHandler property before presenting it. The code
> block receives four parameters: an activityType string describing which activity was chosen (such as
> UIActivityTypePostToFacebook), a Boolean completed parameter that is true if it was successful, an
> array of the data items that were ultimately shared, and an NSError object describing any failure.

The activity choices will be the intersection of what activities are available, what services you have
authorized or configured, and the types of items you're sharing. In Figure 13-3, the choices are pretty
paltry. That's because this app was run on the simulator, which does not have any services like Twitter
or Facebook configured, and the only thing you're sharing is a simple string. I think you can do better.

The More You Share, the More You Get

I admit, sharing a hexadecimal color code probably isn't going to get you a lot of "likes" on
Facebook. In fact, it's pretty boring. When you share a color, what you want to share is a *color*.
You can improve the user experience by preparing as much content as you can for the activity
view controller. Include not just plain-text messages, but images, video, URLs, and so on. The
more, the merrier.

It's a shame you can't attach the image displayed by ColorView. You went to a lot of work
to create a beautiful hue/saturation chart, with the selected color spotlighted. But all that
drawRect(_:) code draws into a Core Graphics context; it's not a UIImage object you can pass to
UIActivityViewController.

Or could you?

If you remember the section "Drawing Images" in Chapter 11, it's possible to create a UIImage object
by first creating an off-screen graphics context, drawing into it, and then saving the results as an
image object. That would let you turn your drawing into a sharable UIImage object! So, what are you
waiting for?

Refactoring drawRect(_:)

Turn your attention to the ColorView.swift file. What you need now is a method that does the
work of drawing the hue/saturation image in a graphics context, separate from your drawRect(_:)
function. Let's call it drawColorChoice(bounds:). This new function will perform the same drawing
work that's currently in drawRect(_:). Your drawRect(_:) function now does little beyond calling
drawColorChoice(bounds:) to draw itself and now looks like the following:

```
override func drawRect(rect: CGRect) {
    drawColorChoice(bounds: bounds)
}
```

The bulk of the code that was in drawRect(_:), with few changes, has been relocated to the drawColorChoice(bounds:) function. You can copy this code from the Learn iOS Development Projects ➤ Ch 13 ➤ ColorModel-2 ➤ ColorModel folder, along with its companion function, hsImage(size:,brightness:).

What you just did might look a little silly, even a waste of time. After all, you just replaced a function with another function that does the same thing and then called it to do exactly what you were doing before. But there's one critical, and strategic, difference between the two. drawRect(_:) draws itself at its current bounds. drawColorChoice(bounds:) draw the hue/saturation field at the rectangle specified. That makes it possible to draw the image with different sizes into different contexts.

Tip   This kind of software change is called refactoring. *Code refactoring* is the art of restructuring your code without changing what it does (see http://refactoring.com/). You refactor to better organize your classes, simplify their interfaces, reduce complexity, or—as in this example—consolidate and reuse code. The key point is that the drawRect(_:) function still behaves the same as it did before the change. But your code is now organized so it's more flexible and reusable.

You did all of this so you can add a new function that returns the hue/saturation graphic as a UIImage object. Add that function now.

```
func colorChoiceImage(# size: CGSize) -> UIImage {
    UIGraphicsBeginImageContext(size)
    let context = UIGraphicsGetCurrentContext()
    var bounds = CGRect(origin: CGPointZero, size: size)

    UIColor.clearColor().set()
    CGContextFillRect(context, bounds)

    bounds.inset(dx: radius, dy: radius)
    drawColorChoice(bounds: bounds)

    let image = UIGraphicsGetImageFromCurrentImageContext()
    UIGraphicsEndImageContext()
    return image
}
```

If you made it through Chapter 11, you shouldn't have any problems understanding this code. It begins by creating an off-screen graphics context, fills it with transparent pixels, calls drawColorChoice(bounds:) to draw the hue/saturation chart and color choice (inset a little so the "loupe" doesn't get clipped), and then turns the finished drawing into a UIImage object. Easy peasy.

Providing More Items to Share

Now if you want to get what the `ColorView` object draws on the screen as an image object, you simply call its `colorChoiceImage(size:)` function. Use this in the `share(_:)` function. Select the `ViewController.swift` file and replace the first two statements with the following code (changes in bold):

```
@IBAction func share(sender: AnyObject!) {
    let shareMessage = "I wrote an iOS app to share a color! ↵
RGB=#\(colorModel.rgbCode) @LearniOSAppDev"
    let shareImage = colorView.colorChoiceImage(size: CGSize(width: 380, height: 160))
    let shareURL = NSURL(string: "http://www.learniosappdev.com/")!
    let itemsToShare = [shareMessage,shareImage,shareURL]
    let activityViewController = UIActivityViewController(activityItems: itemsToShare,
                                              applicationActivities: nil)
    ...
```

Run the app again. This time, you're passing three items (a string, an image, and a URL) to the `UIActivityViewController`. Notice how this changes the interface, as shown in Figure 13-4.

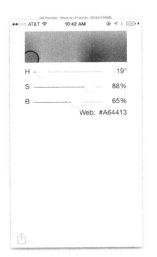

Figure 13-4. Activities with more sharable items

Each activity responds to different kinds of data. Now that you include an image object, activities like Save Image and Assign to Contact appear. Each activity is also free to do what it thinks makes sense for the types of data you provide. The Mail activity will attach images and documents to a message, Facebook will upload images to the user's photo album, while Twitter may upload the picture to a photo-sharing service and then include the link to that image in the tweet. It's completely automatic.

> **Tip**   If you're curious about what activities work with what kinds of data, refer to the UIActivity class documentation. Its "Constants" section lists all of the built-in activities and the classes of objects each responds to.

Excluding Activities

iOS's built-in activities are smart, but they aren't prescient; they don't know what the intent of your data is. Activities know when they can do something with a particular type of data but not if they should. If there are activities that you, as a developer, don't think are appropriate for your particular blend of data, you can explicitly exclude them.

You've decided that printing a color example or assigning it to a contact don't make any sense. (You assume the user has no contacts for Little Red Riding Hood, the Scarlet Pimpernel, the Green Hornet, or other colorful characters.) Return to the share(_:) function in ViewController. swift. Immediately after the statement that creates the activityViewController, add the following statement. You'll find this finished project in the Learn iOS Development Projects ➤ Ch 13 ➤ ColorModel-3 ➤ ColorModel folder.

```
activityViewController.excludedActivityTypes = ↵
                    [UIActivityTypeAssignToContact,UIActivityTypePrint]
```

Setting this property excludes the listed built-in activities from the choices. Run the app again. This time, the excluded activities are, well, excluded (see Figure 13-5). Compare this to Figure 13-4.

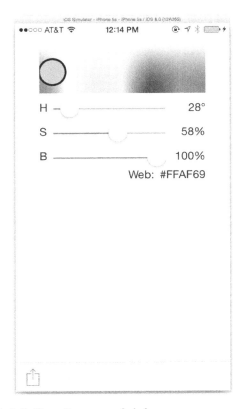

Figure 13-5. Activities with some excluded

The Curse of the Lowest Common Denominator

The activity view controller is a fantastic iOS feature, and it's only gotten better with time. About the only negative thing you can say about it is that it's too easy to use. Its biggest problem is that there's no obvious way of customizing that data items based on what the user wants to do with it.

Case in point: when I was developing the app for the chapter, I initially added a simple rgbCode property to the Color class that returned the HTML code for the color (#f16c14). The problem with this is Twitter. On Twitter, so-called hash tags start with a pound/hash sign and are used to identify keywords in tweets. My color (#f16c14) would be interpreted as an f16c14 tag, which won't be trending any time soon. To avoid this, I rewrote the property so it returns just the hexadecimal portion of the RGB value and purposely left out the # in the message passed to UIActivityViewController. That way, if the user decided to share with Twitter, it wouldn't tweet a confusing message.

> **Note**   Sina Weibo also uses hash tags, but the pound/hash signs bracket the tag (#Tag#). Thus, #f16c14 would not be a hash tag on Weibo.

But that's just the tip of the iceberg. Message length for mail and Facebook can be considerably longer than those on Twitter. Why should your text message or Facebook post be limited to 140 characters?

Providing Activity-Specific Data

The iOS engineers did not ignore this problem. There are several ways of customizing your content based on the type of activity the user chooses. The two avenues iOS provides are as follows:

- UIActivityItemSource
- UIActivityItemProvider

The first is a protocol, which your class adopts. Any object that conforms to the UIActivityItemSource protocol can be passed in the array of data items to share. The UIActivityViewController will then call these two (required) functions:

```
activityViewController(_:,itemForActivityType:) -> AnyObject?
activityViewControllerPlaceholderItem(_:) -> AnyObject
```

The first method is responsible for converting the content of your object into the actual data you want to share or act upon. What's significant about this message is that it includes the activity the user chose in the itemForActivityType parameter. Use this parameter to alter your content based on what the user is doing with it.

For ColorModel, you're going to turn your ViewController object into a sharing message proxy object. Select your ViewController.swift file. Adopt the UIActivityItemSource protocol in your ViewController class (changes in bold).

```
class ViewController: UIViewController, UIActivityItemSource {
```

> **Tip**   If you had a more complex conversion, or multiple conversions, I recommend creating new classes (possibly subclasses of UIActivityItemProvider) that did nothing but perform the transformation. This would make it easy to develop as many different kinds of conversions as you needed.

Now add the first of UIActivityItemSource's two required functions.

```
func activityViewController(activityViewController: UIActivityViewController, ↩
                itemForActivityType activityType: String) -> AnyObject? {
    var message: String?
    switch activityType {
        case UIActivityTypePostToTwitter, UIActivityTypePostToWeibo:
            message = "Today's color is RGB=\(colorModel.rgbCode). ↩
I wrote an iOS app to do this! @LearniOSAppDev"
        case UIActivityTypeMail:
```

```
        message = "Hello,\n\nI wrote an awesome iOS app that lets me share a color ↵
with my friends.\n\nHere's my color (see attachment): hue=\(colorModel.hue)°, ↵
saturation=\(colorModel.saturation)%, brightness=\(colorModel.brightness)%.\n\n↵
If you like it, use the HTML code #\(colorModel.rgbCode) in your design.\n\nEnjoy,\n\n"
        default:
            message = "I wrote a great iOS app to share this color: #\(colorModel.rgbCode)"
    }
    return message
}
```

This function performs the conversion from your object to the actual data object that the activity view controller is going to share or use. For this app, your controller will provide the message (String object) to post.

Your method examines the activityType parameter and compares it against one of the known activities. (If you provided your own custom activity, the value would be the name you gave your activity.) For Twitter and Weibo, it prepares a short announcement, avoiding inadvertently creating any hash tags and including a Twitter-style mention. If the user chooses to send an e-mail, you prepare a rather lengthy message, without a mention. For Facebook, SMS, and any other activity, you create a medium-length message.

Find the share(_:) function and change the beginning of it so it looks like this (removing shareMessage and changing the code in bold):

```
@IBAction func share(sender: AnyObject!) {
    let shareImage = colorView.colorChoiceImage(size: CGSize(width: 380, height: 160))
    let shareURL = NSURL(string: "http://www.learniosappdev.com/")!
    let itemsToShare = [self,shareImage,shareURL]
```

Instead of preparing a message, you now pass your ViewController object with a promise to provide the message. Once the user has decided what they want to do (mail, tweet, message, and so on), your view controller will receive a activityViewController(_:,itemForActivityType:) call and produce the data.

Promises, Promises

You may have noticed the chicken-and-egg problem here. What activities are available is determined by the kinds of data you pass to the activity view controller. But with UIActivityItemSource, the data isn't produced until the user chooses an activity. So, how does the activity view controller know what kind of activities to offer if it doesn't yet know what kind of data your method plans to produce?

The answer is the second required UIActivityItemSource function, and you need to add that now.

```
func activityViewControllerPlaceholderItem(activityViewController: ↵
                            UIActivityViewController) -> AnyObject {
    return "My color message goes here."
}
```

This method returns a placeholder object. While it could be the actual data you plan to share, it doesn't have to be. Its only requirement is that it be the same class as the object that `activityViewController(_:,itemForActivityType:)` will return in the future. Since your `activityViewController(_:,itemForActivityType:)` returns a string, all this function has to do is return any string object.

Caution The object that `activityViewController(_:,itemForActivityType:)` returns should be "functionally equivalent" to the final data object, even if it's not the same data. For example, if you are supplying an NSURL object, the scheme (`http:`, `mailto:`, `file:`, `sms:`, and so on) of the placeholder URL should be the same.

Run the app again and try different activities, as shown in Figure 13-6.

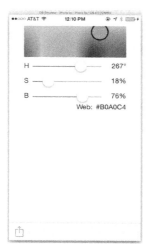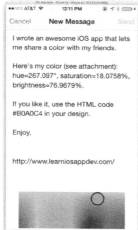

Figure 13-6. Activity customized content

Big Data

The alternative technique for providing activity data is to create a custom subclass of `UIActivityItemProvider`. This class, which already conforms to the `UIActivityItemSource` protocol, produces your app's data object in the background. When the activity view controller wants your app's data, it sets the `activityType` property of your provider object and then requests its `item` property. Your subclass must override the `item` property to provide the desired data, referring to `activityType` as needed.

UIActivityItemProvider is intended for large or complex data that's time-consuming to create, such as a video or a PDF document. It gets an item() function call on a secondary execution thread—not on your app's main thread, which is the thread all of your code in this book has executed on so far. This allows your provider object to work in the background, preparing the data, while your app continues to run. It also requires an understanding of multitasking and thread-safe operations.

In short, if the data you need to share isn't particularly large, complicated, or time-consuming to construct, or you're just not comfortable with multitasking yet, stick with adopting UIActivityItemSource.

Inventing Your Own Activities

It's possible to invent and add your own activities to the items that appear in the activities controller. You have two choices. To create an activity specific to your app—and that appears only in your app—create a concrete subclass of UIActivity. When you're ready to present your activity controller, pass your activity object (or objects, if you've created more than one) in the applicationActivities: parameter. Your custom activities will appear alongside the others.

The exciting addition in iOS 8 is the ability to design an activity that appears in other apps. You design your activity in your app. Any user who has installed your app can then use your custom activity in all the apps that presents a UIActivityViewController. In other words, you can share the sharing. You accomplish this by creating a framework, and you'll create a new activity framework in Chapter 21.

Sharing with Specific Services

I'd like to round off this topic with some notes on other sharing services in iOS and which ones to use.

The UIActivityViewController class is relatively new and largely replaces several older APIs. If you search the iOS documentation for classes that will send e-mail, text messages (SMS), or tweets, you're likely to find MFMailComposeViewController, MFMessageComposeViewController, and TWTweetComposeViewController. Each of these view controllers presents an interface that lets the user compose and send an e-mail message, a short text message, or a tweet, respectively. The latter two don't offer any significant advantages over UIActivityViewController or SLComposeViewController (which I'll explain in a moment), and their use in new apps is not recommended, although they have not been deprecated and are still fully supported.

The MFMailComposeViewController still has a trick or two to offer over UIActivityViewController. Its biggest talent is its ability to create an HTML-formatted mail message and/or pre-address the message by filling in the To, CC, and BCC fields. This allows you to create pre-addressed, richly formatted e-mail, with embedded CSS styling, animation, links, and other HTML goodies.

If you want to present your user with an interface to post to a specific social service—rather than asking them to choose—use the SLComposeViewController class. You create an SLComposeViewController object for a specific service (Twitter, Facebook, or Sina Weibo) using the composeViewControllerForServiceType(_:) function. You then configure that view controller with the data you want to share, as you did with UIActivityViewController, and present the view controller to the user. The user edits their message and away it goes.

Other Social Network Interactions

In ColorModel, we've explored only the sharing side of social networking. If you want your app to get information from your user's social networks, that's another matter altogether. Other types of interactions, such as getting contact information about a user's Facebook friends, are handled by the SLRequest class.

An SLRequest works similarly to the way an NSURLRequest works. You used NSURLRequest objects in Chapter 3 to send a request to the X.co URL shortening service. To use a social networking system, you prepare an SLRequest object in much the same manner, providing the URL of the service, the method (POST or GET), and any required parameters. You send the request, providing a code block that will process the response.

The biggest difference between SLRequest and NSURLRequest is the account property. This property stores an ACAccount object that describes a user's account on a specific social networking service. This property allows SLRequest to handle all of the authentication and encryption required to communicate your request to the servers. If you've ever written any OAuth handling code, you'll appreciate how much work SLRequest is doing for you.

To use other social networking features you must, therefore, prepare the following:

- Service type
- Service URL
- Request method (POST, GET, DELETE)
- Request parameters dictionary
- The user's ACAccount object

The service type is one of SLServiceTypeFacebook, SLServiceTypeSinaWeibo, SLServiceTencentWeibo, or SLServiceTypeTwitter. The URL, method, and parameters dictionary are dictated by whatever kind of request you're making. For those details, consult the developer documentation for the specific service. Some places to start reading are listed in Table 13-1.

Table 13-1. Social Services Developer Documentation

Social Service	URL
Facebook	https://developers.facebook.com/docs/
Sina Weibo	http://open.weibo.com/wiki/
Tencent Weibo	http://dev.t.qq.com/
Twitter	https://dev.twitter.com/docs

Finally, you'll need the ACAccount object for the user's account. Account and login information is maintained by iOS for your app, so your app needs only to request it. Whether the user wants to authorize your app to use their account or they need to sign in, it's all handled for you.

The following are the basic steps to obtaining an account object:

1. Create an instance of the ACAccountStore object.

2. Call the account store's accountTypeWithAccountTypeIdentifier(_:) function to get an ACAccountType object for the service you're interested in. An ACAccountType object is your key to the user's accounts on a specific service.

3. Finally, you call the account store's requestAccessToAccountsWithType(_:) function. If successful (and allowed), your app will receive an array of ACAccount objects for that user.

Services such as Facebook allow an iOS user to be logged into only one account at a time. Twitter, on the other hand, permits a user to be connected to multiple accounts simultaneously. Your app will have to decide whether it wants to use all of the account objects, selected ones, or just one. Once you have an ACAccount object, use it to set the account property of the SLRequest, and you're ready to get social!

Summary

You've learned how to add yet another nifty feature to your app, allowing your users to connect and share content with friends and family around the world—and it took only a smattering of code to get it working. You learned how to tailor that content for specific services or exclude services. If you want more control over which services your app provides, you learned how to use the SLComposeViewController to create a specific sharing interface, along with the SLRequest class that provides a conduit for unlimited social networking integration.

During your journey, you also gained some practical experience in drawing into an off-screen graphics context and refactoring code. In fact, you've been working awfully hard so far. Why not take a break and play a fun game? You don't have one? Well then, read the next chapter and create your own!

Chapter 14

Game On!

Games are a big deal. I'm uncomfortable confessing exactly how many hours I've spent capturing enemy suns or dodging zombies, but let's just say that iOS games can be both engaging and addictive. While this book isn't about game development—there are some great books on the subject—I would like to give you a little taste of how games are created in iOS. In this chapter, you'll learn the following:

- How to create a simple iOS game based on SpriteKit

- How to design a SpriteKit scene

- How to make scene transitions

- How to add image and text content to your scenes

- How to write responder functions to provide user interaction

- How to define the physical behavior of nodes

- How to create physical relationships between nodes using attachments

- How to determine when nodes collide and do something when they do

- How to attach actions to nodes

The design of this game is simple. You're a crewmember on the International Space Station (ISS), and you've been delivered a rare treat: fresh[1] vegetables! Naturally, you want to make a salad. But you only have lab equipment on hand—a beaker and a lab dish—and then there's that pesky problem of microgravity. What you end up with is a bunch of salad parts floating around the cabin. Your job is to herd those ingredients into the beaker using the lab dish, vaguely like the interface shown in Figure 14-1.

---

[1]This, sadly, is pure fantasy. There is no fresh food on the ISS, for fear of bacterial infection or other biological infestation. Maybe someday they'll grow their own.

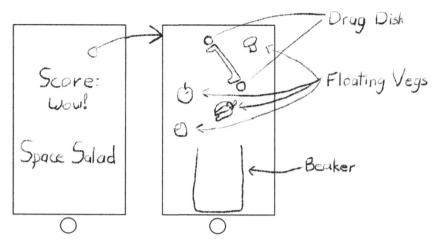

Figure 14-1. SpaceSalad design

To create SpaceSalad, you're going to use SpriteKit. SpriteKit is one of the five key animation technologies in iOS, as described in Chapter 11. Let's get started.

SpaceSalad

Begin by creating a new iOS app. This time, choose the Game app template, as shown in Figure 14-2.

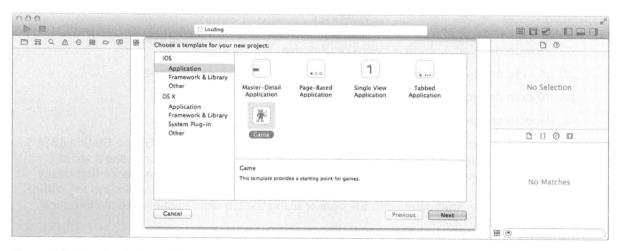

Figure 14-2. Choosing the Game iOS app template

On the next sheet, fill in the app's name (SpaceSalad), enter your Organization Identifier, and choose the Swift language. This template has an additional choice for Game Technology. Pick SpriteKit, as shown in Figure 14-3. The Game template is actually four templates in one. Depending on your Game Technology choice, you'll get a radically different starting point for your app.

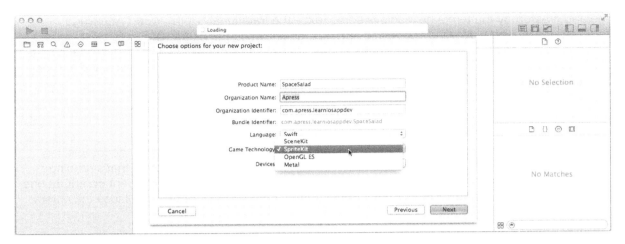

Figure 14-3. *Creating a SpriteKit-based game app*

Click the Create button and choose a location to save your new project. The app template created a fully functional "game" that you can run right now, as shown in Figure 14-4. Go ahead, I'll wait.

Figure 14-4. *Running the SpriteKit template app*

The app created by the template displays some text—the traditional "Hello, World" message. If you tap the screen, a rotating spaceship appears, as shown in the middle of Figure 14-4. As you continue to tap, more and more spaceships appear, all rotating simultaneously. To understand why this is so cool, you need to know a little about SpriteKit and how it differs from `UIView` and similar classes that you've used up to now.

A Brief Tour of SpriteKit

As I explained in Chapter 11, SpriteKit is designed for continuous 2D animation. It accomplishes this by having the graphics-processing unit (GPU) do most of the work. The code that's running your app—in the central processing unit (CPU)—does few of the moment-to-moment computations needed to keep the animation going. It's more of a director. It sets up the scene, places the actors, and yells "Action!" SpriteKit takes it from there.

SpriteKit is designed to be comfortable and as familiar as possible to iOS developers who have been programming with classes such as `UIView`, `UIViewController`, `UIResponder`, and so on. At the same time, there are a number of important differences, many necessary because of the separation of the CPU and GPU and other performance considerations. This makes working with SpriteKit a kind of "Bizarro World" experience, full of recognizable concepts and objects but also awash with inexplicable omissions and puzzling restrictions.

The Familiar

Compared to working with view objects, here's what you'll find familiar:

- SpriteKit *nodes* are like view objects. Each one represents something in the interface.
- A node has a position and a frame.
- Each node defines a local coordinate system.
- A node can be added to another node, becoming its subnode.
- Nodes can be scaled and rotated.
- Nodes can, naturally, be animated.
- Nodes are subclasses of `UIResponder` and can handle all of the standard touch events.

If you substitute the word *view* for *node*, you'll immediately understand these concepts and their relationships. Similarly, a SpriteKit scene and a view controller perform similar roles and tasks.

The Unfamiliar

The big differences between SpriteKit nodes and view objects are as follows:

- Your code does not draw a node's content.
- The origin of a node's coordinate system is at its lower-left, not its upper-left, corner.

- Nodes can have a physics body that describes how it behaves and interacts with other nodes.

- Nodes have a string identifier rather than a numeric tag.

- Nodes appear in a SpriteKit *scene*.

- Scenes are designed in a special Interface Builder scene editor.

- SpriteKit scenes are presented, one at a time, in a SpriteKit view. A SpriteKit view is a `UIView` subclass and can appear anywhere a `UIView` can.

- There is no auto-layout, constraints, or adaption in SpriteKit.

The first difference is the big one. Nodes are drawn (*rendered* in GPU-speak) entirely by the graphics-processing unit. To accomplish this, all of the information needed to draw that node is first transferred to the GPU. Consequently, there is no `drawRect(_:)` function on a node, and you can't use any of the core graphics drawing functions to directly draw your node. Instead, specialized subclasses of `SKNode` render an image (`SKSpriteNode`), text (`SKLabelNode`), or a geometric shape (`SKShapeNode`) in the scene.

> **Note** There are two exceptions to this. First, you can always use core graphics to draw into an off-screen context, capture that as an image, and then supply that image to an `SKSpriteNode`. Second, it's possible to write your own dynamic rendering code that runs in the GPU. But, as I explained in Chapter 11, that's another world and well beyond the scope of this book.

The coordinates system is also vertically flipped from the one used by `UIView` objects. The origin of the coordinate system is in the lower-left corner of a node, and y coordinates increase as they move up.

The second big difference is how nodes are animated. In UIKit, you animate nodes by telling iOS *what* you want animated. You tell it to slide your view from this position to that position, change its scale, and fade in over a period of time. In SpriteKit, you animate nodes by telling iOS *why* they should animate. You give nodes a shape, assign them a mass, define the forces that act on them, and tell SpriteKit what other nodes they collide with. SpriteKit then takes over and continuously animates the nodes, based on your description.

Finally, a SpriteKit scene (`SKScene`) takes on much the same role as a view controller, but it is not a view controller. A SpriteKit view (`SKView`, a `UIView` subclass) is the host for a SpriteKit scene. The `SKView` presents one `SKScene` at a time. It can replace it with a new scene, complete with an animated transition—much the way one view controller presents another view controller. But the host `SKView` and the view controller that owns it never change.

> **Note** In this chapter, *scene* refers to a SpriteKit scene, not a storyboard scene.

Now that you have the general concepts, let's start simple. Begin by creating a SpriteKit scene that displays a single image using a single node. That doesn't sound too hard.

Making the Scene

The Game template creates a typical arrangement for hosting a SpriteKit view. The initial view controller (Game View Controller) contains a single root view object, whose class has been changed to SKView in the storyboard, as shown in Figure 14-5. The view controller does very little beyond acting as a host for the SKView.

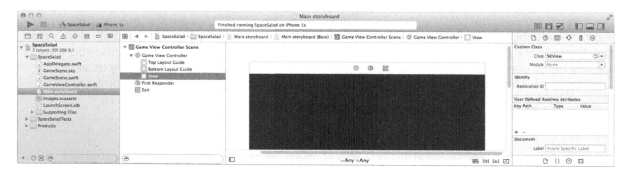

Figure 14-5. View controller hosting a SpriteKit view

Unlike view controllers and storyboards, SpriteKit scenes do not automatically load their scene files. To get the game going, so to speak, the view controller loads the view's initial scene. Let's take a look at that code.

Find the GameViewController.swift file and locate the viewDidLoad() function. Right now, the code there looks something like the following:

```
override func viewDidLoad() {
    super.viewDidLoad()
    if let scene = GameScene.unarchiveFromFile("GameScene") as? GameScene {
        let skView = self.view as SKView
        skView.showsFPS = true
        skView.showsNodeCount = true
        skView.ignoresSiblingOrder = true
        scene.scaleMode = .AspectFill
        skView.presentScene(scene)
    }
}
```

This code calls the unarchiveFromFile(_:) function to load the GameScene object from the GameScene.sks file. An .sks file is a SpriteKit scene file. It then sets some properties of the scene and presents it in the SpriteKit view.

UNARCHIVING A SPRITEKIT SCENE

The unarchiveFromFile(_:) function is not an iOS function. It's actually a little bit of glue, included in the game app template. It's defined as an extension of SKNode. (Extensions can add additional methods to existing classes and are explained in Chapter 20.) You'll find it in the GameViewController.swift file, and it will look something like this:

```
extension SKNode {
    class func unarchiveFromFile(file : NSString) -> SKNode? {
        if let path = NSBundle.mainBundle().pathForResource(file, ofType: "sks") {
            var sceneData = NSData(contentsOfFile: path, options: .DataReadingMappedIfSafe, error: nil)!
            var archiver = NSKeyedUnarchiver(forReadingWithData: sceneData)

            archiver.setClass( self.classForKeyedUnarchiver(), forClassName: "SKScene")
            let scene = archiver.decodeObjectForKey(NSKeyedArchiveRootObjectKey) as SKNode
            archiver.finishDecoding()
            return scene
        } else {
            return nil
        }
    }
}
```

An .sks file is an archive of SpriteKit objects. You'll learn about how objects are archived in Chapter 19. For now, just know that an archive contains all of the data needed to reconstruct a set of objects, restoring their property values and connections.

Interface Builder has a SpriteKit scene editor that lets you create and configure your scene and node objects. These are archived and written to an .sks file that becomes one of your app's resources. To load that scene, you just need to unarchive that file. But unlike storyboards, you can't change the class of an object in the scene editor. The root object is always a standard SKScene object. This is where the unarchiveFromFile(_:) function performs a little sleight of hand.

During the unarchiving process, the class of each object is read from the file and used to construct that object. But you don't want the top-level SKScene object to be a boring old SKScene object. You want it to be your custom subclass of SKScene (GameScene, in this case) with all of your properties and game logic. So, the unarchiveFromFile(_:) function gets the class of the node that's calling this function (GameScene) and passes that to the setClass(_:,forClassName:) function. This function tells the unarchiver to substitute any instance of one class with another.

Now when the .sks file is unarchived and the unarchiver encounters an SKScene object, it constructs a GameScene object instead. When the file is finished loading, it returns your custom GameScene object, prepopulated with the SKNode objects from the file.

So, let's see what's in this magic GameScene.sks file. Select the file in the navigator and take a look. You should see something like what's pictured in Figure 14-6.

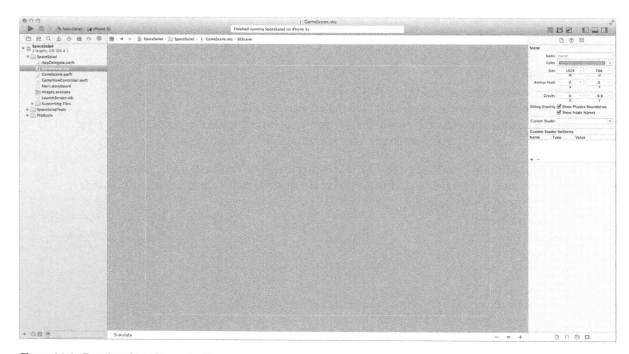

Figure 14-6. Template GameScene.sks file

There's nothing in the GameScene.sks file. That is thoroughly uninteresting—and a little weird, since the template code went out of its way to read it. Where did the text and spaceships come from? Take a look at the GameScene.swift file.

```
override func didMoveToView(view: SKView) {
    let myLabel = SKLabelNode(fontNamed:"Chalkduster")
    myLabel.text = "Hello, World!";
    myLabel.fontSize = 65;
    myLabel.position = CGPoint(x: CGRectGetMidX(self.frame),
                               y: CGRectGetMidY(self.frame));
    self.addChild(myLabel)
}
```

When an SKScene is presented in an SKView, it receives a didMoveToView(_:) call. In the didMoveToView(_:) function provided by the template, it programmatically creates a label node and inserted it into the scene. The mystery is solved. The "Hello, World!" message is created when the scene is presented.

> **Note**   The SpriteKit scene editor is new in Xcode 6. In earlier versions of iOS, all SpriteKit content had to be created programmatically.

While you're here, take a look at where the spaceships come from. The `touchesBegan(_:,withEvent:)` function is received every time you touch the scene. Remember that `SKScene` and `SKNode` are both subclasses of `UIResponder`—the same `UIResponder` you learned about in Chapter 4.

Now that you've had a look around, delete the template code for the `didMoveToView(_:)` and `touchesBegan(_:,withEvent:)` functions. You'll write you own later, but for the moment you don't need them.

Adding Sprites

You want to start by adding a single node to your scene. You could do this in code, as you saw in the template code, but you came here to use the SpriteKit scene editor.

Your content is going to use some image resources, so take a brief pause to add all of the image resources you'll need now. Locate the `Learn iOS Development Projects` ➤ `Ch 14` ➤ `SpaceSalad (Resources)` folder and drag all of the image files into the `Images.xcassets` file, as shown in Figure 14-7.

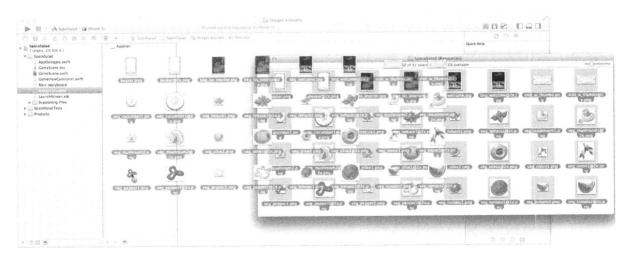

Figure 14-7. Importing image resources

Now select the `GameScene.sks` file. The default scene is in landscape orientation, so begin by switching it to portrait orientation. Select the root `SKScene` object—currently the only object in the scene. Use the node inspector to change its width and height from 1024 by 768 to 768 by 1024. While you're here, set both gravity values to 0. After all, this scene is set in space.

Locate the Color Sprite object in the library, as shown in Figure 14-8. Drop a new sprite node into the scene.

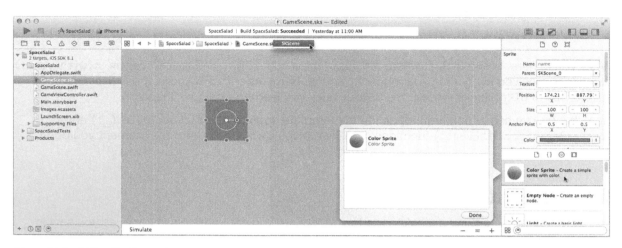

Figure 14-8. Adding the first node

> **Tip** The scene editor has no outline view. To select a node, click its visual representation in the canvas or use the pop-up menu in the scene editor's navigation ribbon, as shown in Figure 14-8.

A sprite node (SKSpriteNode) is a general-purpose node that will display and animate any image or geometric shape. You'll use these a lot.

Set the new node's Name attribute to background and its Texture to bkg_iss_interior.jpg, as shown in Figure 14-9. The sprite will resize itself to match the image resource. Set its Anchor Point attribute to (0,0) and then set its Position attribute to (0,0). The background node will now fill the scene.

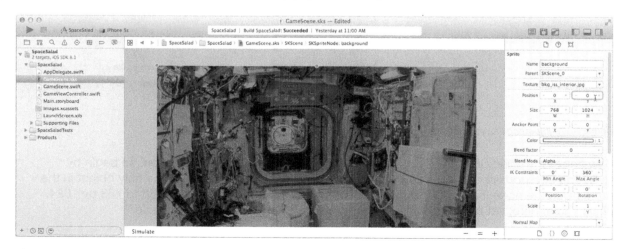

Figure 14-9. Configuring the background node

Sprite nodes have an anchorPoint property that determines the point in the image or shape where the sprite's position property is anchored. It's expressed as a fraction of its height and width. It defaults to (0.5,0.5), meaning the sprite's position will correspond to the center of its image. By setting it to (0,0), the sprite's position will be its lower-left corner. Now when you set background node's position to (0,0), it places the node's lower-left corner at the origin of the scene.

Go ahead and run it. Figure 14-10 shows the app running on an iPad and iPhone. It doesn't do much that could even remotely resemble exciting, but you should be excited; you've successfully created a SpriteKit scene that contains working nodes.

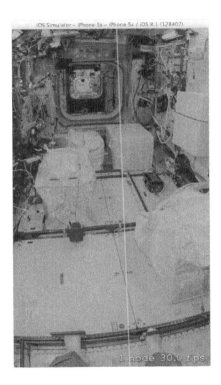

Figure 14-10. The background node in action

Resizing a Scene

One node is great, but you're going to need a lot more before you're done. Stop the app, switch back to the GameScene.sks file, and drag in another color sprite node. Drag it near the lower-left corner of the scene, as shown in Figure 14-11. Set its name to veg and its Texture to veg_cucumber1.png. You've got two nodes now.

Figure 14-11. *Adding the first vegetable node*

Run the app again. It's just about as you would expect. It's still not exciting, but you're getting the hang of adding sprite nodes to your scene. One thing you do notice is that the cucumber is almost off the edge when run on an iPhone, as shown on the right in Figure 14-12.

Figure 14-12. *Running without adaption*

As I mentioned earlier, SpriteKit has no concept of adaption. In fact, a scene doesn't even size itself to fit the SpriteKit view. If you need it to fit the view or adapt its layout to different sizes and orientations, you'll need to roll up your sleeves and do that yourself.

For this app, you want to automatically resize the scene to fit inside its host view. That's actually easy. Select the GameScene.swift file and write a new didMoveToView(_:) function, as follows:

```
override func didMoveToView(view: SKView) {
    size = view.frame.size
}
```

That's all you have to do. When the scene is presented in the host SKView, SpriteKit calls your scene's didMoveToView(_:) function. The code simply resizes the scene so it's the same size as the host view.

Unfortunately, that doesn't accomplish much. You see, there's also no auto-layout or constraints or anything approximating that. The new code resized the scene, but it doesn't alter the size or positions of any of the nodes in the scene. For that, you'll need a little bit more code.

I'm going to provide you with a really simple—some would say naive—solution for repositioning your nodes. Either locate the Learn iOS Development Projects ➤ Ch 14 ➤ SpaceSalad folder and drag the ResizableScene.swift file into your project navigator or create a new ResizableScene.swift file and write the following code:

```
import SpriteKit

class ResizableScene: SKScene {
    let backgroundNodeName = "background"
    override func didChangeSize(oldSize: CGSize) {
        let newSize = size
        if newSize != oldSize {
            if let background = childNodeWithName(backgroundNodeName) as? SKSpriteNode {
                background.position = CGPointZero
                background.size = newSize
            }
            let transform = CGAffineTransformMakeScale(newSize.width/oldSize.width,
                                                  newSize.height/oldSize.height)
            enumerateChildNodesWithName("*") { (node,stop) in
                node.position = CGPointApplyAffineTransform(node.position, transform)
            }
        }
    }
}
```

The ResizableScene class overrides the didChangeSize(_:) function. This function is called whenever your scene is resized, as it will when your scene updates its size property over in didMoveToView(_:). The code looks for a node named background. If it finds one, it makes its size match the scene's size.

It then proportionally translates the position of every node from the old size to the new one. So if a node was positioned at one-third the height and half of the width before, it will be in the same relative position after the resize. Note that the nodes are not resized, just repositioned.

To put this to work for you, change your GameScene class so it is now a subclass of ResizableScene, as follows (modified code in bold):

```
class GameScene: ResizableScene {
```

Run the app again, as shown in Figure 14-13. Compare these results with those in Figure 14-12.

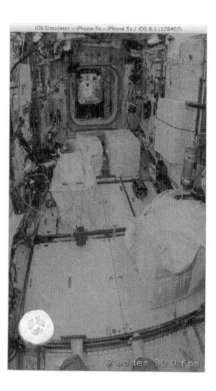

Figure 14-13. Self-resizing scene

And while we're adapting the interface, also take a look at the sprite sizes. That cucumber looks awfully large in the iPhone interface, shown on the right in Figure 14-13. For the GameScene, adapt the sizes of your sprites along with their positions.

Return to the GameScene.swift file. Locate the didMoveToView(_:) function. Just after the statement that sets the size of the scene—indirectly calling the didChangeSize(_:) function—add the following code:

```
let backgroundNode = childNodeWithName(backgroundNodeName) as? SKSpriteNode
let scale = CGFloat( view.traitCollection.horizontalSizeClass == .Compact ? 0.5 : 1.0 )
enumerateChildNodesWithName("*") { (node,stop) in
```

```
    if node !== backgroundNode {
        node.xScale = scale
        node.yScale = scale
    }
}
```

Now on horizontally compact devices, such as iPhones, the size of everything except the background will be half the size. That's enough with resizing and adapting.

Let's Get Physical

You've created a SpriteKit scene, added sprite nodes, and adapted them to various display sizes. But your scene still doesn't do anything yet. The nodes just sit there. So, what does a programmer have to do to get a little action around here?

In the introduction, I said you don't tell SpriteKit nodes *what* to animate; you tell them *why* they should animate. You accomplish this by endowing your nodes with physical attributes such as geometry, mass, resistance, and so on. This is called a *physics body*, defined by the SKPhysicsBody class.

There are three kinds of physics bodies.

- A *dynamic volume* describes a shape with volume and mass that can be animated through forces and collisions. Use this to describe things that move and interact with their environment. A racquetball would be a dynamic volume.

- A *static volume* describes a solid shape that interacts with dynamic volumes but never moves nor is affected by forces or collisions. The wall of a racquetball court would be a static volume.

- An *edge* is an immovable boundary. It acts like a static volume but doesn't enclose a shape. A line describing the ground would be an edge.

A cucumber slice sounds very much like a dynamic volume. It has a shape and a mass, it can move around, and it can bump into things. Select the GameScene.sks file. Select the cucumber node. In the node inspector, locate the Physics Definition section, as shown in Figure 14-14.

Figure 14-14. Adding a physics body to a node

Set the Physics Body attribute to Bounding circle. This creates a physics body whose shape is round. (The shape of the physics body will appear in the scene editor.) Make sure the Dynamic and Allows Rotation options are checked.

Change the Lin. Damping attribute to 0.01 and Restitution to 0.1. Linear damping (linearDamping) acts like drag through air or water, gently slowing the node as it travels. Restitution (restitution) determines how much energy it loses when it bounces off a surface or another node.

Run your app. This time, nothing happens—again. Your node has physical attributes, but there are no forces acting on it. (Remember that you turned off gravity earlier.) If you want your cucumber slice to move around, you need to give it a nudge.

Locate the didMoveToView(_:) function in GameScene.swift. It shouldn't be hard; it's the only function. At the end of the function, add the following code:

```
enumerateChildNodesWithName("veg") { (node,stop) in
    func randomForce( # min: CGFloat, # max: CGFloat ) -> CGFloat {
        return CGFloat(arc4random()) * (max-min) / CGFloat(UInt32.max) + min
    }
    if let body = node.physicsBody {
        body.applyForce(CGVector(dx: randomForce(min: -50.0, max: 50.0),
                                 dy: randomForce(min: -40.0, max: 40.0)))
        body.applyAngularImpulse(randomForce(min: -0.01, max: 0.01))
    }
}
view.ignoresSiblingOrder = true
```

The code then gives the node a little "kick." It applies a variable amount of force in a random direction. It then adds a little "English" by applying a small amount rotational force.

> **Note**   Setting ignoresSiblingOrder to true is an optimization for sprite drawing. When false, it enforces a strict parent-to-child rendering order. This is sometimes important for compound nodes (nodes that contain other nodes) to render correctly. Your app doesn't need that, and setting it to true allows the SpriteKit to render the scene more efficiently.

Now run the app and see what happens. Well, look at that! Your cucumber just drifted off into space—literally. It drifted right off the screen and disappeared! So, you know the physics body is working, and applying a force to the node caused it to move. Now you need to keep it from wandering off, or you're never going to get a meal.

Setting Boundaries

What you need is a barrier or wall of some kind so your cucumber doesn't get away from you. That sounds a lot like an edge physics body. Select the GameScene.swift file. Just before the enumerateChildNodesWithName(...) call you just added to the didMoveToView(_:) function, add the following code:

```
if let background = backgroundNode {
    let body = SKPhysicsBody(edgeLoopFromRect: background.frame)
    physicsBody = body
}
```

This code gets the background node, the one that's filling the background of the scene. It uses its frame to create an edge loop. An *edge loop* is an edge physics body that follows a path—a rectangle, in this case. In other words, it creates four immovable walls. These walls are then added to the scene.

Run your app again. Now the cucumber bounces off the edges and stays in the scene. This is physics bodies and collisions at work.

But one cucumber does not a salad make. Select the GameScene.sks file. Select the cucumber node. Hold down the Option key and drag a copy of the node into the scene. Repeat, 10 more times, until you have 12 nodes in total, as shown in Figure 14-15.

Figure 14-15. *Duplicating the cucumber node*

With each node, select it and set its Texture property to one of the veg_*.png image files so that every node uses a different texture image. Don't select any of the @2x images; those are higher-resolution resources for Retina displays.

Run your app again, and they'll all start drifting around, bumping into the walls and each other, as shown in Figure 14-16. You'll see that they gradually slow down because of drag, resistance, and restitution. This is the real power of SpriteKit. With just a handful of attributes, you can describe a whole world of lifelike objects.

Figure 14-16. Many floating sprites

ENUMERATING CHILD NODES

The enumerateChildNodesWithName(_:,usingBlock:) function is exceptionally useful when working with scenes full of nodes. The function searches for nodes that match the name and passes each one to a code block that can do something with, or to, that node.

Nodes do not need to have unique names. In SpaceSalad, all of the vegetable nodes have the same name (veg). The statement enumerateChildNodesWithName("veg") { ... } processes just the vegetable nodes and ignores the rest.

But the name parameter is actually a search pattern. In your didChangeSize(_:) function, you used an enumerateChildNodesWithName("*") statement to process all the nodes in the scene. And that's just the tip of the iceberg. You can select the nodes to process using globbing patterns such "*_car" (matches "red_car" and "blue_car"), "tire[1234]" (matches "tire1" but not "tire5"), and "pace_car/headlight" (matches a "headlight" node contained in a "pace_car" node).

Search patterns can be quite sophisticated. You'll find a complete description in the *SpriteKit Programming Guide*. Locate the "Searching the Node Tree" section in the "Building Your Scene" chapter.

Adding Obstacles

The app is starting to look lively. Getting back to the design, the goal was to corral the individual salad ingredients into a beaker. The beaker will be a static volume. In other words, it will have a volume and interact with other sprites, but it will never move. This means the player can't knock over the beaker. Maybe you can save that for an advanced level.

The beaker will be a sprite, just like the others. Drag a new color sprite into your GameScene.sks file. Set its Name attribute to beaker and its Texture attribute to beaker.png, as shown in Figure 14-17. Change its Anchor Point attribute to (0.5,0) and then set its position to (384,0), also shown in Figure 14-17.

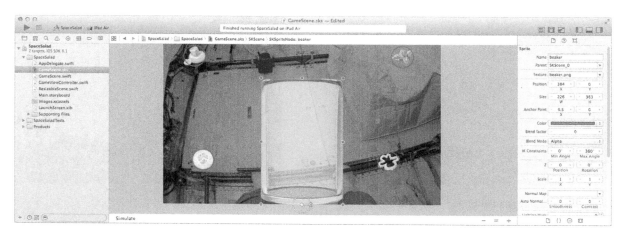

Figure 14-17. Adding the beaker node

> **Caution**   If you now have vegetable nodes that intersect your beaker node, move them so they don't. You don't want to start the physics simulation with the impossible condition of two bodies interpenetrating one another.

The position of the beaker node is at its bottom center, and the position is set to the bottom center of the scene. Because the ResizableScene class moves the node's position proportionally, the beaker will always be sitting at the bottom center of the scene.

Instead of defining a simple physics body using the scene editor, create a more complex shape programmatically. In the GameScene.swift file, add the following code to the didMoveToView(_:) function, just before the code that nudges the vegetables:

```
if let beaker = childNodeWithName("beaker") as? SKSpriteNode {
    if beaker.physicsBody == nil {
        let bounds = BoundsOfSprite(beaker)
        let side = CGFloat(8.0)
        let base = CGFloat(6.0)
        let beakerEdgePath = CGPathCreateMutable()
```

```
        CGPathMoveToPoint(beakerEdgePath, nil, bounds.minX, bounds.minY)
        CGPathAddLineToPoint(beakerEdgePath, nil, bounds.minX, bounds.maxY)
        CGPathAddLineToPoint(beakerEdgePath, nil, bounds.minX+side, bounds.maxY)
        CGPathAddLineToPoint(beakerEdgePath, nil, bounds.minX+side, bounds.minY+base)
        CGPathAddLineToPoint(beakerEdgePath, nil, bounds.maxX-side, bounds.minY+base)
        CGPathAddLineToPoint(beakerEdgePath, nil, bounds.maxX-side, bounds.maxY)
        CGPathAddLineToPoint(beakerEdgePath, nil, bounds.maxX, bounds.maxY)
        CGPathAddLineToPoint(beakerEdgePath, nil, bounds.maxX, bounds.minY)
        let body = SKPhysicsBody(edgeLoopFromPath: beakerEdgePath)
        beaker.physicsBody = body
    }
}
```

It looks like a lot, but what it's doing is really simple. The code gets the beaker node, determines its bounds (its frame in its local coordinate system), and then creates a path that roughly approximates the sides and bottom of the beaker, as illustrated in Figure 14-18. This path then becomes a set of walls that describe the physics body.

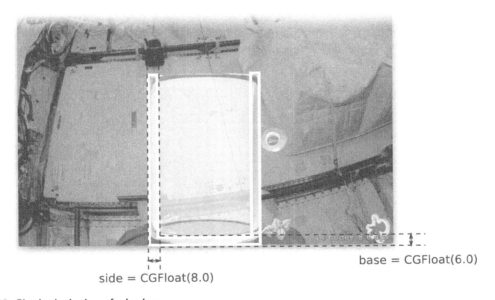

Figure 14-18. Physics body shape for beaker

A physics body shape can be quite complex. SpriteKit provides basic shapes for you (circle, rectangle, polygon, and so on). You can also base a sprite's shape on its image, using the transparent portions of the graphic to determine the sprite's outline. And, as you've just seen, you can create arbitrarily complex paths to describe its shape and volume.

> **Tip** For the best performance, use the simplest body shape possible, which happens to be a circle. Using complex outlines or the shape's image dramatically increases the computations SpriteKit must perform to determine whether a collision has occurred. That, in turn, dramatically reduces animation performance and will limit the number of sprites you can animate simultaneously.

This code uses a utility function to get the sprite's frame in its local coordinate system. Add that function above (or below) your GameScene class, as follows. You'll reuse it later.

```
func BoundsOfSprite( sprite: SKSpriteNode ) -> CGRect {
    var bounds = sprite.frame
    let anchor = sprite.anchorPoint
    bounds.origin.x = 0.0 - bounds.width*anchor.x
    bounds.origin.y = 0.0 - bounds.height*anchor.y
    return bounds
}
```

Now when you run your app, the vegetables bounce off each other, the walls, and the sides of the beaker, as shown in Figure 14-19. If you're lucky, you might even get a few inside the beaker.

Figure 14-19. Vegetables interacting with beaker

But this isn't a game of luck. This is a game of skill, and it's time to add the lab dish so your user can push the vegetables around. That will require some interaction with the player.

Interacting with the Player

The player interacts with a single sprite: the lab dish. So clearly, you need to start by adding a lab dish to your scene. Select the GameScene.sks file and drag in a new color sprite.

Like your beaker, your lab dish is going to need an atypical shape. In the GameScene.swift file, near the code that creates the physics body for the beaker, add the following code. This is a fair bit of typing, so you might want to copy and paste it from the finished project in the Learn iOS Development Projects ➤ Ch 14 ➤ SpaceSalad folder.

```
if let dish = childNodeWithName("dish") as? SKSpriteNode {
    let scale = dish.xScale
    dish.xScale = 1.0
    dish.yScale = 1.0
    let bounds = BoundsOfSprite(dish)
    let minX = bounds.minX
    let maxX = bounds.maxX
    let midY = bounds.midY
    let minY = bounds.minY
    let width = bounds.width
    let bottomThickness = CGFloat(10.0)
    let curveInterpolationPoints = 4
    let dishEdgePath = CGPathCreateMutable()
    CGPathMoveToPoint(dishEdgePath, nil, minX, minY)
    for p in 0...curveInterpolationPoints {
        let x = minX+CGFloat(p)*width/CGFloat(curveInterpolationPoints)
        let relX = x/(width/2)
        let y = (midY-minY-bottomThickness)*(relX*relX)+minY+bottomThickness
        CGPathAddLineToPoint(dishEdgePath, nil, x, y)
    }
    CGPathAddLineToPoint(dishEdgePath, nil, maxX, minY)
    CGPathCloseSubpath(dishEdgePath)
    let body = SKPhysicsBody(polygonFromPath: dishEdgePath)
    body.usesPreciseCollisionDetection = true
    dish.physicsBody = body

    dish.xScale = scale
    dish.yScale = scale
}
```

Just like the beaker, this code gets the bounds of the dish node and uses that to create a path. The path is an irregular polygon, square on one side and roughly concave on the other. You could read the code carefully and try to imagine the shape it's creating. I could also include an illustration. Or, you can get SpriteKit to show it to you.

SpriteKit includes a number of debugging features. You've been looking at two of them since the beginning. In the GameViewController.swift file, the viewDidLoad() function loads the initial scene object and presents it. Before it does, it sets two properties, as follows:

```
skView.showsFPS = true
skView.showsNodeCount = true
```

This causes the scene object to display the number of nodes being rendered and the rate that the scene is being rendered at. See Figure 14-16 for an example. There are additional debugging aides, one of which draws a line corresponding to the physic bodies in the scene. When I turn on features like this, I like to configure them based on a symbolic constant. When I'm done with these aids, I can easily turn them off again. In that spirit, add the following constant, outside the GameViewController class definition:

```
let debugAids = true
```

Now return to the code that sets the debugging aids and change it as follows (modified code in bold):

```
skView.showsFPS = debugAids
skView.showsNodeCount = debugAids
skView.showsPhysics = debugAids
```

Run the app again. This time, SpriteKit will draw the outlines of all the physics bodies in the scene, as shown in Figure 14-20. (The background of Figure 14-20 has been washed out to make the outlines easier to see in print.)

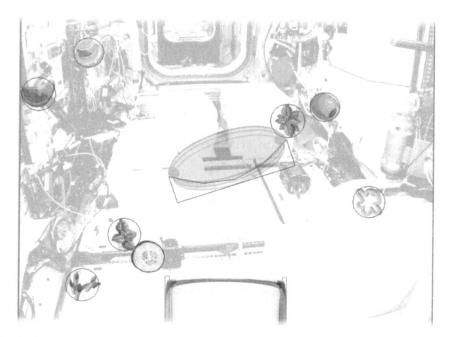

Figure 14-20. *Physics body outlines*

Responding to Touch

SKNode is a subclass of UIResponder. Thus, SKNode can participate in touch events by writing touch event handlers, exactly as you did in Chapter 4. Just like UIView, an SKNode's userInteractionEnabled property is normally set to false. So, by default, no sprites receive touch events, and all the touch events fall through to the SKScene object. For this app, that's perfect.

Your scene object will interpret the touch events and use that to move the lab dish around. This is done in the scene object because you'll respond to touches just outside the dish. If the dish object was the one responding to touches, it would miss those events.

Here's how the interaction with the lab dish node is going to work:

- The dish has two drag locations, centered at opposite ends of the node.
- When the user touches two fingers to the interface and those points are near enough to the thumb drag locations, the user starts dragging the dish.
- The touch positions are matched to the dish's thumb drag locations by proximity. That is, the touch closest to the right end of the dish drags the right end of the dish.
- The dish is dragged around indirectly. The user's touches are used to position two anchor points. These points are connected by attachments to the dish's drag locations.

An attachment, as the name would imply, describes a physical relationship between two nodes or a node and a fixed location, called an *anchor*. An attachment can be inflexible, in which you get a "tow bar" or "pendulum" effect.

An attachment can also be flexible, where it acts like a spring. In this app, the flexible attachment is used with an anchor point. It's as if you nailed the end of a spring to a fixed location and attached the other end to the dish. The physics engine then takes over, moving the dish to follow the forces imposed by the "spring."

The code to do all of that is in Listing 14-1. Save yourself a lot of typing and copy these functions from the finished project in the Learn iOS Development Projects ➤ Ch 14 ➤ SpaceSalad folder.

Listing 14-1. Dish Drag Logic

```
let dragProximityMinimum = CGFloat(60.0)

var dragNode: SKSpriteNode?
var leftDrag: SKNode?
var leftJoint: SKPhysicsJointSpring?
var rightDrag: SKNode?
var rightJoint: SKPhysicsJointSpring?

func dragPoints(dish: SKSpriteNode) -> (leftPoint: CGPoint, rightPoint: CGPoint) {
    let dishSize = dish.size
    let width = dishSize.width/dish.xScale
    let rightThumbPoint = dish.convertPoint(CGPoint(x: -width/2, y: 0.0), toNode: self)
    let leftThumbPoint = dish.convertPoint(CGPoint(x: width/2, y: 0.0), toNode: self)
    return (leftThumbPoint,rightThumbPoint)
}
```

```swift
func attachDragNodes(dish: SKSpriteNode) {
    let thumbs = dragPoints(dish)
    func newDragNode( position: CGPoint ) -> SKNode {
        var newNode: SKNode = ( debugAids ? SKSpriteNode(color: UIColor.redColor(),↵
                                            size: CGSize(width: 8, height: 8))
            : SKNode() )
        newNode.position = position
        let body = SKPhysicsBody(circleOfRadius: 4.0)
        body.dynamic = false
        newNode.physicsBody = body
        addChild(newNode)
        return newNode
    }
    leftDrag = newDragNode(thumbs.leftPoint)
    rightDrag = newDragNode(thumbs.rightPoint)

    leftJoint = SKPhysicsJointSpring.jointWithBodyA( dish.physicsBody,
        bodyB: leftDrag!.physicsBody,
        anchorA: thumbs.leftPoint,
        anchorB: thumbs.leftPoint)
    leftJoint!.damping = 4.0
    leftJoint!.frequency = 20.0
    physicsWorld.addJoint(leftJoint!)
    rightJoint = SKPhysicsJointSpring.jointWithBodyA( dish.physicsBody,
        bodyB: rightDrag!.physicsBody,
        anchorA: thumbs.rightPoint,
        anchorB: thumbs.rightPoint)
    rightJoint!.damping = 3.0
    rightJoint!.frequency = 20.0
    physicsWorld.addJoint(rightJoint!)
}

func moveDragNodes(# touchPoints: [CGPoint], dish: SKSpriteNode) {
    assert(touchPoints.count==2,"Expected exactly 2 touch points")
    var leftLoc = touchPoints[0]
    var rightLoc = touchPoints[1]
    let thumbs = dragPoints(dish)
    if hypot(leftLoc.x-thumbs.leftPoint.x,leftLoc.y-thumbs.leftPoint.y)↵
            + hypot(rightLoc.x-thumbs.rightPoint.x,rightLoc.y-thumbs.rightPoint.y) >
        hypot(rightLoc.x-thumbs.leftPoint.x,rightLoc.y-thumbs.leftPoint.y)↵
            + hypot(leftLoc.x-thumbs.rightPoint.x,leftLoc.y-thumbs.rightPoint.y) {
            let swapLoc = rightLoc
            rightLoc = leftLoc
            leftLoc = swapLoc
    }
    leftDrag!.position = leftLoc
    rightDrag!.position = rightLoc
}
```

```
func releaseDragNodes() {
    if let dish = dragNode {
        physicsWorld.removeJoint(rightJoint!)
        physicsWorld.removeJoint(leftJoint!)
        leftDrag!.removeFromParent()
        rightDrag!.removeFromParent()
        rightJoint = nil
        leftJoint = nil
        rightDrag = nil
        leftDrag = nil
        dragNode = nil
    }
}
```

In a nutshell, the attachDragNodes(_:) function creates the attachment objects and connects them to the ends of the dish node. The moveDragNodes(touchPoints:,dish:) function moves the anchored ends of the attachments to new locations. This creates tension between the dish and the touch positions, causing the dish to move toward and between them. The releaseDragNodes() function deletes the attachment, allowing the dish to float free again.

To drive this process from touch events, add the touch event handler functions in Listing 14-2. If you've read Chapter 4, these should be self-explanatory. The touchesBegan(...) handler looks to see whether the user is touching the interface with two fingers and both of those touch points are within a reasonable distance of the dish node's thumb positions. If all of that is true, it calls attachDragNodes(_:) to start dragging.

Listing 14-2. Touch Event Handlers

```
func points(# touches: NSSet, inNode node: SKNode) -> [CGPoint] {
    return (touches.allObjects as [UITouch]).map() {
        (touch) in touch.locationInNode(node)
        }
}

override func touchesBegan(touches: NSSet, withEvent event: UIEvent) {
    if touches.count == 2 /*&& !gameOver*/ {
        if dragNode == nil {
            dragNode = childNodeWithName("dish") as? SKSpriteNode
            if let dish = dragNode {
                let hitRect = dish.frame.rectByInsetting(dx: -dragProximityMinimum,↵
                                                         dy: -dragProximityMinimum)
                for point in points(touches: touches, inNode: self) {
                    if !hitRect.contains(point) {
                        dragNode = nil;
                        return
                    }
                }
```

```
                    attachDragNodes(dish)
                    moveDragNodes(touchPoints: points(touches: touches, inNode: self),
                                         dish: dish)
                }
            }
        }
}

override func touchesMoved(touches: NSSet, withEvent event: UIEvent) {
    if touches.count == 2 {
        if let dish = dragNode {
            moveDragNodes(touchPoints: points(touches: touches, inNode: self), dish: dish)
        }
    }
}

override func touchesEnded(touches: NSSet, withEvent event: UIEvent) {
    releaseDragNodes()
}

override func touchesCancelled(touches: NSSet!, withEvent event: UIEvent!) {
    touchesEnded(touches, withEvent: event)
}
```

The touchesMoved(...) handler just updates the anchor points with the latest touch positions. Finally, the touchesEnded(...) handler releases the dish. The points(touches:,inNode:) function is a utility that's repeatedly used to extract the touch locations from a set of touch objects and return an array of their positions, in the local coordinates of a given node.

Let's see what you got for all of that code. Run your app. Touch two fingers over the thumb spots on the lab dish. Once you've grabbed it, drag it around to herd the vegetables into the beaker, as shown in Figure 14-21.

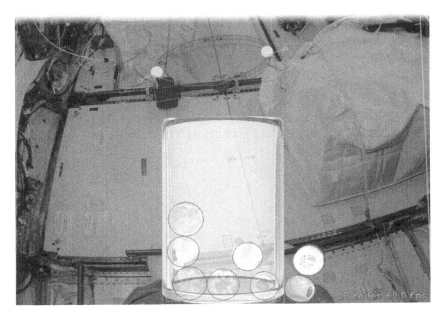

Figure 14-21. Dish node interaction

It's not as easy as it looks, is it? Notice also that the code you added provides its own debugging aids. When debugAids is true, the code that creates the attachment nodes creates visible nodes (SKSpriteNode) rather than invisible nodes (SKNode). This lets you see where your attachment nodes are during debugging.

What you probably didn't notice immediately is that the lab dish gets drawn over the vegetable nodes. Or maybe it doesn't. Or maybe the beaker is drawn underneath some of the vegetables but not others. The problem here is that you haven't established the vertical order of the nodes. Let's attack that next.

Sprites on a Plane

Like UIView, SKNodes have a Z-order. UIViews are drawn in the order they appear in the subviews array. SKNodes, however, have a zPosition property. The greater the zPosition value, the closer the node is to the user. Nodes closer to the user draw on top of nodes that are farther away. The Z-ordering in SpriteKit is completely independent of the order you added the nodes to the scene and can be changed at any time.

If two nodes have the same zPosition value, SpriteKit makes no promises about which one will draw over the other. That can be hazardous at times. For example, your background node has the same zPosition as everything else in your scene. At some point, SpriteKit might decide to draw your background over your vegetables, making your salad disappear! You don't want that to happen.

For SpaceSalad, you want the background to be the farthest sprite in the scene. You then want the dish to draw over the background but behind the vegetables. You want the vegetable to draw over the dish but behind the beaker.

> **Tip**   As a rule, sprites that overlap should have different `zPosition` values. Sprites that don't (or shouldn't) overlap, like your vegetables, can all share the same `zPosition` values.

Organize your sprites into discrete planes by assigning their `zPosition`. Start by adding the following enum to the `GameScene.swift` file, outside of the class definition, as follows:

```
enum GamePlane: CGFloat {
    case Background = 0
    case Clock
    case Dish
    case Vegetable
    case Beaker
    case Score
}
```

This will be useful later when you configure some nodes programmatically. Right now, use it as a guide to change the `zPosition` property of the nodes in your scene file.

Select the `GameScene.sks` file. Select all of the vegetable sprites at once (holding down the Command key to extend the selection) and change their Z Position to 3, as shown in Figure 14-22. Select the dish node and set its Z Position to 2. Select the beaker and set its Z Position to 4. The background already had a Z Position of 0.

Figure 14-22. Setting the Z-order of nodes

Now your vegetables will always be behind your beaker and in front of the background.

Nodes That Go Bump

Once you created physics bodies for the vegetables, beaker, dish, and border, they all started bumping into to each other. These are called *collisions* in SpriteKit. It might seem obvious that everything with a physics body will collide with anything else with a physics body, but this is not the case.

You have a lot of control over what nodes collide with other nodes. Collisions are determined by two properties of the physics body: the category mask (`categoryBitMask`) and the collision mask (`collisionBitMask`).

Each property is an integer value with 32 single-bit flags. You use them by defining up to 32 different categories, assigning each a unique bit. In SpaceSalad, you'll need four categories. Select the `GameScene.swift` file and add this enum outside the class definition, as follows:

```
enum CollisionCategory: UInt32 {
    case Dish =           0b00000001
    case Floaters =       0b00000010
    case Beaker =         0b00000100
    case EverythingElse = 0b00001000
}
```

You then assign each node to one or more of your categories, although a node is typically assigned to only one category. You then set its `collisionBitMask` property with all of the categories it will collide with. In effect, you define a matrix of possible collisions, allowing you to define a node that collides with some nodes and surfaces but not others. For example, your game might have a force field node. Droid and speeder nodes would collide with the field, but energy blast nodes would pass right through it.

You can set the collision categories for your nodes either programmatically or in the SpriteKit scene editor. For example, you could select all of the vegetable nodes and locate the Physics Definitions section in the attributes inspector. Since the physics bodies for the vegetables are defined in the scene editor, set their Category Mask to 2 (0b00000010).

Alternatively, you can assign them programmatically. In the `GameScene.swift` file, find the `didMoveToView(_:)` function. In the block of code that creates the physics body for the background, add the following statement:

```
body.categoryBitMask = CollisionCategory.EverythingElse.rawValue
```

Add similar statements to the code that creates the physics body for the beaker (using the value `CollisionCategory.Beaker`) and the lab dish (using `CollisionCategory.Dish`). If you don't want to set the category values for all of the vegetable nodes in the scene editor, add the following statement to the code block that nudges the vegetable nodes:

```
body.categoryBitMask = CollisionCategory.Floaters.rawValue
```

For SpaceSalad, the categories aren't that important (yet). So far, you're only using categories to determine collisions. By default, the value of the `collisionBitMask` property is `0xffffffff`, which means every body will collide with every other body in any category and is why your nodes have been bouncing around from the beginning.

But collision categories are also used for contact handling. Now that you've assigned your nodes collision categories, put those categories to work.

Contact!

When two physics bodies are touching, they are said to be in *contact*. The contacts that are of most interest are those associated with collisions. When two bodies collide, your game will often want to do something. A brick will explode, a missile will explode, or a tomato will explode. Or maybe something nonexplosive will occur. The point is, your app needs to know when these things happen.

This, too, is remarkably simple. To handle contact events, you must do the following:

1. Create a contact delegate object.

2. Make it the delegate for the physics simulation engine.

3. Define a `didBeginContact(_:)` or `didEndContact(_:)` delegate function, or both.

4. Set the `contactsTestBitMap` in a physics body with the categories that will cause contact events.

First, turn your `GameScene` object into a contact delegate by adding this protocol to your class in `GameScene.swift`, as follows:

```
class GameScene: ResizableScene, SKPhysicsContactDelegate {
```

You then need to make your object the delegate for the physics simulator. In your `didMoveToView(_:)` function, add the following statement:

```
physicsWorld.contactDelegate = self
```

Now add a `didBeginContact(_:)` delegate function to your `GameScene` class, as follows:

```
func didBeginContact(contact: SKPhysicsContact!) {
}
```

You still, however, won't receive any `didBeginContact(_:)` calls. Contact handling only occurs on physics bodies that have set their `contactsTestBitMap` property to a bit mask filled with the categories of the bodies you want to handle contacts with.

For SpaceSalad, that's going to be simple. The goal of the game is to push the vegetables into the beaker and then place the dish on top, to keep them from floating out again. So, the game will end when the lab dish touches the beaker and all of the vegetables are inside the beaker.

Set the contact test category for the dish node. Do this in the `didMoveToView(_:)` function. Locate the block of code that creates the physics body for the dish node, and add the following statement:

```
body.contactTestBitMask = CollisionCategory.Beaker.rawValue
```

Now whenever the dish is dragged down to touch the beaker, your `didBeginContact(_:)` function will be called. The contact object (`SKPhysicsContact`) will contain references to the two bodies that are touching, the coordinate where the contact occurred, and some information about the force and direction of the collision.

SpaceSalad isn't interested in any of that. It just wants to know whether the game has ended. The problem is, your game has surprisingly little game logic so far; there are no timers or scores. With everything else in place, I think it's time to turn this app into a game.

Gamifying SpaceSalad

Let's start making your game act more like a game. One of the things that make a game exciting is setting a time limit and showing a big countdown timer. I tell you, that really gets my heart racing. Since it has a time limit, it means the game must come to an end at some point. This also implies that it must start at some point. Add some logic to start and stop the game and to manage a timer.

Back in `GameScene.swift`, add the following code to your class:

```
let gameDuration = 100.0
var timeRemaining = 0.0
var gameOver = false

func startGame( ) {
    gameOver = false
    timeRemaining = gameDuration
}

func endGame( score: Int ) {
    gameOver = true
    releaseDragNodes()
}
```

You now have a time limit for your game, along with functions to start and stop the game.

> **Tip**   In a larger project, you would isolate your game logic and game state using the Model-View-Controller design pattern. GameScene is your view object. This game logic would be in a separate game controller class (GameController) or isolated in an extension of GameScene. A more complicated game might also warrant a separate game state object, your data model, particularly if you need to save and restore games.

When does the game start? It starts when GameScene is presented. At the end of the
didMoveToView(_:) function, add the following statement:

```
startGame()
```

When does the game end? It ends when all of the salad ingredients are inside the beaker or the time
runs out. And when the game ends, you'll want to compute a score. Wrap all that logic into a single
score() function by adding the following code to the class:

```
func score() -> (score: Int, won: Bool) {
    var capturedCount = 0
    var missing = false
    let beakerFrame = childNodeWithName("beaker")!.frame
    enumerateChildNodesWithName("veg") { (node,stop) in
        if beakerFrame.contains(node.position) {
            ++capturedCount
        } else {
            missing = true
        }
    }
    return (capturedCount*(Int(timeRemaining)+60),!missing)
}
```

This function calculates the score for the game and also determines whether the player has won,
successfully getting all of the vegetables into beaker. It works by getting the frame of the beaker node
and then locating the position of every veg node in the scene. Each captured vegetable counts toward
a winning score. Any vegetable outside the beaker's frame will set the missing flag to true, indicating
that the game isn't over yet. The score is calculated based on the number of captured vegetables and
the amount of time still remaining; the faster you capture them all, the higher your score.

This function gives you everything you need to know when the game has completed. You can
(finally!) write the contact handler from the previous section. Flesh out your contact handler with the
following code (new code in bold):

```
func didBeginContact(contact: SKPhysicsContact!) {
    let outcome = score()
    if outcome.won {
        endGame(outcome.score)
    }
}
```

That was almost anticlimactic. Every time the dish touches the beaker, this code will quickly check
to see whether all of the vegetables are inside the beaker and what the final score is. If the game has
been won, it ends the game with the computed score.

Oh, and there's one tiny detail to attend to. Back in the touchesBegan(_:,withEvent:) function,
modify the first if statement so it reads as follows (modified code in bold):

```
if touches.count == 2 && !gameOver {
```

This simple change prevents the player from grabbing the dish and continuing to play after the game has ended.

Your game will run now, but you have nothing to show for your work. I mean that literally. There's nothing that indicates that the game has started or ended or what the score was. If you want to see your new code in action, set some breakpoints in strategic functions like didBeginContact(_:) and endGame(_:). Xcode will show you what's going on, but you need the player to see it.

Actions in Action

I mentioned adding a timer to your game. Let's do that now. This will, rather conspicuously, show that the game is running and when it's over. Select the GameScene.sks file. This time, drag in a label node, as shown in Figure 14-23.

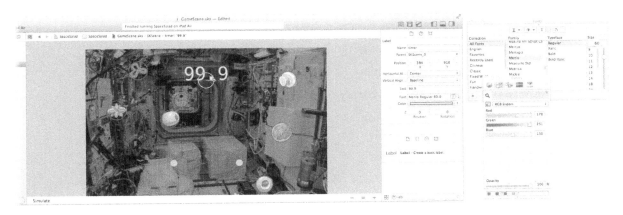

Figure 14-23. Adding a label node

Select the new label node and set its attributes as follows:

- Name: timer
- Position: (384,918)
- Text: 99.9
- Font: Menlo Regular 60.0
- Color: celery green (Red=178, Green=251, Blue=150)
- Z Position: 1 (GamePlane.Clock)

A label node (SKLabelNode) displays some text, just as a sprite node displays an image or color. Like a UILabel object, you can change what it displays simply by updating its text property. For SpaceSalad, you want to update the label every tenth of a second with the remaining time.

If you were doing this with UILabel, you'd probably schedule an NSTimer object to fire ten times a second and have your timer function update the label view. But that's not how you do things in SpriteKit.

In SpriteKit, you animate nodes through actions. An action is an effect or procedure that you attach to a node. Every time SpriteKit has rendered the entire scene—called a *frame*, like a frame in a movie—it performs any pending actions.

The reason for this is because most of what SpriteKit does is done on a background thread, or threads. Actions, collision handlers, and so on, rarely execute on the main thread. To integrate smoothly with what's happening in the scene, you simply create an action that describes what you want the node to do, and at its next opportunity, the node will do it.

> **Caution**   It is important that you don't try to use any classes that aren't thread-safe from your actions. Specifically, don't have an action make changes to any `UIView` or `UIViewController` objects. Remember that many `UIView` changes must happen on the main thread.

There are all kinds of actions you can attach to a node. Here are some examples:

- Move a node to another position
- Move a node, following an arbitrary path
- Rotate
- Change scale
- Hide or reveal a node
- Fade in or out
- Change the texture or color of a node
- Remove a node from the scene
- Wait for a period of time
- Cause an action of another node to run
- Execute an arbitrary block of code
- Perform a sequence of actions
- Perform a group of actions, in parallel
- Perform an action repeatedly

The items at the beginning of this list are your basic animation actions. Remember, earlier, when I said you don't tell nodes how to animate, you tell them why? I overstated this a bit. You *typically* animate nodes using the physics simulator, but you have a full complement of animation actions that you can direct any way you want, and you'll use these in a moment.

The truly open-ended action is the one that executes a block of code. This is where you can attach any logic you want to a node.

The last few actions are where things get really interesting. The sequence and group actions perform a set of other actions, either sequentially or simultaneously. If you want to create an animation sequence (move, then rotate, then fade away, then remove), you create the individual actions, build a sequence action from those, and attach the sequence action to the node. Mixing in the code block action, you can run any logic before, during, or at the end of the sequence.

Finally, the repeat action will perform another action a set number of times or forever. The action it performs could be a sequence or group. Actions can be nested to any depth.

Actions are attached to a node using the `runAction(_:)` function. They run once and are disposed of. The "exception" is the repeat action, which isn't finished until it has run all of its subactions the requisite number of times—or never, in the case of the repeat-forever action.

> **Tip** There is also a special `runAction(_:,completion:)` function that runs an action on a node and then executes a code block. This is equivalent to creating a sequence action that runs an action followed by a code block action.

You're going to use actions to update the timer in the scene. Select the `GameScene.swift` file and find the `startGame()` function. Add the following code:

```
if let label = childNodeWithName("timer") as? SKLabelNode {
    let wait = SKAction.waitForDuration(0.1)
    let decrement = SKAction.runBlock({
        self.timeRemaining -= 0.1
        if self.timeRemaining < 0.0 {
            label.text = "End"
            self.endGame(self.score().score)
        } else {
            label.text = NSString(format: "%.1f", self.timeRemaining)
        }
    })
    let sequence = SKAction.sequence([wait,decrement])
    let forever = SKAction.repeatActionForever(sequence)
    label.runAction(forever)
}
```

The new code gets the timer node you just added to the scene. It then creates a sequence of actions. The first action does nothing (waits) for one-tenth of a second. The second action executes a block of code that gets the time remaining, decrements it by 0.1, and updates the label node, that is, until `timeRemaining` reaches 0.0. Then it sets the timer's text to End and ends the game.

For these actions to run repeatedly, they are first assembled into a sequence action, which is then used to create a repeat-forever action. The repeat-forever action is the one added to the timer node.

> **Tip**   Most actions are immutable and can be reused and run on multiple nodes at the same time. If you have a commonly used action, create it once and reuse it as often as you need.

Since a repeat-forever action never finishes (from the node's perspective), you need to stop it once the game ends. In the `endGame(_:)` function, add the following statement:

```
childNodeWithName("timer")?.removeAllActions()
```

The `removeAllActions()` function does exactly what you think it does.

Now run the app, as shown in Figure 14-24. You see the timer start immediately. If you can successfully get all of the vegetables into the beaker, the game will end, and the timer will stop. If not, the timer will eventually get to 0.0 and will stop the game.

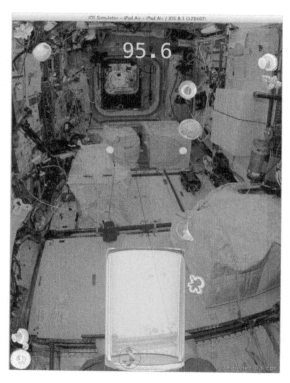
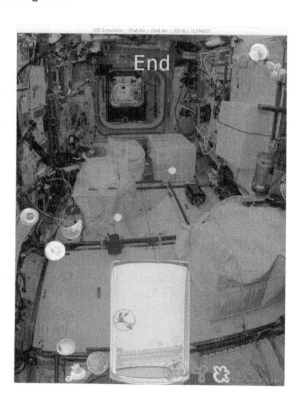

Figure 14-24. Game with timer

Traditional Animation

What's also missing is something to tell the player what their score is. This will bring you full circle, back to straight-up animation sequences.

When the game ends, create a new label node that displays the score. Do that at the end of the endGame(_:) function with the following code:

```
let score = SKLabelNode(text: "Score: \(score)")
score.fontName = "Helvetica"
score.fontColor = SKColor.greenColor()
score.fontSize = CGFloat( view!.traitCollection.horizontalSizeClass == .Compact
                                                        ? 54.0 : 120.0 )
let sceneRect = CGRect(origin: CGPointZero, size: frame.size)
score.position = CGPoint(x: sceneRect.midX, y: sceneRect.height*0.1)
score.zPosition = GamePlane.Score.rawValue
addChild(score)
```

With everything you've learned, this code should be easy to decipher. The code creates a new SKLabelNode, configures its font and text, and positions it in the horizontal center of the scene. Note that it sets the node's zPosition to GamePlane.Score, so it draws on top of all of the other sprites. Finally, the node is added to the scene.

Run your app. Win the game or let it come to an end, and your score will appear.

That's good but boring.

Return to this code. Set the initial scale of the new label sprite to something small by adding the following code to what you just wrote (added code in bold):

```
score.zPosition = GamePlane.Score.rawValue
score.xScale = 0.2
score.yScale = 0.2
addChild(score)
```

Now create actions to restore the size of the label, fade the label in, and move the label up—all at the same time. Immediately after the preceding code, add the following:

```
let push = SKAction.moveToY(sceneRect.height*0.8, duration: 1.0)
push.timingMode = .EaseOut
let grow = SKAction.scaleTo(1.0, duration: 1.2)
grow.timingMode = .EaseIn
let appear = SKAction.fadeInWithDuration(0.8)
let drama = SKAction.group([push,grow,appear])
score.runAction(drama)
```

A group action is an action that starts two or more actions simultaneously. So, the resizing, the movement, and the fade-in effect begin at the same time. Also note that these actions all have different durations. After 1.0 second has elapsed, the label has already completely appeared and has just stopped moving, but it is still growing. The group action finishes when its last action is done.

Now run your game and see how it ends. Yes, that's a lot more interesting. (Sadly, I can't show you the effect in print. You'll just have to run the app yourself.)

Now what? Your game ends, but there's no way to start it again. Yikes! Honestly, most games don't start out right in the game. They usually have a welcome scene where you start the game, access help and settings, and so on. Let's rework SpaceSalad so it has a welcome scene, and you'll also see how easy it is to switch scenes inside a SpriteKit view.

Presenting Scenes

In the file template library, find the SpriteKit Scene template and drag one into your project navigator. Name the file `WelcomeScene`. Now create a welcome scene for your game with the following steps. (Alternatively, you can simply copy in the finished `WelcomeScene.sks` and `WelcomeScene.swift` files from the finished project in the `Learn iOS Development Projects` ➤ `Ch 14` ➤ `SpaceSalad` folder.)

1. Set the dimensions of the scene to (768,1024).

2. Drag in a color sprite and configure it as follows:

    a. Name: background

    b. Texture: bkg_welcome.jpg

    c. Position: (0,0)

    d. Anchor Point: (0,0)

3. Drag in a label node and configure it as follows:

    a. Position: (384,740)

    b. Text: Tap to Play

    c. Font: Helvetica Neue UltraLight 59.0

    d. Color: White

    e. Z Position: 1

4. Drag in another label node and configure it as follows:

    a. Position: (384,657)

    b. Text: Latest Score:

    c. Font: Helvetica Neue Thin 30.0

    d. Z Position: 1

5. Hold down the Option key and drag the last label to duplicate it. Configure the duplicate as follows:

    a. Position: (384,549)

    b. Text: Highest Score:

6. Drag in a new label node and configure it as follows:

    a. Name: latest

    b. Position: (384,608)

    c. Text: none

    d. Font: Helvetica Neue Bold 32.0

    e. Color: White

    f. Z Position: 1

7. Hold down the Option key and drag that last label to duplicate it. Configure the duplicate as follows:

    a. Name: highest

    b. Position: (384,500)

Your welcome scene should look like the one in Figure 14-25.

Figure 14-25. Designing the welcome scene

From the file template library, drag in a new Swift file and name it WelcomeScene. Select and fill it with the following code, assuming you didn't copy the file already.

```
import SpriteKit

class WelcomeScene: ResizableScene {

    override func didMoveToView(view: SKView) {
        scaleMode = .AspectFill
        size = view.frame.size
        if let latest = childNodeWithName("latest") as? SKLabelNode {
            latest.text = "\(GameViewController.latestScore())"
        }
        if let highest = childNodeWithName("highest") as? SKLabelNode {
            highest.text = "\(GameViewController.highestScore())"
        }
    }

    override func touchesBegan(touches: NSSet, withEvent event: UIEvent) {
        if let scene = GameScene.unarchiveFromFile("GameScene") as? GameScene {
            let doors = SKTransition.doorsOpenVerticalWithDuration(1.0)
            view!.presentScene(scene, transition: doors)
        }
    }
}
```

Just like the didMoveToView(_:) function in GameScene, this one resizes its scene to fit the view. It then updates its two labels with the user's latest and highest scores.

The single touch event handler loads the GameScene (just like the view controller is doing now) and presents it. But since there is (or soon will be) a scene already displayed, it adds a transition animation to the presentation.

Now you need to make some changes to your GameViewController. You view controller will keep track of the latest and highest scores. It also needs to be modified so the first scene it presents is the welcome scene.

Select the GameViewController.swift file. Add the following enum outside the class definition:

```
enum GameScoreKey: String {
    case LatestScore = "latest"
    case HighestScore = "highest"
}
```

Now add the following two class functions:

```
class func latestScore() -> Int {
    return NSUserDefaults.standardUserDefaults().integerForKey(GameScoreKey.LatestScore.rawValue)
}

class func highestScore() -> Int {
    return NSUserDefaults.standardUserDefaults().integerForKey(GameScoreKey.HighestScore.rawValue)
}
```

These two functions retrieve the player's latest and highest scores from the user defaults. You'll learn all about user defaults in Chapter 18. For now, just know that the user defaults is a place to store small bits of data that will be remembered between runs of your app.

In the viewDidLoad() function, find the code that loads the initial scene and change it as follows (modified code in bold):

```
if let scene = WelcomeScene.unarchiveFromFile("WelcomeScene") as? WelcomeScene {
    let skView = self.view as SKView
    skView.presentScene(scene)
}
```

While you're here, I think you're done with the debug aids. Find the let debugAids constant and change it to false.

You are almost done, I promise! The app now starts with the welcome scene that shows the latest scores. Tapping it presents the game scene, which starts that game. The only missing piece is when the game ends. The game needs to record the scores and transition back to the welcome scene.

Switch to the GameScene.swift file. Locate the endGame(_:) function and insert the following statement:

```
recordScore(score)
```

After the endGame(_:) function, add that new function.

```
func recordScore( score: Int ) {
    let userDefaults = NSUserDefaults.standardUserDefaults()
    userDefaults.setInteger(score, forKey: GameScoreKey.LatestScore.rawValue)
    if score > GameViewController.highestScore() {
        userDefaults.setInteger( score, forKey: GameScoreKey.HighestScore.rawValue)
    }
}
```

Back in the endGame(_:) function, locate the code that animates the score label. You're going to change it so that once the animation is complete, the node waits for a few seconds and then presents the welcome scene. Add the following code (new code in bold):

```
let drama = SKAction.group([push,grow,appear])
let delay = SKAction.waitForDuration(4.5)
let exit = SKAction.runBlock({
    if let scene = WelcomeScene.unarchiveFromFile("WelcomeScene") as? WelcomeScene {
        let doors = SKTransition.doorsCloseVerticalWithDuration(0.5)
        self.view?.presentScene(scene, transition: doors)
    }
})
score.runAction(SKAction.sequence([drama,delay,exit]))
```

You took the concurrent group of animation actions and made that one step in a sequence of actions, the last one executing a block of code to transition back to the welcome scene. Your finished game should look like the one in Figure 14-26.

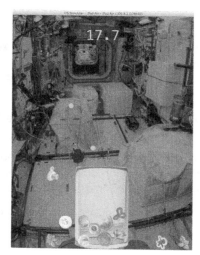

Figure 14-26. Finished SpaceSalad

Beyond SpaceSalad

Congratulations, you've covered a lot of ground in this chapter. SpriteKit is a big world, and you've toured a great deal of it. But you haven't visited everything. In fact, there are a lot of SpriteKit destinations I didn't even mention. It's time to rectify that.

Here are a few topics you might want to explore on your own:

- There are a lot of different ways of creating the texture for a sprite node. For example, you can load or create a single large graphic and then create individual sprites that render portions of that image.

- You can apply Core Graphics filters (blur, saturate, glow, and so on) to sprites. See SKEffectNode.

- As I mentioned at the beginning, it's possible to write your own sprite-rendering logic by writing an OpenGL ES fragment shader program. If you understood that sentence, see the SKShader class.

- Sprites can have a fixed border and will scale their interior, much the way UIButton will resize a graphic so its borders don't look stretched when resized.

- For fine-grained animation control, your scene can execute code at the end of each frame in its update(_:) function. There are also opportunities to process the scene after actions have run (didEvaluateAction()) and after the physics simulator has updated all of the nodes (didSimulatePhysics()).

- The physics simulation engine (SKPhysicsWorld) has a number of interesting features. You can apply speed and gravity to the entire scene, add attachment joints, and find all of the physics bodies that intersect a line.

- There are other kinds of nodes. There are nodes that apply forces and nodes that provide lighting. There are even nodes that create turbulence.

You can read more about all of these topics and more in the *SpriteKit Programming Guide* that you'll find in Xcode's Documentation and API Reference window.

Summary

This is cause for some celebration. This was, by far, the most complex and difficult project in the book, and you did it using technologies you hadn't used before. While SpriteKit shares a lot of similarities with the view classes you've used before and will continue to use, many aspects are radically different. Scene design uses a specialized editor, you must load the scene files yourself, and animation is different, not to mention there are completely new concepts like physics bodies and collisions.

With the momentum you've built up, you can, honestly, coast through the rest of this book. Later chapters are going to introduce you to even more iOS services, such as maps, and there's a lot of practical information about Swift. But all of that is going to seem simple compared to what you've accomplished here.

Speaking of practical information, the next chapter is going to focus on Interface Builder—not so much how to use it as how it works, which is something that's important to understand if you want to be an iOS master developer.

EXERCISE

SpaceSalad is a cute game, but it's sort of jerky. That is, the lab dish often jitters when being dragged around. Try taking a moment to address that.

The behavior of sprites is a combination of all the physics body attributes and their geometry, along with the forces applied to those bodies. There are more than a couple of attributes you can adjust, and every one will have a subtle—or not so subtle—effect on how your sprites behave.

Here are a few things to look into. The "spring" joints between the player's drag position and the thumb nodes of the lab dish have damping and frequency properties. These control the rate at which energy is lost by the spring and how fast it oscillates. Small changes here can have dramatic effects on how the connected nodes interact. A physics body also has a mass property. This is a combination of its area and density properties. Try making the lab dish "lighter" by reducing its density property. Try increasing or reducing the drag (linearDamping) of your vegetables. Play with these and other properties. What happens to game play if you set the veg node's restitution to 0.0? What happens when you assign different restitutions to different nodes? This is a game; have some fun!

Chapter 15

If You Build It...

Interface Builder is Xcode's "secret sauce." It makes the creation of complex interfaces effortless: drag interface elements into a canvas, connect them, click a button, and they become working objects in your app. It's like magic.

Any sufficiently advanced technology is indistinguishable from magic.

—Arthur C. Clarke

"Magic" is often used to describe what we don't understand. Interface Builder can sometimes meet this criteria. It works; you just don't know how. Well, step behind the curtain and prepare to learn those secrets. In this chapter, you will learn the following:

- Learn what Interface Builder files are (exactly)
- Find out how objects in an Interface Builder file become objects in your app
- Discover programmatic equivalents to what Interface Builder does
- Understand how placeholder objects work
- Programmatically load your own Interface Builder files
- Provide your own placeholder objects

You're going to learn what Interface Builder does in a very pragmatic way. I'm going to show you the code that accomplishes what you've been doing in storyboards. Conversely, you'll then take some code you wrote earlier and translate that into an .xib (stand-alone Interface Builder) file.

How Interface Builder Files Work

An Interface Builder file contains a serialized graph of objects. In Chapter 14, you learned a little of what serialization means and some of the challenges involved. In Chapters 18 and 19, you'll learn how to serialize objects and how to create objects that can be serialized (archived). But for now, all you need to know is that "serializing an object" means converting its properties into a transportable array of bytes and eventually reversing the process to get them back again.

> **Note**   I'm still using the term *serialize* in the generic, computer engineering sense. In the language of Cocoa Touch, Interface Builder files are an *archive* of objects. Loading an Interface Builder file consists of *unarchiving* those objects.

So, what's an object graph? An *object graph* is a set formed by an object, all of the objects that object refers to, all of the objects those objects refer to, and so on. The object—or small number of objects—that begins the graph is referred to as the *root* or *top-level* object(s).

Serialization starts at the root object. That object converts its properties into a serialized byte array. If any of its properties refer to other objects, those objects are asked to serialize their property values into the same byte array, and so on, until all of the objects and property values for the entire graph are converted. The finished array of bytes describe the entire set of objects, their properties, and their relationships.

Compiling Interface Builder Files

You use an Interface Builder file by creating one and adding it to your project. You then edit it and build your app.

But the .xib or .storyboard file that you edit in Xcode is not what ends up in your app's bundle. Like your source (.swift) files, your Interface Builder files are compiled. The nib compiler converts the design in your .storyboard or .xib file into serialized data that, when unarchived, will create the objects with the properties and connections you described. This compiled nib file is then added to your app's bundle as a resource file.

> **Note**   Some interface editors take your design and turn it into source code, equivalent to what you drew, which you then compile as part of your app. These tools are called *code generators*. Interface Builder is not a code generator. Interface Builder is an *object compiler*.

Loading a Scene

When your apps needs the objects stored in an Interface Builder file, it *loads* the interface. Figure 15-1 shows the Detail View scene of the Main.storyboard file (from MyStuff in Chapter 7). Figure 15-2 shows the (simplified) graph of objects contained in that scene.

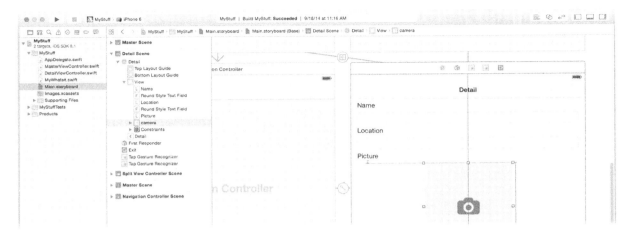

Figure 15-1. *Detail View scene in Interface Builder*

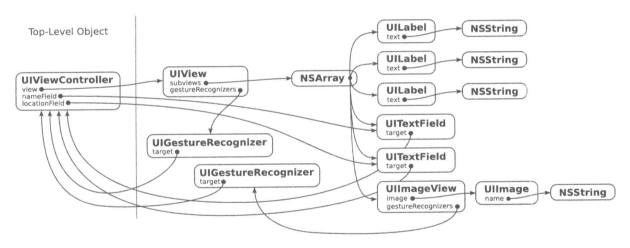

Figure 15-2. *Graph of objects in the Detail View scene*

A storyboard scene consists of at least one top-level object, the view controller. The view controller's view property refers to its single root view object (UIView). This, in turn, contains a collection of subviews (managed by an array). Some of those view objects refer to additional objects, such as NSString, UIImage, and UIGestureRecognizer objects.

The instantiateViewControllerWithIdentifer(_:) function instigates the re-creation (unarchiving) of the view controller and all of its related objects stored in the storyboard scene. This method is invoked automatically when triggered by a segue; or, as you did in the Wonderland app (Chapter 12), you can call it programmatically to create the view controller for a scene when it pleases you.

During deserialization (unarchiving), the property values and connections in the serialized data are used to instantiate new objects, set their properties, and connect them.

Loading an .xib File

Storyboards are the modern method of designing iOS apps. But iOS will also let you design an interface in a separate .xib file. A view controller will load an .xib file automatically, or you can load the objects in an .xib file programmatically. When using an .xib file, the object relationships are subtly different.

Refer again to Figure 15-2. In the storyboard scene, there is only one top-level object (the view controller), and the entire graph of objects is reconstructed by unarchiving that single object. If this interface were stored in an .xib file, its object graph would be a little different, as shown in Figure 15-3.

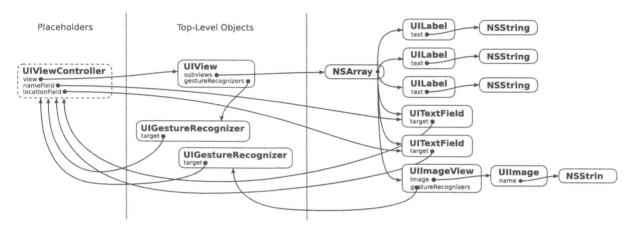

Figure 15-3. Graph of objects in an .xib file

The difference is the placeholder object. *Placeholder* objects—the most important being the file's owner—are objects that already exist when the Interface Builder file is loaded. During the unarchiving process, your existing objects are substituted for the placeholders. The existing objects become part of the object graph but are not created by the .xib file. Outlets in a placeholder can be set to objects created in the file, and objects in the file can be connected to a placeholder. In Figure 15-3, the view and nameField properties in the file's owner (the view controller) are still set to the UIView and UITextField objects.

The important difference to grasp is this: when a view controller is loaded from a storyboard scene, the view controller and all of its connected objects are created for you, en masse. When using an .xib file, it's a two-stage process. The owner object—typically the view controller, but it doesn't have to be—is created first, often programmatically. Then the .xib file is loaded. The .xib file creates all the remaining objects and connects those objects to the existing owner object.

Placeholder Objects and the File's Owner

When an Interface Builder file is loaded, the caller supplies the existing objects that will replace the placeholders in the file. The most common scenario is to use one placeholder object, referred to as the *file's owner*. This is typically the object loading the file; when a view controller loads its Interface Builder file, it declares itself as the file's owner. You can provide any object you choose or none at all, in which case there are zero placeholder objects. Optionally, you can supply as many additional placeholder objects as you want. (Later in this chapter you'll load an Interface Builder file with multiple placeholders.) Think of the file's owner as the "designated placeholder," provided to make the common task of loading an Interface Builder file with one placeholder object as easy as possible.

The important rule to remember is that the class of the file's owner in the Interface Builder file *must* agree with the class of the owner object when the file is loaded. You set the class of the file's owner using the identity inspector in Interface Builder. When you set this, you're making a promise that the actual object will be of that class (or a subclass) when the file is loaded.

Changing the class of the file's owner from UIViewController to UIApplication won't magically give your Interface Builder file access to your app's UIApplication object. It just means that the UIViewController object (the file's real owner) will be treated as if it were a UIApplication object, probably with unpleasant consequences.

> **Caution**   When changing the class of any placeholder object in Interface Builder, ensure that you set it to the class, or a superclass, of the actual object that will be supplied when the file is loaded.

The principle use of the file's owner is to gain access to the objects created in the Interface Builder file. To access any of those objects, you must obtain a reference to them. While it's possible to obtain references to the top-level objects, all other objects must be accessed indirectly, either via properties in the top-level objects or through connections set in the file's owner object. In the example shown in Figure 15-3, the UIView object becomes accessible through the owner object's view property. Without a placeholder object outlet, it would be awkward (sometimes impossible) to access the objects you just created.

When an Interface Builder file loads, only those outlets in the placeholder objects that are connected in the file are set. All other properties and outlets remain the same.

Objects within the Interface Builder file can only establish connections to other objects in the graph or to the placeholder objects. For example, an object being loaded by a view controller cannot be directly connected to the application delegate object. That object isn't in the graph. The exception is the first responder. The first responder is an implied object that could be any object in the responder chain. As you learned in Chapter 4, the responder chain goes all the way to the UIApplication object.

Now that you have a feel for how objects in an Interface Builder file get created, it's time to dig into the details of how objects are defined and connected to one another and what that means to your app.

Creating Objects

Adding an object to an Interface Builder file is equivalent to creating that object programmatically. This is a really important concept to grasp. There is nothing "special" about objects created from Interface Builder files. You can always write code that accomplishes the same results; it's just excruciatingly tedious, which is why Interface Builder was invented in the first place.

In Figure 15-4, an UISlider object is being added to an Interface Builder file. This is borrowed from the ColorModel project in Chapter 8.

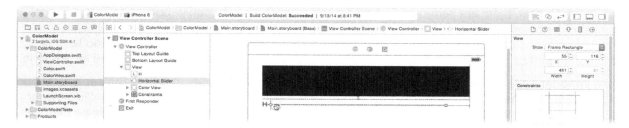

Figure 15-4. Adding an object to an Interface Builder file

The slider will be created with a frame of ((55,116),(506,147)), and it's a subview of the root UIView. The equivalent code (in a view controller) would be as follows:

```
let newSlider = UISlider(frame: CGRect(x: 55, y: 116, width: 451, height: 31))
view.addSubview(newSlider)
```

This code creates a new UISlider object with the desired dimensions and adds it to the view controller's root view object. In both methods (Interface Builder and programmatically), the end result is the same.

> **Note**   Interface Builder understands a few special object relationships and creates those relationships for you. For example, when you add a view object as a subview, it's equivalent to calling addSubview(_:) on the superview. If you add Bar Button Items to a toolbar, the equivalent function would be setItems(_:,animated:). Dropping a new gesture recognizer into a view is the same as calling addGestureRecognizer(_:). Adding constraints is equivalent to calling addConstraint(_:) or addConstraints(_:), and so on.

There's only one, technical difference between how the UISlider object gets created in the Interface Builder file and how you create one programmatically. When you write code to create a view object, you use its init(frame:) initializer function. When an object is unarchived—which is how objects in an Interface Builder file get created—the object is created using its init(coder:) initializer function. The coder parameter contains an object that has all of the properties the new object needs, including its frame. You'll learn all about init(coder:) in Chapter 19.

Editing Attributes

But the frame isn't the only property of the UISlider object. When you created your slider object in ColorModel, you used the attributes inspector to change several of its properties. You changed its maximum range to 360 and checked the Update Events: Continuous option. That was equivalent to writing the following code:

```
newSlider.maximumValue = 360.0
newSlider.continuous = true
```

Again, the resulting object is indistinguishable from the object created by the Interface Builder file, despite subtle differences in how those property values are set.

Creating Custom Objects

You can also ask Interface Builder to create custom objects that you've created, and you've done this several times already. You begin by adding the base class object, like a UIViewController object, to your interface and then use the identity inspector to change the class of the object to the one you want created. In Chapter 4, for example, you changed the root UIView in the Touchy project into a TouchyView object, with all of the methods, properties, actions, and outlets you defined.

What you might not have noticed is an obscure item in the object library named, simply, Object (see Figure 15-5). That's right, it's just an object. By itself, it's nearly useless. But since every object is an object, you can drop one into your design and then use the identity inspector to change its class to just about anything you want.

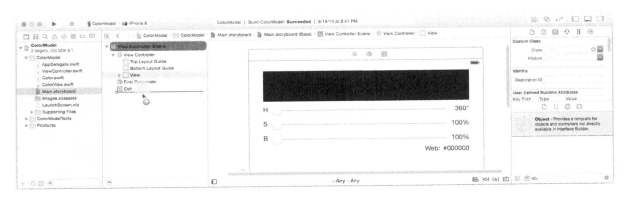

Figure 15-5. Adding an Object object

Let's take the ColorModel project from Chapter 8 as an example. The view controller created the data model object and set its initial property values using the following code:

```
var colorModel = Color()

...

colorModel.hue = 60.0
colorModel.saturation = 50.0
colorModel.brightness = 100.0
```

You can accomplish the same using Interface Builder. Start by adding a generic object to your design, as shown in Figure 15-5. You must drop the object into the outline because an object is not a view object and can't be added to the visual representation of the interface.

Once you've added the object, select it and use the identity inspector to change its class to Color, as shown on the right in Figure 15-6. Now the storyboard will create your data model object when the view controller scene is loaded.

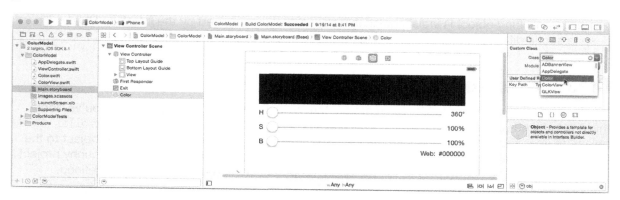

Figure 15-6. *Changing the class of a generic object*

But the object still isn't connected to anything or configured. Interface Builder only makes connections to outlets and actions. Change the data model property in ViewController.swift so it's an outlet, as follows (modified code in bold):

@IBOutlet var colorModel: **Color!**

Now you can connect the view controller to its data model object right in the storyboard file, as shown in Figure 15-7.

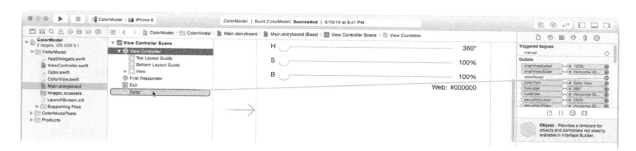

Figure 15-7. *Connection the view controller to the data model*

The only things missing are the Color object's properties. Interface Builder has you covered here too. Open the Color.swift file and add @IBInspectable keywords to all the three properties as follows (new code in bold):

@IBInspectable dynamic var hue: Float = 0.0
@IBInspectable dynamic var saturation: Float = 0.0
@IBInspectable dynamic var brightness: Float = 0.0

The @IBInspectable keyword makes a property editable using the attributes inspector. Now these properties can be set directly in Interface Builder, as shown in Figure 15-8.

Figure 15-8. *Editing custom attributes*

Interface Builder can inspect Boolean, integer, floating point, string, point (CGPoint), size (CGSize), rectangle (CGRect), range (NSRange), and color (UIColor) properties. As of this writing, it cannot edit any other types, most notably attributed strings, nor can it edit enum types, even ones with editable raw values. Ideally, that latter restriction will change someday soon.

@IBInspectable isn't limited to the Object object. You can designate an inspectable property in any class and it will appear in Interface Builder, alongside your actions, outlets, and any inherited attributes.

These simple techniques open up a world of possibilities. You can define all kinds of custom objects and then create, connect, and configure them right in Interface Builder.

> **Tip**   It's also possible to design custom view objects and have them appear in Interface Builder. You do this by creating your custom view in a framework (see Chapter 21) and using the @IBDesignable keyword. Interface Builder will then load the framework and use your custom display code to draw the view—exactly as it will appear in your app—in the Interface Builder canvas. Search the Xcode documentation for sample projects that use the @IBDesignable keyword.

Connections

You've seen how objects and their properties in an Interface Builder file get created, but what about connections? Figure 15-9 shows the hueSlider outlet being connected to a slider object.

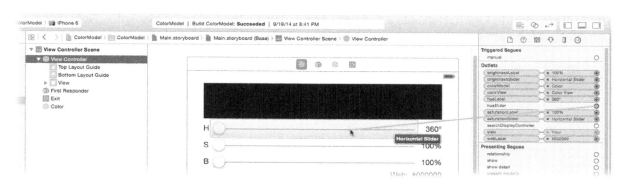

Figure 15-9. *Connecting an outlet in Interface Builder*

Here's the equivalent code:

```
hueSlider = newSlider
```

And this time, when I say "equivalent," I mean "identical." Objects in an Interface Builder file are created in stages. During the first stage, all of the objects are created and have their attributes set. In the next stage, all of the connections are made. Those connections are made using the same methods you'd use to set an outlet property programmatically.

Making Action Connections

Action connections are a little more complicated. An action connection consists of two, and possibly three, pieces of information.

Objects that send a single action (UIGestureRecognizer, UIBarButtonItem, and so on) are connected by setting two properties: the target and the action. The target property is the object (usually a controller) that will receive the call. The action is the selector (play:, pause:, someoneMashedAButton:) that determines which function gets called. Some objects (such as UIGestureRecognizer) can be configured to send actions to multiple targets. You'd connect those objects, programmatically, using code like this:

```
gestureRecognizer.addTarget(viewController, action:"changeColor:")
```

> **Note**   In Shapely, you programmatically created gesture recognizer objects, but you set the target and action when you created the object. That works too.

To connect additional actions, call the addTarget(_:,action:) function again for each. Disconnect an action using removeTarget(_:,action:).

Single-event objects (such as `UIBarButtonItem`) have only a single target property. These objects can only send a single action to one target. You can programmatically make an action connection by setting the `target` and `action` properties individually, like this:

```
barButtonItem.target = viewController
barButtonItem.action = "refresh:"
```

More complex control objects have a multitude of events, any of which can be configured to send action messages when they occur. A `UISlider` object can send action messages when the user touches the control (`.TouchDown`), they drag outside its frame (`.TouchDragOutside`), they release their finger outside its frame (`.TouchUpOutside`), they release their finger inside its frame (`.TouchUpInside`), or the value of the slider changes (`.ValueChanged`). Each of these is identified by an event constant (see `UIControlEvents`). Any event can be configured to send action messages to multiple targets.

In the ColorModel project, you connected the `Value Changed` event of the slider to the `changeHue:` action of the view controller in Interface Builder. The following code creates that same connection:

```
newSlider.addTarget( viewController,
            action: "changeHue:",
    forControlEvents: .ValueChanged)
```

> **Tip** `UIControlEvents` is a set of bits. Combine (OR) multiple constants to attach an action message to multiple events at once.

Sending Action Messages

At this point, you shouldn't be surprised to learn that actions can also be sent programmatically. If you want to send an action, all you have to do is call the `sendAction(_:,to:,from:,forEvent:)` function of your application object (`UIApplication.sharedApplication()`).

Subclasses of `UIControl` send actions by calling their `sendAction(_:,to:,forEvent:)` function. This, incidentally, just turns around and calls `sendAction(_:.to:,from:,forEvent:)` on the application object, passing itself in the `from:` parameter. If you're creating a custom `UIControl` object and it's time to send your control's action, that's the function to call.

> **Tip** If you're sending an action in response to an iOS event (Chapter 4), it's polite to include the `UIEvent` object in the `forEvent:` parameter. Otherwise, pass `nil`.

You can programmatically cause any `UIControl` object to send the actions associated with one or more of its events by calling `sendActionsForControlEvents(_:)`.

In all cases—both when sending action programmatically and when configuring control objects—the target object can be nil. When it is, the action will be sent to the responder chain, starting with the first responder, instead of any specific object (see Chapter 4). To send an arbitrary message up the responder chain, use code that looks like the following:

```
UIApplication.sharedApplication().sendAction( "orderIceCream:",
                                 to: nil, /* responder chain */
                               from: self,
                           forEvent: nil)
```

You now have a good grasp of how Interface Builder works and how objects get created, configured, and connected. You've also learned most of the equivalent code for what Interface Builder does, so you could programmatically create, configure, and connect objects, as you did in the Shapely app.

Forget all of that. Well, don't forget it—you might need it someday—but set it aside for the moment. It's great to know how Interface Builder files work and the code you would write to do that same work. But the point of having Interface Builder is so you don't have to do that work! Instead of writing code to replace Interface Builder, it's time to use Interface Builder instead of writing code.

Taking Control of Interface Builder Files

Now that you understand what Interface Builder files are and how they work, you can easily add new ones to your app and load them when you want. This is the middle ground between the completely automatic use of Interface Builder files by view controllers and creating your view objects entirely with code. In this section, you're going to learn the following:

- Add an independent Interface Builder file to your project
- Programmatically load an Interface Builder file
- Designate multiple placeholder objects that Interface Builder objects can connect to

In Chapter 11 you wrote the Shapely app. Every time a button was tapped, you created a new shape (ShapeView) object, configured it, and attached a slew of gesture recognizers, using nothing but Swift. How much of that code could you accomplish using Interface Builder? Let's find out.

Declaring Placeholders

Starting with the finished Shapely project from Chapter 11, add an Interface Builder file to your project by dragging a View template from the template library into your navigator, as shown in Figure 15-10. Alternatively, you can select the New File command and choose the View template from the template picker. You'll find it under the iOS ➤ User Interface group. Name the file SquareShape. You now have a stand-alone Interface Builder (SquareShape.xib) file that creates a single UIView object.

Figure 15-10. Adding a new Interface Builder file

Your `.xib` file will need an owner object. Instead of using an existing object, let's create one just for this purpose. Add a new Swift class file (from the template library) and name it `ShapeFactory`. Edit the file to create a stub for the class using the following code:

```
import UIKit

class ShapeFactory: NSObject {
    @IBOutlet var view: ShapeView! = nil
    @IBOutlet var dblTapGesture: UITapGestureRecognizer! = nil
    @IBOutlet var trplTapGesture: UITapGestureRecognizer! = nil
}
```

The `ShapeFactory` class will be the file's owner. This is your first placeholder object. To use the owner object, select the new `SquareShape.xib` file in the navigator, select the `File's Owner` in the placeholder group, and use the identity inspector to change its class to `ShapeFactory`, as shown in Figure 15-11. I also edited the object's label so I know what it is.

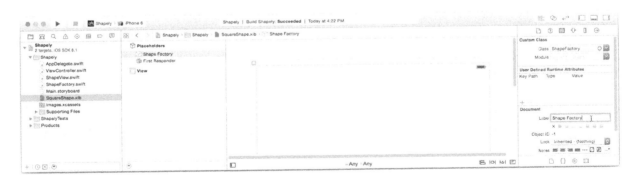

Figure 15-11. Setting the class of the File's Owner

You also need to connect objects—specifically, some gesture recognizers—to your view controller. To accomplish that, you'll need a second placeholder object. From the object library, locate the External Object object and drag it into the outline, as shown on the left in Figure 15-12. An *external object* is a placeholder for an object that you'll provide when you load the .xib file.

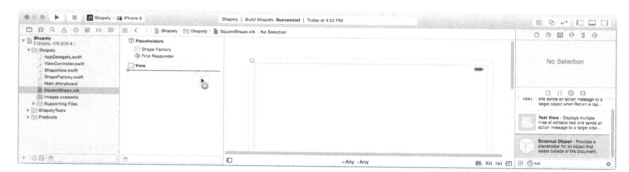

Figure 15-12. Adding an external object placeholder

Select it and change its class to ViewController in the identity inspector. With the external object still selected, use the attributes inspector to assign it an identifier of viewController. Additional placeholder objects are identified by name, so you must assign each a unique identifier string.

You now have an .xib file that creates a UIView object and expects to have access to two existing objects when it loads—a ShapeFactory object and a ViewController object.

The plan is as follows:

1. You're going to change the class of the UIView object so it creates a ShapeView object instead.

2. You'll configure the ShapeView object with the properties you want.

3. You'll connect the shape view to the ShapeFactory's view outlet so the factory object has easy access to the new view object.

4. You're going to design the four gesture recognizer objects in the .xib file, adding them to the ShapeView object and connecting their actions to the view controller placeholder.

5. You'll connect two of the gesture recognizers to the shape factory placeholder so the factory object can do some extra housekeeping that can't be done in the Interface Builder file.

The finished file will look, conceptually, like the object graph in Figure 15-13.

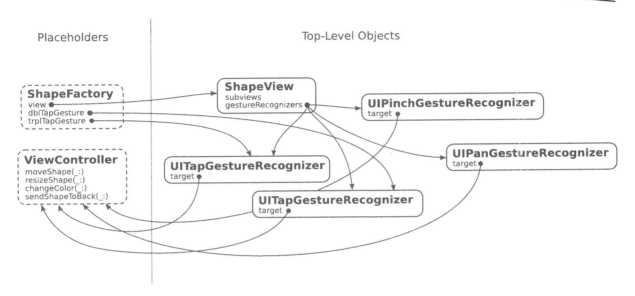

Placeholders   Top-Level Objects

Figure 15-13. *SquareShape.xib object graph*

Designing ShapeView

The first two steps in the plan are to turn the UIView object currently in the .xib file into a completely configured ShapeView object. Select the single view object in the SquareShape.xib file and, using the identity inspector, change its class to ShapeView. Step 1 accomplished.

Switch to the attributes inspector. Xcode doesn't really know what you're going to use the objects in an Interface Builder file for. By default, it assumes that a top-level view object will become the root view of an interface, so it sizes the view as if it were an iPhone or iPad screen and adds a simulated status bar. For ShapeView, that isn't the case, so turn all of these assumptions off. Change the simulated size to Freeform and status bar to None, as shown in Figure 15-14. Now use the attribute and size inspectors to set the following properties:

- Set the background to Default (none).
- Uncheck the Opaque property.
- Make sure Clears Graphics Context is checked.
- Set its size to 100 by 100 points.

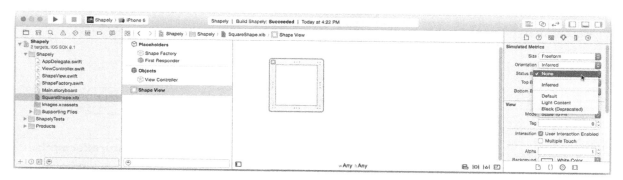

Figure 15-14. *Designing the ShapeView object*

You've now replicated the work of creating a new ShapeView object using an .xib file—all, that is, except for the shape property, which you'll address in a moment.

Select the ShapeView.swift file and make the shape property a variable instead of a constant, with the following code (new code in bold):

var shape: ShapeSelector = **.Square**

This is done because you won't be setting its shape when the object is created (in the .xib file), so it has to be a mutable property. While still in the ShapeView.swift file, make the following changes:

1. Discard the definitions for initialSize and alternateHeight. These were used to define the view's initial size, which is now declared in the .xib file.

2. Delete the entire init(shape:,origin:) initializer function. The view will now be created and configured entirely in the .xib file.

3. You can also delete the init(coder:) initializer function too. Since your view class no longer has any custom initializers, you don't need to declare this one either.

See how much code you've already eliminated? The entire purpose of the init(shape:,origin:) initializer function was to create and configure a new ShapeView object. Most of that work is now being done in your new Interface Builder file.

Connecting the Gesture Recognizers

Back in the SquareShape.xib file, it's time to add the gesture recognizers. From the object library, drag out a Pan Gesture Recognizer and drop it into the Shape View object, as shown in Figure 15-15. Select the recognizer object and use the attributes inspector to set its minimum and maximum touches to 1.

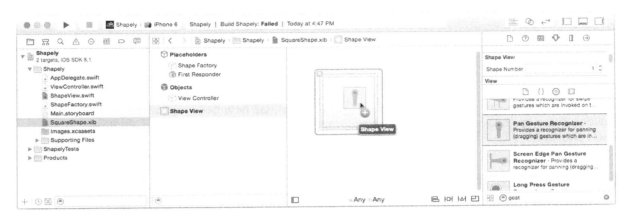

Figure 15-15. Adding the pan gesture recognizer

Switch to the connections inspector and connect its Sent Action to the moveShape: action in the view controller placeholder, as shown in Figure 15-16.

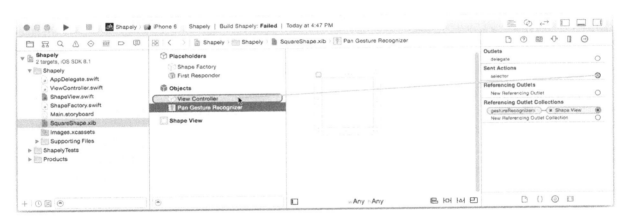

Figure 15-16. Connecting the pan gesture recognizer action

You've now created a pan gesture recognizer that recognizes only single-finger drag gestures. It's attached to the shape view object, and it sends a moveShape: action to the view controller, when triggered. The resulting gesture recognizer object is identical to the one you created, configured, and connected in the addShape(_:) function of ViewController.

Add the other three gesture recognizers, as follows:

1. Drop a Pinch Gesture Recognizer into the shape view.

    a. Connect its sent action to the view controller's resizeShape: action.

2. Drop a Tap Gesture Recognizer into the shape view.

    a. Set its Taps to 2.

    b. Set its Touches to 1.

    c. Connect its sent action to the changeColor: action.

3. Drop a Tap Gesture Recognizer into the shape view.

   a. Set its Taps to 3.

   b. Set its Touches to 1.

   c. Connect its sent action to the `sendShapeToBack:` action.

Much of the code you wrote in the `addShape(_:)` function has now been replicated using Interface Builder. There are two steps that can't be accomplished in Interface Builder; you'll address those in code shortly.

Building Your Shape Factory

Your shape factory object defines outlets that need to be connected to the shape view and selected gesture recognizers. Select the `SquareShape.xib` file, select the File's Owner (or Shape Factory, if you renamed it), and use the connections inspector to connect the `shapeView`, `dblTapGesture`, and `trplTapGesture` outlets to their respective objects, as shown in Figure 15-17. Save the file. (Seriously, save the file by choosing File ➤ Save; it's important.)

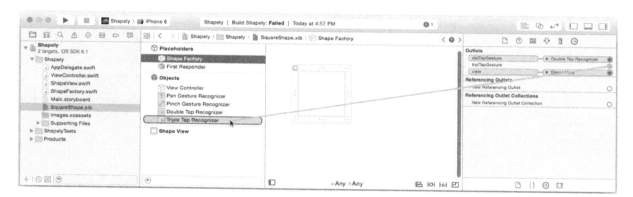

Figure 15-17. Connecting the factory outlets

Tip   Make sure you connect the right gesture recognizer outlet to the correct object because both objects appear as Tap Gesture Recognizer in the outline. If you have Interface Builder objects that might be easily confused, use the identity inspector to change the object's label to something more descriptive. In Figure 15-17, I changed their labels to Double Tap... and Triple Tap... so I can tell which one is which. Object labels are cosmetic and don't alter the functionality of your Interface Builder design in any way.

The one aspect—sorry for the bad pun—that has not been addressed is the difference between the square, rectangle, circle, and oval shapes. If you remember, `init(shape:,origin:)` would produce a 100-by-50-point view for rectangle and oval shapes and a 100-by-100-point view for everything else. In this version, you're going to replicate that logic using two Interface Builder files. `ShapeFactory` will choose which one to load.

Start by creating the second Interface Builder file. Select the SquareShape.xib file and choose the Edit ➤ Duplicate command, as shown in Figure 15-18.

Figure 15-18. Creating the RectangleShape.xib file

Name the file RectangleShape. Select the new file, select the shape view object, and use the size inspector to change the height of the shape view to 50. Now you have two Interface Builder files, one that produces a 100-by-100 view and a second one that creates a 100-by-50 view.

Now switch to the ShapeFactory.swift file. Add a class method that will choose which Interface Builder file (SquareShape or RectangleShape) to load for given shape, as follows:

```
class func nibNameForShape(shape: ShapeSelector) -> String {
    switch shape {
        case .Rectangle, .Oval:
            return "RectangleShape"
        default:
            return "SquareShape"
    }
}
```

Loading an Interface Builder File

You're now ready to create your shape view and gesture recognizer objects by loading an Interface Builder file. (It's about time!) Add the -loadShape:forViewController: method now.

```
func load(# shape: ShapeSelector, inViewController viewController: UIViewController) ↩
                                                        -> ShapeView {
    let placeholders = [ "viewController": viewController ]
    let options = [ UINibExternalObjects: placeholders ]
    NSBundle.mainBundle().loadNibNamed( ShapeFactory.nibNameForShape(shape),
                            owner: self,
                          options: options)
    assert(view != nil, "shape view not connected in xib file")
    view.shape = shape
    dblTapGesture.requireGestureRecognizerToFail(trplTapGesture)

    return view!
}
```

The first two statements prepare the view controller to be a placeholder object when the Interface Builder file is loaded. You may pass as many placeholder objects as you like; just make sure their classes and identifiers agree with the external objects you defined in the Interface Builder file.

The third statement is where the magic happens. The loadNibNamed(_:,owner:,options:) function searches your app's bundle for an Interface Builder file with that name. The name (SquareShape or RectangleShape) is determined by the nibNameForShape(_:) function you added earlier. The owner parameter becomes the file's owner placeholder object. The options parameter is a dictionary of special options. In this case, the only special option is additional placeholder objects (UINibExternalObjects).

When loadNibNamed(_:,owner:,options:) is called, the owner and any additional placeholder objects take the place of the File's Owner and the corresponding external objects defined in the file. The objects in the file are created, the properties of the objects are set according to the attributes you edited, and finally all of the outlet and action connections are established.

> **Tip**   If you have code that needs to execute when your objects are created by an Interface Builder file, override your object's awakeFromNib() function. When an Interface Builder file or scene is loaded, every object it creates receives an awakeFromNib() call. This occurs after all properties and connections have been set.

The function returns an array containing all of the top-level objects created in the file. You can access the objects created by the file either through this array or via outlets that you connected to the placeholders. In this app, you've used the latter technique.

> **Note**   The main reason you created the ShapeFactory class was to provide an owner object with outlets that conveniently provide references to the shape view and recognizer objects you're interested in. Another solution would be to make the view controller the file's owner and dig through the returned array of top-level objects to find the shape view and recognizer objects.

The last two statements take care of the two steps that can't be accomplished in Interface Builder. The shape property of the view is set, and the double-tap/triple-tap dependency is established.

Replacing Code

Switch to the ViewController.swift file. Find the addShape(_:) function and replace the code that programmatically created a new ShapeView object with the following (modified code in bold):

```
@IBAction func addShape(sender: AnyObject!) {
    if let button = sender as? UIButton {
        if let shapeSelector = ShapeSelector(rawValue: button.tag) {
            let shapeView = ShapeFactory().load(shape: shapeSelector,
                                    inViewController: self)
```

> **Note** ShapeFactory is an example of a helper class. A *helper* is an object whose sole purpose is to assist other objects in accomplishing some task. This is often logic that doesn't fit well with the purpose or responsibilities of those other classes.

Now, for the fun part. Find the rest of the code in addShape(_:) that creates, configures, and connects the four gesture recognizers and delete all of it. You don't need any of that now. All four of the gesture recognizers were created, configured, and connected to both the view and the view controller by the Interface Builder file.

Run the finished app and observe the results. You shouldn't be able to tell any difference between this version of Shapely and the one from Chapter 11, which is the point. This exercise bordered on the trivial, but it demonstrated all of the key ways in which you can use Interface Builder files directly, along with their advantages and disadvantages.

- Objects are easy to create, configure, and connect in Interface Builder. This reduces the amount of code you have to write, saving time, and potentially reducing bugs. (This is an advantage).

- There are some properties and object relationships—such as the double-tap/triple-tap dependency—that cannot be set in Interface Builder and must be performed programmatically. (This is a disadvantage).

- You can easily choose between multiple Interface Builder files. Instead of writing huge if/else or switch statements, you can create a completely different set of objects simply by selecting a different Interface Builder file. (This is an advantage).

- You're limited to the configuration and initialization methods supported by Interface Builder. In Shapely, you had to prove a settable shape property in order to "fix" the object after it was created, since you could no longer use the init(shape:,origin:) function. (This is an advantage).

- Interface Builder makes it easy to create complex sets of objects, especially ones like gesture recognizers and layout constraints. It often requires pages of dense, difficult-to-read code to reproduce the layout constraints required for many interfaces. (This is a huge advantage).

- It can sometimes take considerable effort to obtain references to the objects created in an Interface Builder file. You might have to create special placeholder objects or tediously dig through the top-level objects returned by loadNibName d(_:,owner:,options:). In this section you created a class (ShapeFactory) for the sole purpose of providing outlets for the references to the shape view and gesture recognizers. (This is sometimes a disadvantage).

Interface Builder files aren't the best solution for every interface; sometimes a few lines of well-written code are all you need. But in many cases, Interface Builder can save you from writing, maintaining, and debugging (literally) thousands of lines of code. It's an amazingly flexible and efficient tool that can free you from hours of work and improve the quality of your apps. You just needed to know how it works and how to put it work for you.

Summary

Interface Builder is one of the cornerstones of Xcode, and it's what makes iOS app development so smooth. Loading Interface Builder files directly is where the real flexibility of Interface Builder becomes evident. You now know how to define practically any interface, a fragment of an interface, or just some arbitrary objects in an Interface Builder file and load them when, and where, you want. You know how to create any kind of object you like, set its custom properties, and connect it with existing objects in your app. That's an incredibly useful tool to have at your fingertips.

Chapter 16

Apps with Attitude

In a feat of miniaturization that would make Wayne Szalinski[1] proud, most iOS devices are equipped with an array of sensors that detect acceleration, rotation, and magnetic orientation—which is a lot of "ations." The combined output of these sensors, along with a little math, will tell your app with surprising accuracy the attitude the device is being held in, whether it's being moved or rotated (and how fast), the direction of gravity, and the direction of magnetic north. You can incorporate this into your app to give it an uncanny sense of immediacy. You can present information based on the direction the user is holding their device, control games through physical gestures, tell them whether the picture they're about to take is level, and so much more.

In Chapter 4, you used the high-level "device shake" and "orientation change" events to trigger animations in the EightBall app. In this chapter, you'll plug directly into the low-level accelerometer information and react to instantaneous changes in the device's position. In this chapter, you will learn to do the following:

- Collect accelerometer and other device motion data
- Use timers

You'll also get some more practice using affine transformations in custom view objects and use some of the fancy new animation features added in iOS 7. Let's get started.

> **Note**   You will need a provisioned iOS device to test the code in this chapter. The iOS simulator does not emulate accelerometer data.

---

[1]Wayne Szalinski was the hapless inventor in the movie *Honey, I Shrunk the Kids*.

Leveler

The app you're going to create is a simple, digital level called Leveler.[2] It's a one-screen app that displays a dial indicating the inclination (angle from an imaginary vertical plumb line) of the device, as shown in Figure 16-1.

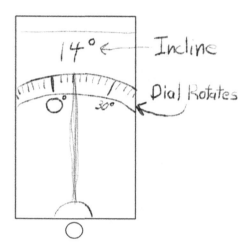

Figure 16-1. Leveler design

Creating Leveler

Create a new Xcode project, as follows:

1. Use the single-view application template.

2. Set the product name to Leveler.

3. Set the language to Swift.

4. Set devices to Universal.

5. After creating the project, edit the supported interface orientations to support all device orientations.

Leveler is going to need some image and source code resources. You'll find the image files in the Learn iOS Development Projects ➤ Ch 16 ➤ Leveler (Resources) folder. Add the hand.png and hand@2x.png files to the Images.xcassets image catalog. In the finished Leveler-1 project folder, locate the DialView.swift file. Add it to your project too, alongside your other source files. Remember to check the Copy items into destination group's folder option in the import dialog. You'll also find a set of app icons in the Leveler (Icons) folder that you can drop into the AppIcon group of the image catalog.

You'll first lay out and connect the views that will display the inclination before getting to the code that gathers the accelerometer data.

---

[2]Look up the word *leveler* for an interesting factoid on English history.

Pondering DialView

The source file you just added contains the code for a custom `UIView` object that draws a circular "dial." After reading Chapter 11, you shouldn't have any problem figuring out how it works. The most interesting aspect is the use of affine transforms in the graphics context. In Chapter 11, you applied affine transforms to a view object, so it appeared either offset or scaled from its actual frame. In `DialView`, an affine transform is applied to the graphics context before drawing into it. Anything drawn afterward is translated using that transform.

In `DialView`, this technique is used to draw the tick marks and angle labels around the inside of the "dial." If you're interested, find the `drawRect(_:)` function in `DialView.swift`. The significant bits of code are in bold. Distracting code has been replaced with ellipses.

```swift
let circleDegrees = 360
let minorTickDegrees = 3
...

override func drawRect(rect: CGRect) {
    let context = UIGraphicsGetCurrentContext()
    let bounds = self.bounds
    let radius = bounds.height/2.0
    ...
    CGContextTranslateCTM(context,radius,radius)
    let tickAngle = CGFloat(minorTickDegrees)*CGFloat(M_PI/180.0)
    let rotation = CGAffineTransformMakeRotation(tickAngle)
    for var angle = 0; angle < circleDegrees; angle += minorTickDegrees {
        ... draw one vertical tick and label ...
        CGContextConcatCTM(context,rotation);
    }
}
```

The `drawRect(_:)` function first applies a translate transform to the context. This offsets the drawing coordinates, effectively changing the origin of the view's local coordinate system to the center of the view. (The view is always square, as you'll see later.) After applying this transform, if you drew a shape at (0,0), it will now draw at the center of the view, rather than the upper-left corner.

The loop draws one vertical tick mark and an optional text label below it. At the end of the loop, the drawing coordinates of the context are rotated 3°. The second time through the loop, the tick mark and label will be rotated 3°. The third time through the loop all drawing will be rotated 6°, and so on, until the entire dial has been drawn. Context transforms accumulate.

The key concept to grasp is that transformations applied to the Core Graphics context affect the coordinate system of what's being drawn into the view, as shown in Figure 16-2. Context transforms don't change its frame, bounds, or where it appears in its superview.

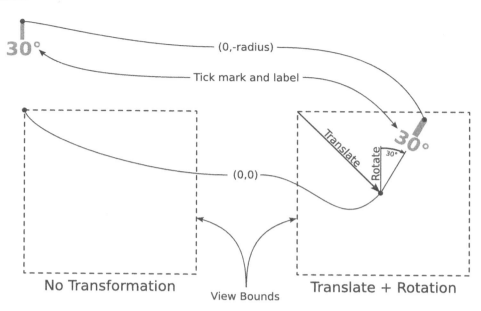

Figure 16-2. *Graphics context transformation*

To change how the view appears in its superview, you set the transform property of the view, as you did in the Shapely app. And that's exactly what the view controller will do (later) to rotate the dial on the screen. This underscores the difference between using affine transforms while drawing versus using a transform to alter how the finished view appears.

Also note that the view draws itself only once. All of this complicated code in drawRect(_:) executes only when the view is first drawn or resized. Once the view is drawn, the cached image of the dial appears in the display and gets rotated by the view's transform property. This second use of a transform simply transcribes the pixels in the cached image; it doesn't cause the view to redraw itself at the new angle. In this respect, the drawing is efficient. This is important because later you're going to animate it.

Creating the Views

You're going to add a label object to the storyboard file and then write code in ViewController to programmatically create the DialView and the image view that displays the "needle" of the dial. Start with the Main.storyboard file.

Drag a label object into the interface. Using the attributes inspector, change the following:

> *Text*: 360° (press Option+Shift+8 to type the degree symbol)
>
> *Color*: White Color
>
> *Font*: System 90.0
>
> *Alignment*: middle

Select the label object and choose Editor ➤ Size to Fit Content. Select the root view object and change its background color to Black Color. At this point, your interface should look like the one in Figure 16-3.

Figure 16-3. *Adding an angle label to the interface*

Select the label and click the pin constraints control. Add a top constraint and set its value to 0, as shown on the left in Figure 16-4. Click the Align Constraints control. Add a Horizontal Center in Container View constraint, as shown on the right in Figure 16-4, also making sure its value is 0.

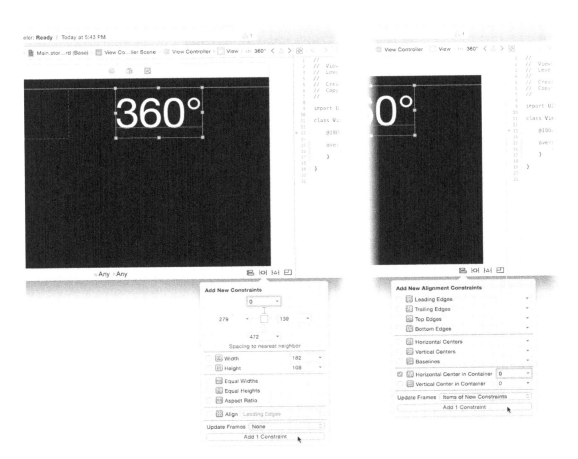

Figure 16-4. *Adding label constraints*

> **Note**   Notice that no constraints for the height, width, left, right, or bottom were set for the label view, yet Interface Builder is perfectly happy with the layout. That's because views like `UILabel` have an *intrinsic size*. For a label, it's the size of the text in the label. In the absence of constraints that would determine the view's size (height and width), iOS uses its intrinsic size, which is enough information to determine its frame.

Switch to the assistant editor. The editing pane will split, and the `ViewController.swift` file will appear in the pane on the right. Add this outlet property to the `ViewController` class:

```
@IBOutlet var angleLabel: UILabel!
```

Connect the outlet to the label view in the interface, as shown in Figure 16-5.

Figure 16-5. Connecting angle label outlet

You'll create and position the other two views programmatically. Switch back to the standard editor and select the `ViewController.swift` file. You'll need the name of the image resource file and some instance variables to keep a reference to the dial and image view objects. Start by adding those to the beginning of the `ViewController` class (new code in bold):

```
class ViewController: UIViewController {
    let handImageName = "hand"
    @IBOutlet var angleLabel: UILabel!
    var dialView: DialView!
    var needleView: UIImageView!
```

Create the two views when the view controller loads its view. Since this is the app's only view controller, this will happen only once. Find the `viewDidLoad()` function and add the following bold code:

```
override func viewDidLoad() {
    super.viewDidLoad()
    dialView = DialView(frame: CGRect(x: 0, y: 0, width: 100, height: 100))
    view.addSubview(dialView)
    needleView = UIImageView(image: UIImage(named: handImageName))
    needleView.contentMode = .ScaleAspectFit
    view.insertSubview(needleView, aboveSubview: dialView)
    adaptInterface()
}
```

When the view is loaded, the additional code creates new `DialView` and `UIImageView` objects, adding both to the view. Notice that `needleView` is deliberately placed in front of `dialView`.

No attempt is made to size or position these views. That happens when the view is displayed or rotated. Catch those events by adding these two functions:

```
override func viewWillAppear(animated: Bool) {
    super.viewWillAppear(animated)
    positionDialViews()
}

override func viewWillTransitionToSize(size: CGSize, ↵
        withTransitionCoordinator coordinator: ↵
        UIViewControllerTransitionCoordinator) {
    coordinator.animateAlongsideTransition( {
        (context) in self.positionDialViews()
        },
        completion: nil )
}
```

Just before the view appears for the first time, you call `positionDialViews()` to position the `dialView` and `needleView` objects. The second function is called whenever the view controller changes size. For a single-view app, like Leveler, that's going to happen only when the device is rotated. In this function, you call `positionDialViews()` again to animate the transition to the new size. This works because the closure block you pass as the first argument is executed as a block-based animation. And as you know from Chapter 11, all you have to do in an animation block is set the view properties you want animated—which is exactly what `positionDialViews()` does.

You'll also want to add this function for the iPhone version:

```
override func supportedInterfaceOrientations() -> Int {
    return Int(UIInterfaceOrientationMask.All.rawValue)
}
```

While you edited the supported orientations for the app, remember (from Chapter 14) that each view controller dictates which orientations it supports. By default, the iPhone's `UIViewController` does not support upside-down orientation. This code overrides that to allow all orientations.

Finally, you'll need the code for `adaptInterface()` (in Listing 16-1) and `positionDialViews()` (in Listing 16-2).

Listing 16-1. adaptInterface()

```
func adaptInterface() {
    if let label = angleLabel {
        var fontSize: CGFloat = 90.0
        if traitCollection.horizontalSizeClass == .Compact {
            fontSize = 60.0
        }
        label.font = UIFont.systemFontOfSize(fontSize)
    }
}
```

Your adaptInterface() function considers the horizontalSizeClass and adjusts the font size of the angle label to 60.0 points for compact devices (iPhone, iPod) and leaves it at 90.0 points for larger interfaces (iPad). The horizontalSizeClass doesn't change during rotation, so adaptInterface() needs to be called once (from viewDidLoad()). If adaptInterface() made other adjustments or Apple releases new devices with a horizontalSizeClass that could change while your app is running, you would need to call it from viewWillTransitionToTraitCollection(...).

Listing 16-2. positionDialViews()

```
func positionDialViews() {
    let viewBounds = view.bounds
    let labelFrame = angleLabel.frame
    let topEdge = ceil(labelFrame.maxY+labelFrame.height/3.0)
    let dialRadius = viewBounds.maxY-topEdge
    let dialHeight = dialRadius*2.0
    dialView.transform = CGAffineTransformIdentity
    dialView.frame = CGRect(x: 0.0,
                            y: 0.0,
                         width: dialHeight,
                        height: dialHeight)
    dialView.center = CGPoint(x: viewBounds.midX,
                              y: viewBounds.maxY)
    dialView.setNeedsDisplay()

    let needleSize = needleView.image.size
    let needleScale = dialRadius/needleSize.height
    var needleFrame = CGRect(x: 0.0,
        y: 0.0,
        width: needleSize.width*needleScale,
        height: needleSize.height*needleScale)
    needleFrame.origin.x = viewBounds.midX-needleFrame.width/2.0
    needleFrame.origin.y = viewBounds.maxY-needleFrame.height
    needleView.frame = CGRectIntegral(needleFrame)
}
```

positionDialViews() looks like a lot of code, but all it's doing is sizing the dialView so it is square, positioning its center at the bottom center of the view, and sizing it so its top edge is just under the bottom edge of the label view. The needleView is then positioned so it's centered and anchored to the bottom edge and scaled so its height equals the visible height of the dial. This is a lot harder to describe than it is to see, so just run the app and see what I mean in Figure 16-6.

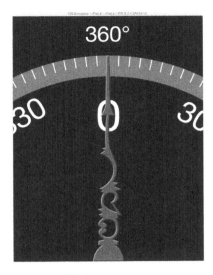

Figure 16-6. *Dial and needle view positioning*

That pretty much completes all of the view design and layout. Now you need to get the accelerometer information and make your app do something.

Getting Motion Data

All iOS devices (as of this writing) have accelerometer hardware. The accelerometer senses the force of acceleration along three axes: x, y, and z. If you face the screen of your iPhone or iPad in portrait orientation, the x-axis is horizontal, the y-axis is vertical, and the z-axis is the line that goes from you, through the middle of the device, perpendicular to the screen's surface, as shown in Figure 16-7.

Figure 16-7. Orientation of accelerometer axes

You can use accelerometer information to determine when the device changes speed and in what direction. Assuming it's not accelerating (much), you can also use this information to infer the direction of gravity since gravity exerts a constant force on a stationary body. This is the information iOS uses to determine when you've flipped your iPad on its side or when you're shaking your iPhone.

In addition to the accelerometer, recent iOS devices also include a gyroscope and a magnetometer. The former detects changes in rotation around the three axes (pitch, roll, yaw), and the magnetometer detects the orientation of a magnetic field. Barring magnetic interference, this will tell you the device's attitude relative to magnetic north. (This is a fancy way of saying it has a compass.)

Your app gets to all of this information through a single gatekeeper class: CMMotionManager. The CMMotionManager class collects, interprets, and delivers movement and attitude information to your app. You tell it what kind(s) of information you want (accelerometer, gyroscope, compass), how often you want to receive updates, and how those updates are delivered to your app. Your Leveler app will use only accelerometer information, but the general pattern is the same for all types of motion data:

1.   Create an instance of CMMotionManager.

2.   Set the frequency of updates.

3.   Choose what information you want and how your app will get it (pull or push).

4.   When you're ready, start the delivery of information.

5.   Process motion data as it occurs.

6.   When you're done, stop the delivery of information.

There's no better place to start than step 1.

Creating CMMotionManager

CoreMotion is not part of the standard UIKit framework. At the beginning of your `ViewController.swift` file, pull in the CoreMotion framework definitions (new code in bold):

```
import UIKit
import CoreMotion
```

You'll need a variable to store your `CMMotionManager` object and a constant to specify how fast you want motion data updates. Add both to your `ViewController` class:

```
lazy var motionManager = CMMotionManager()
let accelerometerPollingInterval: NSTimeInterval = 1.0/15.0
```

The `motionManager` variable is automatically initialized with a `CMMotionManager` object. Notice that the property is `lazy`. Lazy properties in Swift are automatically initialized, but instead of being initialized when your `ViewController` object is created, it waits until someone requests the value for the first time. This defers the construction of the `CMMotionManager` object until it's actually needed.

You've completed the first step in using motion data—a new `CMMotionManager` object will be created and stored in the `motionManager` property.

> **Caution**   Do not create multiple instances of `CMMotionManager`. If your app has two or more controllers that need motion data, they must share a single instance of `CMMotionManager`. I suggest creating a property in your application delegate that returns a singleton `CMMotionManager` object, which can then be shared with any other objects that needs it.

Now perform the second step in using motion data. Locate the `viewWillAppear()` function and add this code to the end of the function:

```
motionManager.accelerometerUpdateInterval = accelerometerPollingInterval
```

This statement tells the manager how long to wait between measurements. This property is expressed in seconds. For most apps, 10 to 30 times a second is adequate, but extreme apps might need updates as often as 100 times a second. For this app, you'll start with 15 updates per second by setting the `accelerometerUpdateInterval` property to 1/15th of a second.

Starting and Stopping Updates

To perform the third and fourth steps in getting motion data, return to the `viewWillAppear()` function and add this statement to the end:

```
motionManager.startAccelerometerUpdates()
```

After creating and configuring the motion manager, you request that it begin collecting accelerometer data. The accelerometer information reported by `CMMotionManager` won't be accurate—or even change—until you begin its update process. Once started, the motion manager code works tirelessly in the background to monitor any changes in acceleration and report those to your app.

Tip   To conserve battery life, your app should request updates from the motion manager *only* while your app needs them. For this app, motion events are used for the lifetime of the app, so there's no code to stop them. If you added a second view controller, however, that didn't use the accelerometer, you'd want to add code to `viewWillDisappear()` to call `stopAccelerometerUpdates()`.

Push Me, Pull You

It might not look you like you've performed the third step in getting motion data, but you did. It was implied when you called the `startAccelerometerUpdates()` function. This function starts gathering motion data, but it's up to your app to periodically ask what those values are. This is called the *pull* approach; the `CMMotionManager` object keeps the motion data current, and your app pulls the data from it as needed.

The alternative is the *push* approach. To use this approach, call the `startAccelerometerUpdates ToQueue(_:,withHandler:)` function instead. You pass it an operation queue and a closure that gets executed the moment motion data is updated. This is much more complicated to implement because the closure code is executed on a separate thread, so all of your motion data handling code must be thread-safe. You really need this approach only if your app must absolutely, positively process motion data the *instant* it becomes available. There are few apps that fall into this category.

Timing Is Everything

Now you're probably wondering how your app "periodically" pulls the motion data it's interested in. The motion manager doesn't post any notifications or send your object any delegate messages. What you need is an object that will remind your app to do something at regular intervals. It's called a *timer*, and iOS provides just that. At the end of the `viewWillAppear()` function, add this statement:

```
NSTimer.scheduledTimerWithTimeInterval( accelerometerPollingInterval,
                            target: self,
                          selector: "updateAccelerometerTime:",
                          userInfo: nil,
                           repeats: true)
```

An `NSTimer` object provides a timer for your app. It is one of the sources of events that I mentioned in Chapter 4 but never got around to talking about.

> **Note**   Making a functioning timer is a two-step process: you must create the timer object and then add it to the run loop. The scheduledTimerWithTimeInterval(_:,target:,selector:,userI nfo:,repeats:) function does both for you. If you create a timer object directly, you have to call the addTimer(_:,forMode:) function of your thread's run loop object before the timer will do anything.

Timers come in two flavors: single-shot or repeating. A timer has a timeInterval property and a function it will call on an object. After the amount of time in the timeInterval property has passed, the timer *fires*. At the next opportunity, the event loop will call the function of the target object. If it's a one-shot timer, that's it; the timer becomes invalid and stops. If it's a repeating timer, it continues running, waiting until another timeInterval amount of time has passed before firing again. A repeating timer continues to fire until you call its invalidate() function.

> **Caution**   Don't use timers to poll for events—such as waiting for a web page to load—that you could have determined using event messages, delegate functions, notifications, or code blocks. Timers should be used only for time-related events and periodic updates. If you want to know why, reread the beginning of Chapter 4.

The code you added to viewWillAppear() creates and schedules a timer that calls your view controller object's updateAccelerometerTime(_:) function approximately 15 times a second. This is the same rate that the motion manager is updating its accelerometer information. There's no point in checking for updates any faster or slower than the CMMotionManager object is gathering them.

Everything is in place, except the updateAccelerometerTime(_:) and rotateDialView(_:) functions. While still in ViewController.swift, add the first function.

```
func updateAccelerometerTime(timer: NSTimer) {
    if let data = motionManager.accelerometerData {
        let acceleration = data.acceleration
        let rotation = atan2(-acceleration.x,-acceleration.y)
        rotateDialView(rotation)
    }
}
```

The first statement retrieves the accelerometerData property of the motion manager. Since you only started gathering accelerometer information, this is the only motion data property that's valid. This property is a CMAccelerometerData object, and that object has only one property: acceleration. The acceleration property contains three numbers: x, y, and z. Each value is the instantaneous force being exerted along that axis, measured in Gs.[3] Assuming the device isn't being moved around, the measurements can be combined to determine the *gravitational vector*; in other words, you can figure out which way is down.

---

[3]G is the force of gravity, equal to an acceleration of approximately 9.81 meters per second every second.

Your app doesn't need all three. You only need to determine which direction is up in the x-y plane, because that's where the dial lives. Ignoring the force along the z-axis, the arctangent function calculates the angle of the gravitational vector in the x-y plane. The result is used to rotate the `dialView` by that same angle. Simple, isn't it?

> **Note** You might have questioned why the arctangent function was given the negative values of x and y. It's because the dial points up, not down. Flipping the direction of the force values calculates the angle *away* from gravity.

Complete the app by writing the `rotateDialView(_:)` function:

```
func rotateDialView(rotation: Double) {
    dialView.transform = CGAffineTransformMakeRotation(CGFloat(rotation))

    var degrees = Int(round(-rotation*180.0/M_PI))
    if degrees < 0 {
        degrees += 360
    }
    angleLabel.text = "\(degrees)°"
}
```

The first statement in the function turns the `rotation` parameter into an affine transform that rotates `dialView`. The rest of the code converts the `rotation` value from radians into degrees, makes sure it's not negative, and uses that to update the label view.

It's time to plug in your provisioned iOS device, run your app, and play with the results, as shown in Figure 16-8. Notice how the app switches orientation as you rotate it. If you lock the device's orientation, it won't do that, but the dial still works.

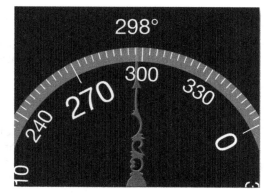

Figure 16-8. Working Leveler app

Herky-Jerky

Your app works, and it was pretty easy to write, but boy is it hard to look at. If it works anything like the way is does on my devices, the dial jitters constantly. Unless the device is perfectly still, it's almost impossible to read.

It would be really nice if the dial moved more smoothly—a lot more smoothly. That sounds like a job for animation. What you want is an animation that makes the dial appear to have mass, gently drifting toward the instantaneous inclination reported by the hardware.

That sounds a lot like the Sprite Kit physics bodies you used in Chapter 14. Unfortunately, Sprite Kit's physics simulation works only with SKNode objects. To use Sprite Kit, you'd have to redesign your entire view around SKView and then re-create the needle, dial, and label using SKNodes. And SKNodes don't draw themselves, so you'll have to rewrite your drawRect(_:) function to draw into an off-screen image and provide that to the SKSpriteNode. Thinking about it, you might as well create a new project and start over.

Another approach would be to smooth out the updates yourself by clamping the rate at which the view is rotated. To make it look really nice, you might even go so far as to add some calculations that gives the dial simulated mass, acceleration, drag, and so on. But as I mentioned in Chapter 11, the do-it-yourself approach to animation is fraught with complications, is usually a lot of work, and often results in substandard performance.

Don't panic! iOS has a solution that will let you build off the work you've already done. It's called View Dynamics, and it's a physics engine for UIView objects. It's simpler than the physics simulator in Sprite Kit, but intentionally so. Like Core Animation, its aim is to make it easy to add simple physical behaviors to UIView objects—not for creating asteroid games.

Like Spite Kit, you use View Dynamics by describing the "forces" acting on a view and let the dynamic animator create an animation that simulates the view's reaction to those forces. Unlike Sprite Kit, these properties are not part of UIView. Instead, you create a set of *behavior* objects that you attach to the views you want animated. Let's get started.

Using Dynamic Animation

Dynamic animation involves three players.

- The dynamic animator object
- One or more behavior objects
- One or more view objects

The *dynamic animator* is the object that performs the animation. It contains a complex physic engine that's remarkably intelligent. You'll need to create a single instance of the dynamic animator.

Animation occurs when you create behavior objects and add those to the dynamic animator. A *behavior* describes a single impetus or attribute of a view. iOS includes predefined behaviors for gravity, acceleration, friction, collisions, connections, and more, and you're free to invent your own. A behavior is associated with one or more view (UIView) objects, imparting that particular behavior to all of its views. The dynamic animator does the work of combining multiple behaviors for a single view—acceleration plus gravity plus friction, for example—to decide how that view will react.

So, the basic formula for dynamic animation is as follows:

1. Create an instance of UIDynamicAnimator.

2. Create one or more UIDynamicBehavior objects, attached to UIView objects.

3. Add the UIDynamicBehavior objects to the UIDynamicAnimator.

4. Sit back and enjoy the show.

You're now ready to add View Dynamics to Leveler.

Creating the Dynamic Animator

You'll need to create a dynamic animator object, and for that you'll need an instance variable to save it in, so add an instance variable for your animator to your ViewController class. While you're here, add some constants and a variable to contain an attachment behavior, all of which will be explained shortly.

```
var animator: UIDynamicAnimator!
let springAnchorDistance: CGFloat = 4.0
let springDamping: CGFloat = 0.7
let springFrequency: CGFloat = 0.5
var springBehavior: UIAttachmentBehavior?
```

Start a new function to create the behaviors. Call it attachDialBehaviors().

```
func attachDialBehaviors() {
    if animator != nil {
        animator.removeAllBehaviors()
    } else {
        animator = UIDynamicAnimator(referenceView: view)
    }
}
```

> **Note**   You can find the finished version of Leveler using View Dynamics in the Learn iOS Development Projects ➤ Ch 16 ➤ Leveler-2 folder.

The first thing you do is to create a new UIDynamicAnimator object, if you haven't yet. When you create a dynamic animator, you must specify a view that will be used to establish the coordinate system the dynamic animator will use. The dynamic animator uses its own coordinate system, called the *reference coordinate system*, so that view objects in different view hierarchies (each with their own coordinate system) can interact with one another in a unified coordinate space. Using the reference coordinate system, you could, for example, have a view in your content view controller collide with a button in the toolbar, even though they reside in different superviews.

> **Note**   You cannot create the dynamic animator in the variable's initialization statement (`var animator = UIDynamicAnimator(referenceView: view)`) because the initializer for `UIDynamicAnimator` needs the view controller's `view` property. During object initialization, the inherited `view` property hasn't been initialized yet and can't be used—a classic chicken-and-egg problem. The solution is to create the dynamic animator outside your object's initializer. The order and rules of object initialization are explained in Chapter 20.

For your app, make the reference coordinate system that of your view controller's root view. This makes all dynamic animator coordinates the same as your local view coordinates. Won't that be convenient? (Yes, it will.)

The first half of the `if` statement discards all added behaviors, in the case where the dynamic animator has already been created. This should never happen, but it ensures `attachDialBehaviors()` starts with a clean slate.

Defining Behaviors

So, what behaviors do you think the dial view should have? If you look through the behaviors supplied by iOS, you won't find a "rotation" behavior. But the dynamic animator will rotate a view if the forces acting on that view would cause it to rotate. Rotating the dial view, therefore, isn't any more difficult than rotating a record platter, a merry-go-round, a lazy Susan, or anything similar: anchor the center of the object and apply an oblique force to one edge.

You'll accomplish this using two attachment behaviors. An *attachment behavior* connects a point in your view with either a similar point in another view or a fixed point in space, called an *anchor*. The length of the attachment can be inflexible, creating a "towbar" relationship that keeps the attachment point at a fixed distance, or it can be flexible, creating a "spring" relationship that tugs on the view when the other end of the attachment moves. To rotate the dial view, you'll use one of each, as shown in Figure 16-9.

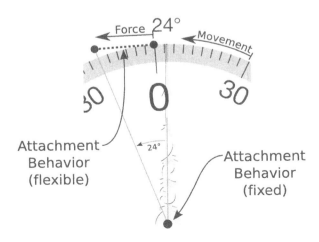

Figure 16-9. dialView attachment behaviors

Return to your new `attachDialBehaviors()` function and create the behavior that will pin the center of the dial view.

```
let dialCenter = dialView.center
let pinBehavior = UIAttachmentBehavior(item: dialView,
                            attachedToAnchor: dialCenter)
animator.addBehavior(pinBehavior)
```

The attachment behavior defines a rigid attachment from the center of the dial view to a fixed anchor point at the same location. When you create an attachment behavior, the existing distance between the two attachment points defines its initial length, which in this case is 0. Since the attachment is inflexible and its length is 0, the net effect is to pin the center of the view at that coordinate. The view's center can't move from that spot.

> **Note**   Most dynamic behaviors can be associated with any number of view objects. Gravity, for example, can be applied to a multitude of view objects equally. The attachment behavior, however, creates a relationship between two attachment points and therefore associates with only one or two view objects.

All that remains is to add that behavior to the dynamic animator. All by itself, this doesn't accomplish much, except to prevent the view from being moved to a new location. Things get interesting when you add a second attachment behavior, using the following code:

```
let dialRect = dialView.frame
let topCenter = CGPoint(x: dialRect.midX, y: dialRect.minY)
let topOffset = UIOffset(horizontal: 0.0, vertical: topCenter.y-dialCenter.y)
springBehavior = UIAttachmentBehavior(item: dialView,
                            offsetFromCenter: topOffset,
                            attachedToAnchor: topCenter)
springBehavior!.damping = springDamping
springBehavior!.frequency = springFrequency
animator.addBehavior(springBehavior)
}
```

The first two statements calculate the point at the top center of the view. A second attachment behavior is created. This time the attachment point is not in the center of the view but at its top-center (expressed as an offset from its center).

Again, the anchor point is the same location as the attachment point, creating a zero-length attachment. What's different is that the `damping` and `frequency` properties are then set to something other than their default values. This creates a "springy" connection between the anchor point and the attachment point. But since the anchor and the attachment point are currently the same, no force is applied (yet).

Of course, none of the behaviors is going to get created until you call `attachDialBehaviors()`. You'll need to do this when the views are initially positioned in `viewWillAppear(_\:)` (new code in bold).

```
override func viewWillAppear(animated: Bool) {
    super.viewWillAppear(animated)
    positionDialViews()
    attachDialBehaviors()
```

You'll need to do it again if the view is ever resized. In this case, you'll want to cancel all of the dynamic animations, let the resize transition complete, and then re-create them for the newly resized views. Edit the code in `viewWillTransitionToSize(...)` so it looks like this (new code in bold):

```
animator?.removeAllBehaviors()
coordinator.animateAlongsideTransition({ (context) in
        self.positionDialViews()
        },
    completion: { (context) in
        self.attachDialBehaviors()
        })
```

Animating the Dial

The stage is set, and all of the players are in place. You've defined a behavior that pins the center of the dial to a specific position, and a second that will "tug" the top-center point toward a second anchor point. The action begins when you move that second anchor point, as shown in Figure 16-9.

Locate the `rotateDialView(_:)` function and delete the first statement—the one that created an affine transform and applied it to the view. Replace that code with the following (new code in bold):

```
func rotateDialView(rotation: Double) {
    if let spring = springBehavior {
        let center = dialView.center
        let radius = dialView.frame.height/2.0 + springAnchorDistance
        let anchorPoint = CGPoint(x: center.x+CGFloat(sin(rotation))*radius,
                                  y: center.y-CGFloat(cos(rotation))*radius )
        spring.anchorPoint = anchorPoint
    }
}
```

Instead of the traditional approach of telling the graphics system what kind of change you want to see (rotate the view by a certain angle), you describe a change to the physical environment and let the dynamic animator simulate the consequences. In this app, you moved the anchor point attached to the top-center point of the view. Moving the anchor point creates an attraction between the new anchor point and the attachment point in the view. Since the center of the view is pinned by the first behavior, the only way the top point of the view can get closer to the new anchor point is to rotate the view, and that's exactly what happens.

Run the app and see the effect. The dial acts much more like a "real" dial. There's acceleration, deceleration, and even oscillation. These effects are all courtesy of the physics engine in the dynamic animator.

Try altering the values of springAnchorDistance, springDamping, and springFrequency and observe how this affects the dial. For extra credit, add a third behavior that adds some "drag" to the dial. Create a UIDynamicItemBehavior object, associate it with the dial view, and set its angularResistance property to something other than 0; I suggest starting with a value of 2.0. Don't forget to add the finished behavior to the dynamic animator. Your code should look something like this:

```
let drag = UIDynamicItemBehavior(items: [dialView])
drag.angularResistance = 2.0
animator.addBehavior(drag)
```

You now have a nifty inclinometer that's silky smooth and fun to watch. Now that you know how easy it is to add motion data to your app and simulate motion using View Dynamics, let's take a look at some of the other sources of motion data.

Getting Other Kinds of Motion Data

As of this writing, your app can use three other kinds of motion data. You can collect and use the other kinds of data instead of, or in addition to, the accelerometer data. Here are the kinds of motion data iOS provides:

- *Gyroscope*: Measures the rate at which the device is being rotated around its three axes

- *Magnetometer*: Measures the orientation of the surrounding magnetic field

- *Device motion*: Combines information from the accelerometer, magnetometer, and gyroscope to produce useful values about the device's motion and position in space

Using the other kinds of motion data is identical to what you've done with the accelerometer data, with one exception. Not all iOS devices have a gyroscope or a magnetometer. You will have to decide whether your app must have these capabilities or can function in their absence. That decision will dictate how you configure your app's project and write your code. Let's start with the gyroscope.

Gyroscope Data

If you're interested in the instantaneous rate at which the device is being rotated—logically equivalent to the accelerometer data but for angular force—gather gyroscope data. You collect gyroscope data almost exactly as you do accelerometer data. Begin by setting the gyroUpdateInterval property of the motion manager object and then call either the startGyroUpdates() or startGyroUpdatesToQueue(_:,withHandler:) function.

The gyroData property returns a CMGyroData object, which has a single rotationRate property value. This property has three values: x, y, and z. Each value is the rate of rotation around that axis, in radians per second.

You must consider the possibility that the user's device doesn't have a gyroscope. There are two approaches.

- If your app requires gyroscopic hardware to function, add the gyroscope value to the UIRequiredDeviceCapabilities of your app's property list.

- If you app can run with, or without, a gyroscope, test the gyroAvailable property of the motion manager object.

The first approach makes the gyroscope hardware a requirement for your app to run. If added to your app's property list, iOS won't allow the app to be installed on a device that lacks a gyroscope. The App Store may hide the app from users who lack a gyroscope or warn them that your app may not run on their device.

You add this key exactly the way you added the gamekit capability requirement in Chapter 14. Find the section "Adding GameKit to Your App" in Chapter 14 and follow the instructions for editing the Required Device Capabilities collection, substituting gyroscope for gamekit.

If your app can make use of gyroscope data but could live without it, test for the presence of a gyroscope by reading the gyroAvailable property of the motion manager object. If it's true, feel free to start and use the gyroscope data. If it's false, make other arrangements.

Magnetometer Data

The magnitude and direction of the magnetic field surrounding your device are available via the magnetometer data. By now, this is going to sound like a broken record.

1. Set the frequency of magnetometer updates using the magnetometerUpdateInterval property.

2. Start magnetometer measurements calling either the startMagnetometerUpdates() or startMagnetometerUpdatesToQueue (_:,withHandler:) function.

3. The magnetometerData property returns a CMMagnetometerData object with the current readings.

   The CMMagnetometerData object's sole property is the magneticField property, which contains three values: x, y, and z. Each is the direction and strength of the field along that axis, in µT (microteslas).

4. Either add the magnetometer value to your app's Required Device Capabilities property or check the magnetometerAvailable property to determine whether the device has one.

Like the accelerometer and gyroscope data, the magnetometerDate property returns the raw, unfiltered, magnetic field information. This will be a combination of the earth's magnetic field, the device's own magnetic bias, any ambient magnetic fields, magnetic interference, and so on.

Teasing magnetic north from this data is a little tricky. What looks like north might be a microwave oven. Similarly, the accelerometer data can change because the device was tilted or because it's in a moving car or both. You can unravel some of these conflicting indicators by collecting and correlating data from multiple instruments. For example, you can tell the difference between a tilt and a horizontal movement by examining the changes to both the accelerometer and the gyroscope; a tilt will change both, but a horizontal movement will register only on the accelerometer.

If you're getting the sinking feeling that you should have been paying more attention in your physics and math classes, you can relax; iOS has you covered.

Device Motion and Attitude

The CMMotionManager also provides a unified view of the device's physical position and movements through its device motion interface. The device motion properties and functions combine the information from the accelerometer, gyroscope, and sometimes the magnetometer. It assimilates all of this data and produces a filtered, unified, calibrated picture of the device's motion and position in space.

You use device motion in much the way you used the preceding three instruments.

1. Set the frequency of device motion updates using the deviceMotionUpdateInterval property.

2. Start device motion updates by calling one of these functions: startDeviceUpdates(), startDeviceMotionUpdatesToQueue (_:,withHandler:), startDeviceMotionUpdatesUsingReferenceFrame(_:), or startDeviceMotionUpdatesUsingReferenceFrame (_:,toQueue:,withHandler:).

    The deviceMotion property returns a CMDeviceMotion object with the current motion and attitude information.

3. Determine whether device motion data is available using the deviceMotionAvailable property.

There are two big differences between the device motion and previous interfaces. When starting updates, you can optionally provide a CMAttitudeReferenceFrame constant that selects a *frame of reference* for the device. There are four choices:

- Direction of the device is arbitrary

- Direction is arbitrary, but use the magnetometer to eliminate "yaw drift"

- Direction is calibrated to magnetic north

- Direction is calibrated to true north (requires location services)

The neutral reference position of your device can be imagined by placing your iPhone or iPad flat on a table in front of you, with the screen up and the home button toward you. The line from the home button to the top of the device is the y-axis. The x-axis runs horizontally from the left side to the right. The z-axis runs through the device, straight up and down.

Spinning your device, while still flat on the table, changes its *direction*. It's this direction that the reference frame is concerned with. If the direction doesn't matter, you can use either of the arbitrary reference frames. If you need to know the direction in relationship to true or magnetic north, use one of the calibrated reference frames.

> **Note** Not all attitude reference frames are available on every device. Use the `availableAttitudeReferenceFrames()` function to determine which ones the device supports.

The second big difference is the `CMDeviceMotion` object. Unlike the other motion data objects, this one has several properties, listed in Table 16-1.

Table 16-1. *Key CMDeviceMotion Properties*

Property	Description
attitude	A CMAttitude object that describes the actual attitude (position in space) of the device described as a triplet of property values (pitch, roll, and yaw). Additional properties describe the same information in mathematically equivalent forms, both as a rotation matrix and a quaternion.
rotationRate	A structure with three values (x, y, and z) describing the rate of rotation around those axes.
userAcceleration	A CMAcceleration structure (x, y, and z) describing the motion of the device.
magneticField	A CMCalibratedMagneticField structure (x, y, z, and accuracy) that describes the direction of the earth's magnetic field.

At first glance, all of this information would appear to be the same as the data from the accelerometer, gyroscope, and magnetometer—just repackaged. It's not. The `CMDeviceMotion` object combines the information from multiple instruments to divine a more holistic picture of what the device is doing. Specifically:

- The `attitude` property combines information from the gyroscope to measure changes in angle, the accelerometer to determine the direction of gravity, and sometimes the magnetometer to calibrate direction (rotation around the z-axis) and prevent drift.

- The `userAcceleration` property correlates accelerometer and gyroscope data, excluding the force of gravity and changes in attitude, to provide an accurate measurement of acceleration.

- The `magneticField` property adjusts for the device bias and attempts to compensate for magnetic interference.

In all, the device motion interface is much more informed and intelligent. If there's a downside, it's that it requires more processing power, which steals app performance and battery life. If all your app needs is a general idea of motion or rotation, then the raw data from the accelerometer or gyroscope is all you need. But if you really want to know the device's position, direction, or orientation, then the device motion interface has it figured out for you.

> **Note**   A device may need to be tilted in a circular pattern to help calibrate the magnetometer.
> iOS will automatically present a display that prompts the user to do this if you set the
> showsDeviceMovementDisplay property of CMMotionManager to true.

Measuring Change

If your app needs to know the rate of change of any of the motion measurements, it needs time information. For example, to measure the change in angular rotation, you'd subtract the current rate from the previous rate and divide that by the time delta between the two samples.

But where can you find out when these measurements were taken? In earlier sections I wrote, "CMAccelerometerData's only property is acceleration," along with similar statements about CMGyroData and CMMagnetometerData. That's not strictly true.

The CMAccelerometerData, CMGyroData, CMMagnetometerData, and CMDeviceMotion classes are all subclasses of CMLogItem. The CMLogItem class defines a timestamp property, which all of the aforementioned classes inherit.

The timestamp property records the exact time the measurement was taken, allowing your app to accurately compare samples and calculate their rate of change, record them for posterity, or use them for any other purpose you might imagine.

> **Tip**   If you need to calculate the change in attitude (subtracting the values of two CMAttitude objects), the
> multiplyByInverseOfAttitude(_:) function will do the math for you.

Summary

In this chapter you tapped into the unfiltered data of the device's accelerometer, gyroscope, and magnetometer. You know how to configure the data you want to collect, interpret it, and use timers to collect it. You also learned how to exploit the device motion data for a more informed view of the device's position in space. There's almost no motion or movement that your app can't detect and react to.

Well, almost. Despite the incredibly detailed information about the direction of the device and how it's being moved around, there's still one piece of information missing: where the device is located. You'll solve that remaining mystery in the next chapter.

Chapter 17

Where Are You?

If you think the accelerometer, gyroscope, and magnetometer are cool, you're going to love this chapter. In addition to those instruments, many iOS devices contain radio receivers allowing them to triangulate their position by timing radio signals they receive from a network of satellites—either the Global Positioning System or the Russian Global Navigation Satellite System. This technology is generically referred to as *GPS*.

What does that mean to you? As a user, it means your iOS device knows where it is on the planet. As a developer, it means your app can get information about the device's location and use that to show your user where they are, what's around them, where they've come from, or how to get to where they want to go. In this chapter, you will do the following:

- Collect location information
- Display a map showing the user's current location
- Add custom annotations to a map
- Monitor the user's movement and offer direction
- Create an interface for changing map options

This chapter will use two iOS technologies: Core Location and Map Kit. Core Location provides the interface to the GPS satellite receivers and provides your app with data about where the device is located, in a variety of forms. Map Kit supplies the view objects and tools to display, annotate, and animate maps. The two can be used separately or together.

Creating Pigeon

The app for this chapter is called Pigeon. It's a utility that lets you remember your current location on a map. Later it will show you where you are and where the marked location is so you can fly back to it. Figure 17-1 shows the design for Pigeon.

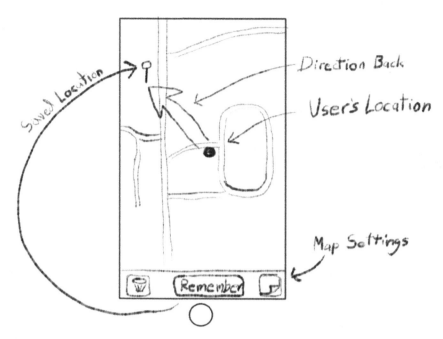

Figure 17-1. Pigeon design

The app has a map and three buttons. The middle button remembers your current location and drops a pin into the map to mark it. When you move away from that location, the map displays where you are, the saved location, and a line showing the direction back. A trash button forgets the saved location, and an info button lets the user change map display options. Let's get started.

Start by creating the project and laying out the interface. In Xcode, create a new project as follows:

1. Use the Single View Application template.

2. Name the project Pigeon.

3. Use the Swift language.

4. Set devices to Universal.

Select the Main.storyboard file. Add a toolbar to the bottom of the interface. Add and configure toolbar button items as follows (from left to right):

1. Add a Bar Button Item and set its identifier to Trash.

2. Add a Flexible Space Bar Button Item.

3. Add a Bar Button Item and set its title to Remember Location.

4. Add a Flexible Space Bar Button Item.

5. Add a Button (not a Bar Button Item) and set its type to Info Light.

From the object library, add a map view object to fill the rest of the interface. Set the following attributes for the Map View object:

1. Check Shows User Location.

2. Check Allows Zooming.

3. Uncheck Allows Scrolling.

4. Uncheck 3D Perspective.

Complete the layout by choosing the Add Missing Constraints to View Controller command, either by selecting the Editor ➤ Resolve Auto Layout Issues submenu or by clicking the resolve auto layout issues button at the bottom of the editor pane. The finished interface should look like Figure 17-2.

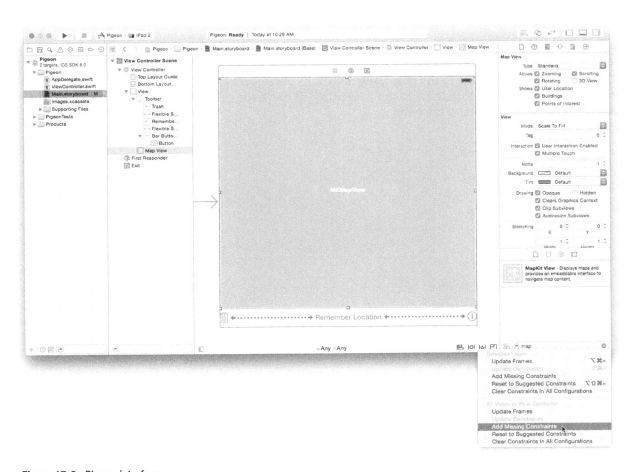

Figure 17-2. Pigeon interface

You'll need to wire up these views to your controller, so do that next. Switch to the assistant editor and make sure ViewController.swift appears in the pane on the right. You'll be using the Map Kit framework, so add an import statement to pull in the Map Kit declarations (new code in bold).

```
import UIKit
import MapKit
```

Add the outlet for the map view and stub functions for two actions to the ViewController class.

```
@IBOutlet var mapView: MKMapView!

@IBAction func dropPin(sender: AnyObject!) {
}

@IBAction func clearPin(sender: AnyObject!) {
}
```

Connect the mapView outlet to the map view object, as shown in Figure 17-3. Connect the actions of the left and center toolbar buttons to the clearPin(_:) and dropPin(_:) functions, respectively. Now you're ready to begin coding the actions.

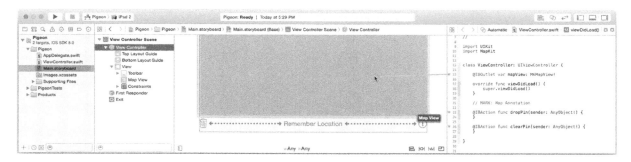

Figure 17-3. *Connecting the map outlets*

Collecting Location Data

Getting location data follows the same pattern you used to get gyroscope and magnetometer data in Chapter 16, with only minor modifications. The basic steps are as follows:

1. If precise (GPS) location information is a requirement for your app, add the gps value to the app's Required Device Capabilities property.

2. Create an instance of CLLocationManager.

3. Declare the reason your app needs location information.

4. Request permission to gather location information.

5. Check to see whether location services are available using the locationServicesAvailable() or authorizationStatus() function.

6. Adopt the `CLLocationManagerDelegate` protocol in one of your classes and make that object the delegate for the `CLLocationManager` object.

7. Call `startUpdatingLocation()` to begin collecting location data.

8. The delegate object will receive function calls whenever the device's location changes.

9. Send `stopUpdatingLocation()` when your app no longer needs location data.

The significant difference between using `CLLocationManager` and `CMMotionManager` is that you can create multiple `CLLocationManager` objects and data is delivered to its delegate object (rather than requiring your app to pull the data or push it to an operation queue).

Another difference is that location data may not be available, even on devices that have GPS hardware. There are a lot of reasons this might be true. The user may have location services turned off. They may be somewhere they can't receive satellite signals. The device may be in "airplane mode," which doesn't permit the GPS receivers to be energized. Or your app may specifically have been denied access to location information. It doesn't really matter why. You need to check for the availability of location data and deal with the possibility that you can't get it.

Finally, there are a number of functions for getting location data depending on the precision of the data and how quickly it's delivered. Knowing that the user moved 20 feet to the left is a different problem from knowing that they've arrived at work. I'll describe the different kinds of location monitoring toward the end of the chapter.

Pigeon needs precise location information that only GPS hardware can deliver. Select the Pigeon project in the project navigator, select the Pigeon target (from the upper-left pop-up menu, as shown in Figure 17-4, or from the target list), switch to the Info tab, and locate the Required device capabilities option in the Custom iOS Target Properties group. Click the + button and add a gps requirement, as shown in Figure 17-4.

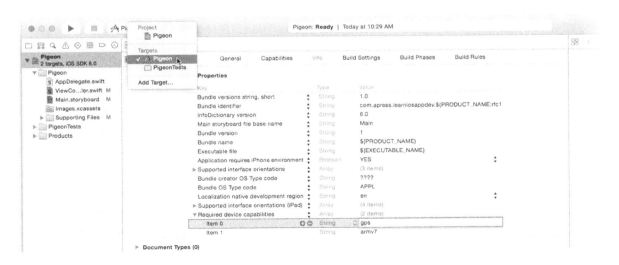

Figure 17-4. Adding the gps device requirement

Asking for Permission

The next two steps are to declare the reason why your app needs to collect location information and ask for permission to get it. Starting in iOS 8, your app must explicitly explain to the user why it's gathering location information and the scope of its collection process.

Your statement of intent is a property of your app. Since you're still in the target's Info section, add that now. Hover over any top-level property, click the + button to create a new property, name the property NSLocationWhenInUseUsageDescription, and type **Pigeon wants to know where you are** for its value, as shown in Figure 17-5.

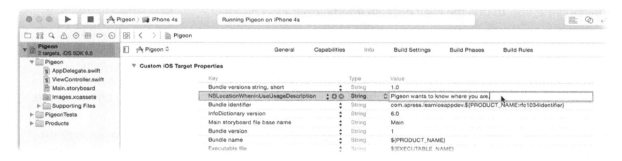

Figure 17-5. Adding a location usage description

The next step is to ask permission. Do this in the AppDelegate class (in the AppDelegate.swift file). Edit the beginning of the class so it looks like this (new code in bold):

```
import UIKit
import CoreLocation

@UIApplicationMain
class AppDelegate: UIResponder, UIApplicationDelegate {
    var window: UIWindow?
    let locationManager = CLLocationManager()

    func application(application: UIApplication!, ↵
        didFinishLaunchingWithOptions launchOptions: NSDictionary!) -> Bool {
        locationManager.requestWhenInUseAuthorization()
        return true
    }
}
```

You added this code to the AppDelegate class because this step is something you're doing for the whole app, not a specific view controller. It's appropriate that it be placed in your app's delegate object. Also, the application(_:,didFinishLaunchWithOptions:) function is one of the earliest opportunities for your code to execute. It's called immediately after the core app initialization is finished but before your app's first view controller appears or the app starts running. It's the perfect place to do things that need to be done early and once.

The first time your app runs, the requestWhenInUseAuthorization() function presents a dialog to the user asking them for access to their location information, as shown in Figure 17-6. Your reason for wanting this information (in NSLocationWhenInUseUsageDescription) is included in that alert.

Figure 17-6. *Location authorization alert*

There are two request authorization functions. You call either requestWhenInUseAuthorization() or requestAlwaysAuthorization(). The former requests permission to gather location information while your app is active. The latter requests permission to gather location information all the time. Since Pigeon uses location information only while it's running, you called the first function.

It's possible for your app to monitor and record location changes when it's not the active app and even when it's not running. I'll discuss alternate location monitoring services later in this chapter.

> **Note**   Technically, the requestWhenInUseAuthorization() and requestAlwaysAuthorization() functions prompt the user only if your app's current authorization status is .NotDetermined. This is true when your app is first installed. If its status is anything else (.Restricted, .Denied, .Authorized, or .AuthorizedWhenInUse), these calls do nothing because your app's authorization (or lack thereof) has already been determined.

Starting Location Collection

You're now probably thinking that I'm going to have you add some code to do the following:

- Make the `ViewController` adopt the `CLLocationManagerDelegate` protocol
- Implement the `locationManager(_:,didUpdateLocations:)` delegate function to process the location updates
- Make the `ViewController` the location manager's delegate
- Call `startUpdatingLocation()` to begin collecting location data

But you're not going to do any of that.

Now I'm sure you wondering why not, so let me explain. Pigeon uses both location services *and* the Map Kit. The Map Kit includes the `MKMapView` object, which displays maps. Among its many talents, it has the ability to monitor the device's current location and display that on the map. It will even notify its delegate when the user's location changes.

For this particular app, `MKMapView` is already doing all of the work for you. When you ask it to display the user's location, it creates its own instance of `CLLocationManager` and begins monitoring location changes and updating the map and its delegate. The end result is that `MKMapView` has all of the information that Pigeon needs to work.

> **Note** Pigeon is a little bit of an anomaly; you'll configure the map view so it always tracks the user's location and the map view is always active. If this wasn't the case, then relying on the map view to locate the user wouldn't be a solution and you'd have to resort to using `CLLocationManager` in the usual way.

This is a good thing. All of that `CLLocationManager` code would look so much like the code you wrote in Chapter 16 that it would make this app a little boring, and I certainly don't want you to get bored. Or maybe you haven't read Chapter 16 yet, in which case you have something to look forward to.

Regardless, all you need to do is set up `MKMapView` correctly. Let's do that now.

Using a Map View

Your map view object has already been added to the interface and connected to the `mapView` outlet. You've also used the attributes inspector to configure the map view so it shows (and tracks) the user's location, and you disallowed user scrolling. There's one more setting that you need to make, and you can't set it from the attributes inspector.

Select the `ViewController.swift` file and locate the `viewDidLoad()` function. At the end, add this statement:

```
mapView.userTrackingMode = .Follow
```

This sets the map's tracking mode to "follow the user." There are three tracking modes—which I'm sure you've seen in places like Apple's Maps app—listed in Table 17-1.

Table 17-1. User Tracking Modes

MKUserTrackingMode	Description
.None	The map does not follow the user's location.
.Follow	The map is centered at the user's current location, and it moves when the user moves.
.FollowWithHeading	The map tracks the user's current location, and the orientation of the map is rotated to indicate the user's direction of travel.

The code you added to viewDidLoad() sets the tracking mode to follow the user. The combination of the showsUserLocation property and the tracking mode force the map view to begin gathering location data, which is what you want.

If you've played with the Maps app, you also know that you can "break" the tracking mode by manually panning the map. You disabled panning for the map view, but there are still circumstances where the tracking mode will revert to MKUserTrackingMode.None. To address that, you need to add code to catch the situation where the tracking mode changes and "correct" it, if necessary.

That information is provided to the map view's delegate. Wouldn't it be great if your ViewController object were the delegate for the map view? I thought so too.

Adopt the MKMapViewDelegate protocol in ViewController (new code in bold):

```
class ViewController: UIViewController, MKMapViewDelegate {
```

Now add this map view delegate function:

```
func mapView(mapView: MKMapView!, didChangeUserTrackingMode mode:↵
                         MKUserTrackingMode, animated: Bool) {
    if mode == .None {
        mapView.userTrackingMode = .Follow
    }
}
```

This function is called whenever the tracking mode for the map changes. It simply sees whether the mode has changed to "none" and resets it to tracking the user.

Of course, this function is called only if your ViewController object is the delegate object for the map view. Select the Main.storyboard file. Select the map view object and use the connections inspector to connect the map view's delegate outlet to the view controller, as shown in Figure 17-7.

Figure 17-7. *Connecting the map view's delegate outlet*

You've done everything you need to see the map view in action, so fire it up. Run your app in the simulator or on a provisioned device. You should see something like what's shown in Figure 17-8.

Figure 17-8. *Testing map view*

The first time your app runs, iOS will ask the user if it's OK for your app to collect location data. Tap Allow, or this is going to be a really short test. Once it's granted permission, the map locates your device and centers the map at your location.

The iOS simulator will emulate location data, allowing you to test location-aware apps. In the Debug menu you'll find a number of choices in the Location submenu (the second image in Figure 17-8). Choose the Custom Location item to enter the longitude and latitude of your simulated location. There are also a few preprogrammed locations, such as the Apple item, also shown in Figure 17-8.

Some of the items play back a recorded trip. Currently the choices are City Bicycle Ride, City Run, and Freeway Drive. Selecting one starts a series of location changes, which the map will track, as though the device was on a bicycle, accompanying a runner, or in a car. Go ahead and try one; you know you want to.

The map can also be zoomed in and out by pinching or double-tapping. You can't scroll the map because you disabled that option in Interface Builder.

While the freeway drive is playing back, add the code to mark your location on the map.

Decorating Your Map

There are three ways of adding visual elements to a map: annotations, overlays, and subviews.

An *annotation* identifies a single point on the map. It can appear anyway you like, but iOS provides classes that mark the location with a recognizable "map pin" image. Annotations can optionally display a *callout* that consists of a title, subtitle, and accessory views. The callout appears above the pin when selected (tapped).

An *overlay* identifies a path or region on the map. Overlays can draw lines (like driving directions), highlight arbitrary areas (like a city park), and note points of interest (like a landmark). Like with annotations, you can draw anything you want on the map, but iOS provides classes that draw simple overlays for you.

A *subview* is like any other subview. MKMapView is a subclass of UIView, and you are free to add custom UIView objects to it. Use subviews to add additional controls or indicators to the map.

Annotations and overlays are attached to the map. They are described using map coordinates (which I'll talk about later), and they move when the map moves. Subviews are positioned in the local graphics coordinate system of the MKMapView object. They do not move with the map.

Your Pigeon app will create an annotation—that is, "put a pin"—at the user's current location when they tap the "remember location" button. The trash button will discard the pin. You already wrote stubs for the dropPin(_:) and clearPin(_:) action functions. It's time to flesh them out.

Adding an Annotation

When the user taps the "remember location" button, you'll capture their current location and add an annotation to the map. I thought it would be nice if the user could choose a label for the location to make it easier to remember what they're trying to remember. To accomplish all that, you'll use a UIAlertController. In ViewController.swift , start by finishing the dropPin(_:) function.

```
@IBAction func dropPin(sender: AnyObject!) {
    let alert = UIAlertController(title: "What's Here?",
        message: "Type a label for this location.",
        preferredStyle: .Alert)
    alert.addTextFieldWithConfigurationHandler(nil)
    let cancelAction = UIAlertAction(title: "Cancel",
                                     style: .Cancel,
                                   handler: nil)
    alert.addAction(cancelAction)
    let okAction = UIAlertAction(title: "Remember",
                                 style: .Default,
                               handler: { (_) in
```

```
            if let textField = alert.textFields?[0] as? UITextField {
                var label = "Over Here!"
                if let text = textField.text {
                    let trimmed = text.stringByTrimmingCharactersInSet(↵
                            NSCharacterSet.whitespaceAndNewlineCharacterSet())
                    if (trimmed as NSString).length != 0 {
                        label = trimmed
                    }
                }
                self.saveAnnotation(label: label)
            }
        })
        alert.addAction(okAction)
        presentViewController(alert, animated: true, completion: nil)
}
```

This function begins by presenting an alert view, configured so the user can enter some text. The code then adds two alert actions (buttons), one to cancel and the other to remember the location. It's the second one that's interesting. If the user taps the remember action, its handler gets the text the user typed in (if any), cleans it up, and supplies a default label if it's empty. The new label is then passed to the saveAnnotation(label:) function.

The other action function is pretty simple.

```
@IBAction func clearPin(sender: AnyObject!) {
    clearAnnotation()
}
```

The work of creating and clearing the annotation falls on the saveAnnotation(label:) and clearAnnoation() functions. Start with the saveAnnotation(label:) function.

```
var savedAnnotation: MKPointAnnotation?

func saveAnnotation(# label: String) {
    if let location = mapView.userLocation?.location {
        clearAnnotation()
        let annotation = MKPointAnnotation()
        annotation.title = label
        annotation.coordinate = location.coordinate
        mapView.addAnnotation(annotation)
        mapView.selectAnnotation(annotation, animated: true)
        savedAnnotation = annotation
    }
}
```

The first step is to get the user's current location. Remember that the map view has been tracking their location since the app was started, so it should have a pretty good idea of where they are by now. You must, however, consider the possibility that the map view doesn't know, in which case userLocation won't contain a value. The user may have disabled location services, is running in "airplane mode," or is spelunking. Regardless, if there's no location, there's nothing to do.

If the map view does know the user's location, it extracts their map coordinates (longitude and latitude) and uses that to create an `MKPointAnnotation` object. This is a simple annotation the marks a location on the map. The annotation is assigned a title and its location, added to the map, and then selected. Selecting the annotation is the same as tapping it, causing the label to appear in its callout.

The app is almost finished; you just need the `clearAnnotation()` function.

```
func clearAnnotation() {
    if let annotation = savedAnnotation {
        mapView.removeAnnotation(annotation)
        savedAnnotation = nil
    }
}
```

That was simple.

Run the app and give it a try. Tap the "remember location" button and enter a label, and a pin appears at your current location, as shown in Figure 17-9.

Figure 17-9. Testing the annotation

Map Coordinates

The coordinates of the annotation object were set to the coordinates of the user's location (provided by the map view). But what are these "coordinates?" Map Kit uses three coordinate systems, listed in Table 17-2.

Table 17-2. Map Coordinate Systems

Coordinate System	Description
Latitude and Longitude	The latitude and longitude, and sometimes altitude, of a position on the planet. These are called *map coordinates*.
Mercator	The position (x,y) on the Mercator map of the planet. A Mercator map is a cylindrical projection of the planet's surface onto a flat map. The Mercator map is what you see in the map view. Positions on the Mercator map are called *map points*.
Graphics	The graphics coordinates in the interface, used by UIView. These are referred to simply as *points*.

Map coordinates (longitude and latitude) are the principal values used to identify locations on the map, stored in a CLLocationCoordinate2D structure. They are not xy coordinates, so calculating distance and heading between two coordinates is a nontrivial exercise that's best left to location services and Map Kit. Annotations and overlays are positioned at map coordinates.

Map points are xy positions in the Mercator map projection. Being xy coordinates on a flat plane, calculating angles and distances is much simpler. Map points are used when drawing overlays. This simplifies drawing and reduces the math involved.

> **Note**   The Mercator projection is particularly convenient for navigation because a straight line between any two points on a Mercator map describes a heading the user can follow to get from one to the other. The disadvantage is that east-west distances and north-south distances are not to the same scale—except at the equator.

Map points are eventually translated into graphic coordinates, so they can appear somewhere on the screen. There are functions to translate map coordinates into graphic coordinates. Additional functions translate the other way.

Adding a Little Bounce

Your map pin appears on the map, and it moves around with the map. You can tap it to show, or hide, its callout. This is pretty impressive, considering you needed only a few lines of code to create it. We do, however, love animation, and I'm sure you've seen map pins that "drop" into place. Your pin doesn't drop; it just appears. So, how do you get your map pin to animate, change its color, or customize it in any other way? The answer is to use a custom annotation view.

An annotation in a map is actually a pair of objects: an annotation object and an annotation view object. An *annotation object* associates information with a coordinate on the map—the data model. An *annotation view object* is responsible for how that annotation looks—the view. If you want to customize how an annotation appears, you must supply your own annotation view object.

You do this by implementing the mapView(_:,viewForAnnotation:) delegate function. When the map view wants to display an annotation, it calls this function of its delegate passing it the annotation object. The function's job is to return an annotation view object that represents that annotation. If you don't implement this function or return nil for an annotation, the map view uses its default annotation view, which is the plain map pin you've already seen.

Add this function to ViewController.swift:

```
func mapView(mapView: MKMapView!, viewForAnnotation annotation: MKAnnotation!)↵
            -> MKAnnotationView! {
    if annotation === mapView.userLocation {
        return nil
    }

    let pinID = "Save"
    var pinView: MKPinAnnotationView!
    pinView = mapView.dequeueReusableAnnotationViewWithIdentifier(pinID)↵
                                        as? MKPinAnnotationView
    if pinView == nil {
        pinView = MKPinAnnotationView(annotation: annotation,↵
                            reuseIdentifier: pinID)
        pinView.canShowCallout = true
        pinView.animatesDrop = true
    }
    return pinView
}
```

The first statement compares the annotation to the map view's user annotation object. The user annotation object, like any other annotation object, represents the user's position in the map. The map view automatically added it when you asked it to display the user's location. This automatic annotation is available via the map view's userLocation property but also appears in the general collection of annotations. If you return nil for this annotation, the map view uses its default user annotation view—the pulsing blue dot we're all familiar with. If you want to represent the user's location some other way, this is where you'd provide that view.

The rest of the code works just like the table view cell code from Chapter 4. The map view maintains a cache of reusable MKAnnotationView objects that you recycle using an identifier. Your map uses only one kind of annotation view: a standard map pin view provided by the MKPinAnnotationView class. The pin is configured to display callouts and animate itself ("drop in") when added to the map.

Tip   If you want to give the user the ability to move the pin they just dropped, all you have to do is set the draggable property of the annotation view object to true.

Run the app again. Now when you save the location, the pin animates its insertion into the map, which is a lot more appealing.

Your `mapView(_:,viewForAnnotation:)` delegate function can return a customized version of a built-in annotation view class, as you've done here. `MKPinAnnotationView` can display pins of different colors, can allow or disallow callouts, can have custom accessory views in its callout, and so on. Alternatively, you can subclass `MKAnnotationView` and create your own annotation view, with whatever custom graphics and animations you want. You could represent the user's location as a waddling duck. Let your imagination run wild.

Showing the Way Home

The second technique for decorating maps employs overlays. Overlays occupy an area of the map, not just a single point. They're intended to represent things such as driving instructions, geographic features, and so on.

Overlays are similar to annotations. There's an *overlay* object that describes where the overlay is on the map—the data model. And there's a companion *overlay renderer* object that's responsible for drawing that overlay—the view.

> **Note**   Both `MKAnnotation` and `MKOverlay` are protocols, not classes. Any class can provide annotation or overlay information for a map view by adopting the appropriate protocol and implementing the required functions. Protocols are explained in Chapter 20.

Unlike annotations, the overlay renderer isn't a `UIView` object. It's a lightweight object that simply contains the code to paint the overlay directly into the map view's graphics context. In brief, it has a `draw...()` function, just like `UIView`'s `drawRect(_:)` function, but nothing else. This means you can't animate an overlay or use any of the standard `UIView` objects.

Also like annotations, iOS provides a set of useful overlay and overlay renderer classes. Let's use the `MKPolyline` and `MKPolylineRenderer` classes to draw a line between the user's saved location and their current location.

Adding Overlays

In Pigeon, you'll dynamically add an overlay whenever the user's location changes. "When does that happen?" you ask. It happens whenever the user moves. "How do I find out about it?" you ask. The map view notifies your delegate whenever the user's location is being displayed in the view *and* their location has changed. Add that delegate function to `ViewController` now—you can find the completed app in the `Learn iOS Development Projects` ➤ `Ch 17` ➤ `Pigeon-2` folder.

```
func mapView(mapView: MKMapView!, didUpdateUserLocation userLocation:
                                              MKUserLocation!) {
    clearOverlay()
    if let saved = savedAnnotation {
        if let user = userLocation {
            var coords = [ user.coordinate, saved.coordinate ]
            returnOverlay = MKPolyline(coordinates: &coords, count: 2)
            mapView.addOverlay(returnOverlay)
        }
    }
}
```

Whenever the user's location changes, start by discarding any existing overlay—it's no longer accurate. Get both the saved location and the user's current location. If both are known, create an MKPolyline overlay data model with two points—the map coordinates of the user and the saved location—and add it to the map. That's it.

> **Note** MKPolyline can describe an arbitrary complex line, much like a Bézier path. It's intended to describe things such as travel routes, geopolitical boundaries, and so on. There's also an MKPolygon class for solid shapes (like shading the area occupied by a national park) and a special MKGeodesicPolyline that's useful for representing very long distances, like the flight path of an aircraft.

Go ahead and knock out that clearOverlay() function and add a variable to save the current overlay.

```
var returnOverlay: MKPolyline?

func clearOverlay() {
    if let overlay = returnOverlay {
        mapView.removeOverlay(overlay)
        returnOverlay = nil
    }
}
```

Providing the Renderer

Unlike annotations, the map view doesn't supply default overlay renderers. To use overlays, you must implement the following delegate function:

```
func mapView(mapView: MKMapView!, rendererForOverlay overlay: MKOverlay!)↵
                                               -> MKOverlayRenderer! {
    if overlay === returnOverlay {
        let renderer = MKPolylineRenderer(overlay: returnOverlay)
        renderer.strokeColor = UIColor(red: 0.4,
                                     green: 1.0,
                                      blue: 0.4,
                                     alpha: 0.7)
        renderer.lineCap = kCGLineCapRound
        renderer.lineWidth = 16.0
        renderer.lineDashPattern = [ 38.0, 22.0 ]
        return renderer
    }
    return nil
}
```

The code asks whether the map view is requesting the renderer for your return path overlay. If so, create an MKPolylineRenderer object and configure it to draw a light green, semitransparent, dashed line with rounded end caps. Note that there's no renderer cache because renderer objects are not reusable; there is one renderer object for each overlay object.

CREATING A CUSTOM OVERLAY RENDERER

Creating a custom overlay renderer is (nearly) as easy as creating a custom UIView, just like the one you wrote in Chapter 11. At a minimum, you create a subclass of MKOverlayRenderer and then override the drawMapRect(_:,zoomScale:,inContext:) function.

Like UIView's drawRect(_:) function, your drawMapRect(...) function is painting into a Core Graphics context. Unlike drawRect(_:), the context is not your own. Your code draws directly into the map view's context, decorating the map with your overlay.

Your object gets its data from the overlay object associated with the renderer object, which you obtain via the inherited overlay property. If you need to display custom data, you would define your own overlay class and then use that object in your custom renderer. The superclass also provides useful conversion functions for turning map points into graphics coordinates, and vice versa.

Renderer drawing does present one complication. Map view drawing is performed on a background thread, for performance reasons. This means that some UIKit drawing objects and functions can't be used because they're not thread safe. They can be avoided by sticking to the Core Graphics functions for all drawing (all of those functions that start with CGContext...()). The documentation for MKOverlayRenderer describes the special steps, and restrictions, needed to draw with UIKit classes.

There's an example of a custom renderer class in the Homer app, which is available for free in the App Store. You can download the source for Homer at https://github.com/JamesBucanek/Pigeon.

Using the simulator or a provisioned device, run Pigeon, save a location, and then move away from that position. The renderer object will draw a fat dashed line between your current location and the saved one, as shown in Figure 17-10, as long as both are known.

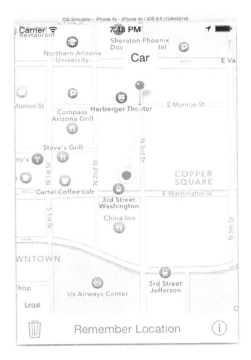

Figure 17-10. Testing the overlay renderer

Annotations and overlays provide almost an unlimited means for adding content to your maps. You can highlight points of interest, provide geographic information, draw travel routes, overlay weather information, promote businesses, or display the location of other players—the possibilities go on and on. If you need more than the basic map pins, lines, and regions provided by iOS, you're free to invent your own annotation views and overlay renderers.

Are you still wondering what the info button in the toolbar is for? I saved that for the exercise at the end of the chapter. Before you get to that, let's take a brief tour of some location services and map features you haven't explored yet.

Location Monitoring

Pigeon is the kind of app that uses immediate, precise (as possible), and continuous monitoring of the user's location. Because of this, it requires an iOS device with GPS capabilities and gathers location data continuously. This isn't true for all apps. Many apps don't need precise location information, continuous monitoring, or to be immediately notified of movement.

For apps with less demanding location requirements, the Core Location framework offers a variety of information and delivery methods. Each method involves a different amount of hardware and CPU involvement, which means that each will impact the battery life and performance of the iOS device in varying ways.

As a rule, you want to gather the *least* amount of location information your app needs to function. Let's say you're writing a travel app that needs to know when the user has left one city and arrived at the next. Do not fire up the GPS hardware (the way Pigeon does) and start monitoring their every movement. Why? Because your app will never get the notification that they've arrived in their destination city because *the user's battery will have been completely drained*! And the first thing the user is going to do, after recharging, is to delete your app. Take a look at some other ways of getting location information that don't require as much juice.

Approximate Location and Non-GPS Devices

Location information is also available on iOS devices that don't have GPS hardware. These devices use location information that they gather from Wi-Fi base stations, cell phone towers, and other sources. The accuracy can be crude—sometimes kilometers instead of meters—but it's enough to place the user in a town. This is more than enough information to suggest restaurants or list movies that are playing in their vicinity.

So, even if you left out the gps hardware requirement for your app, you can still request location information, and you might get it. Consult the horizontalAccuracy property of the CLLocation object for the uncertainty (in meters) of the location's reported position. If that value is large, then the device probably isn't using GPS or it's in a situation where GPS is not accurate.

> **Note**   iOS devices with GPS also use this alternative location information to improve the speed of GPS triangulation—which, by itself, is rather slow—and to reduce power consumption. This system is called *Assisted GPS*.

If your app needs only approximate location information, gather your location data by sending CLLocationManager the startMonitoringSignificantLocationChanges() function instead of the startUpdatingLocation() function. This function gets only a rough estimate of the user's location and notifies your app only when that location changes in a big way—typically 500 meters or more—saving a great deal of processing power and battery life.

The significant location change service also notifies your app even when it's not running—something that regular location monitoring (via startUpdatingLocation()) doesn't do. If you start significant location change updates and your app is subsequently stopped, iOS will relaunch your app (in the background) and notify it of the new location.

> **Note**   Using significant location change notifications, or any other location gathering that would occur while your app isn't running, requires that you request authorization to continuously monitor the user's location using the requestAlwaysAuthorization() function. If you fail to do this or the user explicitly denies your app permission to gather location data in the background, none of these APIs will do anything useful.

Monitoring Regions

Getting back to that travel app, some iOS devices are capable of monitoring significant changes in location, even when the device is idle. This is accomplished using *region monitoring*. Region monitoring lets you define an area on the map and be notified when the user enters or exits that region. This is an extremely efficient (low-power) method of determining when the user has moved.

You could, for example, create a region (`CLRegion`) object encompassing the airport they are traveling to next. You would call the location manager object's `startMonitoringForRegion(_:)` function for each region, up to 20. Then all your app has to do is sit back and wait until the delegate object receives a call to `locationManager(_:,didEnterRegion:)` or `locationManager(_:,DidExitRegion:)`.

Use region monitoring to be notified when the user arrives at work or at their family reunion. To learn more about region monitoring, find the "Monitoring Shape-Based Regions" section of the *Location Services and Maps Programming Guide* that you'll find in Xcode's Documentation and API Reference window. The *Location Services and Maps Programming Guide* also describes how to receive location data in the background when your app isn't the active app, something I haven't discussed in this book.

Reducing Location Change Messages

Another way to stretch battery life is to reduce the amount of location information your app receives. I already talked about receiving only significant changes or monitoring regions, but there's a middle ground between that extreme and getting second-by-second updates on the user's location.

The first method is to set the location manager's `distanceFilter` and `desiredAccuracy` properties. The `distanceFilter` property reduces the number of location updates your app receives. It waits until the device has moved by the set distance before updating your app again. The `desiredAccuracy` property tells iOS how much effort it should expend trying to determine the user's exact location. Relaxing that property means the location hardware doesn't have to work as hard.

Another hint you can provide is the `activityType` property. This tells the manager that your app is used for automotive navigation, as opposed to being a personal fitness app. The location manager will use this hint to optimize its use of hardware. An automobile navigation app might, for example, temporarily power down the GPS receivers if the user hasn't moved for an extended period of time.

Movement and Heading

Your app might not be interested so much in where the user is as in what direction they're going in and how fast. If heading is your game, consult the `speed` and `course` properties of the `CLLocation` object that you obtain from the `location` property of the `CLLocationManager`.

If all you want to know is the user's direction, you can gather just that by calling the `startUpdatingHeading()` function (instead of `startUpdatingLocation()`). The user's heading can be determined somewhat more efficiently than their exact location.

To learn more about direction information, read the "Getting Direction-Related Events" chapter of the *Location Awareness Programming Guide*.

Geocoding

What if your app is interested in places on the map? It might want to know where a business is located. Or maybe it has a map coordinate and wants to know what's there.

The process of converting information about locations (business name, address, city, ZIP code) into map coordinates, and vice versa, is called *geocoding*. Geocoding is a network service, provided by Apple, that will convert a dictionary of place information (say, an address) into a longitude and latitude, and back again, as best as it can. Turning place information into a map coordinate is called *forward geocoding*. Turning a map coordinate into a description of what's there is called *reverse geocoding*.

Geocoding is performed through the `CLGeocoder` object. `CLGeocoder` will turn either a dictionary of descriptive information or a map coordinate into a `CLPlacemark` object. A placemark object is a combination of a map coordinate and a description of what's at that coordinate. This information will include what country, region, and city the coordinate is in, a street address, and a postal code (if appropriate), even whether it's a body of water.

Getting Directions

Another resource your app has at its disposal is the Maps app—yes, the standard Maps app that comes with iOS. There are methods that let your app launch the Maps app to assist your user. This is a simple way of providing maps, locations, directions, and navigation services to your user without adding any of that to your app.

You use the Maps app via the `MKMapItem` object. You create one or more `MKMapItem` objects either from the current location (`mapItemForCurrentLocation()`) or from a geocoded placemark object (`MKMapItem(placemark:)`).

Once created, call the map item object's `openInMapsWithLaunchOptions(_:)` function (for one map item) or pass an array of map items to `openMapItems(_:,launchOptions:)`. The launch options are a dictionary that can optionally tell the Maps app what region of the globe to display, a region on the map to highlight, whether you want it provide driving or walking directions to a given location, what mode to use (map, satellite, hybrid), whether to display traffic information, and so on.

Code examples using `MKMapItem` are shown in the "Providing Directions" chapter of the *Location Services and Maps Programming Guide*.

If you want to provide directions in your app, use the `MKDirectionsRequest` class. You start by creating two `MKMapItem` objects, for the start and end of the trip. You then start an `MKDirectionsRequest`. This object contacts the map servers and returns one or more possible routes. These routes are described by `MKRoute` objects. If you want to display one of those routes in your map, get the `polyline` property of the `MKRoute` object; it's an `MKPolyline` overlay object, ready to add to the map, exactly as you did in Pigeon. You can find more details, along with example code, in the "Providing Directions" chapter of the *Location Services and Maps Programming Guide*.

The Homer app, on the App Store, also performs geocoding and gets directions. You can download the source code for Homer at `https://github.com/JamesBucanek/Pigeon`.

Summary

You've traveled far in your journey toward mastering iOS app development. You've passed many milestones, and learning to use location services is a big one. You now know how to get the user's location, for a variety of purposes, and display that on a map.

Speaking of which, you also learned a lot about maps. You now know how to present a map in your app, annotate it with points of interest, and customize how those annotations look. You learned how to track and display the user's location on the map and add your own overlays.

But you know what? Pigeon still has the same problem that MyStuff has. What good is an app that's supposed to remember stuff if it forgets everything when you quit the app? There should be some way of storing its data somewhere so when you come back to the app it hasn't lost everything. Not surprisingly, there's a bunch of technologies for saving data, and the next two chapters are devoted to just that.

EXERCISE

MKMapView can display graphic maps, satellite images, or a combination of both. It can orient the map to true north or rotate the map based on the orientation of the device. It's rude not to let your user choose which of these options they want to use. Pigeon locked the map view's orientation and display mode. Your exercise is to fix that.

These two aspects of the map display are controlled by two properties: mapType and userTrackingMode. The map type can be set to display graphics (MKMapType.Standard), satellite imagery (MKMapType.Stellite), or a combination of the two (MKMapType.Hybrid). The user's tracking mode can either follow the user (MKUserTrackingMode.Follow) or follow them with heading (MKUserTrackingMode.FollowWithHeading).

The controls you add to the interface are up to you. Some apps add a button right to the map interface that toggles between different map types and tracking modes. For Pigeon, I decided to place the settings on a separate view controller.

You'll find the finished project in the Learn iOS Development Projects ➤ Ch 17 ➤ Pigeon E1 folder. Basically, here's what I did:

1. Create a new Swift class called OptionsViewController, which is a subclass of UIViewController.

2. In the Main.storyboard file, add a new view controller and change the class of the view controller to OptionsViewController.

3. In the new view, add two segmented controls. Configure one to have three segments (Map, Satellite, Hybrid) and the second one to have two segments (North, Heading).

4. Make the background color of the root view slightly tinted and semitransparent.

5. In OptionsViewController, add outlets for the segmented controls and two @IBAction functions to change the settings.

6. Override the viewWillAppear() function and obtain a reference to the MKMapView object from the presentingController. Use the current property values of the map to update the initial selection of the segmented controls.

7. In the two action functions, use the reference to the presenting controller's map view and change the map type or tracking mode based on selected segment.

8. Add a done() function to dismiss the view controller.

9. Connect the segmented controls to the outlets and connect each sent action to the appropriate OptionsViewController action.

10. Add a single-tap gesture recognizer, attach it to the root view, and connect it to the done() function. This will dismiss the view controller.

11. Create a segue from the info button in the toolbar to the new view controller. Set the seque to Present Modally, the presentation to Over Full Screen, and the transition to Cover Vertically.

This is all stuff you learned in Chapters 10 and 12. Here's the finished interface in action:

Chapter 18

Remember Me?

One of the marvelous qualities of iOS devices, which make them such an indispensable part of our lives, is their ability to remember so much stuff: pictures, phone numbers, addresses, appointments, to-do lists, lesson notes, project ideas, keynote presentations, playlists, articles you want to read—the list seems endless. But so far, none of the apps you've developed in this book remembers anything. MyStuff starts with an empty list every time you launch it. Wonderland doesn't even remember what page you were reading. And consider Pigeon, poor Pigeon. Its only task is to memorize one location, and it can't even do that. You're going to fix all of that, and more.

As you might imagine, there are lots of different ways of storing information in iOS. The next two chapters will explore the basic ones. You're going to begin with user defaults (sometimes called *preferences*). This is the technology most often used to remember small bits of information such as your settings, what tab you were viewing, what page number you were last looking at, your list of favorite URLs, and so on. In this chapter, you will do the following:

- Learn about property lists
- Add and retrieve values from the user defaults
- Create a settings bundle for your app
- Store and synchronize property list data in the cloud
- Preserve and restore views and view controllers

The mechanics of property lists and how to use them are simple; it will only take a page or two to explain the whole thing. How best to use them is another matter. Much of this chapter will be focused on the strategies of using property lists, so put on your thinking cap and let's get started.

Property Lists

A property list is a graph of objects, where every object is one the following classes:

- NSDictionary
- NSArray
- NSString
- NSNumber (any integer, floating point, or Boolean value)
- NSDate
- NSData

While a property list can be a single string, it is most often a dictionary that contain strings, numbers, dates, or other arrays and dictionaries. Instances of these classes are called *property list objects*.

Seriously, that's it.

Serializing Property Lists

Property lists are used throughout iOS because they are flexible, universal, and easily serialized. In this case, *serialize* (the Cocoa term) means "serialize" (the computer science term). Cocoa uses the term *serialization* to mean converting a property list into a transportable stream of bytes. You don't often serialize property lists yourself, but they are regularly serialized behind the scenes.

> **Note** A property list can be serialized into two different formats: binary and XML. The binary format is unique to Cocoa. It can be read and understood only by another Cocoa (OS X) or Cocoa Touch (iOS) app. The XML format is universal and can be exchanged with practically any computer system in the world. The advantage of the binary format is efficiency (both size and speed). The advantage of the XML format is portability.

A serialized property list written to a file is called a *property list file*, often a .plist file. Xcode includes a property list editor so you can directly create and modify the contents of a property list file. You'll use the property list editor later in this chapter.

For the Wonderland app, I wrote a Mac (OS X) utility application that generated the Characters.nsarray resource file. That was a property list (an array of dictionaries containing strings), serialized in the XML format, and written to a property list file. Later, you added that as a resource file, which your app turned back into an NSArray object by *deserializing* the file.

> **Tip** If you want to serialize a property list yourself, use the NSPropertyListSerialization class or one of the writeTo(...) methods in NSArray and NSDictionary.

User Defaults

One of the premier uses of property list objects is in the user defaults. The *user defaults* is a dictionary of property list objects you can use to store small amounts of persistent information, such as preferences and display state. You can store any property list value you want into the user defaults (NSUserDefaults) object and later retrieve it. The values you store there are serialized and preserved between runs of your app.

A user defaults (NSUserDefaults) object is created when your app starts. Any values you stored there the last time are deserialized and become immediately available. If you make any changes to the user defaults, they are automatically serialized and saved so they'll be available the next time your app runs.

> **Note**   The user default values are local to your app. In other words, your app can't get or change the values stored by other iOS apps.

Using NSUserDefaults is really simple. You obtain your app's singleton user defaults object using the NSUserDefaults.standardUserDefaults() function. You call "set" function to store values (setInteger(_:,forKey:), setObject(_:,forKey:), setBool(_:,forKey:), and so on). You retrieve values by calling the "get" functions (integerForKey(_:), objectForKey(_:), boolForKey(_:), and so on).

Making Pigeon Remember

You're going to use user defaults to give Pigeon some long-term memory. When you add user defaults to an app, you need to consider the following:

- What values to store
- What property list objects and keys you will use
- When to store the values
- When to retrieve the values

Each decision affects subsequent ones, so start at the top. For Pigeon, you want it to remember the following:

- The remembered map location (duh)
- The map type (plain, satellite, or hybrid)
- The tracking mode (none or follow heading)

The next step is to decide what property list objects you're going to use to represent these properties. The map type and tracking mode are easy; they're both integer properties, and you can store any integer value directly in the user defaults.

The `MKPointAnnotation` object that encapsulates the map location, however, isn't a property list object and can't be stored directly in the user defaults. Instead, its significant properties need to be converted into property list objects, which can be stored. The typical technique is to turn your information into either a string or a dictionary of property list objects, both of which are compatible with user defaults. For Pigeon, you're going to convert the annotation into a dictionary containing three values: its latitude, its longitude, and its title. This is enough information to reconstruct the annotation when the app runs again.

You also have to pick keys to identify each value stored. At the top level, you want to choose keys that won't be confused with any keys iOS might be using. A number of iOS frameworks also use your app's user defaults to preserve information. The simplest technique is to use a prefix that isn't used by iOS. Keys for iOS properties invariably use the two-letter prefix of the classes that store that value. (This is a relic of Objective-C class names.) For example, it's unlikely the keys `HPMapType` and `HPFollowHeading` would conflict with any reserved iOS keys because there are no Cocoa Touch classes with an HP prefix. Keys used for values in subdictionaries can be anything you want.

> **Tip** How do you know if a two-letter prefix is used by a Cocoa Touch class? Open the Documentation and API Reference window. Type in your two letters and see whether any class names appear in the search results.

Minimizing Updates and Code

With the first part out of the way, you can now turn your attention to the much subtler problem of deciding when and where to preserve your values in the user defaults and when to get them back out again.

Tackle the storage problem first. As a rule, you want to make updates to the user defaults as infrequently as practical while still keeping your code simple. The following are the common solutions:

- Capture the value when it changes.
- Capture the value at some dependable exit point.

The first solution is perfect for Pigeon. It saves only three values, and none of those values change that often. The user might change map type and heading from time to time, but they're unlikely to fiddle with those settings a hundred times a minute. Likewise, the user will save a location when they arrive somewhere but won't save another location until they've traveled someplace else.

The reason you want to limit user default updates is that every change triggers a chain of events that results in a fair amount of work occurring in the background. It's something to avoid, as long as it doesn't overly complicate your design. A good design will minimize updates with a minimal amount of code. When you start working with cloud-based storage (later in this chapter), it's even more important to avoid gratuitous changes.

On the other hand, some values you want to preserve might change all the time or in many different places. For example, remembering the playback location of an audio book is something that changes constantly. It would be ludicrous to capture the playback position every second the audio was playing. Instead, it makes a lot more sense to simply note the user's current playback position when they exit the app. You'll explore that technique later in this chapter.

You're going to start by preserving the map type and tracking mode because these are the simplest. Then you'll tackle preserving and restoring the map location.

Defining Your Keys

This tutorial starts with the version of Pigeon in the exercise for Chapter 17. You'll find that version in the Learn iOS Development Projects ➤ Ch 17 ➤ Pigeon E1 folder. If you came up with your own solution to the exercise, you should have no problem adapting this code to your app.

Begin by defining the keys used to identify values in your user defaults. Select the ViewController.swift file and add an enum with three constants.

```
enum PreferenceKey: String {
    case MapType = "HPMapType"
    case Heading = "HPFollowHeading"
    case SavedLocation = "HPLocation"
}
```

Writing Values to User Defaults

Locate the code where the map type and tracking mode get changed. If you're working with the version of Pigeon I wrote for Chapter 17, that code is in OptionsViewController.swift. Find the code where each setting gets changed. In OptionsViewController that happens in the changeMapStyle(_:_ and changeHeading(_:) functions. Change the code so it looks like the following (new code in bold):

```
@IBAction func changeMapStyle(sender: UISegmentedControl!) {
    if let selectedMapType = MKMapType(rawValue:UInt(sender.selectedSegmentIndex)) {
        if let mapView = (presentingViewController as? ViewController)?.mapView {
            mapView.mapType = selectedMapType
            let userDefaults = NSUserDefaults.standardUserDefaults()
            userDefaults.setInteger( Int(selectedMapType.rawValue),
                        forKey: PreferenceKey.MapType.rawValue)
        }
    }
}

@IBAction func changeHeading(sender: UISegmentedControl!) {
    if let selectedTrackingMode = MKUserTrackingMode(rawValue:sender.selectedSegmentIndex+1) {
        if let mapView = (presentingViewController as? ViewController)?.mapView {
            mapView.userTrackingMode = selectedTrackingMode
            let userDefaults = NSUserDefaults.standardUserDefaults()
            userDefaults.setInteger( selectedTrackingMode.rawValue,
                        forKey: PreferenceKey.Heading.rawValue)
        }
    }
}
```

The change is straightforward, and you should have no problem adapting the same idea to your own app. When a setting is changed, the new value is also stored in the user defaults. That's all you have to do. NSUserDefaults takes care of everything else: converting the simple integer value into the appropriate property list (NSNumber) object, serializing the values, and storing them so they'll be available the next time your app runs.

That's the first half. Now you need to add the code to retrieve these saved values and restore the map options when your app starts.

Getting Values from User Defaults

Select the ViewController.swift file and locate the viewDidLoad() function. Replace the mapView. userTrackingMode = .Follow statement with the following code:

```
let userDefaults = NSUserDefaults.standardUserDefaults()
mapView.mapType = MKMapType(rawValue: UInt(userDefaults.integerForKey( ↩
                                      PreferenceKey.MapType.rawValue)))!

if let trackingValue = userDefaults.objectForKey(PreferenceKey.Heading.rawValue) ↩
                                                          as? NSNumber {
    mapView.userTrackingMode = MKUserTrackingMode(rawValue: trackingValue.integerValue)!
} else {
    mapView.userTrackingMode = .Follow
}
```

This new code retrieves the integer values for the map type and tracking mode from the user defaults and uses them to restore those properties before the map is displayed. Now when the user runs the app and changes the map type, every time they launch the app after that, the map type will be the same.

But there's a hitch. The first time the app is run—or if the user never changes the map type or tracking mode—there are no values at all for those keys in the user defaults. If you request the property list object for a nonexistent key, user defaults will return nil. If you request a scalar value (Boolean, integer, or floating-point), user defaults will return NO, 0, or 0.0. Here are three ways of dealing with this situation:

- Choose your values so that nil, false, 0, or 0.0 is the default
- Test to see whether user defaults contains a value for that key
- Register a default value for that key

The map type property adopts the first solution. Conveniently, the initial map type in Pigeon is .Standard, whose integer value is 0. So if there is no value in user defaults for the .MapType key, it returns a 0 and sets the map type to standard—which is perfect.

The tracking mode isn't so lucky. The initial tracking mode Pigeon uses is .Follow, whose integer value is 1. If there's no value for the .Heading key, you don't want to set trackingMode to .None (0) by mistake.

Instead, the code uses the second solution. It first gets the property list (NSNumber) object for that key. If there's no value for that key, user defaults returns nil and you know that a tracking value has never been set. You use this knowledge to either restore the user-selected mode or set the correct default.

> **Tip** Use the method objectForKey(_:) to test for the presence of any value. A property list *object* ultimately represents every value in a property list. The objectForKey(_:) function returns an optional that you can use to test for nil.

That's everything you need to preserve and restore these map settings. It's time to test it, but that will require a little finesse.

Testing User Defaults

Using either a provisioned device or the simulator, run your updated Pigeon app. Tap the settings button and change the map type and tracking mode, as shown in Figure 18-1. This will update the user defaults with the new values, but those values may, or may not, be saved in persistent storage yet. That's because the user defaults tries to be as efficient as possible and may wait for additional changes before beginning the serialization and storage process.

Figure 18-1. Testing the map settings

One way to get its attention is to push your app into the background. Do this by tapping the home button or use the Hardware ➤ Home command in the simulator, shown in the third image in Figure 18-1. When your app enters the background, it doesn't immediately stop running, but it prepares itself for that eventuality. One of those steps is to serialize and preserve all of your user defaults. Take a deep breath and count slowly to five.

With your user defaults safely stored, you can now stop your app and start it running again. Switch back to Xcode and click the stop button. Once the app stops, click the run button. The app starts up again. This time, it loads the map type and tracking mode from the saved user defaults and restores those properties. When the view controller loads, the map is exactly as the user left it last time.

Congratulations, you've learned the basics of preserving and restoring values in the user defaults. In the next few sections you're going to refine your technique a little and deal with the (slightly) more complex problem of preserving and restoring the user's saved map location.

Registering Default Values

The code to restore the tracking mode is awfully ugly. Well, maybe not *awfully ugly*, but it's a little ugly. If you had a dozen of these settings to restore, you'd have a lot of repetitive code to write. Fortunately, there's a more elegant solution.

Your app can register a set of default values for specific keys in user defaults—yes, they're default defaults. When your code requests a value (`userDefaults.integerForKey("Key")`), the user defaults checks to see whether a value for that key has been previously set. If not, it returns a default value. For integers, that value is 0—unless you've specified something else. You do that using the `registerDefaults(_:)` method.

Select the `AppDelegate.swift` file. This is your app's delegate object. It receives a lot of calls about the state of your app. One of those is the `application(_:,willFinishLaunchingWithOptions:)` function. This is the first call your app delegate object receives and is normally the first opportunity for code that you've written to run.

Near top of the file, add the following `import` so your new code can use the Map Kit constants. (You'll find the finished version in the `Learn iOS Development Projects` ➤ `Ch 18` ➤ `Pigeon-2` folder.)

```
import MapKit
```

In your `AppDelegate` class, add the following function (or update it if one already exists):

```
func application(application: UIApplication, willFinishLaunchingWithOptions ↵
                              launchOptions: [NSObject : AnyObject]?) -> Bool {
    let userDefaults = NSUserDefaults.standardUserDefaults()
    let pigeonDefaults = [ PreferenceKey.Heading.rawValue: ↵
                                      MKUserTrackingMode.Follow.rawValue ]
    userDefaults.registerDefaults(pigeonDefaults)
    return true
}
```

The `registerDefaults(_:)` function establishes a backup dictionary for the user default's primary dictionary. The user defaults object actually manages several dictionaries, arranged into domains. When you ask it to retrieve a value, it searches each domain until it finds a value and returns it. The `registerDefaults(_:)` method sets up a domain behind all of the others, so if none of the other domains contains a value for `PreferenceKey.Heading`, this dictionary provides one.

> **Note**   Each domain in the user defaults has its own purpose and properties. The domain into which you store values is persistent; it will be serialized and preserved between app runs. The registration domain is not persistent. The values you pass to `registerDefaults(_:)` disappear when your app quits. You can read about domains in "The Organization of Preferences" chapter of the *Preferences and Settings Programming Guide*.

Now you can clean up the code in `viewDidLoad()`. Return to `ViewController.swift` and replace the code you previously added with this (updated code in bold):

```
let userDefaults = NSUserDefaults.standardUserDefaults()
mapView.mapType = MKMapType(rawValue: UInt(userDefaults.integerForKey( ↩
                                        PreferenceKey.MapType.rawValue)))!
mapView.userTrackingMode = MKUserTrackingMode(rawValue: userDefaults.integerForKey( ↩
                                        PreferenceKey.Heading.rawValue))!
```

Isn't that a lot simpler? Because you've registered a defaults dictionary, your code doesn't have to worry about the situation where there is no value for `.Heading` because now there will always be one.

Now that your map settings are persistent, it's time to do something about that saved map location.

Turning Objects into Property List Objects

The big limitation of property lists is that they can contain only property list objects (`NSNumber`, `NSString`, `NSDictionary`, and so on). Anything you want to store in user defaults (or any property list) *must* be converted into one or more of those objects. Here are three most common techniques for storing other kinds of values:

- ▓ Convert the value into a string
- ▓ Convert the value into a dictionary containing other property list objects
- ▓ Serialize the value into an `NSData` object

The first technique is simple enough, especially since there are a number of Cocoa Touch functions that will do this for you. For example, let's say you need to store a `CGRect` value in your user defaults. `CGRect` isn't a property list object—it's not even an object. You could store each of its four floating-point fields as separate values, like this:

```
let saveRect = someView.frame
let userDefaults = NSUserDefaults.standardUserDefaults()
userDefaults.setFloat(Float(saveRect.origin.x), forKey: "HPFrame.x")
userDefaults.setFloat(Float(saveRect.origin.y), forKey: "HPFrame.y")
userDefaults.setFloat(Float(saveRect.height), forKey: "HPFrame.height")
userDefaults.setFloat(Float(saveRect.width), forKey: "HPFrame.width")
```

And you'd have to reverse the process to restore the rectangle. That seems like a lot of work. Fortunately, there are two functions—NSStringFromCGRect() and CGRectFromString()—that will convert a rectangle into a string object and back again. Now the code to save your rectangle can look something like this:

```
userDefaults.setObject(NSStringFromCGRect(saveRect), forKey: "HPFrame")
```

So if you can find functions that will convert your value to and from a property list object, use them.

The second technique is what you're going to use for the map location. You're going to write a pair of functions. The first will return the salient properties of your MKPointAnnotation object as a dictionary of NSString and NSNumber objects. A second method will take that dictionary and set them again.

Start by adding a new Swift file to your project. Drag a Swift File template from the template library (or choose the New ➤ File... command) and drop it into your project. (You'll find the finished version in the Learn iOS Development Projects ➤ Ch 18 ➤ Pigeon-3 folder.) Name the file PointAnnotationPreservation. Now write the following code in it:

```
import MapKit

enum LocationKey: String {
    case Latitude = "lat"
    case Longitude = "long"
    case Title = "title'"
}

extension MKPointAnnotation {

    var propertyState: [NSObject: AnyObject] {
        get {
            return [ LocationKey.Latitude.rawValue: NSNumber(double: coordinate.latitude),
                     LocationKey.Longitude.rawValue: NSNumber(double: coordinate.longitude),
                     LocationKey.Title.rawValue: title ]
        }
        set {
            let lat = (newValue[LocationKey.Latitude.rawValue] as NSNumber).doubleValue
            let long = (newValue[LocationKey.Longitude.rawValue] as NSNumber).doubleValue
            coordinate = CLLocationCoordinate2D(latitude: lat, longitude: long)
            title = newValue[LocationKey.Title.rawValue] as NSString
        }
    }
}
```

This code defines an extension to the MKPointAnnotation class. It adds a new (computed) property named propertyState. Getting the property returns a dictionary describing the location and title of the annotation. Setting the property updates the annotation's location and title from the values in the dictionary.

> **Note**   An extension adds additional methods or properties to an existing class. You can use them to add new features to classes you didn't write. I explain the ins and outs of extensions in Chapter 20.

This property allows you to get, and set, the relevant properties of an annotation in a form suitable for user defaults. Now let's go use it to save and restore the map location.

Preserving and Restoring savedLocation

Return to `ViewController.swift`. You're going to use the same technique you used to preserve and restore the map settings for the remembered map location. You're going to save the location information (dictionary) when it's established and restore it when the app starts again. The `savedLocation` object isn't, however, a simple integer, so the code is a little more involved. Furthermore, you're now establishing a new location from two places in the code: when the user sets it and when the app starts again. As you know by now, I'm not fond of repeating code, so I'm going to have you consolidate the code that sets the location. This will come in handy later, when you add a third avenue for setting the location.

To summarize, here's what you're going to change:

- Define a `setAnnotation(_:)` function to set or clear the saved location.
- Write `preserveAnnotation()` and `restoreAnnotation()` functions to store, and retrieve, the map location from the user defaults.
- Add code to `saveAnnotation(_:)` and `clearAnnotation(_:)` to preserve the map location.
- Restore any remembered location when your app launches.

Begin by adding the new `setAnnotation(_:)` function to the `ViewController` class:

```
func setAnnotation(annotation: MKPointAnnotation?) {
    if savedAnnotation != annotation {
        if let oldAnnotation = savedAnnotation {
            mapView.removeAnnotation(oldAnnotation)
            clearOverlay()
        }
        savedAnnotation = annotation
        if annotation != nil {
            mapView.addAnnotation(annotation)
            mapView.selectAnnotation(annotation, animated: true)
        }
    }
}
```

This method will be used throughout `ViewController` to set, or clear, the annotation object. It follows a common setter method pattern that handles the cases where the `savedAnnotation` variable is `nil`, the `annotation` parameter is `nil`, both are `nil`, or neither is `nil`. It also deliberately takes no action if the same annotation object is set again.

The next step is to create functions that preserve and restore the annotation object using the user defaults. Add the following code to the ViewController class:

```
func preserveAnnotation() {
    let userDefaults = NSUserDefaults.standardUserDefaults()
    if let annotation = savedAnnotation {
        userDefaults.setObject( annotation.propertyState, ↩
                        forKey: PreferenceKey.SavedLocation.rawValue)
    } else {
        userDefaults.removeObjectForKey(PreferenceKey.SavedLocation.rawValue)
    }
}

func restoreAnnotation() {
    let userDefaults = NSUserDefaults.standardUserDefaults()
    if let state = userDefaults.dictionaryForKey(PreferenceKey.SavedLocation.rawValue) {
        let restoreAnnotation = MKPointAnnotation()
        restoreAnnotation.propertyState = state
        setAnnotation(restoreAnnotation)
    }
}
```

The first function converts the saved location into a property list dictionary using the propertyState getter you just wrote. It then stores that dictionary of values in the user defaults. If there is no saved location, it deliberately removes any previously stored values. The second function reverses the first, obtaining the preserved dictionary from the user defaults, using that to reconstruct an equivalent MKPointAnnotation object, and then sets it as the saved location.

Now you can alter your saveAnnotation(label:) and clearAnnotation() functions so they use the new setAnnotation(_:) and preserveAnnotation() functions (new code in bold).

```
func saveAnnotation(# label: String) {
    if let location = mapView.userLocation?.location {
        let annotation = MKPointAnnotation()
        annotation.title = label
        annotation.coordinate = location.coordinate
        setAnnotation(annotation)
        preserveAnnotation()
    }
}

func clearAnnotation() {
    setAnnotation(nil)
    preserveAnnotation()
}
```

> **Note** This is another example of refactoring. You've consolidated the work of maintaining the `savedAnnotation` variable in a new function but have preserved the behavior of the existing `saveAnnotation(label:)` and `clearAnnotation()` functions.

There's only one thing left to do. In `viewDidLoad()`, add the following statement to the end of the function:

```
restoreAnnotation()
```

Pigeon now has the memory of an elephant! Reuse the test procedure you employed earlier to test the map settings:

1. Run Pigeon.
2. Remember a location on the map.
3. Press the home button to put the app in the background.
4. Stop the app in Xcode.
5. Run the app again.

When the app is restarted, the saved location is still there. Success!

This project demonstrates several common techniques for putting user defaults to work in your app. Remembering user preferences, settings, and working data (such as the saved map location) are all perfect uses for the user defaults.

Another common use is to save your app's display state. When the user selects the Artists tab in the Music app and taps down into an album and ultimately a song, they aren't surprised when they start Music the next day and find themselves at the same track, of the same album, of the same artist, in the Artists tab. That's because the Music app went to some effort to remember exactly what view controller the user left off at and reconstructed it the next time it was launched.

From what you know so far, you might think that you'd have to write code to capture the state of tab view and navigation view controllers, convert those into property list objects, store them in user defaults, and unroll the whole thing again when the app restarts. That's basically what happens, but you'll be happy to know that you don't have to do (much of) that yourself. iOS has a specific mechanism for saving and restoring the state of your view controllers.

Persistent Views

In the section "Minimizing Updates and Code" I said the primary techniques for capturing user defaults were (a) when the value changes and (b) at a dependable exit point. You used technique (a) in Pigeon because it was a perfect fit. The values you were saving were only changed in a handful of places, and they change infrequently. But that isn't always the case.

Some changes occur constantly (such as which view controller the user is in), and some changes occur in a myriad of different ways, making it difficult to catch them all. In these situations, the second approach is the best. You don't worry about trying to monitor, or even care about, what changes are being made. Just arrange to capture that value before the user quits the app, dismisses the view controller, or exits whatever interface they're using. There are two exit points that make good places to capture changes:

- Dismissing a view controller
- The app entering the background

For view controllers, you can capture your values in the code that dismisses the view controller. You might have to do a little extra work in circumstances such as a popover view controller because tapping outside the popover will dismiss it implicitly. You'd want to do something like override your view controller's viewDidDisappear(_:) function so you don't miss that exit route. But for the most part, it's usually pretty easy to catch all of the ways a view controller can be dismissed.

Fading Into the Background

The other great place to capture changes, and particularly the view state, is when the app switches to the background. To appreciate this technique, you need to understand the states an iOS app progresses through. Your iOS app is always in one of these states:

- Not running
- Foreground
- Background
- Suspended

Your app is in the "not running" state before it's launched, or after it's ultimately terminated. Little happens when it's not running.

The foreground state is the one you have the most experience with. This is when your app appears in the device's display and your user is interacting with it. Foreground has two substates, active and inactive, that it jumps between. Active means your app is running. Inactive occurs when something interrupts it (such as a phone call or an alert), but it's still being displayed. Your app's code does not run when it's inactive. The inactive state usually doesn't last long.

Your app moves to the background state when you press the home button, switch to another app, or the screen locks. Your app continues to run for a short period of time but will quickly move to the suspended state.

Your app does not execute any code once suspended. If iOS later decides that it needs the memory your app is occupying or the user shuts down their device, your suspended app will terminate (without warning) and return to the not running state.

But your app might not be terminated. If the user relaunches your app or merely unlocks their screen and it's still in the background state, your app isn't restarted; it's simply activated again. It moves directly to the foreground state and instantly resumes execution. Your app may enter and exit the background state repeatedly over its lifetime.

> **Note**   You can make special arrangements that allow your app to continue to run in the background. For example, you can request to play music or receive user location changes, even while your app is not the foreground app. See the section "Background Execution and Multitasking" in the *iOS App Programming Guide* for further details.

Apps take advantage of this small window of background processing to prepare themselves for termination. This is when the user defaults object serializes its property values and saves them to persistent storage. It's also the perfect time to capture the state of your interface.

Your app can discover when it has entered the background state in two ways. Your app delegate object's applicationDidEnterBackground(_:) function is called. Around the same time, a UIApplicationDidEnterBackgroundNotification notification is posted. Override that function or have any object observe that notification, and save whatever state information you need.

> **Caution**   iOS allots your app approximately five seconds of background processing time to save its state and finish up any work in progress. Your app must wrap up within that time or take explicit steps to enable background processing.

iOS also provides a mechanism to capture, and later restore, the state of your view controllers. This is automatically invoked when your app enters the background state.

Preserving View Controllers

As an example, take the Wonderland app. (I mean that, literally. Go find the finished Wonderland app from Chapter 12. You're going to modify it.) The user can spend all day jumping between tabs, browsing characters in the table view, and flipping through the page view. You want to catch the point when the app switches to the background and remember what tab they had active and what page of the book they were looking at. You'll use this to restore those views the next time the app is launched.

When an iOS app enters the background, iOS examines the active view controller. If properly configured, it will automatically preserve its state in the user defaults. This is a combination of what iOS already knows about the view controller and additional information that your code supplies. Specifically, iOS will remember what tab view was being displayed, the scroll position in a table view, and so on.

To that, you can add custom information that only your app understands. For Wonderland, you're going to remember the page number the user was reading. (Remember that a page view controller has no concept of a page number; that's something you invented for your page view controller data source.)

The first thing to address is the "properly configured" prerequisite. To put iOS to work for you, preserving and restoring your view controllers, you must do two steps:

1. Implement the `application(_:,shouldSaveApplicationState:)` and `application(_:,shouldRestoreApplicationState:)` app delegate functions.

2. Assign restoration identifiers to your view controllers, starting with the root view controller.

The first step tells iOS that you want its help in preserving and restoring your app's view state. These functions must be implemented, and they must return `true`, or iOS will just pass your app by. They also serve a secondary function. If you have any custom, appwide state information that you want to preserve, these are the functions to do that in. Wonderland doesn't have any, so it only needs to return `true`.

Open the Wonderland project from Chapter 12 and select the `AppDelegate.swift` file. Add the following two functions:

```
func application(application: UIApplication, ↵
                shouldSaveApplicationState coder: NSCoder) -> Bool {
    return true
}

func application(application: UIApplication, ↵
                shouldRestoreApplicationState coder: NSCoder) -> Bool {
    return true
}
```

Assigning Restoration Identifiers

Once iOS is given the green light to save your view state, it starts with the root view controller being displayed and checks for a restoration ID. A restoration ID is a string property (`restorationIdentifier`) used to tag the state information for that view controller. It also acts as a flag, inviting iOS to preserve and ultimately restore that view controller's state. If the `restorationIdentifer` property is `nil`, iOS ignores the view controller; nothing gets preserved, and nothing will be restored.

iOS then looks for any view (`UIView`) objects that have a `restorationIdentifier` set and preserves them. If the root view controller is a container view controller, the entire process repeats with each subview controller, capturing the state of each view controller with a restoration ID and ignoring those without.

> **Note**   The search for restorable view controllers skips any view controller that lacks a restoration ID. Thus, to save the state of a table view controller inside a navigation view controller inside a tab view controller, every one of those controllers must have a restoration ID, or else the state of the table view controller won't be captured.

You can set restoration IDs programmatically, but if your view controller is defined in an Interface Builder file, it's simplest to set them there. Select the Main.storyboard file in the Wonderland project. Select the root Tab Bar Controller in the Tab Bar Controller Scene and switch to the identity inspector, as shown in Figure 18-2. Locate the Restoration ID property and set it to RootTabBar.

Figure 18-2. Setting restoration ID property

You've now done everything required to get iOS to save and restore that state of your tab view controller. This, however, won't do you much good. What you want is the subview controller that was visible when the user quit Wonderland to reappear when they launch it again. For that to happen, each of the subview controllers must be restored too. Using the identity inspector, select each of the subview controllers and assign them restoration IDs too, using Table 18-1 as a guide.

Table 18-1. Wonderland View Controller Restoration IDs

View Controller	Restoration ID
Root Tab View Controller	RootTabBar
FirstViewController	Welcome
UINavigationController	CharacterNav
BookViewController	Book

This is enough to remember and later restore the top-level tab the user was viewing when they quit the app. Give it a try.

1. Run the Wonderland app.

2. Choose the character or book tab.

3. Press the home button to push the app into the background.

4. Wait a moment.

5. Stop the app in Xcode.

6. Run the app again.

Restoration ID strings can be anything you want; they just have to be unique within the scope of the other view controllers.

Customizing Restoration

So far, the only view state that gets restored is which tab the user was in. If they were viewing a character's information or had thumbed through to page 87 of the book, they'll return to the character list and page 1 when the app is relaunched.

Deciding how much view state information to preserve is up to you. As a rule, users expect to return to whatever they were doing when they quit the app. But there are limits to this. If the user had entered a modal view controller to pick a song or enter a password, it wouldn't necessarily make sense to return them to that exact same view two days later. You'll have to decide how "deep" your restoration logic extends.

For Wonderland, you definitely want the user to be on the same page of the book. Your users would be very annoyed if they had to flip through 86 pages to get back to where they were reading yesterday. The page view controller, however, knows nothing about the organization of your book data. That's something you created when you wrote the BookDataSource class. If you want to preserve and restore the page they were on, you'll have to write some code to do that.

Each view and view controller object with a restoration ID receives an encodeRestorableStateWithCoder(_:) call when the app moves to the background. During application startup, it receives a decodeRestorableStateWithCoder(_:) message to restore itself. If you want to preserve custom state information, override these two functions.

Select the BookViewController.swift file. Add the following constant and two functions:

```
let pageStateKey = "pageNumber"

override func encodeRestorableStateWithCoder(coder: NSCoder) {
    super.encodeRestorableStateWithCoder(coder)
    let currentViewController = viewControllers[0] as OnePageViewController
    coder.encodeInteger(currentViewController.pageNumber, forKey: pageStateKey)
}

override func decodeRestorableStateWithCoder(coder: NSCoder) {
    super.decodeRestorableStateWithCoder(coder)
    let page = coder.decodeIntegerForKey(pageStateKey)
    if page != 0 {
        let currentViewController = viewControllers[0] as OnePageViewController
        currentViewController.pageNumber = page;
    }
}
```

The first function obtains the current one page view controller being displayed in the page view controller. The OnePageViewController knows which page number it's displaying. This number is saved in the NSCoder object.

> **Note** `NSCoder` is the workhorse of iOS's archiving framework. You use it by storing values and properties, which are converted into serialized data. You'll learn all about `NSCoder` in the next chapter.

When your app is relaunched, the page view controller receives a `decodeRestorableStateWithCoder(_:)` call. It looks inside the `NSCoder` object to see whether it contains a saved (nonzero) page number. If it does, it restores the page number before the view appears, returning the user to where they were when they quit. That wasn't too hard, was it?

Test your new code. Launch Wonderland, flip through a few pages of the book, and then quit the app and stop it in Xcode. Launch it again, and the last page you were looking at will reappear, as if you'd never left.

Deeper Restoration

Exactly how much view state information you decide to preserve is up to you. Here are some tips to developing a restoration strategy:

- `UIView` objects can preserve their state too. Assign them a restoration ID and, if necessary, implement `encodeRestorableStateWithCoder(_:)` and `decodeRestorableStateWithCoder(_:)` functions. Remember that view controller that contains these views must have a Restoration ID for this to occur.

- If you want to restore the state of a data model for a table or collection view, your data source object should adopt the `UIDataSourceModelAssociation` protocol. You then implement two functions (`indexPathForElementWithModel Identifier(_:,inView:)` and `modelIdentifierForElementAtIndexPath(_:,inVie w:)`) that remember and restore the user's position in the table.

- You can encode and restore anything you want in your app delegate's `applicati on(_:,shouldSaveApplicationState:)` and `application(_:,shouldRestore ApplicationState:)` functions. You can use these methods to perform your own view controller restoration or use a combination of the automatic restoration and a custom solution.

The gory details are all explained in the "State Preservation and Restoration" chapter of the *iOS App Programming Guide*, which you can find in Xcode's Documentation and API Reference window.

Pigeons in the Cloud

Cloud storage and synchronization are hot new technologies that make iOS devices even more useful. Set an appointment on one, and it automatically appears on all of your other devices. The technology behind this bit of magic is complex, but iOS makes it easy for your app to take advantage of it.

There are a number of cloud storage and synchronization features in iOS, but the easiest to use, by far, is the NSUbiquitousKeyValueStore object. It works almost identically to user defaults. The difference is that anything you store there is automatically synchronized with all of your other iOS devices. Wow!

There are both practical limits and policy restrictions on what information you should, or can, synchronize between devices. Your first task is to decide what it makes sense to share. Typically, user settings and view states are only preserved locally. It would be weird to change the map type on your iPhone and then suddenly have your iPad's map view change too. On the other hand, if your user were reading *Alice's Adventures in Wonderland* on their iPad, wouldn't it be magic if they could reach for their iPhone and open it up at the same page?

Another reason to carefully choose what you synchronize is that the iCloud service strictly limits how much information you can share through NSUbiquitousKeyValueStore. These limits are as follows:

- No more than 1MB of data, in total
- No more than 1,000 objects
- A "reasonable" number of updates

Apple doesn't spell out exactly what "reasonable" is, but it's a good idea to keep the number of changes you make to NSUbiquitousKeyValueStore to a minimum.

Caution   If you abuse these limits, the iCloud servers may delay your updates or possibly stop synchronizing your data entirely.

Storing Values in the Cloud

Let your Pigeon app spread its wings by adding cloud synchronization. The only piece of information you'll synchronize is the remembered map location—the map type and tracking mode aren't good candidates for syncing. You use NSUbiquitousKeyValueStore almost exactly the way you use NSUserDefaults. In fact, they are so similar that you'll be reusing many of the same strategies and methods you wrote at the beginning of this chapter.

You get a reference to the singleton NSUbiquitousKeyValueStore object via NSUbiquitousKeyValueStore.defaultStore(). Any values you set are automatically serialized and synchronized with the iCloud servers.

Select ViewController.swift and add a variable to hold a reference to the singleton cloud store object. (You'll find the finished version in the Learn iOS Development Projects ➤ Ch 18 ➤ Pigeon-4 folder.)

```
var cloudStore: NSUbiquitousKeyValueStore?
```

Near the beginning of the viewDidLoad() function, add the following statement:

```
cloudStore = NSUbiquitousKeyValueStore.defaultStore()
cloudStore?.synchronize()
```

The first statement gets the cloud store object. The call to synchronize() prompts iOS to contact the cloud servers and update any values in the store that might have been changed by other iOS devices, and vice versa. This will happen eventually, but this hurries the process along when the app first starts and is the only time you'll need to call synchronize().

> **Note**   There's a reason I have you create and store a reference to the single
> NSUbiquitousKeyValueStore object, rather than just use NSUbiquitousKeyValueStore.
> defaultStore() when you need it. It will all make sense by the end of the chapter.

Now update your preserveAnnotation() function so it stores the annotation information in both the user defaults and the cloud (new code in bold).

```
func preserveAnnotation() {
    let userDefaults = NSUserDefaults.standardUserDefaults()
    if let annotation = savedAnnotation {
        userDefaults.setObject( annotation.propertyState,
                        forKey: PreferenceKey.SavedLocation.rawValue)
        cloudStore?.setDictionary( annotation.propertyState,
                            forKey: PreferenceKey.SavedLocation.rawValue)
    } else {
        userDefaults.removeObjectForKey(PreferenceKey.SavedLocation.rawValue)
        cloudStore?.removeObjectForKey(PreferenceKey.SavedLocation.rawValue)
    }
}
```

Cloud Watching

Unlike user defaults, the values in the cloud can change at any time. So, it's insufficient to simply read them when your app starts. Your app has to be prepared to react to changes whenever they occur. In addition, your iOS device doesn't always have access to the cloud. It may be in "airplane" mode, experiencing spotty cell reception, or maybe you're using your device inside a Faraday cage—for a little privacy. No matter what, your app should continue to work in an intelligent manner under all of these conditions.

The preferred solution is to mirror your cloud settings in your local user defaults. This is what preserveAnnotation() does. Whenever the location changes, both the user defaults *and* the cloud are updated with the same value. If the cloud can't be updated just now, that won't interfere with the app. If a value in the cloud should change, you should update your user defaults to match.

That brings you to the task of observing changes in the cloud. So, how do you find out when something in the cloud changes? At this point in the book, you should be chanting "notification, notification, notification" because that's exactly how you observe these changes. Your view controller observes the NSUbiquitousKeyValueStoreDidChangeExternallyNotification notification (which is also the runner-up for being the longest notification name in iOS). You'll create a new function to process those changes, and you'll need to register to receive them.

In your ViewController.swift file, find the viewDidLoad() function and augment the code that sets up the cloud store as follows (new code in bold):

```
cloudStore = NSUbiquitousKeyValueStore.defaultStore()
let center = NSNotificationCenter.defaultCenter()
center.addObserver( self,
          selector: "cloudStoreChanged:",
              name: NSUbiquitousKeyValueStoreDidChangeExternallyNotification,
            object: cloudStore)
cloudStore?.synchronize()
```

> **Caution** You must register to observe change notifications *before* calling synchronize() or your app may miss preexisting changes in the cloud.

The cloudStoreChanged(_:) function will now be called whenever something in the cloud changes. The last step is to write that function.

```
func cloudStoreChanged(notification: NSNotification) {
    let localStore = NSUserDefaults.standardUserDefaults()
    if let cloudInfo = cloudStore?.dictionaryForKey(PreferenceKey.SavedLocation.rawValue) {
        localStore.setObject(cloudInfo, forKey: PreferenceKey.SavedLocation.rawValue)
    } else {
        localStore.removeObjectForKey(PreferenceKey.SavedLocation.rawValue)
    }
    restoreAnnotation()
}
```

Whenever the cloud values change—and there's only one value, so you don't even need to worry about which one changed—it retrieves the new value and copies it into the local user defaults. It then calls restoreAnnotation() to restore the map location from the user defaults, which is now the same as the value in the cloud.

Between preserveAnnotation() and cloudStoreChanged(_:), the user defaults always has the latest (known) location. Should something interfere with cloud synchronization, the app still has a working location in user defaults and continues to function normally.

Finally, consider the restoreAnnotation() function you wrote earlier. It never considered the possibility that there was an existing map annotation. That's because the only place it was sent was when your app started. Now, it can be received at any time, to either set or clear the saved map location. Add an else clause to the end of the method to take care of that possibility (new code in bold).

```
func restoreAnnotation() {
    let userDefaults = NSUserDefaults.standardUserDefaults()
    if let state = userDefaults.dictionaryForKey(PreferenceKey.SavedLocation.rawValue) {
        let restoreAnnotation = MKPointAnnotation()
        restoreAnnotation.propertyState = state
        setAnnotation(restoreAnnotation)
    } else {
        setAnnotation(nil)
    }
}
```

Enabling iCloud

All of your iCloud code is ready to run, but there's just one problem: none of it will work. Before an app can use the iCloud servers, you must add an iCloud entitlement to your app. This, in turn, requires that you register your app's bundle identifier with Apple and obtain an entitlement certificate. These aren't complicated steps, but they are required.

Select the Pigeon project in the navigator. Make sure the Pigeon target is selected (either from the sidebar or from the pop-up menu) and switch to the General tab. Make sure your bundle identifier is a valid—that is, one that you own—reverse domain name that uniquely identifies your app (see "Launching Xcode for the First Time" in Chapter 1). This is the identifier you'll register with Apple's servers, and you can't change it once registered.

Now switch to the Capabilities tab and locate the iCloud section, as shown in Figure 18-3. Turn it on.

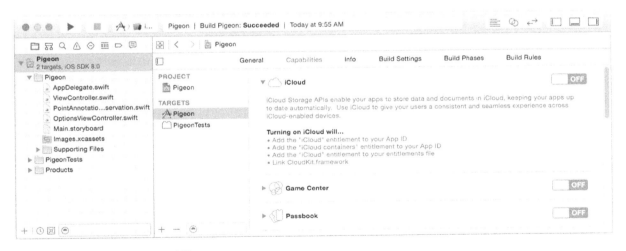

Figure 18-3. Locating iCloud capability

Choose the developer team that will be testing this app and click Choose. Xcode will register your app's unique ID with the iOS Dev Center and enable that ID for use with the iCloud service. It will then download and install the necessary entitlement certificates that permit your app to use the iCloud servers. You should now enable use of the key-value storage, as shown in Figure 18-4, if it isn't checked already. This is the iCloud service that the NSUbiquitousKeyValueStore class depends on.

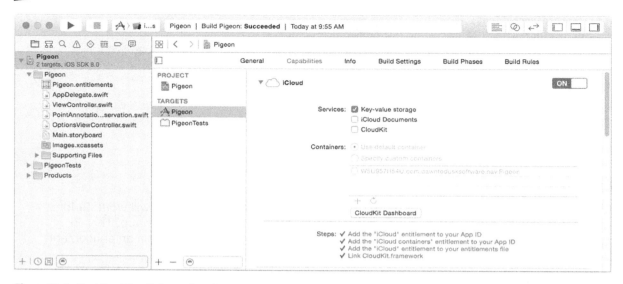

Figure 18-4. *Enabling iCloud's key-value store*

When you enabled the key-value storage, Xcode generates one ubiquity container identifier, shown under Containers in Figure 18-4. This identifier is used to collate and synchronize all of the values you put in `NSUbiquitousKeyValueStore`. Normally, you use the bundle identifier of your app—which is the default. This keeps your app's iCloud values separate from the iCloud values stored by any of the user's other apps.

> **Tip**   You're allowed to share a key-value store identifier used by another app (that you wrote and registered). This allows your app to share a single key-value store with another app. You might do this, for example, if you've created a "lite" version and a "professional" version of your app. Both apps can use the same key-value store to share and synchronize their settings.

Testing the Cloud

To test the cloud version of Pigeon, you'll need two provisioned iOS devices. The iOS simulator cannot access the ubiquitous cloud store. Both devices will need active Internet connections, be logged into the same iCloud account, and have iCloud Documents & Data turned on.

Start the Pigeon app running on both devices. Tap the "remember location" button on one device, give it a name, and wait. If everything was set up properly, an identical pin should appear on the other device, typically within a minute. Try remembering a location on the second device. Try clearing the location.

> **Tip** Even if you have only one iOS device, you can still tell if `NSUbiquitousKeyValueStore` is working by checking the value returned by the call to `synchronize()`. If `synchronize()` returns `true`, then cloud values were successfully synchronized and everything is working. If it returns `false`, then there's a problem. It could be network related. It could also mean your app's identifier, entitlements, or provisioning profiles are not correctly configured.

You don't need to have both apps running simultaneously—but that's just the coolest way to experience iCloud syncing. Launch Pigeon on one device and remember a location. Launch Pigeon on a second device. Start counting, and probably before you get to 20, you'll see the same location appear on the second device. Delete the location on the second device, and—in less than a minute—it will disappear on the first device. This is because the ubiquitous key-value store works constantly in the background, whenever it has an Internet connection, to keep all of your values in sync.

Not everyone will want their map locations shared with all of their other devices. Some users would be perfectly happy with the first, noncloud version of Pigeon. Why not make all of your users happy and give them the option?

Add a configuration setting so they can opt in to cloud synchronization, or leave it off. The question now is, where do you put that setting? Do you add it to the map options view controller? Do you create another settings button that takes the user to a second settings view? Maybe you'd add a tiny button with a little cloud icon to the map view? That would be pretty cute.

There are lots of possibilities, but I want you to think outside the box. Or, more precisely, I want you to think outside your app. Your task is to create an interface to let the user turn cloud synchronization on or off, but don't put it in your app. Confused? Don't be; it's easier than you think.

Bundle Up Your Settings

A *settings bundle* is a property list file describing one or more user default values that your users can set. See, yet another use for property lists. Users set them, not in your app, but in the Settings app that comes with every iOS system. Using a settings bundle is quite simple.

1. You create a list of value descriptions.

2. iOS turns that list into an interface that appears in the Settings app.

3. The user launches the Settings app and makes changes to their settings.

4. The updated values appear in your app's user defaults.

Settings bundles are particularly useful for settings the user isn't likely to change often and you don't want cluttering up your app's interface. For Pigeon, you're going to create a trivially simple settings bundle with one option: synchronize using iCloud. The possible values will be on or off (`true` or `false`). Let's get started.

Creating a Settings Bundle

In the Pigeon project, choose the New ➤ File command (via the File menu or by right-clicking or Control+clicking in the project navigator). In the iOS section, locate the Resource group and select the Settings Bundle template, as shown in Figure 18-5. (You'll find the finished version of this project in the `Learn iOS Development Projects` ➤ `Ch 18` ➤ `Pigeon-5` folder.)

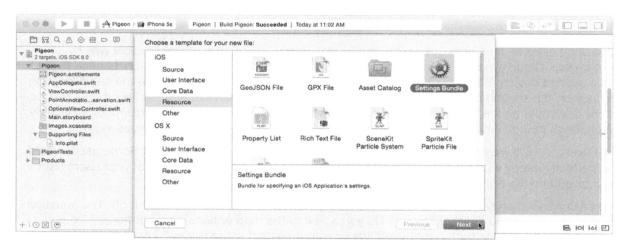

Figure 18-5. Creating a settings bundle resource

Make sure the Pigeon target is selected and add the new Settings resource to your project.

> **Caution**   Do not change the name of the new file. Your settings bundle *must* be named `Settings.bundle`, or iOS will ignore it.

A settings bundle contains one property list file named `Root.plist`. This file contains a dictionary. You can see this in Figure 18-6. The `Root.plist` file describes the settings that appear (first) when the user selects your app in the Settings app.

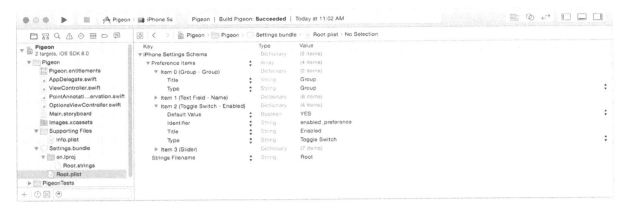

Figure 18-6. *Property list from the settings bundle template*

The dictionary contains an array value for the key `Preference Items`. That array contains a list of dictionaries. Each dictionary describes one setting or organization item. The kinds of setting you can include are listed in Table 18-2, and the organizational items are in Table 18-3. The details for each type are described in the "Implementing an iOS Settings Bundle" chapter of the *Preferences and Settings Programming Guide* that you can find in Xcode's Documentation and API Reference window.

Table 18-2. *Settings Bundle Value Types*

Settings Type	Key	Interface	Value
Text Field	PSTextFieldSpecifier	Text field	A string
Toggle Switch	PSToggleSwitchSpecifier	Toggle switch	Any two values, but YES and NO are the norm
Slider	PSSliderSpecifier	Slider	Any number within a range
Multi-value	PSMultiValueSpecifier	Table	One value in a list of values
Radio Group	PSRadioGroupSpecifier	Picker	One value in a list of values
Title	PSTitleValueSpecifier	Label	Display only (value can't be changed)

Table 18-3. *Settings Bundle Organization Types*

Settings Type	Key	Description
Group	PSGroupSpecifier	Organizes the settings that follow into a group
Child Table	PSChildPaneSpecifier	Presents a table item that, when tapped, presents another set of settings, creating a hierarchy of settings

Your settings bundle can invite the user to type in a string (such as a nickname), let them turn settings on and off, pick from a list of values (map, satellite, hybrid), or choose a number with a slider. If your app has a lot of settings, you can organize them into groups or even link to other screens with even more settings.

The values shown in Figure 18-6 present three settings in a single group named, rather unimaginatively, Group. Those settings consist of a text field, a toggle switch, and a slider.

For Pigeon, you have only one Boolean setting. Select the Root.plist file and use Xcode's property list editor to make the following changes. You're going to discard the slider and text field (you don't need them) and then repurpose the group and toggle switch.

1. Select the row Item 3 (Slider) and press the Delete key (or choose Edit ➤ Delete).

2. Select the row Item 1 (Text Field - Name) and press the delete key (or choose Edit ➤ Delete). Item 2 will now be named Item 1.

3. Expand the row Item 0 (Group - Group).

    a. Change the value of its Title to iCloud.

4. Expand the row Item 1 (Toggle Switch - Enabled) .

    a. Change the Default Value to NO.

    b. Change the Identifier to HPSyncLocations.

    c. Change the Title to Sync Locations.

Your finished settings bundle should look like the one in Figure 18-7.

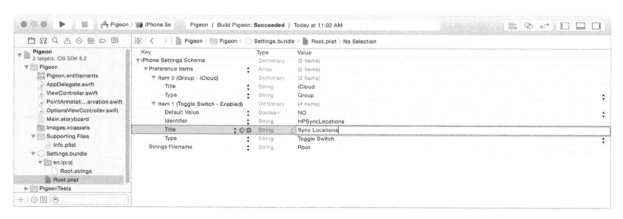

Figure 18-7. Pigeon settings bundle

Using Your Settings Bundle Values

Your settings bundle is complete. All that's left is to put the values you just defined to work in your app. Select the ViewController.swift file and add one more enum case (new code in bold).

```
enum PreferenceKey: String {
    case MapType = "HPMapType"
    case Heading = "HPFollowHeading"
    case SavedLocation = "HPLocation"
    case CloudSync = "HPSyncLocations"
}
```

Locate the viewDidLoad() function, and add the following conditional around your cloud store setup code (new code in bold):

```
if userDefaults.boolForKey(PreferenceKey.CloudSync.rawValue) {
    cloudStore = NSUbiquitousKeyValueStore.defaultStore()
    let center = NSNotificationCenter.defaultCenter()
    center.addObserver( self,
            selector: "cloudStoreChanged:",
                name: NSUbiquitousKeyValueStoreDidChangeExternallyNotification,
              object: cloudStore)
    cloudStore?.synchronize()
}
```

Now your cloudStore object will only get set up and initialized if the user has set the .CloudSync toggle in the Settings app.

That's it! If you're asking "But what about all of those places in the code that store values into cloudStore?" you don't have to worry about those. Your existing code takes advantage of Swift optionals that can ignore functions called on nil objects. If the .CloudSync value is false, cloudStore never gets set and remains nil. When you suffix an object's name with ? before a property or function call (as in cloudStore?.setDictionary(...)), Swift first checks to see whether cloudStore contains a reference. If it's a valid object, it calls the function. But if it's nil, it does nothing and skips to the next statement. The net effect is that, with cloudStore set to nil, Pigeon doesn't make any changes to iCloud's ubiquitous key-value store, and it won't receive any notifications of changes. For a complete explanation, see the "Optional Chaining" section in Chapter 20.

Testing Your Settings Bundle

Run Pigeon, as shown in Figure 18-8. If you still have two iOS devices connected, you can verify that your app is no longer saving the map location to the cloud. Each app is functioning independently of the other.

Figure 18-8. Testing the settings bundle

In Xcode, stop your app(s). This will return you to the springboard (the second image in Figure 18-8). Locate your Settings app and launch it. Scroll down until you find the Pigeon app (the third image in Figure 18-8). Tap it, and you'll see the settings you defined (on the right in Figure 18-8).

Turn your Sync Locations setting on—do this in both devices—and run your apps again. This time, Pigeon uses iCloud synchronization to share the map location.

Summary

Pigeon can no longer be accused of being a bird-brained app! Not only will it remember the location the user saved but also the map style and tracking mode they last set. In doing this, you learned how to store property list values into the user defaults, how to convert non–property list objects into ones suitable to store, and how to get them back out again. More importantly, you understand the best times to store and retrieve those values.

You learned how to handle the situation where a user defaults value is missing and how to create and register a set of default values. You also used user defaults to preserve the view controller states, which gives your app a sense of persistence. You did this by leveraging the powerful view controller restoration facility, built into iOS.

You also took flight into the clouds, sharing and synchronizing changes using the iCloud storage service. iCloud integration adds a compelling dimension to your app that anyone with more than one iOS device will appreciate. And if that wasn't enough, you defined settings the user can access outside of your app.

You've taken another important step in creating apps that act the way users expect. But it was a tiny step. User defaults, and particularly the ubiquitous key-value store, are only suitable for small amounts of information. To learn how to store "big data," step into the next chapter.

EXERCISE

You may have noticed a flaw in the last version of Pigeon—which I cleverly sidestepped by having you stop your app in Xcode before changing the Sync Location setting in the Settings app. Knowing what you now know about app states, the problem should be obvious.

Pigeon only examines the value of the `.CloudSync` value when it first starts. If a Pigeon user switches to the Settings app, changes the Sync Location setting, and then immediately returns to Pigeon, Pigeon is probably still running. It would have been moved the background state and suspended for a bit, but would be reactivated when the user returned. The bug is that Pigeon doesn't check the value of `.CloudSync` again and won't know that it has changed.

There are a couple of ways of solving this. One would be to add code to the `applicationWillEnterForeground(_:)` app delegate function. The solution I picked was to observe the `NSUserDefaultsDidChangeNotification`, posted by `NSUserDefaults`. Remember that the values in a settings bundle make changes to your app's user defaults, and you can observe those changes via the notification center.

You'll find my solution to this problem in the `Learn iOS Development Projects` ➤ `Ch 18` ➤ `Pigeon E1` folder. See if you can think of a third—very similar but more targeted—solution. (Hint, read the documentation for the `applicationWillEnterForeground(_:)` method.)

Chapter 19

Doc, You Meant Storage

If you want your iOS app to store more than a few tidbits of information, you need documents. iOS provides a powerful document framework that brings data storage into the 21ˢᵗ century. The iOS document (UIDocument) class takes care of, or lets you easily implement, modern features such as autosaving, versioning, and cloud storage. In the process, you'll finally learn how to archive objects. In this chapter, you will do the following:

- Create a custom document object
- Use a document object as your app's data model
- Learn how to archive and unarchive your data model objects
- Design a document that can be loaded or saved incrementally
- Handle asynchronous document loading
- Manage document changes and autosaving

You'll find numerous "how-to" guides for using UIDocument because, quite frankly, it's a complicated class to use. There are a lot moving parts and more than a few details you must pay attention to. This has led many developers to ignore UIDocument and "roll their own" document storage solution. I beg you not to do that. Conquering UIDocument isn't *that* hard, and the rewards are substantial.

UIDocument can seem overwhelming—until you understand *why* UIDocument works the way it does. Once you understand some of the reasoning behind its architecture and what it's accomplishing for you, the code you need to write will all make sense. So in this chapter, you'll concentrate not on just the how but the why. By the end, you'll be using UIDocument like a pro.

Document Overview

The word *document* has many meanings, but in this context a *document* is a data file (or package) containing user-generated content that your app opens, modifies, and ultimately saves to persistent storage. We're all used to documents on desktop computer systems. In mobile devices, the concept of a document takes a backseat, but it's still there and in much the same form. In a few apps, like the Pages word processing app, the familiar document metaphor appears front and center. You launch the app, see a collection of your named documents, and choose one to work on; the document opens, and you begin typing. In other apps, it's not as clear that you're using individual documents, and some apps hide the mechanics of documents entirely. You can choose any of these approaches for your app. iOS provides the tools needed for whatever interface you want, but it doesn't dictate one.

This flexibility lets you add document storage and management to your app completely behind the scenes, loosely coupled to your user interface, or echoing the legacy document metaphor of desktop computer systems. Whatever you decide to do with your interface, the place to start is the UIDocument class. Here are the basic steps to using UIDocument in your app:

1. Create a custom subclass of UIDocument.

2. Design an interface for choosing, naming, and sharing documents (optional).

3. Convert your app's data model to and from data that's suitable for permanent storage.

4. Handle asynchronous reading of documents.

5. Move documents into the cloud (optional).

6. Observe change notifications from shared documents and handle conflicts (optional).

7. Implement undo/redo capabilities, or at least track changes to a document.

You're going to revisit the MyStuff app and modify it so it stores all of those cool items, their descriptions, and even their pictures, in a document. There are no interface changes to MyStuff this time. The only thing your users will notice is that their stuff is still there when they relaunch your app!

Where, Oh Where, Do My Documents Go?

So, where do you store documents in iOS? Here's the short answer: Store your documents in your app's private Documents folder and optionally in the cloud.

The long answer is that you can store your documents anywhere your app has access to, but the only place that makes much sense is your app's private Documents folder. Each iOS app has access to a cluster of private folders called its *sandbox*. The Documents folder is one of these and is reserved, by iOS, for your app's documents. The contents of this folder are automatically backed up by iTunes. If you also want to exchange documents through iTunes, your documents must be stored in the Documents folder.

This is somewhat different from what you're used to on most desktop computer systems, where apps will let you load and save documents to any location and your Documents folder is freely shared by all of your apps. In iOS, an app has access only to the files in its sandbox, and these directories are inaccessible to other apps or to the user—unless you deliberately expose the Documents folder to iTunes.

> **Note**   If you're interested in what the other folders in the sandbox are and what they're used for, read the section "About the iOS File System" in the *File System Programming Guide*, which you can find in Xcode's Documentation and API Reference window.

For MyStuff, you're going to store a single document in the Documents folder. You won't, however, provide any user interface for this document. The document will be automatically opened when the app starts, and any changes made by the user will be automatically saved there. Even though you'll be using the standard document classes and storing your data in the Documents folder, the entire process will be invisible to the user.

That's not to say that you can't, or shouldn't, provide an interface that lets your users see what documents are in their Documents folder. A typical interface would display the document names, possibly a preview, and allow the user to open, rename, and delete them. You could do that by using a table view, using a collection view, or even using a page view controller. iOS 8 introduces a standardized interface that does just that. If you want a simple document picker interface, which also works with iCloud Drive, start with the UIDocumentPickerViewController class. If you still want to design your own interface, iOS also provides a new NSURLThumbnail resource—see NSURL.getReso urceValue(_:,forKey:,error:) for retrieving URL resources—that makes displaying your document thumbnails simple.

But, as I said, you don't need to expose the document structure to MyStuff users. You do need to create a custom subclass of UIDocument and define where and how your document gets stored, which sounds like the place to get started.

MyStuff on Documents

Pick up with the version of MyStuff at the end of Chapter 7, where you added an image for each item. Drag a new Swift file from the file template library into your project (or choose the New File command). Name the new file ThingsDocument and make it a subclass of UIDocument with the following code:

```
import UIKit

class ThingsDocument: UIDocument {
}
```

The first thing you're going to add is a constant with the name of your one and only document. Add this outside the ThingsDocument class definition so it's a global constant.

```
let ThingsDocumentName = "Things I Own.mystuff"
```

Now add a computed property to locate your app's Document folder and return your single document file as a URL.

```
class var documentURL: NSURL {
    let fileManager = NSFileManager.defaultManager()
    if let documentsDirURL = fileManager.URLForDirectory( .DocumentDirectory,
                                          inDomain: .UserDomainMask,
                                    appropriateForURL: nil,
                                            create: true,
                                            error: nil) {
        return documentsDirURL.URLByAppendingPathComponent(ThingsDocumentName)
    }
    assertionFailure("Unable to determine document storage location")
}
```

Your new documentURL property returns an NSURL object with the filesystem location of the one and only document used by your MyStuff app, named Things I own.mystuff.

The important method here is the URLForDirectory(_:,inDomain:,appropriateForURL:,create:, error:) function. This is one of a handful of functions used to locate key iOS directories, like the Documents directory in your app's sandbox. The .DocumentDirectory constant tells which one—of the half-dozen or so designated directories—you're interested in. To locate directories in your app's sandbox, specify the .UserDomainMask. The create flag tells the file manager to create the directory if it doesn't already exist. This was gratuitous because the Documents directory is created when your app is installed and should always exist, but it doesn't hurt to say "yes" anyway.

> **Caution**   Do not "hard-code" paths to standard iOS directories, using constants like "~/Documents/".
> Use functions like URLsForDirectory(_:,inDomain:) to determine the path of well-known directories.
> The standard directory locations change from time to time, and you don't want to make assumptions about
> their names or paths.

With the URL of your Documents folder, your code then appends the document's name, creating a complete path to where your document is, or will be, stored.

Now write a function to open your document. MyStuff isn't going to present a document interface. When it starts, it either creates an empty document or re-opens the existing document. Consolidate that logic into a single function, immediately after the documentURL property.

```
class func document(atURL url: NSURL = ThingsDocument.documentURL) -> ThingsDocument {
    let fileManager = NSFileManager.defaultManager()
    if let document = ThingsDocument(fileURL: ThingsDocument.documentURL) {
        if fileManager.fileExistsAtPath(url.path!) {
            document.openWithCompletionHandler(nil)
            }
        } else {
            document.saveToURL(url, forSaveOperation: .ForCreating, completionHandler: nil)
        }
```

```
        return document
    }
    assertionFailure("Unable to create ThingsDocument for \(url)")
}
```

This function creates a new instance of your `ThingsDocument` object at the given (file) URL. If you don't specify a file URL, it defaults to the `documentURL` property you just defined. It uses the file manager to determine whether a document at that location already exists (`fileExistsAtPath(_:)`). If it does, it calls the document's `openWithCompletionHandler(_:)` function to open the document and read the data it contains. If it doesn't exist, it calls the `saveToURL(_:,forSaveOperation:,co mpletionHandler:)` function to save the document. Since the document object was just created, it's empty, and saving it creates a new (empty) document. The opened document object is then returned to the sender.

> **Tip**   The name of MyStuff's document is irrelevant because no one (except its developer) will ever see it. If, however, you do want your users to have access to the documents your app's `Documents` folder, all you have to do is add the `UIFileSharingEnabled` key (with a value of YES) to your app's `info.plist`. This flag tells iTunes to expose the documents stored in the `Documents` folder to the user. Through iTunes, the user can browse, download, upload, and delete documents in that folder. See the "App-Related Resources" chapter of the *iOS App Programming Guide*. Also check out *Technical Q&A #1699* (QA1699). It describes how to selectively share some documents through iTunes, while keeping other documents hidden.

Supplying Your Document's Data

In your subclass of `UIDocument`, you are required to override two functions: `contentsForType(_:,error:)` and `loadFromContents(_:,ofType:,error:)`. These two methods translate your app's data model objects into a form that `UIDocument` can save and later converts that saved data back into the data model objects your app needs.

This is also where implementing `UIDocument` gets interesting. The key is to understand what `UIDocument` is doing for you and what `UIDocument` expects from `contentsForType(_:,error:)` and `lo adFromContents(_:,ofType:,error:)`. There's a strict division of responsibilities.

- `UIDocument` implements that actual storage and retrieval of your document's data.

- `contentsForType(_:,error:)` and `loadFromContents(_:,ofType:,error:)` provide the translation between your data model objects and a serialized version of that same information.

`UIDocument` might be storing your document on a filesystem. It might be storing your document in the cloud. It might be transferring your document over a USB connection. Someday it might store your document on a wireless electronic wallet you carry around on a key fob. I don't know, and you shouldn't care. Let `UIDocument` worry about where and how your document's data gets stored.

When UIDocument wants to save your document, it calls your contentsForType(_:,error:) function. Your implementation should convert your data model objects into data suitable for storage. UIDocument takes the returned data and stores it on the filesystem, in the cloud, or wherever.

When it's time to read the document, UIDocument reverses the process. It first reacquires the data (from wherever it was saved) and passes that to loadFromContents(_:,ofType:,error:), which has the job of turning it back into the data model objects of your app.

The $64,000 question is "How do you convert your data model objects into bytes that UIDocument can store?" That is a fantastic question, and the answer will range from stunningly simple to treacherously complex. Broadly, you have four options.

- Serialize everything into a single NSData object
- Describe a multipart document using file wrapper objects
- Back your document with Core Data
- Implement your own storage solution

The first solution is the simplest and suitable for many document types. Using string encoding, property list serialization, or object archiving (which you'll learn shortly), convert your data model object(s) into a single array of bytes. Your contentsForType(_:,error:) function then returns those bytes as an NSData object that UIDocument stores somewhere. Later, UIDocument retrieves that data and passes an NSData object to your loadFromContents(_:,ofType:,error:) function, which unarchives/deserializes/decodes it back into the original object(s). If this describes your app's needs, then congratulations—you're pretty much done with this part of your UIDocument implementation!

Your MyStuff app is a little more complicated. It's cumbersome to convert all of the app's data—descriptions and images—into a single stream of bytes. Images are big and time-consuming to encode. Not only will it take a long time to save the document, the entire document will have to be read into memory and converted back into image objects before the user can use the app. No one wants to wait ten seconds, and certainly not a whole minute, to open your app!

The solution MyStuff will employ is to archive the descriptions of the items (much like the first solution) into a single NSData object but store the images in individual files inside a package. A *package* is a directory containing multiple files that appears, and acts, like a single file to the user. All iOS and OS X apps are packages, for example.

Wrapping Up Your Data

You might be seeing the glimmer of a conundrum. Or, maybe you don't. Don't worry if you missed it, because it's a really subtle problem. The concept behind contentsForType(_:,error:) is that it returns the raw data that represents your document—just the data. The code in contentsForType(_:,error:) can't know how that data gets stored, nor does it do the storing. Creating a design that states "images will be stored in individual files" is a nonstarter because contentsForType(_:,error:) doesn't deal with files. The returned data might end up being stored in something that doesn't even resemble a file.

So, how does contentsForType(_:,error:) return an object that describes not one, but a collection of, individual data blobs,[1] one of which contains the archived objects and others that contain individual image data? Well, it just so happens that iOS provides a tool for this very purpose. It's called a file wrapper, and it brings us to the second method for providing document data.

A *file wrapper* (NSFileWrapper) object is an abstraction of the data stored in one or more files. There are three types of file wrappers: regular, directory, and link. Conceptually, these are equivalent to a single data file, a filesystem directory, and a filesystem symbolic link, respectively. File wrappers allow your app to describe a collection of named data blobs, organized within a hierarchy of named directories. If this sounds just like files and folders, it should. And when your UIDocument is stored in a file URL, that's exactly what these file wrappers will become. But by maintaining this abstraction, UIDocument can just as easily transfer this data collection over a network or convert the wrappers into the records of a database.

Using Wrappers

Using file wrappers isn't terribly difficult. A *regular file wrapper* represents an array of bytes, like NSData. A *directory file wrapper* (or just *directory wrapper*) contains any number of other file wrappers.

One significant difference between wrappers and files/folders is that a wrapper is not required to have a unique name. A wrapper has a preferred name and a key. Its *key* is the string that uniquely identifies the wrapper, just as a filename uniquely identifies a file. Its *name* or *preferred name* is the string it would like to be identified as. When you create a wrapper, you assign it a preferred name. If you then add it to a directory wrapper and its preferred name is unique, its key and preferred name will be the same. If, however, there is already one or more wrappers with the same name, the directory wrapper will generate a unique key for the just-added wrapper. In other words, it's valid to add multiple wrappers with the same name to the same directory wrapper. Just be aware that adding a wrapper does not replace, or overwrite, an existing wrapper with the same name, as it would on a filesystem. And if you want to refer to it again, you'll need to keep track of its key.

Your contentsForType(_:,error:) function will create a single directory wrapper (docWrrapper) that contains all of the other regular file wrappers. There will be one regular file wrapper with the archived version of your data model objects. Each item that has a picture will store its image as another file wrapper. You'll modify MyWhatsit to store the image in the document when the user adds a picture and get the image from the document when it needs it again.

Incremental Document Updates

Organizing your document into wrappers confers a notable feature to your app: incremental document loading and updates. If your user has added 100 items to your MyStuff app, your document package (when saved to a filesystem) will consist of folding containing 101 files: one archive file and 100 image files. If the user replaces the picture of their astrolabe with a better one, only a single file wrapper needs to be updated. UIDocument understands this. When it's time to save the document again, UIDocument will only rewrite that single file in the package. This makes for terribly fast, and efficient, updates to large documents. These are good qualities for your app.

---

[1]Blob is actually a database term meaning Binary Large Object, sometimes written BLOb.

Similarly, file wrapper data isn't read until it's requested. In other words, file wrappers are lazy. When you open a UIDocument constructed from file wrappers, the data for each individual wrapper stays where it is until your app wants it. For your images, that means your app doesn't have to read all 100 images files when it starts. It can retrieve just the images it needs at that moment. Again, this means your app can get started quickly and does the minimum work required to display your interface.

Constructing Your Wrappers

Select the ThingsDocument.swift file. Start by adding two constants and two instance variables.

```
let thingsPreferredName = "things.data"
let imagePreferredName = "image.png"

var docWrapper = NSFileWrapper(directoryWithFileWrappers: [:])
var things = [MyWhatsit]()
```

The two constants define the preferred wrapper names for the archived MyWhatsit objects and any image added to the directory wrapper. The docWrapper instance variable is the single directory wrapper that will contain all of your other wrappers. For all intents and purposes, docWrapper is your document's data. The things variable is the array of MyWhatsit objects that constitute your data model.

> **Note** Later, you'll replace the things array in MasterViewController with your new ThingsDocument. The document object will become the data model for your view controller.

Now add the crucial contentsForType(_:,error:) function.

```
override func contentsForType(typeName: String, ↵
                    error outError: NSErrorPointer) -> AnyObject? {
    if let wrapper = docWrapper.fileWrappers[thingsPreferredName] as? NSFileWrapper {
        docWrapper.removeFileWrapper(wrapper)
    }
    let thingsData = NSKeyedArchiver.archivedDataWithRootObject(things)
    docWrapper.addRegularFileWithContents(thingsData, preferredFilename: thingsPreferredName)
    return docWrapper
}
```

This function is called when UIDocument wants to create or save your document. The first step handles the second case, where you're overwriting an existing wrapper; it checks to see whether the things.data subwrapper already exists and deletes it. Remember that adding another things.data wrapper won't replace the previous one.

The next step is to archive (serialize) all of the MyWhatsit objects into a portable NSData object. I'll explain how that happens in the next section. The resulting data object is then passed to the addReg ularFileWithContents(_:,preferredFilename:) function. This is a convenience method that creates a new regular file wrapper, containing the bytes in thingsData, and adds it to the directory wrapper with the preferred name. This method saves you from explicitly coding those steps.

Finally, you return the directory wrapper, containing all of the data in your document, to UIDocument. Now you might be asking, "But what about all of the image data? Where does that get created?" That's a really good question. Image data is represented by other regular file wrappers in the same directory wrapper. When the document is first created, there are no images, so the directory wrapper only contains things.data. As the user adds pictures to the data model, each image will add a new wrapper to docWrapper. When your document is saved again, the file wrappers containing the images are already in docWrapper! Each regular file wrapper knows if it has been altered or updated, and UIDocument is smart enough to figure out which files need to be written and which ones are already current.

Interpreting Your Wrappers

The reverse of the previous process occurs when your document is opened. UIDocument obtains that data saved in the document and then calls your loadFromContents(_:,ofType:,error:) function. This function's job is to turn the document data back into your data model. Add this function immediately after your contentsForType(_:,error:).

```
override func loadFromContents(contents: AnyObject,⏎
                    ofType typeName: String,⏎
                    error outError: NSErrorPointer) -> Bool {
    if let contentWrapper = contents as? NSFileWrapper {
        if let thingsWrapper = contentWrapper.fileWrappers[thingsPreferredName]⏎
                                                    as? NSFileWrapper {
            if let data = thingsWrapper.regularFileContents {
                things = NSKeyedUnarchiver.unarchiveObjectWithData(data) as [MyWhatsit]
                for thing in things {
                    thing.imageStorage = self
                }
                docWrapper = contentWrapper
                return true
            }
        }
    }
    return false
}
```

The contents parameter is the object that encapsulates your document's data. It's always going to be the same (class of) object you returned from contentsForType(_:,error:). If you adopted the first method and returned a single NSData object, the contents parameter will contain an NSData object, with the same data. Since MyStuff elected to use the file wrapper technique, contents is an equivalent directory wrapper object to the one you returned earlier.

The first step is to save contents in docWrapper; you'll need it, both to read image wrappers and to later save the document again. The rest of the method finds the things.data wrapper that contains the archived MyWhatsit object array. It immediately retrieves the data stored in that wrapper and unarchives it, re-creating your data model objects.

The loadFromContents(_:,ofType:,error:) function must return true if it was successful or false if there were problems interpreting the document. If the wrapper contained a things.data wrapper and the data in that wrapper was successfully converted back into an array of MyWhatsit objects, the method assumes the document is valid and returns true.

This, almost, concludes the work needed to save, and later open, your new document. There's one glaring hole: the array of MyWhatsit objects can't be archived! Let's fix that now.

OTHER STORAGE ALTERNATIVES

The last two document storage solutions available to you are Core Data and do it yourself (DIY). DIY is one I rarely find appealing. It should be your last resort, because you'll be forced to deal with all of the tasks, both mundane and exceptional, that UIDocument normally handles for you. My advice is work very hard to make one of the first three solutions work. If that fails, you can perform your own document storage handling. Consult the "Advanced Overrides" section of UIDocument's documentation.

One of the most interesting document solutions is Core Data. iOS includes a fast and efficient relational database engine (SQLite) with language-level support. Core Data is far beyond the scope of this book, but it's an incredibly powerful tool if your app's data fits better into a database than a text file. (It's a shame I don't have enough pages because MyStuff would have made a perfect Core Data app.)

One of the huge advantages of using Core Data is that document management is essentially done for you. You don't have to do much beyond using the UIManagedDocument class (a subclass of UIDocument). Many of the features in this chapter that you will write code to support—incremental document updating, lazy document loading, archiving and unarchiving of your data model objects, background document loading and saving, cloud synchronization, and so on—are all provided "for free" by UIManagedDocument.

The prerequisite, of course, is that you must first base your app on Core Data. Your data model objects must be NSManagedObjects, you must design a schema for your database, and you have to understand the ins and outs of object-oriented database (OODB) technology. But beyond that (!), it's child's play.

Archiving Objects

In Chapter 18 you learned all about serialization. Serialization turns a graph of property list objects into a stream of bytes (either in XML or in binary format) that can be stored in files, exchanged with other processes, transmitted to other computer systems, and so on. On the receiving end, those bytes are turned back into an equivalent set of property list objects, ready to be used.

Archiving is serialization's big sister. *Archiving* serializes (the computer science term) a graph of objects that all adopt the NSCoding protocol. This is a much larger set of objects than the property-list objects.[2] More importantly, you can adopt the NSCoding protocol in classes you develop. Your custom objects can then be archived right along with other objects. This is exactly what needs to happen to your MyWhatsit class.

---

[2]All property list objects adopt NSCoding. Property list objects are, therefore, a subset of the archivable objects.

Adopting NSCoding

The first step to archiving a graph of objects is to make sure that every object adopts the NSCoding protocol. If one doesn't, you either need to eliminate it from the graph or change it so it does. In MyWhatsit.swift, change the class declaration so it adopts NSCoding (new code in bold).

```
class MyWhatsit: NSObject, NSCoding {
```

> **Note** You adopt NSCoding by first making your class a subclass of NSObject, the Objective-C base class. You do this for the same reason you did in Chapter 8, making your class compatible with Key-Value Observing; NSObject defines key methods that NSCoding depends on. Note that the @objc Swift keyword would accomplish the same.

The NSCoding protocol requires a class to implement an initializer, init(coder:), and an instance function, encodeWithCoder(_:). The initializer creates a new object from data that was previously archived. The function creates the archive data from the existing object. Both of these processes work through an NSCoder object. The NSCoder object does the work of serializing (encoding), and later deserializing (decoding), your object's properties.

The coder identifies each property value of your object using a key. Define those keys now by adding these constants to your MyWhatsit class.

```
let nameKey = "name"
let locationKey = "location"
```

Now you can write the initializer function.

```
required init(coder decoder: NSCoder) {
    name = decoder.decodeObjectForKey(nameKey) as String
    location = decoder.decodeObjectForKey(locationKey) as String
}
```

init(coder:) initializes all of the new object's properties from the values stored in the coder object. In this case, both of the values are string objects. Besides objects, coder objects can directly encode integer, floating-point, Boolean, and other primitive types. UIKit adds extensions to NSCoder to encode point, rectangle, size, affine transforms, and other commonly encoded data structures. Now write your initializer's mirror image.

```
func encodeWithCoder(coder: NSCoder) {
    coder.encodeObject(name, forKey: nameKey)
    coder.encodeObject(location, forKey: locationKey)
}
```

Translation in the other direction is provided by your encodeWithCoder(_:) function. This function preserves the current values of its persistent properties in the coder object. Your MyWhatsit objects are now ready to participate in the archiving process.

SUBCLASSING AN <NSCODING> CLASS

When you subclass a class that already adopts NSCoding, you do things a little differently. Your init(coder:) function will look like this:

```
required init(coder decoder: NSCoder) {
    super.init(coder: decoder)
    // subclass decoding goes here
}
```

And your encodeWithCoder(_:) function should look like this:

```
override func encodeWithCoder(coder: NSCoder) {
    super.encodeWithCoder(coder)
    // subclass encoding goes here
}
```

Your superclass already encodes and decodes its properties. Your subclass must allow the superclass to do that and then encode and decode any additional properties defined in the subclass.

Archiving and Unarchiving Objects

Once your class has adopted NSCoding, it's ready to be archived. When you want to flatten your object into bytes, use code like this:

```
let data = NSKeyedArchiver.archivedDataWithRootObject(myObject)
```

The NSKeyedArchiver class is the archiving engine. It creates an NSCoder object and then proceeds to call the root object's (things') encodeWithCoder(_:) function. That object is responsible for preserving its content in the coder object. Most likely, it will call its encodeObject(_:,forKey:) function for objects it refers to. Those objects then receive an encodeWithCoder(_:) call, and the process repeats until all of the objects have been encoded. The only limitation is that every object involved must adopt NSCoding.

When you want your objects back again, you use the NSKeyedUnarchiver class, like this:

```
myObject = NSKeyedUnarchiver.unarchiveObjectWithData(data)
```

During the encoding process, the coder recorded the class of each object. The decoder then uses that information to invoke the object's init(coder:) initializer. The resulting object is the same class and has the same property values as the originally encoded object.

> **Note** The predecessor to keyed archiving was *sequential archiving*. You may occasionally see references to sequential archiving, but it is not used in iOS.

The Archiving Serialization Smackdown

Now that you've added both serialization (property lists) and archiving (NSCoding objects) to your repertoire, I'd like to take a moment to compare and contrast the two. Table 19-1 summarizes their major features.

Table 19-1. Serialization vs. Archiving

Feature	Serialization	Archiving
Object Graph	Property list objects only	Objects that adopt NSCoding
XML	Yes	No
Portability	Cocoa or Cocoa Touch apps, or any system that can parse the XML version	Only another process that includes all of the original classes
Editors	Yes	No

Property lists are much more limited in what you can store in them but make up for that in the number of ways you can store, share, and edit them. Use property lists when your values need to be understood by other processes, particularly processes that don't include your custom classes. An example is the settings bundle you created in Chapter 18. The Settings app will never include any of your custom Objective-C classes, yet you were able to define, exchange, and incorporate those settings into your app using property lists. Property lists are the "universal" language of values.

Archiving, by contrast, can encode a vast number of classes, and you can add your own classes to that roster by adopting the NSCoding protocol. Everything you create in Interface Builder is encoded using keyed archiving. When you load an Interface Builder file in your application, NSKeyedUnarchiver is busy translating that file back into the objects you defined. Archiving is extremely flexible and has long reach, which is why it's the technology of choice for storing your data model objects in a document.

Why don't we use archiving for everything? When unarchiving, every class recorded in the archive must exist. So, forget about trying to read your MyStuff document using another app or program that doesn't include your MyWhatsit class—you can't do it. Archives are, for the most part, opaque. There are no general-purpose editors for archives like there are for property lists, and there is no facility for turning archive data into XML documents.

Serialization, Meet Archiving

Now that you have a feel for the benefits and limitations of archiving and serialization, I'm going to show you a really handy trick for combining the two. (You may have already figured this out, but you could at least pretend to be surprised.) NSData is a property list object. The result of archiving a graph of NSCoding objects is an NSData object. Do you see where this is going?

By first archiving your objects into an NSData object, you can store non-property-list objects in a property list, like user defaults! Your code would look like this:

```
let userDefaults = NSUserDefaults.standardUserDefaults()
let data = NSKeyedArchiver.archivedDataWithRootObject(dataModel)
userDefaults.setObject(data, forKey: "data_model")
```

What you've done is archive your data model objects into an NSData object, which can be stored in a property list. To retrieve them again, reverse the process.

```
let modelData = userDefaults.objectForKey("data_model") as NSData
dataModel = NSKeyedUnarchiver.unarchiveObjectWithData(modelData) as DataClass
```

The disadvantages of this technique are the same ones that apply to archiving in general. The process retrieving the objects must to be able to unarchive them. Also, any editors or other programs that examine your property values will just see a blob of data. Contrast this to the technique you used in Pigeon to convert the MKAnnotation object into a dictionary. Those property list values (the location's name, longitude, and latitude) are easily interpreted and could even be edited by another program.

Caution   Don't go crazy with this technique. Services like NSUserDefaults and NSUbiquitousKeyValueStore are designed to store *small* morsels of information. Don't abuse them by storing multimegabyte-sized NSData objects that you've created using the archiver.

I think that's enough about archiving and property lists. It's time to get back to the business of getting MyStuff documentified.

Document, Meet Your Data Model

Where were we? Oh, that's right, you created a UIDocument class and wrote all of the code needed to translate your data model objects into document data and back again. The next step is to make your ThingsDocument object the data model for MasterViewController.

You're doing this because your document needs to be aware of *any* changes to your data model, which I'll explain in the "Tracking Changes" section that follows. Right now, your view controller is the object manipulating your data model (the things array). This isn't good MVC design; your controller is doing some of the data model's job. But it wasn't bad enough to warrant creating another data model class just to encapsulate changes to the things array. With documents in the mix, we just crossed that line, so it's time to refactor. As I've said at the end of Chapter 8, it's OK to venture off the MVC path a little when it keeps your code simple. Just know where you did and be prepared to get back on track when you find yourself in the weeds.

> **Note** In a "big" app, you'd probably create a custom data model class that was separate from your `UIDocument` class. Both the document and view controller would then observe changes to the data model object. In MVC-speak, you'd have a *data model* and a *data model controller* (the document object). Both the document and the view controller would connect to the same data model object. For MyStuff, I'm having you combine the data model and document into a single class for the same reason the data model and view controller were entangled before. It simplifies the design and reduces the amount of code you have to write.

Your current `MasterViewController` is using an array as its data model object. The array object provides a number of methods that the view controller is using to manage it, specifically counting, adding, and removing objects in the array. `UIDocument` doesn't have any of these methods—because it's not a data model. Turn it into a data model by replicating the functions the view controller needs. Select ThingsDocument.`swift` and add the following functions:

```
var whatsitCount: Int {
    return things.count
}

func whatsitAtIndex(index: Int) -> MyWhatsit {
    return things[index]
}

func indexOfWhatsit(thing: MyWhatsit) -> Int? {
    for (index,value) in enumerate(things) {
        if value === thing {
            return index
        }
    }
    return nil
}

func removeWhatsitAtIndex(index: Int) {
    things.removeAtIndex(index)
}

func anotherWhatsit() -> (object: MyWhatsit, index: Int) {
    let newThing = MyWhatsit(name: "My Item \(whatsitCount+1)")
    things.append(newThing)
    return (newThing, things.count-1)
}
```

The purpose of these methods should be obvious. The view controller will now call these functions to count the number of items, get the item at a specific index, discover the index of an existing item, remove an item, or create a new item. The next step is to change your view controller to use this interface. Select your `MasterViewController.swift` file. Replace the `var things: [MyWhatsit]...` declaration with the following:

```
var document = ThingsDocument.document()
```

Your document object is now your data model. You also removed the code that created the fake items for testing. Now that your app is using documents, it will save the items as you create them. Now you need to go through your view controller code and replace every reference to the old `things` array with equivalent code for your document.

> **Tip**   Your file is now awash with compiler errors. Isn't that great? I use this technique all the time. When I need to redefine or repurpose a property value, I deliberately change the name of the property/variable—if only temporarily. Xcode will immediately flag all references to the old name as an error. This becomes my road map to where I need to make my changes. If I liked the original property name, I'll restore it once everything is working.

The rest of the work is mostly replacing code that used `things` with code that will use `document`. Find the `insertNewObject(_:)` function and change it so it reads as follows (modified code in bold):

```
func insertNewObject(sender: AnyObject) {
    let fresh = document.anotherWhatsit()
    let indexPath = NSIndexPath(forRow: fresh.index, inSection: 0)
    self.tableView.insertRowsAtIndexPaths([indexPath], withRowAnimation: .Automatic)
}
```

The document object now takes care of creating a new `MyWhatsit` object—you'll understand why when you work on the code for `MyWhatsit` images. The code also gets the index of the new object from the document, rather than assuming that it was inserted at the beginning or end of the array. This is a smart change because the `anotherWhatsit()` function actually might change its mind someday. And if you ever altered that, this code would still work.

The other "big" change is in the `whatsitDidChange(_:)` function. Alter it as shown (modified code in bold):

```
func whatsitDidChange(notification: NSNotification) {
    if let changedThing = notification.object as? MyWhatsit {
        if let index = document.indexOfWhatsit(changedThing) {
            let path = NSIndexPath(forItem: index, inSection: 0)
            tableView.reloadRowsAtIndexPaths([path], withRowAnimation: .None)
        }
    }
}
```

The loop that looked for the object in the array is replaced with a function call that does the same. The rest of the changes are so mundane that I've summarized them here. (Hint: just follow the trail of compiler errors and replace the `things` statements with equivalent document statements.)

- In `tableView(_:,numberOfRowsInSection:)` the statement

  `things.count` becomes `document.whatsitCount`.

- In `tableView(_:,cellForRowAtIndexPath:)` and `prepareForSeque(_:)` the

  `things[indexPath.row]` expression becomes `document.whatsitAtIndex(indexPath.row)`.

- In `tableView(_:,commitEditingStyle:,forRowAtIndexPath:)` the

  `things.removeAtIndex(indexPath.row)` expression becomes `document.removeWhatsitAtIndex(indexPath.row)`.

Your `ThingsDocument` object is now your app's data model. This is an important step. It's not important that you combined the document and data model into a single object, but it is important that you've encapsulated all of the changes to the data model—counting, getting, removing, and creating items—behind your own methods, rather than simply using array methods. You'll see why shortly.

You might think that you've written enough code that your app would be able to store its `MyWhatsit` objects (at least the name and location bits) in your document and retrieve them again. But there are still a few small pieces of the document puzzle missing.

Tracking Changes

One thing you haven't written is any code to save your document. You've written code to convert your data model objects into something that can be saved, but you've never asked the `UIDocument` object to save itself.

And you won't.

At least, that's not the ideal technique. `UIDocument` embraces the *autosave document model*, where the user's document is periodically saved to persistent storage while they work and again automatically before your app quits. This is the preferred document-saving model for iOS apps.

For autosaving to work, your code must notify the document that changes have been made. `UIDocument` then schedules and performs the saving of the new data in the background. There are two ways to communicate changes to your document: call the `updateChangeCount(_:_` function or use the document's `NSUndoManager` object. As you register changes with the `NSUndoManager`, it will automatically notify its document object of changes.

> **Note** The alternative to using an undo manager and autosaving is to explicitly save the document by calling `saveToURL(_:,forSaveOperation:,completionHandler:)` (or one of the closely related functions). This would imply an interface that works more like legacy desktop applications, where the user must deliberately save their document.

You're not going to embrace NSUndoManager for this app—although it's a great feature to consider and not at all difficult to use. Consequently, you'll need to call your document object's updateChangeCount(_:) function whenever something changes. UIDocument will take it from there.

So, when does your data model change? One obvious place is whenever items are added or removed. Select the ThingsDocument.swift file. Locate the removeWhatistAtIndex(_:) and anotherWhatsit() functions. At the end of removeWhatistAtIndex(_:) and again just before the return statement in anotherWhatsit(), add the following statement:

```
updateChangeCount(.Done)
```

This message tells the document object that its content was changed, and those changes are .Done. There are other kinds of changes (changes because of an undo or redo action, for example), but unless you've created your own undo manager, this is the only constant you need to pass.

The other place that the document changes is when the user edits an individual item. You already solved that problem way back in Chapter 4! Whenever a MyWhatsit object is edited, your object posts a MyWhatsitDidChange notification. All your document needs to do is observe that notification.

Still in your ThingsDocument.swift file, add the following initializer and deinitializer:

```
override init?(fileURL url: NSURL) {
    super.init(fileURL: url)
    let center = NSNotificationCenter.defaultCenter()
    center.addObserver( self,
            selector: "thingsDidChange:",
               name: WhatsitDidChangeNotification,
             object: nil)
}

deinit {
    NSNotificationCenter.defaultCenter().removeObserver(self)
}
```

The initializer registers your document to receive WhatsitDidChangeNotification notifications, and the deinitializer unregisters before your document object is destroyed.

Finally, add the new notification handler method.

```
func thingsDidChange(notification: NSNotification) {
    if indexOfWhatsit(notification.object as MyWhatsit) != nil {
        updateChangeCount(.Done)
    }
}
```

Its only purpose is to notify the document that a MyWhatsit object in this document has changed, and that's what it does.

Testing Your Document

Surely, you've written enough code by now to see your document in action. Run your app, either in the simulator or in a provisioned device. It contains nothing when first launched, as shown on the left in Figure 19-1. Enter the details for a couple of items.

Figure 19-1. Testing document storage

Now either wait about 20 seconds or press the home button to push the app into the background state. When you created a new item, the document was notified of the change. The autosave feature of UIDocument periodically saves the document when the user isn't doing anything else and will immediately save it when your app is moved to the background state.

With your data safely saved in the document, stop the app and run it again from Xcode. You should be rewarded for all of your hard work with the list of items you entered earlier.

What you see, however, is an empty screen, as shown on the right in Figure 19-1.

So, what went wrong? Maybe your document isn't being opened when your app starts? Maybe it didn't get saved in the first place? What you do know is that you've got a bug; it's time to turn to the debugger.

Setting Breakpoints

Switch back to Xcode and set a breakpoint in your contentsForType(_:,error:) by clicking in the gutter to the left of the code, as shown in Figure 19-2. A breakpoint appears as a blue tab.

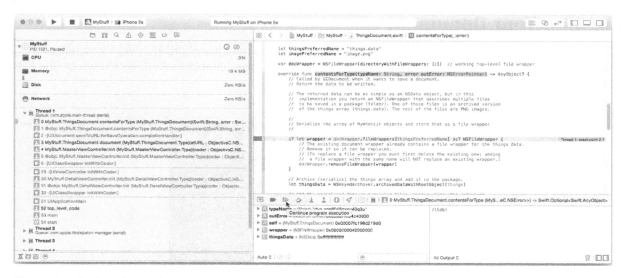

Figure 19-2. Setting a breakpoint in contentsForType(_:,error:)

Uninstall your My Stuff app on your device or simulator. (Tap and hold the My Stuff app icon in the springboard until it starts to shake, tap the delete [x] button, agree to delete the app, and press the home button again.) This deletes your app and any data, including any documents, stored on the device. Run the app again. Xcode will reinstall the app, and it will run with a fresh start.

Almost immediately, Xcode stops at the breakpoint in the `contentsForType(_:,error:)` function, as shown in Figure 19-2. If you look at the stack trace on the left, you can see that the `contentsForType(_:,error:)` function was called from the `document()` function, which was called from `MasterViewController.init()`. This tells you that `contentsForType(_:,error:)` is being sent to create the initial, empty document when no document exists. Remember that when the document doesn't exist, the first thing `document()` does is create one by saving the empty document object.

Stepping Through Code and Examining Variables

So, you know the empty document is getting saved. What about the next step? Click the continue button in the debugger ribbon (also shown in Figure 19-2). The lets your app resume normal execution. Add some new objects and either wait a bit or press the home button to push your app into the background. Again, Xcode will stop at the breakpoint in `contentsForType(_:,error:)`. This tells you your document is being autosaved when you make changes to it. So far, so good.

If your document is getting written correctly, maybe it's not getting loaded correctly. Set another breakpoint in the `loadFromContent(_:,ofType:,error:)` and run your app again, as shown in Figure 19-3. Once Xcode stops in this function, click the Step Over button (right next to the Continue Execution button) to execute one statement at a time. Click it repeatedly until the statement that sets the `things` array has executed, as shown in Figure 19-3.

Figure 19-3. Stepping through contentsForType(_:,error:)

> **Tip**   Step Over executes a complete statement in your source code and stops when it finishes. Step Into executes one statement; if it's a function call, it will move into that function and stop again. Step Out allows the remainder of a function to execute, stopping again when it returns to its caller.

This is the function called to load the contents of your document. It unarchives the data and populates the `things` array. Look in the debugger area at the bottom of the workspace window, and you'll see all of the active variables in this function. One of those is self, the document object being acted upon. Expand it to examine its property values. In it, you'll find a line that says (something like) the following:

```
things = ([(MyStuff.MyWhatsit)]) 2 values
```

That statement says that the `things` property of your document object consists of an array of `MyWhatsit` objects, and it currently contains two objects. This is great! It means your document was successfully read, and the previously serialized data has been reconstructed as two `MyWhatsit` objects.

So, why aren't they showing up in your table view? Let's find out. Locate the `whatsitCount` property and set a breakpoint on its single return statement. (Leave those other breakpoints set.) Run your app again. One of the first things a table view does is get the number of rows in the table from its data source delegate. That function, in turn, reads your `whatsitCount` property. Sure enough, as soon as you run your app, Xcode stops in your `whatsitCount` property getter, as shown in Figure 19-4.

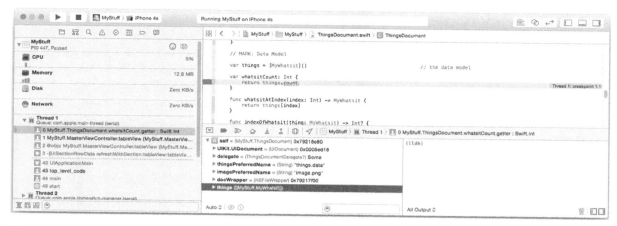

Figure 19-4. *Examining the whatsitCount property*

Again, expand the `self` variable in the debugging pane and look at the things property. This time it's empty. Have you figured out the problem yet? Click the Continue Execution button and let your app run. The next thing that happens is you hit the breakpoint in `loadFromContent(_:,ofType:,error:)`. Have you figured out the problem yet?

Tip   By the way, this is called the "divide and conquer" debugging technique. Decide what your code should be doing, set a breakpoint somewhere in the middle of that process, and see whether that step is happening correctly. If not, the problem either is right there or earlier in your code. If it is happening correctly, the problem is after that point. Choose another breakpoint and repeat until you've found the bug.

Here's the problem. `UIDocument`'s `openWithCompletionHandler(_:)` function (called from `document()`) is *asynchronous*. It starts the process of retrieving your document's data in the background and returns immediately. Your app's code proceeds, displaying the table view, with a still empty data model.

Some time later, the data for the document finishes loading and is passed to `loadFromContents(_:,ofType:,error:)` to be converted into a data model. That's successful, but the table view doesn't know that and continues to display—what it thinks is—an empty list.

What your document needs to do is notify your view controller when the data model has been updated, so the table view can refresh itself. You could accomplish this using a notification, but I think the most sensible solution is to use a delegate function. As a bonus, you'll get practice creating your own protocol.

Tip   Remove a breakpoint by dragging it out of the gutter. Relocate a breaking by dragging it to a new location. Disable or enable a breakpoint by clicking it.

Creating a ThingsDocument Delegate

Define a new delegate protocol. You could add a new Swift file to the project just for this protocol, but since it goes hand in hand with the ThingsDocument class, I recommend adding it right to the ThingsDocument.swift file.

```
protocol ThingsDocumentDelegate {
    func gotThings(document: ThingsDocument)
}
```

This defines a protocol with one function (gotThings(_:)), to be called whenever your document object loads new things from the document. To the ThingsDocument class, add a new delegate property as follows (new code in bold):

```
class ThingsDocument: UIDocument, ImageStorage {
    var delegate: ThingsDocumentDelegate?
```

Find the document(atURL:) function. Change the statement that opens the document to this (modified code in bold):

```
document.openWithCompletionHandler() { (success) in
    if success {
        document.delegate?.gotThings(document)
    }
}
```

The modified code now performs an action after the document is finished loading, which includes the unarchiving of the data model objects. Now it calls its delegate function gotThings(_:), so the delegate (your view controller) knows that the data model has changed.

Switch to the MasterViewController.swift file and make your view controller a document delegate (new code in bold).

```
class MasterViewController: UITableViewController, ThingsDocumentDelegate {
```

Find the awakeFromNib() function and add a statement at the end to make the view controller the document's delegate object (new code in bold).

```
document.delegate = self
```

Finally, write the protocol function gotThings(_:), as follows:

```
func gotThings(_: ThingsDocument) {
    tableView.reloadData()
}
```

Run your app again, as shown in Figure 19-5, and *voilà*! The data in your document appears in the table view.

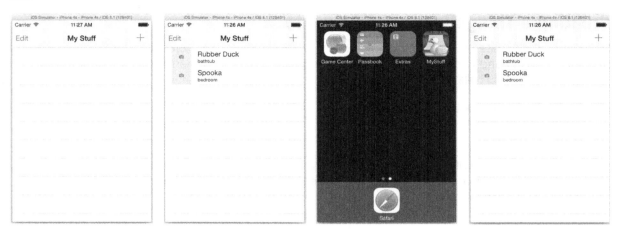

Figure 19-5. Working document

Make changes or add new items. Press the home button to give UIDocument a chance to save the document, stop the app, restart it, and your changes persist. The only content MyStuff doesn't save is any images you add. That's because images aren't part of the archived object data. You're going to add image data directly to the document's directory wrapper, so attack that problem next.

> **Tip**   The Debug ➤ Deactivate Breakpoints command will disable all breakpoints in your project, allowing you to run and test your app without interruption.

Storing Image Files

In the preceding sections, you learned all the basics of serializing your data model objects, storing them in a document file, and retrieving them again. Image data storage takes a different route than the other properties in your MyWhatsit objects. Here is how it's going to work:

- When a new, or updated, image (UIImage) object is added to a MyWhatsit object, the image is converted into the Portable Network Graphics (PNG) data format and stored in the document as a file wrapper. The MyWhatsit object remembers the key of the file wrapper.

- When the document is saved, UIDocument includes the data from all the file wrappers in the document wrapper. The image file wrapper keys are archived by the MyWhatsit objects.

- When the document is opened again, the file wrapper objects for the image data are restored.

- When client code requests the image property of a MyWhatsit object, MyWhatsit uses its saved key to locate and load the data in the file wrapper, eventually converting it back into the original UIImage object.

The key to this design (no pun intended) is the relationship between the MyWhatsit objects and the document object. A MyWhatsit object will use the document object to store and later retrieve the data for an individual image. From a software design standpoint, however, you want to keep the code that actually stores and retrieves the image data out of the MyWhatsit object. The single responsibility principle encourages the MyWhatsit object to do what it does (represent the values in your data model) and the document object to do what it does (manage the storage and conversion of document data) without polluting one class with the responsibilities of the other.

The solution is to create an *abstraction layer*, or *abstract service*, in the ThingsDocument class to store and retrieve images. MyWhatsit will still instigate image management, but the mechanics of how those images get turned into file wrappers stays inside ThingsDocument. Let's get started.

Add a second protocol to the ThingsDocument.swift file, as follows:

```
protocol ImageStorage {
    func keyForImage(newImage: UIImage?, existingKey: String?) -> String?
    func imageForKey(key: String?) -> UIImage?
}
```

This protocol defines a service that will store an image and retrieve an image. The first function will store, replace, or remove an image from storage, returning a key that can later be used to retrieve it. The second function performs that retrieval. Your ThingsDocument class will provide this service, so add it to its repertoire (modified code in bold).

```
class ThingsDocument: UIDocument, ImageStorage {
```

Now modify MyWhatsit to use these methods to save and restore its image property. Select the MyWhatsit.swift file and add two new properties, as follows, one for the image storage provider and a second to remember the image's key in the store:

```
var imageStorage: ImageStorage?
var imageKey: String?
```

Now rewrite the image property. You're going to change it from a simple stored property to a computed property that lazily obtains the image from imageStore when requested and encodes the image in imageStore when set. Rewrite var image as follows (new code in bold):

```
var image: UIImage? {
    get {
        if image_private == nil {
            image_private = imageStorage?.imageForKey(imageKey)
        }
        return image_private
    }
    set {
        image_private = newValue
        imageKey = imageStorage?.keyForImage(newValue, existingKey: imageKey)
        postDidChangeNotification()
    }
}
private var image_private: UIImage?
```

You've refactored the `image` property to store and retrieve its image from an external source, the details of which are known only to `imageStorage`. No code that uses the `image` property changes. As far as the rest of your app is concerned, your `MyWhatsit` object still has an `image` property that can be got or set.

To retrieve the image the next time the document is loaded, your new `MyWhatsit` object must remember the key returned from `keyForImage(_:,existingKey:)`. Modify your `NSCoding` functions, as follows, so the `imageKey` property is also serialized (new code in bold):

```
let nameKey = "name"
let locationKey = "location"
let imageKeyKey = "image.key"

required init(coder decoder: NSCoder) {
    name = decoder.decodeObjectForKey(nameKey) as String
    location = decoder.decodeObjectForKey(locationKey) as String
    imageKey = decoder.decodeObjectForKey(imageKeyKey) as? String
}

func encodeWithCoder(coder: NSCoder) {
    coder.encodeObject(name, forKey: nameKey)
    coder.encodeObject(location, forKey: locationKey)
    coder.encodeObject(imageKey, forKey: imageKeyKey)
}
```

> **Note**   Your `NSCoding` methods do not encode or decode either the image or document property of the object. When the object is unarchived, these property values will be `nil`. This makes them *transient* properties. Properties preserved by archiving are called *persistent* properties.

That concludes most of the changes to the `MyWhatsit` class. Now you have to actually provide the image storage services you promised in the protocol. Select the `ThingsDocument.swift` file. Start by writing the image storage function, as follows:

```
func keyForImage(newImage: UIImage?, existingKey: String?) -> String? {
    if let key = existingKey {
        if let wrapper = docWrapper.fileWrappers[key] as? NSFileWrapper {
            docWrapper.removeFileWrapper(wrapper)
        }
    }
    var newKey: String? = nil
    if let image = newImage {
        let imageData = UIImagePNGRepresentation(image)
        newKey = docWrapper.addRegularFileWithContents( imageData,↵
                                preferredFilename: imagePreferredName)
    }
    updateChangeCount(.Done)
    return newKey
}
```

The newImage parameter is either the image to store or nil if an image should not be stored. The image is stored by converting it into the PNG file format and storing that data in a regular file wrapper.

The existingKey parameter is the key of the previously stored image or nil if there wasn't one. If supplied, the key is used to first discard the previously stored image file.

The function returns the key used to retrieve the stored image (if any). Using different combinations of values and nil, the function can be used to store a new image (image and no key), replace an image (image and key), or remove (no image and key) an image in the document.

That takes care of storing a new image in the document and replacing an existing image with a new one. Now add the code to retrieve images from the document, as follows:

```
func imageForKey(imageKey: String?) -> UIImage? {
    if let key = imageKey {
        if let wrapper = docWrapper.fileWrappers[key] as? NSFileWrapper {
            return UIImage(data: wrapper.regularFileContents!)
        }
    }
    return nil
}
```

This function uses imageKey to find the file wrapper in the document, calls the wrapper's regularFileContents() function to retrieve its data, and uses that to reconstruct the original UIImage object, which is returned to the caller.

> **Note**   The data that a regular file wrapper represents isn't read into memory until you call its regularFileContents() function. File wrappers are just lightweight placeholders for the data in persistent storage, until you request that data.

Sneakily, there's one more place where an image is removed from the document—when the user deletes a MyWhatsit object. Locate the removeWhatsitAtIndex(_:) function. Add code to the beginning of the method to remove the image file wrapper for that item, before removing that item.

But what should this code look like? Just as you don't want your data model classes having intimate knowledge about how images get stored in the document, your document object shouldn't have intimate knowledge about how your data model classes are using ImageStorage. So, let's keep that knowledge located in the MyWhatsit class. Add the following code to your removeWhatsitAtIndex(_:) function (new code in bold):

```
func removeWhatsitAtIndex(index: Int) {
    let thing = whatsitAtIndex(index)
    thing.willRemoveFromStorage()
    thing.imageStorage = nil
    things.removeAtIndex(index)
    updateChangeCount(.Done)
}
```

Instead of removing the image file wrapper for it, you simply let the MyWhatsit object know that you're about to remove it from a document. It will then take care of whatever it needs to do to remove itself. Finally, you disconnect it from your document (image) store so it will behave like a stand-alone MyWhatsit object again.

Oh, you better add that function to your MyWhatsit.swift file, as follows:

```
func willRemoveFromStorage() {
    imageStorage?.keyForImage(nil, existingKey: imageKey)
    imageKey = nil
}
```

All of the mechanics for saving, retrieving, and deleting images from the document are in place. Sadly, none of it will work. The MyWhatsit must be connected to the working ThingsDocument object through its imageStore property for any of this new code to function. At this point, no one is setting that property.

So, where should the imageStore property be set, and what object should be responsible for setting it? The answer is the ThingsDocument object. It should take responsibility for maintaining the connection between itself and its data model objects.

As it turns out, this is an incredibly easy problem to solve because there are only two locations where MyWhatsit objects are created: when the document is unarchived and when the user creates a new item. Start with the anotherWhatsit() function and add a statement to set the new object's imageStore property (new code in bold), as follows:

```
func anotherWhatsit() -> (object: MyWhatsit, index: Int) {
    let newThing = MyWhatsit(name: "My Item \(whatsitCount+1)")
    newThing.imageStorage = self
```

> **Note**   Functions such as anotherWhatsit() are called factory methods. A *factory method* creates new, correctly configured objects for the client. The objects might be different classes or need to be initialized in a special way—like being added to a collection and having their imageStore property set—before being returned. Write factory methods to create objects that need to be created in a way that the sender shouldn't be responsible for.

Locate the loadFromContents(_:,ofType:,error:) function. Immediately after the things array is unarchived, add a loop to assign this document as the image store for all of them (new code in bold).

```
things = NSKeyedUnarchiver.unarchiveObjectWithData(data) as [MyWhatsit]
for thing in things {
    thing.imageStorage = self
}
docWrapper = contentWrapper
return true
```

Your document implementation is finally finished! Give it a spin by running MyStuff. Add some items, attach some pictures, and quit the app, as shown in Figure 19-6. Stop the app in Xcode and start it again. All of the items, along with their pictures, are preserved in the document.

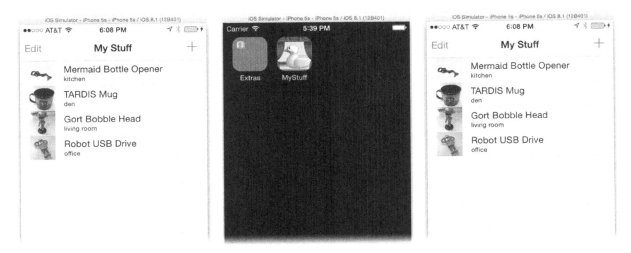

Figure 19-6. *Testing image storage*

Note   In the rush to add image storage to your MyWhatsit object, I wanted to make sure you didn't miss a remarkable fact: you did not change the interface to your data model. None of the code that uses the MyWhatsit object, like the code in DetailViewController, required any modifications. That's because the meaning and use of the image property never changed. The only thing that changed was how that data gets stored. This is encapsulation and refactoring at work.

If you're running MyStuff on a provisioned device, you can see your app's document file(s) in the devices window (Window ➤ Devices) in Xcode. Open the Devices window and select your device, and the applications installed on your device are listed, as shown in Figure 19-7. Select the MyStuff app and choose the Show Container command, also shown in Figure 19-7.

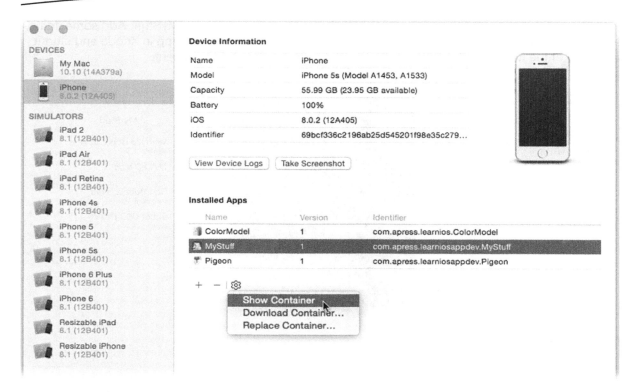

Figure 19-7. *Showing MyStuff's sandbox container*

In the sheet that appears (see Figure 19-8), you can browse the files that make up your app's sandbox. You can clearly see your Things I Own.mystuff document package inside your app's Documents folder. The funny filenames (such as 1_#$!@%!#_image.png) are how UIDocument handles two or more file wrappers with the same preferred name. It gives the files crazy names so they can all be stored in the same directory.

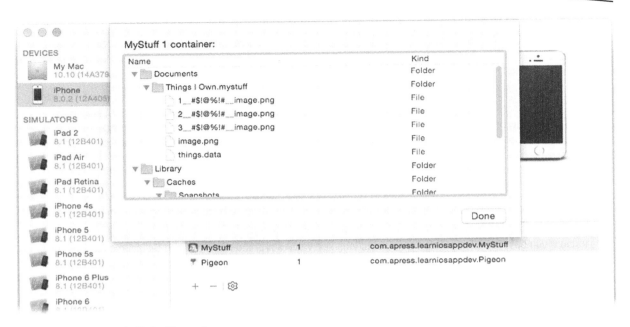

Figure 19-8. The files in MyStuff's sandbox

If you need to get at these files, use the Download Container command instead (see Figure 19-7). Xcode will copy the files from your iOS device to your hard drive, where you can play with them.

Odds and Ends

What you've accomplished in MyStuff is a lot, but it really represents the bare minimum of support required for document integration. There are lots of features and issues that I skipped over. Let's review a couple of those now.

iCloud Storage

You can store your documents in the cloud, much like your stored property list values in the cloud in Chapter 18. Documents, naturally, are a little more complicated.

Apple's guidelines suggest that you provide a setting that allows the user to place all of their documents in the cloud or none of their documents in the cloud. A piecemeal approach is not recommended. When the user changes their mind, your app is responsible for moving (copying) the locally stored documents into the cloud or in the other direction. This isn't a trivial task. It involves multitasking, which I don't get to until Chapter 24.

Once in the cloud, you open, modify, and save documents much the way you do from your local sandbox. All of the code you wrote for contentsForType(_:,error:) and loadFromContents(_:,ofType:,error:) won't need any modification (if you wrote them correctly); you'll just use different URLs. In reality, the data of your "cloud" documents is actually stored locally on the device. Any changes are synchronized with the iCloud storage servers in the background, but you always retain a local copy of the data, both for speed and in case the network connection with the cloud is interrupted.

There are some subtle, and not so subtle, differences between local and cloud-based documents. One of the big differences is change. Changes to your cloud documents can occur at any time. The user is free to edit the same document on another device, and network interruptions can delay those changes from reaching your app immediately.

In general, your app observes the UIDocumentStateChangedNotification notification. If the iCloud service detects conflicting versions (local vs. what's on the server), your document's state will change to UIDocumentStateInConflict. It's then up to your app to compare the two documents and decide what to keep and what to discard. You might query the user for guidance, or your app might do it automatically.

> **Note** The Homer the Pigeon app provides an example of cloud-based UIDocument storage and synchronization. Homer, like MyStuff, allows the user to attach images to their saved locations, resulting in too much data to be shared using the ubiquitous key-value store. You can download the source code for Homer at https://github.com/JamesBucanek/Pigeon.

To learn more about iCloud documents, start with the *Document-Based App Programming Guide for iOS*, which you can find in Xcode's Documentation and API Reference window. It's a good read, and I strongly suggest you peruse it if you plan to do any more development involving UIDocument. The chapters "Managing the Life Cycle of a Document" and "Resolving Document Version Conflicts" directly address cloud storage.

Archive Versioning

When implementing NSCoding, you might need to consider what happens when your class changes. One of the consequences of archiving objects to persistent storage is that the data is—well—persistent. Users will expect your app to open documents created years ago. I'm trying to improve my software all of the time, and I assume you are too. I'm always adding new properties to classes or changing the type and scope of properties. It often means creating new classes and periodically abandoning old ones. All such changes alter the way classes encode themselves and pose challenges when unarchiving data created by older, and sometimes newer, versions of your software.

There are a number of techniques for dealing with archive compatibility. Your newer code might encode its values using a different key. When decoding, your software can test for the presence of that key to determine whether the archive data was created by modern or legacy software. You might encode a "version" value in your archive data and test that version when decoding. Newer software might encode a value in both its modern form and a legacy form so that older software (which knows nothing of the newer form) can still interpret the document data.

There are even techniques for substituting one class for another during unarchiving. (You actually used this in Chapter 14 to substitute your GameScene class for the SKScene class in the archive file.) This can solve the problem of a decoding class that no longer exists. A thorough discussion of these issues and some solutions are discussed in the "Forward and Backward Compatibility for Keyed Archives" chapter of the *Archives and Serializations Programming Guide*.

Summary

Embracing UIDocument adds a level of modern data storage to your app that users both appreciate and have come to expect. You've learned how and where to store your app's documents. More importantly, you understand the different roles that objects and methods play that together orchestrate the transformation of model objects into raw data and back again. You learned how to construct multifile documents that can be incrementally saved and lazily loaded. Along the way, you learned how to archive objects and create objects that can be archived.

You've come a long way, and you should be feeling pretty confident in your iOS aptitude. Adding persistent storage to your apps was really the last major iOS competency you had to accomplish. The next chapter digs into Swift to hone your language knowledge and proficiency.

Chapter 20

See Swift, See Swift Run

As promised, I didn't start out this book with a dry lesson on Swift. You dove right in and started creating apps—and I think that's fantastic. The fact that Xcode empowers even novice programmers to design and create quality iOS apps opens a world of possibilities. But you don't want to stay a novice forever; you don't get the good seats in the monastery's dining hall, and there's never any fan mail. I'm not saying that reading this one chapter will turn you into a Swift guru, but it should definitely up your game.

If you're struggling at all with Swift or are just relatively new to it, give this chapter a good read. It's basically a crash course that will put you on a firm footing. This chapter is not intended to be a definitive guide to Swift. It is, after all, only one chapter. Apple has two excellent guides to the Swift language, which I strongly encourage you to download and keep handy. Both of these books are free. Download them through Apple's iBooks app on your Mac or iOS device.

- *The Swift Programming Guide*
- *Using Swift with Cocoa and Objective-C*

These are Apple's official language guides. The first contains an excellent tutorial as well as a technical description of the language. Think of this chapter as the "Cliff Notes" to *The Swift Programming Guide*. It's a fast-paced tour of all the major features, especially ones you'll use on a daily basis. It's designed to get you using Swift's great features today but not pour over its details. In this chapter, you'll learn the following:

- Learn how classes are declared and objects are created
- Discover Swift's many shortcuts
- Understand the different kinds of properties
- Use protocols and extensions to augment a class
- Master the use of closures
- Learn how best to use optionals and optional chaining

- Explore arrays, dictionaries, structures, enums, tuples, and a host of other basic data types

- Find out how to avoid some memory management traps

There are no projects for this chapter. Instead, you'll use an innovative new feature of Xcode called a playground. A *playground* is a blank page where you can explore the Swift language interactively. Let's get started, and there's no better place to start than the beginning.

The (Short) History of Swift

The history of most computer languages stretches back decades. Swift is an outlier, springing like the goddess Athena fully formed from the forehead of Zeus—or, in this case, Apple. The idea for Swift is only a few years old, and until Apple announced it at its World Wide Developers Conference in 2014, almost no one outside of Apple had even heard of it.

Swift incorporates many modern language features but isn't burdened (at least not yet) with legacy features and syntax. It is a clean, fast, efficient, succinct, safe, modern, and flexible language. Astoundingly, it accomplishes all of this while being binary compatible[1] with existing C, Objective-C, and Objective-C++ code. Let me explain some of these concepts briefly, before you get into the nitty-gritty of using Swift.

Swift is a clean language. By clean, I mean that it's orthogonal and regular—technical terms for being consistent. In a lot of older languages, new features have been bolted on top of other features, which have been bolted on top of the original language. You end up with a patchwork of syntax and rules that aren't always consistent. In Objective-C, for example, you use one syntax for Objective-C string literals, a different syntax for C string literals, and a third syntax for character literals; and the three types aren't compatible with one another. Swift eliminates this kind of inconsistency—as far as it's logically possible.

Swift is fast. Over the past few decades, compiler developers have learned a lot about turning the code you write into efficient machine instructions. One of those lessons is that the more the compiler understands about what the programmer is trying to accomplish, the more efficient it can make the code. Swift's syntax is designed to subtly communicate that information to the compiler. There's a tendency for Swift syntax to describe *what* you want to happen, rather than *how* you want it to happen. This lets the compiler find the best solution for you.

Swift is also a thoroughly modern language, borrowing innovative features from languages such as Rust, Haskell, Ruby, Python, and others. This is not, however, new. The world of software engineering is strewn with the corpses of computer languages that have introduced all manner of powerful new programming paradigms, most developed by computer scientists. The majority of these have fallen by the wayside because they also failed to meet the performance and compatibility demands of the industry. Swift, by contrast, was first conceived and designed by a "compiler guy." Chris Lattner, Apple's lead compiler engineer and one of the principle developers of the LLVM and clang compilers, conceived Swift as a modern language that wouldn't sacrifice speed or compatibility. In other words, you can finally have your software cake and eat it too.

---

[1]*Binary compatible* means that code written in Swift can directly call existing C functions and use Objective-C objects, and vice versa.

Most importantly, Swift is a safe language. Its syntax and rules are designed to prohibit many common, and a few uncommon, programming mistakes that are the bane of software developers everywhere. In 2014, the technology world was rocked by a flaw found in one of the core encryption algorithms used to protect data on the Internet. This flaw was the result of a single misplaced semicolon (;) on a line of C code, a classic mistake that C programmers have been making since the beginning of the language. Swift's syntax is carefully designed to help you avoid making these kinds of simple, yet sometimes catastrophic, mistakes. (That doesn't mean you can't write buggy software; it's just less likely to be Swift's fault.)

Finally, Swift is concise without being terse. By concise, I mean that the same program in Swift is likely to be shorter than the same code written in C, C++, Java, C#, or Objective-C. This means your code is less voluminous, easier to read, and easier to write. That, indirectly, means you have less to write, and what you do write is easier to understand. The following Objective-C statement sorts an array of Person objects into ascending order by date of birth:

```
[people sortUsingComparator:^NSComparisonResult(id l, id r) {
        Person *p1 = (Person*)l;
        Person *p2 = (Person*)r;
        return [p1.birthdate compareDate:p2.birthdate];
    }];
```

Compare that to the same code in Swift:

```
people.sort { $0.birthdate < $1.birthdate }
```

For contrast, a terse language (such as Perl) can accomplish things with astoundingly little code but sacrifices readability. For example, the following is a complete program in Perl:

```
print("".(($line=join("",<>))=~s/.*\n/$h{$&}++?"":$&/ge,$line));
```

If you read that statement and said "Oh yeah, that's reading a file and eliminating all of the duplicate records using a hash table," then you're a natural-born computer language god who can skip the rest of this chapter.

Now that the gods have left the building, I should point out that Swift is very much a work in progress. The version of Swift I'm writing about in October 2014 is, in many ways, substantially different from the one released at Apple's WWDC only a few months earlier. And I expect Swift to continue to change, sometimes dramatically, as it evolves. So, take what you read here with a grain of salt and read up on the latest improvements to Swift. A good place to start is the Swift blog at http://developer.apple.com/swift/blog/. Yes, Swift has a blog.

Classes

You've seen this a hundred times so far, and I explained it in Chapter 6, but here is again, in all its glory. A class in Swift is declared by a class directive, as follows:

```
class ClassName: SuperClassName, ProtocolName {
    private var instanceVariable: Int = -1
    func instanceFunction(firstParam: Int, secondParam: Int) -> Bool {
        return firstParam >= secondParam
    }
}
```

Here are the salient points:

- The class declaration informs the compiler that you're declaring a new class, what class it inherits from, what protocols it adopts, what properties it has, and what methods (instance functions) it defines.

  - The superclass is optional. If your class doesn't inherit from an existing class, the superclass name can be omitted.

  - Protocols are optional. If your class doesn't adopt any protocols, the list of protocol names can be omitted.

- The body of your class consists of its properties and functions. Anything declared inside the class statement belongs to this class.

- You can optionally insert access control directives (public, private, or internal) before property or function declarations.

> **Tip**   By convention, type names start with a capital letter (MyClass, ViewController, Weekday, and so on). Variable names start with a lowercase letter (dataSource, frame, userInteractionEnabled, and so on).

Most of this should all make sense to you by now. The only keywords not mentioned in this book so far are the access control directives. The visibility of a variable or function determines what code is allowed access to them. Table 20-1 lists the choices.

Table 20-1. Access Control Directives

Directive	Meaning
public	Any code can use this property or function.
internal	Only the code in the app or framework where this class is defined can access this property or function.
private	Only functions in this class may access this property or function.

When I say "access," I mean refer to that property, or call that function, in any statement. The `internal` keyword is only interesting when developing frameworks. It's a middle ground between `private` and `public`. For code in the same app or framework, it acts like `public` access. For code outside the app or framework, it acts like `private` access.

> **Note**   If you omit the access control, it defaults to `internal`. Almost all of the time this means that your properties and functions will be `public`. If you start using your classes in frameworks, you'll need to explicitly declare your public interfaces using the `public` keyword.

Playgrounds

But don't take my word for it. Create a new playground and try any of the code snippets in this chapter, or anything else you want to try in Swift. A playground is an interactive Swift document that simultaneously compiles and runs whatever code you put there.

From the Xcode File menu, choose the New ➤ Playground command, or just create a new file and choose the Playground template. Give the playground a file name and save it somewhere. You now have a blank slate to try Swift features, as shown in Figure 20-1.

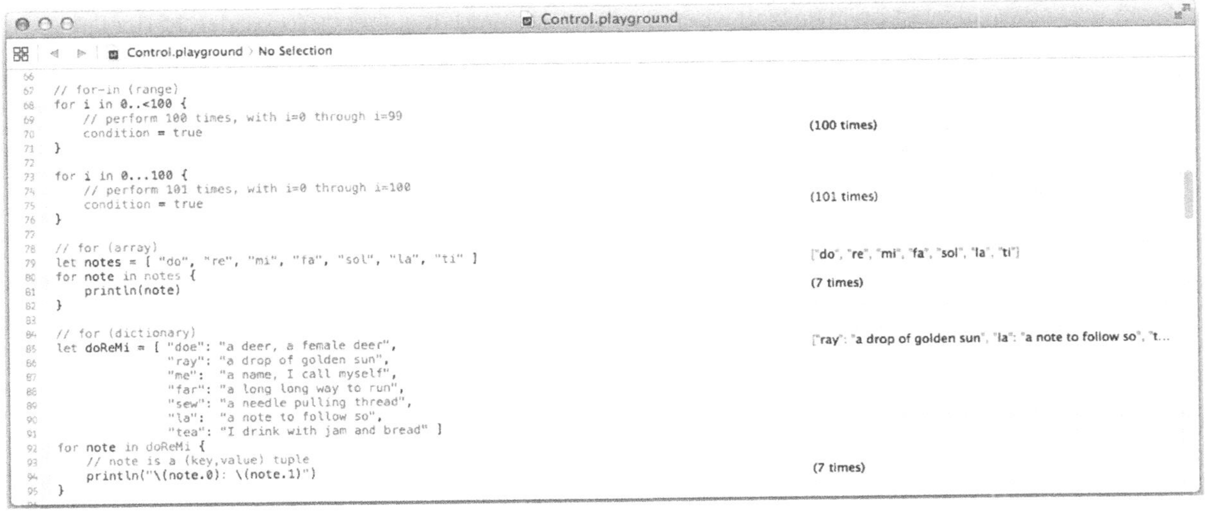

Figure 20-1. Swift playground

You type in code on the left, and the results appear on the right. The right-hand pane will show you what values were set, what an expression evaluates to, how many time a loop ran, the last value returned from a function, and so on. Change your code, and everything is evaluated again.

There are playground files for most of the sections in this chapter. They contain the code snippets described here, along with additional examples and comments. The playgrounds for this chapter can be found in the `Learn iOS Development Projects` ➤ `Ch 20` folder, and all have fairly obvious names. The playground for this section is `Classes.playground`.

Properties

A *property* is a value that belongs to an instance of that class—that is, an object. There are two kinds of properties: stored and computed. A *stored property* allocates variable space within the object to retain a value. You declare a stored property as follows:

```
class ClassStoringProperties {
    let constantProperty: String = "never changes"
    var variableProperty: Int = 1
}
```

A let defines a constant (immutable) property. A var defines a variable (mutable) property. You can obtain the value of either, but you can only change (mutate) the value of a var.

A property has a name, a type, and an optional default value. You can omit the type or the value. If you omit the type, the type is inferred from the value you're setting it to, as follows:

```
let constantProperty = "never changes"
var variableProperty = 1
```

These two properties are identical to the previous two. Their types (String and Int) were inferred from the types of their default values. If you don't specify the type of a property, its type will be the type of the value you set it to.

In Swift, *all* variables must be initialized when they are declared. It is strictly forbidden to declare a variable or constant that is not set with an initial value. This eliminates a whole class of common programming mistakes that arise from uninitialized variables.

Within a class (or structure) you can bend this rule a little. You can declare a stored property that doesn't have a default value, as long as you provide its initial value when the object is initialized. In a class, it's legal to write the following:

```
var uninitializedProperty: Int
```

If you do this, you must provide an initializer function that sets uninitializedProperty to a value before the object can be used. I cover initializer requirements a little later in this section.

Computed Properties

Computed properties, sometimes called *synthetic properties*, are property values that are calculated by a block of code. They have no variable storage associated with them, but they often use other stored properties in their calculations. The following is an example of a computed property:

```
class ClassCalculatingProperties {
    var height: Double = 0.0
    var width: Double = 0.0
    var area: Double {
        get {
            return height*width
        }
        set(newArea) {
```

```
            width = sqrt(newArea)
            height = width
        }
    }
}
```

This class has two stored properties and one computed property. The computed area property can be used just like any other property, as follows, but its value when retrieved is determined by the code in the get block of the property. This is called the property's *getter*. The getter is required.

```
let calculatingObject = ClassCalculatingProperties()
calculatingObject.height = 9.0
calculatingObject.width = 5.0
let area = calculatingObject.area /* area = 45.0 */
```

If you want the property to be mutable, you can also supply a *setter* function, as shown. The parameter to the set(newArea) code block contains the value to be set. If you omit the setter, the property is read-only. It also means you can use a shorthand syntax that drops the get { ... } portion, as follows:

```
var area: Double { return height*width }
```

Even if the value returned by a read-only computed property never changes, you must still declare the property using the var keyword. The logic is that the value could change—there's no way for Swift to know otherwise—so it must be declared to be a variable.

Property Observers

You can also attach code to a stored property. When a stored property is set, you have two opportunities to execute code: a willSet and a didSet code block. You declare these immediately after the stored property, much like a computed property, as follows:

```
class ObservantView: UIView {
    var text: String = "" {
        didSet(oldText) {
            if text != oldText {
                setNeedsDisplay()
            }
        }
    }
}
```

In this example, the code in the didSet(oldText) block executes whenever the text property is assigned. The didSet code block executes *after* the property has been updated; the parameter contains the previous value. Here, it's used to determine whether the string actually changed and redraws the view only if it did.

Similarly, the willSet code block executes *before* the stored property is updated. Its single parameter is the new value to be set. If you want to override the value being set, change the property's value in the didSet function to something other than what was set.

> **Tip**   When writing set, willSet, and didSet code blocks, you can either choose a name for the single parameter or leave it out. If you leave it out, Swift supplies a parameter named newValue, newValue, or oldValue (respectively) for use in your code.

You can't attach code that executes when a stored property is read. And you can't attach property observers to a computed property. The latter would be redundant since the setter code can do anything a property observer could.

Methods

A function in a class is called a *method*, an *instance method*, an *instance function*, or sometimes a *member function*. It's a function that runs in the context of an object. You declare methods as a function in the body of the class, as follows:

```
func pokeUser(name: String, message: String) -> Bool {
    return true
}
```

This method is passed two parameters and returns a Boolean value. You would invoke it with a statement such as the following:

```
let result = object.pokeUser("james", message: "Is that an ice cream truck I hear?")
```

If the function does not return a value, omit the return type that follows the parameter list (-> ReturnType).

Class Methods

A class method is like a global function, but it belongs to the class. A class method does not execute in the context of an object. You declare a class method using the class keyword, as follows:

```
class GoldenAge {
    class func timeRemaining() -> Double { ...
```

You call a class method using the class name (instead of an object reference), as follows:

```
let remaining = GoldenAge.timeRemaining()
```

Because a class method does not execute in the context of an object, you can't refer to any property or instance function of the class directly. This even applies to constants.

Class methods are often used to provide access to global resources, as getters for singletons, or as factory methods to create configured objects.

Parameter names

Every parameter in a function has two names: an *external parameter name* and a *local parameter name*. The following function has three parameters with six names:

```swift
func poke(user name: String, say message: String, important priority: Bool) -> Bool {
    if priority {
        sendMessage(message, toPerson: name)
        return true
    }
    return false
}
```

In this example, every parameter has both an external and a local parameter name, and they are all different. In the function's code, you use the local parameter names (name, message, and priority) to refer to their values.

When calling the function, you use the external parameter names (user, say, important). The following statement will call that function:

```swift
poke(user: "james", say: "Wouldn't some ice cream be great?", important: true)
```

Optional Parameter Names

Both local and external parameter names are optional. If there is no external parameter name, the call's argument list includes only the value. The following function and function call demonstrate this:

```swift
func pokeUser(name: String, message: String) { ... }

pokeUser("james", "I swore I heard the ice cream truck!")
```

If you omit the external parameter name, Swift may use the local parameter name as the external parameter name. For example, the following two method declarations are identical:

```swift
class ExternalNamesInAClass {
    func pokeUser(name: String, message: String) { ... }
    func pokeUser(name: String, message message: String) { ... }
}
```

In both functions, the initial parameter has no external name, while the last one does. In the first function, Swift used the local name of the last parameter as its external name. Both of these functions would have to be called as follows:

```swift
pokeUser("james", message: "I'm going to get ice cream.")
```

So, why does this happen? Swift's expectations about external parameter names vary based on the context of the function as follows:

- A function declared outside a class, structure, or enumeration (sometimes called a *global function*) is not expected to have any external parameter names. If you declare an external name, it will be required to call the function. If you omit it, that argument will be bare.

- A method (a function declared in a class) does not expect an external name for the first parameter but does expect one for all remaining parameters. If you omit an external name, the local name will be used as the external name starting with the second parameter.

- If your parameter provides a default value (see the section "Default Parameter Values"), Swift expects it to have an external name.

- A class or structure initialization function (init()) is expected to have external names for all parameters. If you omit any, the local name is used as the external name.

The first rule makes Swift functions consistent with C, Java, and similar languages. If you don't declare external parameter names, your function calls will look like those legacy languages. You have the option of using Swift's more expressive named parameters, but it's not a requirement.

The second rule is intended to make adopting Objective-C's method naming convention easy within classes. Objective-C doesn't make a distinction between function and parameter names. An Objective-C method name is really just a sequence of tokens that separate the parameters. Consequently, the first token of an Objective-C method typically names the first parameter as well, as in the setBool(_:,forKey:) method (or -setBool:(bool)b forKey:(NSString)key, as it's written in Objective-C). The first parameter is the Boolean value, already identified in the function's name. You wouldn't want to write setBool(bool: true, forKey: "key").

The final rule is to make it easy to create multiple initializers without getting them mixed up. All functions must have a unique signature. Since the function name of all initializers is init, Swift must have unique external parameter names to distinguish between them.

Parameter Name Shortcuts

If you want to specify an external parameter (where Swift does not enforce one) and your external and local parameter names are the same, you can use one name for both by using a # (pound sign or hash) for the external name. The following two function declarations are identical:

```
func function(parameter parameter: Int)
func function(# parameter: Int)
```

Conversely, you can force Swift to *not* use an external parameter name—in those circumstances where it normally would—by replacing the external name with an _ (underscore) character. You can suppress the external parameter name in the poke(_:,message:) function by writing it as follows:

```
func poke(name: String, _ message: String)
```

Now you would call this function simply as object.poke("james","What flavor?").

You can also ignore the local parameter name. Do this when you have no interest in that parameter. For example, the UIControl classes send actions by calling a method whose single parameter is the control object that caused the action. A typical action method looks like this:

```
@IBAction func sendPoke(sender: AnyObject)
```

Quite often, the action method has no use for the sender parameter. You can signal your disinterest by replacing the local parameter name with an _ (underscore) character, as follows:

```
@IBAction func sendPoke(_: AnyObject)
```

The parameter is still there, and the caller is still required to supply it, but the function's code ignores it.

Default Parameter Values

You can supply a default value for one or more parameters. If you do, you can optionally omit that parameter from the function call and the function will receive the default value. You assign default values in a function's declaration, as follows:

```
func pokeUser(name: String, message: String = "Poke!", important: Bool = false )
```

The second and third parameters have default values. Either or both can be omitted from a function call. If you omit the argument in a call, the parameter will be set to the default value. All four of the following statements call this function:

```
defaulter.pokeUser("james")
defaulter.pokeUser("james", message: "Where's my ice cream?")
defaulter.pokeUser("james", important: true)
defaulter.pokeUser("james", message: "The ice cream is melting!", important: true)
```

For clarity, parameters with default values should have external names. Swift assumes this and will use the local name as the external name if you omit it. To avoid ambiguity, any subsequent parameters should also have external names.

Inheritance

A class can inherit from another class. When it does so, it acquires all of the properties and methods of its superclass. The class then augments this foundation with additional properties and methods.

A class can override a method of its superclass. When you do this, you must prefix the method with the override keyword, as follows. This prevents you from accidentally overriding a method because you happened to pick a function name that was already implemented.

```
class BaseClass {
    var lastUserPoked: String = "james"
    func pokeUser(name: String) {
        sendMessage("Poke!", toUser: name)
        lastUserPoked = name
    }
}
```

```swift
class SubClass: BaseClass {
    override func pokeUser(name: String) {
        println("someone poked \(name)")
    }
}
```

A method has a special super variable that refers to the methods and properties of its superclass. Use the super variable to invoke the superclass' method, instead of the one overridden by your class, as follows:

```swift
class SubClass: BaseClass {
    override func pokeUser(name: String) {
        super.pokeUser(name)
        println("someone poked \(name)")
    }
}
```

Overriding Properties

You can also override any property with a computed property. The property you're overriding may be a stored property or another computed property. Again, you use the override keyword to signal your intent. In the following example, the subclass is creating a computed property lastUserPoked that overrides the stored property (lastUserPoked) defined in the base class.

```swift
class SubClass: BaseClass {
    override var lastUserPoked: String {
        get {
            return super.lastUserPoked
        }
        set {
            if newValue != lastUserPoked {
                println("caller is poking a different user")
            }
            super.lastUserPoked = newValue
        }
    }
}
```

Notice how the computed property uses the super.lastUserPoked syntax to access the stored property defined in the base class.

Alternatively, you can override a property observer, as follows:

```swift
override var lastUserPoked: String {
    didSet {
        ...
    }
}
```

The inherited property can be either a stored or computed property, but it must be mutable; property observers are only executed when the value is set.

Blocking Inheritance

If you want to cut out any heirs to your class, methods, or properties, use the `final` keyword. The following class defines a property and method that are final:

```
class ClassWithLimitedInheritance {
    final var trustFundName: String = "Scrooge McDuck"
    final func giveToCharity(amount: Double) {
        if amount > 2.00 {
            println("Too much!")
        }
    }
}
```

You can create a subclass of `ClassWithLimitedInheritance` and extend it, but you cannot override its `trustFundName` property or its `giveToCharity(_:)` method. If you want to prohibit all subclassing, add the `final` keyword to the class itself, as follows:

```
final class EndOfTheLine: ClassWithLimitedInheritance { ...
```

Object Creation

You create a Swift object by writing the class's name as if it were a function call. The following statement creates a new `ClassCalculatingProperties` object and assigns it to `calculatingObject`:

```
let calculatingObject = ClassCalculatingProperties()
```

This syntax allocates a new object and invokes one of the class's initializer functions. In this example, that was `init()`—the initializer with no parameters. You can write your own class initializers. You write one just like a member function with the exceptions that you omit the `func` keyboard, the name of the function is always `init`, and it does not return a value, as follows:

```
class SimpleInitializerClass {
    var name: String
    init() {
        name = "james"
    }
}
```

Every class must have at least one initializer function, else how are you going to create objects? In the following class, all stored properties have default values, and the class doesn't declare any initializers of its own. In this situation, Swift creates an `init()` initializer for you.

```
class AutomaticInitializerClass {
    var name = "james"
    var superUser = true
    // init() supplied by Swift
}
```

You can define as many initializers as you want. They can also include default parameter values, as shown here:

```
class IceCream {
    var flavor: String
    var scoops: Int = 1
    init() {
        flavor = "Vanilla"
    }
    init(flavor: String, scoops: Int = 2) {
        self.flavor = flavor
        self.scoops = scoops
    }
}
```

> **Tip**   If a local variable name has the same name as a property, use the `self` variable to distinguish between them. `flavor` refers to the local parameter. `self.flavor` refers to the object's `flavor` property.

Your initializers are distinguished by their external parameter names (since they all have the same function name). Swift chooses the initializer based on the parameter names, as follows:

```
let plain = IceCream()
let yummy = IceCream(flavor: "Chocolate")
let monster = IceCream(flavor: "Rocky Road", scoops: 3)
```

> **Note**   *All* swift values are created using the same syntax. The expression `CGFloat(1.0)` creates a new `CGFloat` value equivalent to the `Double` constant `1.0`. The expression `Weekday(rawValue: 1)` creates an enumeration value equal to `.Monday`, and so on.

Subclass Initializers

If your class is a subclass, your initializer must explicitly call one of the superclass' initializers. In the following subclass, the initializer sets up its properties and then invokes the superclass' initializer so the superclass can initialize its properties:

```
class IceCreamSundae: IceCream {
    var topping: String
    var nuts: Bool = true
    init(flavor: String, topping: String = "Caramel syrup") {
        self.topping = topping
        super.init(flavor: flavor, scoops: 3)
        }
    }
}
```

Safe Initialization

Swift consistently enforces the rule that you cannot use any value, class, or structure until every variable has been initialized. Swift also lets you defer the initialization of stored properties to your initializer function. This can lead to a bit of a chicken-and-egg problem.

Let me demonstrate the problem by adding an addCherry() function to the IceCream class and then override it in the IceCreamSundae class, as follows:

```
class IceCream {
    ...
    init(flavor: String, scoops: Int = 2) {
        self.flavor = flavor
        self.scoops = scoops
        addCherry()
    }
    func addCherry() {
    }
}

class IceCreamSundae: IceCream {
    ...
    init(flavor: String, topping: String = "Caramel syrup") {
        super.init(flavor: flavor, scoops: 3)  // <-- invalid initializer
    }
    override func addCherry() {
        if topping == "Whipped Cream" {
            ...
        }
    }
}
```

Consider how an IceCreamSundae object gets created. When the initializer for IceCreamSundae starts to execute, the topping property is not yet initialized because it has no default value. You can't call the superclass initializer (super.init(flavor:,scoops:)) yet because there's a possibility that it might call the addCherry() function (which you overrode), which could then access the uninitialized toppings property.

To solve this dilemma, Swift requires all initializers to perform their work in three phases, in the following order:

1. Initialize all stored constants and variables, either explicitly or by relying on the property's default value.

2. Call the superclass initializer to initialize the superclass.

3. Perform any additional setup that would involve calling methods or using computed properties.

The first thing the IceCreamSundae initializer must do is to ensure that all of its properties are initialized. The correct way to write the IceCreamSundae initializer is as follows:

```
class IceCreamSundae: IceCream {
    ...
    init(flavor: String, topping: String = "Caramel syrup") {
        self.topping = topping
        super.init(flavor: flavor, scoops: 3)
    }
}
```

The single self.topping = topping statement satisfies the requirement of the first phase. The topping property does not have a default value and must be explicitly set. The nuts property has a default value; if you don't set it to something else, Swift will set it to true for you. At this point, all subclass properties have been initialized.

Note   Property observers are never executed during object initialization.

This is also the one place in Swift where you can set immutable constants. Even if a property is declared as a constant (let preferDarkChocolate = true), you can set it during the first phase of object initialization.

The second phase must call the superclass initializer. This will initialize all of its properties, its superclass's properties, and so on.

When the superclass initializer returns, the object is fully initialized. It is now safe to call any member function or use any property to prepare the object for use.

Your initializer might be missing some of these phases.

- If the class has no stored properties or all stored properties have default values, the first phase isn't needed.

- If the class doesn't have a superclass, there's no superclass initializer to call, and no second phase.

- If the class doesn't have any initialization beyond Swift's requirements, there won't be a third phase.

Convenience Initializers

The initializers I've described so far are called designated initializers. A *designated initializer* is an initializer that implements the three phases outlined in the previous section.

You can also create convenience initializers. A *convenience initializer* makes it easier to create objects by providing a simplified interface but defers the important work of initializing the object to another initializer *in the same class*. You declare a convenience initializer with the convenience keyword. The following code adds a convenience initializer to the IceCreamSundae class:

```
convenience init(special dayOfWeek: Weekday) {
    switch dayOfWeek {
        case .Sunday:
            self.init(flavor: "Strawberry", topping: "Whipped Cream")
        case .Friday:
            self.init(flavor: "Chocolate", topping: "Chocolate syrup")
        default:
            self.init(flavor: "Vanilla")
    }
}
```

You can now create the ice cream sundae *du jour* with the following statement:

```
let sundaySundae = IceCreamSundae(special: .Sunday)
```

Note the use of self.init(...) to call another initializer in the same class. The called initializer must be in the same class and be either a designated initializer or another convenience initializer that eventually calls a designated initializer.

Inheriting Initializers

Initializer inheritance gets a little tricky. For the complete story, refer to *The Swift Programming Guide* in iBooks, but here are the basic rules:

- If your subclass doesn't define any initializers of its own and all of its stored properties have default values, the subclass inherits all of the initializers from its superclass. (Technically, Swift generates all of the designated initializers for you.)

- If your subclass overrides an initializer, you must prefix it with an override keyword, just like a method or property.

- If your subclass declares any uninitialized stored property variables or constants, you are required to implement designated initializers to set those values.

- If your subclass implements any of its own initializers, it won't automatically inherit any designated initializers. If you want the same designated initializers in your subclass, you must override and re-implement them all.

- You only inherit convenience initializers that call a designated initializer that your subclass also provides (either through inheritance or by overriding it).

As an example, the following BananaSplit class subclasses IceCreamSundae. It doesn't declare any stored properties without default values. If that was all it did, it would have been eligible to inherit all of the initializers from IceCreamSundae. It elected, however, to override the init(flavor:,topping:) designated initializer, as follows:

```
class BananaSplit: IceCreamSundae {
    override init(flavor: String = "Vanilla, Chocolate, Strawberry",
                  topping: String = "Caramel syrup") {
        super.init(flavor: flavor, topping: topping)
        scoops = 3  // Bannana split always has three scoops
    }
}
```

The following code creates a BananaSplit object:

```
let split = BananaSplit(flavor: "Vanilla, Pineapple, Cherry")
```

Because it implemented *at least one* initializer, it won't inherit any other designated initializers. It does, however, automatically inherit the convenience initializer init(special:) because that convenience initializer relies on the designated init(flavor:,topping:) initializer and that one was implemented in this subclass. The following code demonstrates using the inherited convenience initializer to create a banana split:

```
let sundaySplit = BananaSplit(special: .Sunday)
```

Required Initializers

And just to make initializers even more interesting—that is to say, complicated—you can declare that an initializer is required using the required keyword, as follows:

```
required init(flavor: String, scoops: Int) { ... }
```

A required initializer *must* be overridden and re-implemented by a subclass. The subclass has the choice of just overriding the initializer or declaring it as required again. If you simply override the initializer, subclasses of your subclass are not required to implement the initializer again. If you re-require the initializer (using the require keyword again), the subclass of your subclass is required to implement it as well.

The most commonly encountered required initializer is the deserialization initializer in the NSCoding protocol you used in Chapter 19. The init(coder: NSCoder) initializer should be re-implemented in each subclass so that each can properly reconstruct the object from an archive data stream. Your subclass must re-implement init(coder: NSCoder), and you should mark it as required so that any subclasses of your class must do the same.

Closures

A *closure* is an object that encapsulates both a block of code and the variables it needs to execute. Think of a closure as a self-contained bundle of functionality that you can pass around like any other value. The name comes from the way a closure "closes over" the variables it references when it is created. The following code fragment demonstrates the general form of a closure:

```
var externalValue = 2
let closure = { (parameter: Int) -> ReturnType in
    return codeThatDoesSomething(parameter+externalValue)
}
```

A closure is written like a free-floating block of code within a set of curly braces. Here are the salient points:

- Like a function, a closure may have parameters. The caller supplies these values when the closure is executed.

- Closure parameters do not have external names, and they cannot declare a default value.

- A closure's return type must be specified. Use -> Void for closures that don't return a value.

- The closure's parameters and return type are declared before the in keyword. The code of the closure follows the in keyword. A closure with no parameters is written () -> ReturnType.

- A closure may make use of its parameters, variables it declares in its code block, and variables that exist outside the code block. The latter are "closed over" when the closure is created.

- Closures are often referred to as *code blocks*, hearkening back to similar functionality in Objective-C. Many other languages refer to this kind of functionality as a *lambda*.

Normally, a variable ceases to exist once it is out of scope. For example, a function parameter exists only for the lifetime of the function. When the function ends, so do its parameter variables (along with any local variables it created). In the following code, the parameter number gets created when the function is called and disappears again when it returns:

```
func inScope(number: Int) {
    // code that does something with number
}
```

In the following version of inScope(_:), the function returns a closure to its caller. The closure captures the number parameter when it is created.

```
func inScope(number: Int) -> ((Int) -> Int) {
    return { (multiplier: Int) -> Int in
        return number * multiplier
        }
}
```

When the function returns, its number parameter would normally ceases to exist. But since it was "closed over" by the closure, it now also exists in the scope of the closure as well and will continue to exist for the lifetime of the closure.

After the function returns, its reference to the number parameter goes away. The parameter is now, effectively, a private variable in the closure—since there are no other references to it. Each time you call the function, a new parameter variable is created, and a new closure captures that variable, as shown here:

```
let times5 = inScope(5)
let times3 = inScope(3)
```

We can demonstrate this by executing the two closures. You execute a closure by treating the closure variable as if it were a function, as follows:

```
var result = times5(7)   // returns 35 (5*7)
result = times3(7)       // returns 21 (3*7)
```

The two closures each multiply the supplied parameter with the value they captured in the earlier call to inScope().

In another scenario, consider the case where the closure captures a variable and that variable still exists. A closure captures a *reference* to a variable, not its value. (The distinction between values and references is discussed a little later in this chapter.) All the code, inside and outside of the closure, refers to the same variable. To demonstrate that, let's create a persistent variable and a closure that captures it.

```
var multiplier =  3
let sharedVariable = { (number: Int) -> Int in
    return number * multiplier
}
```

When you execute the closure, it multiplies its parameter value with the value of the captured multiplier variable, as follows:

```
result = sharedVariable(4)       // returns 12 (4 * multiplier)
```

If you then modify the multiplier variable, the closure will use the modified value, as follows:

```
multiplier = 5
result = sharedVariable(4)       // returns 20 (4 * multiplier)
```

Capturing self

Swift is full of shortcuts that allow you write only the code needed to express your intent. There are, however, a couple of places where Swift requires you to spell out the obvious so that it's, well, obvious. Closures are one of those places. Consider the following view controller, animating the appearance of a label:

```
class LabelViewController: UIViewController {
    @IBOutlet var label: UILabel!

    override func viewDidAppear(animated: Bool) {
        UIView.animateWithDuration(1.5, animations: { label.alpha = 1.0 })
    }
}
```

Look at the closure carefully and tell me what variable it is "closing over." (Hint, the answer is *not* label.)

That's right, the correct answer is self. Whenever you refer to a property or function within a method, you're implicitly referring to the instance variable or instance function of the context object. Within the context of the viewDidAppear(_:) function, the expression storyboard really means self.storyboard, and the function call setEditing(true, animated: false) is really self.setEditing(true, animated: false).

The distinction in closures can be important. The previous closure captured the self variable (the reference to the view controller object) and not a reference to the specific UILabel object. This is critical because, as you've seen, a closure keeps a reference to the variables it captures.

Let's say I create this closure but then immediately replace the label property with a different UILabel object. When the closure executes, it will use the new UILabel object because it captured self, not the original UILabel object. And this is why Swift won't let you write the preceding code. You must write the closure as follows:

```
override func viewDidAppear(animated: Bool) {
    UIView.animateWithDuration(1.5, animations: { self.label.alpha = 1.0 })
}
```

Swift requires you to write self.label, self.storyboard, and self.setEditing(true, animated: false) when writing a closure. This makes it abundantly clear that you're capturing self and not label or storyboard.

Using Closures

Using closures couldn't be easier. When you create a closure, it becomes a value—one you assign to a variable or pass as an argument. Your use of closures will likely begin as arguments. iOS provides many opportunities to pass a block of code to methods that will ultimately execute that closure to accomplish your tasks. Take almost any project in this book, and you'll see closures in action. In Chapter 16, the code that adapted the display when it was resized passed two closures to the transition coordinator, as follows:

```
coordinator.animateAlongsideTransition( { (context) in self.positionDialViews() },
                              completion: { (context) in self.attachDialBehaviors() })
```

The animateAlongsideTransition(_:,completion:) method takes two parameters, both closures. The first closure is executed to animate your views during the transition, and the second closure executes after the transition is complete.

Notice that the parameter in each closure doesn't have a type. That's because Swift has a lot of shortcuts that let you write concise closures.

Closure Shortcuts

Swift allows you to use a number of shortcuts that simplify your closures.

   ▧   If the parameter and return types of the closure are implied by the parameter or the variable you're assigning it to, you can omit those types.

   ▧   You can omit the parameter names and use their shorthand names.

   ▧   If the code for a closure can be written as a single return statement, you can write just the return expression.

   ▧   If the closure is the last parameter to a function call, you can use the trailing closure syntax.

The first shortcut simplifies the parameters of the closure. In a situation like the animateAlongsideTransition(_:,completion:) method, the description of the closure has already been established by the method. If you look at the method declaration, you'll see something like the following:

```
func animateAlongsideTransition(↵
    _ animation: ((UIViewControllerTransitionCoordinatorContext!) -> Void)!,↵
    # completion: ((UIViewControllerTransitionCoordinatorContext!) -> Void)!) -> Bool
```

This function describes two parameters. Both expect a closure that has one parameter (of type UIViewControllerTransitionCoordinatorContext) and returns nothing (-> Void). The closure you pass as an argument to the call *must* match that description. Because Swift already knows the number and types of the parameters and the type the closure will return, Swift will fill those details in for you. All you have to do is name the parameters, as follows:

```
{ (context) in self.positionDialViews() }
```

The type of the `context` parameter and the return type of the closure are both implied. In this situation, you can also save a few keystrokes by tossing the parentheses, as follows:

```
{ context in self.positionDialViews() }
```

If a parameter is uninteresting, you can replace its name with an _ (underscore), as follows:

```
{ _ in self.positionDialView() }
```

Shorthand Parameter Names

If you don't want to name the parameters, you can use their shorthand names: $0, $1, $2, and so on. If you do that, you can leave out the entire parameters clause at the beginning of the closure. Take the `customActionWithDuration(_:,actionBlock:)` method of `SKAction` as an example. This function is defined as follows:

```
func customActionWithDuration(_ seconds: NSTimeInterval,↩
                  actionBlock block: (SKNode!, CGFloat) -> Void)↩
        -> SKAction
```

The second parameter is a closure that receives two parameters (an `SKNode` and a `CGFloat`). When you call this function, you can write the closure as follows:

```
SKAction.customActionWithDuration( 3.0,
                  actionBlock: {
                      (node, elapsedTime) in
                      if elapsedTime > 0.5 {
                          node.alpha = elapsedTime/3.0
                      }
                  })
```

The closure for the `actionBlock` parameter tests the `elapsedTime` parameter. If more than half a second has elapsed, it sets the node's `alpha` proportionally based on the elapsed time. You could write the same code this way:

```
SKAction.customActionWithDuration( 3.0,
                  actionBlock: { if $1 > 0.5 { $0.alpha = $1/3.0 } } )
```

In the second example, the entire parameter declaration is omitted. Swift assigns the first parameter the shorthand name of $0, the second one $1, and so on. Use these shorthand names exactly as you would the named parameters.

Tip   Limit your use of shorthand names to contexts where the meaning and type of the parameters is obvious. The second example is much less obvious than the first.

Single Expression Closures

There's an even shorter form for closures that return a value. If the code for the entire closure can be expressed in a single return statement, you can omit the `return` statement and write the closure as an expression. This is particularly useful with methods like Swift's `sort(_:)` and `map(_:)` array functions. Let's create a simple to-do item array with the following code:

```
struct ToDoItem {
    let priority: Int
    let note: String
}
var toDoList = [ ToDoItem(priority: 3, note: "Recycle ice cream cups"),
                 ToDoItem(priority: 1, note: "Buy ice cream"),
                 ToDoItem(priority: 2, note: "Invite friends over") ]
```

You can sort this array with the array's `sort(_:)` function. This function accepts a single closure used to compare any two elements in the array. The closure receives two parameters (the two array elements to compare) and returns a Boolean value indicating whether the first (left) parameter should be before the second (right) parameter in the new order. (You'll find examples of this in the `Learn iOS Development Projects` ➤ Ch 20 ➤ `Closures.playground` file.)

Let's sort the array into priority order. Writing this closure with named parameters would look something like the following:

```
toDoList.sort( { (left, right) in return left.priority < right.priority } )
```

As you learned earlier, you can also write the closure using the shorthand parameter names, as follows:

```
toDoList.sort( { return $0.priority < $1.priority } )
```

But since the entire closure is a single return statement, Swift lets you get away with leaving out the `return` and writing the closure as just the expression. The following two statements are equivalent to the previous two:

```
toDoList.sort( { (left, right) in left.priority < right.priority } )
toDoList.sort( { $0.priority < $1.priority } )
```

Trailing Closures

Closures can get even shorter—well, maybe not the closure, but the syntax used to pass a closure as a parameter. If the last argument of a function call is a closure parameter, you can omit that argument and write the closure immediately after the function call. This is called a *trailing closure*. The SKNode class has an `enumerateChildNodesWithName(_:,usingBlock:)` method. The following example shows how you would call that method passing the closure as a regular argument:

```
let scene = SKScene()
scene.enumerateChildNodesWithName("firefly", usingBlock: {
        (node, _) in
        node.hidden = false
    })
```

To write the same code using a trailing closure, omit the last parameter and follow the function call with the closure, as follows:

```
scene.enumerateChildNodesWithName("firefly") { (node, _) in node.hidden = false }
```

Again, this is particularly useful with functions like sort(_:). Using the earlier single expression example, you can ultimately write the sort function as follows:

```
toDoList.sort() { $0.priority < $1.priority }
```

This last example combines type inference, shorthand parameter names, single expression, and the trailing closure shortcuts.

Closure Variables

When you're ready to store a closure in a variable or write a function the takes a closure as a parameter, you'll need to write a closure type. A *closure type* is the signature of the closure (the part before the in keyword) inside parentheses. You write a variable that stores a closure as follows:

```
var closure: ((Int, String) -> Int)
```

This variable stores a closure that receives two parameters, an Int and a String, and returns an Int. Closure parameters don't have external names or default values, so only the parameter types are listed. You can later assign a closure to this variable and later execute it as follows:

```
closure = { (number,name) in return 1 }
closure(7,"deborah")
```

Similarly, a function with a closure parameter is written as follows:

```
func closureAsParameter(key: String, master: ((String) -> Int)) {
    unlockDoor(master(key))
}
```

Since the closure is the last parameter, this function is eligible for tailing closure syntax, like this:

```
closureAsParameter("The Key") { (key) in return key.hash }
```

Protocols

A *protocol* is a set of properties or methods that a class (or other type) can adopt. A protocol is, effectively, a promise to implement a specific set of features. Once your class fulfills that promise, your class can be used in any place that wants a type with that protocol. A class that adopts a protocol is said to *conform to* that protocol.

You declare a protocol much the way you would a class, using the `protocol` keyword. As a simple example, let's create a `Flavor` protocol as follows. These, and other, examples can be found in the `Learn iOS Development Projects` ➤ `Ch 20` ➤ `Protocols.playground` file.

```
protocol Flavor {
    var flavor: String { get }
    func tastesLike(flavor otherFlavor: Flavor) -> Bool
}
```

This protocol requires a `String` property named `flavor` and a function named `tastesLike(flavor:)` that returns a `Bool`.

Your class adopts protocols by listing them after the superclass name (if any), as follows:

```
class IceCream {
    var flavor: String = "Vanilla"
    var scoops: Int = 1
}

class Sundae: IceCream, Flavor {
    func tastesLike(flavor otherFlavor: Flavor) -> Bool {
        return flavor == otherFlavor.flavor
    }
}
```

In this example, the class Sundae is a subclass of IceCream and adopts the Flavor protocol. Adopting the protocol requires that it have a flavor property and a tastesLike(flavor:) function. The first was already inherited from its superclass, so implementing the function is all that's required to adopt this protocol.

> **Note**   Objective-C can define protocols with optional properties and methods. Your class can decline to implement an optional method and will still conform to the protocol. Swift protocols do not have optional members.

The adopting class can fulfill a property requirement with either a stored or a computed property that is implemented, overridden, or inherited. A protocol doesn't care how a class implements the interface, just that it does. Every property in a protocol is followed by either { get } or { get set }. Any property will satisfy the former. If the protocol states the property is { get set }, you must implement a mutable property.

Once Sundae has adopted Flavor, it can be used anywhere there's a variable of type Sundae, IceCream, or Flavor. This allows unrelated classes to be treated as a common type, as long as all adopt the same protocol. In the following example, the completely unrelated class Tofu also adopts the Flavor protocol:

```
class Tofu: Flavor {
    var flavor: String = "Plain"
    var weight: Double = 1.0
```

```
func tastesLike(flavor _: Flavor) -> Bool {
    // Tofu doesn't taste like anything else
    return false
}
}
```

You can now declare variables and parameters of type Flavor and interchangeably use Tofu and Sundae objects as follows:

```
var dessert: Flavor = Sundae()
var chicken: Flavor = Tofu()
if dessert.tastesLike(flavor: chicken) { ...
```

Protocols are regularly used for delegates. A class will use a protocol to define the delegate's interface and then declare a delegate property that can store any object that adopts that protocol. Just look at almost any Cocoa Touch class that has a delegate property.

Extensions

An extension adds properties or methods to an existing class (or other type). You can add methods and computed properties to almost anything, even classes you didn't write. Back in Chapter 7, I told you that adding an imageView property to the MyWhatsit class was poor MVC design because the MyWhatsit class is a data model and the imageView was really a view method. With extensions, you can save your design while still adding an imageView property to MyWhatsit. Start with (a simplified version of) the original class, as follows:

```
class MyWhatsit {
    var name: String
    var location: String
    var image: UIImage?
    ...
}
```

In a separate source file, you can create an extension to MyWhatsit that adds the extra method, as follows. The extension keyword is used to show that you are *extending* the existing class (or other type), not defining a new one.

```
extension MyWhatsit {
    var viewImage: UIImage {
        return image ?? UIImage(named: "camera")!
    }
}
```

Now when you create MyWhatsit objects, they'll all have a viewImage property, just as if you had defined that property in the original class.

```
var thing = MyWhatsit(name: "Robby the Robot")
detailImageView.image = thing.viewImage
```

This preserves MVC separation because the code that manages the data model is separate from the code that deals with view object responsibilities, even though both belong to the same object. In another program, you might reuse the MyWhatsit class in the absence of the extension, in which case the same objects won't have a viewImage property.

Extensions are also handy for adding new functions to common classes. If you need an inKlingon property added to the String type, you can do that in an extension. Then you can write "Hello".inKlingon and Swift will perform your translation, as follows:

```
extension String {
    var inKlingon: String { return self == "Hello" ? "nuqneH" : "nuqjatlh?" }
}
...
let greeting = "Hello"
println(greeting.inKlingon)
```

There are a couple of restrictions to extensions.

■ An extension cannot add stored properties to an existing type. You can only add methods and computed properties.

■ You cannot override an existing property or method in an extension.

Structures

A structure, or struct, in Swift is very much like a class. Unlike most other languages, a Swift structure has more in common with a class than what it doesn't. Here's an example of a Swift structure:

```
struct SwiftStruct {
    var storedProperty: String = "Remember me?"
    let someFixedNumber = 9
    var computedProperty: String {
        get {
            return storedProperty.lowercaseString
        }
        set {
            storedProperty = newValue
        }
    }

    static func globalMethod() {
    }
    func instanceMethod() {
    }
    init(what: String) {
        storedProperty = what
    }
}
```

In Swift, a structure shares the following traits with a class:

- Can define stored properties (and stored properties can have observers)
- Can define computed properties
- Can define methods (instance functions)
- Can define global functions
- Can have custom initializers
- Can adopt protocols
- Can be augmented with extensions

There's very little about these traits that differ—in either capability or syntax—between classes and structures. There are differences, both significant and minor.

- A structure cannot inherit from another structure.
- A structure is a value type, not a reference type.
- A structure does not have a `deinit` function.
- A global function in a structure is declared using the `static` keyword instead of the `class` keyword.

The first is probably the biggest difference. Every structure is an isolated type. Structures do not form an inheritance hierarchy, they cannot participate in subtype polymorphism, and you cannot test their type (which would be pointless because they can only be one type).

Structures are value types. I explain the difference between value and reference types later. For now, just know that a structure is a collection of stored properties. When you assign it to a variable or pass it as a parameter, the entire structure is duplicated. Changes made to a copy do not affect the original.

Like a class, Swift automatically creates a default initializer if all of its stored properties have default values. Unlike a class, a structure also gets a memberwise initializer—assuming it doesn't define any custom initializers of its own. A *memberwise initializer* is an `init` method whose parameters are the names of all of its stored properties. The following example defines a structure with two stored properties. The code that follows creates two instance of the structure using its automatically generated initializers:

```
struct StructWithDefaults {
    var number: Int = 1
    var name: String = "amber"
}

let struct1 = StructWithDefaults()
let struct2 = StructWithDefaults(number: 3, name: "john")
```

Tuples

Tuples are ad hoc, anonymous, structures. Tuples are a convenient way to group a few related values together and treat them as a single value. You write a tuple by surrounding a list of values with parentheses, like this:

```
var iceCreamOrder = ("Vanilla", 1)
```

This statement creates a tuple containing two values, a String and an Int, assigned to the single variable iceCreamOrder. The following example creates the same kind of tuple but also gives its members names:

```
let wantToGet = (flavor: "Chocolate", scoops: 4)
```

The type of a tuple is simply the types of its content. You can assign a tuple to any variable with the same type, as follows:

```
iceCreamOrder = wantToGet
```

> **Note**   There is no practical limit on how many, or what kinds, of values you can include in a tuple. A tuple can be made from floating-point numbers, strings, arrays, objects, structures, enums, dictionaries, closures, and even other tuples.

Tuples are extremely handy for returning multiple values from a function. You used this in Chapter 14 for the score() function; it returned both the player's numeric score and a flag indicating whether the game had been won, in a tuple. In the following example, the nextOrder() function returns a (String, Int) tuple. Play around with these examples in the Learn iOS Development Projects ➤ Ch 20 ➤ Tuples.playground file.

```
func nextOrder() -> (flavor: String, scoops: Int) {
    return ("Vanilla", 4)
}
...
let order = nextOrder()
```

You access the individual values within a tuple much as you would a structure or class. If the tuple members were given names, you can address them as properties, like this:

```
if order.scoops > 3 {
    println("\(order.scoops) scoops of \(order.flavor) in a dish.")
} else {
    println("\(order.flavor) cone")
}
```

If a member of a tuple is anonymous (that is, they don't have member names like the ones in iceCreamOrder), you can still address the member using its index. A *tuple member index* is a number, starting at 0, assigned to each member value in the tuple. You use an index just like a property name, as follows:

```
if iceCreamOrder.0 == "Chocolate" {
    println("\(iceCreamOrder.1) scoops of the good stuff.")
}
```

And there's a third way of addressing the individual values of a tuple. When you assign the tuple, you can *decompose* the tuple into individual variables, as shown here:

```
let (what,howMany) = nextOrder()
if howMany > 3 {
    println("\(howMany) scoops of \(what) in a dish.")
} else {
    println("\(what) cone")
}
```

The first statement declares two new variables, what and howMany. Each is assigned to one value from the tuple. This is a convenient way to assign names to tuples with anonymous members or gain more direct access to each value. If you're not interested in a particular value, replace its variable name with an _ (underscore), just as you would ignore a parameter, as in let (what,_) = nextOrder().

Enumerations

An *enumeration*, or enum, assigns symbolic names to a set of unique literal values. You write an enumeration as a list of the symbols you want to define, as follows:

```
enum Weekday {
    case Sunday
    case Monday
    case Tuesday
    case Wednesday
    case Thursday
    case Friday
    case Saturday
}
```

This defines a new type, Weekday, that can be used much like any other type. The enumeration defines seven unique values. The following statement defines a new variable (dueDay) of type Weekday and assigns it the value Thursday:

```
var dueDay = Weekday.Thursday
```

When Swift already knows the type of the variable or parameter, you can leave out the enumeration type name, like this:

```
dueDay = .Friday
```

This is particularly handy when passing an enumeration value in an argument.

Raw Values

Swift's internal representation of enumeration values is opaque—computer-speak for "you don't know and you can't find out." All you need to know is the values are unique and can be assigned to a variable of that enumeration type.

Optionally, you can define a relationship between the values in an enumeration and values in another type. This alternate value is called the enumeration's *raw value*.

In the following example, an enumeration is defined that has seven values. Each value can be converted to and from a corresponding Int value.

```
enum WeekdayNumber: Int {
    case Sunday = 0
    case Monday
    case Tuesday
    case Wednesday
    case Thursday
    case Friday
    case Saturday
}
```

The choices for a raw value are integer, floating-point number, string, or character. If you choose an integer type, a unique number is automatically assigned to each enumeration value, as shown earlier. You can, optionally, assign specific values to particular cases, as shown with Sunday.

An enumeration value can be converted to its raw value using its rawValue property. Conversely, an enumeration value can be created from a raw value using its init(rawValue:) initializer, both shown here:

```
let dayNumber = WeekdayNumber.Wednesday.rawValue
let dayFromNumber = WeekdayNumber(rawValue: 3)
```

> **Note**   The conversion from a raw value to an enumeration can fail; all enumeration values have a unique raw value, but not all raw values have a corresponding enumeration value. See the "Optionals" section for more about failable initializers.

The dayNumber is an Int with a value of 3. This was obtained by converting the WeekdayNumber. Wednesday value into its raw value. The dayFromNumber is a WeekdayNumber variable containing the value Wednesday, obtained by converting the raw value of 3 into a WeekdayNumber.

Raw values can also be strings or characters. In the following example, an enumeration with string raw values is defined. For non-integer values, you must provide a raw value for every case, and there can be no duplicates.

```
enum WeekdayName: String {
    case Sunday = "Sunday"
    case Monday = "Monday"
    case Tuesday = "Tuesday"
    case Wednesday = "Wednesday"
    case Thursday = "Thursday"
    case Friday = "Friday"
    case Saturday = "Saturday"
}
```

Just as with numeric raw values, you can convert to or from the enumeration value. The following code prints the message "Reports are due on Monday."

```
let reportDay: WeekdayName = .Monday
println("Reports are due on \(reportDay.rawValue).")
```

Associated Values

Each enumeration value can also store a tuple of other values, called *associated values*. This lets you bundle other interesting values with a specific enumeration value. For example, an enumeration of failure reasons might have associated values with information about each particular kind of failure. A .DocumentNotFound value might include the name of the missing document, while the .SessionExpired value might have the time the session ended.

When you add associated values to an enumeration, extra storage space is set aside for the additional tuples. Each tuple is paired with a specific enumeration value. That tuple can only be used when the enumeration variable is set to that value.

It's easier to explain with an example. In the following code, several of the WeekdayChild enumeration values have associated values:

```
enum Sadness {
    case Sad
    case ReallySad
    case SuperSad
}

enum WeekdayChild {
    case Sunday
    case Monday
    case Tuesday(sadness: Sadness)
    case Wednesday
    case Thursday(distanceRemaining: Double)
```

```
    case Friday(friends: Int, charities: Int)
    case Saturday(workHours: Float)
}
```

The .Tuesday and .Saturday values store an associated floating-point number. The .Friday value stores two additional integer values. And the .Thursday value goes completely meta, storing another enumeration value. The other cases do not have associated values; treat those like any other enumeration.

Enumerations and their associated values are constructed through initializers. What follows are some examples, which you can also find in the Learn iOS Development Projects ➤ Ch 20 ➤ Enumerations.playground file.

```
let graceful = WeekdayChild.Monday
let woeful = WeekdayChild.Tuesday(sadness: .ReallySad)
let traveler = WeekdayChild.Thursday(distanceRemaining: 100.0)
let social = WeekdayChild.Friday(friends: 23, charities: 4)
let worker = WeekdayChild.Saturday(workHours: 90.5)
```

> **Tip**   The external names for associated value tuple members are optional. You can leave them out and just use the values, as in WeekdayChild.Friday(23,4).

Oddly, you can't access associated values directly. The only mechanism for retrieving them is through a switch statement, like this one:

```
var child = traveler
switch child {
    case .Sunday, .Monday, .Wednesday:
        break
    case .Tuesday(let mood):
        if mood == .ReallySad {
            println("Tuesday's child is really sad.")
        }
    case .Thursday(let miles):
        println("Thursday's child has \(miles) miles to go.")
    case .Friday(let friendCount, let charityCount):
        println("Friday's child has \(friendCount) friends.")
    case .Saturday(let hours):
        println("Saturday's child is working \(hours) hours this week.")
}
```

You obtain the associated values by decomposing the tuple using let statements within each switch case, as shown earlier. The reason for this odd mechanism is that an enumeration value could, potentially, contain any of the possible enumeration values. But the associated values are only valid when it is set to a specific enumeration value. The switch case ensures that access is only granted to the associated values for that specific enumeration value.

Extended Enumerations

Enumerations are full-blown types, like classes and structures. An enumeration can define computed properties and have static and instance methods. It can adopt protocols, can be extended by extensions, and can have custom initializers. You cannot add stored properties; use associated values for that. The following is an enumeration with computed properties, methods, and a special initializer:

```
enum WeekdayNumber: Int {
    case Sunday = 0
    case Monday
    case Tuesday
    case Wednesday
    case Thursday
    case Friday
    case Saturday

    var weekend: Bool { return self == .Sunday || self == .Saturday }
    var weekday: Bool { return !weekend }
    init(random: Bool) {
        if random {
            nextWeekDayNumber = Int(arc4random_uniform(7))
        }
        self = WeekdayNumber(rawValue: nextWeekDayNumber)!
        nextWeekDayNumber++
        if nextWeekDayNumber > WeekdayNumber.Saturday.rawValue {
            nextWeekDayNumber = WeekdayNumber.Sunday.rawValue
        }
    }
    func dayOfJulienDate(date: NSTimeInterval) -> WeekdayNumber {
        return WeekdayNumber(rawValue: Int(date) % 7 + 2)!
    }
}
var nextWeekDayNumber: Int = WeekdayNumber.Monday.rawValue
```

When writing code that runs in the context of an enumeration, the self variable represents its current value. You establish the enumeration's value in the initializer by assigning a value to self. You'd use any of these features just as you would with a structure or object, as follows:

```
let today = WeekdayNumber(random: true)
if today.weekend {
    clock.alarm.enabled = false
}
```

Numeric Values

Now you're getting down to the simplest types, but there might still be a few surprises waiting for you. Swift has integer and floating-point numeric types. You've been using these throughout this book.

Integer types come in a variety of sizes and signs: Int, UInt, Int8, UInt8, Int16, UInt16, Int32, UInt32, Int64, and UInt64. You'll find examples of these in the Learn iOS Development Projects ➤ Ch 20 ➤ Numbers.playground file.

The vast majority of the time you should use Int, occasionally UInt, and almost nothing else. You'll understand why shortly. The rest of the types are useful only when dealing with specific data sizes, such as binary message formats.

Floating-point numbers come in two flavors: Float and Double. Float is always 32 bits, and Double is always 64-bits.

When running a Swift program on a 32-bit processor, the Int and UInt types are 32 bits wide (equivalent to Int32 and UInt32). When compiled for a 64-bit processor, they are both 64 bits wide. The iOS Foundation library defines the CGFloat type. It is 32-bits (Float) when compiled for 32-bit processors and 64-bits (Double) on 64-bit processors. The Cocoa Touch framework makes extensive use of CGFloat.

Implicit Type Conversion

Swift, quite unlike most computer languages you've probably encountered, has no implicit type conversion. When you assign a variable, pass a value in an argument, or perform an operation on two values, the values you supply must *exactly* match the type expected (with only a few exceptions that I'll get to in a moment). The following example demonstrates this:

```
var signed: Int = 1
var unsigned: UInt = 2
var double: Double = 3.0
var float: Float = 4.0
signed = unsigned // <-- invalid
unsigned = signed // <-- invalid
double = float    // <-- invalid
```

One of the reasons Swift can infer types—relieving you from typing them over and over again—is because there's never any ambiguity about what type a number or expression is, and there's never any possibility of accidentally losing numeric precision through an assignment or conversion. It also means you must intentionally convert any values that aren't the correct type.

This is the reason for my advice to use Int as much as possible. If all your integers are Int, you won't have any conversions to do.

If you have one type and need another, you must explicitly create the type you need. You create integer and floating-point types exactly as you do objects, structures, and enumerations. The following code fixes the impedance mismatch shown earlier by creating new, compatible, types:

```
signed = Int(unsigned)
unsigned = UInt(signed)
double = Double(float)
```

The Int type has initializers that accept every other integer and floating-point type, and vice versa. Generally, these constructors will prevent loss of data by throwing an exception if the conversion cannot be completed. The following example results in an error because the integer value of 300 can't be represented by an 8-bit integer:

```
let tooBigToFit = UInt8(300) // error
```

The exceptions are the integer initializers from floating-point values. These initializers will silently truncate the fractional portion of the value. The expression Int(2.6) will be the integer value 2.

Numeric Literals

Numeric literals, by contrast, are much more flexible. Swift recognizes a variety of number formats, as shown in Table 20-2.

Table 20-2. *Literal Number Formats*

Form	Description
123	Positive integer number
-86	Negative integer number
0xa113cafe	Hexadecimal number
0o557	Octal number
0b010110110	Binary number
1.5	Floating-point number
6.022e23	Floating-point number with exponent
0x2ff0.7p2	Hexadecimal floating-point number with exponent

Any numeric literal can include leading zeros and intermix underscores for readability. Neither changes the value. This lets you write 23_000_000_000 instead of 23000000000. If the type of the literal is not implied or specified, the first five formats in Table 20-2 result in an Int value. The remaining three will be a Double. In the following example, the variable is type Double because the literal defaults to type Double and you didn't specify a type:

```
let avogadroNumber = 6.022_141_29e23
```

However, when you assign a literal to a variable or pass it as an argument, Swift will convert the literal to the receiving type as best it can. This is just about the only time Swift automatically converts types for you. In the following example, an integer literal is being assigned to a Double variable:

```
var double: Double = 3
```

The literal 3 is an integer. But since you're assigning it to a floating-point variable Swift automatically converts the 3 into 3.0, as if you had written var double: Double = Double(3).

Numbers Are Types Too

Unexpectedly, even the simple numeric types are full-fledged types in Swift. A numeric type can have computed properties and methods and can be extended with extensions. The following extension adds a `casualName` property to the `Int` type:

```
extension Int {
    var casualName: String {
        switch self {
            case 0:
                return "no"
            case 1:
                return "just one"
            case 2:
                return "a couple"
            case 3:
                return "a few"
            default:
                return "many"
        }
    }
}
```

Now any `Int` value has a property that can be used like any other property. The following codes print the message "There are a few people here for ice cream."

```
let headCount: Int = 3
println("There are \(headCount.casualName) people here for ice cream.")
```

The standard numeric types already have a number of useful properties. The `min` and `max` properties, for example, return the minimum and maximum value represented by that type. The expression `Int.max` will be the largest positive number you can store in an `Int` variable.

Overflow and Underflow

Swift has the usual suite of mathematical operations: addition (+), subtraction (-), multiplication (*), division (/), reminder division (%), increment (++, both prefix and postfix), and decrement (--, both prefix and postfix). There is also the standard set of reassignment operators: add to (+=), subtract from (-=), multiple with (*=), divide by (/=), and so on. Add to that the bit-shift operators (<< and >>), the bit-wise logical operations (&, |, and ^), and the Boolean logic operators (&& and ||). You should be familiar with all of these. If you have specific questions, refer to *The Swift Programming Guide* in iBooks.

Swift rigorously checks for overflown and underflow in all arithmetic operations. If you increment an integer and the result is too large to be represented by that type, Swift throws a program exception. In the following example, the result of multiplying these two numbers exceeds the value of `Int.max` and terminates the program:

```
let big: Int = 999_999_999
let bigger: Int  = 9_999_999_999
let wayTooBig = big * bigger    // <-- overflow
```

If you have a reason to either embrace or ignore this situation, Swift provides a set of operators that ignore overflow and underflow: multiple ignoring overflow (&*), divide ignoring overflow (&/), remainder ignoring overflow (&%), add ignoring overflow (&+), subtract ignoring overflow (&-), and others.

Strings and Characters

Strings and characters are fundamental types in Swift. A String is swift is a value type. That means if you pass a string as a parameter you're passing a copy of the string, not a reference to the original. Being a value type, a string can be a variable (mutable) or a constant (immutable), as follows:

```
var string: String = "Hello!"
let immutableString: String = "Salut!"
```

String and Character Literals

A string literal is written between double quotes. String literals recognize several escape sequences, all starting with a single \ (backslash) character. Table 20-3 shows the escape codes you can include in a string.

Table 20-3. String Literal Escape Codes

Escape Sequence	Character in String
\\	A single \ character
\"	A single " character
\'	A single ' character
\t	Horizontal tab character
\r	Carriage return character
\0	Null character
\u{*nnnn*}	Unicode scalar with the hexadecimal code of *nnnn*
\(*expression*)	String representation of expression (string interpolation)

Swift uses the same syntax for character literals. The default type of a string literal is the String type. But like numeric literals, Swift will convert a single character string literal into a character literal when it is assigned to a Character type or you explicitly create a Character value. The following examples demonstrate this:

```
let thisIsAString = "String"
let thisIsAlsoAString = "c"
let thisIsACharacter = Character("c")
let thisIsAlsoACharacter: Character = "c"
```

A string literal with a single character is converted to a `Character` type when it's expected to be a `Character`. Otherwise, it will act like a `String`.

If you need to create an empty `String`, use an empty string literal (`""`) or create an empty `String` value (`String()`).

Unicode

Swift fully embraces the Unicode character set. All Swift strings are encoded using Unicode. Furthermore, Swift source files accept Unicode encoding, so you can include any Unicode character right in your program's source file. The following string literal is a perfect example:

```
let hungary = "Üdvözlöm!"
```

Unicode characters are also acceptable in the Swift language. Variable, class, method, parameter, and property names can all include Unicode characters. Basically, any character that is not part of the Swift language is valid in a symbol name. The following two variable names are legal in Swift and can be used anywhere a more pedestrian variable name is used. (See the `Learn iOS Development Projects` ➤ `Ch 20` ➤ `Strings.playground` file for examples of variable names using Emoji characters.)

```
let olá = "Hello!"
let π = 3.14159265359
return π * (r*r)
```

> **Tip**   Swift strings are delimited by the ASCII double quote character (", Unicode 0x22). The more typographical "curly quotes," like the ones around the words "curly quotes," are not recognized as string delimiters. That means you can include single and double curly quotes in your strings without escaping them, like this: `"Rose said "Let's Go!""`.

Unicode encoding is normally transparent, but it can occasionally have odd side effects. Swift uses a particular style of encoding that require some Unicode characters be represented by two or more values. Some string methods will deal with the individual values in your string, while others will interpret the characters in your string. In the following example, the `tricky` value contains a single Unicode character, composed from two Unicode scalars:

```
let tricky = "\u{E9}\u{20DD}" // é
```

If you ask this string what its `length` is, it will return 2. If you ask it how many characters it has, it will return 1. Refer to the sections in *The Swift Programming Guide* on Unicode character encoding and conversion for the details.

String Interpolation

String interpolation is just a fancy name for embedding expressions in a string literal. The expression is converted into a string and becomes part of the resulting string. You've seen this several times in earlier chapters. In the following example, the aboutPi variable is set to "The value of π is approximately 3.14159265359."

```
let aboutPi = "The value of π is approximately \(π)"
let truth = "The character count of \"\(tricky)\" is \(countElements(tricky))"
```

The π variable created earlier was interpreted and converted into a string, which then replaced the \(*expression*) in the string literal. The expression can be anything (formulas, objects, function calls) that Swift can convert into a string.

> **Tip**   To have objects of your custom class convert themselves into strings, override the description property.

While extremely convenient, what string interpolation doesn't provide is any formatting control. Expressions are converted to strings as Swift sees best; you can take it or leave it. If you need to control how values are formatted, say you want an integer value converted into hexadecimal, turn to the NSString class. The following example uses the NSString(format:) initializer to create a string with precise formatting:

```
let aboutPi: String = NSString(format: "The value of %C is about %.4f", 0x03c0, π)
```

The format specifiers, which begin with % (percent sign), can perform a wide variety of conversion, and you have a lot of control over their format. The %f conversion, for example, can limit the number of significant digits after the radix point. In this case, it was capped at four digits. The number 0x03c0 could have been converted into a decimal or octal number but was instead converted to its Unicode character using %C. The resulting NSString is then assigned to the aboutPi variable, which brings us to the next topic.

Strings Are NSStrings

Swift String values are interchangeable with Objective-C NSString objects. You can use a String value wherever an NSString object reference is needed, and vice versa. In the previous section, an NSString object was created and then assigned to the aboutPi: String variable. You can use it like any String and then turn around and pass it to any parameter that expects an NSString.

Swift, however, still treats String values and NSString objects as separate types. If you've created a String value, Swift assumes it only has the methods and properties of a String. If you have an NSString variable, Swift assumes it only has the methods and properties of the NSString class—even though it actually has both. To use NSString methods on a String value, simply cast from one to the other, as shown here:

```
let sparkRange = (string as NSString).rangeOfString("spark")
let objcString = string as NSString
let words = objcString.componentsSeparatedByString(" ")
```

In the first statement, the String value is temporary cast to the NSString type and used to call the rangeOfString(_:) function. In the second statement, the string is again converted to an NSString object but is then assigned to a variable. Since the type of the variable is NSString, you don't have to cast it to use any of the NSString properties or methods. You can also do the reverse, casting any NSString object into a String value.

> **Note** A String, even if it's mutable, cannot be cast to an NSMutableString object.

NSString is a big class and has many useful functions. The String type, by contrast, has very few. By casting your String to NSString, you immediately gain access to the huge repertoire of NSString features. See the NSString class documentation to discover what it offers.

String Concatenation

One feature the String value does offer is string and character concatenation. The + operator will create a new string by concatenating two other strings, as follows:

```
let message = "Amber says " + hungary
```

You can add a string to the end of a mutable string using the += operator. You can also append either a string or an individual character using the append(_:) function, both shown here:

```
var mutableString = "¡Hola!"
mutableString += " James"
let exclamation: Character = "!"
mutableString.append(exclamation)
```

When this code finishes, the mutableString variable contains "¡Hola! James!"

Attributed Strings

You've seen, throughout this book, a number of UIView classes and drawing methods that use attributed strings, instead of regular strings. An *attributed string* associates attribute values with a range of characters within the string. Attributes can express the font the characters are drawn in (font family, size, style), color, typographical adjustments (character spacing), alignment (right justified, superscript, subscript), text decorations (underline, strikethrough), and so on. Attributed strings are flexible and can describe a broad range of complex typography. In concept they're not complicated, although they can be a little tedious in practice.

Attributes are expressed as a dictionary of values. The key identifies the kind of attribute. This dictionary is then associated with a range of characters. The following examples, which you can find in the Learn iOS Development Projects ➤ Ch 20 ➤ AttributedString project, show how attributed strings are constructed:

```
let fancyString = NSMutableAttributedString(string: "iOS ")
let iOSAttrs = [ NSFontAttributeName:            UIFont.italicSystemFontOfSize(80),
                 NSForegroundColorAttributeName: UIColor.redColor(),
                 NSKernAttributeName:            NSNumber(integer: 4) ]
fancyString.setAttributes(iOSAttrs, range: NSRange(location: 0, length: 3))
```

This first block of code creates a mutable attributed string from a plain string. It then creates a dictionary, defining three attributes: the italic system font at 80 points, the color red, and a kerning (inter-character spacing) of 4 points. Those attributes are applied to the first three characters of the string. Note that the space character (fourth character in the string) has no attributes.

This technique used the NSMutableAttributedString class. Use this class when you want to assemble your attributed string piecemeal or you want to assign different attributes to particular ranges within the string. The next example uses a much simpler technique:

```
let shadow = NSShadow()
shadow.shadowOffset = CGSize(width: 5, height: 5)
shadow.shadowBlurRadius = 3.5

let appAttrs = [ NSFontAttributeName:            UIFont.boldSystemFontOfSize(78),
                 NSShadowAttributeName:          shadow ]
let secondString = NSAttributedString(string: "App!", attributes: appAttrs)
```

The second technique creates an attributed string directly from a string and a dictionary of attributes. The appAttrs dictionary describes the system bold font at 78 points. It also applies a drop shadow, defined with an offset of (5.0,5.0) and blur radius of 3.5. When you create an attributed string this way, the attributes apply to all of the characters and the object is immutable.

```
fancyString.appendAttributedString(secondString)
label.attributedText = fancyString
```

Finally, the second attributed string is appended to the first. The appended string retains all of its attributes. The fancyString object now has eight characters, with one set of attributes for the first three, a different set for the last four, and still no attributes for the space between. All attributes have default values, and each character will use the default values for any attributes it's missing.

When the attributed string is assigned to a UILabel, as shown in Figure 20-2, its attributes determine how it is drawn.

Figure 20-2. An attributed string in a label

Here are some tips for using attributed strings:

- An attributed string is *not* a subclass of String or NSString. It has an NSString (its string property), but it isn't an NSString and you can't use it place of a String or NSString.

- If the attributes apply to the entire string, you can create a homogenous, immutable, attributed string using NSAttributedString(string:,attributes:).

- If you want to create an attributed string with a mixture of different attributes, you must create an NSMutableAttributedString and construct it piecemeal.

- Using a mutable attributed string, you can set the attributes for a range of characters (setAttributes(_:,range:)), which replace any previous attributes for that range. You can also add (addAttributes(_:,range:)) or remove (removeAttributes(_:,range:)) attributes. These methods combine with, or selectively remove from, the existing attributes.

> **Caution**   Never change an attribute by altering the value object in an attribute dictionary that's already been assigned to a range. You must always replace the attributes to change them.

Find the *NSAttributedString UIKit Additions Reference* in Xcode's Documentation and API Reference window. The "Constants" section lists all of the attribute keys supported by iOS and what kind of value object to supply for each.

Collections

Swift has two native collection types: arrays and dictionaries. An array is an ordered collection of values. You address individual elements by numeric index. A dictionary maps keys to values. You address each element using its key. Dictionaries are sometimes called *associative arrays*.

You've been using arrays and dictionaries throughout this book. I won't bore you with the details (although many can be found in *The Swift Programming Guide*), but here are some things you should know.

First, all Swift arrays and dictionaries have a type; they are not universal collection objects. An array of [Int] type can store only Int values. For a dictionary, you specify both the type of the key and the type of the value. The preferred method of declaring an array type is with the syntax [Type]. For dictionaries, it's [Type:Type], where the first is the key's type, and the second is the value's. The following examples show some array variables being declared:

```
var emptyArrayOfInts: [Int] = []
var anotherEmptyArrayOfInts = [Int]()
var arrayTypeInferredFromElements = [ 1, 2, 3 ]
var arrayWithADozenPis = [Double](count: 12, repeatedValue: 3.1415926)
```

The emptyArrayOfInts is explicitly declared to be an array of Int values. Its default value is an empty array. The anotherEmptyArrayOfInts variable has the same type, inferred from the type of its default value. This is the syntax you use to create an empty array of a specific type. The arrayTypeInferredFromElements is also an array of Int values. Swift determined its type by looking at the types of the values in the literal array.

Finally, the arrayWithADozenPis variable uses a special array initializer that generates an array of arbitrary size and fills each element with the same value. Now here are some examples with dictionaries:

```
var emptyDictionary = [String:String]()
var dictionaryTypesInferredFromElements = ["red": UIColor.redColor() ]
```

The emptyDictionary contains an empty dictionary that maps String keys to String values. The dictionaryTypesInferredFromElements variable has String keys and UIColor values, inferred from the default value.

The syntax for a literal array is [*element, element*]. A literal array can contain any number (even zero) elements, separated by commas. A literal dictionary is written [*key: value, key: value*]. If you're assigning a collection to a variable or parameter, all of the elements, keys, and values must be compatible with the type of the array or dictionary.

Like String values, arrays are interchangeable with NSArray objects, and dictionaries are interchangeable with NSDictionary objects. Also like String values, arrays and dictionaries are value types. When you pass an array or dictionary as an argument, the entire collection is copied.

> **Note**   Arrays and dictionaries aren't actually copied when you pass them as a parameter. Swift uses a technique of "lazy copying" that waits until the called function actually tries to modify the collection before duplicating it. Since most functions do not change the collections passed to them, Swift avoids the overhead of repeatedly copying the collection while maintaining the illusion that they are always copied.

Here's the crash course on accessing and modifying an array:

- Get the value of an element using subscript syntax: array[1]

- Replace an element by assigning it, using subscribe syntax: array[1] = value

- Append an element to the end of the array with the append(_:) function: array.append(value)

- Append another array to the end of the array using the concatenation assignment (+=) operator: array += [value, value]

- Insert an element at an arbitrary position using the insert(_:,atIndex:) function: array.insert(value, atIndex: 3)

- Remove an element with the removeAtIndex(_:) function: array.removeAtIndex(2)

- Get the number of elements in the array from the count property: array.count

- See whether the array is empty from its isEmpty property: array.isEmpty

Using a dictionary is similar but instead of an index you address each element using its key.

- Get a value using subscript syntax and a key: dictionary["key"]

- Add or replace a value by assignment, using subscript syntax and a key: dictionary["key"] = value

- Add or replace a value, and also determine the value being replaced, using the updateValue(_:,forKey:) function: let previousValue = dictionary.updateValue(value,"key")

- Remove a value by setting it to nil, using subscript syntax: dictionary["key"] = nil

- Remove a value and discover the value being removed using the removeValueForKey(_:) function: let removedValue = dictionary.removeValueForKey("key")

Keys in a dictionary are unique. Setting a value for an existing key replaces the value previous stored for that key. The keys to a dictionary are often strings but can be any type that conforms to the Hashable protocol. Swift's String, Int, Double, and Bool types are all suitable keys. A type that conforms to Hashable must provide the following:

- It implements its == operator so it can be compared with other values of the same type.

- It efficiently implements a hashValue property.

Another thing you're going to want to do is iterate through the values in an array, a dictionary, or even a string for that matter. To do that, you need to know a little about for loops.

Control Statements

Swift, like all C-like languages, has the usual complement of control statements: if, if-else, else-if, for, while, do-while, and switch. The if, if-else, else-if, while, and do-while don't hold any surprises, but there are a couple if cosmetic differences between Swift and similar languages.

- The condition expression does not have to be enclosed in parentheses.

- The condition must be a Boolean expression.

- The curly braces for the conditional code block are required.

Here are a few trivial examples. You'll find these in the Learn iOS Development Projects ➤ Ch 20 ➤ Control.playground file.

```swift
var condition = true
var otherCondition = true

if condition {
    // condition is true
}

if condition {
    // condition is true
} else {
    // condition is false
}

if condition {
    // condition is true
} else if otherCondition {
    // condition is false and otherCondition is true
} else {
    // Both condition and otherCondition are false
}

while condition {
    // Repeat while condition is true
    condition = done
}
```

```
do {
    // Execute once
    otherCondition = done
    // Repeat until otherCondition is false
} while otherCondition
```

Swifts `for` and `switch` statements, on the other hand, have many talents. Let's take a look at `for` loops first.

for Loop

Swift's `for` loop comes in three flavors: traditional, range, and collection. The traditional version is the composed `init`/`while`/`increment` form you see in all C-like languages. Here's an example:

```
for condition = true; condition; condition = false {
}
```

The first statement is executed once to initialize the loop. Then, as long as the condition expression is true, the loop repeats. At the end of each loop, the increment statement is executed, and the condition expression is reevaluated. No surprises here.

The other two forms, often referred to as `for-in` statements, iterate over a range of numeric values or the elements in a collection. The range form looks like the following:

```
for i in 0..<100 {
    // perform 100 times, with i=0 through i=99
}

for i in 0...100 {
    // perform 101 times, with i=0 through i=100
}
```

The `for-in` range loops over a sequence of numbers, described by the range. The *closed-range*, `0...100`, includes all of the value from 0 to 100, inclusive (101 numbers in total). The *half-open range*, `0..<100`, includes the number from 0 to one less than 100. Note that either value in a range can be any numeric expression, such as `0..<inventory.count`.

Caution   The start value of a range must be less than or equal to the end value.

The second `for-in` loop format iterates over contents of a collection. This can be used to loop through the values in an array, dictionary, or string. For arrays and strings (which, in this situation, is treated as an array of characters) the format is simple, as follows:

```
let notes = [ "do", "re", "mi", "fa", "sol", "la", "ti" ]
for note in notes {
    // Loop executes 7 times: note is "do" first time, "re" second time, ...
}
```

```
for character in "When you know the notes to sing, you can sing most anything" {
    // Loop executes 59 times, once for each character in the string
}
```

When used with a dictionary, the loop variable is a tuple containing the (key,value) pair of each entry. You can use a tuple loop variable or decompose it into key and value variables. Both are shown in the following example:

```
let doReMi = [ "doe": "a deer, a female deer",
               "ray": "a drop of golden sun",
               "me":  "a name, I call myself",
               "far": "a long long way to run",
               "sew": "a needle pulling thread",
               "la":  "a note to follow so",
               "tea": "I drink with jam and bread" ]
for note in doReMi {
    // tuple loop variable
    println("\(note.0): \(note.1)")
}

for (noteName,meaning) in doReMi {
    // decomposed variables
    println("\(noteName): \(meaning)")
}
```

Note that you never put a **let**, **var**, or a type for the loop variable. It is always a constant (**let**), and its type is dictated by the range or the collection's element type. Also remember that arrays and strings are always processed in sequential order, but dictionaries are unordered collections, and the order of elements is indeterminate.

switch Statement

Swift's switch statement is a Swiss Army knife of useful tools, far exceeding the capabilities of switch statements you'll find in similar languages. Let's begin with a simple example, which you're undoubtedly familiar with.

```
let number = 9
switch number {
    case 1:
        println("The lonest number")
    case 2:
        println("Enough to tango")
    case 3, 5, 7:
        println("\(number) is prime")
    case 4, 6, 8:
        println("\(number) is even")
    case 13:
        println("Considered unlucky")
```

```
default:
    println("\(number) is a not number I'm familiar with")
}
```

There are a number of features you should be aware of.

- You can switch on most Swift types (integer, string, enumeration, tuple, and any object or struct that conforms to the Equatable protocol).

- Multiple matching conditions can be listed in a single case statement, separated by commas.

- There is no "fall through." Execution of the statement finishes at the end of each case code block. If you want one block to fall through to the next, end the block with the special fallthrough statement.

- Because there is no "fall through," break statements are not required, but you can still use them to exit a block early. If you have a case that has no code, use a single break statement; each case must have a code block, and a break satisfies that requirement.

- All switch statements must be exhaustive, which means they have to cover every possible case. For enumerations, this means you must provide a case for every enumeration value. If your cases aren't exhaustive (or Swift is unable to determine that they are), you must include a default case.

What makes the switch statement so powerful are its case expressions. A case expression is actually a pattern matching mechanism. It can be a constant (as shown earlier), a range, an arbitrary expression, or a tuple containing multiple patterns. You can bind tuple values to new variables or qualify the case expression with arbitrary Boolean conditions. Let's look at these variations, one at a time.

Range Cases

A case can also be a range, as shown in the following example:

```
let testScore = 91
switch testScore {
    case 94...100:
        println("Outstanding!")
    case 86...93:
        println("Very respectable")
    case 75...85:
        println("Pretty good")
    case 60...74:
        println("OK")
    default:
        println("Fail")
}
```

The integer value `testScore` is evaluated against each closed range. "Can the ranges overlap?" you ask. "Can they include variables or expressions?" you ask. Yes, they can. Check out the following `switch` statement:

```
let passingScore = 55
switch testScore {
    case 94...100:
        println("Outstanding!")
    case (100+passingScore)/2...100:
        println("Very respectable")
    case passingScore...100:
        println("Good enough")
    default:
        println("Fail")
}
```

Some of these ranges are determined by variables, and some include expressions. The ranges also overlap. This `case` statement works because of these rules:

- Cases are evaluated in order.
- The first case to match the value is executed.

If you have two overlapping cases, order them so the one with precedence is earlier in the case list.

Switching Tuples

Now take a look at switching on a tuple, as shown in the following example:

```
var sandwich = ("pastrami", "swiss")
var name = ""
switch sandwich {
    case ("tuna", "cheddar"):
        name = "Tuna melt"
    case ("ground beef", "cheddar"):
        name = "Cheeseburger"
    case ("ground beef", _):
        name = "Hamburger"
    case ("steak", "cheddar"):
        name = "Cheesesteak"
    case ("ham", "american"):
        name = "Ham & Cheese"
    case ("ham", "gruyère"):
        name = "Croque-monsieur"
    case ("ham", "swiss"):
        name = "Cuban"
    default:
        name = "\(sandwich.0) with \(sandwich.1)"
}
```

The patterns in each case are applied to the corresponding value in the switch tuple. If all match, the case is executed. In this example, most of the patterns are constants. But any of them could be a variable, an expression, or a range, just like a nontuple `switch` statement.

You can also have a *wildcard* that always matches a value in the tuple. If you want to ignore that value, replace the tuple pattern with _ (underscore), as shown in the ("ground beef", _) case in the previous example. If you want to match all values and also inspect that value in your code, bind the value using a `let` statement, as shown in the following example:

```
sandwich = ("ground beef", "blue cheese")
switch sandwich {
    case ("tuna", "cheddar"):
        name = "Tuna melt"
    case ("ground beef", let cheese):
        name = "Hamburger with \(cheese)"
    default:
        name = "Today's Speical"
}
```

The `let cheese` pattern matches every possible value of `sandwich.1` and then binds that value to the `cheese` variable. You can now use `cheese` and `sandwich.1` interchangeably in that case's code.

Back in the "Enumerations" section, a `switch` statement was also used to access the associated values of an enumeration. With your fresh infusion of `switch` statement knowledge, you might want to look at that example again.

And if that weren't enough flexibility, you can qualify any case with an arbitrary condition—like tacking on an additional `if` statement. You can follow a `case` statement with a `where` expression. If the case pattern matches, the `where` condition is then evaluated. If it's true, then the `case` block is executed. If not, the case didn't match and the next case is considered. The following example demonstrates this:

```
let now = NSDate()
let cal = NSCalendar.currentCalendar()
let when = cal.components(.HourCalendarUnit | .WeekdayCalendarUnit, fromDate: now)
var special = ""
switch when.weekday {
    case 1, 7 where when.hour<13:        // weekend (Sunday or Saturday) before 1 PM
        special = "Eggs Benedict"
    case 1, 7:                           // weekend, the rest of the day
        special = "Cobb Salad"
    case 2 where when.hour<8:            // Monday, before 8 AM
        special = "Ham with Red-eye Gravy"
    case 3, 5 where when.hour<10:        // Tuesday or Thursday, before 10 AM
        special = "Fried Egg Sandwich"
    case 4:                              // Wednesday, all day
        special = "Ruben"
    case 5, 6:                           // Thursday (after 10 AM) or anytime Friday
        special = "Egg Salad Sandwich"
    default:                             // any other time
        special = "Cheeseburger"
}
```

The when variable contains calendar components for the current date and time. Calendar components are understandable time units, like the day of the week, the name of the month, and so on. This case statement uses a combination of patterns to match the weekday, combined with a Boolean expression to qualify the time of day. The expressions could be anything and might also consider if it was a holiday or Friday the 13th.

Optionals

For more than a half-century, programmers have been struggling with a problem: when is a value not a value? There are often situations where a variable, like a date, might contain a valid date object and sometimes it wouldn't. Long ago, programmers settled on the convention of storing a zero for the pointer or object reference value to indicate that it doesn't refer to a valid object. They called this value NULL or nil.

> **Note**   This practice became so widespread that modern computer memory hardware is now designed so there is never any valid memory at, or near, address 0x00000000. This prevents an empty pointer reference from being confused with valid data. (It's also a quick way to crash your program.)

Early programming languages will allow any pointer or object reference can be set to nil. That means that any object reference, in any variable and parameter, in any function could be nil. You either have to test every single incoming value for nil or just hope the caller never sends you a nil reference when you don't expect one. This dilemma is unquestioningly the single most common cause of program crashes on iOS and most other platforms.

The situation gets worse with values like integers. You must reserve one value to mean that the number is not valid. Sometimes this can be as simple as 0 or -1, but if those too are useful numbers, you might have to pick a number like -999 or 9,223,372,036,854,775,807. And there's no convention for this, so if someday -999 turns out to be a usable number, all that code has to change. And it gets worse with smaller types. Consider a Boolean value. Do you pick true or false to mean that it's neither true nor false?

Swift solves this, and a host of other problems, with the optional. An *optional* type is a type that can either hold a value or have no value at all. Every Swift type has an optional type, designated by a question mark (?) following the type name. An Int type always stores an integer value. An Int? type can store any integer value or might have no value at all.

The optional type lets programmers do what they've always needed to do; declare a variable that might have a value or might not. But Swift does it in a very clear and deliberate way and without reserving any values.

More importantly, when you don't use an optional, Swift guarantees that the variable will contain a valid value. Always. No question. If you have an NSDate parameter, that parameter will *always* have a valid date object in it. You never have to test to see whether it's nil, and your program can never crash because you forget to test for nil.

Using Optionals

You declare an optional by suffixing any type with a ?, as shown in the following examples:

```
var sometimesAnObject: NSDate? = NSDate()
var sometimesAString: String? = nil
var sometimesAnInt: Int?
var sometimesAnAnswer: Bool?
```

In the first example, sometimesAnObject can store either an NSDate object or the special value nil. In Swift, nil does not mean zero; it is a special value reserved to mean "no value" and does not equate to any other value. The sometimesAString variable stores an optional string, preset to "no value." When you declare an optional, you don't have to supply a default value; Swift automatically sets it to nil. Both sometimesAnInt and sometimeAnAnswer are pre-initialized to nil.

You can use the "old school" method and test an optional for nil, just as you might test a pointer for NULL in another language. In the following example, the sometimesAnObject is compared to nil and then used accordingly:

```
if sometimesAnObject != nil {
    println("The date is \(sometimesAnObject!)")
} else {
    println("I better not use sometimesAnObject")
}
```

You determine whether an optional has a value by comparing it to nil (either with optional == nil or with optional != nil). In fact, that's the only thing you can do directly with an optional. Once you determine that the variable has a value, you access its value with the optional! syntax. The exclamation point *unwraps* the optional, accessing its underlying value.

And here lies the danger. If you unwrap an optional that doesn't have a value, you can crash your program just as fast as using a NULL pointer in C. To help you avoid the mistakes of the past, Swift provides a special if statement just for dealing with optionals. The following code is equivalent to the previous example:

```
if let date = sometimesAnObject {
    println("The date is \(date)")
} else {
    // This block has no 'date' variable
}
```

The if let variable = optional statement is called *optional binding*, and it does three things in a single step. It first checks to see whether sometimeAnObject contains a value (sometimesAnObject!=nil). If it does, it creates a new constant (let date: NSDate) and then unwraps the optional and assigns it to that constant (= sometimesAnObject!). The code block of the if statement then executes. Since the constant (date) is not an optional, you can freely use it in the body of the block—no unwrapping required.

If sometimesAnObject does not contain a value, nothing happens. The if block doesn't execute. If there was an else block, it executes instead, but there's no date value defined there.

You might be imagining that your code will now be filled with if optional != nil and if let value = optional statements. Don't worry. Swift has a shortcut that simplifies testing for nil in many circumstances, which I'll get to in a moment.

Optionals Carry

An optional is a type, distinct from any other type. When you let Swift choose the type of a variable, you may end up with an optional where you might not expect one. The following is a simple example:

```
var dictionary = [String:String]()
let key = "key"
let value = dictionary[key]        // value: String?
if let existingValue = value {
    println("The value for key \"\(key)\" is \(existingValue).")
} else {
    println("There is no value for key \"\(key)\".")
}
```

The variable value is of type String?. "Why?" you ask. Because the return type of the dictionary subscript accessor is an optional. The dictionary might not have a value associated with that particular key. So, the return type is an optional that can also return "no value" for the answer.

The side effect is that you've created an optional variable (value), and if you want to use the result you must consider the possibility that there is no value for the key "key".

Optional Chaining

The obvious reason for testing to see whether an optional has a value is to avoid accessing the value that's not there or the properties that don't exist, or calling any of the functions that won't work. Swift has an *optional chaining* syntax that tests a variable and performs the next part of the expression (property access, function call, and so on) only if it contains a value. If it doesn't, the expression does nothing. Here's an example:

```
class Cat {
    var quote: String { return "Most everyone's mad here." }
    var directions: String?
    var friend: Hatter?
    func disappear() { println("I'm not all here myself.") }
}
var cheshire: Cat?

cheshire?.disappear()
```

The cheshire variable contains an optional Cat? object. The statement cheshire?.disappear() uses optional chaining. The ? after the cheshire variable says "Check to see if cheshire contains a value and perform the rest of the expression only if it does." That simple statement is roughly equivalent to the following code:

```
if cheshire != nil {
    cheshire!.disappear()
}
```

Optional chaining can also be used to safely set a property, as follows:

```
cheshire?.directions = "Return to the Tulgey woods."
```

When used with properties or the return values of methods, optional chaining will turn any property or return value into an optional. In the following example, the words variable becomes an optional:

```
let words = cheshire?.quote
```

The words constant is a String?. The quote property is not optional, but since it was optionally invoked by chaining, the expression becomes an optional. When cheshire? is evaluated, Swift checks to see whether it is nil. If it is nil, Swift stops evaluating the expression and immediately returns nil. So, even if quote can never return a nil value, cheshire?.quote can. In the next example, optional chaining is compounded with an optional property:

```
let whereToGo = cheshire?.directions
```

The whereToGo variable is still a String?. The directions property is also an optional, but there are no "optional optionals" in Swift. This expression will return either nil or a String. If it returns nil, there's no way (unless you go check) to know whether it was because cheshire was nil or directions was nil. Optional chaining can be as deep as you like, as the following example shows:

```
class Mouse {
    func recitePoem() { }
}
class Hatter {
    var doorMouse: Mouse?
    func changePlaces() { }
}
```

```
cheshire?.friend?.doorMouse?.recitePoem()
```

The last statement will call the Mouse object's recitePoem() function only if cheshire, its friend property, and that property's doorMouse property, all have values. If any don't, the statement does nothing.

It's not obvious, but optional chaining turns *any* statement into an optional. You probably don't think of the recitePoem() function as returning a value, but to Swift it does, and you can use this to your advantage.

This gets a little esoteric, but in Swift the Void type is still a type, and it returns a value, the empty tuple (()), a value with no values. So, while the recitePoem() function doesn't return anything useful, when it becomes an optional, you can test to see whether it returns nothing or nil. (I told you this gets esoteric.) The following example demonstrates this:

```
if cheshire?.friend?.doorMouse?.recitePoem() != nil {
    // cheshire has a friend with a doormouse that recited a poem
}
```

If all of the variables and properties contain a value, the recitePoem() function executes and returns the void tuple (()). If any were nil, the expression stops and results in nil. You can test to see whether you got back a void result or nil, which tells you whether the function executed. See, that wasn't so complicated after all.

Failable Initializers

Initializers can also be optional. These are called *failable initializers*. A failable initializer may decide that it can't create the specific object, structure, enumerator, or whatever you're trying to conjure up. It aborts the construction of the new type and returns nil. You've used failable initializers in earlier chapters. In MyStuff app, you created a UIImage from a resource in your project using code similar to the following:

```
let noSuchImage = UIImage(named: "SevenImpossibleImages")
```

It's entirely possible that a resource named SevenImpossibleImages isn't in your app's bundle. The UIImage can't be constructed, and the noSuchImage optional is set to nil.

You can write your own failable initializer using the init? function name. The following example shows a class that represents a point of interest on a map. It has a database of known locations and their coordinates. If the point of interest isn't known, the object can't be created.

```
class PointOfInterest {
    let name: String
    let location = CLLocationCoordinate2D(latitude: 0, longitude: 0)

    init?(placeName name: String) {
        self.name = name
        if let loc = locationForPointOfInterest(name) {
            self.location = loc
        } else {
            return nil
        }
    }
}

let castle = PointOfInterest(placeName: "Mystery Castle")
```

The initializer function decides whether the object can be created. If not, it deliberately returns nil, signaling that the initializer failed. This makes the return type of the initializer PointOfInterest?.

Implicit Unwrapping

I've saved the worst for last. Swift will let you step right back into the last century by declaring an implicitly unwrapped variable, as follows:

```
var dangerWillRobinson: String!
```

The variable dangerWillRobinson is an optional with none of the normal safeguards. You can still treat it an optional—compare it to nil, conditionally bind it, and use optional chaining—but you aren't required to. If you use the variable by name, it is automatically unwrapped. If it is nil, the results can range from the amusing to the catastrophic.

There's a place for implicitly unwrapped variables, but they should be your last choice. In order of preference:

- Use non-optional variables whenever possible. Swift ensures they will always contain a valid value. This eliminates all ambiguity.

- For values that could legitimately be absent or you need to create the variable well before it can be initialized, use an optional.

- Reserve implicitly unwrapped optionals for values that can't immediately be initialized, but you can reasonably guarantee will be valid before being used.

Interface Builder makes use of implicitly unwrapped variables. Whenever you use the @IBOutlet modifier, it requires the variable to be implicitly unwrapped. You've seen these countless times in the book so far, like this example:

```
@IBOutlet var label: UILabel!
```

The variable can't be set when the view controller object is created. But it will be set by the outlet connection when the scene is loaded from the storyboard. So, by the time your code executes, it will (should!) have a value, and your code can safely assume it has a value.

Unwrapping has some good qualities. It can, if careful used, simplify your code by turning optionals back into non-optional values. Revisiting the UIImage issue, let's say you have an image resource that is a permanent part of your app. There's no reason to assume that the image can't be loaded. You can use unwrapping to turn that back into the regular value that you know it is, as shown in the following code:

```
let placeholderImage = UIImage("placeholder")!
```

The ! blindly unwraps the optional and returns its value, which we trust is always valid.

If you're nervous about an implicitly unwrapped variable, consider adding assert statements to your code. The following code assumes the CheshireCat resource exists but hedges the bet by adding an assert statement:

```
var cheshireImage: UIImage! = UIImage(named: "CheshireCat")
assert(cheshireImage != nil, "Unable to load CheshireCat resource")
catView.image = cheshireImage
```

If the CheshireCat image can't be loaded for some reason, the assert condition will be false, your program will immediately stop, and you'll catch the problem right away—or at least during development.

Type Casting

Occasionally, you'll find yourself with a variable of some base type, like IceCream, that actually has a BananaSplit object in it. You might have a need to interact with that as a BananaSplit object, giving you access to the properties and methods of the specific subclass. Treating one type as if it were another is called *type casting*. Swift has tools to probe the class of a variable and cast it to another type.

If you're simply interested in knowing whether the class of an object is actually a specific subclass, use the is operator. The following example creates objects with three different classes, all compatible with the IceCream class:

```
let cone = IceCream()
let sundae = IceCreamSundae()
let split = BananaSplit()

let mysteryDessert1: IceCream = cone
let mysteryDessert2: IceCream = sundae
let mysteryDessert3: IceCream = split

mysteryDessert1 is IceCreamSundae    // false
mysteryDessert2 is IceCreamSundae    // true
mysteryDessert3 is IceCreamSundae    // true

mysteryDessert1 is BananaSplit       // false
mysteryDessert2 is BananaSplit       // false
mysteryDessert3 is BananaSplit       // true
```

BananaSplit is a subclass of IceCreamSundae, which is a subclass of IceCream. All three were assigned to IceCream variables. The is operator evaluates to true if the object is actually the class, or a subclass, of the given type. cone is neither an IceCreamSundae nor a BananaSplit. sundae is an IceCreamSundae but not a BananaSplit. split is both a BananaSplit and an IceCreamSundae.

> **Note** Swift will not let you write the tautology split is BananaSplit. The split variable is already a BananaSplit type, so it must—by definition—be a BananaSplit object (or a subclass).

Downcasting

Knowing an object's class is interesting, but what you really want to do is to work with the properties and functions of the specific subtype. When you assigned split to mysteryDessert3, Swift *upcast* the object; it took a BananaSplit object and stored it in the more generic (but compatible) IceCream variable. To work with mysteryDessert3 as a BananaSplit object again, you must *downcast* the object, as follows:

```
let mySundae = mysteryDessert2 as? IceCreamSundae
```

The as? operator examines the object and determines whether it's compatible with the type. If it is, it downcasts the object and returns the same object but with the type IceCreamSundae. Now you can do anything with mySundae that you could with sundae. The as? operator, as you might have guessed, returns an optional. If the object can't be safely downcast, it returns nil. Technically, the type of the expression object as? Type is Type?. The following demonstrates the use of downcasting. It's from the Shapely app in Chapter 11.

```
@IBAction func addShape(sender: AnyObject!) {
    if let button = sender as? UIButton {
        ...
    }
}
```

Objective-C doesn't use strong typing the way Swift does. Consequently, a lot of parameters and properties in Objective-C objects are simply AnyObject—a generic type that can hold any object reference. To be useful, you must downcast the value to something interesting. In addShape(_:), the sender parameter is the UIControl that sent the action. We only connected UIButton objects to this action, so the sender should be a UIButton (or some subclass). The if let button = sender as? UIButton checks to make sure it is a UIButton, downcasts it, binds it to the button variable, and runs your code, all in a single statement. If, for some reason, sender isn't a UIButton, your action doesn't do much—but it also doesn't crash.

> **Note** The expression object as? Type will also return nil if object is nil. In the let button = sender as? UIButton statement, sender is an implicitly unwrapped optional. That statement also protects your code from the possibility that sender is nil.

A neat trick is to combine the optional downcast operator with optional chaining, like this:

```
(mysteryDessert2 as? IceCreamSundae)?.nuts = true
```

The downcast operator has a dangerous sibling: the forced downcast operator. It works the same way that as? does, but it doesn't return an optional; it simply assumes the downcast will be successful, the way that ! assumes your optional contains a value. Use it where you are absolutely positive the downcast will work, as follows:

```
let string = "We want ice cream."
let screaming = (string as NSString).uppercaseString

if mysteryDessert2 is IceCreamSundae {
    let mySundae = mysteryDessert2 as IceCreamSundae
    mySundae.nuts = true
}
```

It's always safe to treat a String as an NSString or an Array as an NSArray. In the second example, the if statement has definitively determined that mysteryDesssert2 is an IceCreamSundae, so the expression as IceCreamSundae will always be successful. However, I recommend using binding and optional downcasting to do this because it's shorter, safer, and easier to read.

Downcasting Collections

An array or dictionary is just another type, and you downcast collections the same way you downcast objects. Objective-C arrays and dictionaries are not typed the way Swift's are. Consequently, any time you receive a collection from an Objective-C object it will be a generic [AnyObject] array or an [AnyObject:AnyObject] dictionary. You can downcast it to something more specific, as shown here. (You can find additional examples in the Learn iOS Development Projects ➤ Ch 20 ➤ Casting.playground file.)

```
UIImagePickerController.availableMediaTypesForSourceType(.PhotoLibrary) as [String]
```

The availableMediaTypesForSourceType(_:) function returns a typical [AnyObject] Objective-C array. To use it as an array of String objects, you downcast it to [String].

> **Note**   When you downcast a collection, Swift checks the type of *every* element in the collection to ensure that they are all compatible with that type.

You've already done this in the SpaceSalad project from Chapter 14. A touch event contains a collection of all of the touch points. These are UITouch objects, but since UIEvent is an Objective-C class, allObjects is a generic array. You turned it into the array of UITouch objects with the following expression:

```
let fingers = touches.allObjects as [UITouch]
```

Value vs. Reference vs. Constant vs. Variable

Swift types come in two flavors: value and reference. A *value type* is a variable that stores a value, like an integer or a structure. Simple enough. A *reference type* is a value that stores a reference to a value. Classes are reference types. A variable with a `UILabel` object does not contain that `UILabel` object. The `UILabel` object is allocated somewhere in dynamic memory, and the variable contains a *reference* to that object.

The reason this is a big deal is when you start passing values around in parameters and storing them in other variables. Here are the basic rules:

- Value types are always copied. Pass an `Int` variable in an argument of a function call, and the parameter will be a *copy* of that integer value. You can change the original integer variable, or the parameter, and not affect the other.

- Reference types always refer to the same object. Pass an object variable in an argument of a function call, and the parameter will refer to the same object. Changes to the object are seen by all references to it.

- Even though strings, arrays, and dictionaries are objects (behind the scene— don't tell anyone I told you that), Swift treats them as value types. If you pass an array to a function and modify that array, you're modifying a copy of the array.

Knowing when you're making a copy of a value or passing a reference to the same value is sometimes important. It's particularly important with mutable objects. For example, if you use a collection object like `NSMutableSet`, pass that object to a function, and that function changes the set, when the function returns, your set will have been modified. That won't happen if you'd used an array (value type).

Imaging another situation where you've created an `NSMutableAttributedString` and then use that formatted string for your `UIButton`. The button now has a reference to the same mutable attributed string. What happens if you then modify your attributed string object again?

Actually, nothing happens. The Cocoa Touch framework authors aren't stupid, and they know this can be a problem. There are two techniques for preventing this kind of confusion, and you'll see them throughout iOS.

Many primitive types are immutable. The `UIColor`, `UIFont`, `NSURL`, and many more classes all create immutable objects. Once you have a `UIColor` object you can't change its color. The advantage is that you can use this object's reference in as many places as you like. Because no one can change it, it can't affect anything else that's using it.

Properties like `attributedString` in the `UILabel` class make copies of the object when you set them. So when you set the `attributedString` for the `UIButton`'s title, the `UIButton` object made a copy of your attributed string and kept the copy. You're now free to change the original; it won't affect the button.

Use these same techniques in your code. If you don't want a parameter or property to be affected by later changes to an object, either copy the object when you get it or use immutable objects. Swift has a special `@NSCopying` keyword you can add to stored properties, as follows. It causes a copy of the object to be made when it's set.

```
class SafeClass: NSObject {
    @NSCopying var fancyTitle: NSAttributedString?
}
```

let and var References

In Swift, `let` creates a constant (an immutable value), and `var` creates a variable (a mutable value). So, why can you write the following code?

```
let button = sender as UIButton
button.enabled = false
```

`button` is a constant `UIButton` object. So, why can you modify the `UIButton`? That's because `button` is a constant *reference* to a mutable `UIButton` object. You can change the button object the variable refers to; you just can't change the variable so it later refers to a different `UIButton` object.

Because of this, you'll see `let` used extensively throughout Swift for objects you have every intention of modifying. Conversely, you can't write the following:

```
let companyName = "Yahoo"
companyName.append(Character("!"))    // <-- invalid, companyName can't be modified
```

In Swift, a string is a value type. A `let` string is immutable and can't be changed. The same is true for arrays and dictionaries. This is not true for Objective-C collections. Those are regular objects. A `let` reference to an `NSMutableArray` is still modifiable.

var Parameters

Normally, parameters to a function call are constants. The parameter values cannot be modified in the body of the function. I bet you hadn't even noticed. That's because the parameters to your function are invariably the input for what your function does. You use that input to do something, you rarely do something to your input. But there are two techniques that let you do just that.

The first is to declare a variable parameter using the `var` keyword. It doesn't change how the parameter works, but the parameter's value is mutable in the body of your function. The following is an example from the `Learn iOS Development Projects` ➤ Ch 20 ➤ `References.playground` file:

```
func pad(var # string: String, with char: Character, var # count: Int) -> String {
    while count > 0 {
        string.append(char)
        count--
    }
    return string
}
```

Normally, you wouldn't be able to use the `append(_:)` function on the `string` parameter or decrement the `count` parameter. By specifying that these are var parameters, they become mutable, local variables.

Note that the `string` parameter is a value parameter and still gets copied when the function is called. So, the string you're modifying in the function is not the string that was passed as the argument. You can verify that with the following example:

```
let originalString = "Yahoo"
let paddedString = pad(string: originalString, with: "!", count: 4)
```

After this code executes, `originalString` is still "Yahoo." But what if you did want to modify the original string? There's a way to do that too.

References to Values (inout)

You've already seen how closures create references to your existing values, even value types. You can do something similar in function parameters. If you mark your parameter with the `inout` keyword, it turns your value parameter into a reference parameter. Here's an example:

```
func padSurPlace(inout # string: String, with char: Character, var # count: Int) -> String {
    while count > 0 {
        string.append(char)
        count--
    }
    return string
}
```

The `inout` keyword turns the `string` parameter into a reference to a `String` value. When you call the function, you prefix the variable with an & (ampersand), as follows. This is your visual clue that you're passing a reference to the variable, not a copy of its value.

```
var mutableString = "Yahoo"
padSurPlace(string: &mutableString, with: "!", count: 3)
```

When the `padSurPlace(string:,with:,count:)` function executes, its `string` parameter is referring to the variable you passed in. Any changes made affect the original. After this code executes, the value of `mutableString` will be "Yahoo!!!" This works with any type.

Caution   If you make a parameter `inout`, it can only be used with mutable variables. You can't pass a constant or a literal value for that argument.

Working with C and Objective-C

Swift works so seamlessly with C and Objective-C that there's very little you need to know about either in order to write apps in Swift. In fact, almost everything you've used in this book so far, save what you wrote in Swift, is probably an Objective-C class or C function.

Swift can use any Objective-C class as if it were a Swift class. Objective-C can use most Swift classes as if they were Objective-C classes. If you add Swift to an Objective-C project, or vice versa, Xcode automatically generates translation interfaces that describe your Swift classes to Objective-C and your Objective-C classes to Swift.

There are only a couple of things I want to mention here. If you need to know anything else about how Swift, Objective-C, and C all work together, refer to Apple's *Using Swift with Cocoa and Objective-C*, also available for free in iBooks. This is the companion to *The Swift Programming Language*. It will answer all of your cross-language questions, and probably a few you didn't think of.

The Toll-Free Bridge

In Swift you can seamlessly use Objective-C methods right alongside C functions from Core Foundation. This means you can easily have a mix of Swift values, Objective-C objects, and Core Foundation types. A few of these types overlap and are interchangeable. Table 20-4 lists the Swift, Objective-C, and C types that are equivalent.

Table 20-4. Toll-Free Bridge Types

Swift	Objective-C	C
Array	NSArray	CFArrayRef
	NSAttributedString	CFAttributedStringRef
	NSCharacterSet	CFCharacterSetRef
	NSData	CFDataRef
	NSDate	CFDateRef
Dictionary	NSDictionary	CFDictionaryRef
	NSMutableArray	CFMutableArrayRef
	NSMutableAttributedString	CFMutableAttributedStringRef
	NSMutableCharacterSet	CFMutableCharacterSetRef
	NSMutableData	CFMutableDataRef
	NSMutableDictionary	CFMutableDictionaryRef
	NSMutableSet	CFMutableSetRef
	NSMutableString	CFMutableStringRef
	NSNumber	CFNumberRef
	NSSet	CFSetRef
String	NSString	CFStringRef
	NSURL	CFURLRef

This is not a complete list, but it includes the common ones. You already ran into this in your MyStuff app when setting up the image picker in Chapter 7. The mediaTypes property of the image picker is an array of URI types. These are defined in the Core Foundation as CFStringRef values. To use this in your app, you had to write code like the following:

```
picker.mediaTypes = [kUTTypeImage as NSString, kUTTypeMovie as NSString]
```

The kUTTypeImage symbol is a Core Foundation string value, but you can substitute it anywhere an NSString or String type is expected just by casting it to the desired type.

In another quick example, let's say you've received a CFUUIDRef type (a Core Foundation Universally Unique Identifier) from a framework. You'd prefer that as a Swift String instead. There's a Core Foundation function to convert the CFUUIDRef into a CFStringRef. All you have to do is cast the returned CFStringRef to the type you want, as shown in the following code:

```
let uuid = CFUUIDCreate(nil)
let uuidString: String = CFUUIDCreateString(nil,uuid) as String
```

Method Signatures

Methods in Objective-C and functions in Swift all have a signature. A *signature* is the portion of the function name that identifies it. Signatures are used to match a function call to a function. They are also used as *selectors*, values used to dynamically choose a method to execute.

Swift signatures have their roots in Objective-C signatures, so let's start there. The following method is defined in the Objective-C UIImage class:

```
- (void)drawAtPoint:(CGPoint)point blendMode:(CGBlendMode)mode alpha:(CGFloat)alpha
```

Compare this to the same method in Swift's UIImage class.

```
func drawAtPoint(_ point: CGPoint, blendMode mode: CGBlendMode, alpha alpha: CGFloat)
```

I've highlighted the significant keywords in both. The signature for both of these functions is as follows:

```
drawAtPoint:blendMode:alpha:
```

Notice that local parameter names are not part of the signature. Only the function name and the external parameter names are significant. When you want to unambiguously identify a function in Swift, you write the function using only its name and external parameter names, like this: drawAtPoint(_:,blendMode:,alpha:).

Method signature are still used in the Cocoa Touch framework, although their use is dwindling thanks to closures. If you do need to specify one, you form it as a string. (Swift lacks the special method selector type used by Objective-C.) You did this in the Shapely app in Chapter 11, as follows:

```
let pan = UIPanGestureRecognizer(target: self, action: "moveShape:")
```

The action parameter is a method selector, written as a Swift string, that causes this gesture recognizer to call the moveShape(_:) function when activated.

> **Note** The colons in a selector indicate parameters. If your class has two functions, `setNeedsIceCream()` that takes no parameters and `setNeedsIceCream(_ want: Bool)` that takes one parameter, their signatures are distinguished by the trailing colon: `setNeedsIceCream` vs. `setNeedsIceCream:`.

Memory Management

The fact that I've written this entire book—up to this point—without even mentioning memory management is nothing short of amazing. Memory management in iOS originally placed a great deal of the burden on the programmer. That has since improved, with the recent introduction of Automatic Reference Counting (ARC), but even then there were a significant number of exceptions, restrictions, and caveats.

Swift starts over with a clean slate. iOS, and thus Swift, still uses ARC. But Swift handles ARC so flawlessly that there's really nothing for the programmer to do, except repurpose that portion of their brain they used to dedicate to memory management for something more enjoyable.

This is not to say that you don't need to know anything about memory management in iOS. A cursory understanding is extremely helpful. ARC is a wonderful technology, but is has a Persian flaw. There are situations where you can create memory leaks in your app. And the tools you use to combat those leaks have other, sometimes unwanted, side effects. So, welcome to Memory Management 101. (Don't fret, this is quick course.)

Garbage Collection

In the beginning, there was manual memory management. The programmer was responsible for allocating every block of memory they needed and later releasing it back to the system when they were done with it. As program complexity grew, it quickly became obvious this wasn't an efficient solution. Oh, and programmers got really tired of writing the same code over and over again.

What followed were various forms of automatic memory management. One of those is called garbage collection. *Garbage collection* takes responsibility for recycling the values and objects you are no longer using by returning that memory to the operating system. The next time you need to create an object or concatenate a string, there's memory available to do that.

Conceptually, garbage collection is simple. In the example illustrated in Figure 20-3, you have two button objects. These, in turn, have references to attributed strings that, in turn, have references to strings, dictionaries, and font objects.

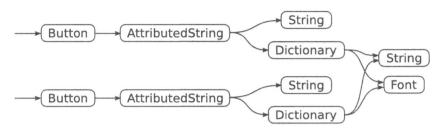

Figure 20-3. Object references in an app

Now you decide to change the title of a button. You create a new attributed string, possibly reusing string and font objects you've used before, and assign the new object to the `attributedString` property of the button, as shown in Figure 20-4.

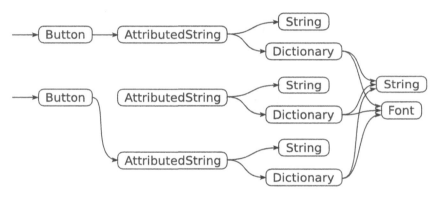

Figure 20-4. Replacing an attributed string object

The question becomes, what does Swift do with the old attributed string object? It's no longer being used. If it, and every other unused object, were allowed to continue occupying memory, your app would soon run out of memory and crash. In fact, just about every app in the world would quickly run out of memory.

What needs to happen is for the objects you're no longer using to be destroyed and their memory recovered. But what does it mean to be "no longer used?" In this example, it's a curious mix. Obviously, the old attributed string object is no longer serving any purpose. Neither are its string and dictionary objects. But the string and font objects the dictionary refers to are still being used by other objects. So, you can't simply destroy the old attributed string object and everything it references.

One solution is to determine the graph of objects that are in use. That consists of the root objects of your application (your `UIApplication` object), all of the objects it references (your view controller objects), all of the objects they reference (view objects), and all of the objects they reference (strings, fonts, colors, and so on). When you're done, you have the complete set of every object your app is using. These are called the *reachable objects*. Everything else is *garbage*, as shown in Figure 20-5.

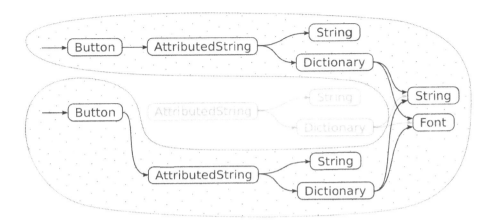

Figure 20-5. *Garbage collection*

This is traditional garbage collection. The awesome feature of garbage collection is that you, the programmer, don't have do to anything. You just create and use the objects you want. As soon as you stop using an object, the operating system disposes of it for you. That sounds a lot like the code you've been writing in Swift. So, Swift must be using garbage collection, right?

Unfortunately, this kind of memory management is too computationally intensive to make an efficient solution for mobile devices. iOS uses a different kind of memory management that tries to accomplish the same thing garbage collection does but with much less overhead.

Reference Counting

iOS uses a technique called *reference counting*. In reference counting, all objects maintain a reference count. The reference count is the number of objects that are still using (have a reference to) that object. If you assign an object to a property, it increments the reference count. When you remove the object from the property, the reference count is decremented. When the reference count hits zero, there are no longer any references to the object and it is destroyed. Swift does this, automatically, for every object reference.

Figure 20-6 shows the same set of objects as those in Figure 20-3, but this time using reference counting. All of the objects have nonzero reference counts and are therefore still in use.

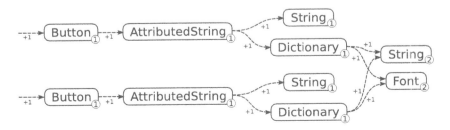

Figure 20-6. *Objects with reference counts*

When you assign a new attributed string to the button, here's what happens. The new object's reference count is incremented and stored as the new property value, as shown in Figure 20-7. This is called a *retain*. While the attributed string was being constructed, it retained all of the objects it references, also shown in Figure 20-7.

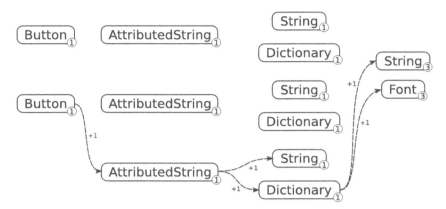

Figure 20-7. *Retaining new objects*

The reference count of the previous property value is then decremented, as shown in Figure 20-8. This is called a *release*. Since the button was its only reference, its count goes to zero, and the object is destroyed. During destruction, it releases any objects it was referencing, and the process repeats.

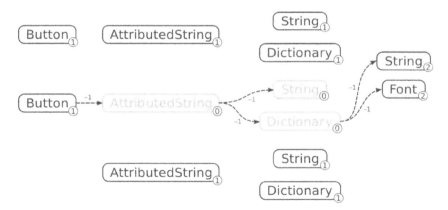

Figure 20-8. *Releasing old objects*

When the whole thing is over, the old attributed string object is gone, as are the string and dictionary objects it was using. But the string and font objects the dictionary was referencing are still with us because they continue to be referenced by other objects.

Reference counting is fast, simple, and efficient, and the end result is the same as garbage collection. Well, it's the same most of the time. There's one situation where reference counting doesn't work so well, and you need to know about it.

Circular Retains

Let's look at a different problem. You're creating an enrollment system. You have Teacher objects and Student objects. The teacher has a reference to each student, and the students all have a reference to their teacher. These objects and their reference counts are shown in Figure 20-9.

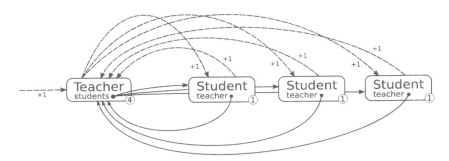

Figure 20-9. *Circular references*

Each Student has a retain count of one (for the teacher's reference). The Teacher has a reference count of four—one from its owner and three from its three students.

The owner is now done with these objects and releases Teacher, as shown in Figure 20-10. This releases the teacher object, decrements its reference count, and then...nothing. The teacher's reference count is still three, so it isn't destroyed. Because it's not destroyed, it never releases its student objects, so they never release their teacher.

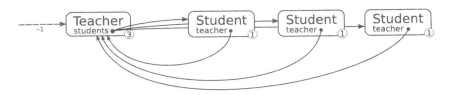

Figure 20-10. *Releasing the Teacher object*

This is called a *circular retain cycle*. It's also called a *memory leak*. These objects will continue to exist forever, and there's no way to get rid of them, short of terminating your app.

There is a way out of this trap. The solution is to not have the Student objects retain the Teacher object. Swift provides a special type called a *weak reference*; it's an object reference that doesn't retain the object it references. The regular kind of reference is called a *strong reference*.

Let's replace the student's `teacher` reference with a weak reference and see what happens, as shown in Figure 20-11.

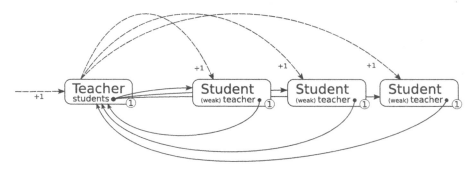

Figure 20-11. *Using weak references*

The weak references still contain Teacher values, but these do not increment its reference count. Now when the teacher object is released, it gets destroyed, and it destroys all of the student objects it was referencing. The following statement declares a weak reference:

weak var teacher: Teacher?

Boom! Problem solved. But you know the old saying, "Every great solution creates its own problem." Or maybe they don't say that; maybe that was just me. Regardless, weak references have their own set of issues. Here's what you need to know:

- A weak reference refers to an object but does not retain it.

- If the object in a weak reference is destroyed, the value is silently set to `nil`.

- A weak reference must be an optional or implicitly unwrapped optional (because it could be set to `nil` at any time).

Weak references are perfect for "tree" or "parent-child" object relationships, where the child maintains a reference to its parent. Another place you'll find weak references used is in delegate and data source properties. In practice—and you've done this throughout the book—an object's delegate object is often itself or its parent object, like a view controller. This creates the same kind of circular retain cycle shown in Figure 20-9. (Yes, an object can retain itself.)

But this too has consequences. You already dealt with this problem in the Wonderland app from Chapter 12. In the `BookViewController.swift` file, you created a property to store your book view's data source, as follows:

```
let bookSource = BookDataSource()
...
dataSource = bookSource
```

Later, you assigned the bookSource to your page view controller's dataSource but kept the same reference in the bookSource property. That's because dataSource is a weak reference. If you don't have at least one strong reference to your BookDataSource object, it will be immediately destroyed, and your page view controller won't have a data source. Believe me, this kind of problem can be maddening to debug.

Retain cycles can be subtle. Another place they can occur is in closures, where the closure refers to the object that owns the closure. There's an extensive section in *The Swift Programming Language* on circular retains. Now that you understand the problem, take a moment to breeze through that section.

And just as the optional has its implicitly unwrapped sibling, weak references also have a dangerous cousin. An *unowned* variable is a non-optional variable with a weak reference. You declare an unowned variable using the unowned keyword, as follows:

```
unowned var teacher: Teacher = ...
```

As you might guess, you'd use this only when you are *absolutely sure* that the object in the reference won't be destroyed before you might use it again. If you use this variable after the Teacher object is destroyed, your app will crash. Worse, it's not an optional; there's no way to test to see whether it's nil. Consider using a weak implicitly unwrapped variable instead.

Even More Swift

But wait, there's more! There is a lot to the Swift language, as witnessed by the length of this chapter—a chapter that's supposed to be a "quick" introduction. And yet, I still didn't get to some of the good stuff. Here are a few more topics you'll want to explore as your Swift skills mature:

- A type alias creates a new name for an existing type, much like C's typedef.

- You can overload operators. A class, for example, can define its own code for the == and != operators, essentially defining what it means for two objects of that class to be "equal."

- You can create your own operators. That's right; you can just make up operators. If you feel that your enumeration needs a +&- operator so that you can write myEnum +&- 3, go for it. (I'm pitying the next programmer who has to figure out what that means.)

- Functions can have variadic parameters. That's a fancy name for a function that accepts a variable number of parameters, like the NSString(format:,_:...) initializer. The ... indicates that you can call the function with as many additional parameters as you want.

- Swift supports generics. A generic is a type that can mutate to deal with different types in a type-safe manner. In English, you can create a class that works with different types of objects. When you use that class, you tell it what type you're working with, and it's as if Swift creates a new subclass of your class just for that type. All of the collection types in Swift are generics. There's only one Array type, but when you declare an array of UITouch objects ([UITouch]), Swift creates an array that only stores UITouch objects and nothing else.

- There's a suite of byte access types that gives you most of the power of C pointers. You can use the byte access types to work with raw data, like image pixel buffers, and interact with C functions that still deal with pointers.

Summary

You've learned a lot about Swift. And I mean, *a lot*—enough to write professional-level iOS apps. I also don't expect you to memorize everything in this chapter the first time around. Most developers, myself included, learned these programming language lessons over the course of many years. Use this chapter as a reference or just come back when things feel fuzzy.

I think it's time to take all of this new Swift knowledge and do something exceptional with it, like create a framework.

EXERCISE

I mentioned in the "switch Statement" section that a tuple cases can contain a combination of constants, expressions, wildcards, bindings, and ranges. Take the switch statement example that used where clauses and rewrite it using just tuple patterns.

You'll find my solution in the Control E1.playground file.

Chapter 21

Frame Up

Now that you've got these mad Swift skills, let's put some of them to use. This final chapter is going to wade a little into the deep end of iOS development. You'll develop an extension—an exciting new feature of iOS 8—and to do that you'll create a framework.

A *framework* is a self-contained bundle of code, resources, and interfaces. A framework can contain compiled code (classes and functions), resources (images, sounds, storyboards), and an API (the list of classes, properties, and functions you're allowed to use). In short, it contains everything you need to use a collection of code that someone else has written. If you've used DLLs or static libraries on other platforms, or possibly Java `.jar` files, you have the general idea.

Frameworks are used extensively in iOS. In fact, iOS is (almost) nothing more than a massive collection of frameworks. A framework makes it easy to bundle together everything needed for a complete programming solution. Take the MapKit framework, for example. It contains the code for classes such as `MKMapView`, it contains resources like the standard push-pin map annotation image, and it contains all of the interfaces that let you use those in your app when you write `import MapKit`.

Starting with iOS 8, Apple now allows app developers to create frameworks and bundle them in their apps. This opens opportunities to include a framework that provides your app with a complete solution. You can now drop in whole frameworks from other developers, share solutions between your own apps, or even create and publish a framework for other developers to use.

Even more exciting, iOS 8 introduces new system-level features that you can extend by packaging your code in a special framework. In this chapter, you will do the following:

- Learn about extensions
- Create an Action extension
- Create a framework
- Share a framework
- Put some of your new closure knowledge to work

You're going to revisit the Shorty app from Chapter 3. Wow, that seems like a long time ago. It's great to have an app that you can browse the Web and then shorten a URL. But what if you're surfing the Web in Safari or Chrome or the new Middle Earth browser (that translates everything into Elvish) and you suddenly need to shorten a URL? What do you do then? You read the rest of this chapter, of course.

Extensions

iOS 8 adds extensions to the app mix. An *extension* is a framework, bundled in your app, that provides a service to enhance the iOS experience outside your app. Currently, there are six kinds of extensions in iOS.

- *Share*: Provide a new way to share information.
- *Action*: Do something novel with the user's information.
- *Today*: Add live, interactive notifications to the lock screen.
- *Photo Editing*: Add new photo filters and effects to other apps.
- *Document Provider*: Give other apps access to your app's documents.
- *Custom Keyboard*: Replace the standard on-screen keyboard with your own.

You're going to create the simplest extension possible, a non-UI Action extension. I did say we were going to be wading into the deep end, not jumping in head first. But don't worry, there's still plenty of work to do. Before you get started, there are a few things about extensions you should understand.

Let's look first at how extensions work. Let's say the user is browsing through their pictures in their Photos app when they find a particularly good picture of Gandalf. They want to share that with the Shire, so they tap the activity button in the interface. Up pops the usual suspects: Facebook, Twitter, Sina Weibo, iMessage, e-mail, and possibly others.

It's the "others" category that's now wide open in iOS 8. The gentlefolk of the Shire use their own social network, ShireShare. iOS 8 discovers a Share extension framework that's been bundled inside the ShireShare app. The extension is loaded and added to the list, right alongside Twitter and the rest. If the user taps the ShireShare button, the code in the extension takes over and presents its sharing interface. This could be its own interface, or it could be built from a standardized interface provided by Cocoa Touch. The extension is then responsible for uploading the picture, along with a message or any other relevant data, to the ShireShare site. The process running the extension is then terminated, and the user resumes browsing their photos.

It's important to note that at no time was the ShireShare app running or was it launched. This entire process occurs while the Photos app is the active app. The Sharing extension in the ShireShare app just provides a new service, one independent of its container app. Other types of extensions provide different experiences.

Creating an Extension

Extensions are packaged in a framework. You build this framework as part of your project, and the compiled framework is included in your app like any other resource. Here are the salient points of interest:

- The *containing app* is your app, the one that contains the extension framework as a resource.

- The *host app* is the app that wants to use your extension.

- The code in your extension is executed in a separate process, isolated from both the containing app and the host app.

- The life cycle of an extension is independent of both the containing and host apps and is usually quite brief.

- Each extension defines one, and only one, kind of service. If you want your app to provide three different services, your app must include three separate extensions.

- Your app can use the code in a framework directly. A framework *cannot* use the code in your app, although it can use code from another framework.

We might as well get started. There's no user interface design for this project because the Action extension doesn't have a UI. Find the Shorty project from Chapter 3. From the File menu, choose the New ➤ Target command. In the target template picker, select the iOS Application Extensions group and pick the Action extension, as shown in Figure 21-1.

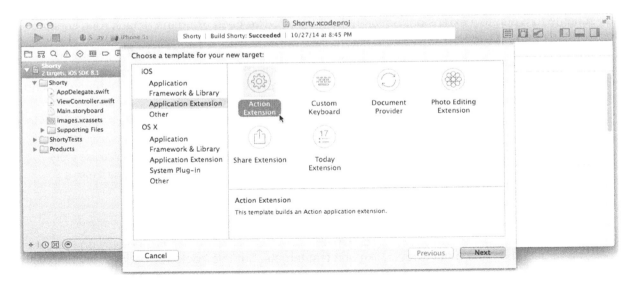

Figure 21-1. Picking the Action extension template

Give the new extension a Product Name of ShortenAction, as shown in Figure 21-2. Make sure the language is Swift. Set Action Type to No User Interface. Xcode automatically offers to make this new target part of your existing app and to embed the framework in your Shorty application. This is exactly what you want.

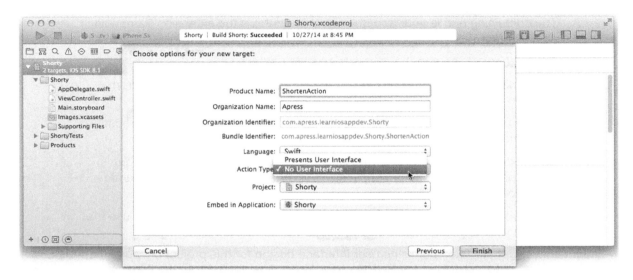

Figure 21-2. Setting the Action extension details

When you click the Finish button, you're likely to see another dialog that says Xcode is preparing a run scheme for your new extension. So far in this book, you've been using the default runs schemes to debug your app on various simulators and devices. To debug an extension, however, you can't just run the extension. Remember that extensions run in a special process and at the behest of another (host) app. Xcode conveniently creates a run scheme that launches another app and prepares Xcode to intercept the code in your extension when that host app loads it. Setting this kind of thing up is tricky, so definitely click the Activate button when Xcode asks.

> **Tip**   The run scheme that Xcode creates for your extension will ask you what host app you want to use every time you run it. If you're using the same host app over and over again, you can edit the scheme so it runs a particular host app instead, so you don't have to pick one every time.

A target produces something in your project. Up until now, you've really been using only one target, your app target. There are other targets, like unit test targets, but this book hasn't done anything with those. Now your project has two significant targets: an app target and an extension target.

Xcode just did quite a bit of work, so before you go too far, let's review what just happened. When you added an extension target, Xcode did the following:

> Xcode created a new target in your project named ShortenAction. That target produces an extension framework named ShortenAction.appex.

> Xcode added the ShortenAction target as a dependent target of the Shorty target. A *dependent target* is a target that must be built before the parent target can be built. This ensures that when you build your Shorty app target, the ShortenAction target also gets built.

> The ShortenAction.appex bundle (the ShortenAction target's product) was added to the list of binaries that get embedded in your Shorty app. An *embedded binary* is a library or framework that contains executable code that gets copied into your finished app as a resource.

> ShortenAction.appex was also added to the list of embedded application extensions. This prepares the embedded framework so it will be recognized as an extension. Without this, iOS won't see your extension.

Connecting Your Extension

All extensions work through an extension point. An *extension point* is a service provided by iOS where extensions will broaden the user's choices. A Share extension adds to the possible sharing options when the user taps the activity button. A Keyboard extension adds to the number of keyboard layouts the user can select from, and so on.

An extension connects to one extension point, specified in its Info.plist file. Select the Info.plist file of your ShortenAction target, as shown in Figure 21-3. You'll find the extension's Info.plist file inside the Supporting Files group of the ShortenAction group. This is the property list for your extension, and it contains important information about what kind of extension it is, determines under what circumstances it should be available, and even determines its display name. Let's tackle the easy one first.

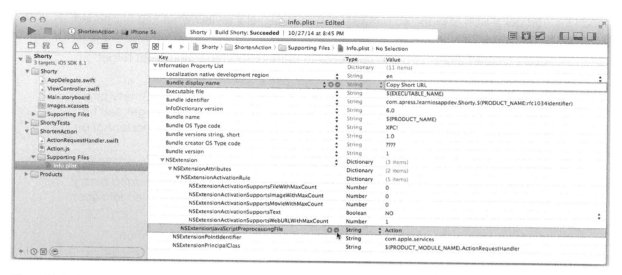

Figure 21-3. Action extension Info.plist

Edit the value of the Bundle display name and change it to Copy Short URL, as shown in Figure 21-3. This is the action's name as it will appear to the user. The next question is "When and how will it appear?" Those answers are in the NSExtension dictionary. Expand that entry to take a look.

The first value used in NSExtension is the NSExtensionPointIdentifier. This tells iOS what kind of extension point your extension works with. The com.apple.service identifier means your extension is a UI-less Action. The rest of the properties are largely dependent on what kind of extension this is.

For a UI-less Action extension, iOS needs to know the class of the object that provides your service. That's stored in the NSExtensionPrincipleClass property, and it's set to ActionRequestHandler. iOS will create an ActionRequestHandler object and then call on it to do the work.

If this was an extension with a user interface, the process is slightly different. The NSExtensionMainStoryboard property would have the name of your extension's main storyboard file. This, in turn, contains the scene with the UIViewController that implements your user interface.

That explains the "how," and now you have to describe the "when." Some extensions are context sensitive. Let's say you've created a Share extension that shares a movie. It would be inappropriate to show that Share extension to the user if they were trying to share a map location or their contact information. You describe the context in which your extension should be used in the NSExtensionActivationRule property. There are two ways to do this. The first, and easiest, is to store a dictionary of predefined rules, also shown in Figure 21-3.

Each value in the dictionary defines a simple rule in which your extension should be used. For example, the NSExtensionActivationSupportsImageWithMaxCount rule is the maximum number of images your extension can work with. If it was set to 3, the user could use your extension to share up to three images at a time. In the template it's set to 0, which means your extension doesn't handle images. You can leave these rules set to 0 or NO in your Info.plist, or you can delete them. It doesn't matter because it means the same thing.

The rule you want is the NSExtensionActivationSupportsWebURLWithMaxCount, and it should be set to 1. This rule activates your extension when the user wants to do something with a single URL.

> **Caution**   Don't confuse NSExtensionActivationSupportsWebURLWithMaxCount with
> NSExtensionActivationSupportsWebPageWithMaxCount. The former activates your extension with a
> URL. The later activates your extension with the contents of a web page—which may, or may not, have a URL.

The other way to determine the "when" is to write an activation rule predicate statement and store it as a String property in NSExtensionActivationRule. If iOS see a string value, it executes the predicate statement to determine whether your extension should be activated. A *predicate statement* is a database-like query that can make all kinds of complex decisions. For example, it could determine that the URL the user wants to share has already been shortened. You could deactivate your extension under that circumstance since there's no point in shortening an already shortened URL. See the *Predicate Programming Guide* for a thorough explanation of the predicate language.

With both the "how" and "when" out of the way, let's move on to actually doing something.

Running your Action

Like all good templates, Xcode creates an Action extension that will run right out of the box. Select the ShortenAction scheme (the one Xcode created for you) and choose a target, as shown in Figure 21-4.

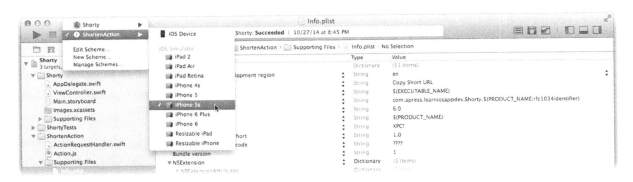

Figure 21-4. Selecting the extension scheme

Run your extension. The run scheme for an extension needs a host app. The host app is the app that will request your extension. Xcode prompts for a host app to launch, as shown in Figure 21-5. For this test, choose Safari.

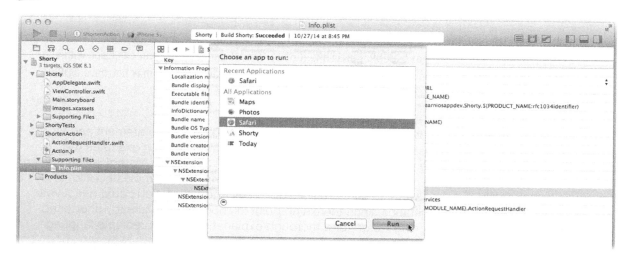

Figure 21-5. Choosing the host app

Safari launches in the simulator, as shown on the left in Figure 21-6. I choose Safari because it's an app that shares URLs, and that's the context your extension works in. Go to any page in Safari and tap the action button. The activity picker appears, also shown in the middle of Figure 21-6. The picker shows both sharing activities and actions. Swipe the actions, and you'll find a new Copy Short URL action, conspicuously missing an icon, as shown on the right in Figure 21-6.

Figure 21-6. The ShortenAction extension appears in the activity picker

Congratulations! Your extension just appeared in Safari. Now if it would only do something useful.

Lights, Code, Action

Stop the running app in Xcode and return to your project. It's time to get familiar with the inner workings of the action.

Select the `ActionRequestHandler.swift` file and take a look at the code. This is where your action happens. For a UI-less Action extension, you define a class that will do the work. It must adopt the `NSExtensionRequestHandling` protocol and implement a `beginRequestWithExtensionContext(_:)` function.

> **Tip** The class that implements your extension can be anything you want. But if you change it, don't forget to update the `NSExtensionPrincipalClass` property in the `Info.plist` to match.

If you look at the code from the template, you'll see it's doing quite a lot. Actually, it's not doing much of anything at all; it's just a demonstration of how you'd do something sophisticated. The template code shows how to run a JavaScript probe against the user's web page. This JavaScript can extract all kinds of information from the page, which your extension could then use. Imagine, for example, an extension in a travel app; it could extract reservation information from a web page and automatically adds it to the user's itinerary. If you need to do something like this, take a good look at the template code.

Your extension doesn't need any of that. You need to gut the `ActionRequestHandling` class and replace it with the code to shorten a URL. Unfortunately, that code is currently baked into the `ViewController` class in your Shorty app.

Every Extension Is an Island

As I mentioned earlier, an extension is a framework. A framework *provides* classes, code, and resources to a consumer, typically an app. It cannot *consume* any classes, code, or resources from the app that contains or hosts it. A framework is an island; if it didn't bring it, it doesn't have it.

The next step, clearly, is to share the code that performs the URL shortening with the extension so both can use it. There are several ways to accomplish this. Here are a couple of obvious ones:

- Hack up a second version of the same code for the extension.
- Reorganize the code so the URL shortening logic is encapsulated in a portable class.

I'm not even going to talk about the first one.

Drag a new Swift file into your app project and name it `Squeezer.swift`. You'll consolidate the URL shortening logic in this class. When adding the new file, make sure you're adding the file to just the Shorty target, as shown in Figure 21-7.

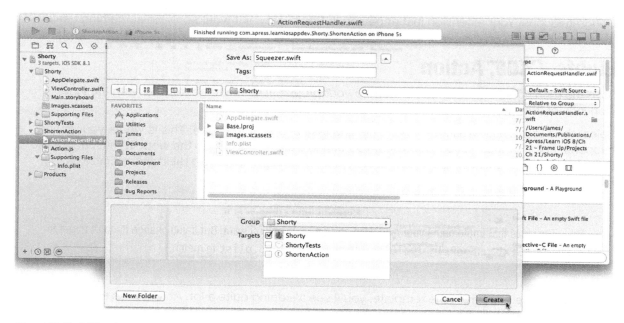

Figure 21-7. Adding Squeezer to the app target

You want to reorganize the URL shortening logic so it can perform the same function for both your app and your extension. Your app needs the URL shortening to occur asynchronously because an app should never block its main event loop. The extension doesn't strictly require this, but it won't hurt. What both need is an easy way to get the shortened URL back when the conversion is done because the app and the extension will want to do different things with the result. Here, then, is the plan:

- The Squeezer class will have a shortenURL(longURL:, completion:) method.

- This function will take the long URL, build the shortening request, start the Internet transaction to convert it, and return immediately.

- When the results are obtained, it will call the completion block supplied by the caller.

- The completion block gets two parameters, the shortened URL or the error that occurred.

This mirrors how the app does it now but repackages the code so it can be easily reused in other ways. The following is the finished Squeezer.swift code:

```swift
import Foundation

let GoDaddyAccountKey = "0123456789abcdef0123456789abcdef"

public class Squeezer {
    public class func shortenURL( # longURL: NSURL,↵
                    completion: ((NSURL?, NSError?) -> Void)) {
        if let absoluteURL = longURL.absoluteString {
            if let encodedURL = ↵
```

```
absoluteURL.stringByAddingPercentEscapesUsingEncoding(NSUTF8StringEncoding) {
    let urlString = ↵
    "http://api.x.co/Squeeze.svc/text/\(GoDaddyAccountKey)?url=\(encodedURL)"
    let request = NSURLRequest(URL: NSURL(string: urlString)!)
    NSURLConnection.sendAsynchronousRequest( request,
                                    queue: NSOperationQueue.mainQueue() ) {
        (_, shortURLData, error) in
        if error == nil && shortURLData != nil {
            var shortURL: NSURL?
            if let data = shortURLData {
                if let short = NSString(data: data,
                                encoding: NSUTF8StringEncoding ) {
                    shortURL = NSURL(string: short)
                }
            }
            completion(shortURL, nil)
        } else {
            completion(nil, error)
        }
    }
}
}
}
}
}
```

Just as in Chapter 3, you'll need to replace the GoDaddyAccountKey value with your X.co account key.

This new version does everything the ViewController class in Shorty was doing. In Shorty, you created an NSURLRequest delegate and data source, started the NSURLRequest asynchronously, and then waited for delegate calls to collect the response data and complete the transaction.

This is such a common task that iOS 8 added a new convenience method that does all of that for you in a single call: sendAsynchronousRequest(_:,queue:,completion:). Instead of defining delegate methods, you supply a closure that's executed once the transaction is complete.

The completion block in shortenURL(longURL:,completion:) examines the results to determine whether it was successful. If it was, it decodes the data of the response and turns it into an NSURL object—just like the app used to do. It then calls the completion closure passed to your shortenURL(longURL:,completion:) function, providing it with the translated NSURL object or an error.

You can now greatly simplify the code in ViewController. Select the ViewController.swift file and make the following changes:

1. Remove the NSURLConnectionDelegate and NSURLConnectionDataDelegate protocols from the class declaration. You don't need these anymore; Squeezer handles all of the communications now.

2. Delete the GoDaddyAccountKey, shortenURLConnection, and shortURLData properties.

3. Delete the connection(_:,didFailWithError:), connection(_:,didReceiveData:), and connectionDidFinishLoading(_:) functions.

4.   Rewrite the shortenURL(_:) action method as follows:

```
@IBAction func shortenURL( AnyObject ) {
    if let toShorten = webView.request?.URL {
        Squeezer.shortenURL(longURL: toShorten) { (shortURL, _) in
            if let urlString = shortURL?.absoluteString {
                self.shortLabel.title = urlString
                self.clipboardButton.enabled = true
            } else {
                self.shortLabel.title = "failed"
                self.clipboardButton.enabled = false
                self.shortenButton.enabled = true
            }
        }
    }
    shortenButton.enabled = false
}
```

Squeezer is now doing all of the communications and URL shortening work. Both the success and failure cases are being handled by the closure.

Take a moment to run your Shorty app—by changing the target scheme back to Shorty—and double-check that it still works. It's always a good idea to retest your app after reorganizing your code.

Obtaining the User's Data

With the shortening logic encapsulated in Squeezer, you can now reuse it to implement your extension. Select the ActionRequestHandler.swift file. Keep the extensionContext property and replace the beginRequestWithExtensionContext(_:) function with the following:

```
funcbeginRequestWithExtensionContext(context: NSExtensionContext) {
    self.extensionContext = context
    for item in context.inputItems as [NSExtensionItem] {
        if let attachments = item.attachments as? [NSItemProvider] {
            for itemProvider in attachments {
                let urlType = String(kUTTypeURL)
                if itemProvider.hasItemConformingToTypeIdentifier(urlType) {
                    itemProvider.loadItemForTypeIdentifier(urlType, options: nil) {
                        (item,error) in
                        dispatch_async(dispatch_get_main_queue()) {
                            if let url = item as? NSURL {
                                self.actionWithURL(url)
                            }
                        }
                    }
                }
            }
        }
    }
}
```

When the user taps your extension, this function gets called. The first thing it does is save the NSExtensionContext in a property. Your code will need it again later.

The NSExtensionContext object contains all of information your extension needs to work with the user's selection. First, it examines the inputItems, an array of NSExtensionItem objects. Each item is a type of data, each of which contains one or more attachments. You need to examine the items and then extract the attachments that your extension wants to work with.

NSEXTENSIONCONTEXT WITH A UI

For non-UI extensions that need an NSExtensionContext, like this one, the extension context is passed as a parameter to beginRequestWithExtensionContext(_:). If your extension has a UI, however, you get the extension context through a different route.

Your interface will be in a storyboard. The extension point loads your storyboard. In the process, the UIViewController that implements your interface is created. Before your view controller is presented, iOS 8 sets its extensionContext property with the active extension context. (This is a new property, added in iOS 8.)

When your view controller code begins execution, you get the information about the items the user wants to work with from your view controller's extensionContext property. Everything after that is the same.

Let's say the user selected two images and a movie to share. The context will contain two items: one for the images and a second for the movie. The image item will contain two attachments, and the movie item will contain one attachment.

Back in your code, the two loops rattle through all of the attachments looking for any that are URLs. It does this using the hasItemConformingToTypeIdentifier(_:) function. You pass this function a universal type identifier (UTI) for a URL—or whatever type you're interested in—and it returns true if the attachment is, or can be converted to, that type.

Once you've found an attachment you want to work with, the next step is to extract it. Attachments can represent large amounts of data—an entire movie, for example. The attachment content is obtained asynchronously using the loadItemForTypeIdentifier(_:,options:,completionHandler:) function. This function procures the contents of the attachment, possibly converting it to the desired type, and then executes a closure when it's ready. Your closure calls the actionWithURL(_:) function, which you haven't written yet.

Before you do, delete any other methods that were included by the template. You can also delete the Action.js file from the project; you won't be using it.

Reusing Squeezer

Add the code for the actionWithURL(_:) function to the ActionRequestHandler class, as follows. This is the function that implements your action.

```
func actionWithURL(url: NSURL) {
    Squeezer.shortenURL(longURL: url) { (shortURL, error) in
        if error == nil {
            if let url = shortURL {
                UIPasteboard.generalPasteboard().URL = url
            }
            self.extensionContext?.completeRequestReturningItems( nil,
                                        completionHandler: nil)
        } else {
            self.extensionContext?.cancelRequestWithError(error!)
        }
    }
}
```

The code reused Squeezer to shorten the URL in the background. When it's done, it executes the closure. The closure checks to see whether the conversion was successful. If it was, it puts the shortened URL onto the clipboard.

Now here's the important part. Once your extension has done whatever it's going to do, you *must* call either the completeRequestReturningItems(_:,completionHandler:) or cancelRequestWithError(_:) function of the NSExtensionContext object you received in the beginning. These calls tell the extension point that your action is complete or that the user (or some unseen force) canceled it.

Timing here is really important. Extensions have to get in, do their thing, and get out. If your extension does something direct and quick, it should do that and then call one of those functions. This Action extension falls into that category. Shortening a URL shouldn't take more than a second or two, at most. Accordingly, your code waits until the URL is converted and then signals that it's done.

On the other hand, if your extension needs to do something time-consuming, such as upload an entire movie to a server, you should start a background upload task and then immediately signal that your extension has completed. The upload will continue in the background while your user gets on with her life. The *App Extension Programming Guide* has a section entitled "Performing Uploads and Downloads" that explains how to set that up.

That's all well and good, but that's not your biggest problem. Xcode it telling you that there's no class named Squeezer, and it's right; there's no class named Squeezer in your extension (framework). Remember, a framework can't access the code or resources in its container app.

You return, once again, to the problem of how to share the URL shortening code with both your app and your extension. One of the simplest is not to share but to duplicate. Select the Squeezer.swift file. Use the file inspector and change the target membership of the file so it is in both the Shorty and ShortenAction targets, as shown in Figure 21-8.

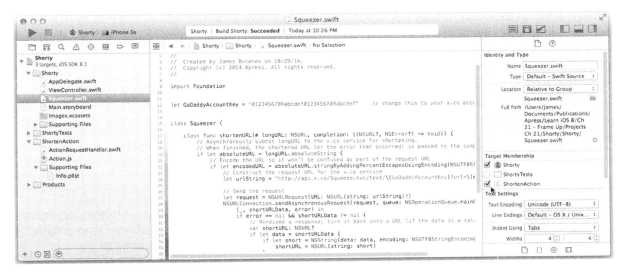

Figure 21-8. *Compiling Squeezer twice*

By making the `Squeezer.swift` file a member of both targets, the file gets compiled twice: once when the ShortenAction framework is built and again when the Shorty app is built. The net effect is that both your app and your extension can use the same class.

Let's take it out for a drive. Select the ShortenAction scheme again (see Figure 21-4) and test it in Safari. Browse to a page, tap the action button, and then tap your Copy Short URL action. If everything is working properly, the URL of the page will be shortened and copied to the clipboard. To verify this, set a breakpoint in the `actionWithURL(_:)` function, as shown in Figure 21-9.

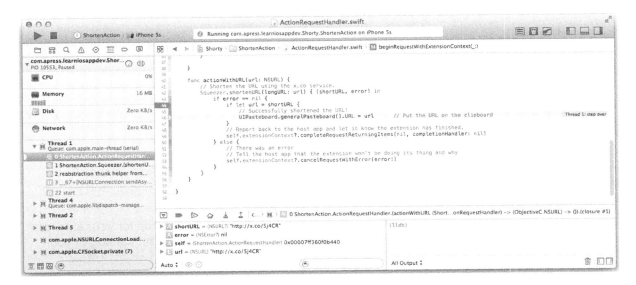

Figure 21-9. *Examining actionWithURL(_:) in action*

When the action executes, it calls `actionWithURL(_:)` to convert the URL. Stepping through the closure code, as shown in Figure 21-9, you can see the successfully shortened URL in the variable pane and step through the code that puts it on the clipboard.

This is pretty amazing. With very little work, you've created a new action that users can use in any of the many thousands of apps that will share an URL. Use the same basic technique to create new sharing services, photo filters, and interactive notifications.

But you're not done just yet. There are cosmetic problems and more serious engineering issues to deal with. So, before you retire this book to your bookshelf, let's take care of those.

Action Icons

Action extensions have their own icon. This is unusual; most extensions appear using their container app's icon. The reason is that action icons aren't icons; they're stencils. A *stencil* is an icon created from the alpha channel (the layer of an image that determines the transparency of each pixel) of an image. The pixel colors are ignored, and the alpha channel is used to create a monochromatic button.

The first step is to add the necessary image files to your project, specifically to the extension's resources. Begin by setting up your extension so it has an icon resource. Select the Shorty project in the project navigator, select the ShortenAction target, and then select the General tab. Locate the App Icons and Launch Images section and click the Use Asset Catalog button next to the App Icons Source, as shown in Figure 21-10.

Figure 21-10. Configuring an icon source for the extension

In the dialog sheet, change the migration option to New Asset Catalog and make sure the "Also migrate launch images" option is not checked. (Extensions don't have launch images, and you don't want to supply one).

Click the Migrate button, and Xcode will create a new asset catalog as a resource for your extension. I suggest changing the name of the catalog so you don't confuse it with the asset catalog of your container app, as shown in Figure 21-11.

Figure 21-11. *Renaming the extension's asset catalog*

If the new asset catalog has an AppIcon group, select it and delete it. With the `ActionImages.xcassets` catalog selected, add a new App Icon, as shown in Figure 21-12.

Figure 21-12. *Adding a new App Icon set*

Locate the `Learn iOS Development Projects` ➤ `Ch 21` ➤ `ShortenAction (Resources)` folder. Drag the four image files into the AppIcon set of the new catalog, as shown in Figure 21-13. These are stencil images whose alpha layer contains the actual design. The color pixels of the image are superfluous but are set to gray just so they don't appear blank while you're working with them.

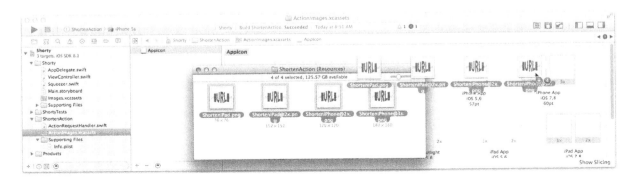

Figure 21-13. *Adding the Action icon stencils*

Test your extension in Safari again, as shown in Figure 21-14. This time, your action will have a stencil-generated icon like the rest of the actions, as shown on the right of Figure 21-14. If you don't see it, try using the iOS Simulator's Reset Content and Settings command and running your test again. This command is equivalent to restoring the iOS device, complete with new car smell. It erases all apps, documents, and any preferences saved on the device. iOS tends to cache information about extensions and might not notice subtle changes made behind the scene. Resetting the simulator forces it to start over.

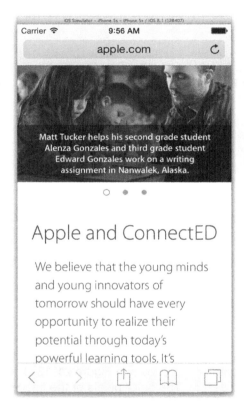

Figure 21-14. Your extension's icon

Your action extension is complete and ready to ship. You could just stop here, or you could take a step into the big league.

Reusing Squeezer, for Real

Compiling the Squeezer class twice is probably fine for a small project like this. But projects don't tend to stay small. As you add more extensions and the capabilities of those extensions grow, what you'll need to share with your app is also going to grow, sometimes substantially. Obviously, you'll need to share all of your data model classes. If you have custom document classes, your extension might want to use those too. And then there's the down-sampling code so your uploaded images aren't too big, the encryption routines so Mordor can't intercept the messages, the code that fetches the current weather forecast for the Shire, and on and on.

What you need is some way to package up compiled code and resources so that both your app and your extension can use them. That, my friend, is the definition of a framework. In this section you'll create a second framework, one just for sharing code, and use that framework in both your app and your extension. Let's get started.

Creating a Framework

Start by adding a new framework target to your project. Select Shorty in the project navigator. If the targets are collapsed, expand them. Click the + button at the bottom of the targets. In the target picker that appears, select the iOS Framework & Library group and then choose to add a Cocoa Touch Framework, as shown in Figure 21-15.

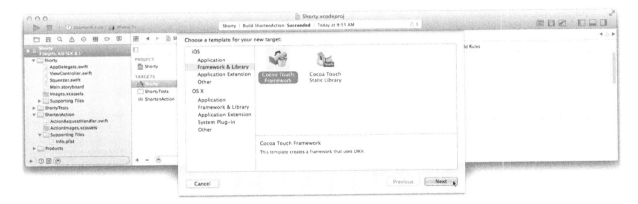

Figure 21-15. *Choosing a framework template*

In the next dialog, name the product SqueezeKit, as shown in Figure 21-16. Make sure both the Project and Embed in Application settings are set to Shorty. This will make the new framework a part of this project and then automatically embed the framework in the Shorty app. It will then be a resource of the Shorty app, just as ShortenAction is now.

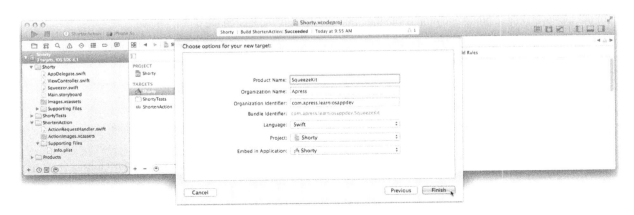

Figure 21-16. *Creating the framework*

Adding Code to a Framework

The next step is to put something in the framework. Select the `Squeezer.swift` file, as shown in Figure 21-17, and use the file inspector to change its target membership. You want the Squeezer class to be compiled in the SqueezeKit target but not in the app or the extension.

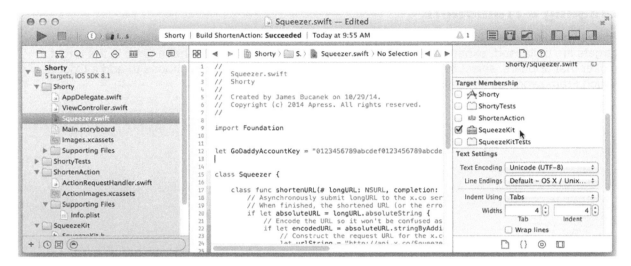

Figure 21-17. *Making Squeezer a member of SqueezeKit*

To make this new relationship clearer, drag the `Squeezer.swift` file from its current location in the project navigator and drop it into the SqueezeKit group.

MOVING SQUEEZER.SWIFT, FOR REAL

You are free to drag around items in your project navigator and organize them any way you like. Your organization in the navigator, however, is independent of the how the files are organized in your filesystem. When you move `Squeezer.swift` from the top-level project group and drop it into the SqueezeKitgroup, the source file doesn't move.

If you're using a source control system or are just a neat freak like me, and you want your project's folder structure to mirror its organization, you'll want to move the source file into the framework's subfolder too. Here's the easiest way to do that:

1. Select the source file.

2. Right-click or Control+click the file and choose the Show in Finder command. Now you know where the real file is.

3. Back in Xcode, delete the file from your project and choose Remove Reference; do not move it to the trash.

4. Back in the Finder, move the file to its new location. In this example, that would be inside the SqueezeKit folder.

5. Drag the relocated file from the Finder back into your project (inside the SqueezeKit group). When Xcode asks, add the "new" file to the just the SqueezeKit target.

While there are ways of relocating files without removing and re-adding them to your project, this technique avoids a lot of the quirks involved in doing that.

Your Squeezer class is now compiled in a framework, and that framework is embedded and linked to your app. You should be able to use it everywhere, right? Not just yet.

Try to build your app and see what happens. In the ViewController.swift file, the compiler is now complaining that there is no Squeezer class. That's because Squeezer is now in a framework. To use the code in a framework, you must import it. At the top of the ViewController.swift file, add an import statement for the SqueezeKit framework, like this (new code in bold):

```
import UIKit
import SqueezeKit
```

Build your app again, and again (!) the compiler is saying that there's no such class. Remember back in the beginning of Chapter 20, where I mentioned access control directives and said that until you start building frameworks you can generally ignore them? You can't ignore them any longer.

The Squeezer class and all of its properties and methods were assigned the default access of internal, which means the class and its members are visible only in the app or framework where it is compiled. When you were compiling it in your app, it didn't matter. Now it does.

Select the Squeezer.swift file and add a public access keyword to both the class and its method, as follows (new code in bold):

```
public class Squeezer {
public class func shortenURL(# longURL: NSURL, ...
```

Compile your app again, and the compiler errors go away! Congratulations, you've created a framework, packed it with useful code, decided what parts of that code are public, and used it in your app.

For Shorty, you're not quite done. Now you're seeing the same errors in the actionWithURL(_:) function of the ActionRequestHandler class. This is the same problem as before. Add a new import statement to beginning of ActionRequestHandler.swift, just as you did for ViewController.swift.

```
import UIKit
import MobileCoreServices
import SqueezeKit
```

Sharing a Framework with an Extension

There's one tiny little detail you should attend to before calling it quits. Extensions run in a controlled environment. To protect that environment, iOS prohibits extensions from using certain Cocoa Touch classes and methods. For example, you can't get the UIApplication object of the process that's running your extension.

Xcode helps you keep from trying to do something you can't with a special compiler flag that will warn you if you try to use something that's out of bounds. The code in your extension is compiled with that flag set. The code in your framework is not. If you're using a framework in your extension, you should set this flag in the framework too. That way, the framework won't let you compile code you can't use from the extension.

Select the Shorty project in the navigator, select the SqueezeKit target, and switch to the Build Settings tab. Make sure you're looking at All settings. Enter the term **safe** into the search field and locate the Require Only App-Extension-Safe API setting, as shown in Figure 21-18. Click the setting value for the SqueezeKit target and change it to YES, also shown in Figure 21-18.

That's it. You're done!

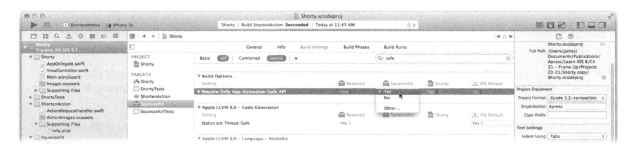

Figure 21-18. *Making SqueezeKit extension-safe*

Summary

Extensions allow your code to enhance into the iOS experience well beyond the bounds of your app. You have the basics, but there's so much more to explore. Give the *App Extension Programming Guide* a good read, and you'll see other ways you can extend your apps.

You've learned a tremendous amount about iOS app development since Chapter 1. It's been an exciting journey and one that's only just begun. With the foundation you have now, you can explore many of the technologies I didn't cover in this book and go deeper into the ones I did.

I hope you've enjoyed reading this book as much as I enjoyed writing it. Use your imagination, apply what you've learned, and promise to write (james@learniosappdev.com) or tweet (@LearniOSAppDev) me when you've written something great. Good luck!

Index

X, Y, Z

Get the eBook for only $10!

> Now you can take the weightless companion with you anywhere, anytime. Your purchase of this book entitles you to 3 electronic versions for only $10.

This Apress title will prove so indispensible that you'll want to carry it with you everywhere, which is why we are offering the eBook in 3 formats for only $10 if you have already purchased the print book.

Convenient and fully searchable, the PDF version enables you to easily find and copy code—or perform examples by quickly toggling between instructions and applications. The MOBI format is ideal for your Kindle, while the ePUB can be utilized on a variety of mobile devices.

Go to www.apress.com/promo/tendollars to purchase your companion eBook.

Lightning Source UK Ltd.
Milton Keynes UK
UKOW07f1939300415

250677UK00004B/247/P